The Game Programmer's Guide to Torque

The Game Programmer's Guide to Torque

Under the Hood of the Torque Game Engine

A GarageGames Book

Edward F. Maurina III

A K Peters, Ltd.
Wellesley, Massachusetts

Editorial, Sales, and Customer Service Office
A K Peters, Ltd.
888 Worcester Street, Suite 230
Wellesley, MA 02482
www.akpeters.com

Set in ITC Slimbach and ITC Eras by Erica Schultz for A K Peters, Ltd.

Cover image and art in the Advanced Maze Runner prototype by Christophe Canon.

Library of Congress Cataloging-in-Publication Data

Maurina, Edward F., III., 1969–
   The game programmer's guide to Torque: under the hood of the Torque Game
Engine / Edward F. Maurina III.
      p. cm.
   "GarageGames book."
   Includes index.
   ISBN 1-56881-284-1 (pbk. : alk. paper)
   1. Computer games—Programming. I. Title.

QA76.76.C672M36   2006
794.8'1526—dc22

                                                              2005056630

Printed in the United States of America

11 10 09 08 07   10 9 8 7 6 5 4 3

This book is dedicated to my wife Teresa, for her encouragement, her advice, and most of all for her tolerance of the odd hours I kept while locked away in my office writing this book.

I must give special thanks to Jerry for acting as an idea bouncing-board and for listening patiently as I discussed chapter ideas over, and over, and....

Of course, I must also thank the many members of the GarageGames community for their unfailing interest in the guide and their encouragement.

Lastly, I would like to thank the GarageGames staff for making the publication of this book possible, giving specific thanks to the "draft reviewers"—Josh Williams, Matt Fairfax, Ben Garney, Matt Langley, and Justin Dujardin.

Contents

Preface

So, you want to make a game? You may be standing in a bookstore holding this book in your hands, or you may be reading this online. Whatever the case may be, some or all of the following thoughts and questions are probably running through your mind:

- **I want to make a game, but can I do it on my own or with a small team?** Making a game is great fun, and a very rewarding experience. You can definitely make a game alone or with a small team as long as you have the right tools available to you. One of those tools is the Torque Game Engine (TGE) and the other is *Game Programmer's Guide to Torque* (GPGT). Using TGE and GPGT, you can create any game that your imagination can encompass and that your skills will allow.

- **TGE sounds good, but will GPGT tell me what I need to know to make my particular game?** TGE is a powerful and flexible game engine that can be used to make any number of different and unique games. You may choose to make single-player or multiplayer games. The game can be a shooter, an adventures, or a role-playing-game, to name just a few. *Game Programmer's Guide to Torque* will teach you the Torque skills you need to create these game types. (See section 1.1, "About the Torque Game Engine," and section 1.2, "What This Guide Contains," to learn more.)

- **Can I get up to speed fast enough to make my game?** Like any other complex and powerful piece of software, Torque can be hard or easy to learn. Everything depends on your approach to the task and whether you have the right resources available to you. With *Game Programmer's Guide to Torque*, with the hundreds of samples that come on the accompanying disk, and with the experience of making the sample game we write while reading this book, you will be able to ramp up very quickly and to move on to your goal—namely, making your own game.

Having been down the path you are just now starting upon, I know how hard it can be to get started and how hard it is to stay motivated in the face of the many challenges involved with learning to use Torque along with the other skills you will need to acquire. I decided to write this guide so that others would not have to struggle to learn Torque.

In closing, this guide is the result of my own need for a better reference and my desire to help other learn about the powerful and flexible Torque Game Engine. It is the culmination of my own game-writing and Torque-using journey. I sincerely hope that it provides you a pleasant beginning to your own game-making adventures.

Introduction

Part I

Chapter 1
Introduction

1.1 About the Torque Game Engine

1.1.1 What Is Torque?

The Torque Game Engine (TGE) is a AAA 3D game engine made available to the indie games community by GarageGames. It is the product of many years of dedicated work and interactive design and development by the staff of Dynamix, a well-known game development company which the founders of GarageGames previously started. As Dynamix made games, they would reuse and refine, taking the best parts of their work to the next generation of the engine. With this engine, they produced games like *Earthsiege*, *Starsiege*, *Tribes*, and eventually *Tribes 2*. All in all, it is safe to say that the code in this engine has its roots in code written as far back as 1995 and perhaps even earlier.

In summary, the Torque Game Engine is a product with man-centuries of development done by proven experts who time and time again used this engine to produce stellar titles. As far as I know, there is no other game engine like this on the market *at any price*.

1.1.2 Why Should I Use Torque?

Educational: One of the best ways to learn programming is to read code written by other developers. If you are going to read code, you might as well have fun and read game code and learn a few tricks in the process.

Resume Building: Mod (modify) the engine to show off your skills to future employers.

MOD Makers: How many times have you gotten stuck trying to mod other engines because they did not support feature X? Now you have the source and can easily add any features you want and truly differentiate your mod from the rest.

To Make Great Games! That's what we all live for, so do it. This is an unprecedented opportunity to build your game using an industry-proven game engine that rocks!

—**GarageGames Site**

One of the beauties of the Torque Game Engine is that you don't have to use it to make games. "What's that, you say?" I repeat, you do not have to use the Torque Game Engine to make games. With the features included in this engine, you can just as easily make a variety of professional, educational, or "your category here" products.

Of course, you must abide by the end user license agreement (EULA), but once you have licensed the engine, the terms of the agreement are pretty free about what you can create. The only real limitation is your own imagination.

1.1.3 Not Just First-Person Shooters

Some people, examining the Torque Game Engine for the first time, may be under the impression that it is only for making first-person shooters (FPS). Nothing could be further from the truth. Yes, it is well suited to the FPS genre, but it can and has been used to make a variety of different game types.

Current Titles

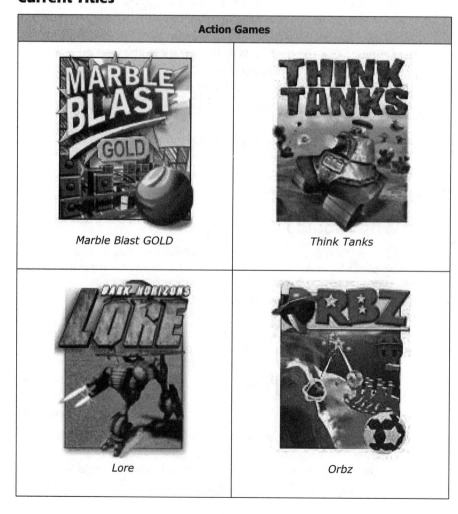

Action Games

Marble Blast GOLD

Think Tanks

Lore

Orbz

Sports	
RocketBowl Plus	*Golden Fairway*

Educational

3-D Language Spain

Upcoming Titles

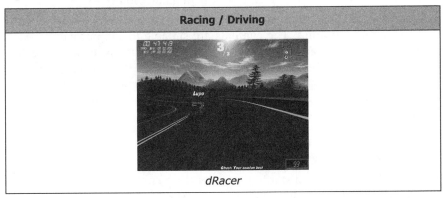

Racing / Driving

dRacer

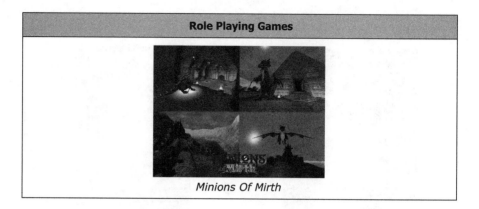

Minions Of Mirth

1.2 What This Guide Contains

By the end of this book, you will understand how to use Torque, and we will even make our own little game in the process. This book aims to fill the following needs.

- **Learning guide.** The guide is designed to quickly walk you through the concepts and learning required to get started on your own games. To that end, it comes with a lesson kit containing complete sets of ready-to-run sample scripts (from discussions) and sample lessons covering all topics discussed.

- **Reference guide.** To make this guide useful even after your preliminary learning experience is complete, the guide is formatted in a way that facilitates looking up specific topics. Also, it comes with quick-reference guides covering all TGE console classes, scripting, script functions and methods, GUI (graphical user interface) controls, etc.

- **Prototyping help.** This guide and the accompanying lesson kit in combination with the resources that come with TGE itself should provide all the materials you will need to create your own game prototypes.

- **Teaching aid.** The guide and associated kit have also been designed with the classroom in mind. The contents are suitable to support game-design courses. A specialized kit is included containing many ready-made lessons/samplers in the following categories: scripts, GUI controls, interfaces, HUDs (heads-up displays), and all of the major 3D/engine topics discussed in the guides. All lessons can be extended, and new lessons can be added with relatively little effort.

1.2.1 Summary

This book is intended as a starting point for the completely new user, but it is also suitable for the user who is moderately experienced with Torque already.

It has the following chapters:

- **Part I: Introduction**
  - **Chapter 1: Introduction**
- **Part II: Engine Overview**
  - **Chapter 2: Torque From 10,000 Feet.** This chapter gives the ten-minute description of Torque and introduces the new user to important concepts and terminology.
  - **Chapter 3: Torque Tools.** Here, we discuss all of the built-in tools and establish an understanding of how to use the TGE kit in editing mode.
  - **Chapter 4: Introduction to TorqueScript.** Here, we introduce the embedded scripting language that comes with TGE. This chapter covers the complete syntax and the major concepts required to work with this scripting language.
- **Part III: Game Elements**
  - **Chapter 5: Torque Core Classes.** This chapter examines the core scripted classes and their importance in the hierarchy, structure, and behavior of the engine.
  - **Chapter 6: Basic Game Classes.** Here we cover the basic classes used to represent shapes, images, and interiors.
  - **Chapter 7: Gameplay Classes.** This chapter reviews the classes through which we implement game interactions that define the gameplay. We also introduce important game-design concepts like the inventory.
  - **Chapter 8: Mission Objects.** TGE provides a myriad of object classes. In this chapter, we discuss all of the mission/game/level placeable objects that have not yet been discussed, excluding special effects.
  - **Chapter 9: Game-Setup Scripting.** Here we work through in-depth discussions of critical scripting classes and features that are associated with setting up and maintaining a game.
  - **Chapter 10: Gameplay Scripting.** In this last scripting chapter, we examine a variety of scripting functions, examining how they work and providing the context in which they contribute to gameplay.
  - **Chapter 11: Special Effects.** This chapter splits out several classes used for audio and visual special effects.
  - **Chapter 12: Standard TGE GUI Controls.** In this chapter, we discuss the 32 most important GUI controls.
  - **Chapter 13: Game Interfaces.** This follow-on chapter builds on the last chapter and walks through the creation of two sets of themed game interfaces. Each set includes a splash screen, a main menu, and a credits screen. We also specify and design three types of HUD to show that complex HUDs can readily be created from basic TGE controls.

- **Part IV: Making The Game**
  - **Chapter 14: Putting It All Together.** Here, we build a complete single-player game prototype. We plan the game; accumulate many of the example scripts, shapes, interiors, and interfaces created in the prior chapters; and glue them all together with a small set of gameplay-specific scripts.
- **Appendices.** In order to facilitate the learning process and to fill the role of reference, an extensive set of appendices is included in electronic form. These appendices include complete references of game class fields and methods, console functions, callbacks, and GUI controls, to name a few.

1.3 What This Guide Does Not Contain

This guide obviously does not contain the answer to every question that every person who uses Torque can come up with. My hope is that it contains enough information and is accessible enough that you can learn how to answer these unanswered questions on your own. However, sometimes that just isn't going to happen, so a "Getting Help" appendix has been included to assist you. First, though, let's determine what you should know before starting.

1.4 What You Should Know Before Reading This Guide

Ah, the fateful question, "What do you, the reader, need to know?" First, understand that this guide is here to help you, but you are going to have to do some real work to learn what it has to tell you.

TANSTAAFL: There ain't no such thing as a free lunch.   **—Robert Heinlein**

Second, since this guide is aimed at a broad audience, I have created a pseudo-matrix below listing topics you should at least be passingly familiar with based on your role in your team.

Who Are You?	Some Stuff You Ought To Know
I'm like, the artist, dude.	• Basic modeling and animation concepts: convex vs. concave, skeletal animations, texture (IFL) animations, blended animations. • At least one modeling tool in this list: MilkShape 3D (MS3D), 3ds Max, Maya, or gameSpace/trueSpace. (Yes, there are other options; see appendix.) • If the only tool (in the prior list) you know is MS3D, then be sure to add QuArK, Cartography Shop, or Hammer to your list. • More? Sorry, this isn't an art guide. In fact, you probably know more about art than I do!

Who Are You?	Some Stuff You Ought To Know
I'm the programmer, man. You got any Dewsky?	• C/C++ • Scripting in Perl, TCL, or perhaps another game-engine scripting language. • Math. If you flinch when I say algebra, geometry, trigonometry, vectors, matrices, or Cauchy-Schwartz inequality (OK, you can flinch on that last one), *MathWorld* (http://mathworld.wolfram.com/) is your friend. • If you are familiar with client-server architectures and simulation concepts, you will have a great head start.
I am the game designer. Enter my world…	• The limitations of your target system(s) as well as **the limit on the speed of light**. Sure, your team can probably make a 4096-player RFMMOTTTG (really freakin' massively multiplayer online tick-tack-toe game), but you probably don't want to. I'm only partly joking here. If this is your first game and you are the idea guy or gal, keep it realistic. There is real work in making a game. • The limits of the tools your team's programmers, artists, and other folks use to implement your ideas.
Me da boss.	• What the…? Why are you reading this… er, I mean you should know of course, Sir/Madam/Other, every member on your team will need two copies of this guide. One for work and one for home. We can't have people getting hernias carrying these back and forth.
Jack of all trades (JOAT), AKA lone wolf.	• This guide is specifically written for you (and for small teams). You will need to know everything on the list above (excluding da boss). Also, be sure to look at the reference appendix and get your hands on some of those books and resources. You've got a real challenge ahead of you, but you can do it!

1.5 How To Obtain Torque (Licensing Torque)

OK, so you're sold. You've bought this book (please tell me you're not standing in the bookstore still deciding…).

Whatever the case, you have decided that this Torque thing sounds like a good deal. To get your hands on this state-of-the-art engine, simply do the following:

1. Visit the GarageGames website: http://www.garagegames.com/.
2. Follow the links to the products page.
3. Add Torque to your cart.
4. Click the "Buy Now" button and follow the instructions.

9

1.6 Getting Started, One Step at a Time ...

On first picking up the Torque Game Engine, you may be somewhat overwhelmed. If asked, most GarageGames members will probably admit that they were, too, and so was I. The fact is, this engine and all the associated files are massive. Just doing a quick count on the current version of the code brings up the following metrics (counts may vary):

- 2329 source files containing 593,930 lines ($\sim$325k lines of code and $\sim$167k lines of comments),
- 322 script files containing 49,856 lines of script ($\sim$37k lines of of script, and $\sim$7k lines of comments), and
- this guide comes with a kit that adds another 187 script files containing 19,566 lines of script ($\sim$11k lines of script, and $\sim$5k lines of comments).

No matter how you twist it, turn it, chop it, or sort it, Torque is big. Big not only in raw size but in features. However, approached with an inquisitive mind, and with the understanding that nothing is free, especially an understanding of the ins and outs of this engine, *you can master Torque.*

1.7 The GarageGames Community and Resources

I've stated this in more than one forum, and I must state it here: the GarageGames community is excellent. I continue to be impressed on a daily basis by how well attended the forums are and how quickly people give answers to questions. The GarageGames site provides several resources.

- **Forums.** These are areas where you can post questions, ideas, general complaints, etc. To date, there have been tens of thousands of posts. At last count (not including forums dedicated to released games), there were 12 major forum categories containing 64 subcategories.
- **Resources.** These are community submitted items including scripts, code, web links, books that are good to read, accumulated references, and more. These resources are organized by date and rating (among other categories).
- **News.** The GarageGames site has a news page and a newsletter. Very cool.

1.8 Conventions

Throughout the guide, I will attempt to align my naming conventions and terminology with those you will encounter in the official Torque SDK (software development kit) documents and elsewhere on the GarageGames site. In the cases where this is not possible, I will make it clear that the names/terms in use are of my own invention.

1.8.1 Icons Legend: Warnings, Notes, and Expert Tips

Throughout this guide, you will be presented with side notes of various forms. Some of these will be warnings of odd or misleading behavior, others will be notes on interesting bits or facts, and some will be expert tips for those who want to explore the edges of Torque's behaviors. You will be able to recognize these side notes by looking for the following icons.

Warning   **Note**   **Expert Tip**

1.8.2 Game-Building Lessons

Throughout the guide, you will find sections marked as one of the following:

1. **Maze Runner Lesson *#123* (90 Percent Step).** If you intend to make the game at the end of the guide, you must complete these lessons. They construct game elements without which the game will not function.

2. **Maze Runner Lesson *#123* (10 Percent Step).** These lessons are considered optional when making the initial version of the game. If you should choose to skip them, the game will still be playable but may be a bit rough around the edges.

These lessons will be largely independent of each other, but if a lesson depends on another lesson, the numeric ID of the lesson, as well as the chapter it is in, will be referenced.

Combined Lessons Appendix

For those who want the entire lesson set in one place, all of the lessons from the printed chapters, up to but not including Chapter 14, are included in the "Combined Lessons" electronic appendix.

Skip Ahead!

To learn about the motivation for the above lesson titles, and to learn what the game will be, please skip ahead to Chapter 14. There, you should read Section 14.1, "Maze Runner: A Simple Single-Player Game," which includes the following.

- **Game Elements.** Here, we will briefly discuss the concept of a *game element*.

- **Game Goals, Rules, and Mechanics.** Next, we will explore the motivation for planning a game's goals, rules, and mechanics before we write the game. Then, we will do this planning for our game.

- **Setting up our workspace.** Before we can start working on the lessons, we need to set up a workspace. In this section, I will instruct you on what steps are required to prepare for the lessons.

- **90 Percent or 10 Percent?** Lastly, I will give you an overview of the 90 percent versus the 10 percent steps and why these ideas matter.

So, skip ahead; it's OK. When you're done, you can come back and start learning about Torque!

Engine Overview

Part II

Chapter 2
Torque from 10,000 Feet

The Torque Game Engine (TGE) has a long legacy. In its various incarnations, it has been used to make both non-networked single-player games and networked multiplayer games. Today, TGE has the following features.

- **Single-player and multiplayer ready.** TGE is based on a standard client-server architecture and is fully scalable to 128 players and beyond.

- **Raster-based graphics.** TGE is not shader based but has the capability to incorporate any features you desire (you have the source code). Furthermore, it is the predecessor to the Torque Shader Engine (TSE), and thus most things learned using TGE will apply to TSE.

- **Event-driven simulation.** TGE is designed around an event-driven simulator. It utilizes separate client and server event loops. Additionally, most game logic and GUI logic is driven by an event system.

- **Memory and network bandwidth efficient.** TGE is designed to have a reduced memory footprint and an accompanying low-bandwidth requirement per connection. It utilizes static datablocks for common information and network compression plus transmission-reduction algorithms.

- **Broad functionality.** Because of its long heritage, TGE comes ready with most of the methods and functions required for standard game calculations, actions, and responses.

- **Fully integrated.** TGE incorporates all the code required to render/play/capture all game elements, including GUIs, sound, 3D graphics, and other I/O (input/output). It also includes a large and expanding set of content creation and debugging tools out of the box.

2.1 TGE Terms and Concepts

When you first start working with TGE, you will come across terms like *interior, shape, datablock, portal, IFL, image,* etc. Some of these words have TGE specific meanings, others are industry-standard terms, and a small set are hybrid terms with meanings in both worlds. Either way, if you are not very experienced, just trying to figure out what these terms are may be a big challenge. To help ease this transition, we will run through some of the more confusing terms and concepts you will encounter while working with TGE. For a more extensive list of terms, see the "Glossary Of Terms" appendix.

2.1.1 Shapes and DTSs (TGE Term)

A shape, also known as a DTS object, is a model created using a polygon (or equivalent) editor. Such models may have

- skeletal animations (see Section 2.1.8, "Animations: Blended vs. Non-Blended"),
- multiple skins (textures),
- animated skins,
- visibility animations,
- multiple levels of detail (see Section 2.1.5, "Level of Detail"),
- translucent and/or transparent components,
- multiple collision boxes (see Section 2.1.6, "Collision Detection"),
- and much more.

This is the first of two model categories used by TGE. DTS, which stands for the Dynamix Threespace Shape, is both the shorthand notation for this concept and the file extension (e.g., player.dts). Shapes are generally used to represent nonstructural entities such as players, power-ups, trees, and vehicles. Shapes can be created with 3ds Max, MilkShape, or Caligari's gameSpace/trueSpace, to name just a few possible content-creation tools. See the GarageGames website to learn how this is done and to find the proper exporter for your content tool(s).

Non-DTS Renderers?

Some users have complained that they would rather use an alternate format instead of being "forced" to use the DTS format. This is entirely possible. Users have already produced alternate mesh renderers to include such formats as 3DS and MS3D. If you have a favorite format and are familiar with how it works, you can simply pick up one of the previously mentioned mesh renderers and modify it for your own format.

Shapes in Our Game

In the prototype for our game, we will need just a few shapes: a player, coins, maze blocks, and fireballs.

- **An avatar or player**. The lesson kit comes with Joe Maruschak's "Blue Guy" (Figure 2.1, left), but we will not be using him beyond a quick introduction. Why? In order to demonstrate the minimum set of animations that need to be included to make the shape work with the Player class, we will make the "Simplest Player" (Figure 2.1, right), a simple geometric shape.
- **Pick-ups, maze blocks, and fireball blocks.** In our game, we will also require shapes to represent coins that we can pick up. Also, we will need

Figure 2.1.
Simple Player shapes.

Blue Guy   Simplest player

Figure 2.2.
Required shapes and blocks.

Coins   Maze blocks   Fireball blocks

a variety of blocks and obstacles (fireball blocks) to build our mazes from (see Figure 2.2).

2.1.2 Interiors and DIFs (TGE Term)

Interiors are models created using convex (see Section 2.1.3, "Convex vs. Concave") brushes.

The InteriorInstance class, frequently referred to simply as Interior(s), is used to display models that represent any structural object, to include such things as buildings, bridges, walls, and other large structures. The motivation for this name comes from the fact that these objects can have an actual inside, i.e., interior.

This modeling technique is used to solve a few technical issues associated with creating large and geometrically complex models that are intended to be entered by other models (or the camera). Some of the biggest technical problems solved by this technique are the following.

- **Efficient collision detection.** Binary space partitioning (BSP) trees are generated and used for detecting collisions against Interior objects. BSP trees provide a very efficient way of determining object collision, one of the most CPU-intensive processes a real-time application performs.

- **Visibility culling.** This technique also provides numerous shortcuts for culling of visibility through the use of portals (see Section 2.1.7, "Portals") so that rooms and terrain that the player can't see don't get sent to the graphics card for rendering. This is a lot harder to do, from a mathematical standpoint, than a nonprogrammer might imagine.

- **Efficient lighting.** Finally, this technique "regularizes" (to abuse the English language a bit) the process of calculating lighting and shading as affected by the presence of the model in the game world.

DIF, which stands for Dynamix Interior Format, is both a shorthand notation for the same concept and the extension for these files (e.g., myBuilding.dif).

Interiors can be created with QuArK, Worldcraft/Hammer, 3ds Max, MilkShape (not advised), or Caligari's gameSpace/trueSpace. See the GarageGames website to learn how this is done and to find the proper exporter for your content tool(s).

2.1.3 Convex vs. Concave (Industry Terms)

In TGE, all collision meshes must be convex, not concave. The trouble is, many people either do not know what these terms are or cannot remember how to identify a convex or concave mesh.

Finding the parts of a mesh that are concave (making it a bad collision mesh) can be frustrating at best. Therefore, you can follow this simple rule when making collision meshes:

If any **line segment** on the mesh, when extended infinitely in both directions, **passes through** the **interior of** your mesh, the **collision mesh** is concave and therefore **bad**.

Or the shorter version:

Line segment passes through interior of collision mesh ... bad (Figure 2.3).

Figure 2.3.

Using line segments to discover concavity.

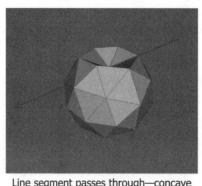

Line segment passes through—concave   Problem solved—convex

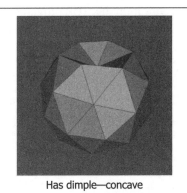
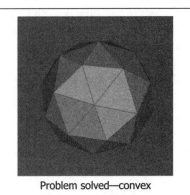

Has dimple—concave   Problem solved—convex

Figure 2.4.
Using dimples to find concavity.

Alternatively, you can examine your mesh and look for dimples, that is, regions where the surface curves inward. (Figure 2.4)

2.1.4 Convex Brush (Industry Term)

A convex brush is a single instance of some regular convex geometry. Convex brushes are combined to create models that can then be converted into an interior. In TGE, any one interior may be composed of many hundreds or even thousands of convex brushes.

2.1.5 Level of Detail (Industry Term)

Often referred to as simply LOD, level of detail pertains to the complexity of a 3D model relative to the current viewing distance to that model. This complexity increases or decreases as the camera (the viewer) moves nearer to or farther from a shape, respectively.

In TGE, both Shapes and Interiors support the ability to automatically substitute new models for a Shape or Interior as the distance from the Shape/Interior changes. These substituted models should have fewer polygons as the distance increases. This has the effect of reducing the rendering load for distant objects, increasing overall frame rates. Properly done, this allows for the creation of complex and densely populated indoor, outdoor, and mixed scenes.

2.1.6 Collision Detection, or COLDET (Industry Term)

Collision detection (COLDET) can loosely be described as the process of detecting when two or more objects (in the simulated world) come into contact with each other. COLDET is a feature that enables interactivity in the game world. TGE (1.4 +) supports a number of unlimited collision detection bounding shapes for polygon models. This means that the level of COLDET

19

interaction is completely under your control. Additionally, TGE provides auto-mated generation of COLDET structures for some Shapes and for Interiors, thus reducing your responsibility while not reducing flexibility.

Collisions in Our Game

Like many games, our game relies on collisions for parts of the interactive experience. In particular, we will want our player to be "killed" if he is struck by a fireball. We will want the player to be able to pick up coins and grenades, which are part of the game's objective.

2.1.7 Portals (Industry Term)

As was noted above when we discussed Interiors, TGE supports portalized rendering of interior models. That is, Interiors support the insertion of portals. These portals will divide an interior into sectors.

In Figure 2.5, we have a single interior with four rooms, numbered 0 through 3. There are three doors in this interior. The thin lines in the picture are portals situated within the doors that connect each room.

In Room 0, there is an observer A, and in Room 2 there is an observer B.

Observer A is facing the door between Rooms 0 and 1. Because a ray cast from Observer A's position can penetrate both the portal between Rooms 0 and 1 as well as the portal between 1 and 3, all three rooms (0, 1, and 3) must be rendered for Observer A, but Room 2 does not need to be rendered.

Observer B is facing the door between Rooms 2 and 3. Because a raycast from Observer B's position can only penetrate the portal between rooms 2 and 3, only these two rooms (2 and 3) need to be rendered for observer B. The other two rooms (0 and 1) do not need to be rendered.

In both of the above cases, if no portals were used, or if the feature were not available, for both Observer A and Observer B, all four rooms would need to be rendered.

2.1.8 Animations: Blended vs. Non-Blended (Industry Terms)

In TGE, meshes (models) are animated using skeletal animation. The engine supports two styles of skeletal animation: absolute (non-blended) and blended.

In simplest terms, absolute animations override all prior animations of all joints that the absolute animation affects. For example, we have an animated arrow. This arrow has a base position, a non-blended animation to the left, and a blended animation to the right. Assume that the left and right anima-tions are equal and opposite each other.

Figure 2.5.

Interior with portals.

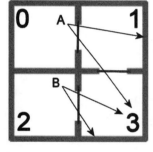

If we play the sequences in Table 2.1, we get the listed results.

Sequence(s)	Result
Non-blended	Arrow leans left.
Blended	Arrow leans right.
Blended followed by non-blended	Arrow leans left.
Non-blended followed by blended	Arrow back in base position (straight up).
Non-blended followed by non-blended	Arrow leans left, just as if it were non-blended only once.
Blended followed by blended	Arrow leans twice as far right as single blended.

Table 2.1.

Blended and non-blended animations.

In Chapter 7, "Gameplay Classes," we will build some real animations, but if you wish to learn more, I suggest perusing some of the online animation docs at GarageGames and/or purchasing BraveTree: Girl Pack (see "Favorite Resources" appendix for details on where to find these).

2.1.9 Image File Lists, or IFLs (TGE Term)

Another kind of animation supported by TGE is texture animation. The premise of this animation style is that the engine will swap the current texture for another at fixed time intervals, thereby animating the texture in question.

This animation is accomplished by specifying texture names in a special way, identifying the texture as an IFL-driven texture (in the model definition). Then, a text file is supplied (by the modeler), specifying the names of the textures to use and the number of frames to play each texture. Beyond this, the animation sequence is played like any other animation.

2.1.10 Callbacks (Industry Term)

For the purpose of this guide, a callback is any console method (scripted function associated with an object in the game world) that is automatically (or directly) called by the engine (or scripts) in response to some event. These callbacks are part of what drives a game.

Callbacks in Our Game

Although we do not strictly focus on callbacks in this guide, several of them will be required to complete our game. Therefore, at the appropriate time, we will take a little time out to discuss and clarify those callbacks that are in fact needed: `onCollision()`, `onPickup()`, and others.

2.1.11 2D and 3D Sound (Industry Term)

In the GarageGames forums, online documentation, and in this guide, you will see references to sound as being either two-dimensional (2D), or three-dimensional (3D). Although odd sounding (no pun intended), these concepts are quite simple.

A 2D sound is a sound that has no apparent origin, and when played, will play equally loud from the left and the right speaker (assuming you have only two).

A 3D sound has (at a minimum) an origin associated with it and is thus transformed and attenuated based on the listener's location relative to the sound's source. That is, 3D sound may play more loudly from one speaker than the other(s).

Please note that 3D sounds can have several other factors associated with them, and that this code exists in the engine. However, all other specialized 3D sound effects are not (by default) compiled into the engine.

Sounds in Our Game

Our game would not be complete without sounds, both for the interfaces and for the game itself. So, we will take time out in later chapters to walk through the setup of the following sounds:

- **Splash-screen music (2D non-networked).** This sound plays when the splash screen is displayed.
- **Button-over and button-press feedback (2D non-networked).** These sounds play to indicate that the mouse has moved over a button, or that a button has been pressed.
- **In-game music (2D non-networked).** We will learn to play music client side.
- **Fireball warning (3D networked).** This sound will be played when a fireball is about to shoot and will give warning in advance of the action. It is the only networked and the only 3D sound we will work on.

2.1.12 Missions (TGE Term)

In the gaming world, there are many words used to described similar things. One of those things is a game level. In Torque, a game may have one level or many. These levels are called missions.

Another way to come to grips with the mission concept is to understand what goes into a mission file. Mission files (stored under the data directory) have the extension .mis. If you were to open one of these files, you would see that it contains a script that is creating and placing content. So in effect, a mission can be thought of as a collection of content that is loaded by the engine upon request. In fact, in most games, the mission is the primary means of loading the initial content such as the terrain, sky, sun, etc. Subsequently, game setup and gameplay scripts may be used to add and remove content, but we get our start by loading a mission.

Do I Have to Use Missions?

Well, you don't actually have to use this construct, but it is the best way to get the base portions of a level/game/etc. loaded. So, if you are expert enough, you can dynamically build the entire level/game/etc., but I do not suggest it.

How Big Can a Mission Be?

It is worth noting that a Torque mission can be extremely large. In fact, I know that one of the GarageGames employees (Matt Fairfax), as part of some research he was doing, loaded all of the interiors from every level in *Quake II*™ simultaneously into a single Torque mission. He mentioned that there was no noticeable dip in frame-rate nor did the engine lag at all. This was in fact a small test of the true power and capabilities of the engine.

Missions in Our Game

Our game will utilize a single mission. It will load a terrain, the sky, a sun (lighting definition), celestial bodies, and various other atmospheric effects.

Subsequent to the initial load, we will be using scripts to dynamically load and unload content from our mission. That is, we will stay in the same mission but use scripts to build and rebuild levels of the game, without ever reloading the mission.

2.1.13 Event-Driven Simulator (Industry Term)

TGE, like all other game engines, is a simulator. If you are at all familiar with the concept of simulation, you will know that there are different types of simulators.

TGE is an event-driven simulator. In other words, all engine actions are caused by some kind of event. There are a variety of events that TGE is aware of and which we will discuss as we continue through this book. These events are enqueued into one of three queues (depending on the event type) and then processed by the engine in the order in which they occurred.

At this point, the important thing to understand is that events drive the game world and thus all of your game scripting, and coding should be designed with that in mind.

2.1.14 Ticks (TGE Term)

In TGE, time is measured in terms of wall-clock time, that is, multiples of milliseconds (ms). Additionally, TGE measures in simulation time. Simulation time is called *tick time* or simply *ticks*.

Because TGE is effectively an event-driven simulator, it cannot always guarantee that events will occur on specific wall-clock time boundaries. Tick time provides a new measure of time that is under the control of the engine itself, allowing it to guarantee that all objects will get their allocated number of ticks and that they will be ticked in the proper order. The elegance of this solution trivializes the significance of this problem. Just understand, without a solution to the guarantee problem, it is for all practical purposes impossible to simulate a multiplayer interactive world, not to mention the problem of handling the additional burden introduced by a networked environment.

Generally speaking, a standard TGE tick is equal to 32 ms, by default. Events occurring on tick boundaries will normally experience an actual tick time of 32 ms, plus or minus 1 to 3 ms.

> Be aware that the granularity of a tick can be changed to suit your own game (or other) needs; i.e., tick times of 2 ms, 16 ms, 64 ms, or even 128 ms are all legal tick times.

2.1.15 Client-Server Architecture (Industry Term)

It is important to understand the architecture used by a game engine as it affects the decisions you, the game designer/programmer/scripter, will make. In the context of a game engine, the term architecture can be loosely translated as, "the organization of the game systems." In other words, "What parts of the engine do what tasks?"

TGE implements a client-server architecture. When we talk about a client-server architecture, we're talking about an organization wherein one part of the engine acts as a sort of controller (the server) and the other part of the engine acts as a controllee (the client).

While executing, the client and the server may either co-exist in the same executable, execute separately on the same machine, or execute separately on separate machines connected over a network.

For a standard client-server architecture, there will always be one server while there may be many clients. The server is aware of all clients, and the clients may or may not be aware of each other.

The client-server architecture is suitable for both single-player and multiplayer games. We will discuss variations on executable "modes" and "interconnects" momentarily.

Why Use a Client-Server Architecture?

This architecture has become common in the game industry for a few reasons.

- First, because it provides a meaningful and understandable way of dividing labor and resources.
- Second, because (as stated previously) it is suitable for both single-player games and multiplayer games. This means that a game can be designed for both single play and multiplay without herculean effort.
- Third, because, in the case of multiplayer games, this architecture scales well for N players, where N can be up to 128 or higher.

This architecture does have *some* drawbacks when writing a single-player game such as unneeded duplication of objects (see Section 2.1.17), and some added control complexity. However, the multiplayer benefits far outweigh these considerations. Also, it cannot be stated too often, having the ability to take a single-player game to the multiplayer arena with few or no changes is well worth the added complexity.

The TGE Client-Server Modes and Connection Schemes

Torque implements the client-server model using a single executable. That is, whenever the engine is run, it contains both a server and a client. In order to implement different game types, the server or the client can effectively be disabled. In essence, the engine can be run in one of the four modes shown in Figure 2.6.

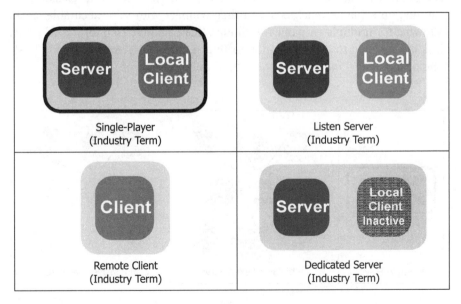

Figure 2.6.
Modes for running Torque

The observant reader will point out, "The single-player and listen-server modes look quite similar." You are in fact correct.

In fact, in the single-player image, the implication is that there is a server, but it has not yet been activated. This activation will not occur until a connection is requested by the client. Also note, in single-player mode, the server will not accept external connection requests. The listen server, on the other hand, does have an active server, and it will accept both internal and external connection requests.

Given these four modes, a game can be interconnected using one of three connection schemes. The connection scheme we select is based on the game type we wish to run.

The simplest game type is the single-player game (Figure 2.7a). This is accomplished by running a single instance of the executable on one machine. In this case, the server and client connect via an internal (local) connection. When this connection is requested, the server becomes active.

The second game type involves a single executable with an active client and an active server running on one machine as a listen server (Figure 2.7b) One player (the hosting player) uses the local client and a local connection. The remaining players use client-only executables, running on separate machines, and connect remotely to the listen server. This mode is appropriate for LAN (local-area network) parties and other cases where a user wants to host a game while participating.

The last game type involves a single executable running as a dedicated server (only the server is active; Figure 2.7c). Multiple client-only executables, running on separate machines, can then connect with this executable, again allowing for multiplayer games. Although this could be used for a LAN party, it is more suited to a professional hosting setup, where your company hosts one or more sessions on a machine used only as a server.

Figure 2.7.

Client-server interconnection diagrams.

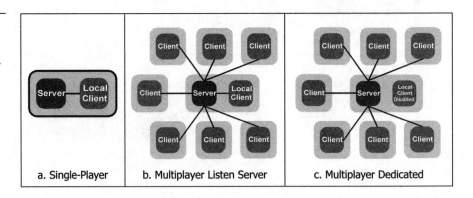

a. Single-Player   b. Multiplayer Listen Server   c. Multiplayer Dedicated

Master Servers (Industry Term)

In the two above multiplayer connection schemes, the remote connections may be on a LAN or across the Internet. In the latter instance, another server is required, namely a master server. It is the job of this specialized server to assist clients in locating game servers.

TGE Client-Server Division of Labor

As was noted above, using a client-server architecture allows one to divide both labor and the location of resources (assets). Table 2.2 shows a summarized listing of the labor division between the TGE client and server.

Task Category	Client Responsibilities	Server Responsibilities
Sound	2D sounds	3D sounds
Input	Capture and pre-process	Post-process and determine response
GUI rendering	All processing and rendering	None
Game rendering	All	None
Animations	Non-authoritative prediction	Authoritative calculations and interactions
Collision detection	Non-authoritative prediction	Authoritative calculations and responses
Game content	• Interfaces • Ownership of content.	• Players, vehicles, weapons, etc. • (Optional) validation of all content
Game decisions and calculations	Limited to things that **do not affect** gameplay, such as particle effect calculations	All decisions regarding object creation, deletion, movement, damage, etc.

Table 2.2.

Division of labor between TGE client and server.

In short, the client is responsible for all tasks *except* those that affect gameplay or those that require spatial calculations in the game world.

Client-Server Communications

This book focuses on making a single-player game and thus does not discuss networking in any great detail. However, it is important to avoid forming bad habits. One of these bad habits is direct manipulation of server data/routines from the client and vice versa. Thus, in Chapter 10 we will talk briefly about how to execute server functions from the client and how to execute client functions from the server.

2.1.16 Objects (Industry Term)

Throughout this guide, you will see the term object being used to refer all kinds of things, including GUI controls, shapes, interiors, and various scripting elements. This may be confusing, but in Torque, all classes used to implement the game are in fact engine objects. Some objects are accessible via the console, and therefore scripts. Some are only accessible internally (by writing C++). In this book, we are only interested in the former.

2.1.17 Ghosts, Control Objects, and Scoping (TGE Terms)

When we are playing a singleplayer or a multiplayer game, all objects are created on the server and then some of these objects are duplicated on the client. These duplicates are called *ghosts* (Figure 2.8).

The duplication of objects as ghosts on the client(s) is controlled by scoping. Each client that attaches to a server must define a single control object. Generally, this control object is some type of avatar (biped, vehicle, or other), but it may also be a camera. Regardless, this control object is responsible for scoping (Figure 2.9).

Scoping, in TGE terms, is the act of determining which objects in the game world are visible, audible, and otherwise required to be present for the current control object to correctly interact with the game world. These objects will be ghosted to the client for that control object and subsequently maintained.

This description trivializes the act of scoping to some degree, but it does describe the essence of what it means and what it does. I will repeat it, but for now be aware that *your game must have a control object*, otherwise it will be unable to render the game world.

Figure 2.8.

Ghosts on the client.

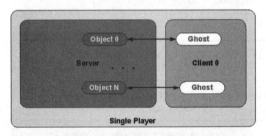

Figure 2.9.

Control objects.

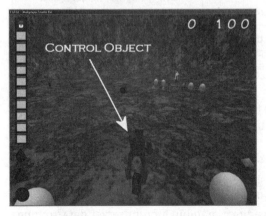

2.1.18 Datablock (TGE Term)

In addition to normal objects, there is a special category of objects called datablocks. Datablocks are special for the following reasons.

- All datablocks are duplicated from the server to each client.
- A datablock XYZ on the server with ID 123 is guaranteed to have the same name XYZ and ID 123 on all clients.
- Datablocks are transmitted to clients at the beginning of a game and not updated after that, making them in effect static.
- Datablocks have special scripting properties, which we will discuss later.
- Because the content of a datablock is controlled by the server and not the client, they are an efficient means of preventing cheating (clients modifying their own game abilities and statistics).

You may ask, "Why do I really need these datablocks?" and that is a valid question. In answer, please consider the following theoretical example.

In game ABC, a multiplayer game, players are allowed to "create" a variety of wheeled vehicles. Each of these vehicles has between four and eight tires, skins, special effects (sounds, dust emitters, etc.), and a rather lengthy list of physical attributes. The complete structure describing these vehicles has a memory size of approximately 2048 bytes (2 KB).

At any time during the game, in which there are up to 32 participants, a player (client) may create a new vehicle. With a client-server architecture, this would require that the server create the object and then ghost all of its data to the player. It is easy to see that in the worst case, where all of the players are within visible range of the other players, the server might have to simultaneously ghost 32 x 2048 bytes of data to *each* of the 32 clients to inform them of the update. This translates to an update of 2 MB of data that would be required nearly *instantly*. In addition to all of the move update information and other ghost updates that would be happening, it can be seen that this game would quickly lag out (halt due to lack of bandwidth).

Now, let us reexamine this example, introducing datablocks. The datablock will predefine all of the vehicle data. This datablock is transmitted once and only once (at the beginning of the game), still accruing the 2 MB penalty. However, to dynamically create a new vehicle, we only need to send a small packet of data, including the ID of the datablock, an initial creation position, and some other miscellaneous data. An estimated size for this packet is roughly 64 bytes. Now, our total simultaneous bandwidth requirement is: 32 x 32 x 64 bytes = 64 KB. This is a much more reasonable number and would be easily handled even on a system using a modem.

Engine Overview

2.2 Finding Your Assets

Game assets are things such as sound files, graphics files, game models, skins for the models, client scripts, server scripts, etc. Deciding how these assets will be organized is one of the most important decisions we will make while planning our game. I kid you not. How we organize our assets can have a significant effect on our productivity as well as our game's final disk footprint.

Unfortunately, deciding on an organizational scheme requires some experience and a plan. So, if this is your first time making a game, it may be a bit hard to do. I suggest you follow the organization used by the FPS Starter Kit to start and then, when you have accrued some experience, draw up your own plan, based on your game's specific needs.

Our sample game will use the Standard TGE Kit as a base.

2.2.1 Finding Assets—TGE FPS Starter Kit

The FPS Starter Kit that comes with TGE has the major directories and directory contents shown in Table 2.3.

Table 2.3.

FPS Starter Kit directories.

The organization of these directories is by no means fixed or in any way magical. As I mentioned earlier, when you become more experienced, you may begin to modify this structure significantly, perhaps doing away with the "common" directory, or incorporating features from other directories where it suits your organizational scheme.

Directory Name	Contents
/	This is the root directory and represents the directory from which the executable was run. This is the highest directory visible to TGE and scripts. It isn't necessarily the same as the root directory on your disk.
/common	This directory contains files that are common between games. The intention here is that these scripts, images, models, etc., are reused at least in prototypes and often in final games.
/creator	This directory contains the built-in tool scripts, GUIs, and other assets.
/starter.fps	This is the game directory (sometimes referred to as a mod directory) and includes all of the scripts, images, models, etc. used in your game. The results of our effort will be stored in subdirectories of this.
/starter.fps/client	This directory contains all of the interface art, GUI definitions, local preference files, and scripts that relate to the client's behavior.
/starter.fps/data	This directory contains models, skins, mission definitions, terrain files, and terrain textures.
/starter.fps/server	This directory contains gameplay scripts.

2.2.2 Finding Assets—Included Lesson Kit

Because the assets that come with this guide are quite extensive and shared between many portions of the kit, the asset chart is too large to print in the guide. Please refer to the "Lesson Kit Assets" electronic appendix for a complete listing and discussion of what assets there are and where they live.

2.3 Sim Hierarchy Overview

As noted previously, TGE is in effect an event-driven simulator. This is made quite clear by the fact that the class structure starts with a class aptly named SimObject (simulation object). This class and its children form the "sim hierarchy." The sim hierarchy can be roughly divided as follows.

- **SimObject.** This is the root class for all simulation objects, that is, all objects that are used to implement a game.
- **SimSet and SimGroup.** Two container classes, the latter acting as base class to the GuiControls and to ScriptGroup.
- **ScriptObject and ScriptGroup.** Two classes used to create scripted classes. These special classes give us the ability to associate fields and methods with scripted classes, thus allowing us to neatly compartmentalize our scripts.
- **SceneObject.** This class is the root class for all objects to be included in the game scene and adds the concepts of position, rendering, and collision.
- **GameBase.** This class is the root to most mission-placeable objects and introduces ticking and datablocks.
- **ShapeBase, ShapeBaseData, and Children.** The ShapeBase classes and children are used to display models. These models are used to represent small world objects, players, vehicles, pick-ups, power-ups, etc. These classes all support complex visible geometry/features and an unlimited number of collision meshes.
- **TSStatic.** This is a lightweight shape-rendering class that does not incorporate any of the ShapeBase features. It merely renders a shape and encapsulates it in a simple object-oriented bounding box. This is the preferred class for noninteractive shapes that are used to add detail in scenes.
- **Interiors.** This class is used to display models that represent any structural object, including such things as buildings, bridges, walls, and other large structures. This class supports standard binary space partitioning of the models. Interiors support portals for more efficient subdivision of rendered spaces.
- **Special Effects.** A last set of classes are supplied that do not fit into either the shape or interior hierarchies. These classes are used to provide a wide set of possible special effects, including audio, visual, and physical (as affects avatars and other game objects) effects.

2.4 TGE I/O Fundamentals

Out of the box, TGE supports inputs from mice and keyboards. With a little work, it will support inputs from gamepads, joysticks, and other input devices as well. TGE also supports basic file I/O out of the box.

2.4.1 TGE Device Input Architecture

When we speak of inputs in the context of TGE, we are talking about user inputs from keyboards, mice, joysticks, and other devices. Although it is possible for there to be other types of inputs, the only ones we are interested in are those that would be used to control gameplay. That said, inputs flow into and through TGE as follows (see Figure 2.10):

- The OS (operating system) processes inputs and passes them to the TGE Platform Layer.
- The TGE Platform Layer identifies and categorizes the inputs, then passes them on to the Game.
- The Game processes the inputs if it can, or ignores them if there are no defined actions associated with them.

Game input processing is the part we are interested in. As can be seen in Figure 2.10, the input is processed as follows:

1. The GlobalActionMap (see below) gets first dibs on the inputs. If it has no mapping for an input, that input is passed on to the GUIs, or more specifically the Canvas.

2. The Canvas attempts to process an input, but passes it on if there is no GUI control(s) programmed to use said input.

3. Lastly, the input is passed to any active (nonglobal) ActionMaps for processing. If none of the currently stacked ActionMaps is coded to use the input, the input is dropped.

Figure 2.10.

Torque input/output architecture.

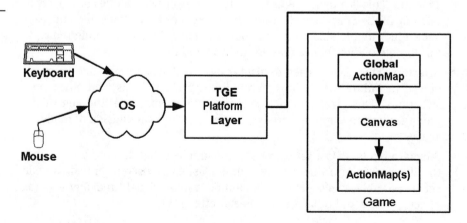

ActionMaps

ActionMaps are a special class designed to capture and redirect inputs. There are two kinds of ActionMap. There is the GlobalActionMap and the normal ActionMap. The main differences between these are:

- **GlobalActionMap.** This is the daddy of input processors and supersedes all other processing methods. This action map should not be popped from the processing stack (see below).
- **ActionMap.** This is a generic action map. It takes lower priority than all other processing methods. These action maps can be pushed and popped from the processing stack as the game's requirements change.

ActionMaps in Our Game

Our game will require some kind of mapping between keyboard and mouse inputs to player movements and behaviors. We will stop briefly and show what these mappings are and discuss how they are attached (indirectly) to the player.

Processing Stack

What the heck is a processing stack, you ask? TGE implements an event queue, which is used to collect all user inputs and various other events. These events are then processed by the engine. The ActionMap is one consumer of these events. Because ActionMaps can be stacked and because they process events on the input queue, I refer to this as the processing stack.

In short, an ActionMap not on the processing stack is not catching and therefore not processing input events.

2.4.2 TGE File I/O

TGE has a file manager that maintains a working list of all the files found in the game directory and all subdirectories. This list is created on start-up. Subsequently, the file manager will locate new files that you add and then attempt to load from the console or via scripts. It will also notice when files have been modified and recompile and load them when requested to do so.

In short, with TGE you can easily add new files and modify existing content without having to restart the engine. This is a huge timesaver when creating new content and while debugging.

> It is worth mentioning that finding new files without restarting is a new feature (introduced in version 1.4). If you are currently using 1.3 or a prior version, you may use the setModpaths() function to find new files. This isn't as nice as an automatic find, but you can still work without restarting.

File I/O and String Manipulation in Our Game

Earlier, when discussing shapes to be used in our game, I alluded to the idea that we would be able to modify the layout of our game. To do that, we will need to create a special level file and then create the scripts to load and parse it. The level file will also specify the starting position of our player, coins, teleport stations, maze blocks, and fireball shooters. By using a separate format, we enable the ability to modify the game and add new levels using a simple text editor. The scripts that do the loading and parsing will exercise several file I/O and string manipulation features.

On a side note, we will also be using file I/O to load the contents of our credits screen.

2.5 Move Along ... Nothing To See Here ... Move Along ...

Well, that was fun. That was a very fast and very dirty coverage of many, but by no means all, of the features in the Torque Game Engine.

Next, we will break out the FPS Starter Kit and start playing around. In the next chapter, I will introduce you to all of the content creation and placement tools that come (built-in) with the Torque Game Engine. You will get to see their power firsthand and to learn about how they work.

Chapter 3
Torque Tools

3.1 What We Are About to Learn

This chapter covers all of Torque's internal (built-in) content creation and placement tools. This includes tools both for building a 3D world and for creation of graphical user interfaces (GUIs).

In addition to learning about these very important tools, we will occasionally pause to test out our newly acquired knowledge in exercises. The results of many of these exercises will turn up in the game we will assemble in the final chapter of this guide.

3.2 Torque's Basic Editors

Torque includes two basic editors, the World Editor and the GUI Editor. The World Editor is further broken down into eight tools. In the following pages, I will be using short names for the individual tools wherever it does not create ambiguity (see Table 3.1).

Editors	Start Editor	Description
World Editor (**WE**)	**F11**	This editor is composed of eight subeditors, each one allowing you to modify and save various aspects of a specific mission. This editor can be used to edit existing missions or to create new ones.
GUI Editor (**GE**)	**F10**	This editor allows you to modify existing GUIs and to create new GUIs, using a simple drag-and-drop interface.
Tools	**Start Tool**	**Description**
World Editor Manipulator (**Manipulator**)	**F2**	This tool allows you to translate, rotate, and scale objects that have already been placed in the world.
World Editor Inspector (**Inspector**)	**F3**	In addition to providing all the capabilities of the World Editor, this editor allows you to view and modify properties of individual mission objects.
World Editor Creator (**Creator**)	**F4**	In addition to providing all the capabilities of the World Editor, this tool allows you to place new objects in the current mission.

Table 3.1.

Torque's basic editors and tools.

Table 3.1 (continued).

Tools	Start Tool	Description
Mission Area Editor (**Area Editor**)	**F5**	This tool allows you to adjust the boundaries of the current mission and provides a means to mirror the current terrain.
Terrain Editor	**F6**	This tool provides the ability to directly manipulate the terrain using the mouse as a multi-operation brush.
Terrain Terraform Editor (**Terraformer**)	**F7**	In addition to providing all the capabilities of the Terrain Editor, this editor allows you to load images as terrain files and to apply various algorithmic generators and filters to the terrain.
Terrain Texture Editor	**F8**	In addition to providing all the capabilities of the Terrain Editor, this tool allows you to select any number of textures and apply them using a set of algorithms to determine blending and placement.
Terrain Texture Painter (**Terrain Painter**)	Window Menu → Terrain Texture Painter	In addition to providing all the capabilities of the Terrain Editor, this tool allows you to select and subsequently to apply up to six different textures to the terrain.

3.3 The World Editor Tools

Let us tackle the World Editor toolset first, as it has the most components and is the most likely place to start when creating a simple mod (modification) or a new game.

As we investigate and learn how to use each of the World Editor tools, please use the GPGT Lesson Kit (provided on the accompanying CD) and run the "World Editor Training" mission.

3.3.1 World Editor Basics

Before leaping into the World Editor tools, let us review some things that hold true for all of the tools. First, we will review the user interface devices. Subsequently, we will discuss the mechanics of movement and viewpoint control, as well as object selection, translation, rotation, and scaling.

3.3.2 World Editor Devices

In this guide, the cursors, menus, and other graphical elements that you encounter in the editors are referred to as devices. Simply stated, these devices provide meaningful feedback to you regarding what action can or should be taken. The terms below are mostly of my own invention, with the exclusion of the appropriately named *gizmo*.

Please note that, while you are editing in the World Editor, you can get help simply by pressing F1. This will bring up a help dialog with descriptions of the tools and their features.

3.3.3 Cursors

Table 3.2 explains what each cursor image means.

Device	Description
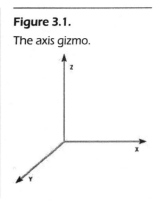 **No-Select Cursor**	When the cursor looks like this, it means that the cursor is not over a selectable object. In other words, you are pointing to an empty space.
Select Cursor	When the cursor looks like this, it means that the cursor is over a selectable object. In other words, you are pointing to an object that can be selected.
Grab Cursor	When the cursor looks like this, it means you have successfully selected an object's gizmo axis in translation mode. In other words, you can move the object around by clicking and dragging when this cursor device appears.
Rotate/Scale Cursor	When the cursor looks like this, it means you have successfully selected an object's gizmo axis in either rotation or scaling mode. It also appears when you have successfully selected a bounding box face for scaling or rotation.

Table 3.2.

Descriptions of cursors.

3.3.4 The Gizmo and Gizmo Scales

The graphic in Figure 3.1 represents the gizmo. The gizmo is a device that is activated when you select one or more objects. It displays the three traditional *x-y-z* axes. Individual axes are selectable and afford the ability to translate, rotate, and scale.

By default, a gizmo axis is dark cyan when not selected and light cyan when the cursor is over it or when it has been "grabbed." Additionally, when a selected gizmo is used for an operation, one of three scales will be shown: the gizmo translation, rotation, or scaling scale.

This scale shows the current position of the object's centroid when you use the gizmo to translate an object.	x: -51.024, y: -127.829, z: 226.473 **Gizmo Translation Scale**
This scale shows the current degrees of rotation around the selected axis when you use the gizmo to rotate an object.	x: 0.000, y: 0.000, z: 1.000, a: 52.519 **Gizmo Rotation Scale**
This scale shows the current height, width, and depth of an object when you use the gizmo to scale it. <w,h,d> correspond to the *x,y,z* axes of the gizmo.	w: 1.2000, h: 1.2000, d: 2.144 **Gizmo Scaling Scale**

Figure 3.1.

The axis gizmo.

3.3.5 Menus and Windows

The World Editor provides a set of traditional menus for selecting the current tool as well as other features (see Figure 3.2).

Please note that all of the menu options will be covered in Section 3.5.3, "World Editor Menus."

Figure 3.2.

World Editor menus.

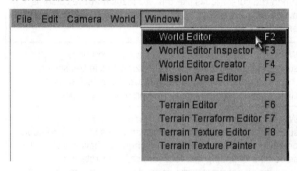

Figure 3.3.

Tool windows.

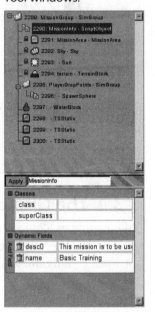

Several of the tools have windows that appear on the right side of the screen (see Figure 3.3). Although these windows have many similarities, it will be better to explain them individually in the respective tool sections below.

3.3.6 Selection Boxes

When selecting a previously unselected object, the selection cursor lets you know when you can select something, and the green selection box (see Figure 3.4) shows which previously unselected object will be selected.

Once you have successfully selected an object, the object will be shown with both a red selection box and a yellow selection box (see Figure 3.5). The red box is object aligned, while the yellow box is world aligned.

The purpose of the yellow box is to show which objects are selected as a group and will therefore be affected by any actions you take. The red boxes are to show which individual objects in the group selection box are actually part of the selection. Notice that, in Figure 3.5, the leftmost and rightmost characters are selected, while the middle character is not.

Once you have successfully selected an object, the selection box will turn blue if your cursor passes over it (see Figure 3.6). Please note that this is not true for drag-select.

Figure 3.4.

Green selection box.

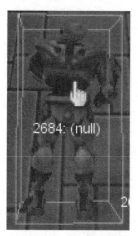

Figure 3.5.

Red and yellow selection boxes.

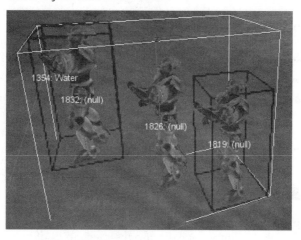

Figure 3.6.

Blue selection box.

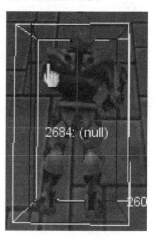

3.3.7 The Handle and Level Grid

Every object in the world displays a handle (see Figure 3.7). The handle has two labels next to it.

1. **A number.** The number signifies which object this is in the mission object list and is the (server-side) ID for the object.

2. **A name.** If the name is "(null)", no name has been assigned to this object. Names are optional but very useful for scripting purposes.

When an object is selected, a faint grid will appear (see Figure 3.8). The grid is parallel to the world's *x-y* plane and passes through the selected object at the handle. When multiple objects are selected, the plane passes through the group handle, which is located at the axis crossing point for the group gizmo.

This device can be used like a ruler for placing objects accurately. Unfortunately, there is no vertical equivalent.

Figure 3.7.

Object handles.

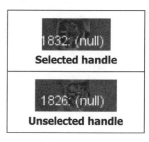

Figure 3.8.

Level grid.

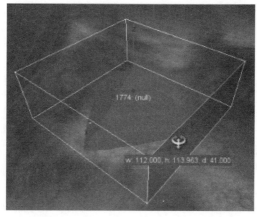

3.3.8 Scale Devices

Figure 3.9.

The scale device.

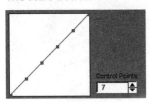

You will see a scale device while editing the terrain and while adjusting terrain parameters (see Figure 3.9). The premise of this device is simple. The 2D scale (line with red dots) represents parameter in two dimensions. Depending on the application, the horizontal spacing may represent elevation, radius, etc. The vertical spacing may represent opacity, blending factor, strength of action, etc. The red dots on the lines are control points. These points can only be moved vertically. All scale interfaces come with a spin box to add or remove control points, thereby increasing horizontal resolution.

Please note that you are better off typing in the value you want, because the spinner changes do not take effect unless you edit the textbox.

3.4　World Editor Mechanics

Now that we have familiarized ourselves with the various devices available in the World Editor, let's discuss the mechanics of how we manipulate objects in the mission using the mouse. We will talk about how to move around the mission, switch camera modes and viewpoints, select objects, and use the mouse to manipulate position, rotation, and scale via the gizmo.

3.4.1　Default Movement and Viewpoint

Table 3.3 gives the keystrokes for moving around the mission and changing camera modes and viewpoint.

Table 3.3.

Moving and changing viewpoint.

Description	Key(s)
Moving around	**W, A, S, D, SpaceBar** (Up, Left, Right, Down, Jump)
Looking around	🖱 + Motion
Zoom	**E** (Zooms when held)
Toggle free-camera vs. player view	**ALT + C**
Toggle 1st vs. 3rd POV (in play mode only)	**TAB**
Free-camera speed (World Editor Only)	**SHIFT + 1 ... SHIFT + 7** (slowest ... fastest)
Drop character at camera	**F7** (play mode after editing only) **ALT + W** (World Editor mode only) **CTRL + F7** (both modes)
Drop camera at character	**ALT + Q** (World Editor mode only)

3.4.2 Object Selection and Translation

Table 3.4 shows how to use the mouse to select and translate objects.

Description	Action	Function
Selection	🖱 on object (see Figure 3.10a)	Selects: • Previously unselected object
	Shift + 🖱 on object (see Figure 3.10a)	Selects: • Previously unselected object Deselects: • Previously selected object
	🖱 on empty space + Drag (see Figure 3.10b)	Selects: • Previously unselected object • Previously selected object Please note that the drag box must enclose an object's centroid (red dot) to select the object.
Object Translation without using gizmo	🖱 + Drag	Translates: • Single previously unselected object • Single previously selected object • Multiple previously selected objects

Table 3.4.

Selecting and translating objects.

Figure 3.10.

Object selection actions.

a.

b.

3.4.3 Using the Gizmo

As described earlier, the gizmo is the aptly named three-axis device that appears when you select either a single object or a group of objects. The gizmo has three individually selectable "handles" that run along the major axes *x, y,* and *z*. These handles gives you the ability to translate, rotate, and scale objects (see Table 3.5).

Function	Mouse	Action
To translate (object-axis)	🖱 gizmo axis	Drag left/right for *x* and *y*, up/down for *z*.
To translate (world-axis)	**SHIFT** + 🖱 gizmo axis	Drag left/right for *x* and *y*, up/down for *z*. In this mode, the gizmo aligns to the world axis and confines translation to translation along the selected world axis.
To rotate	**ALT** + 🖱 gizmo axis	Drag left/right.
To scale (single object only)	**CTRL** + **ALT** + 🖱 gizmo axis	Drag left to grow and right to shrink.

Table 3.5.

Using the gizmo.

Engine Overview

Figure 3.11.

Using the gizmo on single
and multiple objects.

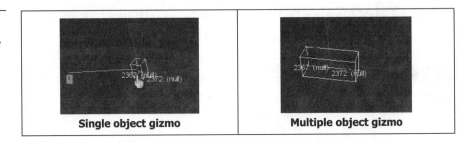

Single object gizmo | **Multiple object gizmo**

Gizmo translations and rotations can be applied to *single* or *multiple* selected objects (see Figure 3.11). Rotations are always about the gizmo axis, which is the handle for single selected objects and the group handle for multiple selected objects.

Gizmo scaling can only be applied to a *single* selected object.

3.4.4 Scaling using Bounding-Box Planes

While experimenting, I accidentally discovered that there is another way to scale objects with the mouse. Not only is this method slightly more intuitive, but it also doesn't require the use of the gizmo. Try the following:

1. Deselect all objects.
2. Find the object you wish to scale and select it.
3. Press and hold **CTRL + ALT.**
4. Click a bounding-box plane and drag the mouse to scale. You'll notice that the selected side of the bounding box is filled with a medium blue hash.

That is all there is to it! Figure 3.12 shows a selected bounding-box face.

Figure 3.12.

Using a bounding-box
plane to scale.

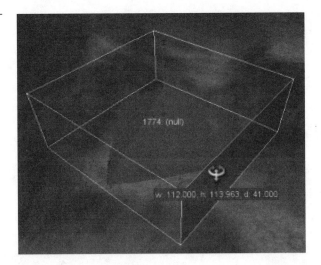

3.5 World Editor (Manipulator)

3.5.1 Starting the Manipulator

1. Start the World Editor by pressing **F11**.
2. Start the Manipulator by pressing **F2**.

3.5.2 The 3D World View Window

The real benefit of the Manipulator tool comes from the fact that you can traverse the world and the 3D world view is not blocked by any dialogs or menus (except for the World Editor menu), giving you an almost-full screen view while you manipulate objects via mouse and hot keys. Upon examination, it can be seen that this tool is very plain (likely as intended). In the sample view in Figure 3.13, we can see the world and its contents. We can apply all standard mouse manipulations as described in Section 3.3, "World Editor Tools".

3.5.3 World Editor Menus

All World Editor tools have a top menu containing the same elements. However, in some tools, certain menu selections will be disabled. Tables 3.6–3.10 give a brief description of each menu and the menus' choices. Some options' descriptions will be deferred until we discuss the specific tool that is affected by said option.

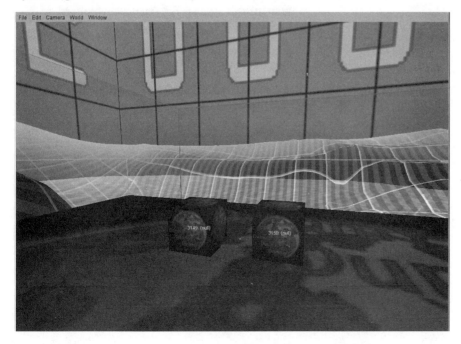

Figure 3.13.
World Editor screen (Manipulator mode).

Table 3.6.

File menu.

Menu Item	Description
New Mission ...	Clicking this option will generate a new mission based on preset values. This generates the same mission every time. **WARNING: This wipes out the current mission. If done at all, it should be done once and only once, before editing.**
Open Mission ... (CTRL + O)	Brings up a dialog to allow you to load an existing mission.
Save Mission ... (CTRL + S)	This saves your current mission.
Save Mission As ...	As with "Save Mission ...", this allows you to save your mission, but in this case, you can specify a name and (existing) directory for the mission file.
Import Terraform Data ...	This feature is deprecated and no longer used.
Import Texture Data ...	This feature is deprecated and no longer used.
Export Terraform Bitmap ...	This choice is enabled by the Terraformer tool. We will discuss it there.

Table 3.7.

Edit menu.

Menu Item	Description
Undo (CTRL + Z)	Undo the last operation. **WARNING: This does not undo all operations, so back up early and often.**
Redo (CTRL + R)	Redoes last operation. As with undo, this does not apply to all operations.
Cut (CTRL + X) Copy (CTRL + C) Paste (CTRL + V)	Standard cut-copy-paste. Can be applied to single and multiple objects.
Select All (CTRL + A)	Selects all objects (shapes and interiors) in the mission.
Select None (CTRL + N)	Deselects previously selected terrain. This does not deselect objects.
Relight Scene (ALT + L)	Causes the engine to relight the current terrain and apply shadow maps. This trips up a lot of beginners. I will discuss this further when we learn about adding interiors.
World Editor Settings ...	This brings up the World Editor Settings dialog. (Discussed below.)
Terrain Editor Settings ...	This feature relates to the Terrain editor and will be discussed there.

Menu Item	Description
Render Plane	Show plane when objects are selected.
Render Plane Hashes	Show hashes when objects are selected.
Render Object Text	Show objects' names and IDs.
Render Object Handle	Show objects' handles (red dot).
Render Selection Box	Show selection boxes.
Plane Extent	Length by width dimensions of plane (floating point OK).
Grid Size	Hash spacing for grid (floating point OK).
Show Mouse Popup Info	Show mouse popup scales when moving-rotating-scaling.
Move Scale **Rotate Scale** **Scale Scale**	These values increase or decrease mouse sensitivity for individual mouse actions (move, rotate, scale).
Planar Movement	Checked: Object will move along plane when dragged. Unchecked: Object will *attempt* to follow terrain when dragged.
Collide with Object's Bounding Box	If checked, object can be selected by placing cursor anywhere on object's bounding box.
Objects Use Box Center	If checked, handle is in object center; otherwise at lower limit of object bounding box.
Axis Gizmo Active	Enable gizmo.
Min Scale Factor **Max Scale Factor**	Determine minimum and maximum multiple by which objects can be scaled from original size.
Visible Distance	Minimum distance within which object handles are visible/selectable. (This has nothing to do with visible distance during gameplay. Examine the Sky object for that.)
Gizmo Screen Len	Gizmo axis length in screen pixels.
Project Distance	Ray length for selection cursor.

Table 3.8.

World Editor settings.

To modify the World Editor settings, click Edit → World Editor Settings…, then change the appropriate setting.

Menu Item	Description
Lock Selection	Disable mouse actions (drag, rotate, scale) on current selection(s). This does not prevent changes via the Inspector window although a 🔒 will show up in the World Editor tree.
Unlock Selection	Re-enable mouse actions on current selection(s).
Hide Selection	Hide (i.e., do not render) current selection(s).

Table 3.9.

World menu.

Table 3.9 (continued).

Menu Item	Description
Show Selection	Un-hide previously hidden object(s). Use the Inspector to select these objects. They have a 🔒 next to them in the World Editor tree.
Delete Selection	Delete current selection(s).
Camera to Selection	Move camera to centroid of current selection(s).
Reset Transforms	• Un-rotate selected objects that are rotated (i.e., align to objects' default alignment). • Un-scale selected objects that are scaled (i.e., scale all objects' dimensions to 100% of default scale). • Works for multi-select. • This is not the same as Undo.
Drop Selection	Make currently selected object(s) drop according to drop current rule (see Table 3.10).
Add Selection to Instant Group	We will discuss this feature when we discuss the Inspector.
Drop at …	We will discuss these in Table 3.10.

Table 3.10.

"Drop At…" menu item.

In the World menu drop-down, there is a group of "Drop at xyz…' radio-selections (only one can be selected). Before you start placing objects in the Creator, you should understand what these settings are going to do for you.

Menu Item	Description
Drop at Origin	This causes new or pasted objects to be created at the World Origin.
Drop at Camera	This causes new or pasted objects to be created at the current location of the current camera. You could think of there being three cameras: • one in the character's head during 1st POV (Point of View) viewing, • a second in the following camera position during 3rd POV, and • the third being the actual free-floating camera. Figure 3.14 shows an object dropped in 1st and 3rd POV to clarify this.
Drop at Camera w/Rot	This does the same as "Drop at Camera" with the addition that the object will have the camera's rotation.
Drop below Camera	In this mode, new objects are created somewhere below the current camera.
Drop at Screen Center	This is the default "drop at" mode. I think this mode's title is a bit of a misnomer. It seems that this behaves more in the following fashion: Cast ray from camera eye: • On collision with object bounding box, water, or terrain, drop the object at point of collision. • If ray extends beyond "Project Distance" (set in World Editor dialog), drop object at camera eye (position).
Drop at Centroid	This option allows you to select multiple objects and have the newly created object placed in the virtual centroid of the group.

Menu Item	Description
Drop to Ground	Objects are dropped to the ground at mission center. I wouldn't use this if there is any possibility that there could be an overlapping interior at the mission center, because dropping another interior there will crash the editor.

Table 3.10 (continued).

Figure 3.14.
Drop at camera (ouch!).

The Window menu is probably the most easily understood. It allows you to select which of the World Editor tools you wish to use. The only important thing to remember is that you must use this menu to select the Terrain Texture Painter tool since there is no hot key for it.

3.6 World Editor Inspector (Inspector)

3.6.1 Starting the Inspector

1. Start the World Editor by pressing **F11**.
2. Start the Inspector by pressing **F3**.

3.6.2 Examining the Inspector

The Inspector tool (Figure 3.15) allows you to select an object and manipulate its script-exposed parameters via text boxes, spinners, radio buttons, checkboxes, etc. These parameters will vary based on the object. Later, we will examine specific parameters for water, terrain, the character, the sky, etc. Now, for the purpose of learning about this tool, we will work with a simpler object, namely the SpawnSphere. The purpose of this object is unimportant at this time. The key thing is that it is easily located and manipulated.

To begin, look directly overhead. You should see a gray object. Select it and you should have a view similar to Figure 3.16.

Taking a quick inventory of the screen elements, we see the World Editor menu at the top, the 3D World View window which takes up nearly two-thirds of the screen, the World Editor tree window in the upper right, and finally the World Editor Inspector window in the lower right.

3.6.3 World Editor Tree

Before we jump into the relatively straightforward World Editor Inspector, let's discuss the World Editor tree and some important organization features it provides.

First, expand the list in the World Editor tree window. The initial list is completely collapsed, which doesn't do us a lot of good when we're trying to manipulate objects.

Engine Overview

Figure 3.15.

World Editor screen
(Inspector mode).

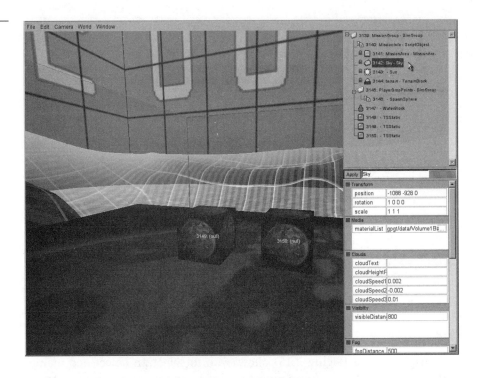

Figure 3.16.

The Inspector screen
elements.

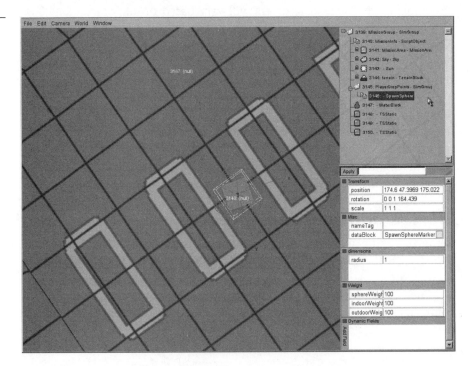

1. Expand the MissionGroup SimGroup by clicking the [+] next to the text "####: MissionGroup – SimGroup." See Figure 3.17; numbers may vary from illustration.

2. Expand the PlayerDropPoints – Sim-Group.

Figure 3.17.
World Editor tree window.

You should now have something similar to Figure 3.17. If for some reason the SpawnSphere entry is not highlighted, please click on it once to select it.

Locked Items

You will notice that some entries in the tree have a lock icon next to them. This means that the entry is "locked" and cannot be edited. You may lock an item by creating a dynamic field (see "Inspector—Dynamic Fields" in Section 3.6.6) named "locked" and then setting that field to true. You may unlock an entry by deleting this field, or by setting it to false.

3.6.4 SimGroups

At this point, you may be asking, "What is a SimGroup?" Subsequent chapters in Part III will get into the nitty gritty details about SimGroups, SimSets, and SimObjects. For now, we'll simply describe SimGroups as a means by which we organize objects. This is both useful from an organization sense, i.e., knowing where to find things while you are editing, and for scripting purposes. By predefining a consistent set of SimGroups and by organizing your objects within them, your current job as a mission/level designer will be greatly simplified. Your script writers will thank you also. If that is your job, too, then pat yourself on the back.

As can be seen from the current view of the World Editor tree, SimGroups, as well as particular entities (SimObjects), can be nested within SimGroups. In fact, every mission entity is present in this list and will be found nested within a SimGroup.

So, how exactly do we place objects within a SimGroup? Let's find out. First, make a duplicate copy of the SpawnSphere. We already have it selected, so all you need to do is type **CTRL + C** (to copy) followed by **CTRL + V** (to paste). Alternately, you can use the Edit Menu → Copy/Paste operations.

Now that you've created a new SpawnSphere, you need to locate it in the World Editor tree. If you've followed the instructions above, you will find the new SpawnSphere at the bottom of the tree (see Figure 3.18). We would much rather have it in the PlayerDropPoints – SimGroup with the rest of the SpawnSpheres. So, let's manually move this one to the correct spot and then learn how to place objects in the right SimGroup the first time.

Figure 3.18.

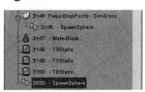

Figure 3.19.

Figure 3.20.

Figure 3.21.

Moving Existing Objects into a SimGroup (Add-Group or Instant Group)

The new SpawnSphere should already be selected, but if it isn't, please click on it to select it. Now, use the slider on the right side of the World Editor tree and find the PlayerDropsPoints – SimGroup. Select this as the Add-Group through the key/mouse combination: **ALT +** 🖱. The Add-Group should now be selected with a gray background (see Figure 3.19).

Now, select the menu item World → Add Selection to Instant Group. *Voilà!* The SpawnSphere is in the PlayerDropPoints – SimGroup (see Figure 3.20).

These steps will work in all versions of Torque, but in version 1.4 and later, you may simply drag and drop objects from SimGroup to SimGroup.

Creating Objects in a Preexisting SimGroup (Add-Group)

OK, so that was a hassle. How do we get objects to place in the correct Sim-Group when we create them? Simple. You already have a SpawnSphere in your copy buffer, and you already have the Add-Group selected (see above). Paste another SpawnSphere and it should show up in the PlayerDropPoints – SimGroup (Figure 3.21). Easy as pie! The trick is to select your instant group before pasting objects and they will automatically be placed in that SimGroup.

3.6.5 World Editor Key Stroke/Mousing List

Table 3.11 is a summary of operations you may perform on SimGroups and Objects with the mouse and key combinations.

Table 3.11.

Mouse	Action	Function
ALT + 🖱	On SimGroup	Set current Add-Group.
CTRL + 🖱	On SimGroup	(De)select all members in SimGroup.
CTRL + 🖱	On Object	(De)select object(s).
SHIFT + 🖱	On Object	Select multiple objects.

3.6.6 World Editor Inspector Window

Now let's address the World Editor Inspector. This is, of course, the window from which this tool gets its name. The purpose of this window is to allow you to inspect and modify parameters for individual objects. If you play around a bit and click on different objects, you will begin to see that different object types have different parameters. For now, we'll address the more common values, add new values, and finish off with some tips on using the interface effectively. We will leave a detailed inspection of individual objects' parameters for Chapter 8, "Mission Objects."

Inspector—Common Fields

Table 3.12 describes the common fields used in the World Editor Inspector.

Field	Description
Position (X,Y,Z)	Three floating-point values representing the coordinates of the selected object in world space.
Rotation (X$_m$,Y$_m$,Z$_m$,A)	Four floating-point values where the first three are multipliers and the fourth value is the angle (in degrees) of the rotation(s). Example: rotation 0 1 0 90.0 means the object is rotated 90 degrees about the y-axis, relative to the world-axis.
Scale (X$_m$,Y$_m$,Z$_m$)	Three floating point values representing a relative scaling. The values act as multipliers of the object's default dimension(s) in the indicated axes. Example: scale 1 1 2 means that this object will be twice as tall as the default when loaded into the world. Please note that these values correspond indirectly to those you see when mouse scaling. Mouse-scaling values are actual world dimension.
shapeName (shapes only)	This parameter's name is a misnomer. It actually gives the relative path and filename of the selected shape.
interiorFile (interiors only)	This parameter gives the relative path and filename of the selected interior.
Object Name	There isn't actually a parameter tag for "Object Name," but there is an editable text field for it. The text field is located to the right of the Apply button. You can type just about anything in this field, though no spaces are allowed. Click Apply to name your object. Please note that objects can be given the same name. We'll leave further discussion of object naming for a later chapter. Just remember that this is how you change it from the Inspector.

Table 3.12

Common fields in Inspector.

Inspector—Dynamic Fields

I won't explain what dynamic fields are yet, but rather I will explain a way that they can be added to objects. To add a dynamic field:

- select the object to which you wish to add a field,
- click the Add button found in the Dynamic Fields section of the World Editor inspector window (see Figure 3.22), and

Figure 3.22.

Engine Overview

Figure 3.23.

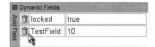

- give the field a meaningful and unique name and an initial value.

To modify the value of a dynamic field, follow the same steps as changing the value of any other field. Just modify the contents of the text field next to the dynamic field name and click Apply.

To delete the dynamic field click on the garbage-can icon next to the dynamic field (see Figure 3.23), and the field will be removed permanently. **This cannot be undone**.

3.7 World Editor Creator (Creator)

3.7.1 Starting World Editor Creator

1. Start the World Editor by pressing **F11**.
2. Start the Creator by pressing **F4**.

3.7.2 World Editor Creator Window

The Creator (see Figure 3.24) tool is used to create (or place) new content. From the World Editor Creator, we can select objects to insert into our current mission. Figure 3.25 shows the Creator's top-level folders.

Figure 3.24.

World Editor screen
(Creator mode).

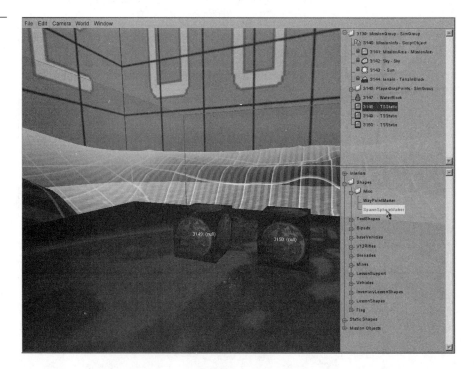

- **Interiors**. Buildings and other interiors.
- **Shapes**. Animatable shapes.
- **Static Shapes**. Lightweight inanimate shapes.
- **Mission Objects**
  - Environmental stuff like the sky, sun, water.
  - Mission stuff like MissionArea, Triggers, and Cameras.
  - System stuff like SimGroups.

Placing (Creating) New Objects

Creating new objects is much like pasting objects. Simply

1. move to the location in the mission area where you would like to place the object;
2. look approximately where you want to place the object;
3. find the object you wish to place by looking in the World Editor Creator tree; and
4. click once on the object in the list.

Once an object is placed in the world, you can freely manipulate its position, rotation, and scale via the mouse. If, however, you want to change object parameters, you'll need to switch back to the Inspector.

Adding Objects to Creator Tree

When the engine is first started, it creates a list of all files found in the mod directory. Later, when we start the Creator, the Interiors tree is populated with all known DIF files, and the Static Shapes is populated with all DTS files found. In both cases, the original directory hierarchy for the mod is maintained (see "abcshack" sample below).

The Shapes tree is populated with ShapeBase objects created in scripts. We'll defer discussing these shapes until Part III, "Game Elements." For now, let's learn how to get basic interiors and shapes into their respective trees.

Adding Interiors to the Creator Tree

Torque needs the following files to create an Interior:

- **DIF**. Once an Interior has been properly generated, there will be a file named interior_name.dif, where interior_name is whatever you chose to name your interior object.
- **Graphics file(s)**. An Interior will have at least one graphics file. By default, the graphics files used for the Interior need to be located in a directory above the Interior's DIF file or in the same directory as the DIF file.

Figure 3.25.
World Editor Creator top-level folders.

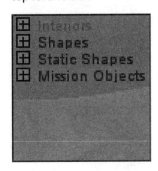

Spaces in a folder name will make the parts after spaces show up like a subdirectory.

```
Bobs Room\room.dif
```
produces:
```
[-]-□ Bobs
    [-]-□ Room
        └ room
```

53

Figure 3.26.

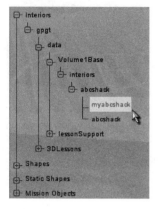

Example:

1. In the directory "example\gpgt\data\GPGTBase\interiors\abcshack" you will find a file named abcshack.dif. Make a copy of this file and rename it myabcshack.dif.

2. Completely exit the GPGT Lesson Kit, reload it, and start the World Editor Creator again.

3. Now, in the Creator tree, under Interiors → gpgt → data → GPGTBase → Interiors → abcshack, you will see a new Interior named myabcshack (see Figure 3.26).

Adding Static Shapes to the Creator Tree

Torque needs the following files to create a Static Shape:

- **DTS.** Once a shape has been properly generated, there will be a file named shape_name.dts, where shape_name is whatever you chose to name your shape object.

- **Graphics file(s).** A shape will have at least one graphics file. By default, the graphics files used for the shape need to be located in the same directory as the shape's DTS file.

- **DSQ(s) (optional).** For an animated shape created in 3ds Max, there is a third type of file, containing animation data. For simplicity's sake, this will not be discussed here, other than to note that they may exist. By default, the DSQ file(s) used for the shape need to be located in the same directory as the shape's DTS file.

Figure 3.27.

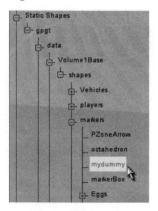

Example:

1. In the directory "example\gpgt\data\GPGTBase\shapes\markers" you will find a file named dummy.dts. Make a copy of this file and rename it mydummy.dts.

2. Completely exit the GPGT Lesson Kit, reload it, and start the World Editor Creator again.

3. Now, in the Creator Tree, under "Static Shapes → gpgt → data → GPGTBase → shapes → markers" you will see a new Shape named mydummy (see Figure 3.27). Try placing it.

You might be wondering why the object showed up in Static Shapes instead of Shapes. Objects under Static Shapes are lightweight objects (created with TSStatic). Objects under the Shapes tree are created using the ShapeBase hierarchy. ShapeBase adds several capabilities, including animations, sounds, rendering effects, etc. This requries the creation of a datablock. We will discuss creating ShapeBase objects and their datablocks in Chapter 6, "Basic Game Classes."

3.8 Mission Area Editor (Area Editor)

3.8.1 Starting the Mission Area Editor

1. Start the World Editor by pressing **F11**.
2. Start the Mission Area Editor by pressing **F5**.

3.8.2 The Mission Area Editor Window

In the upper right corner of the screen, you will see a blue and white image (see Figure 3.28). This image represents the mission map. The Mission Area Editor provides the ability to select the size and location of the mission bounds (or area). Interestingly, it also provides a terrain editing feature.

Editing the Mission Area

The Mission Area Editor is very simple to use. Simply click the Edit Area checkbox, and handles will appear on the mission area box. Now drag and resize to your heart's content. You will be able to see the effect of your changes in the 3D World View window also. One thing to keep in mind is that the image is inverted; that is, the top of the image is what most would consider south, the bottom north, and the left and right, respectively, west and east. This could quickly become cumbersome to remember, so the creators of the Area Editor

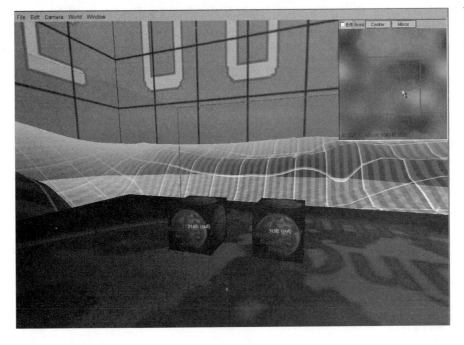

Figure 3.28.
Mission Area Editor screen.

Figure 3.29.

Mission Area Editor details.

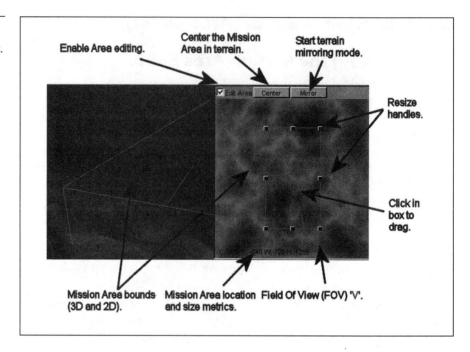

provided a device to give you a better hint as to where you are looking when you edit. The device I'm speaking of is the Field Of View (FOV) 'V'. Look at the labeled example in Figure 3.29.

Before moving on, there are a couple of things that you should know.

- You can use the Area Editor window to rapidly relocate your character/ camera. Simply be sure that the Edit Area button is *not* checked and click in the window. Your character/camera (depending on view mode) will "jump" to that point.
- If you have made modifications to your terrain using the Terraformer or the Terrain Editor, those changes will not automatically be reflected in the Area Editor image. To refresh the image, do the following.

  1. Make your terrain changes.
  2. Start the Area Editor and make sure Edit Area is checked.
  3. Drag the mission area off center.
  4. Recenter by clicking the Center button. The updated terrain should now be reflected in the Area Editor image.

The moral of this story is to edit your terrain topography first, then edit your mission area. And do all this before placing interiors, shapes, or other mission objects.

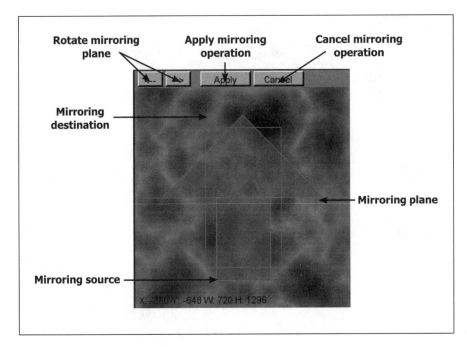

Figure 3.30.

Mirror in Mission Area
Editor.

Mirroring the Mission Area

As I mentioned above, the Mission Area Editor also provides what I would
label a "terrain editing feature"—namely, the ability to mirror the terrain. This
is very useful if you wish to create a balanced (in terms of terrain obstacles)
mission area. To use this feature, click on the "mirror" and you will see something similar to Figure 3.30. The application of this tool is simple:

• select the orientation of the mirroring plane (with <-- --> buttons) and

• click Apply to mirror copy the source onto the destination.

3.9 Terrain Editor

3.9.1 Starting The Terrain Editor

1. Start the World Editor by pressing **F11**.

2. Start the Terrain Editor by pressing **F6**.

3.9.2 The Terrain Editor Window

When you start the Terrain Editor, you will see a shot like the one in Figure
3.31. This looks very much like the view in the Manipulator, except that there
are no windows obscuring your view. However, if you look closely, you'll

Figure 3.31.

Terrain Editor screen.

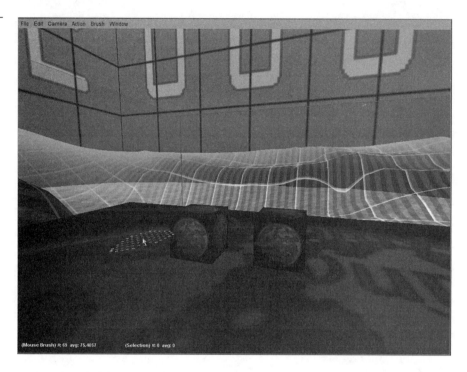

notice some odd squares following your cursor around while you move your mouse. These squares are yet another Torque user-interface device, the purpose of which is to give you feedback on what terrain area will be affected when you choose to manipulate it and, to some degree, how it will be affected. Before we jump right into learning how to edit the terrain, let's look at the other two devices on the screen.

The Over Vertex Brush Scale

I refer to the text beside the label "(Mouse Brush)" in Figure 3.32 as the Over Vertex Brush Scale. The purpose of this scale is twofold.

1. It shows how many vertices are currently under the brush. In Figure 3.32, we have 69 vertices under the brush.
2. It shows the average elevation of the vertices under the brush.

The Selected Brush Scale

I refer to the text beside the label "(Selection)" in Figure 3.33 as the Selected Brush Scale. The purpose of this scale is twofold.

1. It shows how many vertices are currently selected. (We'll learn about selecting below.)

2. It shows the average elevation of these selected vertices.

Figure 3.32.
The Over Vertex Brush Scale.

Figure 3.33.
The Selected Brush Scale.

3.9.3 Editing

There are two basic modes for editing via the Terrain Editor:

1. **Brush mode.** The default mode, which I call brush mode, is a free-floating 9 × 9 vertex brush. You can adjust the shape and hardness of the brush as well as change its size by rough increments. In addition, this mode provides several operations.

2. **Selection mode.** The second mode, which I use less frequently, but which can do things that you cannot do in brush mode, is what I call the selection mode. In this mode, you select arbitrary blocks of terrain. Then, you can perform a single operation upon them—modify their height via mouse movement.

Editing in Brush Mode

I think it is fair to say that most of your editing is going to be in brush mode, and because it is the default mode, I'll discuss it first. As mentioned previously, you can modify the brush shape, hardness, and size. Figure 3.34 describes the details that are modifiable in the Brush menu.

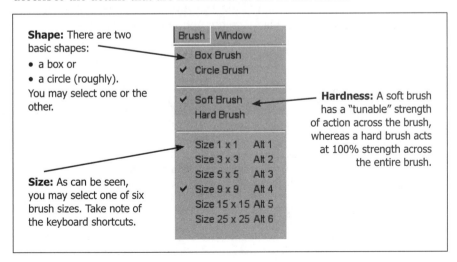

Figure 3.34.
Details of the brush menu.

Shape: There are two basic shapes:
- a box or
- a circle (roughly).
You may select one or the other.

Hardness: A soft brush has a "tunable" strength of action across the brush, whereas a hard brush acts at 100% strength across the entire brush.

Size: As can be seen, you may select one of six brush sizes. Take note of the keyboard shortcuts.

59

Engine Overview

Basic Brush Editing Actions

OK, now that we know about basic brush manipulation, what about the operations? In Table 3.13, let's take a look at the action menu (shown in Figure 3.35).

Table 3.13.
Action menu descriptions.

Figure 3.35.
Action menu.

Operation	Meaning
Add Dirt *	Raises terrain under brush.
Excavate *	Lowers terrain under brush.
Adjust Height *	Temporarily selects vertices under brush. • Mouse Up—raises vertices • Mouse Down—lowers vertices.
Flatten	Sets all vertices under brush to average height of vertices under brush.
Smooth *	Does a nearest-neighbor elevation average on vertices under brush.
Set Height	Sets all vertices to preselected height. (See "Terrain Editor Settings" section for setting this value.)
Set Empty **	Removes the terrain between the outer edges of the brush.
Clear Empty **	Puts terrain back in spots where it was previously removed.
Paint Material	Paints vertex with currently selected texture. (See Section 3.12, "Terrain Texture Painter.")
* This action is affected by brush hardness settings.	
** Not a vertex operation per se. These operations modify the block of terrain between a set of vertices.	

Selection in Brush Mode

All right, so what about this other mode, selection? There isn't really much to it. To get into selection mode, just open the Action menu (see Figure 3.35) and click Select. Now, you can select terrain as explained in Table 3.14.

Table 3.14.
Making selections.

Action	Result
Previously Unselected Vertex	Selects vertex.
Previously Selected Vertex	May increase strength of action (see discussion of brush hardness below) if the selection cursor has a stronger value than the currently selected vertex's action strength.
CTRL + Previously Selected Vertex	De-selects vertex.

Having selected the terrain blocks that we wish to modify, we can open the action menu and click Adjust Selection. Now, we can 💾 and drag up/down to raise/lower the elevation of the selected blocks.

To leave selection mode, select any other operation in the Action menu. Also, once selected, vertices stay selected, regardless of mode. If you wish to deselect all selected vertices, press **CTRL + N** or click Select None in the Edit Menu.

Brush Hardness

Brush hardness has been mentioned several times but not completely explained. When the brush hardness is set to Soft, the action strength along the diameter of the brush can be modified. In simple terms, if the strength of action is set low, then the value change for that part of the brush is also low. If the strength of action is set high, the value change for that part of the brush will be high. This attenuation is in relation to the movement of the mouse. The brush gives strength of action feedback through coloration (see Table 3.15). Brush coloration is a continuous scale from red to green. You can manipulate this hardness in the Terrain Editor Settings dialog found under the Edit menu. See Figure 3.36 for examples.

Color	Relative Hardness (Strength of Action)
Red	Hardest (100%)
Orange	Hard (> 50%)
Yellow	Soft (< 50%)
Green	Softest (almost 0%)

Table 3.15.

Brush hardness and coloration.

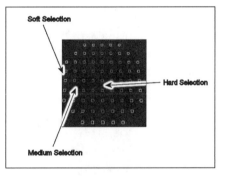

Figure 3.36.

Brush hardness results.

Terrain Editor Settings

Earlier, I deferred a discussion of these settings. Now is the time to understand them. The Terrain Editor Settings... (see Figure 3.37), found under the Edit menu, gives us some additional control beyond brush shape, hardness, and size. Table 3.16 gives further explanation of the settings found in this dialog box.

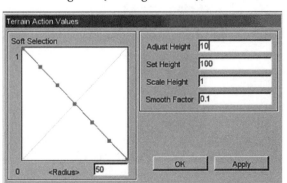

Figure 3.37.

Terrain Editor Settings dialog box.

Table 3.16.

Terrain Editor settings.

Dialog Area	Purpose
Soft Selection spline	This spline scale modifies the brush hardness. Left is the center of the brush and right is the outer edge.
<Radius>	See "Selection and <Radius>" section.
Adjust Height	Increment by which the height of fully selected (hard) terrain is adjusted per mouse tick.
Set Height	Height to set selected terrain to when Set Height operation is used.
Scale Height	Increment by which height is scaled when using scaling operations.
Smooth Factor	Strength of smoothing operation. Higher values smooth more aggressively but may produce less interesting terrains as a result.

Selection and <Radius>

Instead of attempting to explain <Radius> with words, I give a pictorial example in Figure 3.38. In the following sequence, I have changed to selection mode and am using a 1 × 1 brush. I then select four separate vertices. Next, after opening the Terrain Editor Settings dialog, I change the radius values to those shown and hit Apply. See how the selection changes?

Figure 3.38.

Example of using <Radius>.

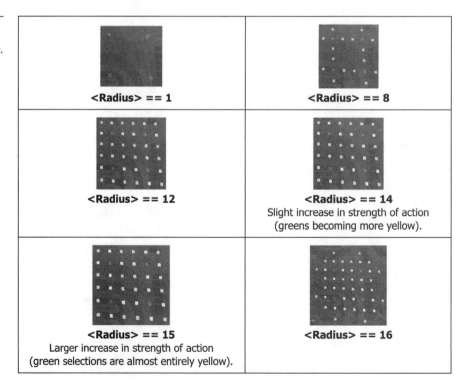

<Radius> == 1

<Radius> == 8

<Radius> == 12

<Radius> == 14
Slight increase in strength of action
(greens becoming more yellow).

<Radius> == 15
Larger increase in strength of action
(green selections are almost entirely yellow).

<Radius> == 16

3.10 Terrain Terraform Editor (Terraformer)

3.10.1 Starting the Terraformer

1. Start the World Editor by pressing **F11**.
2. Start the Terraformer by pressing **F7**.

3.10.2 The Terraformer (An Overview)

Of all the in-game editor tools, the Terraformer is probably the most elaborate and complicated. The shortest explanation of the Terraformer is that it is a tool to algorithmically build terrains. You may ask why you would want to use this tool to build terrains. The number one reason I can think of is that it is a fast way to create interesting terrains.

In this section, I provide the following details about the Terraformer:

- description of Terraformer windows,
- summary of all operations,
- rundown on how operations are applied,
- brief descriptions of the individual operation interfaces, and
- a list of important Terraformer factoids.

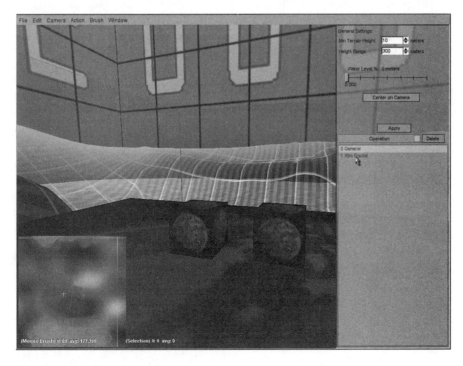

Figure 3.39.

Terraformer screen.

Engine Overview

3.10.3 The Terraformer Preview Window

If you are reading this guide from front to back, this will be the first time that you have seen the window in Figure 3.40. You'll note that it is similar to the Mission Area Editor window. In fact, this window displays very similar data. For the purpose of this discussion, we'll focus on the following aspects.

1. **Center marker.** There is a faint white + in the preview window. This marks the center of the map. Every time you apply Terraformer operations, this is where the camera will be moved to.

2. **FOV marker.** There is a red V that is always in the center of the window. This shows your current field of view, i.e., area in your view relative to the map.

3. **Boundary marks.** In addition to the center marker, there are faint horizontal and vertical lines, representing the boundaries of the current heightmap.

Figure 3.40.

Terraformer window.

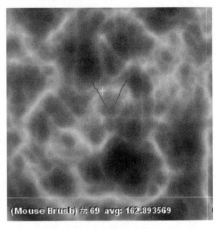

4. **Heightmap image.** Although it may not be obvious at first, the image in the preview window is a translation of the heightmap. The funky coloring can be interpreted very easily. The darker an area is, the lower it is; likewise, the lighter an area is, the higher it is.

Figure 3.41.

a. Terraformer operations tree.

b. Terraformer operations pull-down menu.

3.10.4 Terraformer Operations Tree

In the lower right corner of the screen, you will find the Terraformer operations tree. There is a button labeled Operations and clicking on this will bring up a pull-down menu with all the operations (see Figure 3.41). When you select an operation, it is added after the currently highlighted operation (so you can insert new operations into the middle of a list of existing operations).

Terraformer Operations

Each of the Terraformer operations has its own settings. These can be accessed in the upper right window. Before we cover these, let's quickly enumerate and describe the general properties of the operations.

In his *Tribes* editing guide, *Editing Maps and Missions in Tribes 2*, Tim Hammock appropriately categorizes the operations as either "generators" or "filters." In addition, I would like to add the category "base". Table 3.17 gives a summary of the base, generator, and filter operations.

Table 3.17.

Base, generator, and filter Terraformer operations.

Base	Summary
General	This is the default operation. It cannot be removed from your list of operations. The values set in this operation are used by subsequent generators and filters.
Generator	**Summary**
fBm Fractal	The random **f**ractional **B**rownian **m**otion generator (if you were wondering what the acronym means) is a basic terrain generator. It produces rolling hills with various steepness based on settings. It tends to produce smoothly topped hills but can produce jagged peaks.
Rigid MultiFractal	Another fractal-based generator, this tends to produce hills with serrated (or sharp) peaks.
Canyon Fractal	This fractal-based generator produces a series of troughs (canyons). It can produce shallow to deep canyons that run straight or twist.
Sinus	This generator would probably be impossible to get a handle on without the code. However, a quick peek shows that this generator creates terrain by iteratively adding the scaled sum of a sine and cosine pair with some basic noise for flavor. Just remember that, ignoring the noise element, all terrains produced with this generator have the same base shape. Your choice of settings will determine how this shape is applied to progressively smaller sections of the terrain. I'll give more details below.
Bitmap	This operation allows you to import an image file as your terrain heightmap.
Filter	**Summary**
Turbulence	This filter erodes and redeposits terrain features and kind of reminds me of the smudge brush applied algorithmically. It seems to erode more than it redeposits. Both of these actions are done in a swirly, turbulent (therefore the name) fashion. This filter significantly alters the look of your terrain.
Smoothing	This is a simple nearest-neighbor averaging filter. It will tend to remove jagged areas in your terrain.
Smooth Water	This is like the smooth filter but is limited to smoothing terrain that is at or below the level of global water height (set under General operation). No smoothing is done for features above the water height.
Smooth Ridges/ Valleys	As the name implies, this filter affects specific regions based on their characteristics. Plateaus with jagged edges will be rounded at the edges while retaining their original steepness. Deep dimples in valleys will be filled in—how much depends on settings.
Filter	This filter allows you to adjust groups of like elevations globally. In other words, terrain heights are divided into discretely modifiable groups, from lowest elevation to highest elevation.
Thermal Erosion	This is a very aggressive eroding filter. You can rapidly remove materials from sloped areas of your terrain with this. The official docs say this uses a "thermal erosion" algorithm.
Hydraulic Erosion	This is a very weak eroding filter. The official docs say this uses a "hydraulic erosion" algorithm.
Blend	This filter allows you to combine two existing operations via a set of mathematical operations, blending them together. We will look at an example of this shortly.

How Operations Are Applied

Operations are applied to the terrain in the order they appear in the list, top to bottom. This means that if you apply two generators in a row, the second generator's results are the only ones that will be seen. More interestingly, you can apply filters in different orders for different results. The best way to learn about these operations is to experiment.

Operations' Settings

I'll give a quick rundown of the various operations' settings and then set you loose.

General

- **Min Terrain Height** (0..500). Defines the lowest possible point in the map. Tools and generators will not be allowed to create terrain elevations lower than this.
- **Height Range** (5..500). Defines the maximum difference between min height and max height. Therefore, max height = = min height + range.
- **Water Level.** A global value used as input to subsequent filters. It does not place water.
- **Center on Camera.** Sets the map origin to the current camera location.

fBm Fractal

> **fBm Fractal Tips:**
>
> • If your height range is large (say 350+), you will tend to have jagged hills, regardless of other settings.
>
> • With a default height range (300), Very High Detail will tend to create knife-edged hills, even for low Hill Frequencies (8).

- **Hill Frequency** (1..24). Indirectly determines number of hills. Higher values create more hills.
- **Roughness** (0.0..1.0). Determines roundness of hills. Lower values tend to create more rounded hills, while higher values create taller and more pointy hills, i.e., steeper slopes.
- **Detail** (Very Low..Very High). In terms of visual results, higher values produce more jagged peaks (knife edges).
- **Random Seed.** Seed that feeds into random portion of generator. Using the same value for subsequent generations produces the same sequence of numbers.
- **New Seed.** Creates a new seed.

Rigid MultiFractal

- **Hill Frequency** (1..24). Indirectly determines number of hills. Higher values create more hills.
- **Roughness** (0.0..1.0). Determines roundness of hills. Lower values tend to create more rounded hills, while higher values create taller and more pointy hills, i.e, steeper slopes.

- **Detail** (Very Low..Very High). In terms of visual results, higher values produce more jagged peaks (knife edges).
- **Random Seed.** Seed that feeds into random portion of generator. Using the same value for subsequent generations produces the same sequence of numbers.
- **New Seed.** Creates a new seed.

Canyon Fractal

- **Canyon Frequency** (4..10). Number of canyons to produce.
- **Chaos** (0.0..1.0). A value of zero will produce very artificial-looking and straight canyons. A value of one will produce squirrelly features, almost unrecognizable as canyons.
- **Random Seed.** Seed that feeds into random portion of generator. Using the same value for subsequent generations produces the same sequence of numbers.
- **New Seed.** Creates a new seed.

Sinus

- **Scale** (on..off). Although the scale implies there are ranges of values for each control point, values are either on or off. Dragging a control point to the bottom turns it off. Any other vertical position is on.
- **Random Seed.** Seed that feeds into random portion of generator. Using the same value for subsequent generations produces the same sequence of numbers.
- **New Seed.** Creates a new seed.
- **Control Points.** Controls number of points on scale. Type values into this field. More control points mean more detail, i.e., higher levels of subdivision and iteration.

As mentioned before, the Sinus generator builds the terrain using a combination of sinusoidal values and noise. If you want to see the underlying structure, set the seed to 0. Now, poking around with the control points will produce something that looks like Figure 3.42.

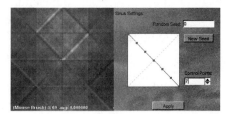

Figure 3.42.

Sinus generator with seven control points.

Now set the number of control points to 3. Notice in Figure 3.43 that the overall structure is still recognizable.

Figure 3.43.

Sinus generator with three control points and various point scales.

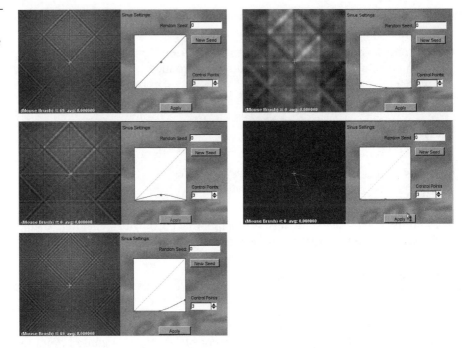

Turbulence

- **Turbulence Factor** (0..1.0). Determines strength of action. Lower values mean less displacement and less variation in height. Higher values mean vigorous swirling and modifications to height.
- **Radius of Effect** (1..40). Determines filter size. 1 equals a 3×3 filter, 2 equals a 4×4 filter, etc., up to a 42×42 filter.

Smoothing

- **Iterations** (0..40). Determines number of smoothing passes to run.
- **Aggressiveness** (0.0..1.0). A relative factor, determining how much material to remove.

Smooth Water

- **Iterations** (0..40). Determines number of smoothing passes to run.
- **Aggressiveness** (0.0..1.0). A relative factor, determining how much material to remove.

Smooth Ridges/Valleys

- **Iterations** (0..40). Determines number of smoothing passes to run.
- **Aggressiveness** (0.0..1.0). A relative factor, determining how much material to remove.

Filter

- **Scale.** Each control point corresponds to a specific height (see below for calculation). Subsequent applications change these values.
- **Control Points.** Determines now many elevation bands there are.

You can make significant and rapid changes to your terrain with this filter. Understanding how this works can be kind of tricky. At first, you might think that the ranges will be based on the Min Terrain Height and Height Range set in the General settings. This may or may not be true. If your current terrain extends to the lowest and highest points, then, yes. However, let's say your Min Terrain Height is set to 0, but your lowest elevation is 100. Also, Height Range is set to 200, but your highest elevation is only 200 (i.e., half the range). Then, the elevation bands are determined as follows:

- Lowest elevation: 100 world units
- Highest elevation: 200 world units
- Control points: 5
- Width of each elevation band: $(200 - 100)/5 == 20$ world units
- Resultant elevation bands (left-to-right in scale):

Control Point 1	Control Point 2	Control Point 3	Control Point 4	Control Point 5
100..119 meters	120..139 meters	140..159 meters	160..179 meters	180..200 meters

Moving a control point is like grabbing all elevations in that band and raising or lowering them by a relative amount. Additionally, there is a push-pull relationship between bands of elevation; that is, by modifying one band, you also (slightly) modify all other elevation bands. Figure 3.44 shows some sample changes so you can judge for yourself. This tool rapidly changes the face of your terrain, so caution is the word.

Please note that, by default, the scale comes up looking like Figure 3.44a (only it has seven control points). If left like this, no changes will be made.

In Figure 3.44b, we raise the low elevation band as much as possible. Remembering that lighter values are higher elevation, notice that some previously dark regions are now very light. Also, notice that, overall, the total elevation of the map seems to have been lowered.

In Figure 3.44c, we lower the high elevation band as much as possible. Lo and behold, previously high areas are now completely dark, but what else has happened? The rest of the map seems to have raised.

In Figure 3.44d, we've lowered all bands except for the middle band. As can be easily seen, we've basically said, "make the middle band the highest range."

Engine Overview

Figure 3.44.

Sample changes using control points.

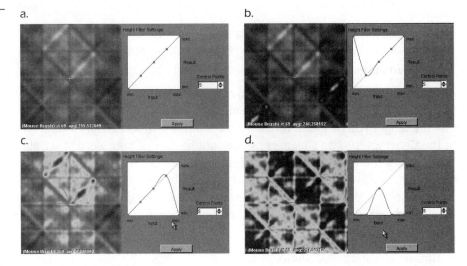

Thermal Erosion Tips:

• For multiple iterations, if a slope falls below the Min Erosion Slope, erosion no longer affects that area.

• The Material Loss value is a bit misleading. A 100% loss does not mean, "set this value to lowest height." Instead it means something like, "set this value to lowest nearby height."

• This is a very vigorous filter, quickly removing large quantities of material.

Thermal Erosion

• **Iterations** (0..50). Determines number of smoothing passes to run.

• **Min Erosion Slope** (0.0..89.0 degrees). Defines a cutoff slope value. What this is saying is, do not apply this erosion to slopes with a current value lower than that set here; i.e, if a slope has a 15 degree inclination and this value is set to 45, no changes will be made to that part of the map.

• **Material Loss** (0..100). The relative percentage of material that should be removed per pass.

Hydraulic Erosion

• **Scale.** No effect.

• **Iterations** (0..50). Determines number of erosion passes to run.

• **Control Points.** No effect.

Hydraulic Erosion Tips:

• This is one of those cases where having access to the code shortens research drastically. The scale (filter) is passed in to the erosion method but not used. So, whatever changes you make to it are going to be ignored. Since control points are part of the same mechanism, you can ignore these, too. The only thing you need to modify is Iterations.

• This sweet little filter fills one duty: erode the channels, or low points, between steep hills. It erodes wide flat basins, too, but the effects are not as noticeable. You've got to admire the person who coded this. To write an algorithm that consistently targets a specific terrain feature for erosion? Brilliant!

Blend

The parameters to this filter modify the blending equation above the Apply button. Easy as pie. Just remember that Source A is always the operation prior to this blend. (Yes, it can be a blend of a blend of a ... well, you get the idea) Figure 3.45 shows the recreation of a nice terraformer sample from the *Tribes 2* days. It nicely demonstrates the power of the Blend filter.

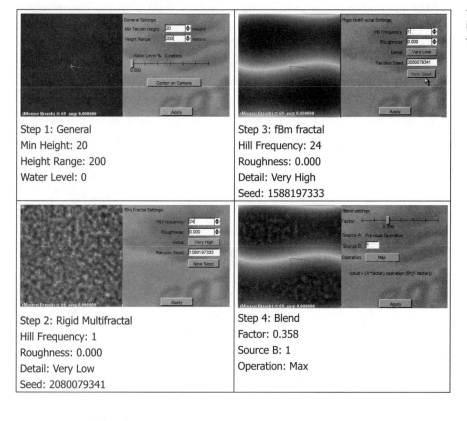

Step 1: General
Min Height: 20
Height Range: 200
Water Level: 0

Step 3: fBm fractal
Hill Frequency: 24
Roughness: 0.000
Detail: Very High
Seed: 1588197333

Step 2: Rigid Multifractal
Hill Frequency: 1
Roughness: 0.000
Detail: Very Low
Seed: 2080079341

Step 4: Blend
Factor: 0.358
Source B: 1
Operation: Max

Figure 3.45.
The Blend filter.

Loading a Bitmap

I have purposely deferred a discussion of loading your own bitmaps until the end. Of all the questions I see asked over and over in the forums, one of the most repeated is, "How do I load a bitmap as my terrain?" As you would imagine, doing this is relatively simple. Once you have the PNG file you wish to use as your terrain bitmap, simply place it anywhere in the current mod directory (gpgt\data\heightFields, for example). Now, in the Terraformer, select the bitmap operation and choose the newly placed bitmap as the operation's source file. Click Apply, and you're done.

Although "loading a bitmap" seems to imply a BMP file, you must actually use PNG files.

Loading a Terrain File

Similar to loading a bitmap is the operation to load a previously created terrain file. When you select this operation, the engine will pop up a dialog from which you may select any currently available terrains.

Be warned that this operation will completely replace your current terrain. Also, if you are missing textures that are used in the to-be-loaded terrain (or the textures are in a new location), your terrain painting may start off white. To resolve this problem, please read the section "Fixing Broken Terrain Paths" at the end of Section 3.12, "Terrain Texture Painter."

> If you have not yet followed the steps in Section 14.4, "Setting Up Our Workspace," please do so before doing Lesson #1.

3.10.5 Maze Runner Lesson #1 (90 Percent Step)— Terrain for Our Game

Here is the first of several lessons in which we'll apply the massive amount of knowledge we're gaining in a practical situation, building our own simple game step by step. In this first quick lesson, we'll create a terrain for our game to be played out on. Follow the simple steps in this section to get started.

Copy Required Files

From the accompanying disk, please copy the "\MazeRunner\Lesson_001\ heightFields" directory into "\MazeRunner\prototype\data".

Generate New Terrain

To generate the cauldron for our game terrain, do the following (see Figure 3.46).

1. Quit the Lesson Kit and start up the Maze Runner prototype.
2. Start the Maze Runner mission.
3. Start the Terraformer.
4. Use the Bitmap operation to generate a terrain using the file "\MazeRunner\prototype\data\heightFields\mazerunner.png".

After applying the generator, the terrain should be shaped like a cauldron. Save the mission.

Adjust Spawn Point

Now we have a simple terrain. You might also want to use the Inspector to remove all but one spawn point and to position it at "0 0 100" so we don't have such a long way to fall when we spawn into the mission again. Now, don't forget to save your changes.

Figure 3.46.

a. Terrain preview.

b. Terraformer settings.

And with that, we have taken the first small step towards making our little Maze Runner game!

3.11 Terrain Texture Editor

3.11.1 Starting the Terrain Texture Editor

1. Start the World Editor by pressing **F11**.
2. Start the Terrain Texture Editor by pressing **F8**.

3.11.2 The Terrain Texture Editor Preview Window

After the Terraformer, the Terrain Texture Editor is probably the second most complicated tool in the World Editor tool kit. Again, we're faced with an array of operations that can be performed, based on various factors and settings. When all is said and done, this tool's main goal is to allow us to place textures on our terrain via selection algorithms and calculations. The end result of said placement can be a very natural- or unnatural-looking landscape. Like the Terraformer, we have the preview window, operations tree, and settings window (see Figure 3.47). In addition, we have a textures list, snuggled between the settings window and the operations tree.

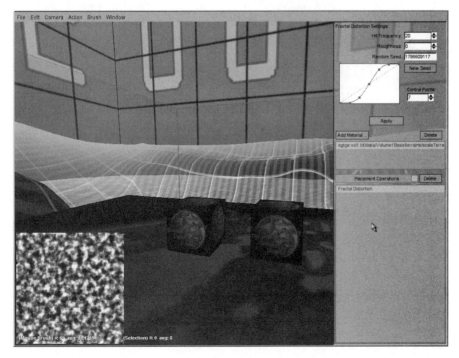

Figure 3.47.

Terrain Texture Editor screen.

3.11.3 The Texture Editor Textures List (Loading Textures)

Figure 3.48.

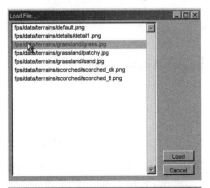

Before we can start texturing our terrain, we need to decide which textures will be part of our palette. To load a terrain, simply click the Add Material... button and select a terrain from the dialog that comes up (Figure 3.48).

Figure 3.49.

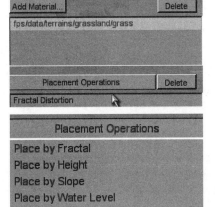

The Terrain Texture Editor places our textures in layers. The first (topmost) texture in the texture list is the base layer. This is the texture that is visible if no other textures get applied to a point on the terrain. In this case, we have selected the grass texture as our base texture (Figure 3.49).

Figure 3.50.

Subsequently added materials are always placed at the end of the list. These textures are applied based on an algorithm and settings (or placement operations). See Figure 3.50.

In the case that two textures (besides the base texture) are applied to the same pixel on the terrain, they are blended.

3.11.4 Terrain Texture Editor Operations

Fractal Distortion (Base Filter)

Every texture gets a base filter called Fractal Distortion, the purpose of which is to provide randomness to the way the textures are placed. The interface is very similar to the Terraformer's fBm generator. The major difference is the scale interface. The math behind the filter and the interface controls are somewhat complicated to describe. Honestly, the easiest way to understand what this filter does is to simply play around with it a bit and observe what happens with various settings.

Place by Fractal

The Place by Fractal filter is also complex to describe, and in my opinion, not incredibly important for your day-to-day game-development needs. Here again, if you're interested in learning about this filter, the best way to understand it is to experiment, testing different settings and values, and noting their effects.

Place by Height

This filter has a simple purpose. It places textures at certain delineated elevation bands and blends them based on the vertical setting for that band. I'll show the result of this in Figure 3.51.

Place by Slope

As with the Place by Height filter, this filter is relatively straightforward. The left side of the scale represents less steep terrain and the right side represents more steep terrain. Again, the vertical scale is the blending factor.

Place by Water Level

This last filter allows us to place a texture at or below the water level we set in our Terraformer. This is useful if you are building an island or have a large lake, but I suggest avoiding it otherwise. Instead, for smaller bodies of water, you can hand paint using the Texture Painter, which we'll be talking about in Section 3.12.

Because it is said that a picture is worth a thousand words, Figure 3.51 includes some sample pictures of the Terrain Texture Editor in use.

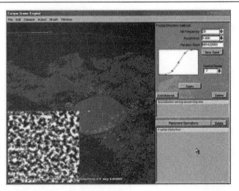

Base layer of grass only.

Operation: Fractal Distortion
Fractal Distortion Settings:
  Hill Frequency: 20
  Roughness: 0.0
  Random Seed: 801422093
Control Points: 7
Material: Grass

Figure 3.51.

Samples of Terrain Texture Editor.

Engine Overview

Figure 3.51 (continued).

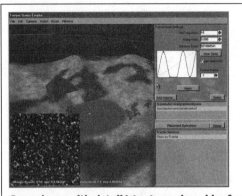

Operation: Place By Fractal
Fractal Mask Settings:
  Hill Frequency: 16
  Roughness: 0.0
  Random Seed: 821699541
Control Points: 7
Material: detail1

Grass base with detail1 texture placed by fractal.

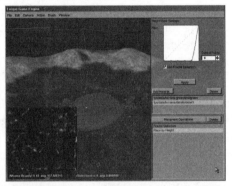

Operation: Place By Height
Height Mask Settings:
Control Points: 6
Use Fractal Distortion: true
Materials: Grass, detail1

Grass base with detail1 applied by height. Notice height setting set to place only at highest elevation band.

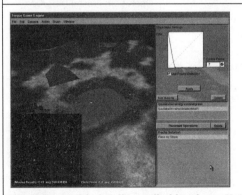

Operation: Place By Slope
Slope Mask Settings:
Control Points: 7
Use Fractal Distortion: true
Materials: Grass, detail1

Grass base with detail1 applied by slope. Notice slope setting set to place only on least steep (flattest) areas.

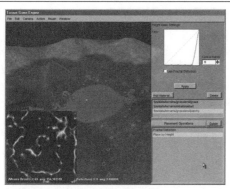

Operation: Place By Height
Height Mask Settings:
Control Points: 6
Use Fractal Distortion: false
Materials: Grass, detail1, patchy

Figure 3.51 (continued).

Grass base with detail1 and patchy set to apply at same elevation (by height). Notice blending of detail1 and patchy.

3.12 Terrain Texture Painter (Terrain Painter)

3.12.1 Starting the Terrain Texture Painter

1. Start the World Editor by pressing **F11**.
2. Select Terrain Texture Painter from the Window menu.

Figure 3.52.
Terrain Texture Painter screen.

3.12.2 Examining the Terrain Painter

The last of the tools we will examine in this section is the Terrain Painter. Among all the tools, this is probably the most straightforward. If you have successfully loaded the Terrain Painter, you will see something like the image in Figure 3.52. If you have used any tools like Worldcraft, Wally, or any of a number of other content-creation tools, you will be familiar with the concept of a palette, but just in case, I will describe it.

The Terrain Painter Palette

Currently, the palette is limited to six textures. Also, the palette texture "spots"

Figure 3.53.

"Load File..." dialog box.

must be loaded in counterclockwise order. In other words, if you tried clicking on the Add... button in the upper right corner right now, nothing would happen. Try clicking the Add... button in the middle left. Load the patchy.png texture.

When you click either an Add... button or a Change... button, the Load File... dialog pops up (see Figure 3.53). The tool will automatically find files in either of the following two formats:

1. Portable Network Graphics (*.png)

2. JPEG (*.jpg)

I strongly suggest using PNG files. Also, you should adhere to strict rules regarding the dimensions and color content of your graphics files.

Dimension	Required: 256 × 256 pixels
DPI or PPI	Suggested: 72
Pixel Depth/Colors	Suggested: 24/16 million
Alpha Layer	Suggested: none

On the right side of the screen, you should see a window that looks similar to Figure 3.54. In this image, there are two of six allowed textures enabled. The purpose of this window is to act as a sort of painter's palette for textures. Simply by dabbing your cursor on (clicking on) a loaded texture, you can use that texture to paint the terrain with the now familiar brush. As with the Terrain Editor, you can change the shape, size, and hardness of the brush. In this case, the hardness will affect blending. A softer brush provides a softer stroke,

therefore less of the new texture is applied per stroke, with more of the underlying texture showing through. Give it a try. Click on the "patchy" texture and
paint some lines, swirls, whatever. Cool, eh?

Fixing Broken Terrain Paths (All White Terrain)

Sometimes, we will find it necessary to move our terrain files (*.ter) and/or
our terrain textures. As a result, the next time we relight our terrains, they may
render without textures. TGE embeds relative texture paths within the body of
the terrain file, so when we move the terrain file, we break these paths.

Fixing this problem is relatively painless. Simply follow these steps.

1. Load the mission with the broken terrain. The terrain will be all white (see
   Figure 3.55).
2. Open the Terrain Painter tool. If you examine the painter palette, you will
   see that all of the texture slots are blank, even though they do have the
   texture name listed (see Figure 3.56).
3. One by one, click on the Change... buttons and relocate the matching
   texture (as is listed by the blank palette chip) using the Texture Selection
   dialog (see Figure 3.57).
4. Finally, save the terrain, and your terrain file will be fixed!

Figure 3.54.

The palette.

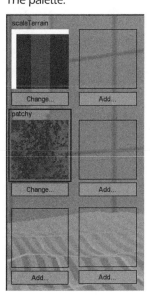

Figure 3.55.

Broken terrain; shows up as white.

Figure 3.56.

Blank palette texture slot.

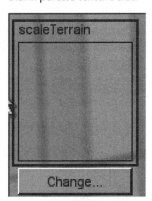

Figure 3.57.

Texture Selection dialog.

bump0.png
bump1.png
default.png
grass.jpg
patchy.jpg
sand.jpg
scaleTerrain.png

3.13 World Editor Quick Tips

3.13.1 Manipulator (F11 + F2) Tips

- **Translating rotated objects.** To move a rotated object, press and hold **SHIFT** before selecting the object's gizmo. This will force the gizmo to align to the world axes, thus making it easier to move the object about.

- **Quick scaling.** Select the object to be scaled. Press and hold **CTRL +ALT**, then hover the mouse over the side to be scaled. A blue hash will appear. Clicking on this and moving the mouse scales in the selected dimension.

- **Quick move.** Select an object with the mouse and then, being sure the gizmo is not highlighted, click on the object's bounding box and hold the left mouse button. Now you can move the object about the world plane in *x* and *y* directions.

- **Better placement (snap-to).** Turn on the editor's snap-to by opening the console (~) and typing "snapToggle();". Now, open the WorldEditor Settings dialog (under the Edit menu) and set the Move Scale to the value you want snaps to happen on. While moving objects with the gizmo, movements will snap to this increment.

3.13.2 Inspector (F11 + F3) Tips

- **Staying organized.** Make sure to add SimGroups before placing objects, and then be sure to place objects in them when populating the mission.

- **Locking objects.** To make editing simpler and safer, objects can be locked. A locked object cannot be translated, rotated, or scaled using the mouse. However, changes can still be applied via the Inspector pane. To lock an object, simply select the object in the Inspector and add a dynamic field named `locked`. If `locked` is set to `true`, the object will be mouse-modification immune. To unlock the object, delete the variable or set it to `false`.

3.13.3 Creator (F11 + F4) Tips

- **New Interiors are black (relighting the scene).** In versions prior to TGE 1.4, interiors started out black and needed to be "relit" to get their textures. To get the textures to render and to get the shadow for this DIF baked into the terrain, you need to relight the scene. Simply type **ALT + L**. In version 1.4 and beyond, all newly placed interiors will be draft-lit. This means that the interior will be lit, but no self-shadowing or terrain shadowing will be done. To see the final lighting results, you will still need to relight the scene. Draft lighting was added to save time and give better feedback while editing.

3.13.4 Area Editor (F11 + F5) Tips

- **Quick camera/player movement.** To quickly move the camera/player to a point on the map, open the Area Editor and click on the preview map. The camera/player will be moved to that point on the map.

3.13.5 Terraformer (F11 + F7) Tips

- **Setting map to zero elevation (perfectly flat).** To create a map at zero elevation, open the Terraformer, add the operation Terrain File, do not select a terrain file, and apply the operation. Because no terrain file was selected, the loader will flatten the terrain to zero elevation.

- **Setting map to non-zero elevation (perfectly flat).** To create a flat map at a set elevation, open the Terraformer, then:
  - remove all current operations;
  - add a Sinus operation;
  - click on General and set Min Terrain Height to desired height;
  - type 0 in Height Range (clicking roller buttons does not allow this, only typing);
  - click on previously added Sinus operation; and
  - click Apply.

3.13.6 Terrain Painter (Windows → Texture Painter) Tips

- **Increasing texture count.** Search the GarageGames website for a resource titled "8 terrain textures instead of 6" that provides an easy solution for increasing the number of textures the Terrain Painter palette can hold.

3.13.7 General Editing Tips

- **Better placement (use the grid).** Use the grid like a ruler when placing objects. Don't forget that the grid size can be adjusted in the World Editor Settings dialog. Using this feature in addition to snap-to can simplify placement greatly.

- **Reduce visual clutter while editing.** When the number of objects in a mission is significant, too many labels (centroid + object ID) may be visible. To alleviate this, either disable "render object text" (in the World Editor Settings dialog), or reduce the "visible distance" (a field in the Sky object).

- **Exact scaling.** When you want to scale an object by an exact factor, use the min/max scale factor settings found in the World Editor Settings dialog. By simply setting these factors to the same number, then applying a scale operation, the object will scale to the exact value.

- **Stop selecting far objects accidentally.** Along with visual clutter, sometimes it occurs that far objects get selected by mouse movements; i.e., while attempting to select a near object, a far object is alternately or additionally selected. Simply reduce the "project distance" for the pointer (World Editor Settings dialog), or reduce the "visible distance" (a field in Sky object).

- **Stop objects falling through terrain during placement.** To keep objects from falling through the terrain while you place them, open the World Editor Settings dialog and uncheck "Planar movement", then uncheck "objects use box center". Now sliding objects around with the mouse will be less likely to cause them to fall through the terrain.

- **Speed up scene relight.** When editing, we don't necessarily care if the scene lighting is perfect. To speed up scene relights (**ALT + L**), open the console (~) and type

```
$pref::sceneLighting::terrainGenerateLevel=0;
```

Now relights will be done with the lowest precision. In general, this is still pretty good, and it may be all right to leave it here. Note that the highest value is 4, but this setting can take 50 or more times the length of time it takes to relight with a setting of 0.

3.14 The GUI Editor

3.14.1 Starting the GUI Editor

1. Select the GUI you wish to start editing in:
   - Main Menu (for now start here);
   - In-Game (playGui); or
   - other... anywhere else in your game.
2. Start the GUI Editor by pressing **F10**.

3.14.2 Examining the GUI Editor

If you have just started the GPGT Lesson Kit and then pressed **F10**, you will see pretty much what is shown in Figure 3.58 *except* the Content Editor will contain the Main Menu.

The GUI Editor can get confusing quickly if you don't know what you're doing, or if you don't pay attention to what you've done. As Figure 3.58 shows, there are four areas to the GUI Editor. In clockwise order from the top left, they are as follows.

1. **Content Editor.** This is the place where you will be mouse-interacting with your GUI(s).

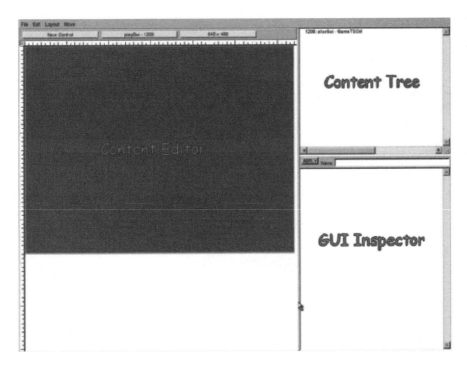

Figure 3.58.

The GUI Editor *screen.*

2. **Content Tree.** This will display the hierarchical (parent-child) relationship of the controls in the current GUI.

3. **GUI Inspector.** This inspector is similar in function to the World Editor Inspector in that it is used to display all the data about a chosen object. In this case, the object is a selected GUI control (a window, button, slider, etc.).

4. **Toolbar** (at top, not labeled). The toolbar provides several major functions, which will be described shortly.

This all may seem simple enough, but there are a few things to beware of and a few things you should know before you start.

3.14.3 Things to Beware!

• **Hosing up is so easy to do.** Please understand that it is very easy to completely hose up an interface if you are not cautious. That said, it is an excellent idea to make frequent backups of your project.

• **I can't see jack...** The minimum resolution for editing GUIs is 800 × 600, but if at all possible, I suggest editing at 1024 × 768. You will find that the Content Tree and Inspector are much easier to use and read at this resolution.

- **I'm stuck!** It is easy to get stuck while editing GUIs. That is, you may find yourself in a situation in which you are unable to exit the GUI Editor. This will happen less and less as you become more familiar with the tool and its operation. If you do get stuck, you can kill the application.

- **Duplicate GUIs (backups).** If you edit like I do, you may be accustomed to creating backup copies of your files as you work. You may continue to do this, but you should not leave them in the current game directory hierarchy. If you do, TGE will find them. Subsequently, when you go to save, this will confuse the save dialog when it tries to find the best place to save the GUI you are editing.

- **Start and stop the editor from the same parent GUI.** The most common mistake I made when I started playing around with the GUI Editor was starting the editor and then later trying to exit after having switched to a different GUI. For example, try the following.

  1. Start the GPGT Lesson Kit and press **F10**.
  2. 🖫 on MainMenuGui and switch to playGui.
  3. Try to exit by pressing **F10**.
  4. Huh? Now the mouse is locked, and the screen didn't change. Hmmm...
  5. Press **F10** (should be able to move mouse now).
  6. 🖫 on the button with playGui displayed.
  7. Switch back to MainMenuGui.
  8. Try to exit again by pressing **F10**.
  9. *Voilà!* Back to the Main menu.

So what happened there? Well, **F10** gets us in and out of the editor, but if we have changed the current menu, it exits into the new editor in order for us to test it. The reason the screen seemed to lock up was because the playGui was not properly activated. The important thing to remember is this: when you are finished editing GUIs, switch back to the GUI you started from, and then exit the GUI Editor.

3.14.4 GUI Editor Basics

We will review the user-interface devices. Then, we will discuss the mechanics of control manipulation, GUI navigation, how to add new controls to an existing GUI, and how to create a new GUI.

GUI Editor Devices

As with the World Editor, there are graphic controls that provide you with feedback while editing. There are far fewer of these devices in the GUI Editor, but it is important to give them a quick review (see Table 3.18).

Device	Description
Single Select	When you have a single control selected, eight black squares will show up. The little squares are handles that allow you to resize the control.
Multi-Select	Similar to the single select is the multi-select. When you have multiple objects selected, each object will have eight squares along the perimeter of the object. The difference is that when the squares are white, it means that you cannot resize. Only dragging is allowed.
APPLY OK	When you have a single control selected and are editing fields in the Inspector, the handles turn gray. If they have a white outline, it means APPLY will take effect if clicked.
APPLY OK	When you have multiple controls selected and are editing fields in the Inspector, the handles on all selected controls turn gray. If they have a black outline, it means APPLY **will not** take effect if clicked. Think of the black outline as a warning. Sometimes it isn't obvious when objects get crowded together.
Add Parent	The final device is the Add Parent box. Hierarchy in your GUI is an important concept. In order to create hierarchy (add controls to existing controls vs. to the top parent), you must select an Add Parent. The Add Parent box gives feedback, showing which control is the current Add Parent.

Table 3.18.

GUI Editor graphic controls.

3.14.5 Control Manipulation

Now that we've covered the basic GUI Editor devices, let's talk about how we manipulate controls; i.e., how do we resize, move, etc. See Tables 3.19, 3.20 and 3.21. Unlike the World Editor, the GUI Editor has no menu, so you have to use hot keys to cut, copy, and paste. Naturally, these hot keys are the same in both editors.

Table 3.19. Moving and resizing (mouse and keyboard).	**Mouse Resizing**	🖱 an object(s) in either the Control Editor or the Content Tree. (Multi-select only works in the Control Editor.) AND 🖱 a handle and drag.
	Mouse Moving	🖱 an object(s) in either the Control Editor or the Content Tree. (Multi-select only works in Control Editor.) AND 🖱 a selected object(s) (not on a handle) and drag.
	Keyboard Moving	🖱 an object(s) in either the Control Editor or the Content Tree. (Multi-select only works in Control Editor.) AND (Up, Down, Left, or Right) **Arrow Key** moves *one* pixel in selected direction. OR **SHIFT +** (Up, Down, Left, or Right) **Arrow Key** moves *ten* pixels in selected direction.

Table 3.20. Moving and resizing (Layout menu).	**Align Left (CTRL + L)** Align all selected controls' left edges to left edge of leftmost-selected control. 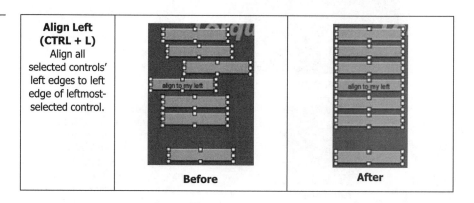

Table 3.20 (continued).

Align Right (CTRL + R) Align all selected controls' right edges to right edge of rightmost-selected control.	**Before**	**After**
Align Top (CTRL + T) Align all selected controls' top edges to top edge of topmost-selected control.	**Before** **After**	
Align Bottom (CTRL + B) Align all selected controls' bottom edges to bottom edge of bottommost-selected control.	**Before** **After**	
Center Horizontally Centers all selected controls horizontally within rectangle defined by edges of outermost-selected controls.	**Before**	**After**

Table 3.20 (continued).

Space Horizontally Evenly spaces controls horizontally within bounds of leftmost and rightmost edges.	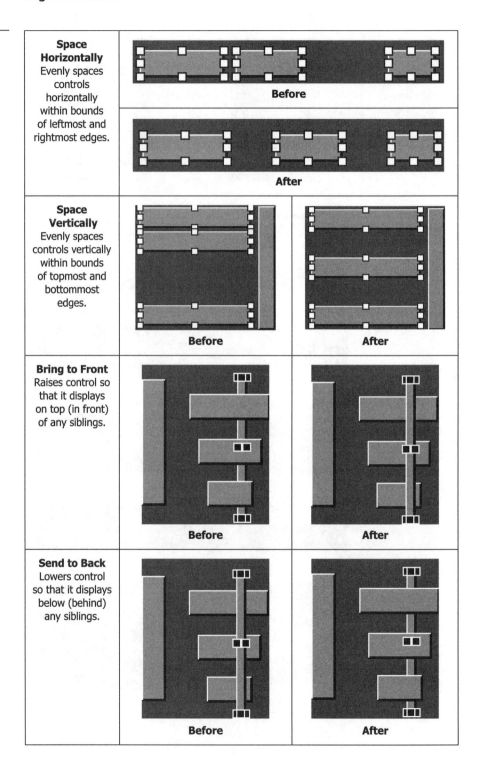
Space Vertically Evenly spaces controls vertically within bounds of topmost and bottommost edges.	
Bring to Front Raises control so that it displays on top (in front) of any siblings.	
Send to Back Lowers control so that it displays below (behind) any siblings.	

Cut	**CTRL + X**	Single or multiple controls OK.
Copy	**CTRL + C**	Single or multiple controls OK.
Paste **(to current Add Parent)**	**CTRL + V**	Please note that, if controls are selected, the paste will happen (to currently selected Add Parent), but you will not see the pasted objects if they are not normally visible unless selected.

Table 3.21.

Cutting, copying, and pasting.

Add Parents

I've mentioned the term Add Parent a few times now, but to be absolutely clear, I'm going to discuss it one more time. In order to add a new control as a child of another control (parent), you must have selected the parent control by right-clicking it. If properly done, the control that you wish to be the parent will get a yellow and a blue outline (the yellow might look green). Now, any added controls will automatically become children of the Add Parent control. There is no mouse-only method of moving a child into a parent. You'll either have to:

1. cut, select Add Parent, and paste, or
2. edit the GUI file by hand later.

GUI Navigation

In order to edit an existing GUI, we need to know how to get to it; i.e., we need to know how to load a GUI into our Content Editor. If you have been following this guide in order, you have already done this. However, even if you have, there are a few ways to do it.

- If you want to edit the Main menu, simply start the GPGT Lesson Kit and open the GUI Editor.

- If you want to edit the playGui, simply start the GPGT Lesson Kit, load the "World Editor Training" mission, and open the GUI Editor.

What, however, do you do if you want to edit a GUI that isn't easy to get to work with the Load Mission dialog, for example? Let's say we want to add a label to the existing Create New GUI dialog. How would we get to it if we started editing in the Main menu? Assuming that you are at the Main menu:

- open the GUI Editor (**F10**), and
- 🖫 NewGuiDialog from the middle pull-down (above Content Editor).

New Control	NewGuiDialog - 1112	640 x 480

At this point, the Create new GUI dialog should be visible in the Content Editor (see Figure 3.59). That is basically it. Just select whatever GUI you need to edit, and there you are.

Figure 3.59.

Create New GUI dialog.

Engine Overview

Figure 3.60.

Content Tree.

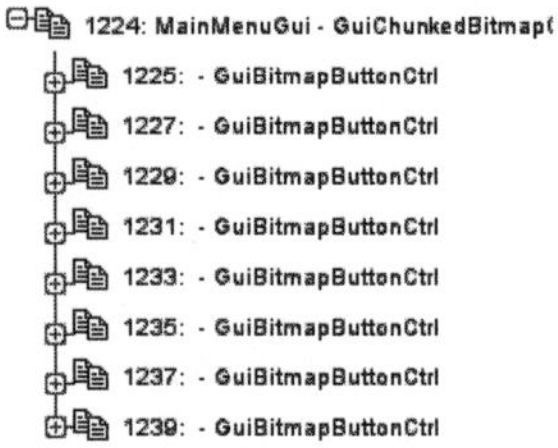

Figure 3.61.

New button.

Before we move on, get yourself back to the MainMenuGui and close the GUI Editor (**F10**).

3.14.6 Adding Controls to an Existing GUI

Adding a new control to an existing GUI is very simple. That is, adding the graphical portion is simple. We'll cover hooking scripts to your new controls a little later. For now, do the following.

- Start the GPGT Lesson Kit.

- Open the GUI Editor (**F10**).

- Expand the Content Tree by clicking on the [+].

- 🖫 on MainMenuGui (top of tree) to select it as your Add Parent. Your Content Tree will look something like Figure 3.60. Also note that the main window now has a yellow and a blue outline, meaning it is the Add Parent.

- 🖫 on the New Control button and select GuiButtonCtrl from the pop-up list.

- A new button will appear in the upper corner of the Content Editor. Drag it so that it is on the right side of your Quit button (see Figure 3.61).

- In the Inspector, give your new button the name "My First Button." 🖫 on APPLY and verify that the button now appears in the Content Tree and that it has a name (Figure 3.62).

- Now, in the Inspector, make the command equal to "quit();" and 🖫 on APPLY again (see Figure 3.63).

- Now, to save your work select File → Save GUI, select MainMenu.gui, then 🖫 on the Save button in the dialog (see Figure 3.64).

Figure 3.62. "My First Button."

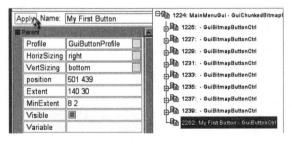

Figure 3.64. Saving the GUI.

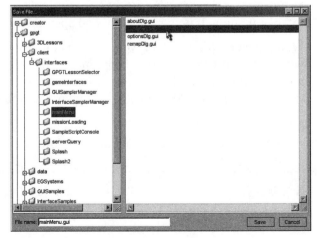

Figure 3.63. Quit command.

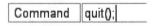

At this point, your changes to the GUI are final. Let's test it.

- Get out of the GUI Editor (**F10**).
- Exit the GPGT Lesson Kit.
- Restart the GPGT Lesson Kit.
- What happened? If you followed the instructions above, you placed spaces in the name of your new button. This is a no-no. If you restarted without deleting the DSO files (as instructed), the old menu is now showing, and the new button is not showing. If you deleted the DSO files and then restarted, the splash screen hung when switching to the main menu. In the former case, you can simply press the Quit button and keep reading. In the latter case, open the console by pressing the tilde (~) key, and then type `quit;` followed by **ENTER**.

All right, so we've killed the game, but we still have to fix our problem. To do so, follow these steps.

1. Open the file "gpgt\client\Interfaces\mainMenu\mainMenu.gui".
2. Search for "new GuiButtonCtrl(My First Button) {".
3. Replace it with "new GuiButtonCtrl(MyFirstButton) {".
4. Start the GPGT Lesson Kit.
5. Click your new button, and the GPGT Lesson Kit quits.

If you are observant, at this point you have a big question. Namely, why did the button (seem) to move from where you put it to somewhere else? That is, we placed it near the Quit button, but then when we ran the app it, well, … it moved! This brings us to the important discussion of horizSizing and vertSizing.

horizSizing and vertSizing

In general, these settings define how a control will be resized or repositioned when the control's parent container is resized. As a general rule, you can assume that the root container (the Canvas) will have a starting size of 640 × 480, and it (and all of the controls it contains) will be resized/repositioned from this state.

As any container is resized, all of its child controls are resized and/or repositioned according to the horizSizing and vertSizing properties of each control. If any of those controls are containers with children of their own, they too will be resized and/or repositioned in the same fashion. This behavior cascades down the parent-child tree of controls. This provides a basic layout capability.

The basic settings for these two properties are: center, relative, left/top, right/bottom, and width/height. Each is explained below.

- **Center.** This setting will center the control in its container. Only the control's position is altered—the control's extent (width and height) remains the same.

- **Relative.** When this setting is applied, the control in question will be resized and repositioned to maintain the same size and position relative to the parent container. For example, if the parent doubles in size, so will this control; additionally, the space between the control and the parent's borders will double.

- **Left/Top and Right/Bottom.** These settings only affect position. Extent is unaffected. Simply put, the change in size of the parent is applied to the distance between the control and the specified edge of the screen. This means that the control will maintain its distance from the opposite edge.

- **Width/Height.** These settings result in changes to the extent of the control only. The difference in size of the containing control is applied directly to the extents of the control itself.

3.14.7 Creating a New (Parent) GUI

Now, we'll learn how to create a new GUI. I warn you in advance that there is more to this topic than might seem apparent. For now, I'll demonstrate the mechanics of creating a new page. In later chapters, I'll go into greater detail on how the GUI system works.

Let's create a new dialog box. The dialog will have a label and a single button.

The Parent

Figure 3.65.

Creating a parent.

- Start the GPGT Lesson Kit.

- Open the GUI Editor (**F10**).

- Select File → New Gui.

- In the dialog that comes up, rename the GUI to MyFirstGui (no spaces) and 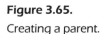 on Create (see Figure 3.65).

That's it for creating the parent. Now let's add some controls.

The Dialog

If you have not yet read through Section 3.14.6, "Adding Controls to an Existing GUI," please stop and do so. If you have, then do the following.

- Add a new GuiWindowCtrl control and, using the Inspector, modify the following parameters as indicated.
  - Name: MyFirstWindow
  - position: 200 100
  - extent: 350 250

- Select the MyFirstWindow control as the Add Parent.
- Add a new GuiTextCtrl control and using the Inspector modify the following parameters as indicated.
  - Name: MyFirstLabel
  - position: 145 5
  - extent: 60 20
  - text: My First Gui (notice the spaces)
- Add a new GuiButtonCtrl control and, using the Inspector, modify the following parameters as indicated.
  - Name: MySecondButton
  - position: 150 100
  - extent: 50 50
  - command: `Canvas.setContent(mainMenuGui);`
  - text: Cool
- Save this GUI under the name MyFirstGui.gui in the "gpgt/client/interfaces" directory.

Now, quickly test your new GUI by pressing **F10**. Note that earlier I warned you not to do this. In fact, it is OK to do so, but you must understand what is happening. We're not really trying to quit the editor. We want to temporarily suspend it so we can test our GUI. It just so happens that this suspending quits the GUI Editor if we press **F10** while editing the same page we entered the GUI Editor on. It can be confusing. Your new dialog should look like the one in Figure 3.66.

The next step is hooking up our dialog so we can load and unload it in the GPGT Lesson Kit.

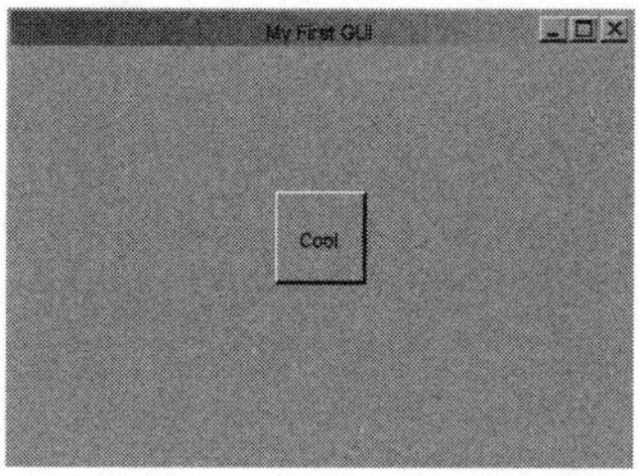

Figure 3.66.
Creating a dialog box.

3.14.8 Loading New GUIs

Now that we've successfully created our first dialog box, let's make it available in the GPGT Lesson Kit. In other words, let's use it. If you have been following the guide in order, you have already created a new button in the Main menu. Using what you have already learned, please make the following changes to the button.

- Select the existing GuiButtonCtrl control named MyFirstButton and, using the Inspector, modify the following parameters as indicated.
  - command: `Canvas.setContent(MyFirstGUI);`
  - text: Open Dialog
- Save the GUI.

Let's test it by pressing **F10** to exit the GUI Editor.

- 🖫 on the relabeled button Open Dialog should start our new dialog GUI.
- 🖫 on the button Cool should return you to the Main menu.

Notice that I said *should* above. If you quit the GPGT Lesson Kit between the sections "The Dialog" and "Loading New GUIs," then when you 🖫 on the Open Dialog button, nothing will happen. Why? Because it didn't get loaded. In order for any GUI to be available, it needs to be loaded before you try to wake it. This loading is done in various places. The organization of GUI loading scripts is beyond the scope of this section, but for completeness, I'll show you how to get your new GUI loaded.

Open the file "GPGT LessonKit\gpgt\client\init.cs" and search for the following code.

```
// Load up the shell GUIs
    exec("./interfaces/mainMenu/loader.cs");
```

Modify the code so it looks like this:

```
// Load up the shell GUIs
exec("./interfaces/mainMenu/loader.cs");
exec("./interfaces/MyFirstGUI.gui");
```

Save the file. Restart the GPGT Lesson Kit. Now, you can switch back and forth between the newly created dialog and the Main menu.

3.14.9 Summary

We started this chapter by learning that TGE provides two basic editors, the World Editor for editing the game world, and the GUI Editor for editing interfaces. Next, we summarized the eight tools contained in the World Editor.

After the introduction, and for the bulk of the chapter, we worked our way through the individual World Editor tools.

- **The Manipulator.** A full-screen editor made for tweaking the scene arrangement.
- **The Inspector.** A partial-screen editor created for tweaking the properties of existing objects in the scene.
- **The Creator.** A partial-screen editor with an object selection tree used to create new objects.
- **The Area Editor.** A partial-screen editor used to adjust the mission boundaries, to mirror the terrain, and for quick navigation of the camera/player position within a mission.

- **The Terrain Editor.** A partial-screen editor using various brushes to directly manipulate terrain geometry.

- **The Terraformer.** A partial-screen editor containing algorithmic base, generator, and filter elements used to create (or import) complex terrain geometries.

- **The Terrain Texture Editor.** A partial-screen editor utilizing sophisticated algorithmic generators and filters to paint the terrain with stunning detail.

- **The Terrain Painter.** A partial-screen editor utilizing a palette and brushes for making modifications to generated terrain textures, and/or for the wholesale editing of terrain textures by hand.

Having completed the long World Editor tools discussions, we ended the chapter with a detailed walk-through discussing the use of the GUI Editor. In this discussion, we learned about creating and saving new interfaces. We learned about placing controls and modifying their dynamic scaling and anchor behaviors. Finally, we made a simple interface to exercise and cement our newfound knowledge.

At a few points along the way, we took the time to make use of TGE editors/tools to create content for the prototype of the game we will be completing at the end of this guide.

All in all, we accomplished quite a lot in this chapter. At this point, you should already be able to open the kit, start the editors, and with some confidence in your results, poke about and start to create the worlds in your mind.

Chapter 4
Introduction to TorqueScript

This chapter offers an introduction to the Torque Game Engine scripting language, often referred to simply as TorqueScript. Besides introducing the TorqueScript language itself, this chapter will provide a foundation to build on when discussing other TGE topics.

Before starting, please understand that it is assumed you are familiar with some basic programming concepts. You do not need to be a guru, but having a basic familiarity with C/C++ and object-oriented programming principles will greatly facilitate learning TorqueScript.

4.1 TorqueScript Concepts and Terminology

4.1.1 To Script or Not To Script?

A frequent question I've seen in the forums is, "Do I need to use scripts?" No, you really don't need to use the built-in scripting language if you don't want to, but I'm 99 percent sure that, once you do start to use TorqueScript, it will be apparent that scripting in Torque is by far easier and more efficient than coding and recompiling every change you wish to make.

Even though the engine is written in C++ and assembly language, most of your game will be programmed in TorqueScript, denoted by files with the *.cs extension. The advantages of using a scripting language instead of coding everything in C++ are that your game does not have to be recompiled every time you make a change; it's a more-targeted, higher-level game language than C++; and you don't have to worry about memory management. A popular misconception is that scripts are slow; this is not necessarily true. TorqueScript is compiled into byte-code before being executed and is surprisingly fast. While C++ code will always be faster, the flexibility of scripting is superior for most gameplay-related functions.

Perhaps you doubt me? Or, maybe you aren't familiar with scripting in general. In either case, let's talk about scripting, and I'll see if I can set you on the right course.

What Is Scripting?

What exactly is a scripting language? What can you do with scripts? And why are they used so much in modern game development?

Scripting languages are programming languages designed to enable scripting. Scripting is the act of using preexisting [engine] components to accomplish new tasks. In other words, we use a scripting language to access features in the engine and then use those features to provide a game experience.

Generally, scripting languages are interpreted, not compiled (like C++ and other languages). This makes scripted tasks somewhat slower than compiled tasks, but we make this trade in order to gain flexibility and visibility, as well as ease of use. Because scripting languages also allow you to modify your program without having to recompile it, we are able to rapidly prototype and repair code. This speeds development significantly.

Often, scripting languages allow you to write code without worrying about nitty-gritty details like data types or memory management. This is both a boon and a bane. It is a boon as it simplifies many programming tasks, but a bane because it allows us to make mistakes that a strict compiled language and its compiler would find.

Given the above, it should be easy to see why scripting languages are used so heavily in modern games. However, if you are not convinced, consider these possible uses for a scripting language.

- **Prototyping.** During the development of your game, you will often need to test out ideas. New gameplay features might come up, or features in the original design might not work as well as envisioned and will need to be modified or replaced. To be efficient, you will need the ability to quickly test all these ideas, so you can decide whether to keep or modify each of them. Creating these quick tests is called *prototyping*. Scripts are great for prototyping because they are so quick to code with, test, and modify. After you prototype in script, performance-critical functionality can be ported over to C++ for final inclusion in the game.

- **Debugging.** Scripts are great for debugging, too. Because scripts are easily modified (on the fly), you can identify problems, address them, and retest without having to recompile and, in some cases, without even having to restart the game. Scripts can also be used to quickly create test units that stress other pieces of code to identify otherwise hard-to-find problems.

- **Game customization and tweaking.** The look and feel of a game's interface and many of its gameplay mechanics normally go through tweaks and revisions during the course of development. Thus, it is best to place most code related to these areas in script. This helps to rapidly test different looks and gameplay behaviors, as mentioned in the point on prototyping, above. There is a side benefit to developing your game this way as well. Having code related to your interface and gameplay in scripts allows end-users to customize your game to their liking (but only to the extent you choose to allow them when playing the official version of your game). Also, these types of script changes are the basis of many game mods. Mods are very popular in games like *Unreal, Quake,* and *Tribes.* Taking *Tribes 2* as an example, *War 2002, Renegades,* and *Team Aerial Combat* are all script-based mods. From a coding perspective, mods can be very simple to implement when working with games that incorporate flexible scripting languages and use them for much of the game's code. Implementing your game in such a fashion can obviously be a big draw for potential players that are interested in playing and/or creating mods. This allows user communities to breathe new life into your game, extending its shelf life.

- **Writing non–performance-critical functionality.** Really, *any* piece of functionality that won't have a big impact on performance can be coded in script. Writing render pipelines in script isn't a good idea, but writing code to modify the behavior of an existing pipeline is perfectly feasible and quite common.

Scripting makes sense in many more situations. The inclusion of scripting languages is a powerful feature of modern game engines, and developers are wise to leverage the advantages of scripting at every sensible opportunity.

4.1.2 Features We Need

If you accept that scripting is useful, what should you be looking for in a scripting language? What functionality should it provide? At minimum, a scripting language for use in a game should provide the following features.

- **Basic programming-language features.** The scripting language should provide all of the basic features common to modern programming languages, such as powerful variable types, basic operations (addition, subtraction, etc.), standard control statements (`if-then-else`, `for`, `while`, etc.), and subprograms (functions, file inclusion).

- **Access to engine structures.** This is a critical feature. For a game engine's scripting environment to be of use, it must provide some kind of interface to manipulate the core engine functionality and structures. The scripting system should allow access to the rendering, audio, physics, AI, and I/O systems. It must also allow the creation and deletion of objects and the definition of new functions.

Some other (very) nice features to have are the following.

- **Familiar and consistent syntax.** Ideally, the syntax of a scripting language is familiar, meaning it is similar to the syntax of a language many programmers are already familiar with, for example, C or C++.

- **Object-oriented functionality.** Object-oriented programming has been a revolution in the art and science of software engineering. Scripting languages that provide object-oriented functionality offer many benefits, including the following.

- **Encapsulation.** Provides a means of limiting access to code and data (not directly supported in TorqueScript).
- **Inheritance**. Provides a means of creating new objects from the definitions of existing engine objects and/or scripted objects.
- **Polymorphism**. Allows us to override the default behavior of derived object code, whether the object is derived from engine objects or other scripted objects.

- **On-demand loading and scoping.** Why have all the code in memory at once when it can be loaded as needed? Besides saving memory, scripting languages that allow the dynamic loading and unloading of pieces of code also make it easy to override a program's functionality on the fly.
- **Means of speeding up scripted code.** As noted above, scripted code is not usually compiled—it is simply interpreted at run time. A feature that many common scripting languages (Perl, Tcl, VBScript, Java) provide is the ability to compile scripts into byte-code. This byte-code is then executed on a virtual machine. The benefits of this are size and speed. Byte-code is (normally) smaller than and executes faster than interpreted code.

4.2 What about TorqueScript?

All right, enough generalities. What is Torque's scripting language like? Torque-Script is a strong and flexible language with syntax similar to C++. It provides all of the features listed above, including those on the "would be nice" list. The remainder of this chapter is dedicated to script-only functionality.

Please note that all the pertinent functions both for scripting and for exposing engine features to the console are covered in the "TorqueScript Quick Reference" appendix.

4.2.1 The Console and Sample Scripts

In order to facilitate your learning experience, many sample scripts are included with the GPGT Lesson Kit. These scripts are organized by chapter. Furthermore, all labeled scripts (labeled in the text of this document) can be run from the console simply by typing the supplied function name.

For example, the following sample script:

```
//bt99();
```

```
echo( "Torque Rocks" );
echo ( 1 + 1 );
```

can be run by typing `bt99();` into the console command line and then pressing **ENTER**.

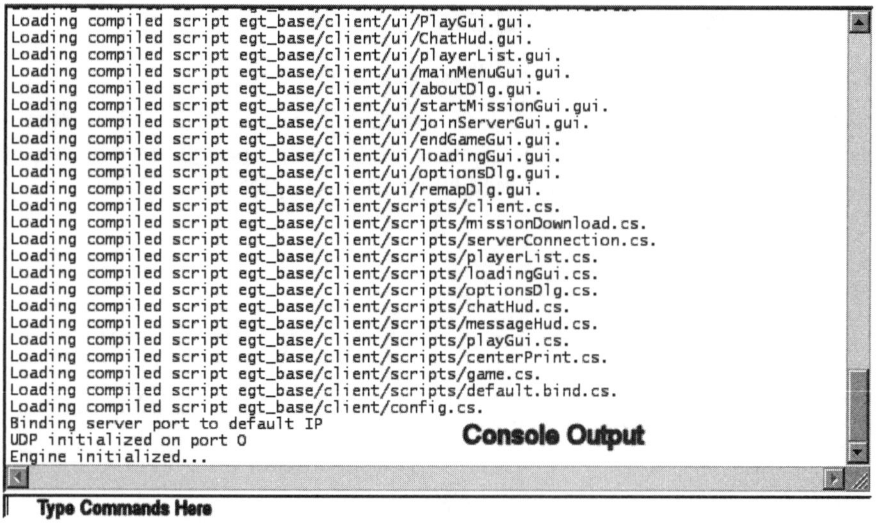

```
Loading compiled script egt_base/client/ui/PlayGui.gui.
Loading compiled script egt_base/client/ui/ChatHud.gui.
Loading compiled script egt_base/client/ui/playerList.gui.
Loading compiled script egt_base/client/ui/mainMenuGui.gui.
Loading compiled script egt_base/client/ui/aboutDlg.gui.
Loading compiled script egt_base/client/ui/startMissionGui.gui.
Loading compiled script egt_base/client/ui/joinServerGui.gui.
Loading compiled script egt_base/client/ui/endGameGui.gui.
Loading compiled script egt_base/client/ui/loadingGui.gui.
Loading compiled script egt_base/client/ui/optionsDlg.gui.
Loading compiled script egt_base/client/ui/remapDlg.gui.
Loading compiled script egt_base/client/scripts/client.cs.
Loading compiled script egt_base/client/scripts/missionDownload.cs.
Loading compiled script egt_base/client/scripts/serverConnection.cs.
Loading compiled script egt_base/client/scripts/playerList.cs.
Loading compiled script egt_base/client/scripts/loadingGui.cs.
Loading compiled script egt_base/client/scripts/optionsDlg.cs.
Loading compiled script egt_base/client/scripts/chatHud.cs.
Loading compiled script egt_base/client/scripts/messageHud.cs.
Loading compiled script egt_base/client/scripts/playGui.cs.
Loading compiled script egt_base/client/scripts/centerPrint.cs.
Loading compiled script egt_base/client/scripts/game.cs.
Loading compiled script egt_base/client/scripts/default.bind.cs.
Loading compiled script egt_base/client/config.cs.
Binding server port to default IP
UDP initialized on port 0                Console Output
Engine initialized...
```

Type Commands Here

Figure 4.1.
Script console.

To bring up the console, first, start the GPGT Lesson Kit, then hit the tilde key (~) in the upper left corner of the US-standard keyboard (next to the 1). The console will come right up (Figure 4.1).

Some of the sample scripts rely on the presence of datablocks. Thus, it will be necessary for you to first load the "3D Lessons" mission, before running them. As a reminder, the prewritten scripts will print a warning if you are not running the lessons mission:

```
Note: If you are not running the Lesson Sampler
Mission,  some examples may not work. Please click
'Start Mission..' from the GPGT Main Menu and select '3D
Lessons' mission.
```

4.2.2 The Sample Script Console

In addition to prewritten scripts, you may at any time bring up a special application supplied with the Lesson Kit, the Sample Script Console. This application has an editor window where you can type (or paste) a script and then execute it at the push of a button. The sample console will execute your script and show you the results.

To start this application, just run the Lesson Kit and press the Sample Script Console button.

4.3 TorqueScript Features

This scripting language has the following features.

- **Type-insensitive.** In TorqueScript, variable types are converted as necessary and can be used interchangeably. TorqueScript provides several basic literal types, which are described later in this chapter.

```
//bt00();

if( "1.2" == 1.2 ) {
  echo( "Same, TorqueScript is type-insensitive" );
}
else {
  echo( "Different, what!?" );
}
```

The code above will echo "Same, TorqueScript is type-insensitive."

- **Case-insensitive.** TorqueScript ignores case when interpreting variable and function names.

```
//bt01();

$a = "An example";
echo($a);
echo($A);
```

This code will echo "An example" twice.

- **Statement termination.** Statements are terminated with a semicolon as in many modern programming languages (C++, Java, JavaScript, etc.).

```
$a = "This is a statement";
```

If you do not include the semicolon at the end of a TorqueScript statement, an error will be echoed to the console.

- **Full complement of operators.** The complete list of TorqueScript's operators is given in the appendix. TorqueScript provides all the basic operators common to most programming languages, along with a few more advanced operators.

- **Very complete set of supplemental string, math, and other functions.** In addition to the built-in operators, TorqueScript comes with a very complete set of console functions that handle various string, math, and other operations. Table 4.1 lists some of the most commonly used functions. Please note that these functions are fully described later in the book (in Chapter 9, "Game-Setup Scripting," and Chapter 10, "Gameplay Scripting"), *and* a quick-reference with complete syntax, description, and sample usage is provided in electronic form with this guide.

Strings			
getSubStr	ltrim	rtrim	strchr
strcmp	stricmp	stripChars	stripTrailingSpaces
strlen	strlwr	strpos	strreplace
strstr	strupr	trim	
Words, Records, Fields			
detag	firstWord	getField	getFieldCount
getFields	getRecord	getRecordCount	getRecords
getTag	getWord	getWordCount	getWords
NextToken	removeField	removeRecord	removeWord
restWords	setField	setRecord	setWord
Files			
expandFileName	fileBase	fileExt	fileName
filePath	findFirstFile	findNextFile	getFileCount
getFileCRC	isFile	isWriteableFileName	
Vectors			
VectorAdd	VectorCross	VectorDist	VectorDot
VectorLen	VectorNormalize	VectorOrthoBasis	VectorScale
VectorSub			
Matrices			
MatrixCreate	MatrixCreateFromEuler	MatrixMulPoint	MatrixMultiply
MatrixMulVector			
Random Numbers			
getRandom	getRandomSeed		setRandomSeed
Math			
mAbs	mAcos	mAsin	mAtan
mCeil	mCos	mDegToRad	mFloatLength
mFloor	mLog	mPow	mRadToDeg
mSin	mSolveCubic	mSolveQuadratic	mSolveQuartic
mSqrt	mTan		

Table 4.1

Commonly used Torque console functions.

- **Full complement of control structures.** As with any robust language, TorqueScript provides the standard programming constructs: `if-then-else`, `for`, `while`, and `switch`.

```
//bt02();

for($a=0; $a<5; $a++) {
 echo($a);
}
```

- **Functions.** TorqueScript provides the ability to create functions with the optional ability to return values. Parameters are passed by value and by reference (see Section 4.3.5 for a detailed description and examples).
- **Provides inheritance and polymorphism.** TorqueScript allows you to inherit from engine objects and to subsequently extend or override object methods (see Section 4.3.6 for a detailed description and examples).
- **Provides on-demand loading and unloading of functions.** TorqueScript supports a very cool feature that allows you to load and unload functions as needed (see Section 4.3.8 for a detailed description and examples.)
- **Provides namespaces.** Like C++, TorqueScript supports the concept of namespaces. Namespaces are used to localize names and identifiers to avoid collisions. This means, for example, that you can have two different functions named `doIt()` that exist in two separate namespaces, but which are used in the same code (see Section 4.3.9 for a detailed description and examples).
- **Compiles and executes byte-code.** As a bit of icing on the cake, the TorqueScript engine compiles scripts prior to executing them, giving a speed increase as well as providing a point at which errors in scripts can be reasonably found and diagnosed. This compilation is done just-in-time and results in p-code, which is not the same as compilation of C++ or C, which result in machine code.

With this overview of TorqueScript's features, we can begin taking a detailed look at how TorqueScript works. We'll start by examining how TorqueScript handles the basics—variables, operators, and control statements. With these topics covered, we'll move on to cover in detail the more advanced features of TorqueScript.

4.3.1 Variables

Variables come in two flavors in TorqueScript: local and global. Local variables are transient, meaning they are destroyed automatically when they go out of scope. And what is scope? *Scope* is a term used to refer to the block of code a variable is defined in. For example, if we have a function, and we declare a local variable inside of that function, the local variable will be destroyed as soon as the function is done processing. When this happens, we say the variable has "gone out of scope." So, local variables only exist in their local scope—the function they are defined in. A piece of code inside a different function is not able to see the local variable. Global variables, on the other hand, are permanent and exist throughout the entire program they are defined in.

TorqueScript specifically marks local and global variables with special characters so that they are easy to tell apart. The syntax is as follows.

```
%local_var = value1;
$global_var = value2;
```

In TorqueScript, variables do not need to be declared before you use them. If a piece of code attempts to evaluate a variable that was not previously created, TorqueScript will declare the variable automatically.

//bt03();

```
for( 0 ; %a < 5 ; %a++ ) {
   echo( "%a == " , %a );
}

echo( "%a == " , %a );
```

Let's take a closer look at what this code does. On its first pass through the loop, the above code creates a new variable named %a. It must do so because %a has not yet been created when the loop tries to use it for the first time.

1. The echo() command inside the loop will print the value contained in the variable %a four times, echoing the values "", 1, 2, 3, 4, and 5 as the loop iterates and %a's value increases. "" is known as the null string. The first time through the above loop, %a is not yet defined, so TGE prints the null string.
2. After the loop finishes, %a will be echoed once again, by the line after the loop.

That is a basic description of how local and global variables work in TorqueScript. However, we have not yet discussed the rules for naming variables.

Variable names may contain any number of alphanumeric (a..z, A..Z, 0..9) characters, as well as the underscore (_) character. However, the first character in a variable's name cannot be a number. You may end variable

> In computer-science classes, we are taught time and time again that global variables are bad.
>
> Used to replace or circumvent a feature of the language you are programming in, they are bad.
>
> In languages like C, we have the ability to pass values between various levels of scope (either file or function) using pointers and references.
>
> As a scripting language, TorqueScript does not support these constructs: everything is passed by value. Instead, the global variable construct is supplied. Its purpose is to make data available across any and all scopes and contexts. In short, globals are not bad, and you should use them while writing scripts for Torque.

names with a number, but if you do, you must be especially careful with array names. For further explanation, see "Arrays" in Section 4.3.2.

Lastly, local and global variables can have the same name but contain different values. The following code will echo GPGT , GPGT 1, GPGT 2, and GPGT 3.

```
//bt04();

$a="GPGT";

for( 0 ; %a < 4 ; %a++ ) {
 echo( $a , " " , %a );
}
```

4.3.2 Data Types

TorqueScript implicitly supports several variable data types: numbers, strings, Booleans, arrays, and vectors. Each type is detailed below.

Numbers

Nothing mysterious here. TorqueScript handles your standard numeric types.

```
123      (integer)
1.234    (floating point)
1234e-3  (scientific notation)
0xc001   (hexadecimal)
```

Strings

This is for string data.

```
"abcd" (string)
'abcd' (tagged string)
```

Standard strings, in double quotes, behave as you would expect. Try these examples:

```
//bt05();

echo("Hello!");
echo("1.5" + "0.5");
```

Strings that appear in single quotes, 'abcd', are treated specially by TorqueScript. These strings are called *tagged strings,* and they are special in that they contain string data but also have a special numeric tag associated with them. Tagged strings are used for sending string data across a network. The value of a tagged string is only sent once, regardless of how many times you actually attempt the sending. On subsequent sends, only the tag value is sent. Tagged values must be detagged when printing.

Try the following examples.

//bt06();

```
$a="This is a regular string";
$b='This is a tagged string';
echo("Regular String: " $a);
echo("Tagged String: " $b);
```

Now that we know how to name strings and assign them values (normal or tagged), let's take a look at the special string operators TorqueScript offers.

> You may find it odd that the last line shows a blank. This is because, although we have created the tagged string, it has not been transmitted to us. You can only detag a tagged string that has been passed to you.

String Operators

There are four string operators.

```
@    (concatenates two strings)
TAB  (concatenation with tab)
SPC  (concatenation with space)
NL   (newline)
```

To concatenate two strings means, simply, to stick them together. For example, if we concatenate the strings "Hi" and "there", we end up with a big string reading "Hithere".

The basic syntax for these string operators is "*string1*" *op* "*string2*".

//bt07();

```
echo("Hi" @ "there.");
echo("Hi" TAB "there.");  // Note: TAB prints as ^ in console
echo("Hi" SPC "there.");
echo("Hi" NL "there.");
```

Escape Sequences

There is one last area you need to know about in order to work with strings in TorqueScript: escape sequences.

```
\n       (newline)
\r       (carriage return)
```

```
\t        (tab)
\c0..\c9 (colorize subsequent text)
\cr       (reset to default color)
\cp       (push current color on color stack)
\co       (pop color from color stack)
\xhh      (two digit hex value ASCII code)
\\        (backslash)
```

As in C, TorqueScript allows you to create a new line and tabs using the tried and true backslash character. These are called *escape sequences*. Escape sequences are used to indicate to the string-processing system that a special character is being read.

Additionally, for data that is printed to the console and GUIs, you can colorize by using \c*n*, where *n* is a value between 0 and 9, representing a predefined set of colors.

//bt08();

```
echo("\c2ERROR!!!\c0 => oops!");
```

The code above prints the line ERROR!!! => oops! with the first part in red and the second part in black. Going into detail about console output colorizing is beyond the scope of this chapter, but a little experimentation will go a long way toward helping you understand how the system works.

Booleans

Like most programming languages, TorqueScript also supports Booleans. Boolean variables have only two values—true or false.

```
true   (1)
false  (0)
```

Again, as in many programming languages, the constant true evaluates to the number 1 in TorqueScript, and the constant false evaluates to the number 0. Be careful, however, when comparing numeric values to the Boolean values true and false: *only the values 1 and 0 will compare correctly*. That is, in TorqueScript, the following statement will echo 0.

```
echo( 100 == true );
```

Numbers, strings, and Booleans: those are the basic data types in many programming languages, and TorqueScript supports them all. Next, we'll look at higher-level variable data types: arrays and vectors.

Arrays

It is a common misconception that TorqueScript does not support multi-dimensional arrays. This is not true, as the code below shows. The reason many people get confused about multidimensional arrays in TorqueScript is that there are multiple ways to address the array. As you can see, you can separate the dimension indices (M and N) with commas or underscores.

```
$MyArray[N]          (one-dimensional array)
$MyMultiArray[N,N]  (multidimensional array)
$MyMultiArrayM_N     (multidimensional array)
```

You must understand that in TGE all variables are eventually interpreted as strings. Furthermore, square brackets are removed, and commas are converted to underscores during the interpretation process. Underscores remain untouched. The real purpose of the brackets, commas, and underscores is that they function as "composers;" i.e., they help build the string from its various components. This is where the power of TorqueScript's arrays comes in to play. Consider the following code.

//bt09();

```
$TestVarEDO = 10;
$substring = EDO;
echo($substring); // prints EDO
echo($TestVar[$substring]); // prints 10
```

What we have done here is use the square brackets to compose a variable name on the fly.

There are a couple more things to know about TGE arrays.

1. $a and $a[0] are *separate and distinct variables.*

   //bt10();

   ```
   $a = 5;
   $a[0] = 6;
   echo("$a == ", $a);
   echo("$a[0] == ", $a[0]);
   ```

   Run this code, and you will see that $a and $a[0] are distinct in the output.

2. $MyArray0 and $MyArray[0] are *the same.* It may be surprising, but TorqueScript allows you to access array indices without using the common bracket [] syntax.

> The use of the square bracket operator to concatenate (compose) variable names on the fly is very useful in TorqueScript, but it should only be used when the usage does not obfuscate or otherwise render the script unreadable to others.
>
> We will in fact take advantage of this scripting feature in the guide, but I will explain my reasoning before doing so.

```
//bt11();
```

```
$MyArray[0] = "slot 0";
echo ( $MyArray0 );
$MyArray[1] = "slot 1";
echo ( $MyArray1 );
$MyArray[0,0] = "slot 0,0";
echo ( $MyArray0_0 );
```

Now that we have a basic understanding of arrays, it's time to move on to vectors.

Vectors

This helpful data type is used throughout Torque.

"1.0 1.0 1.0 1.0" **(4 element vector)**

For example, many fields in the World Editor take numeric values in sets of 3 or 4. These are stored as strings and interpreted as *vectors*. There is a whole set of console operations for manipulating vectors. Also, vectors are taken as input for many game methods. In the following example, two vectors are added together using the console function VectorAdd().

//bt12();

```
$srcRay = "1.0 0.0 1.0";
$destRay = "1.0 6.0";
echo( VectorAdd( $srcRay , $destRay ) );
```

Remember, TorqueScript does not support pointers or references. This means that all functions return values. In the above code, VectorAdd() is taking two vectors as inputs and returning a new vector as an output.

We could alternately write the above code as follows.

```
$srcRay = "1.0 0.0 1.0";
$destRay = "1.0 6.0";
$resultVec = VectorAdd( $srcRay , $destRay );
echo( $resultVec );
```

Either of the above code snippets will output 2 6 1, which represents the vector <2 , 6 , 1>, the result of adding the vectors <1.0 , 0.0 , 1.0> and <1.0 , 6.0>.

Bad Vector Math

A common mistake among beginning Torque scripters is something like the following.

```
echo( "1 2 3" + "4 5 6" ); // Wrong!
```

The inexperienced scripter might expect the resultant output to be 5 7 9. Instead, the output will simply be 5. Why? Because the built-in operators only look at the first element of each vector. To correctly add (or otherwise manipulate) vectors, use the supplied vector functions (full syntax given later and in the appendices): `VectorAdd`, `VectorCross`, `VectorDist`, `Vector-Dot`, `VectorLen`, `VectorNormalize`, `VectorOrthoBasis`, `VectorScale`, and `VectorSub`.

4.3.3 Operators

A complete listing of TorqueScript's operators can be found in the "Torque-Script" appendix. Refer to the appendix for detailed information. In general, operators in TorqueScript behave very similarly to operators in C-derived languages. However, there are two commonly encountered caveats when working with TorqueScript's operators.

- Syntactically, the `++` and `--` operators are only post-fix operators (i.e., `++%a;` which is a pre-fix operation, does not work; only `%a++`, which is a post-fix operation, will work).

```
$a = 15;
echo( $a++ ); // Prints 16
```

- String comparisons are of the following form:

```
$=    (string equal to operator)
!$=   (string not equal to operator)
```

In TorqueScript, the equivalent of 0 for strings is the null string "".
However, one has to be very careful when using the comparison operators.
If you use the numeric operator == to compare zero (0) and a null string (""),
you will get a return value of **true**.

```
echo( 0 == "" ); \\ Will print 1 to console.
```

However, if we use the string comparison operator $=, the same comparison will return **false**.

```
echo( 0 $= "" ); \\ Will print 0 to console.
```

4.3.4 Control Statements

We'll now take a look at TorqueScript's control statements—branching and looping structures. TorqueScript supports all the common control statements.

Branching Structures

We compare three branching control statements.

- **if-then-else.** The general structure of the if-then-else statement is the following.

```
if(expression) {
   statements;
} else {
   alternate statements;
}
```

Things to know:

- Brackets ({}) are optional for single-line statements. (Many programmers find it more helpful to always use brackets.)
- Compound if-then-else-if-then-... statements are perfectly legal. (Many programmers find switch statements easier to read for large blocks of related if cases).

- **switch.** The general structure of the switch statement is as follows:

```
switch(expression) {
case value0:
   statements;
   break;
case value1:
   statements;
   break;
...
case valueN:
   statements;
   break;
default:
   statements;
}
```

Things to know:

- switch only (correctly) evaluates numerics. There is a special statement, switch$, for strings.

- `break` statements are superfluous. TorqueScript will only execute matching cases.
- In TorqueScript, `switch` statements are no faster than `if-then-else` statements.
- **switch$**. This statement behaves exactly like the `switch` statement with one important exception: it is only for strings.

Looping Structures

We look at two looping control statements.

- **for.** The general structure of the `for` loop is the following.

```
for(expression0; expression1; expression2) {
   statement(s);
}
```

Here is an example.

//bt13();

```
for(%count = 0; %count < 5; %count++) {
   echo(%count);
}
```

As you can see, this is identical to the `for` loop in C++.

- **while.** The general structure of the `while` loop is the following.

```
while(expression) {
   statement(s);
}
```

Here is an example.

//bt14();

```
%count = 0;
while (%count < 5) {
   echo(%count);
   %count++;
}
```

Again, this is very similar to the looping structure in C++.

If you are a C or C++ coder, you may be used to taking advantage of the fall through in a `switch` statement. For example, in C, the following code will print the same message for values 1, 2, and 3, but not for 4:

```
// C code
switch( val ) {
case 1:
case 2:
case 3:
  printf( "Hello" );
case 4:
  printf( "World\n" );
}
```

In this sample, the cases 1 through 3 will print `Hello` and fall through case 4 to print `World\n`, in the end producing `Hello World\n`.

You cannot do this in TorqueScript. In the following similarly structured example, nothing will print for cases 1 or 2, and we will get `Hello` for 3 and `World` for 4:

```
// TorqueScript
switch( %val )
{
case 1:
case 2:
case 3:
  echo( "Hello" );
case 4:
  echo( "World" );
}
```

Remember: switch statements do not fall through in TorqueScript.

As you can see, TorqueScript supports the standard set of control statements and handles them very similarly to familiar languages like C++.

In the next section, we continue our detailed examination of TorqueScript's standard features. We'll be looking at how TorqueScript handles functions (it's similar to C++, but more flexible).

4.3.5 Functions

Basic functions in TorqueScript are defined as follows.

```
function func_name([arg0],...,[argn]) {
  statements;
  [return val;]
}
```

Here is an example.

//echoRepeat();

```
function echoRepeat (%echoString, %repeatCount) {
  for (%count = 0; %count < %repeatCount; %count++) {
    echo(%echoString);
  }
}

echoRepeat("hello!", 5);
```

The code above will echo the string `hello!` five times to the console.

TorqueScript functions can take any number of arguments, each separated by commas. Functions may return a value by using the `return` statement, just as in C++.

Things to know:

• If you define a function and give it the same name as a previously defined function, TorqueScript will completely override the old function. Even if you define the new function with a different number of parameters, if its name is exactly the same as another function, the older function will be overridden. This is important to note: TorqueScript does not support function polymorphism in the same way C++ does. However, TorqueScript provides packages (see Section 4.3.8), which can get around this problem.

• *For functions defined in TorqueScript,* if you call a function and pass fewer parameters than the function's definition specifies, the unpassed parameters will be given an empty string as their default value. Similarly, if you pass too many parameters, the extras will be dropped.

- *For functions defined in C++*, if you call a function and pass fewer parameters than the function's definition specifies, the engine will complain, and the call will fail. The same goes for passing too many arguments.

- TorqueScript supports recursion, and it behaves just as in C++. The following example is a rewrite of the `echoRepeat()` function we used above, but this version uses recursion instead of a `for` loop:

```
//echoRepeatRecurse();

function echoRepeatRecurse (%echoString, %repeatCount) {
  if (%repeatCount > 0) {
    echo(%echoString);
    echoRepeatRecurse(%echoString, %repeatCount--);
  }
}

echoRepeatRecurse("hello!", 5);
```

4.3.6 Objects

Having covered the basics of the language, it's time to examine some of TorqueScript's more powerful details.

In Torque, every item in a game is a SimObject, or a subclass of SimObject, and all of these objects can be accessed via script. For example, Player, WheeledVehicle, and Item are all accessible via script, although they are defined in C++.

Objects are created in TorqueScript using the following syntax (see Table 4.2).

```
%var = new ObjectType(Name : CopySource, arg0, ..., argn) {
  <datablock = DatablockIdentifier;>

  [existing_field0 = InitialValue0;]
  ...
  [existing_fieldM = InitialValueM;]

  [dynamic_field0 = InitialValue0;]
  ...
  [dynamic_fieldN = InitialValueN;]
};
```

Let's create a first object, with no initialization.

115

Table 4.2

Definitions of object syntax elements.

Syntax Element	Description
`%var`	The variable where the object's handle will be stored.
`new`	A keyword telling the engine to create an instance of the following ObjectType.
`ObjectType`	Any class declared in the engine or in script that has been derived from SimObject or a subclass of SimObject. SimObject-derived objects are what we were calling "game world objects" earlier in this book.
`Name` (optional)	Any expression evaluating to a string, which will be used as the object's name.
`CopySource` (optional)	The name of an object that is previously defined somewhere in script. Existing field values will be copied from CopySource to the new object being created. Any dynamic fields defined in CopySource will also be defined in the new object, and their values will be copied. Note that if CopySource is of a different ObjectType than the object being created, only CopySource's dynamic fields will be copied.
`arg0, ..., argn` (optional)	A comma-separated list of arguments to the class constructor (if it takes any).
`datablock`	Many objects (those derived from GameBase, or subclasses of GameBase) require datablocks to initialize specific attributes of the new object. Datablocks are discussed in Section 4.3.10.
`existing_ fieldN`	In addition to initializing values with a datablock, you may also initialize existing class members (fields) here. Note that if you wish to modify a member of a C++-defined class, the member must have been exposed to the console.
`dynamic_fieldN`	Lastly, you may create new fields (which will exist only in script) for your new object. These will show up as dynamic fields in the World Editor Inspector.

```
// Create a SimObject w/o modifying any fields
$example_object = new SimObject();
```

Then create a second object using an initialization block.

```
// Create a SimObject w/ dynamic fields
$example_object = new SimObject() {
  a_new_field = "Hello world!";
};
```

Now let's create a datablock definition.

```
// Create a StaticShape using a datablock
datablock StaticShapeData( MyFirstDataBlock ) {
  shapeFile = "~/data/shapes/player/player.dts";
  junkvar = "helloworld";
};
```

Then make an object that uses that definition.

```
new StaticShape() {
 dataBlock = "MyFirstDataBlock";
 position = "0.0 0.0 0.0";
 rotation = "1 0 0 0";
 scale = "1 1 1";
};
```

In the Expert Tip on p. 111, I mentioned that == and $= will return opposite results when the operands are 0 and "". Specifically, == will compare them as being equal and $= as not equal. This is important to remember when you check for the nonpresence of a dynamic field.

The safest way to check for a nonpresent field is the following.

```
$y = new StaticShape() {
 dataBlock = "MyFirstDataBlock";
 position = "0.0 0.0 0.0";
 rotation = "1 0 0 0";
 scale = "1 1 1";
};
if( $y.myField == 0 ) {
 echo( "myField is not initialized (not present)" );
}
```

This is the safest method of comparing, because it will continue to compare correctly for:

- field not initialized,
- field set to 0,
- field set to "".

In other words, we can forget (or goof) later and preinitialize the field with a value equivalent to logical `false` and this code will still work.

Of course, if you are really sharp and don't make mistakes, you can compare for uninitialized fields as follows:

```
if( $y.myField $= "" ) {
 echo( "myField is not initialized (not present)" );
}
```

Just remember that this comparison can fail if the field is later preinitialized to 0.

Engine Overview

Handles and Names

Every object in the game is identified and tracked by two parameters.

- **Handle**. Every object is assigned a *unique* numeric ID upon creation. This is generally referred to as the object's handle.
- **Name**. Additionally, all objects *may* have a name.

In most cases, handles and names may be used interchangeably to refer to the same object, but a word of caution is in order: handles are always unique, whereas multiple objects *may* have the same name. If you have multiple objects with the same name, referencing that name will find one and only one of the objects.

Fields and Console Methods

TorqueScript object fields and console methods are the equivalents of C++ object members and methods. Objects instantiated via script may have data members (referred to as *fields*) and functional methods (referred to as *console methods*). In order to access an object's fields or console methods, one uses the standard dot notation, as in C++.

```
// Note: The scripts below assume we have an object with a
//  handle of 123, and a name of AName

// Directly access via handle
//
123.field_name = value;
123.command_name();

// Directly access via name
//
AName.field_name = value;
AName.command_name();

// Indirectly access via a variable
// containing either a name or a handle
//
%AVar.field_name = value;
%AVar.command_name();
```

To get a picture of how this works for real, do the following.

- Start the GPGT Lesson Kit.
- Run one of the missions.

- Start the World Editor Inspector (press **F11**).
- Switch to camera view (press **ALT + C**; on a Mac, you may need to select Camera View from the Camera menu) and select the character (hold down the right mouse button to look around; drag the mouse down until your player comes into view).
- Give the character a name, such as myGuy (type *myGuy* in the textbox next to the Apply button, and then click the Apply button).
- Open the console (press the ~ key).
- Then, run the following sample.

```
//bt16();

$player_name = "myGuy";
$player_id = $player_name.getID();
echo( $player_name.position );
echo( $player_name.getID() );
echo( "myGuy".getID() );
echo( myGuy.getID() );
```

In the above example, `getID()` returns the unique ID of the player object.

Dynamic Fields

In addition to normal fields (object fields exposed to script by the engine), TorqueScript allows you to create dynamic fields. Dynamic fields are associated with a single instance of an object and can be added and removed at will.

Adding a dynamic field in TorqueScript is automatic. If you try to read an object field and the field is not found, TorqueScript will simply return an empty string, and no dynamic field will be created. However, if you try to write to an object field that doesn't exist, TorqueScript will automatically create a matching dynamic field for the object, and assign it the value you indicated.

```
//bt17();

// new_var will not be created because we are only
// 'reading' it
echo( $player_id.new_var );

// new_var2 will be created and initialized to "Hello"
$player_id.new_var2 = "Hello";

echo( $player_id.new_var2 );
```

> Dynamic fields, if created, are only visible by the server. When objects and datablocks are sent to the clients, only those fields that are exposed by the engine will be sent to the clients. This can be a little confusing until you understand that the engine does not have any context for dynamic fields and thus cannot send them across the network.
>
> If you find yourself needing to add new fields to existing objects or datablocks, and if you want them to be transmitted to clients, you may either write networking scripts to do this, or you may edit the code and recompile the engine. Unfortunately, these are both advanced topics beyond the scope of this book. For now, just remember:
>
> **Dynamic fields are not networked!**

119

4.3.7 Console Methods

In addition to supporting the creation of functions, TorqueScript allows you to create methods within the scope of the console (not requiring you to use C++ to add them). These are called console methods and are like functions, except that they are associated with a specific namespace (see Section 4.3.9, "Namespaces").

```
function classname::method_name(%this, [arg0],...,[argn]) {
    statements;
    [return val;]
}
```

Table 4.3.

Definitions of console method syntax elements.

Syntax Element	Description
function	A keyword telling TorqueScript we are defining a new function.
classname::	The class type this function is supposed to work with.
func_name	The name of the function we are creating.
%this	A variable that will contain the handle of the "calling object."
...	Any number of additional arguments.

At a minimum, console methods require that you pass them an object handle. You will often see the first argument named %this. People use %this (contains object ID of object calling this method), but you can name it anything you want. As with console functions, any number of additional arguments can be specified separated by commas. Also, a console method may optionally return a value.

When a console method is called by the engine, or on the handle or name of an object, the ID of the object is passed automatically as the first argument.

Being associated with a namespace, console methods may be called on an instance of any object in that namespace. *Calling on an instance* means that the method is called using dot (.) notation in one of the following three ways:

```
// Aname is the object's name
AName.methodName( [ arguments ] );
```

or

```
// 123 is is the object's numeric ID
123.methodName( [ arguments ] );
```

or

```
// %var contains the object's name or ID
%var.methodName( [ arguments ] );
```

Here are some examples.

```
function Goober::hi(%this) {
  echo("Goober Hello ", %this);
}
```

Assuming our player handle is 1000, if we type:

```
1000.hi();
```

we get the following.

```
<input> (0): Unknown command hi.
Object (1000) Player->ShapeBase->GameBase->SceneObject->
NetObject->SimObject
```

What has happened is that Torque has searched the entire hierarchy of Player and its parent classes, looking for a function called `hi()` defined in the context of one of those classes. Not finding one, it prints the above message. To demonstrate that Torque does search the class hierarchy of Player, try the following next.

```
function NetObject::hi(%this) {
 echo("NetObject Hello ", %this);
}
```

Typing:

```
1000.hi();
```

we get the following.

```
NetObject Hello 1000
```

Next, if we define:

```
function Player::hi(%this) {
 echo("Player Hello ", %this);
 Parent::hi(%this);
}
```

we can type:

```
1000.hi();
```

and get the following:

```
Player Hello 1000
NetObject Hello 1000
```

Do you see what happened? Torque found `Player::hi()` first, but we also wanted to execute the *previous definition* of `hi()`. To do this, we used the `Parent::` keyword. Of course, not finding a ShapeBase instance, which is Player's literal parent, Torque then searched up the hierarchy of the chain until it came to the NetObject version.

Lastly, we can force Torque to call a specific instance as follows.

> Defining subsequent console methods with the same name as prior console methods overrides the previous definition permanently, unless the redefinition is within a package (see Section 4.3.8, "Packages").

```
NetObject::hi(1000);
```

gives us:

```
NetObject Hello 1000
```

and:

```
ShapeBase::hi(1000);
```

also gives us:

```
NetObject Hello 1000
```

since there is no ShapeBase instance of `hi()` defined.

4.3.8 Packages

Packages provide dynamic function polymorphism in TorqueScript. In short, a function defined in a package will override the prior definition of a same named function when the package is activated. Packages have the following syntax.

```
package package_name() {
  function function_definition0() {
    [statements;]
  }
  ...
```

```
function function_definitionN() {
   [statements;]
}
};
```

Things to know:

- The same function can be defined in multiple packages.
- Only functions can be packaged.
- Datablocks (see Section 4.3.10) cannot be packaged.

Packages can be activated as follows.

```
ActivatePackage(package_name);
```

Packages can be deactivated as follows.

```
DeactivatePackage(package_name);
```

Packages are managed on a stack. Each call to `ActivatePackage(package_name)` pushes its argument onto the stack, and it is always the topmost package that will be active.

The easiest way to get a feel for packages is with an example. The following example is the most detailed we've looked at so far in this guide, but don't worry. It will make perfect sense when we're done.

The following code has been provided with the GPGT Lesson Kit. Simply start the Lesson Kit, open the console (~), and follow the instructions below.

```
//test_packages( N ); // N == 0, 1, or 2

// Define an initial function: demo()
//
function demo() {
   echo("Demo definition 0");
}

// Now define three packages, each implementing
// a new instance of: demo()
//
package DemoPackage1 {
    function demo() {
        echo("Demo definition 1");
    }
};
```

Engine Overview

```
package DemoPackage2 {
    function demo() {
        echo("Demo definition 2");
    }
};

package DemoPackage3 {
  function demo() {
        echo("Demo definition 3");
        echo("Prior demo definition was=>");
        Parent::demo();
  }
};

function test_packages(%test_num) {
    switch(%test_num) {
    // Standard usage
    case 0:
        echo("------------------------------------------");
        echo("A packaged function overrides a prior");
        echo("definition of the function, but allows");
        echo("the new definition to be \'popped\' ");
        echo("off the stack.");
        echo("------------------------------------------");
        demo();
        ActivatePackage(DemoPackage1);
        demo();
        ActivatePackage(DemoPackage2);
        demo();
        DeactivatePackage(DemoPackage2);
        demo();
        DeactivatePackage(DemoPackage1);
        demo();

    // Parents
    case 1:
        echo("------------------------------------------");
        echo("The Parent for a packaged function is");
        echo("always the previously activated ");
        echo("packaged function.");
        echo("------------------------------------------");
        demo();
        ActivatePackage(DemoPackage1);
        demo();
        ActivatePackage(DemoPackage3);
```

```
        demo();
        DeactivatePackage(DemoPackage3);
        DeactivatePackage(DemoPackage1);
        echo("--------------------------------------");

        demo();
        ActivatePackage(DemoPackage1);
        demo();
        ActivatePackage(DemoPackage2);
        demo();
        ActivatePackage(DemoPackage3);
        demo();
        DeactivatePackage(DemoPackage3);
        DeactivatePackage(DemoPackage2);
        DeactivatePackage(DemoPackage1);

    // Stacking oddities
    case 2:
        echo("--------------------------------------");
        echo("Deactivating a \'tween\' package will");
        echo("deactivate all packages \'stacked\' after");
        echo("it.");
        echo("--------------------------------------");
        demo();
        ActivatePackage(DemoPackage1);
        demo();
        ActivatePackage(DemoPackage2);
        demo();
        DeactivatePackage(DemoPackage1);
        demo();
    }
}
```

The standard way to use a package is to define a previously defined function inside the package, activate it as needed, and then deactivate it to go back to the default case for the function. To see this in action, type: `test_packages(0);`.

TorqueScript provides a useful keyword, `Parent::`. By using the `Parent::` keyword in a packaged function, we can execute the function that is being overridden. To see this in action, type: `test_packages(1);`.

It is important to understand that packages are, essentially, stacked atop each other. So, if you deactivate a package that was activated *prior* to other packages, you are in effect automatically deactivating all packages that were activated after it. To see this in action, type `test_packages(2);`.

125

Things to know:

- Packages may define new functions. Remember that when you deactivate a package, these functions become undefined.
- The `Parent::` keyword is not recursive, i.e., `Parent::Parent::fun()` is illegal.
- Again, deactivating packages activated prior to other more recently activated packages deactivates all subsequently activated packages.

4.3.9 Namespaces

As previously mentioned, namespaces are provided in TorqueScript. The way they work is quite simple. First, all objects belong to a namespace. The namespace they belong to normally defaults to the same name as their object's class name. Players belong to the `Player::` namespace, vehicles to the `Vehicle::` namespace, etc.

```
// Player class namespace
Player::
```

Also as previously mentioned, these namespaces provide separation of functionality, such that one may have functions with the same name but belonging to separate namespaces. To use one of these functions, either you must manually select the appropriate namespace, or in some cases this is done automatically for you.

It is important to understand that the `::` is not magical in any way. In fact, you can create functions with `::` in their name. This doesn't mean they belong to a namespace. If the expression prefixing the `::` is not a valid class/namespace name, in effect, all you have done is create a unique name.

```
// Not really namespaces
function Ver1::doIt() {
  ...
};

function Ver2::doIt() {
  ...
};
```

Now, there is more to namespaces that you need to understand, but before we can address that, we need to learn about some other topics. So, we will revisit namespaces below in the appropriately titled Section 4.4, "Datablocks, Objects, and Namespaces Revisited."

4.3.10 Datablocks

Of all the features in TorqueScript, datablocks are probably the most confusing. To make things worse, they are central to the creation of most objects, which means you need to understand them relatively early.

"Datablocks are special objects that are used to transmit static data from server to client" (from engine.overview.txt).

This definition, although true, doesn't really tell us much. Some searching turns up additional definitions.

"A datablock is an object that contains a set of characteristics which describe some other type of object" (from Joel Baxter, in the GarageGames forums).

Better, but this is still a little blurry on the purpose and use of datablocks.

"A datablock is a(n) object that can be declared either in C++ engine code, or in script code … Each declared datablock can then be used as a "template" to create objects …"(from Liquid Creations, Scripting Tutorial #2).

Very good. So, datablocks are templates, and we use them to create new objects with the attributes specified by the template. But how do we do this? Well, for the answer to that question, you'll have to wait. First, we need to discuss a few other important topics, and then we will revisit datablocks and give them the thorough coverage that they deserve.

The Object-Datablock Connection

The Torque novice may stumble along for a bit, playing with the examples that are provided with Torque. Eventually, the question arises, "Why are some objects made with datablocks and others not?"

The answer, from a practical standpoint, is because otherwise you won't have a working game; specifically, any GameBase object, or subclass of GameBase, must be made with a datablock, otherwise the script will not compile.

To understand the philosophical reasons, we first observe that objects placed in the game world will fall into three broad categories.

- The object does not have much associated data and/or has few parameters.

- The object does have a lot of parameters, but these parameters are likely to be unique, or must be allowed to be unique, between instances of the object.

- The object has a lot of data or parameters, but it is OK for these data/parameters to be shared between instances.

The first two categories fit the class of objects that do not need and are therefore not created from datablocks. Conversely, the third category fits the class of objects that could benefit from using datablocks. Why? How? Recall that, unlike normal objects, you are only allowed to have a single instance of any one datablock. Furthermore, objects that are created from datablocks all share the same instance of that datablock.

I can sense that some folks will be shaking their heads at this point, so let's look at Table 4.4, which should clarify the relationship.

In the code snippets in Table 4.4, we make two physical zones, independent of each other. For each, we needed to specify all field values. We also made two StaticShapes. Each StaticShape has unique attributes, but they both share one datablock, which is used to describe the model they render and (as we'll see later) many more attributes.

Now, let's examine the creation of non–datablock-created objects in detail, followed by datablock-created objects.

Table 4.4.

Comparison of non–datablock-based and datablock-based objects.

Non-Datablock-Based Object	Datablock-Based Object
• Created directly from a C++ class in the console • Contains fields • May contain dynamic fields	• Created directly from a C++ class in the console • Contains fields • May contain dynamic fields • *Requires* an additional datablock field, which is assigned a previously defined datablock.

<pre>new PhysicalZone(firstPhysicalZone) {
 position = "371.851 322.83 218";
 rotation = "1 0 0 0";
 scale = "1 1 1";
 velocityMod = "1";
 gravityMod = "1";
 appliedForce = "0 0 0";
 polyhedron = "10 10 10 1 0 0 0 -1 0 0 0 1";
};
 	
new PhysicalZone(secondPhysicalZone) {
 position = "671.851 125.83 218";
 rotation = "1 0 0 0";
 scale = "1 1 1";
 velocityMod = "1";
 gravityMod = "1";
 appliedForce = "0 0 0";
 polyhedron = "10 10 10 1 0 0 0 -1 0 0 0 1";
};</pre>
	<pre>datablock StaticShapeData(SimpleTarget0) {
	 category = "Targets";
	 shapeFile = "~/data/…/simpletarget.dts";
	};
	
	new StaticShape(firstTarget) {
	 dataBlock = "SimpleTarget0";
	 position = "360.17 325.775 219.906";
	 rotation = "1 0 0 0";
	 scale = "1 1 1";
	};
	
	new StaticShape(secondTarget) {
	 dataBlock = "SimpleTarget0";
	 position = "460.17 325.775 219.906";
	 rotation = "1 0 0 0";
	 scale = "1 1 1";
	};</pre>

Creating Non–Datablock-Based Objects

I've provided the syntax for creating objects previously, but let's go ahead and create some variations of non-datablock objects to clarify the use of that syntax. We will use physical zones (p-zones) in all our examples.

```
new PhysicalZone() {
};
```

The above example creates a p-zone but doesn't specify a name or any of the parameters; therefore, it will take the default value provided by the C++ class's constructor.

```
new PhysicalZone(SpeedupZone) {
 position = "0 0 0";
 velocityMod = "2";
};
```

The above example will create a p-zone named "SpeedupZone," positioned at < 0,0,0 >. This particular p-zone will multiply the player's velocity by two when the player enters the zone.

```
new PhysicalZone(SpeedupZone2 : SpeedupZone) {
 position = "10 10 10";
};
```

The above example will create a p-zone named "SpeedupZone2," positioned at < 10,10,10 >. Aside from position, which has been redefined, it will inherit (by copying) all the fields in the previous datablock definition, SpeedupZone. However, the only field that will be different from the default is `position`. Thus, the above p-zone creation statement, using inheritance, is equivalent to the following p-zone creation statement, not using inheritance.

```
new PhysicalZone(SpeedupZone2) {
 position = "10 10 10";
 velocityMod = "2";
};
```

Creating Datablock-Based Objects

Like non–datablock-created objects, when we create new instances of data-block-created objects, we can inherit (copy) fields from previously defined datablock-created objects.

We will talk about physical Zones (p-zones) in Chapter 8, "Mission Objects," but for now, let me say that a p-zone is a rectangular object that can be placed in the world to change physical characteristics in that zone.

For example, a p-zone can be used to change the gravity and/or apply a force and/or modify an object's current velocity when the object passes into or through the area encapsulated by the physical zone's bounds.

In essence, I'm saying that the syntax rules for object creation are universal. To assure you of this, I will show you two examples of datablock-created objects, one normal and one with inheritance.

```
new StaticShape(TestTarget) {
 position = "0 0 0";
 rotation = "1 0 0 0";
 scale = "1 1 1";
 dataBlock = "SimpleTarget0";
};
```

The above example creates a StaticShape named "TestTarget." It defines the position, rotation, and the scale. Additionally, it tells the engine to use datablock "SimpleTarget0" to initialize this object's datablock. Subsequently, this object will always be associated with the datablock "SimpleTarget0."

```
new StaticShape(TestTarget2: TestTarget) {
 position = "0 10 0";
};
```

The above example creates another StaticShape. This one is named "Test-Target2." It inherits all the fields of TestTarget and overrides the position. The important thing to understand is that it shares datablock "SimpleTarget0" with the other instance of StaticShape, "TestTarget"; i.e, we have two instances of StaticShape that share one instance of the datablock "SimpleTarget0."

Declaring Datablocks

So far, we have clarified the connection between objects and datablocks. We have demonstrated that only a single instance of any datablock can be created and shared between any number of datablock-using objects. We have shown that the rules for creating objects are the same between those objects that use datablocks and those that do not. The only thing remaining for us to discuss is the declaration of datablocks. So, let's get to it.

We declare datablocks similarly to the way we create objects. Datablock declaration syntax is as follows.

```
// In TorqueScript
datablock DataBlockType(Name [: CopySource]) {
  category = "CategoryName";
  [datablock_field0 = Value0;]
  ...
  [datablock_fieldM = ValueM;]
```

```
[dynamic_field0 = Value0;]
...
[dynamic_fieldN = ValueN;]
};
```

As you can see, this is almost identical to the syntax used to create console objects. Let's break it down bit-by-bit anyway in Table 4.5.

Syntax Element	Description
datablock	A keyword telling the engine that this is a datablock object.
DataBlockType	Any datablock class declared in the engine that has been derived from GameBaseData or a subclass of GameBaseData.
Name	Any expression evaluating to a string, which will be used as the datablock's name.
: CopySource (optional)	A previous datablock definition from which to inherit values.
category	A keyword that tells the engine where to place this object in the World Editor Creator Tree (see Chapter 3, "Torque Tools"). If the CategoryName does not exist in the tree, it will be created.
datablock_fieldM	You may initialize any and all existing fields in the datablock.
dynamic_fieldN	As with objects, you may add fields to the datablock that are not defined in the C++ version. Unlike objects, however, once defined, these values are static.

Table 4.5.

Definitions of datablock declaration syntax elements.

Now, let's do a few examples.

```
datablock StaticShapeData( MyTargets ) {
 category = "Targets";
 shapeFile = "~/data/shapes/targets/simpletarget0.dts";
};
```

The above example declares a datablock of the type StaticShapeData named "MyTargets." Additionally, we have specified that this StaticShape should be located in the "targets" folder in the World Editor Creator Tree. Lastly, it will be drawn using the shape file located at "~/data/shapes/targets/simpletarget0. dts."

```
datablock StaticShapeData(SimpleTarget0 : MyTargets) {
 StartHidden = 1;
};
```

The above example creates declares a datablock of the type StaticShapeData named "SimpleTarget0" that inherits all the data from MyTargets. In addition, this declaration adds a new variable named "StartHidden" and sets it to 1.

Accessing Datablock Fields

Remember that datablocks are SimObjects, and we can access (read) their fields like any other object. However, changing a datablock field after the datablock is created and transmitted to all clients will have no effect on the client copies of the field(s) you have changed.

You may only get useful results from changing datablock fields in a single-player game, because both the client and the server are sharing the same datablock. In all other scenarios, you should consider the datablock object to be a read-only object.

> You might be using this guide in a classroom setting, or in another instructional venue. In that case, you might be using the console to load files containing datablocks, scripts, etc. Later, when using the Lesson Kit on your own, you might be surprised to find that the datablocks you were experimenting with are suddenly gone.
>
> The thing you must remember is that things that you do in the console are transient and (generally) do not affect the setup of the kit. Thus, if you quit and reload, any files you brought into context by loading via the console are now not loaded.
>
> So, to ensure that datablocks, scripts, etc. are loaded, you must modify the appropriate loader to bring them in.
>
> For example, by default, the datablocks for a mission are loaded in the function `onServerCreated()`, located in the file game.cs under the current game's "server" subdirectory (e.g. example/myGame/server/game.cs).
>
> Simply add an `exec` statement to the list of others you see there to load your datablock-containing file, and you'll be back in business.

Maze Runner Lesson #2 (90% Step)—Loading Datablocks

As we work on the Maze Runner game, we are going to need several datablocks and the accompanying scripts that were created for your use in this game and in your future creations. So, let's take the time now to get them loading. From the accompanying disk, do the following.

1. Copy the "\Base\Scripts\GPGTBase" directory into "\MazeRunner\ prototype\server\scripts".
2. Now, edit the function `onServerCreated()` in the file "\MazeRunner\ prototype\server\scripts\game.cs" to look like the following (bold lines are new or modified).

```
exec("./marker.cs");
exec("./player.cs");
exec("./GPGTBase/loadGPGTBaseClasses.cs");
```

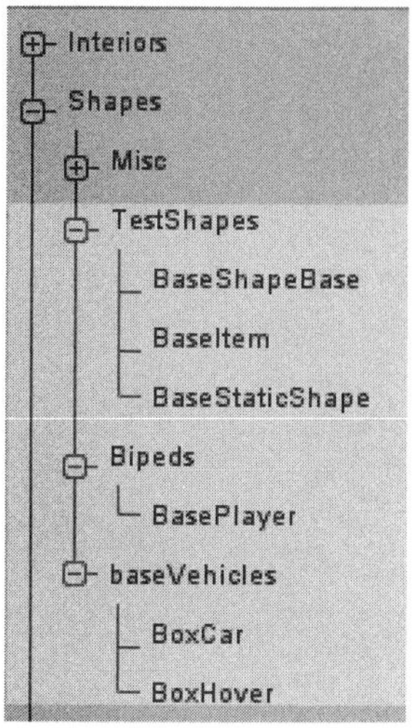

Figure 4.2
Creator directory.

In the above script, we are loading all of the GPGT base datablocks (classes) after all the other datablocks that FPS normally includes. We also add the data files that go with the datablocks.

To test for a successful load, simply start your prototype and load the "MazeRunner" mission. Then run the Creator tool, and you should have directories in the Creator as in Figure 4.2.

4.4 Datablocks, Objects, and Namespaces Revisited

For every SimObject in Torque, there is a namespace. Additionally, namespaces are chained. This means that, when the engine starts to search for something in the namespace, it begins at the entry point associated with the current object and seeks upward through all the parents' namespaces until it either finds what it is looking for or fails out. "Yes, yes," you say, "we've covered this, but how do we use this feature?" To answer that question, we'll look at some examples, starting with the simple stuff.

4.4.1 Object Namespace Hierarchies

When we wish to create a new method for the namespace of an object, we do something like the following.

```
function GameBase::DoIt(%this) {
  echo ("Calling StaticShape::DoIt() ==> on object" SPC %this);
}
```

The function `DoIt` is being declared in the GameBase namespace. This means that we can call this function on any object created from the GameBase class or its children. Here is an example.

```
//bt18(a);

%myTarget = new StaticShape( CoolTarget ) {
  position = "0 0 0";
  dataBlock = "BaseStaticShape";
};

%myTarget.DoIt();
```

Assuming the ID in `%myTarget` is 100, the above call would produce the following output in the console.

```
Calling StaticShape::DoIt() ==> on object 100
```

You'll notice a couple of things.

1. When we called `DoIt()`, we did so without passing an argument explicitly, but when the console message printed, it did in fact get an argument with the value 100.
2. The one argument `DoIt()` does take is named `%this`.

Regarding number 1, because we used the handle to call the function [`%myTarget.DoIt()`], the ID of this object gets passed implicitly to the function (see Expert Tip, page 120). That said, all of the following calls will produce the same result. Note that because this sample is in a function and because we create a new object each time we run it, the ID of the object will change for every run.

```
//bt18(b);

%myTarget.DoIt();
StaticShape::DoIt(%myTarget);
CoolTarget.DoIt();
"CoolTarget".DoIt();
100.DoIt()
"100".DoIt()
StaticShape::DoIt(100);
```

As you can see, there are various ways to call the same function, all of which are useful in different scenarios. Please note that, in the cases where we use the name of the object, the name will be passed as the ID. Torque automatically does look-ups for names; thus, in most cases, names can be used interchangeably with IDs, as long as the names are unique.

We've discussed the most basic use of namespaces. Now let's talk about datablock namespaces.

4.4.2 Simple Datablock Namespaces

As previously mentioned, datablocks are nothing more than objects themselves. They exist in the console alongside regular objects, and they too have their own namespaces. For example, if we wish to create a new method for the ItemData namespace, we can do something like the following.

```
function ItemData::GetFields( %ItemDbID ) {
 echo ("Calling ItemData::GetFields () ==> on object" SPC %ItemDbID);
 echo (" category  =>" SPC %ItemDbID.category);
 echo (" shapeFile =>" SPC %ItemDbID.shapeFile);
 echo (" mass      =>" SPC %ItemDbID.mass);
 echo (" elasticity =>" SPC %ItemDbID.elasticity);
 echo (" friction  =>" SPC %ItemDbID.friction);
 echo (" pickUpName =>" SPC %ItemDbID.pickUpName);
}
```

The function `GetFields` is being declared in the ItemData namespace. BaseItem is an instance of ItemData.

```
// from GPGT Lesson Kit = Item.cs (edited)
datablock ItemData( BaseItem ) {
   category = "TestShapes";
   shapeFile = "~/data/GPGTBase/shapes/markers/dummy.dts";
   mass = 10.0;
   elasticity = 0.05;
   friction = 0.7;
   pickUpName = "Default Item";
};
```

We could call our new function on BaseItem as follows.

//bt19();

```
==>BaseItem.GetFields();

   Calling ItemData::GetFields () ==> on object BaseItem
   category                       => TestShapes
   shapeFile                      => gpgt/data/GPGTBase/shapes/markers/dummy.dts
   mass                           => 10
   elasticity                     => 0.0498534
   friction                       => 0.698925
   pickUpName                     => Default Item
```

Now, this may seem completely trivial, but it is important to understand that a majority of the interesting methods that are called by the engine as a response to user action, like `onCollision()`, `onAdd()`, `create()`, etc., are not called on instances of objects. They are called on the datablocks of instances of objects that use datablocks. This is crucial, because we can do some very special things with datablocks and their namespaces.

When the engine calls a method that is scoped to a datablock, the engine will **always** pass the datablock ID as the first argument and the object ID as the second argument.

```
function CrossbowAmmo::doIt( %DB, %Obj ) {
 echo( "DB: " , %DB , "Obj: " , %Obj );
}
```

Also, we can manually call console methods scoped to datablocks in three ways.

```
$ammo = new Item( ) {
 datablock = CrossbowAmmo;
}
// 1 - Direct call, must pass Datablock and Obj ID
// Output: DB: 123 Obj: 456.
Crossbowammo::doit( Crossbowammo , $ammo );
// 2 - Call on datablock name, must pass Obj ID
// Output: DB: Crossbowammo Obj: 456.
Crossbowammo.doit( $ammo );
// 3 - Call on stored datablock ID, must pass Obj ID
// Output: 123 Obj: 456.
$DBID= $ammo.getDatablock();
$DBID.doit( $ammo );
```

In the first case, we are using the syntax rules of TorqueScript to treat the method-scoped function like a flat function. We call it directly and pass both the datablock ID and the object ID.

In the second case, we refer to the datablock by name and pass the object ID.

In the third case, we acquire the ID of the datablock with another console method `getDatablock()` and call the method on it, again passing the ID of the object.

4.4.3 Inserting Datablock Namespaces (ClassName)

Datablocks provide a hook with which to manipulate the namespace calling sequence. The hook is the `className` field. It works as follows.

```
datablock ItemData(CrossbowAmmo) {

    . . .
  className = "Ammo";

    . . .
};
```

What this is doing is adding a new namespace between CrossbowAmmo and ItemData, so that the namespace calling sequence will look like this: CrossbowAmmo → Ammo → ItemData → etc. We could define two functions as follows.

```
function Ammo::onPickup(%AmmoDB, %AmmoOBJ, %Picker, %Amount) {
   echo ("Calling Ammo::onPickup () ==> on ammo DB" SPC %AmmoDB);
   %AmmoDB.DoIt();
}

function Ammo::DoIt(%AmmoDB) {
 echo ("Calling Ammo::DoIt () ==> on ammo DB" SPC %AmmoDB);
}
```

Then we could collide with an ammo item. This would then automatically call the onPickup() callback, and we would expect to see the following message (assuming the datablock ID is 66).

```
Calling Ammo::onPickup () ==> on ammo DB 66
Calling Ammo::DoIt () ==> on ammo DB 66
```

This powerful feature allows us to insert a special namespace that we can use for several different datablocks. In other words, we could define two more ItemData datablocks as follows.

```
datablock ItemData(FlamingCrossbowAmmo) {
    ...
  className = "Ammo";
    ...
};

datablock ItemData(ExplodingCrossbowAmmo) {
    ...
  className = "Ammo";
    ...
};
```

> ⚠ You cannot legally specify a className that is the same as the current datablock name.

We would then have the structure shown in Figure 4.3.

Later in our code, objects derived from the three different datablocks CrossbowAmmo, FlamingCrossbowAmmo, and ExplodingCrossbowAmmo can all use the same onPickup() and DoIt() functions as declared in the Ammo:: namespace. This cuts way down on the amount of code we need to write.

Figure 4.3.

Sharing namespace with
`className` keyword.

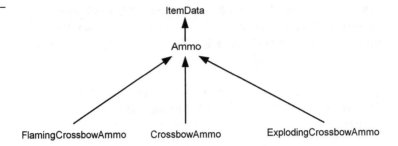

4.4.4 Namespace Inheritance?

You might wonder at some time whether namespace hierarchies can be inherited. The answer is no. If we do this:

```
datablock ItemData(CrossbowAmmo) {
  // ...
};

datablock ItemData(FlamingCrossbowAmmo : CrossbowAmmo) {
  // ...
};
```

the namespace calling sequence for CrossbowAmmo will be CrossbowAmmo → ItemData → etc., and for FlamingCrowssbowAmmo it will be Flaming-CrossbowAmmo → ItemData → etc. (see Figures 4.4 and 4.5). If we want FlamingCrossbowAmmo to use the CrossbowAmmo namespace, we have to do the following.

```
datablock ItemData(CrossbowAmmo) {
  // ...
};
```

Figure 4.4.

CrossbowAmmo namespace not inherited.

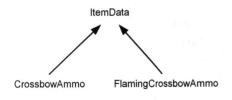

Figure 4.5.

CrossbowAmmo namespace added.

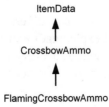

Figure 4.6.

`className` inherited, then overridden.

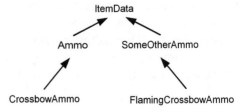

```
datablock ItemData(FlamingCrossbowAmmo) {
  // ...
  className = "CrossbowAmmo";
  // ...
};
```

Please note that if you do define a `className` field in a datablock, subsequent children datablocks will copy that value to their own `className` field unless it is overridden in the child's definition, as follows (see Figure 4.6).

```
datablock ItemData(CrossbowAmmo) {
  // ...
  className = "Ammo";
  // ...
};

datablock ItemData(FlamingCrossbowAmmo : CrossbowAmmo) {
  // ...
  className = "someOtherAmmo";
  //
};
```

4.4.5 A Parting Reminder (Datablock versus Object Namespaces)

Before closing this chapter, I want to take a moment to remind you that, when you create new objects that use datablocks, the majority of the functions that are called by the engine are called on the datablock of the object, not the object itself. I've seen questions time and again in the forums that have their root in confusion about this topic. So, save yourself a headache later and make sure you get this idea down firmly!

4.4.6 Helping Yourself

The console supplies a few helpful functions and method that can be used to get extra information about objects and the functions that are available to you.

dump() and tree()

If you have an object or a datablock and want to know what fields it has and what methods are scoped to it, type the following in the console (assuming the ID of the object or datablock is stored in $Obj).

```
$Obj.dump();
```

To see a listing (inspector) of all the objects that are currently loaded, type:

```
tree();
```

This will bring up a special debugging tool that functions much like the Inspector.

4.5 Summary

It has been a long chapter, but you made it through. It is doubtful that anyone could fully absorb all of the information presented in this chapter after just one reading. So, while you work with Torque and encounter problems, use this chapter as a resource, revisiting sections that were not clear on the initial pass.

To recap, and as a reference, here is what we covered.

- First, we talked about what game-engine scripting languages are and why they're useful. We talked about the features a good scripting language should have and discovered that TorqueScript has all of them.

- With the introductory analysis out of the way, we dug into the meat of TorqueScript, studying each of the features of the language in detail. We talked about TorqueScript's variables at length—studying variable naming and scoping and the numeric, string, Boolean, array, and vector datatypes.

- Continuing with the detailed overview of the language, we looked at TorqueScript's operators, control statements, and functions.

- We then covered how to use objects in TorqueScript, looking at their handles and names, fields and commands, dynamic fields, and console methods.

- Next, we quickly introduced packages, namespaces, and datablocks. We covered these sections briefly at first, needing to understand more about the interaction between the engine and the script console before we could go into further detail.

- After a detailed look at the engine-console interface mechanisms in Torque, we came back to datablocks, objects, and namespaces. For datablocks in particular, we found out how datablocks and objects are related to each other and found out how to declare datablocks. Studying namespaces, we learned that they can be tricky but discovered object namespace hierarchies, learned how to create simple datablock namespaces, and then became datablock namespace masters.

- We ended with a quick discussion of how to help yourself, covering a few more features of Torque that enable debugging.

Game Elements

Chapter 5
Torque Core Classes

All right! We've finished going through the engine overview and now it is time to jump into the guts of some important TGE classes. As was previously mentioned, at its core, TGE is an event-driven simulator. This simulator has defined a hierarchy of classes, based on the aptly named class SimObject.

In this chapter, we will be inspecting the SimObject class, and some of the other core classes. Each of these core classes is a major branch in the SimObject hierarchy, off of which many other classes hang. We will discuss those (hanging) classes in the subsequent chapters.

The following specific classes are covered in this chapter.

- **SimObject**. The root class for all other SimObjects. Understanding this class is fundamental to understanding how TGE classes interact.
- **SimDataBlock**. The base datablock class. We have already discussed this class, but we will revisit it to ensure that we are ready to move on to subsequent classes.
- **SceneObject**. The base class for almost all scene-placeable objects.
- **GameBase and GameBaseData**. These (otherwise minor) classes represent the first object-datablock pairing and act as parents to all subsequent classes with this kind of relationship.

5.1 SimObject

5.1.1 SimObject Features

SimObject has the following features.

- **Identification**
  - Object name (alphanumeric)
  - Object ID (numeric)
  - Group ownership
- **Saving**
  - Save to file

- **Self-Documentation**
  - Object information dumping
- **Classification**
  - Class Name
  - Object Type (a bitmask)
- **Destruction**

5.1.2 SimObject Description

As one would expect of a root class, this class forms the basis for the organization and usage of all subsequent classes. Its major responsibility is to track standard data about an object, such as the object's name, ID, what SimGroup it belongs to (if any), and what type of object it is. It also handles saving itself to file, deleting itself, scheduling actions on itself, and dumping a list of console methods and fields associated with itself.

5.1.3 Name and ID, Please...

An object will always have a unique ID and may optionally have an alpha-numeric name. Furthermore, objects may be referenced by name or by ID. ID referencing is the preferred method because it is unambiguous. Multiple objects may share the same name, and references by name always retrieve the first object found to have the specified name.

Examine the following code to see how using names instead of IDs can lead to confusion.

//ts00();

```
// The following code demonstrates the issue that occurs
// when giving multiple objects the same name.

%obj0 = new SimObject( test ); // a SimObject named 'test'
%isSame = ( %obj0 == test.getID() );
echo( "%obj0 == test.getID() => ", %isSame );

%obj1 = new SimObject( test );
%isSame = ( %obj0 == test.getID() );
echo( "%obj0 == test.getID() => ", %isSame );

%isSame = ( %obj1 == test.getID() );
echo( "%obj1 == test.getID() => ", %isSame );
```

The following results for the above code show that the engine finds the last instance of a named object when searching by name.

```
%obj0 == test.getID() => 1
%obj0 == test.getID() => 0
%obj1 == test.getID() => 1
```

5.1.4 Class Name and Type Information

Every object is created from a class, and every class has a unique class name. This information can be retrieved via script and is useful for categorizing objects. Additionally, every object stores information about its inheritance structure, that is, its type.

```
//ts01();

%obj = new Player( SuperGuy ) {
 datablock = BasePlayer;
};

// will echo ==> Player
echo( %obj.getClassName() );

// will echo ==> SuperGuy
echo( %obj.getName() );

// will echo ==> PlayerData
echo ( %obj.getDatablock().getClassName() );

// will echo ==> BasePlayer
echo ( %obj.getDatablock().getName() );
```

What about type information? In TGE, each mission-placeable object derived from SimObject has the ability to store and retrieve a mask value that shows the object's inheritance structure. For example, a WheeledVehicle, being far down the chain, will have bits for WheeledVehicle, Vehicle, ShapeBase, and GameBase set. Why are there no bits for the hierarchy between SceneObject and SimObject? It is implied. You cannot place an object that is not a SceneObject, and SceneObject is a child of SimObject.

The actual bit values are declared in objectTypes.h, but to make scripting simpler, they are exposed as named variables (done in main.cc). The following types are currently defined.

$TypeMasks::StaticObjectType	$TypeMasks::EnvironmentObjectType
$TypeMasks::TerrainObjectType	$TypeMasks::InteriorObjectType
$TypeMasks::WaterObjectType	$TypeMasks::TriggerObjectType
$TypeMasks::MarkerObjectType	$TypeMasks::GameBaseObjectType
$TypeMasks::ShapeBaseObjectType	$TypeMasks::CameraObjectType
$TypeMasks::StaticShapeObjectType	$TypeMasks::PlayerObjectType
$TypeMasks::ItemObjectType	$TypeMasks::VehicleObjectType
$TypeMasks::VehicleBlockerObjectType	$TypeMasks::ProjectileObjectType
$TypeMasks::ExplosionObjectType	

To check the type of an object, we use the `getType()` method and use bit-wise operators to compare return value against the above masks.

```
//ts02();

%obj = new Vehicle() {
  datablock = BoxCar;
};

if( %obj.getType() & $TypeMasks::VehicleObjectType ) {
  echo("Yup, it's a vehicle...");
}
else {
  echo("Sorry, but that is not a vehicle...");
}

%obj.delete();

%obj = new Player() {
  datablock = BasePlayer;
};

if( %obj.getType() & $TypeMasks::VehicleObjectType ) {
  echo("Yup, it's a vehicle...");
}
else {
  echo("Sorry, but that is not a vehicle...");
}

%obj.delete();
```

Object type masks are used in a variety of other ways, so you might want to bookmark this page.

5.1.5 Saving and Deleting

Removing an object from the world is as simple as telling that object to delete itself.

```
%obj.delete(); // Ahh! I kill myself... ;)
```

Objects are able to clean up their own fields and otherwise cleanly remove themselves from the world. However, as a general rule, objects do not automatically delete other objects that they may logically own. Fortunately, there are callbacks and SimGroups to help us out here. These are both topics for a later chapter, so for now just read on.

5.1.6 Dumping Information

At the end of Chapter 4, we introduced the dump() function. This function is introduced by the SimObject and can therefore be called by any child of this class.

The dump() function prints all the following information associated with an object to the console:

- **Engine-registered console methods**. All methods registered as being associated with the dumping object's class or one of its parents.
- **Console-registered console methods**. All scripted methods associated with the dumping object's class or one of its parents.
- **Member (nondynamic) fields**. Fields permanently exposed for this class (by the engine).
- **Tagged (dynamic) fields (for this object)**. Fields created in the dumping object during or subsequent to its creation.

You will probably use this function quite a bit, so let's give it a quick try to get you started.

```
//ts03();

%obj = new SimObject();
%obj.dump();
```

5.1.7 Group Membership

We have not discussed them yet, but Torque has two (base) container classes, SimSet and SimGroup. The latter has a special property, wherein any object stored in a SimGroup is guaranteed to only be stored in that SimGroup and no other SimGroup. SimSets offer no such guarantee.

We will discuss this in some detail later, but for now, let's just remember that an object can only be in any one SimGroup (container) at any one time. Given this restriction, it is possible that we might want to know what SimGroup our object is in. If we have the name of an object, or if we have its ID, we can simply "ask" the object what container it is in.

```
%obj.getGroup()
```

The above code will return either –1, or a nonnegative numeric value. If the value –1 is returned, the object is not stored in a group; otherwise, the numeric ID that is returned is the ID of the SimGroup container that currently "owns" this object.

5.1.8 SimObject Methods

SimObjects have several useful built-in methods, described in Table 5.1.

Table 5.1

Summary of SimObject methods.

Method	Description
delete()	Delete this object.
dump()	Dump information about this object to the script console.
getClassName()	Return this object's C++ class name.
getGroup()	Get the ID of the group this object is stored in, or else return –1.
getID()	Get this object's numeric ID.
getName()	Get this object's alphanumeric name.
getType()	Get this object's type bitmask.
save(fileName)	Save this object to the file specified in fileName.
schedule()	Described later in Chapter 9, "Gameplay Scripting."
setName(newName)	Change the name of this object to value in newName.

5.2 SimDataBlock

5.2.1 SimDataBlock Features

SimDataBlock features include the following.

- Initialization
- Scoping

SimDataBlock is the root class of all datablock classes. We have talked about datablocks quite extensively already. However, I would like to quickly revisit a few important datablock features, ending with a lead-in to the topic of callbacks.

5.2.2 Datablock-Object Pairing

Remember that almost all GameBase-derived objects are paired with a like-named SimDataBlock-derived class. Table 5.2 shows the current complete (alphabetic) list of pairings.

Datablock Class	Object Class	Datablock Class	Object Class
CameraData	Camera	PathCameraData	PathCamera
DebrisData	Debris	PathedInteriorData	PathedInterior
ExplosionData	Explosion	PlayerData	Player
FlyingVehicleData	FlyingVehicle	PrecipitationData	Precipitation
fxLightData	fxLight	ProjectileData	Projectile
GameBaseData	GameBase	ShapeBaseData	ShapeBase
HoverVehicleData	HoverVehicle	ShapeBaseImageData	- none -
ItemData	Item	SimDataBlock	- none -
LightningData	Lightning	SplashData	Splash
MissionMarkerData	MissionMarker	StaticShapeData	StaticShape
ParticleData	- none -	TriggerData	Trigger
ParticleEmitterData	ParticleEmitter	VehicleData	Vehicle
ParticleEmitterNodeData	ParticleEmitterNode	WheeledVehicleData	WheeledVehicle

Table 5.2

Datablock-object pairings.

5.2.3 Namespace Rules

Chaining and Building

All SimObject-derived classes have a namespace calling chain. SimDataBlock-derived classes add to the namespace chain in two ways. First, they add the name of the datablock to the chain. Second, they have a mechanism for adding an additional namespace by using the `className` keyword.

The `className` keyword should not be confused with a class's name (from SimObject). It serves a different purpose and does not affect the output of `getClassName()`.

```
datablock PlayerData( myPlayerDatablock ) {
  className = myPlayerDataBlockParent;
};
```

The above datablock produces a namespace chain like the following.

myPlayerDataBlock → myPlayerDataBlockParent → PlayerData → ...

The class name above could have been any string not already in the chain. I chose "myPlayerDataBlockParent" so that the hierarchy would be clear, but I could just as well have called it "Freddie" and gotten the following chain.

myPlayerDataBlock → Freddie → PlayerData → ...

We can later use this datablock to build an instance of the Player class as follows.

```
%myPlayer = new Player( TorqueDude ) {
 datablock = "myPlayerDatablock";
};
```

Noninheritable

In standard TGE, namespaces are noninheritable in the console. This means that, if we create a new datablock myPlayerDatablock2 and inherit (copy) the fields from myPlayerDatablock, as follows:

```
datablock PlayerData( myPlayerDatablock ) {
  className = myPlayerDataBlockParent;
};

datablock PlayerData( myPlayerDatablock2 :
                      myPlayerDatablock ) {
  // Copies: className = myPlayerDataBlockParent;
  // from myPlayerDatablock
  // ...
};
```

the new datablock will not have the myPlayerDatablock name in its namespace. Instead, its namespace will look like the following.

myPlayerDataBlock2 → myPlayerDataBlockParent → PlayerData → ...

It does inherit the added namespace specified by `className`, but the parent datablock namespace is lost.

Scoping

As a direct result of this namespace business and due to the way TGE is designed, we can create console methods (functions scoped to a console class) as follows.

```
function myPlayerDataBlockParent::DoIt( %theDB , %optionalArgs, ... ) {
  // ..
};
```

As can be seen from this example, the function `DoIt()` has been scoped to the myPlayerDataBlockParent namespace, using the namespace resolution operator `::`. Thus, we now refer to `DoIt()` as a console method (or method, for short).

This (noncallback) method takes a minimum of one argument and may have as many additional arguments as we deem necessary. The required argument is often named `%this`, but in our example it has been given the more meaningful name `%theDB`. Why? Well, as you probably recall, when the method is called (properly), the engine will pass, as the first argument, the ID of the datablock associated with the object that caused the method to be fired.

We can certainly call methods directly, or on a datablock name/ID if we want to, but most of these methods are called by the engine as the result of some event. Recall (from earlier) that methods called as the result of some event are called callbacks.

5.3 SceneObject

5.3.1 SceneObject Features

SceneObject features include the following:

- **Transforms**
  - Position
  - Rotation
  - Scale
  - Transform
  - Forward vector
- **Collision Detection**
- **Volumes**
  - Object box
  - World box

> Remember that, when the engine automatically calls a method on a datablock, the method is referred to as a callback. All callbacks scoped to datablocks receive two default arguments, not the single argument a regular datablock method gets. The first argument is the ID of the datablock, and the second argument is the ID of the object that the callback is being called for. Torque implements a great number of callbacks. For the most part, we do not discuss them in this guide. However, those callbacks that will affect our efforts to write a single-player game will be discussed.

Game Elements

5.3.2 SceneObject Description

A SceneObject is an object capable of appearing in a scene. It can be rendered. It may be moved, rotated, and scaled. It may be collided with, and it takes up space within the game world.

5.3.3 Position, Rotation, and Scale

All SceneObject-derived objects provide three basic fields.

- **Position.** A three-element floating-point field describing the object's initial placement position in the world.
- **Rotation.** A four-element floating-point field specifying the shape's rotation as a quaternion.
- **Scale.** A three-element floating-point field specifying the *x-y-z* scaling factors for a shape.

```
%obj = new Player( Blockman ) {
  position = "0 0 0"; // start at world-zero
  rotation = "1 0 0 0"; // quaternion giving zero rotation
  scale = "1 1 2.5"; // 2.5 times as tall as standard version
};
```

These fields are used during the creation of an object to set the object's initial position, rotation, and scale. Not a big surprise.

The real surprise comes later, if you try to modify these fields directly. If you are using the Inspector to make these changes, they will *always* take effect, but if you are using scripts, your results will vary. This is because some objects regularly mark these fields as dirty and retransmit them to the client ghosts while other classes never mark them as dirty so the changes go unheeded.

This is not a bug. You are not supposed to modify these variables directly, but rather use access methods. These access methods are described in Table 5.3.

Table 5.3.

Access methods.

Method	Description
getPosition()	Returns the object's current position.
getScale()	Returns the object's current scale.
setScale(newScale)	Sets the object's scale to newScale.

The access methods described might not seem like enough. This is because the makers of the engine have combined the position and orientation information into a composite vector called a *transform*.

5.3.4 The Transform

An object's transform is a composite vector containing both *position* and *rotation* information.

```
"posX poxY posZ rotX rotY rotZ rotTheta"
```

The access methods used to get and set transform are defined in Table 5.4.

Method	Description
getTransform()	Returns the object's transform vector.
setTransform(newTransform)	Sets the object's transform to newTransform and marks this information as dirty so that all ghosts are updated.

Table 5.4.

Access methods to get and set transform.

In the following example, we want to translate an object by 10 meters along the world *x*-axis. Using a couple of string functions we extract the position and rotation vectors as well as the rotation theta about the rotation vector. Then, we add "10 0 0" to the position vector. After re-assembling the vector, we translate the object's position by passing in the new transform to a setTransform() call. Simple.

```
%myTransform = %obj.getTransform();
%myPosition = getWords( %myTransform, 0 , 2 );
%myRotationVec = getWords( %myTransform, 3 , 5 );
%myRotationTheta = getWord( %myTransform, 6 );

// Move shape +10 in X direction
%myNewPosition = vectorAdd( %myPosition , "10 0 0");
%obj.setTransform( %myNewPosition );
```

The methods getWords(), getWord(), and vectorAdd() will be described in Chapter 9, "Gameplay Scripting".

5.3.5 Collision Detection

This class introduces the ability to interact with the world via collisions. SceneObjects can collide with other objects and can be collided with. Collision detection and response is a complex and advanced topic, which we won't be able to cover in detail; however, as with callbacks, those collisions that we need to discuss will be discussed briefly prior to writing any of the required code for our game.

For some objects, it is actually possible to modify the object's position field and then to rescale the object to its current scale. This will cause the scale and position to be marked as dirty, allowing us to move an object that might otherwise ignore even the transform update. One example of this is the ParticleEmitterNode object, which we will discuss in Chapter 8, "Mission Objects."

I don't generally encourage people to use hacks, and this is a hack, but this little tip is really quite useful.

5.3.6 Object Boxes and World Boxes

Every scene object has an object box and a world box. These two boxes serve unique purposes.

The object box is an object-oriented box whose coordinates are relative to the object's centroid. The extents of this box are the non-scaled $<x\ y\ z>$ bounds of the shape. The purpose of this box is to provide an unscaled basis for bounding and scaling calculations done in script.

The world box is a (world) axis-aligned bounding box. The coordinates of the world box are real-world and do not need to be translated or scaled. This box tells us (approximately) how much space a shape is taking up in the world and where. It is useful for placement calculations and obstacle-avoidance checks, among its many other uses.

We can get these useful bits of data with these methods in Table 5.5.

Table 5.5.

Methods for getting object- and world-box data.

Method	Description
`getObjectBox()`	Returns the six-element floating-point vector representing this object's object box. The first three values represent the lower left corner, and the latter three values represent the upper right corner.
`getWorldBox()`	Returns the six-element floating-point vector representing this object's world box. The first three values represent the lower left corner, and the latter three values represent the upper right corner.
`getWorldBoxCenter()`	Returns the three-element floating-point vector representing the center of this object's world box.

5.3.7 The Forward Vector

It is frequently important to know which direction a shape is facing. We can retrieve this information by asking for the object's forward vector.

The forward vector is a normalized vector representing the orientation of the shape's y-axis relative to the world axes (in Torque, $+z$ is up, $+y$ is forward, and $+x$ is left). The `getForwardVector()` method provides a quick means of retrieving this value.

```
%playerFacing = %player.getForwardVector();
echo("Player's forward vector is:" SPC %playerFacing );
```

A frequently seen beginner's mistake is to assume that the forward vector and the rotation vector from the object's transform are the same.

They are **not** the same, and you should not treat them as such. Each of them has a separate purpose and use.

5.4 GameBase and GameBaseData

5.4.1 GameBase Features

GameBase features include the following:

- **Ticking**
- **Datablocks**

5.4.2 The Foundation Game Classes

All GameBase objects are built using datablocks; thus, it is not surprising that the majority of what this class does is focus on datablock functions. It is also the first object to experience ticks. This is just something to put under your hat for now, but it is important to know. Only GameBase objects and their children are ticked.

Datablocks are used to store static data as well as to scope many important methods and callbacks. In order to allow us to access the data these objects contain, we first require a method of obtaining an object's datablock. Of course, Torque supplies us a method to do this. Given that we know the object for which we want the datablock, we can get that object's datablock as follows.

```
%myDataBlock = %obj.getDatablock();
```

Additionally, we may change an object's datablock at any time with a call like the following.

```
%obj.setDatablock( Blockman2 );
```

What exactly does changing the datablock do for us though? Well, the obvious thing it does is change the source of subsequent datablock data retrievals; i.e., datablock values retrieved (by us and by the engine) in the future will get their content from the newly specified datablock. This is pretty cool, but there is another more important (and more subtle) thing that this does. By changing the datablock of an object, we are effectively changing that object's namespace (the console method calling chain). Consider the following code.

```
function BlockMan::doit( %DB ) {
  echo( "In BlockMan::doit(" SPC %DB SPC ")" );
}
```

Game Elements

```
function BlockMan2::doit( %DB ) {
  echo( "In BlockMan2::doit(" SPC %DB SPC ")" );
}
%obj = new Player( BlockMan ) {
  // ...
};

%obj.doit(); // Calls BlockMan::doit

%obj.setDatablock( BlockMan2 );

%obj.doit(); // Calls BlockMan2::doit
```

If you stop and think about it, this is an extremely powerful tool and can be used for some heavy-duty coding. Note also that objects that render a shape will render the new shape as defined by the new datablock, so this is a quick way to change an object's entire mesh.

5.5 Summary of Core Classes

This is a rather short chapter, but it is very important because these classes form the basis for almost all scripting that we will do in the future. In almost every gameplay-related script we write, we will touch at least one of these classes' features.

Chapter 6
Basic Game Classes

6.1 Shape and Interiors

In this chapter, we will discuss all of the fundamental classes that are used to create models in our game world. Excluded from this discussion are any classes that are normally used as avatars.

Torque supplies a large set of classes used to display two fundamental categories of models: shapes and interiors.

6.1.1 Shapes

In TGE, shapes are normally nonstructural objects. More exactly, shapes should not be used to represent an object that must have both an interior *and* an exterior that can be accessed via another shape. The reason for this is simple: shapes have only exterior collision.

Shapes are created and rendered either with the children of ShapeBase or ShapeBaseImageData, or with TSStatic.

In this chapter, the two children of ShapeBase that we will be discussing are the following.

- **Item.** Used to represent interactive items like coins, pickups, and power-ups.
- **StaticShape.** Used to represent objects that are stationary or have limited movement/interaction capabilities.

We will defer a discussion of the following ShapeBase children classes until the next chapter because they are normally used as avatars and require special attention.

- **Player**
- **Vehicle, WheeledVehicle, HoverVehicle,** and **FlyingVehicle**

Additionally, we will discuss the following high-level topics in the next chapter.

- **GameView/POV.** We discuss how the interactions of several classes combine for our GameView and determine the point of view.
- **Inventories.** A nearly universal construct is the inventory. We will discuss the basic elements of the one that is included with this guide.

6.1.2 Interiors

Interiors are used to display models that represent any structural object, including such things as buildings, bridges, walls, and other large structures. The motivation for this name comes from the fact that these objects can have an actual inside. This type of model supports arbitrary collision with both inside surfaces and outside surfaces.

The class used to represent interiors implements a standard BSP collision scheme. Thus, it supports dividing models/meshes into n-dimensional convex partitions that can be entered. Additionally, interiors can use portals to cull hidden geometry.

Some other features supported by interiors are self-shadowing, terrain shadowing, and light maps. Interiors will self-shadow and, when the relighting phase executes, the engine will back a shadow texture into the terrain based on the location of each interior. Interior shadowing and lighting are accomplished with the use of precalculated light maps. The basic exporter produces pretty nice light maps. Additionally, there is a radiosity exporter available for creating smoother lighting.

Most of what you will need to know about interiors is art-based and includes such things as placing portals correctly, creating BSP-acceptable geometry, adding lights and textures, and preparing multiple level of detail (LOD) versions of meshes.

Interior lighting and shadowing is pretty nice, but if you wish to have more control over this, and if you want these lights to affect nonstatic objects like the player, you should pick up the Torque Lighting Kit for TGE or consider moving up to the Torque Shader Engine.

6.2 ShapeBase/ShapeBaseData

These are the root classes in the ShapeBase class hierarchy. The ShapeBase class itself cannot be used to create objects in the world. It should be considered a "virtual" class. Instead, use the children classes. ShapeBaseData is the datablock class associated with ShapeBase.

6.2.1 ShapeBase and ShapeBaseData Features

ShapeBase and ShapeBaseData have the features shown in Table 6.1. As can be seen, these classes have a significant burden for providing shape functionality. As a side effect, ShapeBase-derived objects have a significant network weight. Thus, if you do not need any of the features in Table 6.1 for a shape, consider using TSStatic instead (see Section 6.5).

6.2.2 Rendering

In order to be rendered, a shape must provide a model (mesh). Additionally, we might wish to allow a shape to be cloaked and/or to render an environmental map. These features are provided by the ShapeBaseData datablock.

Category	Features
Rendering	• Environmental mapping • Cloaking • Fading • Hiding • Skinning
Damage	• Damage level tracking • Damage states • Self-repairing • Invincibility • Damage flashes and whiteouts • Explosions
Energy	• Energy level tracking • Recharging
Physical Parameters	• Mass • Density • Drag • Velocity • Impulses
Eye Transforms	
Camera Settings	• Field of view • Point of view • Range and angle limits
Animations	• Four threads
Sound	• Four independent threads
Mounting	• Shape-to-shape • Image-to-shape

Table 6.1.

In the following example, we are creating a StaticShapeData datablock named "FadeEgg":

```
// Fade Egg from Rendering
datablock StaticShapeData( FadeEgg )
{
  category = "LessonShapes"
  shapeFile =
      "~/data/Shapes/Lessons/GeneralLessonShapes/egg.dts";
};
```

Game Elements

Later, we can create an instance as follows.

```
%theEgg = new StaticShape {
  datablock = FadeEgg;
};
```

Environmental Mapping

If we set the "emap" datablock parameter to `true`, the shape will use the environmental mapping texture specified for the sky object, if it was specified.

Cloaking

ShapeBase-derived shapes have the ability to cloak. When a shape is cloaked, it is reskinned with the `cloakTexture` specified in its datablock. Furthermore, this skin is rendered at a fixed overall alpha (specified in the engine). The `cloakTexture` does not need an alpha channel for the cloak to succeed, however, if the fixed alpha used by the engine is not low enough, you can further reduce it by using a `cloakTexture` with an alpha channel. Shapes that are cloaked behave just like uncloaked shapes in all other respects.

In order to cloak an object, first define a datablock with a cloak texture, as follows.

```
datablock StaticShapeData( CloakEgg ) {
  category = "LessonShapes";
  shapeFile =
     "~/data/Shapes/Lessons/GeneralLessonShapes/egg.dts";
  cloakTexture =
  "~/data/Shapes/Lessons/GeneralLessonShapes/testskin.png";
};
```

If you choose to **not** specify a `cloakTexture` and then you cloak a shape, that shape will get a default white texture. This is actually pretty nice and gives a reasonable cloaking effect. You might consider trying this before working too hard on a special texture for cloaking.

Then, having created an instance, enable cloaking as follows.

```
%theEgg.setCloaked(true);
```

Fading and Hiding

ShapeBase-derived shapes have the ability to fade in and out of view as well as to be hidden. While a shape is fading in or out, its collision mesh is still active. In fact, once a shape is completely faded out, its mesh is still active and can still be collided with. You must hide an object to disable its collision mesh.

```
// Fade this egg from view, over a 1.5 second period,
// starting immediately
%theEgg.startFade( 1500 , 0 , true );

// Schedule the egg to be 'hidden' in 1.6 seconds
// (disables collision mesh)
%theEgg.schedule( 1600 , setHidden , true );
```

Skins

ShapeBase-derived shapes are allowed to have multiple skins. In order to use this feature, the skins to be used for a shape must follow some simple rules. First, a texture (skin) is required to group the skins for this shape. It has a name of the form `base.setName.suffix`.

- **base.** The engine looks for this special prefix and uses it to 'group' textures by setName.

- **setName.** This string identifies the skins that are in this group.

- **suffix.** This is any acceptable TGE image format: PNG, JPG, etc. (see Appendix for complete list).

Subsequently, any textures to be included in the set for multiskinning must have names of the form `skinName.setName.suffix`.

- **skinName.** This is the optional part of the skin name and is used in the `setSkinName()` method (see below). This name can be any arbitrary string you wish to use. Skin names are stored as tags.

For example, if you wish to have a shape with three skins, you could use the following textureNames.

```
base.skin.png       // Apply this texture to the shape.
skin0.skin.png      // First Skin
skin1.skin.png      // Second Skin
skin2.skin.png      // Third Skin
```

Subsequently, we could change the skin for a shape as follows:

```
%obj.setSkinName("skin2"); // automatically converted to a tag

// OR

%obj.setSkinName('skin2'); // The tag itself.
```

   The question will arise, "Can I do this for multiple textures on the same mesh?" Yes, you can have multiple texture groups on one mesh, but when you flip one texture, all the other textures will revert to their base texture. So, if you need to change multiple textures, you might want to consider using IFLs (image file lists) as an alternative to multiskinning. In fact, IFLs may be better anyway if:

- you wish to animate a texture rapidly, and/or
- you wish to change the texture on only a small part of the shape, and
- you are willing to give up one animation slot (per playing IFL).

6.2.3 Damaging, Disabling, Destroying, and Exploding!

ShapeBase-derived objects can be damaged, disabled, and eventually destroyed. Upon destruction, a shape may continue to render, or it may explode and leave behind debris.

Damaging

To allow a shape to take damage, we must define some key values in our datablock:

```
datablock StaticShapeData( SelfHealingBlock ) {
  // ...

  maxDamage = 100;
  disabledLevel = 80;    // Disabled at 80 or greater points
  destroyedLevel = 100; // Destroyed at maxDamage
  repairRate = 0.05;     // Repair @ 1.6 points per second
};
```

What we have said here is that this object can take up to 100 damage points and that it should be considered disabled at 80 points and destroyed when it hits 100. If we wished, we could set either of these values higher than max-Damage, which is the same as saying "cannot be disabled" or "cannot be destroyed," respectively. The last value repairRate tells the engine to apply 0.05 points of "repair" every tick until damage equals zero.

Setting Up Repairs

This seems pretty simple so far, but a few things need to be clarified. Although we have specified values for damage, our shape will not do anything automatically. We are responsible for applying damage, changing the damage state of the shape, and setting the repair rate. Until the repair rate is set by calling setRepairRate(), a shape will not self-repair.

Thus, when we create our object, we want to use `setRepairRate()` to enable self-repair. An ideal place to do this is in the shape's `onAdd()` callback:

```
function SelfHealingBlock::onAdd( %DB , %theShape ) {
  %theShape.setRepairRate( %DB.repairRate );
}
```

Damaging

Later, we may wish to apply damage to our shape. To do so we would use code similar to the following.

```
%theShape.applyDamage( %someDamage );
```

Repairing Manually

In addition to a damage method, a method is supplied to repair a shape as follows.

```
%theShape.applyRepair( %someRepair );
```

There is, however, a slight trick to making this work. If we have chosen to allow our shape to self-repair (by calling `setRepairRate()` with a nonzero value), we cannot apply repairs at a greater rate than the specified rate.

In other words, if you want to repair an object that is able to self-repair, you will need to do the following.

```
// Turn off self-repair
%theShape.setRepairRate( 0 );

// Do the repair
%theShape.applyRepair( %someRepair );

// Turn self-repair back on
%theShape.setRepairRate(%theShape.getDatablock().repairRate );
```

Of course, if a shape is not automatically repairing, then we simply call `applyRepair()`, and we're good to go.

Damage States

It is up to us (through the use of scripts) to take responsibility for tracking the damage level of our shape and for setting its damage state. What is a damage state, you ask?

A normal shape can be in any one of three (damage) states: enabled, disabled, or destroyed. A sample method to deal with this might look like the following:

In addition to the three standard states, players (which we have not yet discussed) can also be "dead," which is equivalent to being disabled and destroyed.

```
function ShapeBase::determineDamageState( %theShape ) {
%curDamage = %theShape.getDamageLevel();
%disabledDamage = %theShape.getDatablock().disabledLevel;
%destroyedDamage = %theShape.getDatablock().destroyedLevel;

if( %curDamage >= %destroyedDamage ) {
  %theShape.setDamageState( Destroyed );
}
else if( %curDamage >= %disabledDamage ) {
  %theShape.setDamageState( Disabled );
}
else {
  %theShape.setDamageState( Enabled );
}
}
```

Invincibility

It is possible to make a shape invincible, either permanently or temporarily. To do so permanently, we use the `isInvincible` keyword in the datablock.

```
datablock StaticShapeData( InvincibleBlock :
                            SelfHealingBlock) {
  // ...
  isInvincible = true;
};
```

If we only want this invincibility to be temporary, we can use the `setInvincibleMode()` method.

```
%theShape.setInvincibleMode( time , speed );
```

This method works as follows.

- The shape on which this is called will be invincible for a period of time specified by the floating-point value `time`, as measured in seconds.
- The screen will flicker blue if it is the control object that has been made invincible.

The flickering effect is used to indicate to a player that his or her avatar is invincible. Furthermore, this flicker rate will change and the flicker will become increasingly translucent as the time elapses.

The rate of this flicker is controlled by the floating-point value speed. apeed can be between 0 and 1. If it is set to 0, there is no flickering. If it is set to 1, the flickering is very fast. Generally, lower values are nicer.

Postdestruction Rendering

This leads us to a final damage topic, which is postdestruction rendering; that is, does the shape render subsequent to destruction? This, too, is determined by the datablock.

```
datablock StaticShapeData( ExplodeGears ) {
  // ...
  renderWhenDestroyed = false;
};
```

In this instance, we have instructed the engine to stop rendering the shape when it is in the "destroyed" state. Unfortunately, there is a catch. Even if the engine stops rendering the shape, the collision box will remain active; i.e. collisions will still happen. Therefore, if you wish to entirely remove the object from interaction, you should either delete it subsequent to destruction or hide it.

Damage Flashes and Whiteouts

What are damage flashes? Well, in your game, the player may at some time take damage or be blinded by a bright light. In order to express this concept to the person playing your game, you can use the following console methods.

```
// Show red-haze to imply massive damage to player
%cam = %player.client.camera;
// We need the camera ID to do flashes
%cam.setDamageFlash( 1.0 );

// Show Whiteout to imply slight and temporary blinding.
%cam = %player.client.camera;
// We need the camera ID to do whiteout
%cam.setWhiteOut( 0.5 );
```

These two effects can be applied together.

It is important to understand that these methods must be called on the camera for the effect to be shown. Calling this on other shapes has no effect.

Lastly, there is also a blackout function in the engine, but it is not hooked up with a console method. However, if you have the source code, hooking this up would be as easy as 1...2...3.

Explosions

If you have specified an `explosion` datablock for your shape and the shape is destroyed (`setDamageState()` is called with the argument `Destroyed`), the shape will create an explosion object at the current location of the shape. The explosion will then play and delete itself when finished. It is that simple.

In addition to the `explosion` field, there is an `underwaterExplosion` field. This field is used to specify an alternate explosion that should be played when the shape is destroyed underwater. If no `underwaterExplosion` is specified and the shape is underwater, then the normal explosion will be played.

```
datablock StaticShapeData( ExplodeGears ) {
  // ...
  explosion = "GearsExplosion";
  underwaterExplosion = "GearsUnderwaterExplosion";
};
```

Debris

As with explosion datablocks, if a debris datablock has been specified for your shape and the shape is destroyed, the shape will create a debris object at the current location of the shape. Debris represents the refuse left behind by a destroyed shape. Debris can behave in a wide variety of ways and therefore merits its own discussion. If you are interested, please skip ahead to Chapter 11, "Special Effects."

```
datablock StaticShapeData( ExplodeGears ) {
  // ...
  debris = "GearsDebris";
};
```

6.2.4 Energy

ShapeBase-derived objects can have energy. This energy can be used for various purposes such as powered movement, weapons, vehicles, etc. Initially, shapes start out de-energized (energy level == 0). We may choose to provide an initial charge at creation time and/or to enable recharging. Before we can do either of these, however, we must set up the datablock as follows.

```
datablock StaticShapeData( FireTube ) {
  // ...
  maxEnergy = 20;
  rechargeRate = 0.05; // 1.6 points per second
};
```

The above datablock tells the shape that its maximum energy is 20 points and that, when the energy is below maximum, it will recharge at a rate of 0.05 points per tick (about 1.6 points per second). As with self-repair, we need to enable recharging with a method call.

To give a shape an initial charge, and then to enable recharging, we can do the following.

```
function FireTube::onAdd( %DB , %theShape ) {
  // Start with maxEnergy
  %theShape.setEnergyLevel( %DB.maxEnergy );

  // Enable recharging
  %theShape.setRechargeRate( %DB.rechargeRate );
}
```

Unlike with self-repair and manually applied repairs, we may manually add energy to our shape even if it is recharging.

6.2.5 Physical Parameters

Being in the world, most shapes will need the ability to interact. In real-world terms, interactions are based on physics. As this is only a simulation of reality, a minimal set of physical parameters is supplied for all shapes via a shape's datablock. All shapes have the concept of mass, density, and drag. These can be considered unitless, but it is often nice to treat mass and density as metric units (kilograms and kilograms per cubic meter, respectively).

```
datablock PlayerData( BlockManPlayer ) {
  // ...
  mass = 90; // Kilos
  density = 10; // Kilos/cubic meter
  drag = 0; // Unitless 'air' resistance
};
```

Applying a velocity to a StaticShape will do you no good. It is static and can only be moved by using the `setTransform()` method.

Velocity

At any time, a shape may be in motion. Thus, it is handy to have a means of getting and setting the current velocity of a shape.

```
%obj.getVelocity();
%obj.setVelocity( velocity );
```

Impulses

If we wish, we can apply an impulse to any shape with mass. An impulse is an application of force, causing an instantaneous change in velocity.

Take a look at the following example to see how we apply an impulse:

```
// Give this player a whack (10x mass) straight up

%objectMass = %player.getDatablock().mass;

%impulseVector = vectorScale( "0 0 1" , %objectMass * 10 );

%player.applyImpulse( %obj.getWorldBoxCenter() ,
                            %impulseVector );
```

Varying Impulse Position

The astute reader will notice that the impulse method takes a position vector. The question that arises in the curious mind is, "What happens if I apply an impulse to a position that is not in the center of a shape?" The answer: Results may vary.

The reason to allow an off-center impulse is to allow us to spin an object. However, only vehicles will spin. All other classes will ignore any offset and treat the impulse as if it is applied to the shape's centroid.

Applying impulses to StaticShapes and to items with the `static` parameter set to true, will do nothing. These shapes cannot be moved by impulses.

6.2.6 Eye Transforms and Vectors

In addition to the transform and the forward vector inherited from Scene-Object, ShapeBase and children provide the following positions and vectors.

- **Eye point.** A point in three-space, representing the position of the shape's eye.
- **Eye vector.** A vector representing the pointing direction of the shape's eye.
- **Eye transform.** A transform, not for the shape but for the shape's eye.

Each of the above quantities are available if the mesh used by the shape has defined a skeletal node with the name "eye." To acquire these quantities, we use the following methods.

```
// Eye Point
echo( %obj.getEyePoint() );

// Eye Vector
echo( %obj.getEyeVector() );

// Eye Transform
echo( %obj.getEyeTransform() );
```

It is possible to call these methods on a shape without an eye node, as the engine will use the shapes centroid as the eye in this case. Just be aware that this is what is happening.

6.2.7 Camera Settings

The ShapeBase camera settings are part of a larger discussion that encompasses the GameView and the player's point of view, so we will come back to this class when we talk about those topics.

6.2.8 Animations

ShapeBase-derived shapes have the ability to run up to four simultaneous animations. These animations can be any of the supported animations:

- nonblended (absolute) skeletal,
- blended skeletal,
- image file list, and
- visibility.

These animations are applied in the order of the threads they occupy, which is important to keep in mind for blended skeletal animations.

Cyclic Animations

TGE supports the concept of a cyclic animation. A cyclic animation is nothing more than an animation that cycles. When an animation cycles, it progresses as follows: frame 0, frame 1, ... frame n, frame 0 ..., ad infinitum until paused or stop.

Playing

To play an animation, we must have the name of the animation and a free thread to play it in.

```
%obj.playThread( 0 , "someAnimation" );
```

In this sample, we've decided to play an animation named "someAnimation" in thread 0. As soon as this statement is executed, the animation will begin to play and will continue to play until it hits the end of its sequence. Upon hitting the end of its sequence, an animation can do one of two things. If it is noncyclic, it will stay in the "playing" state and hold on the last frame of the animation. If it is cyclic, the animation will start over at the first frame of the animation.

We have not talked about POV yet, but if you are at all familiar with games, you will already know that a camera can be in 1st POV (looking through the eyes of the player) or in 3rd POV (somewhere external to the player). The above eye quantities are all relative to a 1st POV viewpoint, so if your game is running in 3rd POV, all three quantities will be unchanged by the movement of the camera; i.e., the eye will still be in its 1st POV position, and the eye vector will not track the camera. To learn more about this topic, see the camera discussion in Chapter 7, "Gameplay Classes."

If there were already an animation present in thread 0, the playing script shown would normally stop that animation and start the new animation. For the exceptions, see "Animation Oddities".

Direction

Animations have the concept of a direction. They can be played forward or in reverse. All animations start playing in the forward direction. To change an animation's direction, we use the method below.

```
%obj.setThreadDir( 0 , true ); // Play thread 0 FORWARD

// OR

%obj.setThreadDir( 0 , false ); // Play thread 0 REVERSE
```

Pausing and Stopping

So far, we know how to play and reverse a thread, but what if we need to pause our thread or stop it entirely? Both of these options are available to us. We can toggle pause; i.e., if the thread is playing it will pause, and if it is paused it will start playing again.

```
%obj.pauseThread( 0 ); // Toggle pause for thread 0
```

We can also stop an animation.

```
%obj.stopThread( 0 ); // Stop the animation in thread 0
```

Stopping an animation resets the joints affected by this animation to their pre-animation positions; i.e., the animation transforms are no longer applied. You need to do this if you want to re-pose a noncyclic thread that has reached its end.

Animation Oddities

It is worth noting that, when using the animation methods to control animation threads, there is some latency involved. So, you may run into some strange issues while playing threads.

Noncyclic Threads Remain in Play State at End of Sequence

When a noncyclic animation is played, it eventually completes. However, TGE does not automatically stop the thread. Instead, the thread remains in the "play" state. If you have a noncyclic thread that you wish to "re-play," you would think you could simply type:

```
%obj.playThread( 0 , "someAnimation" );
```

Unfortunately, this will not work. Nor will the following.

```
%obj.stopThread( 0 );
%obj.playThread( 0 , "someAnimation" );
```

Instead you'll need to do one of two things. You can schedule a stop after starting the thread, as follows.

```
%obj.playThread( 0 , "someAnimation" );
%obj.schedule( time , stopThread, 0 );
// time > animation length in ms
```

Otherwise, you'll have to delay the restart as follows.

```
%obj.stopThread( 0 );
%obj.schedule( 100 , playThread, 0 , "someAnimation" );
```

Damage Animations

All ShapeBase-derived objects will automatically play two different animation sequences based on the shape's damage state.

"Visibility" Sequence

The first of the two sequences that is auto-played is the "Visibility" sequence. This should be a blended animation. It will assume one of two positions; i.e. it is either off or on and does not actually play an animation sequence. When the shape's damage state is not destroyed, the shape plays position zero (0) of this sequence. When the shape is destroyed, it plays position one (1) of the thread.

"Damage" Sequence

The second of the two sequences that is auto-played is the "Damage" sequence. This sequence can be blended or nonblended. This thread plays as follows.

If `damageLevel > = destroyedLevel`,

If `damageState = = ` "Destroyed," play "Damage" sequence position zero (0).

If `damageState ! = ` "Destroyed," play "Damage" sequence position one (1).

If `damageLevel < destroyedLevel`, play thread at position `damageLevel / destroyedLevel`.

In short, this sequence advances as damage is accumulated, until the shape is destroyed. This thread/sequence is used to create a damage effect on shapes and may involve IFLs, geometry animation, visibility animations, etc.

By now, you've seen the method `schedule()` a few times and have probably begun to wonder what it is. Although we will discuss this in Chapter 10, "Gameplay Scripting," let me summarize what it is now. The `schedule()` method is used to schedule either a function or a method call in the future. The variety we have used thus far schedules methods. In this example, we scheduled a method named `stopThread` to execute in *time* milliseconds. This method will be called on the object `%obj` that scheduled it and will be passed a 0. That's it.

6.2.9 Sound

ShapeBase-derived objects have the ability to control up to four simultaneous sound threads. Sounds themselves are declared using audio profiles (AP) and audio descriptions (AD) (see Chapter 11, "Special Effects"). Playing a sound declared with the audio profile named "SomeAudioProfile" is as simple as the following.

```
%obj.playAudio( 0 , SomeAudioProfile );
```

How this sound plays is up to the AP and the AD. It may play forever or it may play only once. However, if we wish to stop this sound from playing, we can do so with the following code.

```
%obj.stopAudio( 0 );
```

6.2.10 Mounting

ShapeBase-derived shapes have the ability to mount other shapes and ShapeBaseImages. In total, eight shapes, eight ShapeBaseImages, or any combination of up to eight total can be mounted to any single shape.

Mounting is tracked through the use of mount slots. Mount slots should not be confused with mount nodes.

- **Mount slots** are the indices into the shape's mount list.
- **Mount nodes** are positions on the shape corresponding to named joints/nodes in the model. These names are mount0 … mount31 (TGE supports a maximum of 32 mount nodes).

To clarify the difference between nodes and slots, let's look at the images in Figure 6.1 from one of my own game prototypes. In the game, eight shields are attached to this tower, all of them attaching to the mount0 node (Figure 6.1a). In Figure 6.1b, you can see three of the shields. In Figure 6.1c, three of the shields have been attached to mount0.

Figure 6.1a.

Tower with mount0 node.

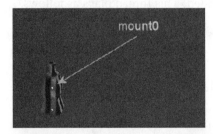

Figure 6.1b.

Individual shields with mountPoint node.

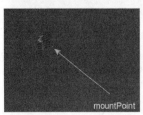
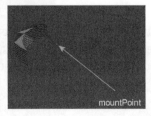
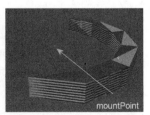

The important takeaway is that, although all three shields are attached to the same node (mount0), they are each in their own slots. Assuming they were mounted from innermost to outermost shield, those slots would be Slot 0—Inner Shield, Slot 1—Middle Shield, Slot 2—Outer Shield.

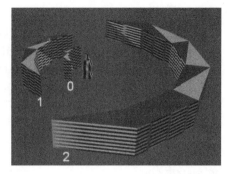

Figure 6.1c.

Shields mounted to tower at mount0.

Things to Know

You should be aware of the following.

- Mounted shapes and images will translate and rotate with the node that they are mounted to.
- If a mount node is animated, the shape/image mounted to that node will follow the node through its animation.
- Multiple objects/images can be mounted to the same mount node but not in the same slot.
- Images do not have collision meshes and will therefore not collide with objects when the shape they are mounted to moves.
- Shapes that are mounted to other shapes retain their collision meshes.

There is a pretty hefty set of console methods dedicated to dealing with mounting tasks. We will not be covering them all here, but never fear, they are all listed in the "Console Fields and Methods" Section of Appendix A with descriptions that should clarify their purposes. For now, we'll do a simple example showing what it takes to mount a shape to a shape, and then an image to a shape.

Mounting Shape-to-Shape

In the following examples, we will be discussing two shapes, shapeA and shapeB. In all instances, shapeB will be mounted onto shapeA.

For the mount to succeed, shapeA must have a numbered mount node (i.e., mount0 ... mount31) defined in the DTS file. Additionally, shapeB must have a node named "mountPoint" (also defined in the DTS file). Given this, mounting is as simple as the following.

```
%shapeA.mountObject( %shapeB , 10 );
```

Once this code executes, `%shapeB` should now be attached to `%shapeA` at mount node 10. However, if shapeA does not have a mount10 mount node, or if shapeB does not have a node named "mountPoint," then the mount will

Game Elements

probably either be shapeB center to shapeA center or shapeB center to shapeA foot (this happens with bad mounts to the player).

Assuming that the mount worked, shapeB will now translate and rotate with shapeA's numbered mount node. This means that any translation or rotation of the numbered mount node (including those caused by animations of the node) will rotate and translate shapeB. Additionally, shapeA's collision box remains active and will record collisions.

Well, that's all fine and dandy, but some time in the future, we may wish to detach these two shapes from each other. To do this, simply use the following code.

```
%shapeA.unmountObject( %shapeB );
```

Mounting Image-to-Shape

In the following examples, we will be discussing the mounting of a Shape-BaseImageData datablock (Image) to a ShapeBase object (Shape). We will refer to the Shape as shapeA and the Image as imageA. To be absolutely clear, imageA is being mounted to shapeA.

As with shape-to-shape, shapeA must define a numbered mount node (i.e., mount0...mount31) in its DTS file, and imageA must define a mount node named "mountPoint." As an additional requirement, the datablock definition for imageA must specify which numbered node in shapeA it will mount to. In other words, every ShapeBaseImageData datablock predefines which numbered mount node it can attach to.

```
datablock ShapeBaseImageData( imageA ) {
  // ...
  mountPoint = 15; // ONLY mounts to mount mode 15
};
```

Having properly made our DTS files and having declared a datablock for imageA with a mountPoint field, we mount the Image to the Shape as follows.

```
// Mount imageA to shapeA on mount mode 15,
// using slot 0 (of 8)
%shapeA.mountImage( %imageA , 0 );
```

If you examine this code closely, you will notice three things.

First, imageA is being mounted to shapeA.

Second, when we called `mountImage()`, we passed it the name of the Image datablock as the first argument. Remember that Images are datablocks, and datablocks each have a unique ID. Also, remember that TGE can use either IDs or names. Thus, as long as the name is unique (as it is for all datablocks), you are guaranteed to get the proper object, which is in this case the imageA datablock.

Third, the second argument to the `mountImage()` method is 0. When mounting an image to a shape, we must specify the slot that the mounting will be recorded in. This is important because, if by some chance you mount two images to the same shape and the second image uses the same slot as the first image, the first image will be dismounted. Images can be mounted to the same numbered node on a shape, but the mount information must be tracked in different mount slots.

Finally, to detach imageA from shapeA, we use the following code.

```
%shapeA.unmountImage( %imageA );
```

6.2.11 Miscellaneous—CRC and `aiAvoidthis`

ShapeBaseData provides a couple of miscellaneous fields. The first is "computeCRC." This field, if true, tells the engine to do some error checking when loading this shape. If the error checking fails, we will get an error message complaining that the shape could not be loaded, and the game will fail out to the menu. Why do this? Well, for one thing, this ensures that the server and all clients are using the same version of a shape. The CRC (cyclic redundancy code) is calculated on the server, and thus if a client in a multiplayer scenario has a nonmatching CRC, that client will fail out.

The other miscellaneous field is named `aiAvoidthis` and has no function at this point. You may use this in your scripts to indicate that an AI should avoid the object. The only benefit this has over using a server-side dynamic field is that this field is networked, allowing clients to observe it, too.

6.3 Item and ItemData

These classes are used to represent items, specifically, items that the player will interact with. These are things like weapons, power-ups, traps, mines, etc. Item and ItemData have all the features of their parents, ShapeBase and ShapeBaseData.

6.3.1 Item and ItemData Features

Item and ItemData add the following features to those inherited from ShapeBase and ShapeBaseData.

- **Rendering**
  - Light emission

- **Physics**
  - Stationary (Static) + nonstationary placement
  - Auto-rotation (spinning animation)
  - Elasticity
  - Velocity limits
  - Stickyness
  - Friction
  - Gravity modification
- **Collisions**
  - Collision timeouts
- **Dynamic typing**

Items are used to represent objects that are to be picked up or otherwise interacted with. They are special in that they can be walked through but still signal a collision event.

6.3.2 Item Rendering

Items add one new trick to the rendering feature set: dynamic lights!

Lights, Camera, ... Action

Items can emit light in three ways: none, constant, and pulsing. In order to create an item with a light, specify the datablock as follows.

```
datablock ItemData( ConstantLightEgg ) {
  // ...
  lightColor = "1 0 0 1.0";
  lightRadius  = 6.0;
  lightType  = "ConstantLight";
};
```

When an item is made from this datablock, it will emit a constant red light with a radius of 6 world units.

The three names for the light types are `NoLight`, `ConstantLight`, and `PulsingLight`.

The lighting of an item can be further modified such that, if the item is nonstatic, it does not render a light.

```
datablock ItemData( ConstantLightEggStaticOnly ) {
  // ...
  lightOnlyStatic = true;
};
```

6.3.3 Item Physics

A fun thing about items is that they display all kinds of interesting physical attributes. They can be made to stay put or move around, to rotate, to bounce, to slide, to fall and fly at varying rates, or to float away.

Static Items

When we create an item, we can set the `static` field in the object (not the datablock) to true or false.

```
%theEgg = new ItemData() {
   datablock = "ConstantLightEgg";
   static = false;
};
```

Setting this field to `true` tells the engine that this item will stay put once it is placed. If we want to allow it to move after placement, we set `static` to `false`. This parameter can be set in the `create()` method for ItemData, in the `onAdd()` callback for the datablock that is used to create the item, or as we have done above, in the object creation statement.

If we wish to change the `static` field later, we can do so. We can also check the current value as follows.

```
if( %theEgg.isStatic() ) {
   echo("This egg is static. It won't move now.");
}
```

Rotating Items

Items are often used to represent objects that the player is meant to pick up. A common hint that an object is meant to be picked up is that the object rotates. This is often seen in arcade games and first-person shooters. Thus, TGE provides the ability to cause an item to rotate. This is done by setting the `rotate` field in the object (not the datablock) to `true`.

```
%theEgg = new ItemData() {
   datablock = "ConstantLightEgg";
   rotate = true;
};
```

The rotating state of an item can be modified at any time, and we can check it by using the following method:

```
if( %theEgg.isRotating() ) {
   echo("This egg is rotating.");
}
```

Bouncy Items

As noted above, items can be made elastic, causing them to bounce when dropped. The field `elasticity` can take both positive and negative values. A positive value of 1 is not guaranteed to be equal to 100 percent elasticity, due to rounding errors. Also, if you choose to use a negative value, be aware that, if you don't limit the velocity (see `maxVelocity` below), eventually a bouncing item will crash the engine when the instantaneous change in velocity becomes too high.

```
datablock ItemData( BouncyEgg ) {
  // ...
  elasticity   = 0.7;
};
```

The datablock above will produce an item that bounces for a while then settles down.

Maximum Velocity (`maxVelocity`)

Because we have various ways of causing an item to move and perhaps to increase its velocity, because the engine does not handle very high velocities and accelerations well, and for practical playability reasons, we need a way to limit the velocity an item can achieve. This is done quite simply as follows:

```
datablock ItemData( LimitedVelocityEgg ) {
  // ...
  maxVelocity = 1000; // Limited to 1000 world units / s
};
```

Sticky Items

It may be that sometimes we would like an item to stick when it hits the ground. This can be achieved by making the item sticky.

```
datablock ItemData( StickyEgg ) {
  // ...
  sticky = true;
};
```

An item made with the above datablock will stick to the terrain when it falls to the ground. This overrides elasticity.

When an object sticks to the terrain, we can get both the position of the item and the normal at that point as follows.

```
%lastPos = %myItem.getLastStickPos();
%lastNormal = %myItem.getLastStickNormal();

if ( 100000 < vectorLen( %lastPos ) ) {
  echo("This item did not stick yet.");
} else {
  echo("This item stuck at: ", %lastPos,
       " with a normal of: ", %lastNormal);
}
```

hasStuck()

Before version 1.4 of the engine, it was hard to tell if an item had stuck yet. However, with the official release of 1.4, a new method has been provided:

```
%stuck = %stickyEgg.hasStuck();
```

This method will return `true` if the item has in fact stuck to something.

Sliding Items

If some velocity has been imparted to an item, or if it has fallen to the ground in a sloped area, we may wish for this item to eventually stop sliding. TGE provides a `friction` field which can be made either negative or positive. Low values equal low friction, and high values equal high friction. A negative value will actually cause the item to accelerate. Again, we need to use caution with negative values; as with `elasticity` values greater than 1.0, a negative friction will eventually cause the engine to crash.

Interestingly, we can use a negative `friction` with a `maxVelocity` to create an item that stays in perpetual motion at about the same velocity.

```
datablock ItemData( PerpetualMotionEgg ) {
  // ...
  friction = -10; // Accelerate rapidly to our limit
  maxVelocity = 20; // Limited to 20 world units / s
};
```

Modifying Gravity (gravityMod)

Items have the ability to "experience" their own gravity; that is, we can modify the way gravity affects individual items. This is done through their datablocks as follows.

```
datablock ItemData( LowGravityEgg ) {
  // ...
  gravityMod = 0.25;
};
```

An item made with the above datablock will only experience one quarter the gravity normally experienced by an item.

We can also make our `gravityMod` values negative. If you do so, be sure to limit the velocity, or else the object will fly away and eventually crash the engine. Also, such an item should be moved back to a starting point or eventually destroyed, otherwise it will float off and be of no use to the player.

6.3.4 Item Collisions

Items are intended to represent objects that the player interacts with in the world, usually by running over them and picking them up.

Consider that eventually we may wish to drop items that we have picked up. We'll cover this in all its gory detail in the "Inventories" section in Chapter 7, but basically we create a new instance of the to-be-dropped object and then drop it where the player is or toss it away from the player.

Now, consider that, if we don't have a way to disable the collision features, we'll just pick the object up again as soon as it is created. Thus, collision timeout for items exists.

Collision Timeout

Individual items can be told to ignore collisions with one specific object for a short period of time. We simply do the following.

```
%itemHandle.setCollisionTimeOut( %objectToIgnore );
```

In the above example, we've told the item represented by `%itemHandle` to ignore collisions with `%objectToIgnore`. It will honor this request for approximately a half second and then re-enable collisions with the to-be-ignored object.

6.3.5 Items and `dynamicType`

A `dynamicType` field is specified for StaticShapeData and ItemData datablocks. In both cases, it provides the ability to further differentiate an object's type by providing a value that will be added to the result of `getType()` when called on this object.

If you'll recall our earlier discussion of the `getType()` method (Section 5.1.4), you'll remember that each mission-placeable object has an associated bit-mask. We use these masks to differentiate objects when doing ray casts, radius searches, etc. The proper way to deal with `dynamicType` is to specify a new mask (in objectTypes.h) and export it to the console (in main.cc). Subsequently, you can use this value in `dynamicType`, and then `getType()` for these objects (and their children) will also have your new bit position set.

Having said that, if your purpose is *only* to use this in scripts, you can specify new `$TypeMasks::` values in script and use them. However, the best and safest way to do this is within the engine framework, where you will benefit from the checking your compiler does for you.

6.3.6 Maze Runner Lesson #3 (90 Percent Step)— Game Coins

In this lesson, we will examine the game coin's datablock definition. Later, we will implement scripts to pick up these coins, but for now, all we need to do is talk about the coin's geometry, the datablock definition, and the creation script.

Copy Required Files

From the accompanying disk, please copy the file \MazeRunner\Lesson_003\ coins.cs into \MazeRunner\prototype\server\scripts\MazeRunner.

Now, edit the function `onServerCreated()` in the file \MazeRunner\ prototype\server\game.cs to look like the following.

```
exec("./GPGTBase/loadGPGTBaseClasses.cs"); // MazeRunner
exec("./MazeRunner/coins.cs"); // MazeRunner
```

Please note that, until this step, the directory \MazeRunner\prototype\server\ scripts\MazeRunner did not exist, so you need to create it yourself.

> You may be tempted to try mounting an item to some other shape. If you try this, you will discover that it is not supported. In fact, items cannot be mounted to other shapes, but other shapes can be mounted to items.
>
> This is quite useful, as such mounted shapes can temporarily shield an item from contact and thus from pickup.

Coin Geometry

The geometry for this coin is very simple and can be found in the file \Maze-Runner\prototype\data\MazeRunner\Shapes\Items\coin.ms3d", where we copied it earlier. If you load the file in MilkShape 3D, you will see that it is nothing more than a thin disk. It has one render mesh and no collision mesh. Because this model is used for an item, a collision mesh will automatically be generated by TGE.

The skin was generated using Ultimate Unwrap 3D. It's simple and does the job. Now, all we need is a datablock and a creation script, `onAdd()`.

The Coin Datablock

The datablock for our coins is very simple. If we look at the file we just copied, we will see the following datablock definition.

```
datablock ItemData( Coin : BaseItem ) {
    shapeFile = "~/data/MazeRunner/Shapes/items/coin.dts";
    category = "GameItems";
```

Game Elements

```
  sticky = true;
  lightType = NoLight;
  mass = 1.0;
  respawn = false;
};
```

The coin item has the following attributes.

- It is an instance of Item (just to be clear about this).
- It is derived from BaseItem (there are base datablocks for all of the classes we discuss in this guide).
- We'll be able to find this object under Shapes/GameItems in the Creator menu.
- It is sticky and will stay put when it hits terrain or an interior.
- It does not emit light.
- As a rule, I never create a massless object. This avoids any future difficulties should I choose to apply an impulse to the shape. So, this coin gets an arbitrarily chosen mass of 1.
- When this coin is picked up we don't want it to be respawned. So, we set the field `respawn` to `false`. This won't mean anything to you yet, but when we discuss the Simple Inventory sytem in Chapter 7, "Gameplay Classes," this will become clear.

The Coin onAdd()

We have mentioned callbacks only briefly thus far, and we will discuss them in Chapter 9, "Gameplay Scripting." For now, just know that all SimObject instances and all instances of children of SimObject call the `onAdd()` callback after the object is created and initialized.

Later, when we write the scripts to place objects, it will become clear that we want objects to stay put when they are placed. Coins have the option of being static (don't move on their own), or nonstatic (affected by gravity and other forces). Therefore, we need to force the coin to be static by making a suitable `onAdd()` callback. Find the following code at the end of the file we just copied.

```
function Coin::onAdd( %DB , %Obj ) {
  Parent::onAdd( %DB , %Obj );
  %Obj.static = true;
  %Obj.rotate = true;
}
```

The callback does the following.

- Calls the `Parent::` version of this callback to allow it to do any work it needs to do (optional and based on your design methodology).
- Sets the object as static. Now, it won't fall (due to gravity) or be affected by impulses.
- Makes the coin rotate. Now the render code will rotate the coin. Please note that this only rotates the render mesh, not the collision box that TGE generates.

Testing

To verify that our changes worked, you can:

1. restart the prototype,
2. open the "Maze Runner" mission,
3. start the Creator,
4. look under Shapes and find the folder GameItems, and
5. open the GameItems folder to find a new placeable shape, Coin.

If this did not work, check your console for errors (typos, files not found, etc.).

6.4 StaticShape and StaticShapeData

These classes are used to represent any world object that needs to allow moving objects to collide with it *and* needs at least some of the other features provided by ShapeBase and ShapeBaseData. If you want to make a completely stationary object that has a simple collision mesh and requires no interaction features, use TSStatic instead (see Section 6.5).

StaticShape and StaticShapeData do not provide many new features. In fact, their main purpose is to act as a concrete instance of the ShapeBase and ShapeBaseData classes. In other words, you can create instances of these where you cannot create instances of ShapeBase.

6.4.1 StaticShape and StaticShapeData Features

StaticShape and StaticShapeData have all the features of their parents ShapeBase and ShapeBaseData. Additionally, these classes provide the following *new* shape features.

- Powered state tracking
- Dynamic typing

6.4.2 Powered State

StaticShape adds the concept of powered vs. nonpowered. In truth, this is just a flag to be used by us in our scripts. The engine does nothing different based on this information.

Using two new console methods, we can set and get the powered state of a StaticShape:

```
%myStaticShape.setPoweredState( true );
  // Shape is now 'powered'

if( %myStaticShape.getPoweredState() ) {
  echo("This shape is powered!");
} else {
  echo("This shape is NOT powered!");
}
```

6.4.3 dynamicType

This field behaves exactly like the same named field found in the Item class. Please refer to Section 6.3.5, "Items and dynamicType," for a description.

6.4.4 Maze Runner Lesson #4 (90 Percent Step)— Fade and Fireball Blocks

In our game, we are going to have two kinds of special maze blocks. The first one will be a block that can be faded in and out of view (Figure 6.2a), and the second will be a block that shoots fireballs (Figure 6.2b). Both of these blocks require features from the ShapeBase hierarchy. The fade block uses the fading and hiding features. The fireball block uses the reskinning property.

In this lesson, we will concentrate on the mesh properties and the data-blocks that go with these two blocks. Later, we will write the scripts to fade the fade blocks and to shoot fireballs from the fireball blocks.

Figure 6.2

a. Fade block.

b. Fireball block.

Copy Required Files

From the accompanying disk, please copy:

1. the file \MazeRunner\Lesson_004\fadeblock.cs into \MazeRunner\ prototype\server\scripts\MazeRunner, and

2. the file \MazeRunner\Lesson_004\fireballs.cs into \MazeRunner\ prototype\server\scripts\MazeRunner.

Then, modify onServerCreated() in \MazeRunner\prototype\server\ scripts\game.cs to include these lines (bold lines are new):

```
exec("./MazeRunner/coins.cs"); // MazeRunner
exec("./MazeRunner/fadeblocks.cs"); // MazeRunner
exec("./MazeRunner/fireball.cs"); // MazeRunner
```

Block Geometry

The blocks will both have the same geometry, namely a single render mesh and a single collision mesh. To see this geometry, open the file \MazeRunner\prototype\ data\MazeRunner\Shapes\MazeBlock\blockA.ms3d using MilkShape. You will see that this model has a render mesh named "block0" and a single collision mesh named "collision-1".

To enable reskinning, we need to do something special with the model's skin.

Reskinning

Still in MS3D, if you look at the material named "skin", you will see that we are using a texture named "base.skin.png". (It only shows as "base" on the MS3D button, but trust me, the file is named "base.skin.png".) By using a skin with this name, we will later be able to change the skin on this model.

To clarify, the rules for reskinning are as follows.

1. Skin your mesh with a texture named "base.*XYZ*.png", where *XYZ* can be anything you choose. The important thing to notice is that "base" is at the start of the skin. This tells TGE that this is a reskinnable mesh.

2. Create as many extra textures as you need, as long as they have the name "*LMN.XYZ*.png", where *XYZ* is the same name from step 1 and *LMN* is a name to make your texture name unique.

3. Reskin a shape at any time by writing the following code.

```
%obj.setSkinName( "LMN" );
```

The above code tells the mesh to use the texture "*LMN.XYZ*.png" instead of "base.*XYZ*.png".

Self-Illuminating

Because we are using a sort of cartoon/platform theme in our game, we will want all of the blocks to self-illuminate. This means that they will not be affected by the in-game lighting. To do this, we simply choose the self-illuminating option when exporting (using the DTS-Plus exporter). Please see Figure 6.3.

Datablocks

All right, these base blocks are pretty much good to go. Let's just create some datablocks and we can move on.

Figure 6.3

Making material self-illuminating.

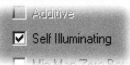

Fade Blocks Datablock

For the fade block, please open the file \MazeRunner\prototype\server\scripts\ MazeRunner\fadeblocks.cs. In this file, find the following lines of script.

```
datablock StaticShapeData( FadeBlock ) {
  category = "FadeBlocks";
  shapeFile = "~/data/MazeRunner/Shapes/MazeBlock/blockA.dts";
  isInvincible = true;
};
```

> Not shown, but present in the completed copy of this file (as written by me), there is another bit of code at the top. It is a reloader. Reloaders are little scripts that are used to reload the file, thus reloading the datablock definitions and any scripts in the file. In single-player mode, I use reloaders to reload files I have changed while the mission is still running. This way, I can make minor tweaks to scripts, etc., and not have to reload the entire mission.
>
> The reloader for the fadeblocks.cs file is as follows.
>
> ```
> function rldfade() {
>    exec("./fadeblocks.cs");
> }
> ```

This datablock has the following attributes.

- These blocks will go in a special group (in the Creator tree) named Fade-Blocks.
- It loads the mesh for the model we just discussed.
- It is invincible and thus takes no damage. We want this so that fireballs striking a fade block will not damage it.

Fireball Blocks Datablock

For the fireball block, please open the file \MazeRunner\prototype\server\ scripts\MazeRunner\fireball.cs. In this file, find the following lines of script.

```
datablock StaticShapeData( FireBallBlock ) {
  category = "FireBallBlocks";
  shapeFile = "~/data/MazeRunner/Shapes/MazeBlock/blockA.dts";
  isInvincible = true;
};
```

As you can see, this datablock is identical (except for the name) to our fade-block datablock. The behavior differences are entirely script based, and the reason we need another datablock is because, later, we will want to associate some methods with the fade block but not the fireball block.

6.5 TSStatic

This class is not a child of the ShapeBase hierarchy and does not use a datablock. It is used for any shape that will not be moved and will not need to be animated or make sounds.

6.5.1 TSStatic Features

TSStatic has the following features.

- Basic rendering
- Simple collision

   TSStatic objects are very lightweight objects used to render meshes that are used for scene filling and to render meshes that do not need any of the features provided by the ShapeBase hierarchy.

6.5.2 Rendering

TSStatic will render a standard mesh (just like a ShapeBase derivative), but it cannot play any animations, reskin, cloak, etc. It just renders.

6.5.3 Collision

If you wish for these shapes to be collideable, you must create a collision mesh as part of the model. This gives you the freedom to choose which items are collideable and which are not. The shape supports multiple collision meshes.

   The TSStatic object will not register collisions, nor will it respond, but all other active colliders (objects that can collide with other objects) will register their own collision with a TSStatic object.

6.5.4 Creating TSStatic Shapes

Creating and placing a new TSStatic shape is simplicity itself:

```
%object = new TSStatic() {
  position = "0 0 0"
  rotation = "1 0 0 0";
  scale = "1 1 1";
  shapeName = "~/data/Shapes/Lessons/GeneralLessonShapes/egg.dts";
};
```

6.5.5 Moving and Scaling

The basic `position`, `rotation`, `scale`, and `shapeName` datablock fields behave in the same way as they do for a ShapeBaseData-derived object. Also, being a a child of SceneObject, the TSStatic class can be scaled using `setScale()` and moved/reoriented using `setTransform()`.

6.5.6 Maze Runner Lesson #5 (90 Percent Step)— Maze Blocks

The primary geometry of our maze consists of blocks and groups of blocks. Later, when we discuss the level-loading scripts (Section 9.5.10), we'll talk about how these blocks are placed. For now, we will restrict ourselves to the creation of these blocks.

The maze blocks share the same geometry and skin setup as the fade blocks and fireball blocks from Lesson #4 (Section 6.4.4). So, if you have not completed that lesson, please do it first.

Block Geometry

In addition to the single-block geometry we produced for the prior blocks, we need several additional variations for the maze blocks. In theory, we could build our entire level out of single blocks. However, I don't advise this as we do pay a penalty (network and processing) for each block in the scene. So, knowing in advance that we will have various structures in our levels combining several blocks, we will make a few larger meshes. This way if we need an area the size of say nine (3 × 3) blocks, we can place just one big block.

If you look in the \MazeRunner\prototype\data\MazeRunner\Shapes\ MazeBlock directory we created earlier, you will see that there are blocks A through J. The geometries of those shapes can be seen in Figure 6.4. There are four square blocks and three each of the horizontally oriented and vertically oriented linear blocks. It may not be apparent immediately, but with these

Figure 6.4.

Geometries of blocks A through J.

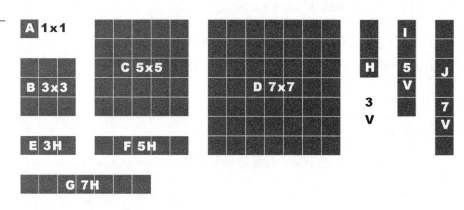

188

blocks, we can create symmetrically laid out levels without needing to reorient the blocks at placement time.

Placing Blocks

We aren't writing the code to place these blocks yet, but when we do, it will look something like this:

```
new TSStatic() {
  shapeName = "~/data/MazeRunner/Shapes/MazeBlock/block" @
              %blockType @ ".dts";
  position = %actX SPC %actY SPC $CurrentElevation;
  scale = "1 1 1";
};
```

This code snippet is actually from our level builder, and as you can see, we will be dynamically selecting the mesh to use as well as calculating the position as we place the block.

Examine the Blocks

This guide does not discuss modelling, nor does it cover the various modelling tools. However, as the blocks have already been created for you, I suggest that you examine a few to see how they are constructed. Pay particular attention to blocks E through J.

Don't forget that all of the maze blocks have been copied over to our data directory already at "\MazeRunner\prototype\data\MazeRunner\Shapes\ MazeBlock". You can open any of the block models (*.ms3d) with a copy of MilkShape 3D.

6.6 ShapeBaseImageData (Images)

ShapeBaseImageData objects (commonly referred to as just Images) are lightweight objects that can only be attached to ShapeBase objects and are used to render, animate, and script weapons, backpacks, flags, and other mounted objects. These are used instead of ShapeBase objects because they require much less network bandwidth to manage and transmit to clients. In addition, they supply a unique set of capabilities.

6.6.1 ShapeBaseImageData Features

ShapeBaseImageData has the following features.

- **Rendering**
  - Environmental mapping

- Light emission
- POV dependent rendering
- Camera offsets
- **Mounting**
  - Can mount to any ShapeBase class or child
  - Engine-event transitions
  - Timed transitions
  - User-defined transitions
  - Hooks for lighting, particle emission, sounds, and animations
- **Scriptable state machines**
  - Up to 31 user-defined states
  - Engine-event transitions
  - Timed transitions
  - User-defined transitions
  - Hooks for lighting, particle emission, sounds, and animations
- **Physical parameters**
  - Mass
- **Collisions**
  - No collision box

6.6.2 Rendering Options

POV and Offsets

As noted above, ShapeBaseImage supplies some fields for manipulating how an image is rendered.

- **firstPerson.** If true, this image is rendered in both 1st POV and 3rd POV. It is sometimes useful to not render an image in 1st POV, and this field allows you to disable rendering if necessary.
- **eyeOffset.** When rendering an image in 1st POV, the image may not be in what looks like the correct position. To remedy this for the player's view only, you can apply this offset to adjust the position of the weapon in the player's first person view of the world. This does not affect third-person rendering and is not seen by other players.
- **eyeRotation.** Similarly to position, when rendering an image in first POV, the image may not be in what looks like the correct orientation. To remedy this for the player's view only, you can apply this rotation to adjust the rotation of the weapon in the player's first-person view of the world. This does not affect third-person rendering and is not seen by other players.

Lighting

When mounted, an image can emit no light, a constant, or a pulsing light. This lighting feature is controlled by the following ShapeBaseImageData fields.

- **lightType.** This string specifies what type of light the image emits: `NoLight`, `ConstantLight`, or `PulsingLight`.

- **lightColor.** This three-element floating-point vector determines the color of the light. Individual elements must be in the range [0.0, 1.0] and represent the red, green, and blue components of the light color in that order.

- **lightRadius.** This floating-point value specifies the radius of the light sphere.

- **lightTime.** For pulsing lights, this integer value specifies the light's period in milliseconds.

6.6.3 Mounting

ShapeBaseImageData has three parameters affecting how the image is mounted.

- **mountPoint.** This field is a numeric value in the range [0, 31] and corresponds to a numbered mount point on the receiving shape. When an image is mounted to a shape, it is the responsibility of the image mesh to supply a specially named joint/node: mountPoint. When instructed to mount this image to a shape, TGE will calculate a mount transform using the receiving shape's numbered mount point and the image's named mountPoint.

  - If the numbered mount point does not exist in the receiving shape's mesh, the receiving shape's centroid will be used instead (in the player, this further offsets to the foot position).

  - If the image does not specify a mountPoint joint/node, its centroid will be substituted for that part of the mounting transform calculation.

- **offset.** This field is used to apply a position offset to the mount transform.

- **rotation.** This field is used to apply a rotation offset to the mount transform. This is especially handy when a weapon mounts at the wrong angle. This can easily happen if a player's mount0 joint/node has gotten rotated during the creation or animation/posing process. Instead of attempting to resolve this problem in the mounting shape's mesh/skeleton (which can be tricky), just apply a `rotation` to the image's mount transform.

> You can only mount one instance of an image to a shape. More than one instance of the same ShapeBaseImageData, mounted to the same ShapeBase object, violates the engine mounting protocol.

6.6.4 Weapon-Related Features

We will not be dicussing weapons-related ShapeBaseImageData features here; however, all fields and methods are listed and documented in the appendix that comes with this guide.

6.6.5 State Machines

The most powerful (and to some degree the most complicated) facet of ShapeBaseImageData-derived images is their state machines. Each image can define a unique state machine with up to 31 states. These state machines are designed to be used with weapons but can be used for other purposes, too.

Before proceeding, you should already understand what a state machine is. However, if you do not, the following summary may help.

A state machine, in the context of a game engine, is a mechanism by which action-reaction events can be scripted or programmed. Essentially, an object (in this case a weapon image) starts in a known state. Based on pre-defined input events, the state machine may transfer to a new state. Each state has a purpose, although the purposes may be varied and can include playing an animation, playing a sound, running a script, etc. Additionally, each state may define multiple exit paths.

States

There are 30 fields associated with the various states, state transitions, state triggers, state actions, etc., that the Image state machine handles. Because most of these are associated with weapons, a complete discussion of these states is not given here. For now, we will focus on how the basic state-machine mechanism works.

A listing of all the state fields appears in Table 6.2. A complete listing of states with descriptions is provided in the Fields and Methods appendix.

Table 6.2.

State fields.

stateAllowImageChange	stateDirection	stateEjectShell
stateEmitter	stateEmitterNode	stateEmitterTime
stateEnergyDrain	stateFire	stateIgnoreLoadedForReady
stateLoadedFlag	stateName	stateRecoil
stateScript	stateSequenceRandomFlash	stateSequence
stateSound	stateSpinThread	stateTimeoutValue
stateTransitionOnNotLoaded	stateTransitionOnTriggerDown	stateTransitionOnTriggerUp
stateTransitionOnAmmo	stateTransitionOnLoaded	stateTransitionOnNoAmmo
stateTransitionOnNoTarget	stateTransitionOnNotWet	stateTransitionOnWet
stateTransitionTarget	stateTransitionTimeout	stateWaitForTimeout

Defining States

We can define up to 31 states in our Image state machines. To do so, we simply name them as follows.

```
datablock ShapeBaseImageData( SimpleStates ) {
  // ...
  stateName[0] = "Preactivate";
  stateName[1] = "GreenLight";
  stateName[2] = "YellowLight";
  stateName[3] = "RedLight";
};
```

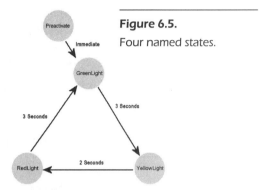

Figure 6.5.

Four named states.

This code produces four named states: `Preactivate`, `GreenLight`, `YellowLight`, and `RedLight`. So far, we haven't connected the states, so we don't know how the machine "flows." Thus, our state picture would look something like Figure 6.5.

Required States?

If it isn't obvious by the names of these states, we'll be making a traffic light with this state machine. However, you may wonder at the choice of state zero (`Preactivate`).

Generally speaking, you must define a state for the machine to start in. Traditionally, that state is named `Preactivate` and is numbered zero. This state will not execute scripts, animations, or sounds. The most it can do is give TGE a place to start the machine and wait for a bit before transitioning to the first active state.

Transitioning

There are several ways to transition from one state to another. In addition, we can make multiple paths out of any one state. For now, we'll focus on making a single transition for each state. We want these transitions to look like Figure 6.6.

Furthermore, the transitions we would like to use for our stoplight are timed transitions. It is possible to make states timeout and then transition to a named state. For example, if we wanted to create this sequence:

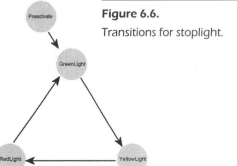

Figure 6.6.

Transitions for stoplight.

- `Preactivate` → `GreenLight` (immediate)
- `GreenLight` → `YellowLight` (3 seconds)
- `YellowLight` → `RedLight` (2 seconds)
- `RedLight` → `GreenLight` (3 seconds)
- repeat ...

193

we would code our state machine as follows.

Figure 6.7.

Timed transitions for stoplight.

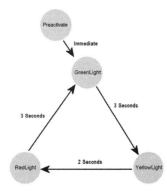

```
datablock ShapeBaseImageData( SimpleStates ) {
    // ...
    stateName[0] = "Preactivate";
    stateTransitionOnTimeout[0] = "GreenLight";

    stateName[1] = "GreenLight";
    stateTransitionOnTimeout[1] = "YellowLight";
    stateWaitForTimeout[1] = true;
    stateTimeoutValue[1] = 3.0;

    stateName[2] = "YellowLight";
    stateTransitionOnTimeout[2] = "RedLight";
    stateWaitForTimeout[2] = true;
    stateTimeoutValue[2] = 2.0;

    stateName[3] = "RedLight";
    stateTransitionOnTimeout[3] = "GreenLight";
    stateWaitForTimeout[3] = true;
    stateTimeoutValue[3] = 3.0;
};
```

This produces the state machine in Figure 6.7.

Making States Do Work

Great! Now, we have a state machine that will transition: `Preactivate` → `GreenLight` → `YellowLight` → `RedLight` → `GreenLight` → ... ad infinitum. Wait a second, though. It isn't doing any work! Well, as with transitions, state machine states can do lots of different kinds of work. They can run scripts, play sounds, trigger particle emitters, etc. Pretty cool.

Now, for our example we want the stoplight to change the light colors repeatedly. How the heck are we going to do that? Here are some ideas.

- Run a script and change the image skin? Nope. Images don't support skin switching.
- Run a script and replace the image itself? Naw. You could do this, but it's really messy.
- Use an IFL and switch animation states? Yeah. That's what we'll do.

IFL is the acronym we use when talking about an image file list. A TGE supported feature we have not yet talked about is animated textures. It is possible to create a model that takes a base image and then changes skins using an animation sequence. It is kind of like the ShapeBase skin-switching idea, but it is more flexible and can get higher frame rates than that method.

Running Animations

So, we've chosen to run an animation to change the light. How do we do it? Like this.

```
datablock ShapeBaseImageData( SimpleStates ) {
  // ...
  stateName[0] = "Preactivate";
  stateTransitionOnTimeout[0] = "GreenLight";

  stateName[1] = "GreenLight";
  stateTransitionOnTimeout[1] = "YellowLight";
  stateTimeoutValue[1] = 3.0;
  stateSequence[1] = "GreenLightOn";

  stateName[2] = "YellowLight";
  stateTransitionOnTimeout[2] = "RedLight";
  stateTimeoutValue[2] = 2.0;
  stateSequence[2] = "YellowLightOn";

  stateName[3] = "RedLight";
  stateTransitionOnTimeout[3] = "GreenLight";
  stateTimeoutValue[3] = 3.0;
  stateSequence[3] = "RedLightOn";
};
```

This example tells TGE to switch the animation sequence for this image to the named states when the state machine transitions into the state. At this point, our work is done. We have defined our state machine.

Running Scripts

Because you might want to do more than just run an animation, I'll get you started on running scripts and then let you investigate the other states yourself. To run a script when we transition into a state, we do the following.

```
datablock ShapeBaseImageData( SimpleStates ) {
  // ...
  stateName[0] = "Preactivate";
  stateTransitionOnTimeout[0] = "GreenLight";

  stateName[1] = "GreenLight";
  stateTransitionOnTimeout[1] = "YellowLight";
```

```
    stateTimeoutValue[1] = 3.0;
    stateScript[1] = "doSomething";
    // ...
};
```

Then, we must be sure we've created a function doSomething() in the namespace of our image.

```
function SimpleStates:doSomething( %this ) {
 // ...
}
```

Physical Parameters

If tracking physical properties is important to your game, then it will be worth noting that ShapeBaseImageData provides a mass field to represent the mass of a mounted shape. It can be extracted directly from the ShapeBaseImage mass field. There is no getMass() equivalent.

Mass can be used for various purposes, ranging from calculating a player's cumulative mass (with weapons, etc.) to determining if a weapon is too heavy for the player to carry or mount.

Collisions

An interesting thing about ShapeBaseImageData images is that they do not have a collision box. Therefore, no collisions occur. However, you may notice that very large weapons will push back when they are mounted and the weapon is pushed up against an interior or another object with a collision mesh.

This pushing back occurs if the mesh that the image uses defines a special node named retractionPoint. The engine will see that retractionPoint has collided with the boundary of a collision mesh and push the weapon back to prevent it from penetrating walls and other objects. If you do not want this behavior, simply do not create this node in your models.

Image Animations

Images support multiple animations, mostly related to weapons, but there is one animation sequence that is somewhat generic, namely the ambient animation.

ambient Sequence

If you wish, you may define a cyclic animation for images, named ambient. This sequence will play continuously. It may be blended or nonblended depending upon your needs.

6.6.6 InteriorInstance

This section of the chapter is mostly informational. Except for basic rendering and placement, all features related to interiors require art skills not discussed in this guide. However, I want you to know what features are available to those who are interested in learning more about the "art" aspects of interiors. You may skip this section if you are not interested in this kind of discussion.

Terrain Inside

When you create a new interior (that is, when you place one in the world), you may set a special field named `showTerrainInside` to `true` or to `false`.

If this field is set to `true`, terrain will show up inside the interior.

If this field is set to `false`, all rooms bounded by portals will turn off any terrain that might normally poke throught the floor of the bounded room(s).

Remember that, if there are no portals bounding a room, the `show-TerrainInside` field will have no effect.

Activating and Deactivating Lights

TGE supports the ability to enable and disable individual lights in an interior. To check for these triggerable lights, use the following method.

```
%myInterior.echoTriggerableLights();
```

Or, if you already know what your light names are, you can activate and deactivate the lights as follows.

```
%myInterior.activateLight( lightName );
%myInterior.deactivateLight( lightName );
```

Using `alarmMode`

TGE supports another Interior lighting feature. This is a sort of hanger-on from the days of *Tribes*. In *Tribes 2*, when a power supply got knocked out, the lights in an interior would turn red. This was the `alarmMode` setting for that light; i.e., you would have a `normalMode` and an `alarmMode` light in the same spot, and `alarmMode` of the InteriorInstance would dictate which light was on. The method to switch the `alarmMode` on and off is as follows.

```
%myInterior.setAlarmMode( "On" );
%myInterior.setAlarmMode( "Off" );
```

Notice that, instead of Booleans, this method takes the actual strings "On" and "Off".

Levels of Detail

In order to create an interior that supports multiple levels of detail (LOD), you must make several instances of the same interior and manually modify them to have less and less detail. Then, following the instructions for you particular exporter, export these interiors together. TGE can then use this multiple LOD interior. It will automatically modify the LOD for you.

Manual LOD

You may also manually set the LOD for an interior using scripts. First, you can query the InteriorInstance for the number of levels it supports.

```
// Returns number of LOD levels in this DIF
%myInterior.getNumDetailLevels();
```

Then you may select one of those levels.

```
%myInteior.setDetailLevel( 0 ); // Set LOD to 0
```

Selecting a nonexistent LOD will default to LOD 0.

Disabling LOD

You may wish to disable LOD changing for various reasons. To do so, simply set the global variable `$pref::Interior::detailAdjust` to false.

Mirrors

A very cool feature supported by InteriorInstance is the mirror object. Using the various BSP tools supported by Torque, simply drop a mirror entity into your model and *voilà!*

Yes, before you ask, mirrors will reflect the outside world too, not just the inside of an interior and its contents.

I'll mention it again later, but if your player shape is set to **not** render while in 1st POV, you will not be able to see yourself in mirrors while in 1st POV. To fix this, simply enable rendering of the player shape while in 1st POV.

6.7 Summary

We started this chapter restating the fact that Torque has two broad categories of model rendering objects, the shape and the interior. We spent a short time discussing the general purpose of the shape category and then listing the various shape classes as well as mentioning their primary uses. Next, we briefly discussed the purpose of the interior category.

Having finished summarizing and bullet listing, we jumped into a discussion of shapes and the ShapeBase hierarchy. First on this stop were the base classes ShapeBase and ShapeBaseData. We covered the primary features supplied by these classes, giving detailed descriptions for rendering, damage, energy, physical parameters (like mass and density), eye transforms, shape animations, sounds attached to shapes, shape and image mounting, and the deployment helper functions.

Next up on the list of shapes were Item and ItemData. Again, a detailed discussion of features followed. We covered the cool rendering, lighting, physics, and collision features, ending with a short discussion of dynamic typing. Along the way we stopped and created some assets (coins) for our game.

After Item and ItemData came a very short discussion of the simple StaticShape and StaticShapeData classes, which are basically concrete implementations of the virtual ShapeBase and ShapeBaseData classes.

TSStatic came next. We learned that this is not a derivative of ShapeBase but rather a lightweight class used for rendering models that don't need a lot of features besides basic rendering and simple collisions. Here, we made two new resources for our game, the fade block and the fireball block.

Really rolling now, we jumped into an introductory talk about the ShapeBaseImageData class. We learned about its various features, including rendering, mounting, per-image state machines, physical parameters, and collisions (the lack of them). As an introduction to the image state machine, we implemented a simple stoplight using the image state-machine features.

After images, we moved on to a short discussion of interiors. Here, we learned about terrain interactions, lights and lighting, LOD, and mirrors.

Overall, this was a fairly short chapter, but it still packed in a lot of useful information that you may wish to refer to again. Additionally, to supplement this information, there is a complete appendix that documents all of the console classes, including shapes and interiors. The descriptions in the appendix are succinct but complete, covering all fields, methods, and callbacks for every console class we discuss.

Chapter 7
Gameplay Classes

7.1 Gameplay?

Gameplay is probably one of the most nebulous terms (besides *fun*) used when discussing games and game design. For the purpose of this chapter (and subsequent chapters), we are less interested in the definition of gameplay than we are interested in the elements of gameplay.

One such element is *interaction*. In fact, it is safe to say that gameplay cannot exist without interaction. Futhermore, I will propose that interaction is in fact a major element of gameplay. To that end, this chapter focuses on the primary classes that are used to enable and implement interaction within our games.

The following classes are discussed in this chapter.

- **Camera.** This provides us with our view on the world.
- **Player.** This class supports a variety of features and is intended to be used to represent bipedal, multipedal, and other types of avatars.
- **Vehicles.** TGE provides three implementable vehicle classes: FlyingVehicle, HoverVehicle, and WheeledVehicle. These, like the Player class, are meant to be used as avatars or as transport for the avatar.

This chapter also focuses on a topic that is not centered in any one class, but operates on and with several classes to provide a very commonly found interaction construct, the *inventory*. Inventories form the basis for common game interactions, namely picking up, storing, using, and dropping objects.

So, the last topic in this chapter is about an inventory system that is supplied with the guide. It is a standalone inventory system that (unavoidably) utilizes some scripting topics that we have not yet discussed. Thus, you may wish to stop before reading that part of the chapter and quickly review Chapter 9, "Game Setup Scripting" and Chapter 10, "Gameplay Scripting." Then, when you are properly briefed, return here and finish the chapter.

7.2 Camera and CameraData

Together and in cooperation with other gameplay classes, Camera and CameraData define our game view.

Game view is a generic term I am using to consolidate several view-related topics. Some of these topics are listed in Table 7.1.

Topic	Description
Point of View (POV)	There are two basic POVs we are concerned with. • First person, which is the case where the camera is looking out of the player's head or eye. • Third person, which is the case where the camera is looking down on the player from a distance.
Field of View (FOV)	Field of view is a camera term that has to do with the angle of coverage (or angle of view). When we talk about FOV in TGE, we are measuring an angle on either side of an imaginary vector coming straight out of the camera and pointing into the world in the direction we are looking. For an FOV of 45 degrees, our view angle is 90 degrees (45 degrees to each side of the vector). If we think for a moment, we'll come to the conclusion that an FOV of 180 degrees would mean we can see all around the point of viewing (360 degrees of coverage). A standard FOV for first-person views is 90 degrees (180 degrees of coverage) or less.
Control Object	In Torque, there always has to be a control object, scoping our position in the game world and thus allowing the engine to determine what is visible to us. Any of the classes in this chapter are approriate control objects.
Free Camera	In addition to having the camera tied to one of the other gameplay classes, it is possible for the camera to roam freely, in effect taking over the role of avatar (although without any visible representation, of course).
Zooming	What we call zooming in TGE is actually a foreshortening of the FOV. That is, as our FOV decreases, it seems visually as if our view is zooming in and bringing far objects nearer. Likewise, as our FOV increases, objects seem to move away.

Table 7.1.

Game view topics.

7.2.1 Camera and CameraData Features

Camera and CameraData have the following features.

- Point of view
- Field of view
- Render scoping

The Camera class is really quite lightweight and derives almost all of its behavior from the ShapeBase class. In fact, as you will soon discover, there are times when a camera is not even required, and another ShapeBase-derived class can handle the Camera class's duties. However, let's not get ahead of ourselves. Instead, let's first learn more about the game view.

7.2.2 Parts of the Whole

In order to control the current game view, we will (at times) involve several classes' fields, methods, console functions, and console variables. Table 7.2 summarizes all TGE elements involved with game view.

TGE Element	Description
Engine Defined Console Functions	
setDefaultFov(defaultFOV)	Sets default FOV to specified value if it is between the current min/max.
setFov(defaultFov)	Sets current FOV to specified value if it is between the current min/max.
setZoomSpeed(speed)	Sets the zoom speed (milliseconds per 90 degree FOV delta).
Globals	
$cameraFov	Global variable showing current camera's current FOV. Updated every frame.
$camera::movementSpeed	Defines current speed of free camera in world units per second. Set in scripts, used by engine.
$firstPerson	A global variable used solely for tracking the current first-person status of the camera.
GameConnection:: Console Methods	
setFirstPerson(FirstPerson)	Sets this game connection to first- or third-person view based on the Boolean value of the argument firstPerson.
Camera:: Console Methods	
setFlyMode();	Sets camera to free-camera (fly) mode; i.e., camera is not attached to an object.
setOrbitMode(orbitObject, transform, minDistance, maxDistance, curDistance, ownClientObject);	Attaches camera to arbitrary ShapeBase object and causes it to be in orbiting mode.
ShapeBaseData:: Fields	
cameraDefaultFOV	Defines default FOV for camera "viewing through" this shape.
cameraMaxDist	Defines max distance for camera "viewing through" this shape.
cameraMaxFOV	Defines max FOV for camera "viewing through" this shape.
cameraMinDist	Defines min distance for camera "viewing through" this shape.
cameraMinFOV	Defines min FOV for camera "viewing through" this shape.

Table 7.2.

TGE elements involved with game view.

203

Table 7.2 (continued).

TGE Element	Description
firstPersonOnly	Declares that the camera attached to this shape may only view in first person.
observeThroughObject	Declares that the camera attached to this shape should use the shape's field parameters for FOV and Distance.
useEyePoint	This tells the camera to use the controlling object's camera transform.
ShapeBase:: Methods	
setCameraFOV(fov);	Set FOV to new value fov. Automatically clamped to curent min/max. Does not take effect immediately, only when camea switches modes.
getCameraFOV();	Returns current camera FOV for this shape, which may or may not be the same as the current FOV.
PlayerData:: Fields	
maxFreeLookAngle	Total radians of rotation (about player) allowed when in "free look" mode.
maxLookAngle	Maximum upward rotation of camera about player in radians. 0.0 is straight forward. 1.57 is straight up.
minLookAngle	Minimum downward rotation of camera about player in radians. 0.0 is straight forward. −1.57 is straight down.
VehicleData:: Fields	
cameraDecay	Rate at which camera returns to default position (post-lag). Measured in seconds (floating point).
cameraLag	How much the camera lags a vehicle that is accelerating.
cameraOffset	Camera's vertical offset from vehicle in world units.
Model Nodes	
eye	Location for first-person camera to attach to this shape.
cam	Location for third-person camera to attach to this shape.

As can be seen by this list, setting up the game view can be somewhat complicated. We will examine each of the TGE elements individually, in the order listed in Table 7.2. Then, we will take these elements and combine them (by example) into commonly encountered game views.

The Control Object (An Aside)

Before we can proceed, we have to briefly discuss the control object. As previously noted, the client requires that there be (at all times) a control object. This object is used to determine many things, but in the context of game view, we only care whether the camera is the control object or another shape is the control object. Changing the control object is as simple as a single function call. For an example of this, let's look at the camera-toggling command that comes with both the TGE Demo and the GPGT Lesson Kits.

The sampler that comes with this guide has a lesson that explores game views by allowing you to mix and match different player, vehicle, and camera settings. This lesson is named "Game Views."

```
function serverCmdToggleCamera(%client) {
  if ($Server::ServerType $= "SinglePlayer") {
    %control = %client.getControlObject();
    if (%control == %client.player) {
      %control = %client.camera;
      %control.mode = toggleCameraFly;
    }
    else {
      %control = %client.player;
      %control.mode = observerFly;
    }
    %client.setControlObject(%control);
  }
}
```

As can be seen, by simply passing the handle of a ShapeBase object (or a camera) to the method `setControlObject()`, we can change the current control object.

The control object affects the game environment in several ways, but for the most part these are advanced topics. For now, we will limit our discussion to the differences between having a camera, a player, or a vehicle as the control object.

FOV and Zoom Console Functions

There are two FOV console functions and one zoom function. The `setDefaultFOV()` and `setFOV()` methods do basically the same thing. They will change the current FOV to a new FOV. This change will occur either immediately or over a short duration (based on the current zoom speed).

Game Elements

However, there is a slight difference in the way these two functions operate. If the FOV is currently adjusting and we call setDefaultFOV(), it will be ignored. On the other hand, calls to setFOV() are never ignored.

The setZoomSpeed() function is used to set the time it takes to zoom per 90 degrees of FOV. Here are some examples.

```
setZoomSpeed( 0 );          // Transition FOV's immediately

setFOV( 45 );               // Set FOV to 45 degrees (takes
                            // network latency time only)

setZoomSpeed( 4000 );       // Transition of 90 degrees FOV
                            // requires 4 seconds

setFOV( 90 );               // Set FOV to 90 degrees
                            // (takes two seconds)
```

The Globals

There are three globals that may at times be involved in game-view decisions.

The first of these globals is $cameraFOV. It should be treated as a read-only global used to reflect the current FOV settings as the engine sees them.

The second of these globals, $camera::movementSpeed, can be read and modified. It is used to adjust how fast the camera moves in free-fly mode.

The third and last of these globals, $firstPerson, can also be read and modified. However, it changed its behavior after version 1.3. In version 1.3, changes to this global change the POV between 1st and 3rd POV. Starting in version 1.4, this global is used by scripts to track the current POV, but changes to the value do not affect the behavior of the engine. Only calls to GameConnection::setFirstPerson() do this, as you will see shortly.

GameConnection::setFirstPerson()

As I just mentioned, in versions 1.3 and earlier, the 1st and 3rd POV transition is controlled by the global variable $firstPerson. In versions 1.4 and later, this functionality is handled by the console method setFirstPerson(). For either the TGE Demo or the GPGT Lesson kit, if you search the file " ~ /client/scripts/default.bind.cs" you will find the following code:

```
function toggleFirstPerson( %val ) {
  if ( %val ) {
    $firstPerson = !$firstPerson;
    ServerConnection.setFirstPerson( $firstPerson );
  }
}
```

This code now uses $firstPerson to track the current POV (1st or 3rd) and tells the server to switch to whatever POV we have selected.

Camera Methods

When the camera is not attached to a shape (when it is the control object), it can be in one of two modes.

- **Free-fly mode.** Camera is free to fly anywhere in the world.

- **Orbiting mode.** Camera is "tethered" to an object and follows the object if it moves.

  To clarify these concepts, let's look at some sample code.

```
%client.setControlObject(%camera);
%camera.setFlyMode();
$camera::movementSpeed = 25;
  // limit camera velocity to 25 world units/s
```

The above code makes the camera the control object, places the camera in free-fly mode, and then sets the camera's current movement rate to 25 world units per second, using the global $camera::movementSpeed.

```
%client.setControlObject(%camera);
%camera.setOrbitMode( %player , %player.getTransform() ,
                   10.0 , 15.0 , 10.0 );
```

The second piece of code makes the camera the control object and then tethers it to the player, where it will be allowed to orbit. It is told to orbit the player and use the camera's current transform. Furthermore, the orbit "tether" is limited to a length of between 10 and 15 world units, starting at 10 world units.

ShapeBaseData Fields

ShapeBaseData has eight fields that contribute to our game view.

The FOV and Distance Fields

The first five ShapeBaseData fields are related to the FOV and viewing distance. We may specify a default FOV and constrain FOV within a minimum and a maximum bound by specifying degree values (between –360.0 and 360.0) for cameraDefaultFOV, cameraMinFOV, and cameraMaxFOV, respectively. We may also define a minimum and maximum distance between the "camera" and the current control object by setting cameraMinDist and cameraMaxDist, respectively.

observeThroughObject

This field is used to tell the engine which FOV and distance values to use when a camera is in orbit mode. When the engine detects that the camera is in orbit mode, it will query the object that the camera is orbiting and use that object's datablock for the observeThroughObject field setting. If the field is set to true, the engine will place the camera directly behind the shape it is orbiting and use that object's datablock's FOV and distance values. If the field is set to false, then the engine will use the FOV values in the camera's datablock and the distance value specified in the setOrbit() call.

firstPersonOnly

This field is used to restrict the view (when a camera is attached to a shape) to 1st POV only. This is done by setting the control object's datablock field firstPersonOnly to true. If this field is false, the camera is allowed to assume either 1st POV or 3rd POV.

useEyePoint

Sometimes, the player will mount another shape, such as a vehicle. At times like this, we may want the camera to now use the vehicle's camera nodes (eye and/or cam). By setting the useEyePoint field to true, we are instructing the engine to do this. If this field is false, the engine will continue to use the FOV and distance values it was already using (in the vehicle's datablock).

ShapeBase Methods

There are two FOV methods scoped to the ShapeBase class. These are used for setting and getting the current FOV of a shape. I suggest, however, that you do not use the setcameraFOV() method. It almost always gets overridden or ignored. The getCameraFOV() method is useful, though, because it is the only way to get the current FOV for a non-camera object. Remember that, for the current camera, you can just observe the global variable $cameraFov.

PlayerData Fields

When the camera is attached to a player and in 1st or 3rd POV, we can restrict the angles (pitch and yaw) that the camera may assume.

minLookAngle/maxLookAngle (Pitch)

By setting the minLookAngle and maxLookAngle fields, we can restrict the up-down rotation (pitch) of the camera. These fields take values in radians. In the following example, the camera can pitch all the way around in either direction.

```
datablock PlayerData( testAvatar8: testAvatar2 ) {
  minLookAngle = -3.141593;
  maxLookAngle = 3.141593;
};
```

In the following example, the camera can pitch straight down to straight up.

```
datablock PlayerData( testAvatar8: testAvatar2 ) {
  minLookAngle = -1.57;
  maxLookAngle = 1.57;
};
```

maxFreeLookAngle (Yaw)

In addition to pitch, we can limit the left-to-right (yaw) of the camera when it is attached to a player. This is done by setting the `maxFreeLookAngle` field. Again, this field takes values in radians. In this example, the camera can yaw a complete 360 degrees in either direction (left or right).

```
datablock PlayerData( testAvatar8: testAvatar2 ) {
  maxFreelookAngle = 3.141593;
};
```

Notice the name of this field: **maxFreeLook**Angle. The implication is that this (also) controls the angle of free-looking.

Free-looking is a special mode where the camera is in 3rd POV and it rotates around the player without rotating the player's body. The head may rotate if an appropriate animation is provided (see Section 7.3, "Players"). This free-looking is used for looking around without changing aim-point and for other purposes.

To get into free-look mode, the camera must be in 3rd POV, then we set the global variable `$mvFreeLook` to `true`. When this variable is `false`, the camera and player will behave normally.

VehicleData Fields

Besides players, the camera can be attached to a vehicle. The vehicle data-block adds a few more fields to make the camera behave nicely. For example, when a vehicle accelerates, the camera can lag behind. Then, the camera can catch back up. Also, we can choose the current distance between the camera and the node on the vehicle it is currently attached to.

Lagging and offset are controlled by three VehicleData fields.

Lagging

To enable lagging, we set the VehicleData field `cameraLag` to a positive value. Likewise, we must set the `cameraDecay` value to a positive value.

```
datablock WheeledVehicleData( testVehicle ) {
   // ...
   cameraLag = 0.1; // Lags by 10% of delta while accelerating
   cameraDecay = 0.75; // Recovers 75% of lag per second
};
```

Offset

We can force the camera to be vertically offset from the camera node it is attached to by setting `cameraOffset`.

```
datablock WheeledVehicleData( testVehicle ) {
   // ...
   cameraOffset = 1.5; // Vertical offset of 1.5 world units
};
```

Your Meshes and Special Nodes

We'll touch on this again when we talk about players and vehicles, but if you want the camera to attach properly to a model, the model must have two specially named nodes (joints): `eye` and `cam`.

`eye` is the 1st POV camera mount, and `cam` is the 3rd POV camera mount.

If one or both of these is not present and the current POV needs it, the default mounting point will be the centroid of the shape.

7.2.3 Basic Game Views Cookbook

At this point, you should have a pretty good idea of what is going on with individual elements that affect game view. However, you might still be fuzzy on the big picture, so I will provide some cookbook examples for the most commonly used game views.

The recipes in this section only apply to version 1.4 and later. If you are working with version 1.3 or earlier, you will either want to upgrade or change all code referencing the `setFirstPerson()` method to statements that change the value of the global `$firstPerson` instead. For example, instead of `ServerConnection.setFirstPerson( true )`, you would have `$firstPerson = 1`.

1st POV Only—Standard (90-Degree) FOV

To force the engine to use only 1st POV, have the player use the following datablock and make the player the control object.

```
datablock PlayerData( firstPOVOnly ) {
   firstPersonOnly        = true;
   observeThroughObject   = true;

   cameraDefaultFOV       = 90.0;
   cameraMinFOV           = 90.0;
   cameraMaxFOV           = 90.0;
};
```

Forcing 1st POV Only—Alternate Method

There is another way to force a 1st POV. First, disable the `toggleFirst-Person()` function by unmapping it (from actionmap) or gutting it.

```
function toggleFirstPerson(%val) {
   //  removed entire body of function
}
```

Now, in the file " ~ /server/scripts/clientConnection.cs" at the very end of the function `GameConnection::onConnect()` add the following code.

```
ServerConnection.setFirstPerson( true );
```

Forcing 3rd POV Only

Follow the steps we used (above) to disable the `toggleFirstPerson()` function and make sure that your player datablock has the following values.

```
datablock PlayerData( thirdPOVOnly ) {
   firstPersonOnly        = false;

   observeThroughObject   = true;
   // ...
};
```

Now, in the file " ~ /server/scripts/clientConnection.cs" at the very end of the function `GameConnection::onConnect()` add the following code.

```
ServerConnection.setFirstPerson( false );
```

1st or 3rd POV Capable

To allow the game view to be either 1st or 3rd POV, have the player use the following datablock and make the player the control object.

```
datablock PlayerData( firstOrThirdPOVOK ) {
   firstPersonOnly = false;
   observeThroughObject = true;

   // average FOV freedom
   cameraDefaultFOV = 90.0;
   cameraMinFOV = 45.0;
   cameraMaxFOV = 120.0;

   // average looking freedom
   minLookAngle = -1.57;    // straight down
   maxLookAngle = 1.57;     // straight up
   maxFreelookAngle = 2.1; // 2/3 rotation
};
```

Enabling Orbit Mode

To enable orbit mode, the datablock for the object that the camera will be tethered to should be configured similarly to the following example.

```
datablock PlayerData( useCameraSettings ) {
   observeThroughObject    = false;
   firstPersonOnly         = false;

   // Average Looking Freedom
   minLookAngle = -1.57;    // straight down
   maxLookAngle = 1.57;     // straight up
   maxFreelookAngle = 2.1; // 2/3 rotation
};
```

Additionally, the camera should have a datablock definition that defines FOV values.

```
datablock CameraData ( fixedFOVDistanceCam ) {
   // Standard FOV
   cameraDefaultFOV = 90.0;
   cameraMinFOV = 90.0;
   cameraMaxFOV = 90.0;
};
```

Use Vehicle's Eye Node on Mount

To have the game view automatically use a vehicle's eye and cam nodes when a player mounts the vehicle, edit the vehicle's datablock as follows.

```
datablock wheeledVehicleData( theVehicle ) {
  // ...
  useEyePoint = true;
  // ...
};
```

> One thing that people often forget is that the camera is derived from SceneObject and therefore has all of its attributes. One of these attributes is the transform. It is often nice to have a camera dropped into the game in exactly a certain place with a specific orientation. One way to do this is to move the camera to the place you want to spawn, orient it, and then grab the camera's transform.
>
> ```
> $camTransform = %cameraID.getTransform( );
> ```
>
> With this information in hand, simply place a single spawn point in the game and then force it to assume the saved transform.
>
> ```
> $spawnPointID.setTransform( $camTransform );
> ```
>
> Last, save the mission. Now, the next time you load up and drop into the world, your free-camera position and orientation will be exactly correct.

7.3 Player and PlayerData

The Player and PlayerData classes derive from ShapeBase and ShapeBaseData, respectively. Therefore, they inherit all the features of those classes. Additionally, they add the following features.

- Rendering
  - First POV enable
- Forces and factors
  - Max speeds
  - Energy drain
  - Delays
  - Resistance factors
  - Angle limits
  - Step height
- Velocity parameters

- Programmable pickup radius
- Look-angle limits
- Impacts (vs. collisions)
- Special effects
  - Foot puffs
  - Footprints
  - Splashes
  - Bubbles
  - Sounds
- Standard animations

7.3.1 Player Rendering (POV)

As we've seen, when the camera is attached to a player, we can view our game in either 1st POV or 3rd POV. In additon to the features restricting camera yaw and pitch, there is one more field of interest: `renderFirstPerson`.

renderFirstPerson

When we are viewing in 1st POV, it may be neccesary to disable rendering of the player mesh (on the player's client only); that is, we might not want the player to be able to see his body in 1st POV. Rendering of the player's body (mesh) in 1st POV can be disabled using the `renderFirstPerson` field, as follows.

```
datablock PlayerData( doNotRenderin1stPOV ) {
  // ...
  renderFirstPerson = false;
};
```

Please remember (from the Expert Tip in Section 6.6.6), if you have an interior with mirrors and you are playing in 1st POV with `renderFirstPerson` set to `false`, your player will not render in the mirror. To fix this, set `renderFirstPerson` to `true`.

7.3.2 Player Special Effects

The player comes with a ton of special effects, including particle effects and sound effects. For ease of consumption, these have been divided into categories.

Foot Puffs and Footprints

The player can be made to emit particles representing foot puffs while walking on terrain by specifying the following.

```
datablock PlayerData( makeFootPuffs ) {
  // ...
  footPuffEmitter = "myDustPED";
  footPuffEmitterNumParts = 15;
  footPuffRadius = 0.25;
  // ...
};
```

The above sample specifies that "myDustPED" will be used by the player's foot-puff emitter. Furthermore, it will emit 15 particles. The location of the foot-puff emitter is automatically determined by the engine.

Besides foot puffs, we can have footprints. Footprints are rendered using decals, so please see Chapter 11, "Special Effects," for declaring decals. In order to use a declared decal for a footprint, do the following.

```
datablock PlayerData( renderFootPrints ) {
  // ...
  decalData = "PlayerFootprint"; // Decal Datablock
  decalOffset = 0.1; // Alternate decals left-right offset
};
```

Besides the decal datablock, an offset is specified. This offset is the distance from center (in world units) that alternating decals are rendered. In other words, for the above code, the left-decal is rendered 0.1 world units to the left of center, and the right is 0.1 world units to the right of center. This makes the distance between the decals 0.2 world units.

We could specify the PlayerFootprint datablock as follows.

```
datablock DecalData(PlayerFootprint) {
  sizeX = 0.25;
  sizeY = 0.25;
  textureName = "~/data/shapes/player/footprint";
};
```

The PlayerFootprint specifies that the footprint should be 0.25 by 0.25 world units square and use the image in Figure 7.1. This image measures 32×32 pixels. It could be larger for greater detail, but changing the size of the image file does not change the resultant footprint size.

Figure 7.1.

Player footprint.

Splashes and Bubbles

When the player enters and/or moves through the water, the engine can optionally produce splashes and bubbles. To create a splash when the player enters the water (near) vertically, do the following.

```
datablock PlayerData( splashAndBubble ) {
  // ...
  // 1 world unit/s or greater causes splash
  splashVelocity = 1.0;
  // Particle Emitter DB for splash
  splash = "splashPED";
  // Angle of incidence <= 45 for splash
  splashAngle = 45.0
};
```

In this sample, if the player is moving at 1 world unit per second or greater and the angle of incidence (entry angle) with the water is less than or equal to 45 degrees, the splash PED will play. This means a splash requires a near vertical drop to happen.

To make the player emit splashes while moving through the water, do the following.

```
datablock PlayerData( splashWhileMovingHorizontally ) {
  // ...
  // Splash at 0.25 world unit/s or greater
  splashVelEpsilon = 0.25;
  // Splash Particle Emitter DB #0
  splashEmitter[0] = "splashPED0";
  // Splash Particle Emitter DB #1
  splashEmitter[1] = "splashPED1";
};
```

To produce bubbles for a period of time each time the player moves in water, do the following.

```
datablock PlayerData( bubbleDuringAndAfterMoving ) {
  // ...
  // Bubble Particle Emitter DB
  splashEmitter[2] = "bubblePED";
  // Ticks to froth (bubble) for (1/3 sec)
  bubbleEmitTime = 10.0;
};
```

Sounds and Sound Modifiers

In addition to particle emission, the player can produce a series of sounds. Here is an example.

```
datablock PlayerData( exitWaterSoundSample ) {
  // ...
  // Make sound when exiting at 2+ world units/s
  exitSplashSoundVelocity = 2.0;
  exitingWater = "myExitSoundAudioProfile";
};
```

In this sample, the trigger event is exiting water at a velocity greater than `exitSplashSoundVelocity`. When this event occurs, the `exitingWater` audio profile is played.

In addition to the above sound and its sound modifier, there are many, many more such pairs. Each of these pairs follows the same behavior as the one we just examined. A sound will be played if an audio profile for the sound is specified, and if the conditions of the sound's modifier are met. Please refer to Appendix A.3, "Console Objects' Fields and Methods Quick Reference," for a complete listing of the various player sound fields and their associated triggers and/or modifiers.

Property Maps

There is a file named "propertyMap.cs" located under the data subdirectory. In this file, you'll find statements like the following.

```
addMaterialMapping( "grass" , "sound: 0" , "color:
    0.46 0.36 0.26 0.4 0.0" );
```

This statement associates some data with a texture (material) named "grass". One of these bits of data is the sound number associated with this material. You can add materials as suits your needs. The complete list of possible sounds are in Table 7.3.

Table 7.3.

Sound types.

Sound	Sound Type
0	Soft
1	Hard
2	Metal
3	Snow

7.3.3 Player Physics

The Player class adds a new set of physical parameters on top of those inherited from ShapeBase and ShapeBaseData.

Forces and Factors

In this section, we'll briefly discuss the fields that limit player motion. Somewhat later (Section 7.4), we'll talk about how the player is made to move.

Game Elements

These forces and factors are all relatively straightforward. We'll discuss the less obvious ones in Table 7.4. All velocities are in world units per second.

Table 7.4.

Forces and factors limiting player motion.

Force/Factor	Purpose
Forward and Backward Motion	
maxForwardSpeed	Maximum forward velocity.
maxBackwardSpeed	Maximum backward velocity.
Sideways Motion	
maxSideSpeed	Maximum sideways velocity.
General Horizontal Motion	
horizMaxSpeed	Maximum horizontal velocity on ground, in air, or in water.
horizResistFactor	Delta factor used to determine how much of horizResistspeed is removed from current velocity.
horizResistSpeed	Velocity at which horizontal resistance kicks in.
Jumping	
jumpDelay	Forced delay between jumps (in ticks).
jumpForce	Force applied to player on jump. Should be less than 40,000 * mass.
jumpEnergyDrain	Drain this many energy points for every jump.
jumpSurfaceAngle	Cannot jump if surface angle equal to or greater to this many degrees.
maxJumpSpeed	Cannot jump if running faster than this.
minJumEnergy	Cannot jump if energy lower than this.
Running	
runEnergyDrain	Drain this much energy per tick while running.
runForce	Accelerate player by this much per tick as a result of a move (command). Should be less than 40,000 * mass.
runSurfaceAngle	Cannot accelerate if surface angle equal to or greater to this many degrees.
Upward Motion	
upMaxSpeed	Maximum velocity allowed in the positive z direction.

Force/Factor	Purpose
upResistFactor	Delta factor used to determine how much of upResistSpeed is removed from current velocity.
upResistSpeed	Velocity at which vertical resistance kicks in.
Underwater Motion	
maxUnderwaterForwardSpeed	Maximum underwater forward velocity.
maxUnderwaterBackwardSpeed	Maximum underwater backward velocity.
maxUnderwaterSideSpeed	Maximum underwater sideways velocity.
Recovery	
recoveryDelay	Number of ticks to stay in recovery mode after hard fall.
recoveryRunForceScale	Scale factor to apply to horizontal motion while in recovery mode.

Table 7.4 (continued).

Resist Factors

The resist factors in Table 7.4 may not be entirely clear at first glance. TGE provides resist factors for horizontal and upward vertical motion. These are in addition to the drag field provided by ShapeBaseData. The general equation for these resist factors is as follows.

```
if (velocity > resistVelocity ) {
currentVelocity -= resistVelocity * resistFactor * timeDelta;
}
```

In other words, once resist speed is achieved, resistance is applied by a factor of that resist speed.

Recovery Delays

When the player falls from a great distance, the landing is considered to be hard. TGE treats hard landings in a special way. As soon as a hard landing occurs, the player switches into "recovery mode." This recovery mode lasts for recoverDelay ticks. During this time, the player's run acceleration is modified by a factor of recoveryRunForceScale. The general equation for this is as follows.

```
if ( ElapsedTimeSinceHardFall <= recoverDelay ) {
  currentVelocity += currentAcceleration * recoveryRunForceScale;
}
```

Impacts

The player can collide with objects just like any other ShapeBase-derived object. In addition to this collision detection, a new kind of collision has been added. These collisions are called *impacts*. There are two kinds of impacts, those with the ground and those with other objects.

General Impacts

A velocity threshold can be set, above which a collision is determined to be a general impact.

```
datablock PlayerData( generalImpact ) {
  // ...
  // Collision is Impact at >= 10 world units/s
  minImpactSpeed = 10.0;
};
```

Impacts with the Ground

A velocity threshold can be set, above which a collision is determined to be a ground impact.

```
datablock PlayerData( groundImpact ) {
  // ...
  groundImpactMinSpeed = 8.0;
  groundImpactShakeAmp = "8.0 8.0 12.0";
  groundImpactShakeDuration = 1.0;
  groundImpactShakeFalloff = 0.5;
  groundImpactShakeFreq = "10.0 10.0 10.0";
};
```

In the above sample, any impact at over 8 world units per second is considered to be a ground impact and thus fires the ground shake effect. The camera is shook with the specified amplitude and frequency, falling off by a factor of 50 percent per tick to nothing over 1 second.

Impacts and Recovery (Mode)

As with a hard fall, impacts will automatically cause the player to enter recovery mode. If the player is squatting every once in a while for no particular reason, it is probably because the impact velocity settings are too low.

Step Height

There is a factor named `maxStepHeight` that limits how great a positive change in elevation must be before a player cannot step up. If the elevation change in a particular direction is greater than this value, the player will not be able to walk in that direction. The only way to get over this step is by trying to jump over it.

7.4 Controlling The Player

So far, we've talked about how the motion of the player is limited and parameterized by fields in the PlayerData datablock. Now, let's talk about how we control our player's translations and rotations in the world.

7.4.1 Movement Globals

TGE has a set of global variables that interact to determine if the control object translates or rotates. Additionally, the translation factors are further modified by a common global while the rotation factors are modified by the current FOV (via script).

Translations

All translations are modified (in script) by the global variable $movementSpeed. This value is a multiplier that affects the input value and is later multiplied by the various speed factors discussed above to give a final acceleration. The general equation of how the translations are calculated in script is as follows.

```
// Result is clamped [0.0, 1.0]
$mvActionValue = %value * $movementSpeed;
```

Later, inside the engine, our acceleration is calculated as follows.

```
acceleration = $mvActionValue * speedFactor * timeDelta
```

Subsequently, maximum velocity (ignoring drag and other factors) is as follows.

```
maxVelocity = $mvActionValue * speedFactor
```

The specific global variables (named action values corresponding to $mvActionValue in the first equation) are as shown in Table 7.5. To see some

A frequently asked question is, "Is there a way to dynamically scale my player's velocity?" I've seen folks answer this with a "no." It should be clear from this discussion that that answer is wrong. To scale your player's velocity, simply scale the value in $mvActionValue. This value can be between 0.0 and 1.0.

Action Value	Description
$mvLeftAction	Move left.
$mvRightAction	Move right.
$mvForwardAction	Move forward.
$mvBackwardAction	Move backward.
$mvUpAction	Move upward.
$mvDownAction	Move downward.

Table 7.5.

Keyboard translation global action values.

examples of the variables in use, examine the file "default.bind.cs" in either the TGE Demo or the GPGT Lesson Kit.

Keyboard Rotations

If we so choose, we can add key mappings to enable camera/player/vehicle yawing and pitching via keyboard instead of mouse. Each of these actions is modified by the preference variable $Pref::Input::KeyboardTurnSpeed. The general equation showing how these rotations are calculated in script is as follows.

```
$mvActionValue = %value * $Pref::Input::KeyboardTurnSpeed;
```

The TGE Demo and GPGT Lesson Kit do not use these features, but they are easy to hook up. Table 7.6 describes the global action values for keyboard rotations.

Table 7.6.

Keyboard rotation global action values.

Action Value	Description
$mvYawRightSpeed	Yaw right.
$mvYawLeftSpeed	Yaw left.
$mvPitchDownSpeed	Pitch down.
$mvPitchUpSpeed	Pitch up.

Mouse Rotations

All mouse rotations are modified (in script) by a script (provided in the TGE Demo and GPGT Lesson Kit) named getMouseAdjustAmount(). This is done to keep mouse yawing and pitching consistent across FOVs.

This function produces a multiplier that is used as follows.

```
$mvActionValue += getMouseAdjustAmount(%val);
```

The specific yaw and pitch global variables (named action values) are described in Table 7.7.

Table 7.7.

Yaw and pitch global action values.

Action Value	Description
$mvYaw	Yaw camera by this amount.
$mvPitch	Pitch camera by this amount.

7.4.2 The MoveMap

We're doing pretty well so far. We know how to define a player so that it has the forces and factors we want, and we know how to tell TGE to translate/rotate our character. Now, how do we attach that code to the keyboard and/or mouse?

In Chapter 9 we will discuss the ActionMap class, but to summarize its purpose for now, the ActionMap is a class whose job it is to convert device inputs into function calls. In both the TGE Demo and GPGT Lesson Kit, a special action map has been defined. Its name is `moveMap`. `moveMap` is automatically loaded when we start a mission. By default, it has been configured to connect our keyboard actions to function calls which then calculate movements using the global variables we discussed above. If you are curious about this process, I suggest you skip ahead to Section 9.4, "Device Inputs and Action Maps," and then open the "default.bind.cs" file you will find in either the TGE Demo or the GPGT Lesson Kit.

We've talked enough now about the Player and PlayerData classes to jump into the actual creation of our test player. The accompanying disk contains several player models, including the default Torque Orc and Blue Guy. Additionally, it includes Simplest Player, which is a non-bipedal player with no animations or other special features.

7.4.3 Maze Runner Lesson #6 (90 Percent Step)— Simplest Player

For our game, we will need to make a very simple player. This player is nothing more than a ball with three nodes (joints): floor, eye, and cam (Figure 7.2).

Figure 7.2.
Simplest Player.

Copy Required Files

From the accompanying disk, please copy the file "\MazeRunner\ Lesson_006\mazerunnerplayer.cs" into "\MazeRunner\prototype\server\scripts\ MazeRunner".

Now, edit the function `onServerCreated()` in the file "\MazeRunner\ prototype\server\game.cs" to look like this (bold lines are new or modified):

```
exec("./MazeRunner/fireballs.cs"); // MazeRunner
exec("./MazeRunner/mazerunnerplayer.cs"); // MazeRunner
```

Simplest Player Skeleton

Because we're not going to animate this player, it doesn't need very many nodes (joints) in its skeleton. In fact it only needs a root node and the two camera mount points (see Table 7.8).

Node	Description
floor	The root node, specifying the physical bottom of the mesh.
eye	The 1st POV camera node.
cam	The 3rd POV camera node.

Table 7.8.
Simplest Player nodes.

Root Node

In this model, the *root* node is located at the bottom of the player, and the eye and cam nodes are attached to it. This node defines the bottom of the player and is where the mesh contacts the ground. The engine uses the lowest node it finds in a mesh's skeleton as the bottom of the shape; thus, if this node were placed in the middle of the player, the player would sink into the ground.

Eye and Cam Nodes

The next node is the *eye* node. It is located on the "forehead" just above and between the eyes. This is where the 1st POV camera will be mounted.

The last node is the *cam* node. This is located behind and above the model. It doesn't necessarily need to be here, but this model was designed (in part) to show the difference between an eye mount and a cam mount. As you've probably guessed, this is where the 3rd POV camera will mount.

Simplest Player Geometry

Visible Mesh

There isn't much to say about this. It's a ball. The player has one mesh and one skin. We're not using any IFLs or other fancy features.

Collision Mesh

We do not need to define a collision mesh for instances of the Player class, as the engine does this automatically.

Simplest Player Animations

Earlier I said that this player is not animated. I lied. OK, I didn't exactly lie. For any player to work, the root animation needs to be exported at a minimum. Then, to get rid of some annoying warnings, you'll need to export the other animations (shown in Table 7.9). Since the player isn't going to need these animations, I've left them blank and just exported the same sequence for each.

The sequences for these animations are shown in Table 7.10, which includes the following information.

- **Animation.** This is the (required) name for the animation sequence in question.
- **Start Key/End Key.** These are the frames in which the named animation begins and ends.
- **FPS.** This is the base frame rate at which the animation should be played.
- **Cyclic.** This indicates whether the animation should be played once or in a cycle.

Animation	Description
root	A default animation that plays while the player is at rest.
run	Forward running animation.
back	Backwards running animation.
side	Sideways stepping animation.
jump	Moving jump animation.
standjump	Stationary jump animation.
fall	Long falling animation, which starts about 1 second after fall starts.
land	Hard landing animation (played while in recovery-mode).

Table 7.9.

Animation descriptions.

Animation	Start Key	End Key	FPS	Cyclic	Blended
root	1	2	1	Y	N
	seq: root=1-2, fps=1, cyclic				
run	1	2	1	Y	N
	seq: run=1-2, fps=1, cyclic				
back	1	2	1	Y	N
	seq: back=1-2, fps=1, cyclic				
side	1	2	1	Y	N
	seq: side=1-2, fps=1, cyclic				
jump	1	2	1	N	N
	seq: jump=1-2, fps=1				
standjump	1	2	1	N	N
	seq: standjump=1-2, fps=1				
fall	1	2	1	N	N
	seq: fall=1-2, fps=1				
land	1	2	1	N	N
	seq: land=1-2, fps=1				

Table 7.10.

Sequences for animations.

The default MS3D exporter does not support blending and many of the other cool special features that DTS supports. So, I suggest that you visit the GarageGames site and download the "DTS Plus" exporter (resource).

- **Blended.** This indicates whether the sequence should be blended or not.

Finally, for each sequence there is a combined line something like "seq: root = 1-2, fps = 1, cyclic." This is what you would type in for the default exporter, but since we're using the DTS Plus exporter, you will enter the values via that exporter's dialog.

Simplest Player's Datablock

Because the datablock for this shape is a bit long, only the pertinent portions are listed here.

```
datablock PlayerData( MazeRunner : BasePlayer ) {
  shapeFile = "~/data/MazeRunner/Shapes/Players/MazeRunner.dts";
  boundingBox = "1.6 1.6 2.3";
  invincible = true;
  groundImpactMinSpeed = 1000;
  ImpactMinSpeed = 1000;
  renderFirstPerson = false;
  observeThroughObject = true;
  // ...
};
```

This player has the following notable attributes.

1. It derives (copies) from the BasePlayer datablock that comes with the GPGT Lesson Kit.

2. As would be expected, the mesh we just built (or copied) is used.

3. The shape is a little bigger than the normal character, so we've increased the dimensions of its bounding box from "1.2 1.2 2.3" to "1.6 1.6 2.3," adding an extra three-tenths of a world unit in the *x* and *y* dimensions.

4. The player is marked as invincible because we are not going to use damage to determine if it is "dead." Instead, we'll kill it immediately if the mesh is hit by a fireball or if it falls in the lava.

5. Impacts are effectively disabled by setting the velocity factors to values greater than any velocity the player will be able to achieve in this game.

6. `renderFirstPerson` is disabled, meaning the mesh will not render while the game view is 1st POV.

7. The camera has been instructed to use the player's camera settings (`observeThroughObject` is `true`).

Loading the Datablock

Now, edit the "\MazeRunner\prototype\server\scripts\game.cs" file and update `onServerCreated()` to contain the following code (new code is bold).

```
exec("./MazeRunner/fireball.cs"); // MazeRunner
exec("./MazeRunner/MazeRunnerPlayer.cs"); // MazeRunner
```

Using This Player

Now, to use this player instead of the Blue Guy we have been using thus far, edit the "\MazeRunner\prototype\server\scripts\game.cs" file and modify the highlighted code (below) in `GameConnection::createPlayer()` to look like the following.

```
function GameConnection::createPlayer(%this, %spawnPoint) {
  //...

  // Create the player object
  %player = new Player() {
    dataBlock = MazeRunner; // Change this line
    client = %this;
  };

  //...
}
```

7.5 Vehicles

So far, we have talked about game view, cameras, and players (the first category of avatars). Now we will discuss vehicles, the second category of avatar. TGE provides classes for making the following vehicle types.

- **Wheeled vehicles.** Ground vehicles with four, six, or eight tires.
- **Hover vehicles.** Ground vehicles with no tires.
- **Flying vehicles.** Science-fiction–style air vehicles. We do not discuss this vehicle type here (although a working sample is provided).

7.5.1 Vehicles Overview

Vehicles share many traits, and all three vehicle types derive from the same base class. So, we'll talk about vehicle geometries, nodes, particle emissions, and animations as a group. We will follow this with a discussion of the base classes VehicleData and Vehicle. Then, we'll talk about mounting and dismounting vehicles.

There are working samples of each type of vehicle included in the GPGT Lesson Kit, and a full explanation of how they were created is included in the appendices. All of these vehicles were created and animated with MilkShape 3D, a reasonably featured and low-cost tool.

Vehicle Geometries (Meshes)

Just as the player must have some kind of geometry (mesh or meshes), so must a vehicle. Each type of vehicle has a minimum set of required geometries. These basic geometries are described in Table 7.11.

Besides visual geometry and the one collision mesh, another kind of geometry can be included in your models—a second type of collision mesh named LOS (line of sight). See Table 7.12.

Game Elements

Table 7.11.

Vehicle geometries.

Geometry	Description
Chassis	The body of the vehicle. This can be complex or very simple.
Collision-1	A simple nonconcave collision mesh. This is the primary collision mesh used for the vehicle. It is suggested that this mesh not have more than 20 vertices because collision calculations are quite CPU-intensive and the time required increases with the complexity of the mesh.
Tire	This is only required for the WheeledVehicle class.

Table 7.12.

Line-of-sight collision mesh.

Geometry	Description
LOSCol-9 .. LOSCol-16	Line-of-sight collision meshes. These meshes are used for registering the impact of projectiles and other line-of-sight–dependent collisions like ray-casts.

In practice, you may specify more than one collision mesh, but this is not suggested. However, multiple LOS meshes are acceptable and quite normal to encounter.

General Vehicle Nodes

Another part of a model's construction is the set of nodes (or joints) to which the mesh attaches. In TGE, the majority of these nodes are used by the engine to attach particle effects, and the remaining two are used for attaching the camera (Table 7.13).

Not all nodes are used by all vehicles and not all vehicles have all nodes (Table 7.14).

As previously mentioned, some of the nodes are used to mount particle emitters. Table 7.15 specifies what particle-emitter field (in a datablock) is associated with what node.

The emitters attached to a vehicle will activate at various times. Table 7.16 specifies when the emitters will be activated (not all these emitters are attached to nodes).

Vehicle Animations

Vehicles can have several animations. In addition to the damage animations that are inherited from the ShapeBase classes, vehicles have the new animations in Table 7.17.

All of these animations are blended. Not all animations are available in all vehicles. Table 7.18 specifies which vehicles use which animations. Additional animations can be provided but must be activated from script.

Node(s)	Description
cam	Third-person camera position.
contrail0 .. contrail3	Particle-emitter mount. Simulates contrails.
eye	First-person camera position.
hub0 .. hub7	Helper nodes that specify the location of the tires.
JetNozzle0 JetNozzle1	Particle-emitter mount. Simulates thrusters in rear of vehicle.
JetNozzle2 JetNozzle3	Particle-emitter mount. Simulates thrusters in front of vehicle.
JetNozzleX	Particle-emitter mount. Simulates thruster on bottom of vehicle.
mount0 .. mount31	General mount points that can be used for anything. However, 0 is normally the driver mount-point, and 1..10 are passengers, gunners, turrets, etc.

Table 7.13.

Vehicle nodes.

Node	Wheeled	Hover	Flying
cam	optional	optional	optional
contrail0 .. contrail3	—	—	optional
eye	optional	optional	optional
hub0 .. hub7	optional	optional	optional
JetNozzle0 JetNozzle1	—	optional	optional
JetNozzle2 JetNozzle3	—	optional	optional
JetNozzleX	—	optional	optional
mount0 .. mount31	optional	optional	optional

Table 7.14.

Use of nodes by vehicle type.

Although the cam and eye nodes are labeled "optional," you must have at least one of them. If neither is present, the camera will mount to the centroid of the vehicle.

Also, be aware that all nodes can be animated, including the cam and eye nodes.

Node	Hover	Flying
contrail0 .. contrail3	—	`trailEmitter`
JetNozzle0 JetNozzle1	`forwardJetEmitter`	`forwardJetEmitter`
JetNozzle2 JetNozzle3	`backwardJetEmitter`	`backwardJetEmitter`
JetNozzleX	`downJetEmitter`	`downJetEmitter`

Table 7.15.

Particle-emitter fields associated with nodes.

Game Elements

Table 7.16.

Activation of emitters.

Node	Wheeled	Hover	Flying
contrail0 .. contrail3	—	—	When velocity exceeds `minTrailSpeed`.
JetNozzle0 JetNozzle1	—	On forward thrust.	On forward thrust.
JetNozzle2 JetNozzle3		On backward thrust.	On backward thrust.
JetNozzleX	—	On upward thrust.	On upward thrust.
dustTrailEmitter	—	Velocity > 0 && Elevation <= `triggerTrailHeight` Emits from rear of vehicle.	—
tireEmitter	While moving from tires.	—	—
dustEmitter	When vehicle is within `triggerDustHeight` of ground. Please note that this emitter uses colors specified for terrain in propertyMap for that terrain texture, or all white if not found. Dust rises from ground beneath vehicle to `dustHeight`.		
damageEmitter[0] damageEmitter[1] damageEmitter[2]	If vehicle has sustained damage percentage greater than `damageLevelTolerance[n]`, then damageEmitter[n] is activated for emitters 0 and 1. Emitter 2 is only activated if the vehicle is damaged and underwater. Damage particles are emitted at a random point at a distance of `damageEmitterOffset` from the vehicle's centroid. Additionally, `numDmgEmitterAreas` specifies if we have 1 or 2 emitters specified.		

Table 7.17.

Vehicle animations.

Animation	Description
activateBack	An animation that occurs when the vehicle is thrusting (accelerating) forward.
activateBot	An animation that occurs when the vehicle is thrusting (accelerating) upward.
brakelight	An animation to turn the brake lights on and off. Usually implemented with an IFL.
maintainBack	An animation that occurs when the vehicle is gliding forward.
maintainBot	An animation that occurs when the vehicle is gliding upward.
spring0 .. spring7	Blended animations used to animate the suspension for wheeled vehicles.
steering	Blended animation to turn the steering wheel when wheeled vehicles turn.

Animation	Wheeled	Hover	Flying
activateBack	—	optional	optional
activateBot	—	—	optional
brakelight	optional	—	—
maintainBack	—	optional	optional
maintainBot	—	—	optional
spring0 .. spring7	optional	—	—
steering	optional	—	—

Table 7.18.

Use of animations by vehicle type.

7.5.2 Vehicle and VehicleData

These classes are virtual parents to the three concrete classes used for wheeled, hover, and flying vehicles. The Vehicle class has no fields, variables, or methods. So, we only need to discuss the datablock.

Vehicle Physics

In general, vehicle physics can be quite difficult to understand and to manipulate. So, I'll give a short description of the various fields and their purposes, then I'll supply sample vehicles with working values in the GPGT Lesson Kit. After that, you'll need to experiment.

Integration

The integration field tells the engine how many times to try to resolve the current motion. The value in this field determines the time slice used. Larger values equal smaller time slices and more iterations. Choosing a value for this field is a tradeoff of stability vs. time. Smaller time slices mean a more stable evaluation, but we pay for these multiple updates in computing time.

In short, a value of about 4 is good for hover and wheeled vehicles, but you may need a higher value for flying vehicles or high-velocity vehicles. Experimentation will tell.

Friction and Restitution

The bodyFriction field determines how much velocity is lost to rubbing on impact with a surface. This can have some odd side effects, however, so you may want to make this value either very small or zero (in the case of flying vehicles).

The bodyRestitution tells us how much the vehicle will "bounce back" when it hits something. This field should be less than 1. A good value is between 0.4 and 0.5.

contactTol and collisionTol

The field contactTol is compared to the result of a dot-product calculation to determine if a collision occurred. Thus, if you want to cause collisions to be largely ignored, this value should be near to 1.0. However, this value is normally about 0.1, which is an angle of incidence of about 6 degrees; i.e., any contact at an angle betweeen about 6 and 90 degrees registers as a collision.

The field collisionTol is a value that specifies the "don't care" distance for a collision. If the possibly colliding points are farther apart than collisionTol, the collision doesn't happen. This, too, is usually set to 0.1 (world units).

massBox and massCenter

The mass of a vehicle is treated as if it is evenly distributed within a sphere. The diameter of the sphere is normally equal to the distance between opposite corners of the vehicle's world bounding box. However, for wheeled vehicles, if the massBox field is greater than 0, this value is used instead. This way, we can compact the mass or spread it out as meets our needs.

The massCenter field is a three-element floating-point vector specifying an offset from the vehicle's centroid. This is used to move the massBox away from the vehicle's centroid.

minDrag and maxDrag

In addition to the normal drag value provided by ShapeBaseData, we can specify a minDrag and maxDrag. However, these values are only used for flying vehicles. minDrag is the minimum drag that will always be applied to the vehicle. maxDrag is now a dead variable and not used at all.

Steering

We can specify a maxSteeringAngle in radians for all vehicle types. This will limit how quickly we can steer in a new direction. Smaller values equal slower turns, and larger values equal faster turns.

Jetting

Interestingly, all vehicles can use a jetForce, which is a generic forward thrust value (in the case of wheeled vehicles, applied in addition to frictional forces).

Jetting is activated when move trigger three is nonzero ($mvTrigger-Count3 > 0).

In order to jet, the vehicle must have more energy than minJetEnergy (by default this is 1). Lastly, when jetting, jetEnergyDrain energy is removed from the vehicle per tick. The default for jetEnergyDrain is 0.8.

Impacts and Impact Sounds

Like the player, vehicles can have impacts. Likewise, there are sounds associated with these impacts. Because I've talked about this concept in Section 7.3.2, I will not discuss it further and just refer you to Appendix A.3, "Console Objects' Fields and Methods Quick Reference," for specifics.

The Camera

We have already discussed our ability to control the camera in Section 7.2: the camera can lag the vehicle when it accelerates and will do so when we set `cameraLag` to a positive value. This lag is recovered at a rate of `cameraDecay`.

The other thing we can do to the camera is offset it (vertically) by `cameraOffset` world units from the 3rd POV mount point (cam).

`collDamage` fields

Neither the `collDamageThresholdVel` nor the `collDamageMultiplier` field is used by the engine. These are for scripting purposes only.

That is it for our discussion of the VehicleData class. Now, let's discuss the general topic of mounting and dismounting, as well as how to use a vehicle as the player.

7.5.3 Vehicle Mounting

A vehicle can either be mounted (player sits on or in it) or it can substitute for a player. Furthermore, any of the following actions can occur.

1. Player mounts vehicle on collision or in response to other action.
2. Player starts in the mounted position.
3. Player is replaced with vehicle on collision or in response to other action.
4. Player starts as vehicle.

Each of these cases requires a set of console methods and some dynamic fields in the vehicles/players. Because there are innumerable correct ways to handle these cases, it might seem a bit daunting the first time you have to solve this problem. So, sample flows and source code are provided with the GPGT Lesson Kit to handle cases 1, 3, and 4. We won't cover case 2 directly, but it can be derived from the other cases.

Mounting Vehicles

In the GPGT Lesson Kit, when a collision occurs between a Player object and a Vehicle, the engine will attempt to fire the `onCollision()` callback for both datablocks. The `playerData::onCollision()` method provided with the Lesson Kit will then attempt to mount this player to the vehicle, if the vehicle is mountable and if the player is not already mounted to another vehicle (Figure 7.3).

- **PlayerData::onCollision().** Fires on a collision and calls the `Player-Data::doVehicleMount()` if the collided object is a vehicle, it is mountable, and the player is not already mounted to a vehicle.

- **PlayerData::doVehicleMount().** Handles the work of mounting the player to the vehicle. This method also manually notifies the vehicle that an object (the player) is being mounted to it by calling the vehicle's `onPlayerMount()` method.

- **VehicleData::onPlayerMount().** This method is called by `doVehicle-Mount()` in the case that a player gets mounted to the vehicle. The purpose of this method is to do any special animations or other actions you might require in the case of a mounting.

- **PlayerData::onMount().** This is automatically called by the engine as a result of `PlayerData::doVehicleMount()` calling the engine `mount()`

Figure 7.3.

Mounting vehicles.

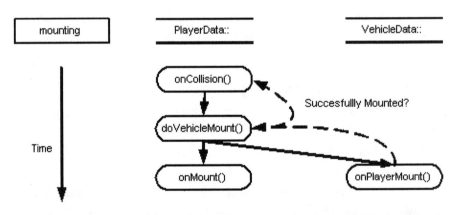

Table 7.19.

Dynamic fields for mounting.

Player Object Dynamic Field Name	Description	Range
canMount	A Boolean value specifying whether the player is allowed to mount a vehicle.	[true , false]
isMounted	A Boolean value denoting whether the player is already mounted to something.	[true , false]
Vehicle Datablock Dynamic Field Name	**Description**	**Range**
isMountable	A Boolean value determining if this vehicle can be mounted.	[true , false]

console method to mount the player object to the vehicle. In this code, we do some cleanup work on the player, like resetting the transform, placing the player in the sitting pose, and setting the vehicle as the new control object.

Mounting Dynamic Fields

In order to do the work of mounting or substituting, we require that there be a few dynamic fields present in the player object and the vehicle's datablock (Table 7.19).

Dismounting Vehicles

Assuming that the player is mounted to a vehicle, we may wish to allow for dismounting to occur. The GPGT Lesson Kit provides source code to handle this as a result of a key press, but dismounting can easily be made to result from other actions, too (Figure 7.4).

- **User Action.** The user requests a dismount via mouse click or button press. (See the "Vehicle Action Maps" section below.)
- **`PlayerData::doDismount()`.** Attempts to dismount from the current mount point. This method manually calls the `VehicleData::onPlayerDismount()` method to notify the vehicle that the dismount is occuring.
- **`VehicleData::onPlayerDismount()`.** This method is provided so that the vehicle can play a special animation or do other work when the player dismounts.

Vehicle Action Maps

It is important to know that TGE has code that automatically checks to see if a player is mounted to an object. When this is true and when a moveTrigger two event (`$mvTriggerCount2 > 0`) is received, the engine will automatically call the `doDismount()` callback. In both the TGE Demo and GPGT Lesson Kit, the spacebar is tied to `$mvTriggerCount2`. So, you do not need to modify or add an action map unless you wish to remap the trigger to something besides the spacebar.

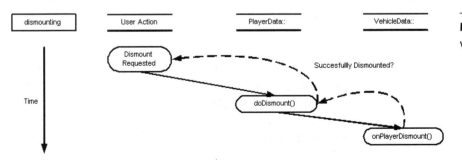

Figure 7.4.

Vehicle dismounting flow.

Game Elements

7.5.4 Wheeled Vehicles

Now that we've discussed general vehicle information, we'll discuss the specific vehicle types supported by TGE. The first of these is the wheeled vehicle. Wheeled vehicles in TGE support 4, 6, and 8 tires. The chassis of the vehicle is represented by the WheeledVehicleData and WheeledVehicle classes, the tires by the WheeledVehicleTire class, and the suspension by the Wheeled-VehicleSpring class. We'll talk about each of these in turn.

WheeledVehicleData and WheeledVehicle

These classes inherit all the fields in the VehicleData and Vehicle classes, respectively. In addition, the WheeledVehicleData class brings some new fields and features.

The Engine

A wheeled vehicle is moved by its engine. The power of this engine is defined by the `engineTorque` field. Also, the engine can be used to slow the vehicle. That is, when the engine is not engaged in accelerating or maintaining the vehicle's current velocity, it can apply a braking force. Simply set `engine-Brake` to a positive value, and the engine will slow the car by this factor.

Braking

In addition to engine braking, we can actually apply a braking force. The brake force is set using the `brakeTorque` field. It uses equivalent units (applied oppositely) to engine torque.

There is a small catch to braking. Braking is caused by `$mvTrigger-Count2` being nonzero. This is the same trigger associated with player jumping. So, braking will not work if the player is mounted to a vehicle.; i.e., only vehicles used as the player will brake.

The Wheels

We need to specify a maximum angular velocity (rotational rate) for our tires. This keeps them from over- or underrotating and is used to tune the look of our tires. It does not affect how the vehicle drives. This effect is controlled by the `maxWheelSpeed` field.

Sounds

Our vehicles can make noises under various circumstances. When the engine is engaged, TGE will try to play the `engineSound` audio profile. When jetting (`$mvTriggerCount3 > 0`), TGE will play the sound specified by `jetSound`. If the vehicle skids or the tires otherwise break friction, TGE will attempt to play the sound specified by `squealSound`.

WheeledVehicleTire

A wheeled vehicle can specify a different tire datablock for each tire if we so choose. The tire datablock is named "WheeledVehicleTire" and has the following features.

Friction

Tires exhibit both static and dynamic friction. If you have not studied dynamics, this may mean nothing to you. In real life dynamics, there are two kinds of friction: static and kinetic (some texts will say there are three: static, kinetic, and breaking).

Static friction is the friction found between two surfaces when both surfaces are stationary. Static friction is what keeps the objects stationary. When a force is applied that overcomes static friction, the object to which the force is applied will begin moving. This is named `staticFriction` in TGE.

When an object is moving, it usually has a different friction. This friction is known as kinetic friction, and is named `kineticFriction` in TGE. Normally (for most materials), static friction is higher than kinetic friction.

So, what does this mean in TGE terms? Well, TGE simplifies real-world physics, but it does respect these two factors. While a tire is either stationary or moving and has not yet slipped, `staticFriction` is applied. However, when the torque applied by the engine results in a force higher than `staticFriction`, the tire will begin to slip. At this point, TGE starts to use `kineticFriction` in its calculations.

In short, with a lower `kineticFriction`, a tire that is slipping will continue to slip until the applied force is reduced or removed.

Longitudinal Forces and Factors

A tire exhibits forces in two directions (springs handle the third for TGE). The forward/backward force is known as longitudinal force (Figure 7.5, left). In TGE, this force is defined by the `longitudinalForce` field.

There are two additional longitudinal factors that act in concert with `longitudinalForce`. Their purpose is to produce a more realistic tire action. Real tires are like springs and deform slightly when forces are applied to them. However, they only deform so much before acting rigid (or exploding, which they do not do in TGE). The springiness of a tire is set using `longitudinalDamping`. This damping is attenuated by a factor `logitudinalRelaxation` (Yes, this field is misspelled. It has been and will remain spelled this way to prevent breaking people's scripts).

To make your tires behave like rubber, make `longitudinalDamping` about 10 percent of the value of `longitudinalForce`, and you can adjust this by making `logitudinalRelaxation` between 0.0 and 1.0.

Figure 7.5.

Longitudinal and lateral forces.

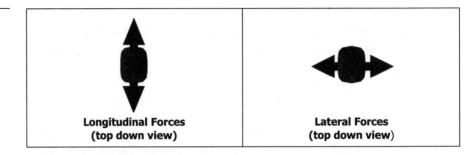

Figure 7.5.

Longitudinal and lateral forces.

Lateral Forces and Factors

The next force tires produce is side-to-side or lateral force (Figure 7.5, right). Lateral force is determined by the field `lateralForce`. Similarly to longitudinal forces, we have `lateralDamping` and `lateralRelaxation` factors.

Physical Parameters

Beyond forces, tires themselves have both a mass and a radius. The `mass` of each tire contributes to the vehicle's total mass. The `radius` field is important because it defines the bounding-box size for the tire. By default, the radius is 0.6 world units. So, if you make an abnormally large or small tire, be sure to adjust this value.

Restitution

The `restitution` field in tires is no longer used.

WheeledVehicleSpring

The final component in a wheeled vehicle is the suspension. The suspension is defined by the WheeledVehicleSpring datablock. As with tires, each tire location can have a unique spring. These springs have the following features.

Upward Force and Damping

Figure 7.6.

Upward force and damping.

To frame the discussion of this next force, think of the tire as being on the ground. Then, the third force component is the force that pushes up on the vehicle, keeping it off of the ground (Figure 7.6). This pushing force is defined by the field `force` in the spring datablock.

By default, the spring will push with all its force when the spring is fully compressed, and with no force when it is fully extended. The force varies linearly between these two extensions.

This spring force can be attenuated when the tire is traveling up and down. If we specify a value for the `damping` field, this force will be factored into the spring force. A good ratio for `damping` is about 20 percent of force.

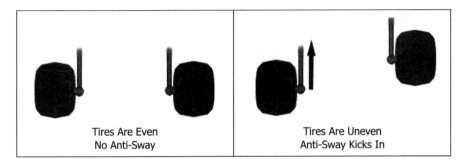

Figure 7.7.
The anti-sway factor.

Tires Are Even
No Anti-Sway

Tires Are Uneven
Anti-Sway Kicks In

The Anti-Sway Effect

An odd thing can occur when one tire hits a stone or some other obstacle. It can temporarily cause that part of the car to be higher than the rest of the car; i.e., the car is now off kilter. To compensate for this, TGE provides an anti-sway factor (see Figure 7.7). The anti-sway force, specified by the `antiSway-Force` field, is used to rebalance the vehicle (at least partially). In general, if the anti-sway value is lower than the normal force (`antiSwayForce < force`), the car will tilt away from the raised tire. If the values are equal, the opposite spring will try to equalize the force, levelling the car. It can only do so to the extent of the difference between the two springs' extensions. The anti-sway force equation is as follows.

```
antiSway = (oppositeWheelExtension - wheelExtension) *
   spring->antiSwayForce;
```

Length of Travel

Lastly, we can specify the length of our spring. This length limits the distance the tire hub may travel from its topmost position to its bottommost position (Figure 7.8). The length is specified by the field length and cannot be zero.

Figure 7.8.

Length of travel of hub.

Powered Wheels

The motivational force, the force that moves your vehicle, comes from the tires. By default, all wheels are enabled and thus produce motivational force during the game, but at any time after the creation of a vehicle, we may choose to disable or re-enable individual wheels. This will have an effect on how the vehicle steers and drives in general. To set the power on a wheel, simply use the following method.

```
// De-power left-front tire
%vehicle.setWheelPowered( 0 , false );
```

The tire locations on a wheeledVehicle are numbered 0 through 7 and are ordered left-to-right and front-to-back. So, for a four-wheeled vehicle, the tire positions are: 0—left-front, 1—right-front, 2—left-rear, and 3—right-rear.

Remember, wheels are ordered front left, front right, second front, ..., left rear, right rear. Also, trying to power or depower a wheel that does not exist will cause an error, so be sure your script is aware of the tire count for the vehicle it is modifying.

7.5.5 Hover Vehicles

The next category of vehicles is the hover vehicle. This vehicle is a ground vehicle that remains a short way above the ground. It has no tires to move or turn and instead uses "thrusters" for these maneuvers. There are only two classes involved in making these vehicles: HoverVehicleData and HoverVehicle.

HoverVehicleData and HoverVehicle

These classes inherit all the fields in the VehicleData and Vehicle classes, respectively. In addition, the HoverVehicleData class brings some new fields and features.

Horizontal Motion

The motion of the hover vehicle in the horizontal plane is controlled by three forces: `mainThrustForce`, `strafeThrustForce`, and `reverseThrust-Force`. The first force is applied to forward motion, the second to left-right motion, and the third to reverse motion.

Drag

There is a field named `dragForce` that modifies the maximum rate of the hover vehicle. Setting this value too high will cause the vehicle to not move at all. Experimentation is required, but a good starting value is 1, then move upward.

vertFactor and FloatingThrustFactor

The first of these two factors (`vertFactor`) is multiplied into the vertical component of drag. It defaults to 0.15 but may be increased to produce more drag in the vertical direction.

The second factor (`FloatingThrustFactor`) is used to modify general thrust strength depending on whether the vehicle is floating (*not* in contact with water, terrain, or interior). If the vehicle is *not* floating, 100 percent of the force is applied. However, if the vehicle is floating, the general force equation becomes the following.

```
force = FloatingThrustFactor * force;
```

This factor can be between 0.0 and 1.0 and defaults to 0.25, meaning that floating thrust is only one-quarter that of nonfloating thrust. The purpose here is to keep the vehicle reasonably powered while in the air, but to make the thrust very strong while in contact with water, terrain, or an interior.

Floating Gravity

When a hover vehicle is not in contact with water, the terrain, or an interior, the total amount of gravity applied to the vehicle will be as follows.

```
gravityForce = local gravity
```

However, once the vehicle contacts any of the aforementioned obstructions, we can reduce the force of gravity by a factor of `floatingGravMag` (can be between 0.0 and 1.0). This gives us the following gravity force equation.

```
gravityForce = local gravity * floatingGravMag
```

The purpose of this is to allow a nonfloating vehicle to get back in the air more easily.

Hovering

There is a force called `stabSpringConstant`. This field must be set to a value equal to two times the mass of the vehicle or higher, or the vehicle will sink to the ground. The field `stabDampingConstant` acts to keep the hover vehicle from bouncing around too much and can be higher than `stabSpringConstant`. In fact, the higher it gets, the less bounce there is when hovering over terrain with abrupt elevation changes.

Jetting Around

If jetting is active (`$mvTriggerCount3 > 0`), the `turboFactor` is applied. The current calculated thrust is multiplied by the value in this field if it is nonzero.

Stabilizers

The hover vehicle has a nonvisible bounding box that is used to "stabilize" it. This box grows as the velocity of the hover vehicle increases and shrinks as the vehicle reduces speed. We can limit the bounds of this box by using the two fields `stabLenMin` and `stabLenMax`.

Rolling and Pitching

When the hover vehicle rolls and pitches, it can optionally glide in the direction of the roll or pitch. Simply set the fields `rollForce` and `pitchForce` respectively to some nonzero value and the vehicle will move toward the roll/pitch until it rotates back to vertical.

Game Elements

Keeping the Vehicle Upright

Because hover vehicles may travel over hilly and bumpy terrain, it is possible that the vehicle may want to tip over. Therefore, the engine provides a force for keeping the vehicle upright. This force is specified using the `normal-Force` field. When a hover vehicle is tilted or canted, this force is applied to right the vehicle so that it is parallel to the surface below it. It is not a strong contributor, so keeping this high is a good idea.

Steering

There are two forces involved in steering our vehicle. The first is named `steeringForce` and is the value applied in the direction of our turn. The second is `gyroDrag`. This is a resistive force that trys to stop the turn.

Stay Put!

When the vehicle is not thrusting and should be sitting still, it may still slide about, especially if there is a slope. To prevent the vehicle from constantly sliding away, we can set two fields to nonzero values. First, we set a threshold velocity `brakingActivationSpeed`. When the vehicle is not thrusting, autobraking will begin to activate as soon as the speed of the vehicle is lower than this. Once braking is activated, the force `brakingForce` will be applied until the vehicle comes to rest.

Special Effects

The hover vehicle supports three new sounds: `jetSound`, `engineSound`, and `floatSound`. These sounds play while jetting, thrusting, and hovering, respectively.

7.5.6 Alternate Mounting Positions

In our discussions, we have only talked about mounting to mount0, but it is completely possible to mount to another mount node. We can blindly mount our players to nodes, but the best way to handle multiple mountings is to check to see if a node is available. To do this, you can use this piece of code (slight modification of script found in the forums):

```
function findEmptySeat( %vehicleObj , %mountPoints, %startNode ) {
  if ( 0 >= %startNode )
    %count = 0 ;
  else
    %count = %startNode ;
  for ( 0 ; %count < %mountPoints ; %count++ ) {
```

```
%node = %vehicleObj.getMountNodeObject(%i);
if (%node == 0) {
return %i;
}
}
return -1;
}
```

This method iterates from 0 to %mountPoints and returns the number of the first mount point with no passenger. We can just mount our player to this point, or we can go a step further and find the closest node and mount to it.

```
function findNearestEmptySeat( %playerObj , %vehicleObj , %mountPoints ) {
%nearest = 1000;
%mountNode = -1;
for( %count = 0 ; %count < %mountPoints ; %count++ ) {
%node = %vehicleObj.getMountNodeObject(%i);
if (%node == 0) {
%distVec = vectorSub( %player.getWorldBoxCenter() ,
getWords( %vehicleObj.getSlotTransform( %node , 0 , 2) ) );
%nodeDist = vectorLen( %distVec );
if( %nodeDist < %nearest ) {
%nearest = %nodeDist;
%mountNode = %node
}
}
}
return %mountNode;
}
```

This function behaves much in the same way as the prior seat finder, but it will return the node number for the nearest empty passenger position. Please note that, for this to work, your nodes *must* be numbered 0 through 7.

7.6 Inventories

It would be fair to say that most games implement some kind of inventory system. The purpose of these systems is to provide a set of mechanisms for storing game items and for later retrieving them. The functions of an inventory are varied, but at their most basic, they must provide the following minimal set of features.

- **Must be able to store items.** This seems obvious, but what does it mean? It means that, when an inventory item is encountered in the world, the inventory system must provide a means of removing it from the world and storing it for later retrieval.

- **Must be able to retrieve items.** Given that the system has stored an item, we will likely need to retrieve the item some time later. The inventory system must provide a mechanism for retrieving the item from storage and placing it back into the game world.

In addition to these mandatory features, it is usually beneficial to be able to do the following.

- **Use an item.** What is the use of having an item in inventory if it can't be used for anything? The bulk of responsibility for using should rest with the item itself, but the inventory system must provide a means of getting at the item's use methods.

- **Flexibly handle different item types.** The inventory system should be flexible. For example, it would be nice if the system could easily be programmed to do the following:

  1. pick up a coin and store it;
  2. when a health power-up is encountered, use it if it is needed and store it if not;
  3. automatically mount and prepare weapon items if the player doesn't have an active weapon.

- **Limit item carrying.** Lastly, an inventory system should be able to just say no. That is, depending on the game genre, an inventory should not allow certain items to be stored, or it should limit how many/much of an object can be placed in it.

The TGE FPS Demo comes with a scripted inventory system that does some of the above tasks as follows.

- Objects are stored in the player object (the control object).
- The responsibility for storing, retrieving, and using items is split between the control object, the control object's datablock, and the object being stored/retrieved.
- Storable items must be predeclared. That is, the control object must be told what inventory items it can store.
- Storable items are declared and accessed using datablocks as indices into inventory arrays. This allows for item-specific behavior as well as a simple way of referring to inventory slots.
- It doesn't use the same methodology, nor is it as easily expanded, but the basic TGE FPS Kit inventory can also be maximum-count constrained.

Having summarized the TGE inventory system, we will not be discussing it further. Instead, we will be discussing the Simple Inventory System.

7.7 The Simple Inventory System (SimpleInventory)

The Simple Inventory System (subsequently referred to as SimpleInventory) is provided in a fully functional state with the guide, so you could skip this chapter and just use it. However, you'll learn a lot more if you continue reading.

SimpleInventory has the following attributes.

- It is script-based and will work with any TGE game.
- It is implemented with ScriptObjects and can be placed in any object or stand alone. In effect, this allows any object to have an inventory or inventories, further compartmenting and structuring game interactions.
- It is a generalized inventory system, designed to store nonunique items referenced by their datablock names.
- Items are stored and referenced by their datablock, and thus items with unique properties can be stored, but their uniqueness will be lost.
- An inventory can store any number of any type of datablock-identified item.
- A maximum count limit can be set for any specific inventory item.
- All methods that operate on SimpleInventory are scoped under the `SimpleInventory::` namespace.
- Inventory methods are provided for `ShapeBaseData::` to enable a basic set of SimpleInventory interactions:
    - `doPickup()`—pick up one instance of an object,
    - `doThrow()`—throw or drop one instance of an object from inventory, and
    - `doUse()`—use an object from inventory.
- Inventory methods are provided for `ItemData::` and `Item::` classes to complete the inventory functionality.

7.7.1 Designing SimpleInventory

Over the course of the next few pages, we will succinctly discuss the design of SimpleInventory. This will reinforce some scripting topics we have discussed previously as well as give insight into the system such that changing it (if you should choose to) will not be too tedious.

Inventory Builder

Generally, it is better to use a builder (constructor, for you C++ folks), than to hand-build complicated objects. So, we will use one for our inventory system:

Game Elements

```
newSimpleInventory( %name )
```

```
Creates a new simpleInventory object, with optional %name.
Prints error message(s)
Returns 0 if inventory failed to instantiate.
```

```
%myInventory = newSimpleInventory( "backpack" );
```

The inventory object returned by our inventory builder has the structure shown in Figure 7.9.

- The inventory itself is a Script-Object.

- It has an optional name (as provided to the builder function).

- It contains a SimSet named knownItemTracking. This Sim-Set is used to contain the IDs of all items (datablocks) ever stored in the inventory (this is used to simplify content tracking).

Figure 7.9.

Structure of inventory.

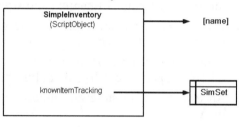

Specifying Stored Objects

We have a way to create our inventory object, now we want a way to identify an inventory (storable) item.

As we said above, SimpleInventory should be able to store items specified/identified by datablocks. This means we would like to be able to specify our item datablocks something like the following.

```
datablock ItemData( bullet ) {
  // specific internal fields not important (yet)
};
```

Simple. The above datablock is no different from any other ItemData datablock we would normally specify. This is good because it means we don't need to change our content-creation flow or remember any special rules.

Initial Contents

Next, we need to add a method for initializing the contents of our inventory.

```
setInventoryCount( %theInventory , %objectName , %numObjects )
```

```
Set total number of %objectName objects in the inventory to
%numObjects.
Returns number of items succesfully set.
```

If you're not examining the code as you read, now would be a good time to open a browser and take a quick peek at the code for this method (found in "SimpleInventoryGeneral.cs"). This code is fully commented and should be easy to follow. Feel free to peruse this in depth at a later time. For now, please take note of the following important points.

- In order to avoid painful bugs, the SimpleInventory system validates arguments and enforces some rules. This is a good practice in general and specifically when dealing with datablocks.
- Since it will do the same check frequently, the validation code is separated out into a method that does the following.
  - Verifies that `%objectName` (item to be inventoried) is both an object (exists) and is an ItemData datablock. This inventory system will only inventory ItemData-derived objects, so this is a safe restriction.
  - Forces the `%objectName` into string format (vs. ID). Why? Recall that datablock names are automatically converted to IDs in some cases. Because we don't want to worry about this, during our day-to-day usage of the inventory system, we'll just make sure that the system itself watches for this and handles it. We need to be consistent when using datablocks as indices. In this case, we're always going to use names because they are easier to identify (than numbers) when using `dump()` and because we generally use names when referring to datablocks in script.

Limiting Inventory Counts

We said above that this inventory system allows limits to be placed on individual inventory item counts. To do this we need another inventory method.

```
setInventoryMaxCount( %theInventory , %objectName , %maxObjects )
```

  Limits storage of **%objectName** objects in the inventory to **%maxObjects**.
  %maxObjects can be: "", 0, or N > 0. A value of "" clears any prior limit.

The limiting methodology used by SimpleInventory is not elaborate. Basically, a limit can be unspecified ("" meaning no limit), zero (0), or some positive value (N).

Remaining Basic Features

To this point, we have discussed how to create an instance of SimpleInventory, how to specify an inventory (storable) item, how to initialize an inventory instance, and how to limit inventory counts. What is left? Well, we still need the following features.

- A means of getting an inventory count for any specific object.

```
getInventoryCount( %theInventory , %objectName)
---------------------------------------------------------------------------
 Purpose:
 Get total number of %objectName objects in the inventory.
 Returns 0 if none found.
---------------------------------------------------------------------------
```

- A means of adding new items to the inventory.

```
addObject( %theInventory , %objectName [ , %numobjects ] )
---------------------------------------------------------------------------
 Purpose:
 Add one [or %numObjects] %objectName items(s) to the
 inventory. Returns number of items succesfully added.
---------------------------------------------------------------------------
```

- A means of retrieving an item(s) from the inventory.

```
removeObject( %theInventory , %objectName [ , %numobjects ] )
---------------------------------------------------------------------------
 Purpose:
 Remove [or %numObjects] %objectName item(s) from the
 inventory. Returns number of items succesfully removed
 (which may be less than requested count).
---------------------------------------------------------------------------
```

As can be seen, there really isn't much to the design of a simple inventory system. Next we'll address how to use this inventory system.

7.7.2 Using SimpleInventory

SimpleInventory Callback Flows

TGE provides a set of callbacks that "fire" in response to various game events. These callbacks are nothing more than console methods that are scoped to a particular class' datablock. One of these callbacks is the onCollision() method. onCollision() is called for all ShapeBase derivates and Projectiles when a collision occurs in the game. For now, we will limit our discussion to collisions between ShapeBase-derived objects (Player objects specifically) and Item objects.

Picking Up Objects

When a collision occurs between a ShapeBase object and an Item object, the engine will attempt to fire the onCollision() callback for both objects' datablocks. The SimpleInventory system uses the ShapeBaseData::on-

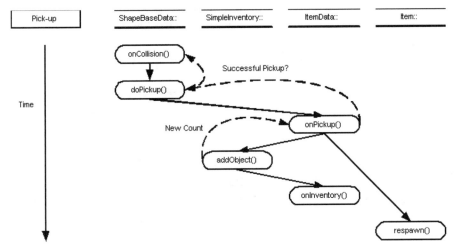

Figure 7.10.

Flow of pickups after collision.

Collision() callback to initiate pickups. Said pickups follow the flow shown in Figure 7.10.

- **ShapeBaseData::onCollision().** Fires on a collision and calls the ShapeBaseData::doPickup() if the collided object is an Item.

- **ShapeBaseData::doPickup().** Checks to see if the owner object has an inventory. If so, it calls the item's ItemData::onPickup() method.

- **ItemData::onPickup().** This method will try to place itself in the inventory using the SimpleInventory::addObject() method. If the item is successfully added to ShapeBase object's inventory, onPickup() will call Item::respawn() to temporarily remove (hide) the object from the world.

- **ItemData::onInventory().** Often it will be beneficial to have a place to do some extra processing after picking up an item. For example, when picking up a weapon, we would like to use the default flow (to reduce redundant code) but have a simple way of handling mounting, ammo loading, etc. In theory this could be done in the onPickup() by overriding, calling the Parent::, etc. However, this will quickly become an intractable solution for large games. Better is to have an item-specific callback that is executed every time the inventory count for that item is modified. The ItemData::onInventory() method fills this role.

- **Item::respawn().** Depending on the game type we're writing, objects that are picked up should either be respawned or removed permanently from the world. The simple inventory system handles both of these cases. If the dynamic field respawn is set to true in the item's datablock, the item is respawned. If not, the item is permanently removed from the world if the pickup succeeds. The Item::respawn() method does the respawning work. Items will respawn (become visible again) in $Item::Respawn-Time milliseconds.

249

Figure 7.11.

Flow after a throw request.

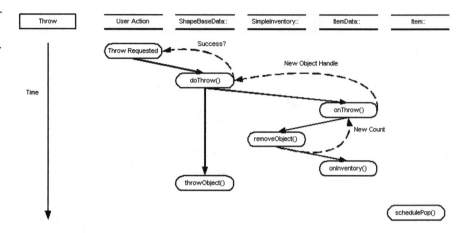

Throwing/Dropping Inventoried Objects

Assuming we have an item(s) in our inventory, we may at some time wish to throw (drop) it. This kind of action can be accessed through a key press (as well as a myriad of other ways). Key presses are handled by action maps. When the action map dictates that a throw has been requested, it will use a `commandToServer()` call to call the `shapeBaseData::doThrow()` method to start the throw flow (Figure 7.11).

- **Throw requested.** The user requests a throw via mouse click or button press. The action map is programmed to convert this client action into a server action via the `commandToServer()` function (see "InventoryLesson.cs" and "ServerCommands.cs").

```
lessonMap.bindCmd( keyboard, "t", "",
"commandToServer(\'throw\', InventoryItem.getID() );");
```

- **ShapeBaseData::doThrow().** Checks to see if the owner object has an inventory. If so, it calls the `ItemData::onThrow()` method. If the `Item-Data::onThrow()` method returns a new object handle, the `ShapeBase-Data::throwObject()` method is used to do the throwing.

- **ItemData::onThrow().** This method will try to extract one instance of the item from the owner's inventory using the `SimpleInventory::removeObject()` method. If an intstance is acquired, `onThrow()` will instantiate (build) a new copy and pass the items handle back to the `doThrow()` method.

- **ShapeBaseData::schedulePop().** As with the pick-up flow, if the dynamic field `respawn` is set to `true` in the item's datablock, the item is meant to be transient and so should be popped from existence after throwing. The `ShapeBaseData::schedulePop()` method does this work. The

250

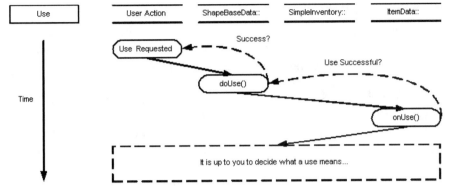

Figure 7.12.

Flow after a use request.

item will pop from existence in $Item::PopTime milliseconds after being thrown (dropped).

- **ItemData::onInventory().** See pickup flow above.

- **ShapeBaseData::throwObject().** As noted above, this method actually "throws" the newly instatiated item object. This method handles both 1st POV (along eye vector) throws and 3rd POV (arc along forward vector) throws. Throw force is defined in the owner object's dynamic field throw-Force.

Using Inventoried Objects

Assuming we have an item in our inventory, we may at some time wish to use it. This kind of action can be accessed through a key press (as well as a myriad of other ways). Key presses are handled by action maps. When the action map dictates that a use has been requested, it will use a commandTo-Server() call to call the shapeBaseData::doUse() method to start the use flow (Figure 7.12).

- **Use requested.** The user requests a use via mouse click or button press. The action map is programmed to convert this client action into a server action via the commandToServer() function (see "InventoryLesson.cs" and "ServerCommands.cs").

```
lessonMap.bindCmd( keyboard, "u", "",
    "commandToServer(\'use\', InventoryItem.getID() );");
```

- **ShapeBaseData::doUse().** Checks to see if the owner object has an inventory. If so, it calls the ItemData::onUse() method.

- **ItemData::onUse().** The coding of this method is entirely dependent upon what the use action means.

Item-Specific Responses

For an inventory system to be useful, it has to be somewhat flexible. Simple-Inventory was written to be flexible without being too complicated as a first inventory example. The flexibility comes in several flavors.

Pickup Substitutions

Sometimes the pickup object needs to be different from the object we collide with. For example, we might decide to have grenades in our game. We'd like these grenades to come in packages of three grenades. We'd like the following to be true:

- grenade packs are used for `onCollision()` to start a grenade pickup flow,
- individual grenades are stored in the inventory, and
- individual grenades are thrown.

SimpleInventory allows this by adding an optional dynamic field named `InventoryItem` to datablocks that need to do a substitution.

```
datablock ItemData( Grenade ) {
  // ...
};

datablock ItemData( GrenadePack ) {
  InventoryItem = Grenade; // Store grenade, not grenade pack
  // ...
};
```

With the above datablock, we can place grenade packs in the world, but when we pick them up, we get grenades. As noted, `InventoryItem` is optional, and if not specified, the datablock name is stored instead.

The observant will notice one small flaw. We haven't specified how many grenades a grenade pack is worth. This leads to the next topic: variable pickup values.

Variable Pickup Values

When we pick up objects, we sometimes want the pickup to be worth one (1) instance, and other times we want it to be worth N instances, where N is nonzero. SimpleInventory allows this by supporting an optional dynamic field named `InventoryValue`. When this field is present in an item's datablock and that item is picked up, `InventoryValue` items will be stored. By default, one item is stored.

For example, the following code will use the trick we learned above in combination with this new trick to store three grenades when picking up a grenade pack.

```
datablock ItemData( GrenadePack ) {
  InventoryItem = Grenade;
  // Store 3 grenades instead of 1 grenade pack
  InventoryValue = 3;
  // ...
};
```

Variations on `onPickup()`

The prior two variations were useful tricks, but what do we do when we want the pickup flow to be completely different? Answer: we write a new `onPickup()` method.

Let's say you have a coin item and a health power-up in your game. For the coin, the default pickup is acceptable, but we would like the health power-up to be automatically applied if the player needs it, and placed in the inventory if not. In order to do this, a new `onPickup()` method will need to be defined for the health power-up.

```
datablock ItemData (NormalHealthKit) {
  healValue = 20;
};


// New onPickup() for NormalHealthKit
function NormalHealthKit::onPickup(%pickupDB,%pickupObj,%ownerObj) {
  // Check if player needs healing and apply kit if necessary, else store kit.
}
```

So, what about if we have multiple varieties of the health power-up? Is there a way to program this functionality just once? The answer is an emphatic yes. Recall that the `className` keyword can be used to add an additional level to the namespace of a class. We can use this to create a generic namespace for all health power-ups as follows.

```
datablock ItemData (NormalHealthKit) {
  className = "HealthKit";
  healValue = 20;
};


datablock ItemData (MegaHealthKit) {
  className = "HealthKit";
  healValue = 100;
};


// New onPickup() for all Health Kits
function HealthKit::onPickup(%pickupDB,%pickupObj,%ownerObj) {
```

```
    // Check if player needs healing and apply kit if
    // necessary, else store kit.
}
```

Alternate to `onPickup()`

Recall that, in the flows, the `onInventory()` method was mentioned as a place to put "extra" code. This is still true and is in fact often the place where problems like the health kit above should be solved. It is up to you, but I suggest deferring changes in the flows until after `onPickup()`, `onThrow()`, and `onUse()`. In the end, this will keep your code cleaner and allow you to reuse other flows.

For example, we solved the health-kit problem above by writing a new `onPickup()`. Alternatively, we could have added an `onInventory()` that would then call the `onUse()` method if the player needed to heal. We would already need to write the `onUse()`, so it would be better not to rewrite similar code for healing in an `onPickup()`, too.

```
// New onInventory() for all Health Kits
function HealthKit::onInventory( %inventoryDB , %ownerObj,
                                 %amount ) {
   // If the player needs healing, call the onUse() flow.
}
```

Non-Pickup Variations

We've discussed the pickup flow to death. What about the other two flows? Both throw and use can be item specific, too. The key is to program variant functionality in the namespace of the object that normally is responsible for deciding what the action means. For throws, it is the ShapeBaseData class that normally decides what a throw is. For uses, it is the ItemData class. Therefore, normally variations of a throw will be programmed in the `doThrow()` method, and variations on use will be programmed into `onUse()`.

Finally, any time the inventory count for an item changes, the `onInventory()` method is called, with the inventory DB (datablock), owner ID, and amount (of change). Consider this as a possible place to do your special coding.

Constraining SimpleInventory

As previously mentioned, SimpleInventory does not constrain object pickups. Any item can be picked up, and any number of items can be stored. It is easy to see that this is too simplistic for most uses, but it can quickly be improved upon by adding any or all of the following constraints.

- **Allowed Items.** Add code to predeclare the types of items that can be stored.
- **Disallowed Items.** Add code to predeclare the types of items that cannot be stored.
- **Item Count Limit.** Add code to limit the maximum number of a specific item that can be carried in the inventory.
- **Total Count Limit.** Add code to limit the maximum number of cumulative items (of all types) that can be carried in the inventory.
- **Mass Limit.** Add code to track and limit the total mass for all items in the inventory. Please remember that all ShapeBase-derived objects have a mass indicator in their datablock.
- **Bulk Limit.** Add a new field to the item's datablock denoting how bulky an item is. Then, add code to the inventory to limit total bulk.

Even with these changes, the inventory system may be too restrictive, as it relies on datablocks to index items. This means that only objects using datablocks can be inventoried (not a big restriction), and all data in the object instances themselves are lost (can be a big problem). If you are programming a role-playing game (RPG) or similar game, it will be useful to allow object instances to be unique; e.g., this is Bob's sword, or these boots are damaged. Therefore, it will be absolutely required that objects that are stored in the inventory be faithfully re-created at a later date, and if you want to stick with a script-only system, you must find a way to determine the fields in an object and then to store them. This will require coding an extension into the engine.

7.7.3 General Inventory Tips and Gotchas

While coding up SimpleInventory, I ran into some issues. So, rather than let you stumble on them, too, I'm supplying them here.

- **Datablock names as indices and arguments.** Remember that Simple-Inventory uses datablock names both to index arrays of inventory items and as arguments in all the functions. Also, remember that the engine may automatically convert these names to ID numbers. This can cause a mismatch in the inventory lookup. So, when in doubt, use the `getName()` method. For an example of how this is used, see the `SimpleInventory::verifyArgs()` method.
- **Item Behaviors.** Remember that inventory items are based on the Item class. For items to work appropriately as an inventory item, they must be properly configured.
  - `Item.static.` If you intend to be able to throw an object, this must be `false`; otherwise, the object will stay where it was spawned.

- `ItemData.sticky`. If you want a thrown object to stop when it hits the ground, set `sticky` to `true`.

- `ItemData.friction`. Setting `friction` to a value of about 0.7 will cause a thrown object to arrest its motion quickly.

- `ItemData.mass`. If you intend to throw the object, it must have a positive mass. Using `applyImpulse()` on a ShapeBase object with zero mass will crash the engine.

- **Motivation for using ScriptObject**. Perhaps this should have been explained earlier, but as SimpleInventory uses script objects, they can be placed anywhere and in anything, including in other inventories. Also, why just have one?

7.7.4 Inventory Validation

SimpleInventory comes with code to validate that the basic functions of the inventory system are working properly. This code is located in "SimpleInventoryValidation.cs" and is run every time the GPGT Lesson Kit is started. This code may be disabled, but it is a short test and won't affect anything after running. To see if the system is working, search for the words "Validating Simple Inventory System" and check for error messages.

Also, if you do decide to edit the system, you can cause it to reload the inventory system scripts and to rerun the validation scripts by typing the following in the console.

```
sris();
```

7.7.5 Maze Runner Lesson #7 (90 Percent Step)— Preparing Our Game Inventory

In this short lesson, we will examine the steps required to get our player (MazeRunnerPlayer) to use the SimpleInventory system to pick up coins.

Loading the Inventory System

In order to use our inventory system, we must ensure that it is getting loaded. In fact, we have already done this first step. When we set up our "MazeRunner" directory and copied the Maze Runner prototype directory into it, we modified the file "\MazeRunner\prototype\main.cs". We had it load the inventory system's main script file, as follows.

```
function onStart() // in main.cs {
    // MazeRunner
    exec("./EGSystems/SimpleInventory/egs_SimpleInventory.cs");
```

```
// MazeRunner
exec("./EGSystems/SimpleTaskMgr/egs_SimpleTaskMgr.cs");
//..
```

This then loaded the other script files that comprise this system.

```
// in egs_SimpleInventory.cs
exec("./SimpleInventoryBuilder.cs");
exec("./SimpleInventoryGeneral.cs");
exec("./SimpleInventoryValidation.cs");
```

Adding an Inventory

With the inventory system being loaded, we now have to hook it to any classes that wish to "own" an inventory. The simplest way to do this is to have each class add an inventory system to the object when the object's onAdd() callback is executed.

Take a look in the file "\MazeRunner\prototype\server\scripts\GPGTBase\Player\PlayerDataMethods.cs". It contains the definitions for all of the important callbacks used by a player class. All of these callbacks are scoped to PlayerData::, ensuring that they will be called unless a new datablock, deriving from PlayerData::, redefines the callbacks.

We are already loading this script file, so we get the benefit of all of these callbacks already. One of these callbacks is PlayerData::onAdd(), which, among the other things that it does, creates an inventory and saves a reference to it in the player object.

```
function PlayerData::onAdd(%DB,%Obj) {
  // 1
  Parent::onAdd(%DB,%Obj);

  // 2
  %Obj.enableMountVehicle = true;

  // 3.
  %Obj.myInventory = newSimpleInventory();

  %Obj.myInventory.setOwner(%Obj);
}
```

This means that we do not have any work to do. We do not have to implement a new version of onAdd() scoped to MazeRunnerPlayer::, but if we wanted to, we could write one like this:

```
function MazeRunnerPlayer::onAdd( %DB , %Obj ) {
  // Usually called first
  Parent::onAdd( %DB , %Obj );

 // Other statments here ...
}
```

Removing an Inventory

It is normal to destroy objects created in the onAdd() callback when the onRemove() callback is executed.

Again, this is taken care of for us by the base code we are using from the GPGT Lesson Kit. The following is the onRemove() callback from the same file we just examined above.

```
function PlayerData::onRemove(%DB,%Obj) {
  // 1
  if( isObject( %Obj.myInventory ) ) %Obj.myInventory.delete();
  // 2
  Parent::onRemove(%DB,%Obj);
}
```

Easy as pie! Of course, we could again write a specialized version of the onRemove() callback and just be sure to call the Parent:: version at some point (normally last).

```
function MazeRunnerPlayer::onRemove( %DB , %Obj ) {
  // Other statements here ...

  Parent::onRemove( %DB , %Obj ); // Usually called last
}
```

What About Constraining?

In our game, we don't want to constrain the inventory, but if we wanted, for some reason, to prevent the player from picking up coins, we could simply modify the onAdd() callback to look like the following.

```
function MazeRunner::onAdd( %DB , %Obj ) {
  Parent::onAdd( %DB , %Obj );

  // No coins for you!
  %obj.myInventory.setInventoryMaxCount( Coin , 0 );
}
```

In Review

I know you're disappointed that there was no work to do in this lesson. So, let's just summarize the steps instead. This way you will know what they are when you are on your own.

1. Load inventory system scripts.
2. Ensure that the `onAdd()` callback adds an inventory to the object when it is created.
3. In your own `onAdd()`, be sure to constrain the inventory system as is required by your game. Use the contraint methods included with the inventory system.
4. Make sure that the `onRemove()` callback deletes the inventory.

7.8 Gameplay Classes Summary

We started this chapter by discussing the idea of gameplay. I proposed that interaction is a major element of gameplay, setting the stage for our discussion of the gameplay classes (classes implementing player interaction with the world). We closed the introductory material by summarizing the primary gameplay classes: Camera, Player, and Vehicle.

Our first gameplay discussion was centered on the Camera and CameraData classes but cast a wide net about other concepts which we generally labeled *game view* (a combination of POV, FOV, control object, free camera, and zooming). We talked about game view for a bit, observing the fact that other classes interacted with the camera to define the concept. We then discussed the individual game view components in detail, describing each of them. We also discussed the side topic of render scoping and the fact that it is controlled by the control object. Having warmed up properly, we looked into class interactions in detail and closed our game view discussion with six (cookbook) examples of game view control, including:

- two methods to force 1st POV (one with a limited FOV),
- forced 3rd POV,
- a method of enabling 1st or 3rd POV,
- the correct settings to allow a camera to use its own parameters instead of those from the object it is attached to, and
- the way a camera can be made to switch to using a vehicle's view settings (not the player's) upon player-to-vehicle mounting.

Our next discussion included the Player and PlayerData classes. We learned about all of the features provided by this important set of classes, including rendering features, forces and factors (speeds, delays, resistance, etc.), pickup radius, looking angle limits (restrictions on view angles for cameras attached to players), the difference between an impact and a collision, special effects, and the standard player animations. We ended the discussion by making a simple player for use in our game.

After Players, we discussed the various Vehicle classes, and to start the discussion off properly, we talked about general vehicle attributes.

- **Geometries.** Chassis, tires, and collision meshes.
- **Nodes.** Camera, tire, and special effect nodes.
- **Animations.** Back, bot, brakelight, spring, and steering.

Once the most general discussion of vehicles was completed, we talked about the base classes for all vehicles: Vehicle and VehicleData. We discussed the features these classes brought to the table, including physics, steering, jetting, impacts, camera features, and emitters. We ended with a general discussion on mounting players to vehicles.

Done with the general vehicle discussions, we talked about the Wheeled-Vehicle and WheeledVehicleData classes. We learned about how to program the basic engine and braking parameters as well as about controlling the look of the wheel rotation animation.

The WheeledVehicle class uses several datablocks, including the Wheeled-VehicleTire and WheeledVehicleSpring datablocks. We discussed these in order and learned about the following properties for each.

- **WheeledVehicleTire.** We learned that we can implement up to eight tires per wheeled vehicle using this class to represent the tires. Also, we saw that it is acceptable to mix tires on a vehicle.
  - **Friction.** We learned that the tires provide all vehicle friction as long as the chassis is not in contact with the ground.
  - **Motivational forces.** We discussed the fact that tires provide both longitudinal (forward-and-backward) and lateral (side-to-side) forces, which act together to move our wheeled vehicles and to maintain their heading.
  - **Tire radius.** We examined this attribute and saw that it is important that it should match our tire model for correct visual behavior.
- **WheeledVehicleSpring.** We learned that this class represents the "shocks" for our wheeled vehicles.
  - **Damping forces.** We learned about how damping is used to control the expansion and contraction rates for our springs and therefore the tires. These forces allow us to create very soft to very hard springs with varying rates of recovery.
  - **Anti-sway.** We learned how the anti-sway force in the springs helps keep the vehicle's chassis level relative to the surface below the vehicle.

- **Length of travel.** Here we learned how to reduce the distance a tire hub may travel.

We closed our wheeled vehicle discussion by talking about powered wheels and their effect on driving performance, followed by a set of examples showing how to choose alternate mounting positions.

Next up, we talked about hover vehicles. We learned how to control our horizontal motion and how to implement a certain amount of drag in order to slow a travelling hover vehicle. We then discussed some factors that affect the vehicle when it comes into contact with the ground, water, or an interior versus when it is floating free of obstructions. We discussed hovering and jetting, as well as how to stabilize the vehicle and ensure that it remains upright. We talked about steering and ended with a discussion of how to keep our parked hover vehicles from floating away down a hill (the same method applied to stopping an unmanned vehicle).

The final section in this chapter took a sharp turn and talked about a concept instead of a particular class. That concept is the inventory (or inventory system). We talked about what an inventory system is and why it is needed. Then we compared the features provided by the inventory system that comes with this guide (SimpleInventory) against the one implemented in the TGE FPS Demo. Once we were done with explanations and motivations, we jumped into a review of the implementation and usage of SimpleInventory. This discussion included detailed flows of pickups, throws/drops, and uses, discussing the scripts and classes involved as well as laying out motivations for the way the inventory behaves. To complete our discussion of inventories, we talked about various means of modifying the standard flow and ways to improve upon the system.

This chapter contained no shortage of difficult to understand and even harder to remember details about interaction. Unfortunately, to successfully create your game, you need to undestand what we have discussed, so I suggest rereading this chapter and reviewing the samples that come with the GPGT Lesson Kit. When you are well educated in these topics, you will be a long ways toward succesfully creating a game.

Chapter 8
Mission Objects

8.1 Mission Objects

This mega-chapter covers most of the objects that can be placed using the Mission Editor Creator. I call this a mega-chapter because it encapsulates a large series of object descriptions as well as tips on using and/or scripting them.

If you are reading this chapter first, some of what you read here may not make a great deal of sense due to some holes in your TGE education. Those holes are filled in the prior chapters. So, if you do find this material confusing, please go back and read (or at least scan) the chapters that precede this one. Be warned: some of the objects described in this chapter are not simple. You will need to experiment with them to fully understand their capabilities, but this chapter should get you started down the right path. The primary goal here is to familiarize you with these objects and some of their attributes as well as to help you with any peculiarities. I won't necessarily cover every attribute of these objects in this chapter. Instead, an appendix is supplied, giving details on each object.

Finally, it is assumed that you are familiar with the built-in tool set. If not, go back and read Chapter 3, "Torque Tools." When you are ready, come back and check this chapter out.

> Throughout this guide and therefore in this chapter, we have exclusively used the term "world unit" instead of meter. However, in the GarageGames forums and on the Torque IRC channel, you may see people refer to things in terms of meters. Because some standard measurements such as acceleration due to gravity are set at metric standard values (9.81 world units per second squared) it is easy to fall into the belief that the system is actually metric and that distances are measured in meters. In fact, the engine is unitless with respect to most measurements excluding time. However, as the engine has been given metric-like values for all important constants, this discussion of meters versus world units becomes a question of semantics. Because I wanted to insure that this guide would always be accurate with reference to measurements, I have chosen to use world units instead of meters, but you should not be confused when you see other sources of information on Torque reference meters.

8.2 Terrain

In Torque, terrain is represented by an infinitely repeating heightmap. The heightmap itself is usually represented by a 256 × 256 full-color (24-bit) PNG

Figure 8.1.

Terrain repeating.

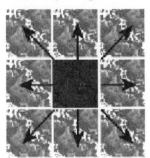

image. The engine uses this single image as a home tile, which is edge-blended and infinitely repeated in the world plane (Figure 8.1). The default real-world measure of the home tile is 2048 world units on edge.

8.2.1 Terrain Features

Terrain has the following features.

- **Detail texture.** A texture used to give more detail to locally visible terrain.
- **Bump mapping.** The terrain supports emboss-style bump mapping, using a single source texture.
- **In-game editing.** With the Terrain Editor and the Terrain Painter, you can hand modify the shape and texturing of your terrain without leaving the game. This is described in Chapter 3.
- **Algorithmic generation.** The Terraformer provides a tool-set of algorithms for generating terrains. This is described in Chapter 3.
- **Algorithmic painting.** The Terrain Texture Editor provides a tool-set of algorithms for applying textures to the terrain. This is described in Chapter 3.
- **Alternate sizing.** Although it is advisable, one does not need to stick to a 2048-world unit square home tile.
- **No terrain.** Finally, if not needed, the terrain can be removed entirely.

8.2.2 The Detail Texture

When you first start working with the terrain, it is easy to be overwhelmed and to miss an interesting yet important feature, namely the detail texture. If you open up the Inspector and select the terrain, you will see that there is a field named `detailTexture` under the Media SimGroup. This field provides the path to a texture that will be used to add detail to the local terrain. This additional texture is rendered once every world unit for n world units. Additionally, it is blended with the underlying textures with a ratio that falls off to zero at about 64 world units from the camera. Look at the screen shots in Figure 8.2 to see the difference between terrain with and without a detail texture. I think you'll agree that the one with a detail texture is much nicer.

Great, right? Well, yes and no. Yes, because the terrain definitely looks better with a detail texture. No, because you can only have one per mission, which means all terrain in any single mission will have a fundamental sameness to it. For the most part, this is not a big deal, and most players won't even notice. However, you need to realize that your choice of detail texture can have a big impact on the visual quality of your terrain, and you should probably count on having different textures for different levels/missions, as this is a subtle way of creating distinct ambiences from level to level.

Terrain with Detail Texture | Terrain without Detail Texture

Figure 8.2.
Detail texture.

Detail textures may be any size between 1 × 1 pixels and 512 × 512 pixels as long as they follow the standard rules for textures used by Torque. See Appendix D.1, "TGE Must-Know Facts," for information on TGE's texture rules.

8.2.3 Bump Mapping

This feature is controlled by four terrain parameters and a preference variable. It is simplest to edit the terrain parameters using the Inspector (Figure 8.3).

- **bumpTexture.** Specifies a texture to use as the emboss map. Must follow Torque scaling standards for bitmaps, should be a mixture of blacks and whites, and it should tile. You must save the mission and reload for this to take effect. The engine uses this texture to create the two textures required for embossing. One is the original; the second is the inverted original.

Figure 8.3.
Editing terrain parameters.

- **bumpScale.** Determines how stretched the bump-map texture is. In other words, small numbers cause the emboss map to cover a very small area, giving a more finely detailed bump mapping.

- **bumpOffset.** Is the diagonal offset between the two textures that make up the emboss bump-map effect.

- **zeroBumpScale.** Controls the bump-mapping radius. If you consider that bump mapping is only enabled within this radius (centered about camera), then it will be easy to understand that smaller values will cause the bump

Game Elements

mapping to cease nearer to the camera, while larger values will make it stretch further into the visible distance.

As noted, there is one preference variable.

- **pref::Terrain::enableEmbossBumps**. Allows you to disable this feature, which could be necessary on a slow machine or an older video card.

Figure 8.4 illustrates the effects of these variables.

Figure 8.4.

Changing terrain parameters.

8.2.4 More about Terrain Painting

Although it might seem obvious, I'll say explicitly that the textures used to paint the terrain should be seamless. Why? Well, because the textures are repeated every `squaresize` world units. This means that, with a default `squaresize` of 8, a painting texture repeats after only 8 world units. Regardless, if your textures are not seamless, it will be noticeable.

8.2.5 Alternate Terrain Sizing

Interestingly, when people start playing with Torque, they soon realize that the terrain tiles. Then, after asking around, they realize that the map is "only" 2 km × 2 km. A percentage of these people have in mind making some kind of game that would require a much larger terrain, say a massively multiplayer online role-playing game (MMORPG). They immediately focus on the problem of making the terrain bigger. In fact, if you are reading this, I imagine that you might be one of those people.

Now, I'm not going to say that you cannot scale the terrain, nor am I going to say that you cannot expand the tiling feature to include multiple unique tiles. You can do these things, but they are not trivial.

I will provide two suggestions to the alternate terrain sizing problem and then leave the hard work to you.

Modifying `squaresize`

The easiest means (although not very robust) of modifying the terrain size is to change the terrain object's `squaresize` parameter. This parameter can be edited in the Inspector and can be found in the terrain's Misc SimGroup.

What does changing the value do? If you will recall, the terrain heightmap is really nothing more than a two-dimensional array of values. Furthermore, we normally represent height maps as a bitmap that (in Torque) is 256 pixels on a side. `squaresize` is a multiplier that specifies how many world units apart the pixels are in the heightmap. Sounds simple, right? In a sense, it is. Legal values for `squaresize` are between 2 and 64 and are not strictly limited to multiples of two, meaning you can have the map sizes shown in Table 8.1.

`squaresize`	Map (Home Block) Dimensions
2	512 world units squared
4	1024 world units squared
8 (default)	2048 world units squared
9	2304 world units squared
...	...
64	16,000 world units squared (this is 256 million square world units!)

Table 8.1.

Map sizes.

This seems good at first, but once we start playing around with it, we start to see problems. The one most people notice right away is "water holes." At nonstandard square sizes, water blocks will sometimes exhibit holes—that is, a square region where there should be water, but no water is rendered. This is very annoying. Another problem is collision. Terrain collision is affected negatively by larger square sizes. This can be so serious that the player may actually fall through the terrain in some places. Finally, we run into the more subtle issues of memory usage and texture bandwidth. Varying `squaresize` modifies both memory usage and texture bandwidth associated with terrain rendering. I have personally noticed that a `squaresize` of 2 severely reduces frame rate.

So, given all these bad things, should you use this method? Sure, but only if you want to go up or down by a factor of 2. Then, this is a good partial solution. I say partial because there are ways of solving the problems noted above. However, I'm going to leave this as an exercise for the reader.

Atlas

OK, I admit it. Changing the `squaresize` is not that great an idea. Sure, it works in limited cases, but what if you want to make that really big MMORPG? Well, I must suggest that you move up to the Torque Shader Engine (TSE). TSE is a child of TGE that encompasses several new sets of features. The first, and most obvious, of these is shaders, hence the name. Less well known is the use of Atlas.

Atlas is the terrain-engine manager for TSE. It can handle any size terrain, and I mean any size. So, if you really, really, really must make a big terrain, go ahead and try out TSE and Atlas.

However, although I do encourage you to move up to TSE, I don't necessarily suggest that you start off making an MMORPG as a first game. Read on to understand my reasoning.

8.2.6 Big Terrains: Don't Do It!

I want you to stop and consider this simple question: How are you going to populate this very large world you wish to make? This might seem like a silly question, but let me assure you that it is not.

I once read something to the effect that the people who made *Tribes 2* were a bit worried about the map size being a limitation but quickly realized that it is very difficult to actually fill four square kiloworld units of space. In fact, most missions in *Tribes 2* are much smaller than the maximum map size.

OK, you may still be thinking something like: Yeah, but I can walk all the way across the map in, like, no time flat! In fact, traveling at top speed, it will take you just shy of 2.5 minutes to walk from one side of the map to the other. This would make the Torque character pretty darned fast. In fact, the default maximum (unmodified) speed for the character is 68 kiloworld units per hour. Normal humans sprint at somewhere near 30 kiloworld units per hour maximum, but it just feels too slow to make the character walk and run at normal human speeds.

This information is important for the following reasons.

1. You are going to have a heck of a time populating 4 square kiloworld units, which is equivalent to about 400 square city blocks (there is no official dimension for a city block, but they average between 100 to 200 world units on end).

2. There are other solutions.
   - Just use the tiled terrain. Who is going to notice that it repeats if it takes 2.5 minutes to run across it?
   - Slow the character down and tighten up spacing on objects. This is easier to do than increasing the size of the terrain. Guaranteed!

3. This is really going to hurt and you don't want to do it. OK, I'm not exactly telling the truth, but I can say that it is not simple to do this.

8.2.7 No Terrain?

If you wish to have a terrainless mission, it is entirely possible. However, you may have to edit the mission file to do this.

Trying to delete the terrain from the Inspector is a bit tricky. You have to unlock the terrain (set dynamic field `locked` to `false`), and then you have to delete it.

My suggestion is that you simply open your mission file in any handy text editor, find the block named TerrainBlock, and delete the entire thing.

Oh, you might want to put something in the world for your player to stand on, or the next time you open the mission, the player will fall forever.

8.3 Water (Blocks)

After terrain, water is another hot forum topic. Fortunately, water has gotten a lot of attention from community members. However, this additional attention has had the side effect of making water seem complicated to use. In reality, most options are just that—optional. You can place and set up water in just seconds, or if you want to go for a specific effect, you can spend hours tweaking the parameters.

For the sake of brevity, I will give the quick setup instructions first, then I'll cover the advanced options.

8.3.1 Basic Water (Quick Setup)

OK, get your stopwatch out. Start it. Now follow these instructions:

1. Start the GPGT Lesson Kit.
2. Open the World Editor training mission.
3. Start the Mission Editor.
4. Switch to the Creator tool.
5. Switch to free-camera mode and move the camera up a few world units.
6. Look somewhere near your character.
7. Insert a new water block (Mission Object → Environment → Water).
8. Just Click OK for the dialog that comes up.
9. Switch to the Inspector tool.
10. Click on the water block.
11. Click the Expand All button.
12. Change Media → `SurfaceTexture` to "gpgt/data/GPGTBase/water/howwater0".
13. Make sure Debugging → `UseDepthMask` is not checked.
14. Set Surface → `surfaceOpacity` to 1.0.
15. Set Surface → `envMapIntensity` to 0.0.
16. Click Apply.

Done! Depending on the speed of your machine, that should have taken about 60 seconds or less.

8.3.2 Water Features

Water has the following features.

- **Discrete scaling.** Because of the algorithmic nature of the water in Torque, water blocks are scaled in fixed increments. By default, this is 32 world units.
- **Discrete positioning.** Again, as a byproduct of its algorithmic nature (and due to a sometimes overlooked terrain relationship), water is positioned in fixed increments. By default, this is 8 world units, i.e., `squaresize`.
- **Various texture-based effects.**
  - **Basic surface texture.** Plain-Jane base texture for water.
  - **Shore texture.** An additional texture for shorelines.
  - **Over and under environmental maps.** Static environmental reflections on the surface of water from above and below.
  - **Specular reflections.** Simulates perturbed specular reflection from water surface.

- **Underwater fog.** Torque provides a static fog for when the camera is underwater.

- **Underwater texturing**. Under certain circumstances, up to two additional caustic textures will be rendered over the view.

- **Waves.** Torque supports sinusoidal waves.

- **Viscosity and density.** These two real-world characteristics affect the characters and objects that encounter the water.

- **Predefined water types.** Torque provides several predefined types of water that give you various ready-made effects.

- **Flow.** Torque can visually simulate flowing water.

- **Distortion.** If the above visual effects are not enough, you can use distortion parameters to make the water yet more realistic or unrealistic if you so choose

- **Multiple blocks.** Last, you may have multiple independent blocks of water.

8.3.3 Advanced Water

All right, unless you are just goofing around and learning the engine, it is likely that you will want to make your water look a little more interesting. No problem there. Water blocks can do some very cool things.

Position and Scale

Before we jump into the cool stuff, let's briefly discuss basic positioning and scaling. Unlike most objects, you cannot position or scale water blocks arbitrarily. Instead, the x and y components of both position and scale are adjusted in discrete steps. Position $<x, y>$ is adjusted in steps of 8, and Scale $<x, y>$ is adjusted in steps of 32. For both position and scale, the z parameter can be adjusted continuously.

On a side note, if you have been reading this guide straight through, you may recall that the default terrain `squaresize` is also 8. It is no coincidence that both position and scale are adjusted in multiples of `squaresize`. If you are going to play with nonstandard terrain sizes, or if you are going to make modifications to the way water blocks work, you'll have to remember that terrain and water are closely related. Kissing cousins, you might say.

It is very important to note that the z parameter should *not* be zero. Most people make the mistake of not adjusting this parameter. Most of the time, this will seem OK, but if the camera will ever be under the surface of the water, then you must have a positive value for z. More accurately, you must adjust the z parameter of a water block, such that the lower boundary of the water block is below the lowest point in the terrain, for all points in the terrain covered by the block. Why? If you do not do this, you may encounter a strange bug where the water fog disappears at certain viewing angles. This can destroy any suspension of disbelief you have managed to accrue, and it is very distracting.

The Various Textures (Media)

The water block has progressed greatly since the day Torque was first released. With this progression has come a profusion of new parameters, including a multitude of texture parameters. Fortunately, these parameters are simple to understand.

- **surfaceTexture.** This texture is used to define the base water layer(s). This texture is rendered in two layers, with one layer reoriented at a 45-degree angle (about *z*, of course). This makes the water more interesting.

- **shoreTexture.** We'll talk more about shorelines in a moment, but Torque has the ability to render shorelines differently. When it renders the shoreline, it blends this texture with surfaceTexture, giving a nice visual effect.

- **envMapOverTexture.** If environmental mapping (see "Reflections and Specular Masks" below) is enabled, this texture is rendered when looking down onto the water from above. This represents an environmental reflection on the water's surface.

- **envMapUnderTexture.** As with envMapOverTexture, this represents an environmental reflection, but this is the texture you will see if looking up from beneath the water.

- **submergeTexture0 and submergeTexture1.** These two textures are only used when liquidType is one of the lava types (Lava, HotLava, or CrustyLava). These two textures are rendered perpendicular to the viewing plane. Additionally, they are animated. A suggestion I was given, which I'll pass along, is to use two high-quality (say 512 × 512 instead of the normal 256 × 256) grayscale caustics for these. Note: By making some simple changes to the source code, you can colorize the resultant output to the screen.

- **specularMaskTex.** This texture is used to make the surface of the water look as if it is reflecting light. Again, this should be some kind of caustic grayscale. The engine does take into account the position and elevation of the sun when rendering the specular effect.

Makin' Waves

The water would not be very interesting if it were just a flat plane. Fortunately, Torque supports a wave feature. The bad part is that it is a simple sinusoidal function. Nonetheless, it does a good job and looks good for most purposes. If you wish to have waves, set the WaveMagnitude parameter to a nonzero value. Bigger values equal bigger waves. Note that it is best not to attempt to place two water blocks side by side if you are using waves. Because the algorithms for each block are calculated separately, you will get visible seams and discontinuities. Also note that there is one disappointing thing about waves. If your player is floating in water (see "Sinking and Floating" below), the waves will not lift the player; that is, the water motion does not affect the player's vertical position, nor will splash effects occur from water hitting a motionless player.

Sinking and Floating

You may be wondering about how to make a character float, or perhaps you would like to make the water more viscous, say like quicksand. Well, Torque supports two water parameters for these effects:

- **density.** The default water density is 1. Meanwhile, the default character density is 10. This means that the character will sink upon entering the water. Therefore, if you want the character to be more buoyant, you can adjust either or both parameters. Just remember the following rules:

  water density < player density → Player sinks.

  water density = = player density → Player neither sinks nor floats.

  water density > player density → Player floats.

- **viscosity.** In addition to choosing whether a character will float or sink in water, we can indirectly adjust how quickly this occurs by changing the viscosity of the water. A thicker fluid like, say, honey has a high viscosity, whereas plain water will have a low viscosity. By increasing this value, you create an effect where the player will require more time to float or sink.

> This also affects the player's ability to walk through water. If the viscosity of the water is high and the player is hip-high (model's centroid is submerged) or further submerged, the player will begin to slow appreciably while walking.

Liquid Types

The liquidType parameter was mentioned briefly above. Out of the box, Torque supports several water types. They are legacy types from the *Tribes 2* days. Unfortunately, they are not all distinct any longer. Now you have three basic categories.

- **Basic water types**. All these behave similarly: Water, OceanWater, RiverWater, and StagnantWater.
- **Lava types**. These cause damage when the player enters the water block, but not while the player is submerged. It is up to you to write scripts that apply damage while the player is submerged. The reason for this is flexibility. Instead of forcing a fixed iterative damage on users, the creators of TGE decided to leave subsequent iterative damage up to us. When the water type is one of the three lavas, submergeTexture0 and submergeTexture1 will be rendered if you have specified them.
  - Lava. Damage parameter is $DamageLava.
  - HotLava. Damage parameter is $DamageHotLava.
  - CrustyLava. Damage parameter is $DamageCrustyLava.

> By default, all three lava types apply the same damage, but you can change this by specifying your own values in the $DamageLava, $DamageHotLava, and $Damage-CrustyLava parameters. Please note that your own scripts will have to use these settings to apply damage.

- **Quicksand.** This behaves just like water, except that the underwater fog does not render. Any other behaviors are up to us and our scripts.

For most purposes, a `liquidType` of either Water or Lava will suffice.

Underwater Fog

So, what is underwater fog? It is the effect of water coloration and dimming that can be attributed to the physical effect of light passing through water.

Until version 1.4, TGE employed a fixed color for water fog, which could not be adjusted via script. If you are still working with version 1.3 or prior, I suggest exposing the parameter that affects fog color to the console. As of this time, that code exists at about line 900 in "game.cc". Just look for the following code.

```
glColor4f(.2, .6, .6, .3);
```

Fortunately, if you are using version 1.4 of the engine, a color vector is now exposed under the name `underwaterFog` and can be modified from the Inspector and from scripts.

Water Flow

So far, we've talked about how to make waves, but what about horizontal effects, like water flow? Torque supports this too. You can cause specific textures to translate over time, giving the illusion of water flow. The following parameters are involved.

- **FlowRate.** If this value is nonzero, water flow will be enabled. The higher the value, the more quickly textures will translate. The following textures flow.
  - nonoriented `surfaceTexture`.
  - `shoreTexture`.
- **FlowAngle.** This parameter (in degrees) determines the direction of the translation. The following values demonstrate the direction of flow based on angle.
  - 0°. Textures will translate in the negative direction along the world *x*-axis.
  - 90°. Textures will translate in the negative direction along the world *y*-axis.
- **SurfaceParallax.** When `FlowRate` is non-zero, the flow rate of the oriented `surfaceTexture` is controlled by this value as shown in Table 8.2.

SurfaceParallax	surfaceTexture vs. oriented surfaceTexture
Magnitude greater than 1	Nonoriented surfaceTexture flows more slowly than oriented surfaceTexture.
Magnitude equals 1	Nonoriented surfaceTexture and oriented surfaceTexture flow at same rate.
Magnitude less than 1	Oriented surfaceTexture flows more slowly than nonoriented surfaceTexture.
Magnitude equals 0	Oriented surfaceTexture remains stationary.
Negative values	Oriented surfaceTexture counterflows.

Table 8.2.

Flow rate of surfaceTexture.

Water Distortion

In addition to supporting waves and water flow, Torque supports a distortion feature. It is difficult to classify this effect, because by varying the distortion parameters, you can get wildly different effects. However, the basis for these effects is simply the stretching and squeezing of the surfaceTexture's and shoreTexture's *uv* coordinates across a defined grid. The following parameters are involved.

- **DistortGridScale.** You don't normally need to vary this from its default value unless you have scaled your water. This allows you to adjust distortion such that the effect is the same between a large water block and a small water block.

- **DistortMag.** If this value is nonzero, distortion is enabled. Generally, the magnitude of this value should be less than 1 or the distortion behaves strangely. Both positive and negative values are legal.

- **DistortTime.** As you might guess, this is the period of the distort function. It is inversely proportional to the distortion's rate of change. In other words, larger values mean slower distortions and smaller values mean faster distortions. A value of zero is illegal and will cause the texture rendering to fail gracefully.

Realistic Shoreline Rendering

We've mentioned the shoreTexture several times now but avoided discussing how and when it is used. TGE multitextures the shoreTexture with the surfaceTexture based on the depth at that location and the following parameters.

- **ShoreDepth.** Shore rendering is determined by a ray cast at distinct points across the surface of the water block. The result of this ray cast returns the distance between the top of the water and the terrain directly below that point on the surface. If this value is greater than or equal to ShoreDepth,

Figure 8.5.

Depth versus alpha curves.

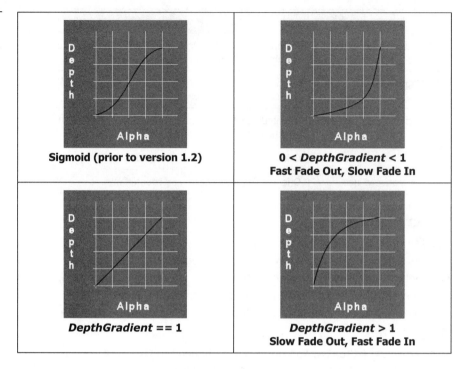

the engine is instructed to render the `shoreTexture`. If you choose to set this value to zero, the `shoreTexture` will not render at all.

- **MinAlpha/MaxAlpha**. As might be intuited, these two parameters determine the minimum and maximum alpha to use while rendering `shoreTexture`. This directly affects the multitexturing equation involving the `surfaceTexture` and `shoreTexture`.

- **DepthGradient**. Controls the slope between `MinAlpha` and `MaxAlpha`. In older versions of the engine, this was implemented as a sigmoid function, but since version 1.2, it has been implemented using the (more involved) gamma-correction function. This gives us the depth versus alpha curves shown in Figure 8.5.

Reflections and Specular Masks

TGE doesn't support real-time reflections (out of the box), but it does support the next best thing, which is a static environment map. In fact, as noted above, it supports two maps, one for above the water and the other for below. In addition to being able to specify these two environment maps (using `envMapOverTexture` and `envMapUnderTexture`, respectively), you determine how they blend by adjusting the `envMapIntensity` parameter. Legal values are between 0 and 1.

In addition to environmental mapping, TGE supports specular masks to simulate highlights. The specular mask is used to make the surface of the water shiny, that is, to provide interesting looking highlights. When you use a specular mask, the engine will render highlights, based on the texture you provide (`specularMaskTex`), the position of the sun, the elevation and inclination of the camera, and two additional specular parameters.

- **specularPower.** This determines how large an area is shiny. Lower values cause more of the specular map to be rendered; larger values will tend to show just a spot of highlighting.

- **specularColor.** This can be used to change both the color of the resultant highlight and its intensity. This parameter takes a 4-tuple floating-point vector "r g b a."

The `specularMaskTex` should be a grayscale caustic for a natural-looking water highlight.

Texture Scaling

Two parameters have been provided to allow you to modify the scale of the `surfaceTexture` and the `shoreTexture` rendering. These are named `TessSurface` and `TessShore`, respectively. Low values result in the textures covering large areas of water prior to repeating, whereas large values cause the textures to repeat over shorter distances. Some caution is in order when using these parameters. First, extremely small values can cause the textures to become distorted. Second, extremely large values can cause texture aliasing even when the camera is very near the water. Just remember, if you cause your graphics card to have to downscale the texture when the camera is near the water, you are wasting your artists' time.

Tying Up Loose Ends

In addition to the water-block parameters covered thus far, there are a few additional ones. First, there may be several under the Dynamic SimGroup. You can remove all of these. None of these parameters is hooked to anything in Torque 1.2 and beyond. The remaining parameters are the following.

- **rotation.** Water blocks cannot be rotated.
- **UseDepthMask.** Caution is in order regarding this parameter. You may crash the engine if you attempt to change this in the Inspector or from the console. So, if you want to experiment, change the mission file directly. Simply stated, if your value is `false`, only the `envMapOverTexture` will be rendered on the top of the water. All other surface textures will be disabled.
- **surfaceOpacity.** This affects how opaque the combination of `surfaceTexture` and `shoreTexture` is. A value of zero is not transparent, just

Game Elements

very translucent. A value of one is quite opaque. You'll have to adjust this to meet your needs.

- **removeWetEdge**. Setting this value as true tells the engine to (attempt to) clip the edges of water that protrude from beneath terrain features. Results will vary when using this feature.

8.3.4 Maze Runner Lesson #8 (10 Percent Step)— Lava in the Cauldron

The game will have lava at the bottom of the cauldron. Falling into this lava kills the avatar and causes it to be respawned in its original spawn position. For now, we're only worried about getting the visual part done (the lava). We'll handle the interactions later. Please do the following.

1. Start up your Maze Runner prototype, run the "Maze Runner" mission, and start the Creator tool.

2. Create a water block (Mission Objects → Environment → Water), only providing the name "Maze-RunnerWater" when the creator dialog appears (Figure 8.6).

3. Using the Inspector, be sure that the water has the settings shown in Table 8.3.

Figure 8.6.

Creating a water block.

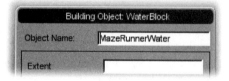

OK, so it doesn't look exactly like lava, but it gets the point across. You can tweak this to your heart's content after we get the game running. For now, let's move on.

Table 8.3.

Water settings for lava.

Parameter	Value
position	< −256 −256 55 >
scale	< 512 512 15 >
UseDepthMask	true
surfaceTexture	prototype/data/GPGTBase/water/lava.png
shoreTexture	prototype/data/GPGTBase/water/lava.png
specularMaskTex	prototype/data/GPGTBase/water/lavaspecmask.png
specularColor	< 1 1 1 0.2 >
specularPower	12
All others	Use defaults

8.4 Sky

In standard Torque, the sky object renders a sky box. In addition to the six sides of the box, you may specify up to three textures for cloud layers and three separate fog layers.

8.4.1 Sky Features

The sky has the following features.

- **Configurable sky box.** As noted above, the sky is represented by a sky box. It offers such features as disabling the bottom texture and render bans.
- **Three cloud layers.** With the standard Torque sky, you can have up to three cloud layers, each individually configured.
- **General fog and three layers of fog.** In addition to the generalized fog supported by the Sky object, you can define three additional layers of fog.
- **Visibility distance.** The Sky object is the place you go when you want to modify (the camera's) maximum view distance.
- **Wind.** The Sky object owns and controls the wind vector, which is used by other mission objects.
- **Environmental map.** It may seem strange, but when you are seeking the environmental map that is used on characters and objects with environmental mapping enabled, this is the place you go. It is part of the sky box's texture list.

8.4.2 The DML File

The DML file is the place you specify your skybox and cloud textures. The file itself can be placed anywhere you wish below the game root directory, since you can specify the relative path in the field `materialList`. A sample file would look something like the following.

```
gpgt_base1
gpgt_base2
gpgt_base3
gpgt_base4
gpgt_base5
gpgt_base6
env_map
layer0
layer1
layer2
```

In this example, `gpgt_base1` .. `gpgt_base4` represent the side textures, `gpgt_base6` is the top of the box, and `gpgt_base5` is the bottom of the box.

279

The first five textures are required if `useSkyTextures` is true and `render-BottomTexture` is `false`. The sixth texture is required if `renderBottom-Texture` is `true`.

The next texture in the DML file is `env_map`. This texture is used for any environment mapping applied to shapes. This texture is optional if you are not doing any environment mapping and do not intend to have clouds.

Finally, the last three textures in the DML file specify texture names for the cloud layers. The ordering of these textures has nothing to do with the cloud height. Cloud height is controlled by `cloudHeightPer[3]`. We'll talk more about this in Section 8.4.4.

Please note that I've stated above that this or that texture is optional based on decisions you make. However, until you get rolling, I suggest that you always specify six textures for the sky box and one additional texture for the environment map. This way, you won't run into any difficulties. Note also that the file is positional. Therefore, for example, if you want clouds, you must have specified the seven prior textures, even if they are dummy textures that won't be used.

8.4.3 The Sky Box and Render Bans

"When it [noRenderBans] is false, the engine will draw fog onto the sky box [directly]. It does this so 3D objects that are fogged out (say all white) don't stand out against an unfogged background (the sky box). If the camera enters an area of fog (a 'band') the skybox will be appropriately fogged too."

—Ben Garney, September 15, 2005

In general, by setting `noRenderBans` to `false`, we ensure that rendering looks good with fog. Of course, we may not always want this behavior and can thus enable render bans by setting the field to `true`. To get a visual perspective on this, take a look at the two images in Figure 8.7. It should be noted that the effect of this choice is especially evident from a height.

Figure 8.7.

Use of render bans.

noRenderBans == true   noRenderBans == false

Figure 8.8.
Cloud textures.

| One Texture:
`cloudHeightPer == 0.8` | One Texture:
`cloudHeightPer == 0.5` | One Texture:
`cloudHeightPer == 0.2` |

8.4.4 Clouds

As mentioned above, the cloud layers are specified by textures eight, nine, and ten in the DML file. All cloud layers are optional.

cloudHeightPer

Texture eight corresponds to `cloudHeightPer[1]`, nine to `cloudHeight-Per[2]`, and ten to `cloudHeightPer[3]`. These parameters (`cloudHeight-Per`) are used to control the central height of the cloud meshes. The cloud meshes themselves are a nine-faced hemisphere. The `cloudHeightPer` parameter specifies the height of the upper plane of this hemisphere. Figure 8.8 has some sample images to demonstrate the `cloudHeightPer` parameter. A value of 0.0 will cause the cloud mesh not to render, and values above 0.8 poke through the sky box causing visible artifacts.

Multiple Layers

In terms of viewing, Layer 2 is rendered first, and Layer 0 is rendered last, meaning that Layer 0 will look like it is in front of Layer 2 regardless of `cloudHeightPer`.

Cloud Motion

Cloud motion is described by two parameters. All clouds move in the same direction, specified by the (misnamed) parameter `windVelocity`, which is an *x-y-z* vector. The *x* and *y* components control the direction of the wind and therefore the clouds. Putting a nonzero value in *z* breaks the cloud renderer, so don't do it. You can control the velocity of the flow with the `cloudSpeed` parameter. Yes, velocities can be negative, so clouds can counterflow.

8.4.5 Fog

Clouds are cool, but sometimes you need fog in addition to, or instead of, clouds. No problem. Fog is supported in Torque by a general fog, and by up to three fog layers.

General Fog

The first type of fog affects visibility regardless of your location. The field `fogDistance` is used to determine this. Low values indicate low visibility, and high values indicate high visibility. Values greater than or equal to `visibleDistance` are equivalent to 100 percent visibility (unless you have `noRenderBans` unchecked).

Fog Layers

As noted above, there are three layers. Layer 1 is always the lowest, and Layer 3 is always the highest. Each layer has a field `fogVolumeN` associated with it. This field takes three parameters: visible distance, bottom elevation, and top elevation.

The visible distance determines the distance from the camera at which visibility is (near) zero. Bottom and top elevations determine where the layer (or band) of fog begins and ends, respectively. To enable a band, visible distance must be greater than zero and top elevation must be greater than bottom elevation. Also, do not forget that, if you are going to enable more than one layer of fog, they must not overlap each other, or rendering will be messed up. They may touch but not penetrate. Here are some sample settings.

```
fogVolume1 = "250 0 50";
fogVolume2 = "350 50 150";
fogVolume3 = "25 200 500";
```

- The first layer starts at 0 world units and stops at 50 world units, with a visible distance of 250 world units.
- The second layer starts at 50 world units (touching layer one) and stops at 150 world units, with a visible distance of 350 world units.
- The third layer starts at 200 world units and stops at 500 world units, with a visible distance of only 25 world units.

8.4.6 Visibility

We've seen that fog can affect our visibility, but how do we determine our maximum view distance? This question is critical and can affect performance as well as aesthetics; `visibleDistance` is the parameter we are looking for. It measures in world units and can be set to just about any value. A word of caution, though: extremely large distances can kill performance big time.

8.4.7 Rendering Issues

If you are having rendering problems, you may wish to check the following.

1. Get the latest drivers for your video card.
2. Set quality settings to their highest values for D3D or OpenGL, depending on which application programming interface (API) you are using.
3. Be sure that bit depth is 32 (both in your driver settings, and under Options → Graphics → Bit Depth from the main menu).

If you still encounter issues, talk to someone on the Torque Internet Relay Chat (IRC) channel (IRC server: irc.maxgaming.net; IRC port: 6667; channel: #GarageGames), or post a descriptive thread (after searching the forums, of course).

8.4.8 Sky Scripting

Storm Fog

Storm fog is a scripting feature used to fade a layer of fog in and out over a period of time. In order to enable this features, the sky must have been created with the `fogStorm[1,3]` checkboxes checked. You must have correctly defined the visible distance and low and high values for the fog layer. For example, if we wished to fade in and out just one layer, we could define something like in Figure 8.9.

Notice that `fogStorm1` is selected. Subsequently, we could fade layer 1 of our fog to 50 percent over a 5 second period, using the following code.

```
Sky.stormFog( 0.5 , 5 );
```

Or, we could turn it entirely off instantly using the `stormFogShow()` method.

```
Sky.stormFogShow( 0 );
```

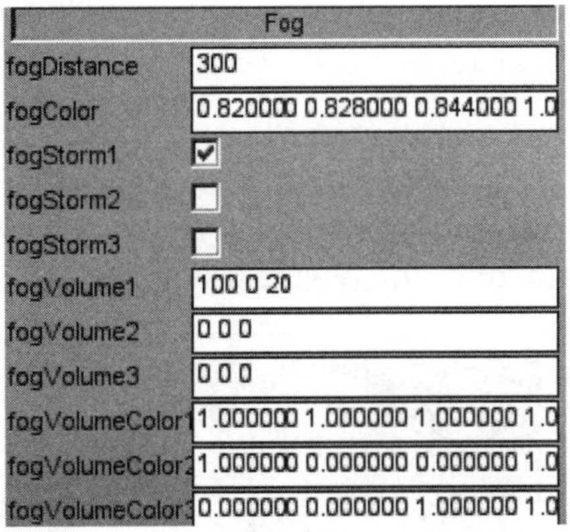

Fog	
fogDistance	300
fogColor	0.820000 0.828000 0.844000 1.0
fogStorm1	☑
fogStorm2	☐
fogStorm3	☐
fogVolume1	100 0 20
fogVolume2	0 0 0
fogVolume3	0 0 0
fogVolumeColor1	1.000000 1.000000 1.000000 1.0
fogVolumeColor2	1.000000 0.000000 0.000000 1.0
fogVolumeColor3	0.000000 0.000000 1.000000 1.0

Figure 8.9.

Storm-fog definitions.

Note that fog layers fade in layer by layer, starting with Layer 1 and ending with Layer 3. They fade out in the opposite order.

Please note that, if you enable `fogStorm` and the storm is inactive (or deleted), your fog will disappear.

Storm Clouds

Storm clouds is a scripting feature similar to storm fog, except for the three cloud layers. Because clouds are defined differently from fog, we can't disable the feature for certain layers, so all layers that are defined will be affected when using the `stormClouds` method. That said, if we wanted to fade our clouds out over a 10 second period, we would write the following code.

```
Sky.stormClouds( 0 , 10 );
```

8.4.9 Maze Runner Lesson #9 (10 Percent Step)— Starry Night

If you are building the Maze Runner game while you read this guide, the original sky is a bit too bright for our game, so we will need to do the following to create a starry night instead.

1. Start up your Maze Runner prototype, run the "Maze Runner" mission, and start the Inspector tool.
2. Find the Sky object and change the DML file to one you will find in /Maze-Runner/prototype/data/GPGTBase/skies/starrynight/starry_sky.dml. This file contains the following list of texture names.

   ```
   stars0
   stars1
   stars2
   stars3
   stars4
   stars5
   stars6
   cloud1
   ```

The textures used in this file are just a set of five generated starfields, a placeholder for the seventh texture, and a randomly (noise) generated translucent cloud texture (Figure 8.10).

Figure 8.10.

Sky textures.

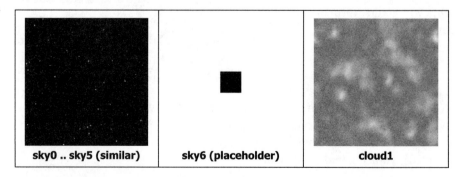

| sky0 .. sky5 (similar) | sky6 (placeholder) | cloud1 |

Parameter	Value
materialList	prototype/data/GPGTBase/skies/starrynight/starry_sky.dml
cloudHeightPer[0]	0.5
cloudHeightPer[1]	0
cloudHeightPer[2]	0
cloudSpeed1	0.0005
cloudSpeed2	0
cloudSpeed3	0
visibleDistance	1000
fogDistance	2000
fogVolume1	< 550 0 300 >
fogVolume2	< 0 0 0 >
fogVolume3	< 0 0 0 >
All others	Use defaults

Table 8.4.

Sky settings for starry night.

3. Using the Inspector, be sure that the sky has the settings shown in Table 8.4.

8.5 Sun (Mission Lighting)

The Sun object has a simple job, namely to determine how the mission will be lit. Initially, you may or may not find this particular mission object simple to use, but with a little help, this should be no big deal. Please note that this object does not have a visible representation; that is, you can't actually see the Sun mission object. If you need a visual representation of your sun(s), use the fxSunlight mission object.

8.5.1 Sun Features

A sun has the following features.

- **Configurable light source.** Using the Sky mission object, you may configure the position of the light source and coloration (both direct and ambient) of the light it emits.
- **Object shading.** Objects are darker on the side opposite the sun's position.
- **Shadows**. Shadows are supported, but there are issues. See Section 8.5.2, "Shadows and Sun Direction."
- **No sun and multiple suns.** You can have 0, 1, 2 … well, you get the idea.

8.5.2 Shadows and Sun Direction

Torque supports shadows and pseudo–self-shadowing. When I say pseudo–self-shadowing, I mean that objects are darker on the side facing away from the sun. This is done correctly for the terrain, shapes, and interiors. Unfortunately, shadows cast by objects onto other objects are a little buggy. Both terrain and interiors properly cast shadows onto other objects, but shapes do not. What do I mean by properly? Well, shadows should be calculated based on the azimuth and elevation parameters. If I say a shadow is cast correctly, I mean it adjusts based on these parameters. Table 8.5 should clarify things.

Table 8.5.

Shadowing and self-shadowing.

Mission Object	Shadows?	Self-Shadows?
Terrain	• Does adjust based on sun parameters. • Does affect other mission objects. • Self-shadowing is baked.	Yes
Interiors (.dif)	• Do adjust based on sun parameters. • Do affect other mission objects. • Are baked into terrain.	Yes
Shapes (.dts)	• Adjust orientation and length based on sun parameters. • Do affect other mission objects. • Are dynamic.	Yes

Please note that, while you are reading this chapter, it is likely that you are using the demo version of TGE. In order to show the engine's best face, the demo includes some features from the Torque Lighting Kit (TLK). While this is nice, it may cause some confusion if a feature that I describe here does not match the demo. So, instead of trying to document both TGE and TLK here, I will be describing the standard version of the Torque Software Development Kit (SDK). This way, you will know exactly what you are getting when you buy the SDK while also knowing (from the demo) what TLK can do for you.

Baked shadows are calculated once during the lighting phase of a mission load and are static until/unless the mission is relit.

Better Lighting

Although lighting in the base version of TGE is good, it cannot compare to the extended ranges and other features provided by the Torque Lighting Kit. Neither can it compare to the almost unlimited set of effects you can get by using the Torque Shader Engine. So, if you're looking for more intense or dazzling lighting effects, remember that you have options that keep you in the Torque family and thus retain all of the other great features Torque provides.

Azimuth and Elevation

Once you grasp the concept of azimuth and elevation, they are quite easy to work with, but describing them directly is a bit of a chore. I'm sure there is a succinct mathematical way of describing these terms, but not being a mathematician, and wanting to be clear to those similarly handicapped, I will instead describe them simplistically.

Imagine, if you will, that we have a magic arrow (yes, a vector). The base of this arrow is stuck to the world axis. Magically, the head of the arrow always points at the sun. Given this, our magic arrow will behave as shown in Table 8.6.

Azimuth (degrees)	Elevation (degrees)	The Arrow
0	0	Points down the *y*-axis and lies in the *x-y* plane.
45	0	Makes a 45-degree angle between *x* and *y* and lies in the *x-y* plane.
90	45	Points down the *x*-axis, making a 45-degree angle between *x* and *z*.

Table 8.6.

Azimuth and elevation following the sun.

In all cases above, *x*, *y*, and *z* are the world axes.

Both azimuth and elevation can theoretically take any value between 0 and 360, but in practice, there are certain values that do not work well.

Azimuth

- Legal range: [0, 360).
- At 90 and 180 degrees, shadows stop rendering.

Elevation

- Legal range: [0, 360).
- Suggested range: [0, 90).
- Engine will crash if this is set to 90 degrees.
- Values greater than 180 are below the terrain and may produce odd effects.

8.5.3 Color and Ambient Parameters

OK, enough about where the sun is, but what about the color and ambient parameters? First, both of these parameters affect the scene lighting in different ways. Briefly, color is the part of the light that is cast directly onto shapes, interiors, and the terrain. It accounts for the shadows that interiors and terrain features cast. The ambient parameter is the portion of the light that is scattered by the environment and appears to come from all directions. Both parameters account for the total lighting of the terrain, the character, and interiors. Changes to the ambient portion of lighting are most easily noticed, but you should experiment with both factors (ambient and color) to achieve the results you need.

Both parameters take four arguments, $< r\, g\, b\, i >$, where *i* is the intensity. Currently, intensity has no effect for either parameter.

Game Elements

8.5.4 Multiple Suns?

You may have more than one sun, but be aware that the following is true.

- Mission lighting will take significantly longer.
- Lighting is cumulative and clamped, meaning you can saturate your lighting.
- Shadows do not behave as you would expect with two or more light sources; instead, you'll likely end up mauling your shadows.

The number one reason for adding multiple light sources is to get cool shadowing effects. Since this doesn't really work as expected, you are probably better off just sticking with one sun.

8.5.5 No Sun?

This has been an on-again, off-again feature. Currently, you must specify a sun or your game will crash (TLK handles this case without crashing). However, if you want a totally dark mission, you can achieve this with a sun present. Just set the two color parameters (`color` and `ambient`) to "0 0 0 0". In the end, this is safer than removing the sun, even if it does work for you now.

8.5.6 Maze Runner Lesson #10 (10 Percent Step)— Low Lighting

If you are building the Maze Runner game while you read this guide, the original sun (lighting) is a bit too bright for our game, so we will need to do the following to match our night sky.

1. Using the Inspector, lower the lighting values for the Sun object to the values in Table 8.7.
2. Now, relight the scene (**ALT + L**) to see the values take effect.

Table 8.7.

Lighting values for low lighting.

Fields	Values
elevation	90
azimuth	90
color	< 0.5 0.3 0.3 1 >
ambient	< 0.2 0.2 0.2 1 >

8.6 Precipitation and Lightning

A couple of nice effects to be able to add at will are precipitation (i.e., rain, snow, hail, etc.) and lightning. These are actually separate mission objects (one for precipitation, and two possibilities for lightning), but I'll address them together because they are relatively small and have at least a tangential relationship.

8.6.1 Precipitation Features

Precipitation has the following features.

- **Variable density.** You can choose between a light shower and a downpour. Additionally, the density of rainfall varies randomly over time to give it a more organic feel.
- **Variable velocity.** Since real raindrops do not all fall at the same rate, Torque supports the ability to randomly vary the velocity of individual drops.
- **Drop coloration.** For an additional degree of realism, you can modify the coloration of individual drops by providing up to three colors.
- **Multiple textures.** Because having just one texture for the drop would be boring, Torque supports 16.

8.6.2 Lightning Features

There are two different objects that can be used for lightning. First, there is the Lightning object, which supplies the following features.

- **Generated lightning.** Based on LightningData fields you set, the engine generates jagged lightning bolts.
- **Targetable strikes.** You can, to some degree, target where lightning begins and where it will strike.
- **Fade color.** You can choose what fade color is used for the bolts. The fade color is used to simulate the effect of seeing a lightning strike.
- **Fogging.** You can enable fogging features to make the lightning extra impressive, but this feature requires hardware support.
- **Thunder.** You can supply a sound datablock to provide thunder with the lightning.

Second, there is a recent addition, WeatherLightning, which supplies the following features.

- **Textured lightning.** Based on WeatherLightningData fields you set, the engine renders your supplied lightning textures.
- **SkyFlash and fuzzing effects.** Based on WeatherLightningData fields you set, the engine renders flashes in the sky and an afterimage for each bolt.
- **Thunder.** You can supply a sound datablock to provide thunder with the lightning.

8.6.3 Let There Be Rain

Setting up a precipitation object requires that we consider several facets of the rain storm's behavior, including the density of the storm, the speed at which individual drops fall, drop coloration, and the images that should be used for our raindrops. As you will see, all of this is quite straightforward.

Precipitation Density

Precipitation density is a measure of how many raindrops we have in a certain area. We can vary the precipitation density by varying `maxRadius`, `maxNumDrop`, and `percentage`. Together, `maxNumDrops * percentage` determines the current number of drops falling. We can spread these drops out by selecting various values for `maxRadius`. A low value of, say, 30 will cause drops to fall within 30 world units of the camera, and a value of 125 will cause them to fall as far away as 125 world units.

Precipitation Velocity

In order for our precipitation to look more realistic, we'll want it to fall at varying rates. To do this, simply set `minVelocity` to a nonzero value lower than `maxVelocity`. Now, drops will fall at some random speed between `minVelocity` and `maxVelocity`. Additionally, setting `offsetSpeed` to a nonzero value adds a bit of horizontal velocity to the drops. Don't overdo it on this parameter, though, as high values can make the precipitation look a bit unnatural.

Varying Drop Colors

The base color of your drops is determined by the texture(s) you use for your precipitation (see below), but you can modify this with the `color[3:1]` parameters. As far as I can tell, 33 percent of the drops are either `color1`, `color2`, or `color3`. So, setting the `< r g b >` portion of these to something other than `< 1 1 1 >` will cause the textures to be shaded that color. Note that the alpha channel (fourth value) does nothing.

Precipitation Media

By default, any individual drop is a billboard.[1] For the sake of this discussion, think of a billboard as a polygon that automatically orients itself to be facing a specific direction. These billboards are textured using 1/16th of a texture supplied in the PrecipitationData field `dropTexture`. That is, you supply the relative path to a PNG file in `PrecipitationData.dropTexture`. This texture should be a 4 × 4 grid containing a raindrop image in each of the sixteen resulting grid blocks (see Figure 8.11). When the engine gets ready to produce a new drop, it will randomly select one of the 16 subtextures and use it as the precipi-

---

[1] If you want to learn all about billboards, pick up a good book like Akenine-Möller and Haines, *Real-Time Rendering, Second Edition* (A K Peters, Ltd., 2002).

tation billboard. You may use JPG or PNG files for precipitation, but I suggest using PNG, as JPG does not support the transparency that you will likely need.

8.6.4 It Was a Dark and Stormy Night...

What would a storm be without a little lightning and thunder? Well, fortunately you don't need to find out, because Torque comes with two different classes that each display different styles of lightning and play thunder sounds, too. We will discuss both in this section, starting with a discussion of Lightning and then segue into a discussion about WeatherLightning.

Lightning (and WeatherLightning) objects are blocks like water. This means that you can place multiple blocks of lightning throughout your mission, or if you choose, you can have just one big block covering the whole mission. Blocks may overlap. You can freely scale the lightning block using the Inspector and the mouse.

8.6.5 Lightning Strikes!

First, it is important to understand what a strike is. When the engine gets ready to draw the lightning, it decides whether it is going to strike the ground, the highest local object, or if there will be a miss.

When there is a miss, the lightning is drawn at an angle, sometimes even parallel to the ground. These misses give the lightning a more realistic look. So, how does the engine determine if there will be a miss or a strike, and when there is a strike, how is it determined if an object or the ground will be hit?

First, the zone where anything can be hit is determined by the location of the lightning box as well as the `strikeRadius`. Bolts will strike objects or the ground within `strikeRadius` of the lightning object. To determine if an object will be hit, or if the ground will be struck, the engine grabs a list of all damageable objects in the strike zone and does a sort, looking for the highest object. It can randomly choose an object that is not the highest, but it prefers the highest object (as does real lightning). Finally, the engine rolls the dice, so to speak, and if the value it gets back is less than or equal to `chanceToHit` (remember those good old AD&D days?), that object is hit. If the value is higher than `chanceToHit`, then the bolt hits a random location on the ground.

We can control the number of lightning strikes (this includes misses) per minute with the parameter `strikesPerMin`. This is not the inverse of the strike period but instead a rough number of strikes per minute. Increasing this value increases the number of strikes in any period, but strikes can happen very rapidly or with short pauses between them. This just gives it a more random feel. You can't predict a lightning strike.

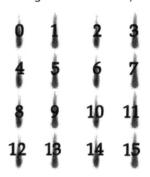

Figure 8.11.

Precipitation texture (a 4 × 4 grid of subtextures).

Game Elements

So, what about `strikeWidth`? Well, this determines the width of the bolt on a strike. Bolts all have a default width for misses, but for strikes, you can control the width. Do you want a fat strike or a narrow one?

Lightning Color

The textures you choose for your lightning are used as a mask, but the coloration comes from the `color` and `fadeColor` parameters. The bolts are drawn first, using `color`, and then over a short period, they are faded out. While this fade occurs, the bolts are colored `fadeColor`. This gives a nice heated plasma effect and mimics the behavior of the eye when it sees a lightning bolt. When you see an actual lightning strike or any focused bright light, most of the receptors in the eyeball fire for the area where the bolt is focused by your eye's lens. This temporarily uses up all the available chemicals that make sight possible. In other words, those receptors are temporarily turned off by the overload. The effect is a phantom bolt that fades over a short time.

Leaning Lightning?

In addition to controlling the strike zone, we can control where the lightning bolts start. If we set `boltRadius` to zero, then all bolts will radiate from the topmost center position of the lightning box. We can also set the value to something big, like 500. Now, all the bolts will seem to be coming from far away and angling towards the strike zone (assuming a small strike zone).

Ooh... Pretty Lightning!

Finally, if you set `useFog` to `true` and if the user's graphics card supports both multitexturing and fog-coordinate extensions (a pretty good bet for cards two or fewer years old), the engine will do a nice bit of texturing with local fog (i.e., fog around the camera).

Two Ways to Create Lightning

The engine supplies two means of making lightning. The first type is generated (Lightning object) and uses no textures. The second way uses textures instead of generation (WeatherLightning object) for more spectacular effects.

Generated Lightning (Lightning Objects)

In order to create generated lightning, we must still create a datablock for our lightning.

```
datablock LightningData(LightningExample) {
  // Play this sound when lightning strikes!
  strikeSound = LightningStrikeSound;
```

```
    // Up to eight thunder sounds can be defined
    thunderSounds[0] = ThunderSound0;
    thunderSounds[1] = ThunderSound1;
};
```

This datablock specifies zero textures, a strike sound, and two of the eight possible thunder sounds.

Now, we can place a lightning object in our mission using this datablock or create one via script.

```
new Lightning() {
    position = "0 0 180;
    scale = "100 100 500";
    dataBlock = "LightningExample";
    strikesPerMinute = "90";
    strikeWidth = "0.25";
    chanceToHitTarget = "100";
    strikeRadius = "25";
    boltStartRadius = "100";
    color = "1.000000 1.000000 1.000000 1.000000";
    fadeColor = "0.100000 0.100000 1.000000 1.000000";
};
```

This sample will produce a lightning storm centered at an < x y > of "0 0" and starting at an elevation of 180 world units. Up to 90 bolts will strike per minute, all of which will be fairly narrow and striking within a radius of 25 world units of "0 0", but starting at a radius of 100 world units; that is, these lightning bolts will lean in. Finally, the bolts will start off completely white and fade to a dark blue.

Textured Lightning (WeatherLightning Objects)

Alternatively, we could use the WeatherLightning object and specify a WeatherLightning datablock as follows.

```
datablock WeatherLightningData(TexturedLightningExample) {
    strikeTextures[0] = "./data/lightning1frame1";
    strikeTextures[1] = "./data/lightning1Frame2";
    strikeTextures[2] = "./data/lightning1Frame3";

    flashTextures[0] = "./data/flash";

    fuzzyTextures[0] = "./data/lightningFuzzframe1";
    fuzzyTextures[1] = "./data/lightningFuzzFrame2";
    fuzzyTextures[2] = "./data/lightningFuzzFrame3";
```

293

```
    strikeSound = LightningStrikeSound;

    thunderSounds[0] = ThunderSound0;
    thunderSounds[1] = ThunderSound1;
};
```

This datablock uses three textures for lightning bolts, one texture for a bolt-origin flash (in the sky), and three textures for after-bolt fade images. In each case, we could have specified up to eight textures for the three effects. In addition to these visual effects, like Lightning, WeatherLightning can play a strike sound and up to eight thunder sounds (although we only specified two).

At this point, you might be a little confused about what you get with Lightning objects and what you get with WeatherLightning objects, so let's summarize their features.

Lightning Features Revisited

In summary, the Lightning object is used to create generated lightning effects. It gives us various controls over how that lightning is generated, including the width of the bolt, the starting location of the bolt, the ending location of the bolt, its initial color and ending color, and finally the number of bolts per minute. In addition to these Lightning field controlled features, the LightningData datablock has the fields and features shown in Table 8.8.

WeatherLightning Features Revisited

In summary, the WeatherLightning object is used to create textured lightning effects. It gives us fewer controls over the bolts than the Lighting object. In fact, we can only control the number of bolts per minute, using the strikes-PerMin field. However, this object does have the benefit of producing very nice bolt effects. These effects are specified using the WeatherLightningData datablock and supplies the features shown in Table 8.9.

8.6.6 Maze Runner Lesson #11 (10 Percent Step)— Stormy Weather

If you are building the Maze Runner game while you read this guide, we are now going to add some rain, lightning, and thunder to our scene. The game is meant to have a "cartoon spooky" theme, and these elements will add to that.

Adding the Rain

1. Start up your Maze Runner prototype, run the "Maze Runner" mission, and start the Creator tool.

Field Name	Description
strikeSound	An audio profile to use for the strike noise. Should be 3D audio profile created with datablock keyword.
thunderSounds[8]	Eight audio profile slots for thunder/lightning strike sounds. Should be 2D audio profile created with datablock keyword.

Table 8.8.

Fields in Lightning datablocks.

Field Name	Description
strikeTextures[8]	Eight texture slots for relative paths and names of lightning texture files.
flashTextures[8]	Eight texture slots for relative paths and names of lightning origin-flash texture files.
fuzzyTextures[8]	Eight texture slots for relative paths and names of lightning fade textures.
strikeSound	An audio profile to use for the strike noise. Should be 3D audio profile created with datablock keyword.
thunderSounds[8]	Eight audio profile slots for thunder/lightning strike sounds. Should be 2D audio profile created with datablock keyword.

Table 8.9.

Fields in WeatherLightning datablocks.

Parameter	Value
minSpeed	1
maxSpeed	1.5
rotateWithCameraVel	true
numDrops	2000
boxWidth	200
boxHeight	100
doCollision	0
All others	Use defaults

Table 8.10.

Settings for rain.

Figure 8.12.

Adding rain.

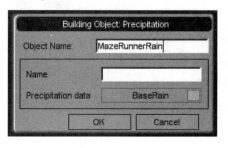

Figure 8.13.

Adding lightning.

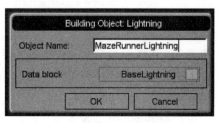

Table 8.11.

Settings for lightning.

Parameter	Value
position	< 0 0 300 >
scale	< 256 256 250 >
strikesPerMinute	6
strikeWidth	1.5
strikeRadius	128
color	< 0.89 0.8 0.42 1 >
fadeColor	< 0.5 0.9 0.9 1 >
chanceToHitTarget	0
boltStartRadius	32
All others	Use defaults

2. Select a precipitation object (Mission Objects → Environment → Precipitation), giving it the object name "MazeRunnerRain" and choosing the datablock BaseRain (Figure 8.12).
3. Open the Inspector and give the new rain object the settings in Table 8.10.

Adding Lightning

1. Go back into the Creator tool.
2. Select a lightning object (Mission Objects → Environment → Lightning), giving it the object name "MazeRunnerLightning" and choosing the datablock BaseLightning (Figure 8.13).
3. Open the Inspector and give the new lightning object the settings in Table 8.11.

8.7 Audio Emitters

So far, we've focused on visible environmental objects. What about sounds? Audio emitters are objects that you can use for placing positional sounds. Audio emitters have the ability to turn themselves on and off based on a trigger. This trigger can be modified in size and shape to meet your needs. Let's take a look, or perhaps I should say, let's have a listen?

8.7.1 Audio Emitter Features

Audio emitters have the following features.

- **2D sound.** This is sound with no apparent source. In other words, it is neither directional nor positional.

- **3D sound.** This is sound with a specific source. Furthermore, this type of sound is modulated by distance from and facing angle to the sound source.

- **Looping and nonlooping sounds.** Emitters can be programmed to loop a variable number of times or as one-time emitters.

- **Triggers.** 3D sound emitters have the ability to turn themselves on and off based on a cut-off distance.

8.7.2 2D Sound

2D sound is very simple. All 2D sound emitters are turned on at the earliest opportunity (shortly after they are created). If looping is enabled, audio emitters will not stop playing until all loops have been exhausted; otherwise, they will play once and then stop.

You can specify a 2D audio emitter with the following settings.

- **Media**
  - `description`. Set this to the relative directory + filename for the sound file. Either WAV or OGG files are acceptable formats.
  - `type`. A value between 1 and 8, corresponding to the audio group this emitter should belong to (see "2D Gain" below).

- **Sound**
  - `volume`. Between 0.0 (0 percent gain) and 1.0 (100 percent gain).
  - `outsideAmbient`. Should be checked.

- **Looping.** Set looping parameters based on your requirements (see "Looping" below).

- **Advanced**
  - `is3D`. Should be unchecked.

2D Gain

Gain determines how loudly your sound will play. The gain equation for 2D emitters is as follows.

```
2D gain == game master volume * audio group gain * emitter gain
```

Game master volume is controlled from the main menu under Options → Audio. Audio group gain is controlled by the field Media → `type`.

- Valid values for type are 1..31. By default, only 1..8 are set up.
  - **0.** Is reserved.
  - **1.** GUI audio type (Options → Audio → Shell Volume)
  - **2.** Sim audio type (Options → Audio → Sim Volume)
  - **3..8.** Set to 0.8 (search for `channelVolume` in scripts).

- The purpose of this gain is to allow you to adjust the gain for a group of emitters in one step.

  Emitter gain is controlled by the field Sound → `volume` parameter.

Looping

If you haven't already guessed, the looping parameters allow you make an emitter (2D or 3D) play the sound file between one and infinite times. To enable looping, make sure Looping → `isLooping` is checked. Then, set your loop count. Loop counts work as follows.

- `loopCount` = = −1. Loop infinitely.
- `loopCount` = = 0. Loop once and only once.
- `loopCount` = = 1. Loop once, possibly twice.
- `loopCount` = = (n > 1). Loop n times.

On rare occasions, a value of 1 will cause *two* loops. So, if you really want only one loop, use a loopCount setting of 0.

Loop Gaps

The loop gap parameters control the delay between subsequent loops. `minLoopGap`, as you would imagine, defines the lower boundary for delays and `maxLoopGap` the upper. Torque randomly chooses a value between these two. Loop gaps are approximately equal to $2n$ milliseconds, where n is the `LoopGap` value selected. Please note that loop gaps can be used to do some interesting things (see Table 8.12).

Table 8.12.

Use of loop gaps.

minLoopGap	maxLoopGap	Action
0	0	Sound turns on, but won't turn off (2D and 3D)
0	1	Sound turns on immediately and turns off at end of loop or upon exiting 3D region (see below).
1	0	Sound does not turn on, ever.
N > 1	N > 1	Normal behavior.

By using the settings `minLoopGap` = 1 and `maxLoopGap` = 0, you can tell the emitter to not play at load time. Once the load is completed, you can have a script set the gap values to whatever delay you need, or you can hook the sound up to a trigger.

2D Visual Feedback

Visual feedback in 2D mode is simple. While editing, you can see the emitter as a small cube. The cube will be black while not playing and green while playing (Figure 8.14).

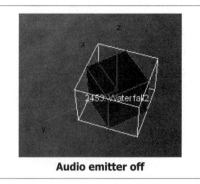

Audio emitter off

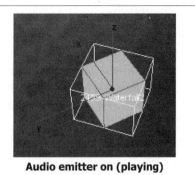

Audio emitter on (playing)

Figure 8.14.
Audio visual feedback.

8.7.3 3D Sound

In real life, sound radiates from a source to a listener. Additionally, sound is attenuated by several factors, including distance, angle, occlusion, etc. Torque simulates the behavior of real-world sound with OpenAL's 3D sound features. 3D audio emitters support distance and angular attenuation. How they support these features can be a little confusing, so we will treat this topic like a puzzle and examine each puzzle piece individually to see how it fits into the complete picture.

Sound Zones and Sound Cones

In practice, audio emitters support four zones of sound (Table 8.13 and Figure 8.15).

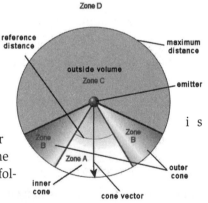

Figure 8.15.
Sound cones.

Zone A—Inner Cone

As noted above, gain in the inner cone is a function of distance from the emitter (source). To determine the physical volume of the inner cone, we must specify the following.

Zone	Description	Gain attenuation
A	Listener in inner cone.	Gain is a function of linear distance from source.
B	Listener in outer cone.	Gain is a function of linear distance from source and angular distance from inner cone edge.
C	Listener in area outside outer cone.	Gain is a constant value determined by outside volume.
D	Listener beyond maximum distance from source.	Emitter is deactivated.

Table 8.13.
Four zones of sound.

- `is3D` must be checked to enable 3D sound.
- `position` specifies the tip of the cone and the base of the `coneVector`.
- `rotation` specifies the direction in which `coneVector` points.
- `maxDistance` specifies the base of the cone. `coneVector` is a unit vector, but you can image a line passing through the vector, starting at `position` and ending at `position + coneVector * maxDistance`, and this is the position of the cone base.
- `coneInsideAngle` specifies the inner cone sweep.

To specify the gain of the inner cone, we must specify the following.

- `volume`. Emitter gain.
- `referenceDistance`. This specifies the distance (from the emitter) at which 3D gain $==$ 0.5.

Inner cone gain works as shown in Table 8.14.

Zone B—Outer Cone

Gain in the outer cone is a function of inner-cone gain and the angle from the outer edge of the inner cone. To determine the physical volume of the outer cone, we must specify the following.

- inner cone.
- `coneOutsideAngle`, which specifies the outer cone sweep.

The outer cone shares all the parameters of the inner cone including the axis. To specify the gain of the inner cone, we must specify one additional parameter.

- `coneOutsideVolume`, which is the gain at and beyond the outer edge of the outer cone. *Important!* If this value is 0, the outer cone will be disabled and there will be no sound except inside the inner cone.

Outer-cone gain works as shown in Table 8.15.

Zone C—Outside Volume

If `coneOutsideVolume` is nonzero, the area outside of the outer cone has a gain between `coneOutsideVolume` and zero, based on the distance from the emitter. Outer-volume (zone) gain works as shown in Table 8.15.

Zone D—Beyond `maxDistance`

The `maximumDistance` can be used to draw an imaginary sphere around the emitter. If the camera enters that sphere, the emitter is told to load its sound. Additionally, if the camera is inside an enabled sound zone, the emitter is told to play the sound. Conversely, if the camera moves from within the sphere to outside the sphere, the sound is told to stop playing.

Listener Position	Emitter Gain	
P < R	0.5 * P/R	where
P == R	0.5	P = | listener position – emitter position | R = `referenceDistance`
M > P > R	~ R/P	M = `maxDistance`

Table 8.14.

Inner cone gain.

Listener Position	Emitter Gain	
Ca == Ia	Ig	where
Ca < Ia < Oa	Ig → Ov (as a function of angle)	Ig = inner cone gain at current distance from emitter Ca = (coneOutsideAngle – Current Angle) / 2 Ia = coneInsideAngle / 2
Ca == Oa	Ov	Oa = coneOutsideAngle / 2 Ov = coneOutsideVolume

Table 8.15.

Outer cone gain.

Listener Position	Emitter Gain
P	`coneOutsideVolume` → 0 (as a function of distance)
where P = | listener position – emitter position |	

Table 8.16.

Outer volume gain.

3D Visual Feedback

Before we jump into examples, let's discuss the visual feedback associated with 3D audio emitters. Because there are more audio concepts to express, the visual feedback is a little more complex than for 2D emitters, but only marginally (Figure 8.16 and Table 8.17). You can specify a 3D audio emitter as follows:

- **Media**
  - `description`. Relative directory + filename for the sound file. Only WAV format is supported. Mono and stereo formats OK.
  - `type`. 1 through 8 (see "2D Gain" above).
- **Sound**
  - `volume`. Between 0.0 (0% gain) and 1.0 (100% gain).
  - `outsideAmbient`. Should be checked.
- **Looping**. Set looping parameters based on your requirements (see "Looping" above).

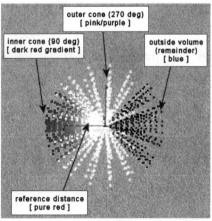

Figure 8.16.

Visual feedback for 3D audio.

Table 8.17.

Audio emitter—3D visual
feedback.

Inner cone	Red fading to black. Fade starts at `referenceDistance`.
Outer cone	Pinkish-purple.
Outside volume	Blue.
On/Off indicator	Same as 2D (not visible in Figure 8.16).

- **Advanced**
  - `enableVisualFeedback`. Should be checked. Please note that, even if this is not checked, visual feedback renders when a 3D emitter is selected.
  - `is3D`. Should be checked.
  - `coneInsideAngle`. Set to your preference.
  - `coneOutsideAngle`. Set to your preference. 0 to disable.
  - `coneOutsideVolume`. Set to your preference. 0 to disable all but inner cone.
  - `coneVector`. Don't touch this. It is set automatically when you adjust rotation. Typed changes will be overridden.

Audio Descriptions and Profiles

Audio descriptions and profiles are an alternate way of (pre-) specifying the specifics of an audio emitter. These will be discussed in Chapter 11, "Special Effects." For now, it is perfectly suitable to define the parameters for an audio emitter using the Inspector.

8.7.4 3D Emitter Examples

Figure 8.17 gives examples of 3D audio emitters.

8.8 Particle Emitter Nodes

One of the more time-consuming mission objects to place is the particle emitter—not because it is particularly hard to understand, but because it offers a venerable cornucopia of features. Moreover, it is just plain fun to play with! In fact, if you don't approach it knowing the basics of how to use it and with a good idea of the result you want, you could burn several hours goofing around. While I can't help you focus on a particular idea, I can help you understand the basics of using it.

I must warn you before we start: we are going to depart from using the mission editor alone. In order to build emitters, we need to write some script datablocks. For now, you can just use my examples directly, and you should not get into too much trouble. Later, you may experiment and write your own.

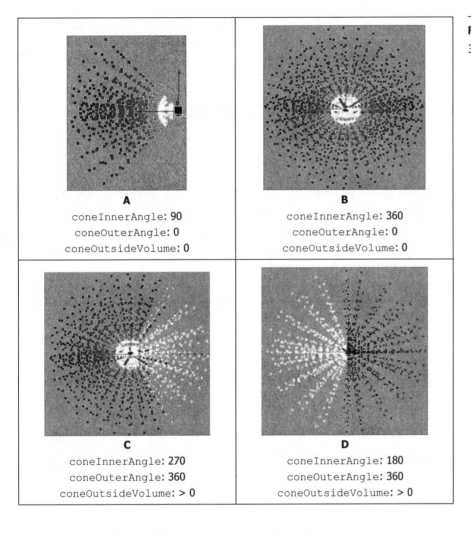

Figure 8.17.
3D audio emitters.

8.8.1 What Is a Particle Emitter Node?

Particle emitter nodes (PENs) are static objects (that is, they don't normally move) that can be used to provide special effects such as smoke, fire, waterfalls, fireflies... you name it. They do this by emitting—you guessed it—particles. As is commonly[2] the case in 3D systems, these particles are billboards. In the case of particles, these billboards are usually textured with a partially opaque and partially translucent texture and are usually facing the camera. What this means is that, when you look at any particular particle, it will normally be facing you, and you will likely be able to see through parts of it.

So, what do we have so far? In Torque, particles are billboards, and they are shot out of PENs. However, particles don't just shoot out of PENs. In fact,

[2] Some common particles are billboards, pixels, and lines.

we (the game designers) choose how many particles there are, what kinds of visual effects they have, how fast they shoot, whether they are affected by wind, gravity, etc. All these factors make PENs useful. Most important of all, we can create some awesome effects at a low cost.[3]

8.8.2 Particle Emitter Data Blocks

As I mentioned above, we need to build a few datablocks before we can play with particle emitters. Specifically, we will need a minimum of three datablocks.

- **ParticleEmitterNodeData (PEND).** Think of this as the base for the emitter. It controls one aspect of the particle emitter—time.
- **ParticleEmitterData (PED).** This is used to describe the behavior of the PEN itself. It controls how many particles are emitted, how fast, and in what position/direction.
- **ParticleData (PD).** This describes individual particles. It controls coloration, fade, spin, drag, velocity, acceleration, and whether gravity, particle life, and a few other things affect a particle.

The GPGT Lesson Kit (and the prototype content on the accompanying disk) comes with several predefined particle datablocks, including the following.

- **baseSmokePD0.** A ParticleData datablock used to represent smoke.
- **baseSmokePD1.** A ParticleData datablock used to represent smoke. Uses same parameters as `baseSmokePD0` with new texture.
- **baseFirePD0.** A ParticleData datablock used to represent simple fire.
- **baseFirePD1.** A ParticleData datablock used to represent a nicely animated fire.
- **baseSparkPD0.** A ParticleData datablock used to represent sparks.
- **baseBubblePD0.** A ParticleData datablock used to represent bubbles.
- **baseDustPD0.** A ParticleData datablock used to represent dust.
- **basePED.** A ParticleEmitterData datablock using `baseSmokePD0`.
- **basePEND.** A (default) ParticleEmitterNodeData datablock.

If we wanted to use some of the above datablocks in script, we could do the following:

```
new ParticleEmitterNode(PEN_Test0) {
  position = "0 0 0";
  rotation = "1 0 0 0";
  scale = "1 1 1";
  dataBlock = "basePEND";
  emitter = "basePED";
```

```
    velocity = "1";
};
```

8.8.3 ParticleEmitterNodeData (PEND) Datablock Parameters

The PEND datablock specifies a time multiplier for an individual PEN (Table 8.18). This time is used subsequently in certain calculations, which we'll cover in Section 8.8.7.

8.8.4 ParticleEmitterData (PED) Datablock Parameters

The PED datablock specifies the behavior of a PEN, including what particles it emits, at what rate, in what direction, with how much velocity, and for how long (Table 8.19). It also describes how particles will be oriented.

8.8.5 ParticleData (PD) Datablock Parameters

The PD datablock describes an individual particle, including how things like wind, drag, gravity, and an acceleration factor affect it (Table 8.20). It also describes physical parameters of the particle including color, size, spin, and lifetime. Lastly, it describes advanced features, like alpha inversion and animation.

8.8.6 PEN Parameters

In order to specify a PEN in your mission, you can add it with the World Editor (WE) (**F11**→ **F4**; Mission Objects → environment → particleEmitter), or by hand-editing your mission file. In order to do this, we need to specify the parameters in Table 8.21.

8.8.7 PEN Equations

As promised, I'll describe some important equations below. Armed with these and the subsequent descriptions of theta and phi, orientation, and animation, you should be able to prespecify approximate values before you start to experiment and tune, which should save lots of time.

Parameter	Range	Description
timeMultiple	[0.01 , 100.0]	Time multiplier, used to increase or decrease elapsed time by a ratio. Affects ejection period, ejection position calculation.

Table 8.18.

PEND datablock parameters.

Table 8.19.

PED datablock parameters.

Parameter	Range	Default	Description
ejectionPeriodMS	[1 , inf)	100	Milliseconds between last and next particle ejection.
periodVarianceMS	(0, ejectionPeriodMS]	0	Amount to vary ejection period by.
ejectionVelocity	[0 , inf)	2.0	Initial velocity imparted to particles.
velocityVariance	[0 , ejectionVelocity]	1.0	Amount to vary initial velocity by.
ejectionOffset	[0 , inf]	0.0	Particle ejections begin at ejectionOffset distance from emitter.
thetaMax	[0 , 180] [thetaMin , 180]	90.0	Modifies emitter ejection up and down. This modifies the PEN up vector. 0 = fully up, 180 = fully down
thetaMin	[0 , 180] [0 , thetaMax]	0.0	Modifies emitter ejection up and down. This modifies the PEN up vector. 0 = fully up, 180 = fully down
phiReferenceVel	[0 , 360]	0.0	Causes emission point to rotate clockwise phiReferenceVel degrees per second about the PEN UP vector.
phiVariance	[0 , 360]	360.0	Separate from phiReferenceVal, this parameters enables a random ejection between 0 degrees and phiVariance.
overrideAdvance	false		Always false (legacy code).
orientParticles	[true , false]	false	If true, face emission direction. If false, face camera.
orientOnVelocity	[true , false]	true	If true and if orientParticles == true, face direction of motion. If false, use orientParticles setting.
particles	PD name(s)		List of PD datablocks to use/emit.
lifetimeMS	[0 , inf)	0	Length of time to eject particles before stopping (in milliseconds). lifetimeMS == 0: Always on lifetimeMS > 0: lifetimeMS milliseconds
lifetimeVariance	[0 , lifetimeMS)	0	Amount to vary lifetimeMS by.
useEmitterSizes	false		Not used for PENs. These apply to particle emitters attached to a particle emitter object.
useEmitterColors	false		

Table 8.20.

PD datablock parameters.

Parameter	Range	Default	Description
dragCoefficient	(0.0 , 1.0)	0.0	Factor determining velocity subtracted per second.
windCoefficient	[0.0 , 1.0]	1.0	Percentage of wind vector added to particle vector.
gravityCoefficient	(-inf , inf)	0.0	Gravitational acceleration for particle. Negative values cause particles to rise.
inheritedVelFactor	[0.0 , inf)	0.0	Multiplier determining how much of the PED ejectionVelocity is added to the initial velocity of the particle.
constantAcceleration	(-inf , inf)	0.0	Incremental velocity added to particle velocity on a per-second basis.
lifetimeMS	(100 , inf)	1000.0	Particle life in milliseconds. At the end of its life, the particle is deleted.
lifetimeVarianceMS	(100 , lifetimeMS)	0.0	Amount to vary lifetimeMS by.
spinSpeed	(-10000 , 10000)	0.0	Speed at which particle rotates about its facing vector. Only valid when PED orientParticles == false.
spinRandomMin	(-10000 , 10000)	0.0	Minimum random value added to spinSpeed.
spinRandomMax	(-10000 , 10000)	0.0	Maximum random value added to spinSpeed.
useInvAlpha	true or false	false	Inverts interpretation of texture alpha.
animateTexture	true or false	false	Sequence between additional textures, specified in animTexName[50].
framesPerSec	(1 , 200)	1	Frame frequency for animated textures.
textureName	"Path + File Name"	""	Texture path and filename (PNG only). Must be <= 255 characters long.
animTexName[50]	"Path + File Name"	""	Additional texture path and filenames (PNG only). Used when animateTexture == true. animTexName[0] same as textureName.
colors[4]	"r g b i"	"1.0 1.0 1.0 1.0"	Color interpolation values. Please note that only these values determine particle color. The texture is used as an alpha map, not for coloration.
sizes[4]	[0 , inf)	1	Size interpolation values.
times[4]	[0 , 1]	0.0, 1.0, 1.0, 1.0	Key frames. These affect interpolation rates over life of particle.

Table 8.21.

PEN parameters.

Group	Field Name	Description
Transform	position	Used to set location of PEN.
	rotation	Values have no effect.
	scale	Values have no effect.
Misc	nameTag	Not used by engine.
	dataBlock	PEND datablock name.
	emitter (*Particle data* in WE)	PED datablock name.
	velocity	Initial ejection velocity for this emitter.

Some of the datablocks below produce vectors. Those vectors are calculated from a series of vectors and scalars (from the datablocks and internally from the engine). In order to be clear, I will *italicize vectors* and **bold scalars**. Velocities are in world units per second, and unless otherwise specified, input vectors are unit vectors.

Particle Initial Velocity

Each particle is given an initial velocity vector at ejection time. The velocity vector is determined as follows:

```
emitAxis * PEN.velocity * ejectionAxis * (
PED.ejectionVelocity + PED.velocityVariance * 2.0 *
rand[0.0,1.0] - PED.velocityVariance ).
```

emitAxis is always < 0, 0, 1 > (in practice you can ignore this factor). ejectionAxis depends on orientation, theta, and phi. rand[0.0,1.0] produces a random value between 0 and 1.0.

Particle Post-Ejection Velocity Changes

After being ejected, a particle may or may not have its velocity modified.

```
NextVelocity == CurrentVelocity *
  ( (PD.constantAcceleration * InitialVelocity) -
    (CurrentVelocity * PD.dragCoefficient) -
    (WindVelocity * PD.windCoefficient) +
    (<0.0, -9.81> * PD.gravityCoefficient) )
```

Please note that there is a time delta component not shown.

Particle Lifetime

Particle lifetimes are a simple concept. If a particle is created at time n, at time n + lifetime, the particle will be deleted. Lifetimes affect interpolation, which will describe next. The PD.lifetimeVarianceMS allows us to randomly vary individual lifetimes, which makes things seem less artificial when viewed. Lifetimes are in milliseconds.

```
PD.lifetimeMS + ( rand[-1,1] * PD.lifetimeVarianceMS )
```

8.8.8 Particle Interpolations

Particles are subject to two types of interpolation: color and size. Color interpolation is the ability to modify the particle color over its lifetime. Similarly, size interpolation is the ability to modify the particle size over its lifetime.

Interpolation is controlled by key frames (PD.times[4]), of which Torque allows up to four. The minimum value for a key frame is 0.0, and the maximum value is 1.0. Key frames should be used in order, and unused key frames should be set to 1.0.

This is probably all still sounding rather mysterious, so I'll give some examples and explain what they do.

```
PD.color[0] = "1.0 1.0 1.0 1.0";
PD.color[1] = "1.0 1.0 1.0 0.0";
PD.color[2] = "1.0 1.0 1.0 0.0";
PD.color[3] = "1.0 1.0 1.0 0.0";

PD.size[0] = 1.0;
PD.size[1] = 1.0;
PD.size[2] = 1.0;
PD.size[3] = 1.0;

PD.time[0] = 0.0;
PD.time[1] = 1.0;
PD.time[2] = 1.0; // Unused
PD.time[3] = 1.0; // Unused
```

The above example tells the particle to remain at size 1.0 for its entire lifetime and to fade smoothly from bright white to transparent.

```
PD.color[0] = "1.0 0.2 0.2 1.0";
PD.color[1] = "0.2 1.0 0.2 1.0";
PD.color[2] = "0.0 0.2 1.0 1.0";
PD.color[3] = "0.0 0.2 1.0 1.0";
```

```
PD.size[0] = 0.5;
PD.size[1] = 1.0;
PD.size[2] = 1.5;
PD.size[3] = 2.0;

PD.time[0] = 0.0;
// 1/3 time here framed by time[0] and time[1]
PD.time[1] = 0.33;
// 1/3 time here framed by time[1] and time[2]
PD.time[2] = 0.66;
// 1/3 time here framed by time[2] and time[3]
PD.time[3] = 1.0;
```

The above example causes the particle to smoothly increase from a size of 0.5 to 2.0 over the particle's lifetime. Additionally, the particle's color is interpolated from a shade of red, to green, then to blue, where it stays for the last one-third of its lifetime.

Interpolation takes some practice getting used to, but it's a nice touch that gives us some cool variations on particles.

8.8.9 PEN Lifetimes

Just as particles have lifetimes, so can particle emitter nodes. A PEN can be told to emit particles forever or for a fixed duration.

```
// Emit forever after being created
PED.lifetimeMS = 0;

// Emit for five seconds plus or minus 1.5 seconds
// after being created
PED.lifetimeMS = 5000;
PED.lifetimeVarianceMS = 1500;
```

8.8.10 PEN Particle Ejection Frequency

The PEND and PED datablocks give us three parameters in total to adjust the rate at which particles are emitted.

- **PEND.timeMultiple.** This changes the simulation time versus real time ratio. All events occur in simulation time. With the addition of this parameter, the particle emitter will view time as passing at the rate of PEND. timeMultiple * real time. This feature allows us to use the same PED in two (or more) different emitters and vary the rate of emission. It also gives us a nice way to tune the overall rate of our effects.

- **PED.periodMS.** This is the base time between particle ejections.
- **PED.periodvarianceMS.** This is the amount to vary the base time between ejections.

Given these three parameters, the particle emitter will eject particles at random intervals, where the time between ejections is (1/PEND.timeMultiple) * (PED.periodMS - PED.periodVarianceMS) and (PEND.timeMultiple) * (PED.periodMS + PED.periodVarianceMS). To clarify this, let's look at some examples.

```
// Emit a new particle every 200 milliseconds with no variation
PEND.timeMultiple = 1.0;
PED.periodMS = 200;
PED.periodVarianceMS = 0.0;
```

In the above example, the particle emitter will see time passing at the normal rate, so that one second of real time is equal to one second of simulation time.

```
// Emit a new particle every 400 milliseconds with no variation
PEND.timeMultiple = 0.5;
PED.periodMS = 200;
PED.periodVarianceMS = 0.0;
```

In the above example, the particle emitter will see time passing at half the normal rate, so that two seconds of real time are equal to one second of simulation time.

```
// Emit a new particle every 100 milliseconds +/- 25 ms
PEND.timeMultiple = 2.0;
PED.periodMS = 200;
PED.periodVarianceMS = 50;
```

In the above example, the particle emitter will see time passing at twice the normal rate, so that one second of real time is equal to two seconds of simulation time.

8.8.11 Theta and Phi Explained

ParticleEmitterData has four fields: thetaMin, thetaMax, phiReferenceVel, and phiVariance. Together, they control the direction in which our emitter ejects particles. Although they have scary-sounding names, these fields are really quite easy to use. To show this, let's start with the theta fields, and then we'll discus the phi fields.

Figure 8.18.

Theta ejection vectors.

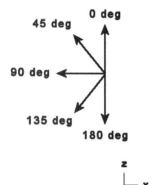

thetaMin **and** thetaMax

Theta controls the up and down of the emitter's ejection vector. Imagine, if you will, that you are standing to the side of an emitter. If we play with the theta parameters, we can make the emitter eject particles anywhere straight up and straight down (Figure 8.18).

Torque supplies the two parameters PED.thetaMin and PED.thetaMax. These act as boundaries. We point the emitter in a specific direction such as 90 degrees (straight out) by setting PED.thetaMin to 90 and PED.thetaMax to 90. Alternatively, if we wish to spread our particles out, we can set PED.thetaMin to 0 and PED.thetaMax to 90. Now, particles will be randomly ejected with an ejection vector pointing between straight up and straight out.

Figure 8.19.

Phi ejection vectors.

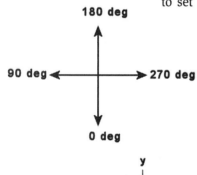

phiReferenceVel **and** phiVariance

Since theta was so simple, you might jump to the conclusion that phi controls the left and right. If you did, you would be both right and wrong. The phi parameters do control the ejection vector's left to right pointing, but not like the theta parameters. Whereas PED.thetaMin and PED.thetaMax were used to set the minimum and maximum up-down ejection angles, our minimum phi angle is always zero degrees and PED.phiVariance controls the upper angle. This means we cannot point our phi in the same way we can theta. (See Figure 8.19.)

So, what about PED.phiReferenceVel? This strange parameter causes the emitter to spin clockwise about its up vector. PED.phiReferenceVel is measured in degrees per second.

OK, let's summarize what the theta and phi parameters do for us. PED.thetaMin and PED.thetaMax allow us to control the up-down pointing of our ejection vector. Furthermore, we can specify a range of up-down positions between which the ejection vector will randomly vary. Next, PED.phiVariance allows us to change the right-left pointing of our ejection vector, but we can only adjust the right direction of the ejection vector. Left is always stuck at 0 degrees. Finally, PED.phiReferenceVel can be used to cause the emitter to spin clockwise about its up vector at phiReferenceVel degrees per second.

8.8.12 Orientation Explained

We've covered orienting the ejection vector, but what about the particle itself? First, remember that the particle is actually a billboard. Initially, I said that these billboards would normally face the camera. The PED orientation parameters give us the ability to choose between various billboard orientations. Table 8.22 summarizes particle orientation options.

PED.orientParticles	PED.orientOnVelocity	Resulting Orientation
false	don't care	**Screen oriented.** Particle always faces screen (camera).
true	false	**Face ejection.** Face along ejection vector.
true	true	**Face motion.** Face along trajectory.

Table 8.22.

Particle orientation options.

8.8.13 Animated Textures

Among the other cool features supported by Torque's particle emitter is the ability to animate a particle via multiple textures. In Torque, you can specify up to 50 separate textures.[4] Then, while the particle is being displayed, Torque will cycle through these images.

It's really quite simple to do this. Take a look at the following example.

[4] If you're willing to edit the engine, you can set this value to anything you want (within reason).

```
PD.animTexName[0] = "~/path_to_texture/texture0";
PD.animTexName[1] = "~/path_to_texture/texture1";
...
PD.animTexName[49] = "~/path_to_texture/texture49";
PD.framesPerSec = 1; // Play one frame per second
```

In the above example, we've specified 50 distinct textures for use in our sequence. Then, we specified that they must be played one (frame) per second. When the sequence gets to the end, it will begin to repeat. It's really that simple.

8.8.14 Multiple Particles?

You might recall that we could specify more than one particle for the `PED.particles` parameter. If you specify multiple particles for an emitter's PED, the emitter will eject the particles in order and then repeat. The following reasonable questions arise.

1. How do I specify more than one PD?

2. How many can I specify?

Here are three examples of the syntax for specifying three particles for a PED.

```
particles = PD_Name0 TAB PD_Name1 TAB PD_Name2;
// OR
particles = PD_Name0 SPC PD_Name1 SPC PD_Name2;
// OR
particles = "PD_Name0 PD_Name1 PD_Name2";
```

Basically, `PED.particles` needs to be a whitespace-separated string of PD names. You may specify as many particles as you need.

8.8.15 Holy Popping Particles!

An interesting problem I initially had while playing with particles was a disturbing popping effect when the particles' `PD.lifetimeMS` limit was hit. This can have several sources, but if you study the effect, it should be apparent that the cause is simply the fact that a very visible object is suddenly popping out of existence.

To make this transition subtler, just use the particle interpolation parameters. Here are some suggestions:

- Be sure your interpolations are smooth; i.e., don't use values like 0.1, 0.5, 0.6, 1.0 unless you are looking for a shuddering effect.
- Fade particles by lowering the fourth `PD.colors` parameter (which represents intensity or alpha) over the lifetime of the particle.
- Shrink particles in the latter part of their life.

8.8.16 Can I Mount Emitters?

A common question in the forums is, "Can I attach an emitter to my XYZ?" Unfortunately, you may not attach a particle emitter to an arbitrary shape or node in a shape. Many shapes provide specialized nodes for particular emitter effects, but TGE does not support arbitrary mounting of particle emitters.

8.8.17 Can I Move Emitters?

Another question I often see is, "Can I move an emitter after I place it?" Often, the answer I see given to this questions is, "No." However, this is not true. There is a way to move particle emitters. If you want to move a particle emitter after it is placed in the world, do the following.

1. Store the ID of the emitter you want to move in a global variable or in another appropriate location.
2. In script, modify the `position` field of the particle emitter node. Yes, modify the `position` field.
3. Last, to move the PEN, simply rescale the PEN, using its current scale.

```
$myPEN =      // ... create the PEN and store its ID
$myPEN.position = "10 10 10";
              // We want to move to < 10 10 10 >
$myPEN.setScale( $myPEN.getScale() );
```

Sure, it's a bit of a hack, but it gets the job done.

8.8.18 Maze Runner Lesson #12 (90 Percent Step)—Teleport Station Effect

If you are building the Maze Runner game while you read this guide, we are now going to create the datablocks for a set of particle emitters that will be used later to mark the position of our teleport stations.

We will need three distinct versions of this emitter. So, our strategy will be to create a base ParticleData datablock and a base ParticleEmitterData datablock using the previous ParticleData datablock. Then, we will use the inheritance feature of TorqueScript to create two copies of each datablock with minor modifications. This will give us a total of six datablocks. For the ParticleEmitterNodeData datablock, we'll just use the `basePEND` datablock that comes with this guide.

Copy Required Files

From the accompanying disk, please copy the file "\MazeRunner\Lesson_012\ teleporters.cs" into the directory "\MazeRunner\prototype\server\scripts\ MazeRunner".

Now, edit the function `onServerCreated()` in the file "\MazeRunner\ prototype\server\game.cs" to look like the following (bold lines are new or modified).

```
exec("./MazeRunner/mazerunnerplayer.cs"); // MazeRunner
exec("./MazeRunner/teleporters.cs"); // MazeRunner
```

ParticleData (TeleportStation_PD0)

We want our particles to be nebulous particles of medium size with a red, green, or blue coloration.

```
datablock ParticleData(TeleportStation_PD0) {
  dragCoefficient = 0.0;
  gravityCoefficient = -0.50;
  inheritedVelFactor = 0.0;
  constantAcceleration = 0.0;
  lifetimeMS = 400;
  lifetimeVarianceMS = 100;
  useInvAlpha = false;
  textureName = "~/data/GPGTBase/particletextures/smoke";
  colors[0] = "0.7 0.1 0.1 0.8";
  colors[1] = "0.7 0.1 0.1 0.4";
  colors[2] = "0.7 0.1 0.1 0.0";
  sizes[0] = 0.1;
  sizes[1] = 0.3;
```

You may have noticed that the Teleport-Station_PD0 datablock definition only supplied array elements 0, 1, and 2 for of each of the colors[], sizes[], and times[] arrays. You may wonder why I did not specify array index three for each of these arrays. The reason for this is simple. Interpolation occurs between times 0.0 and 1.0, and since times[2] is defined as 1.0, the interpolation will automatically stop when it gets to colors[2], sizes[2], and times[2]. This is not to say that we could make times[3] less than 1.0 and add more entries, but rather that we don't need to use all of the array elements.

Game Elements

```
      sizes[2] = 0.3;
      times[0] = 0.0;
      times[1] = 0.5;
      times[2] = 1.0;
};
```

As can be seen,

- this particle will float upward since it has a negative gravity coefficient;
- it has a short lifetime between 300 and 500 milliseconds;
- the particle it uses is nebulous (see negative image in Figure 8.20);
- it fades from medium red to dark red evenly; and
- it starts off small and triples in size over time.

ParticleEmitterData (TeleportStation_PED0)

```
datablock ParticleEmitterData(TeleportStation_PED0) {
    ejectionPeriodMS = 1;
    periodVarianceMS = 0;
    ejectionVelocity = 2.0;
    ejectionOffset = 0.5;
    velocityVariance = 0.5;
    thetaMin = 0;
    thetaMax = 80;
    phiReferenceVel = 0;
    phiVariance = 360;
    overrideAdvance = false;
    particles = "TeleportStation_PD0";
};
```

As can be seen,

- this particle emitter ejects a new particle every millisecond, meaning we'll have up to 500 particles alive at any time (per emitter);
- it ejects particles at 1.5 to 2.5 world units per second starting at the center to 0.5 world units out;
- the ejection vector will be anywhere about the center and starts from slightly upward to straight up; and
- of course, it uses the particle we just made.

Duplicate Datablocks

The last step before trying these emitters out is to duplicate them so we have three sets. As you can see when looking at the code, we have taken advantage of TGE's datablock inheritance:

Figure 8.20.

Smoke particle

```
datablock ParticleData(TeleportStation_PD1 : TeleportStation_PD0 ) {
  colors[0] = "0.1 0.7 0.1 0.8";
  colors[1] = "0.1 0.7 0.1 0.4";
  colors[2] = "0.1 0.7 0.1 0.0";
};

datablock ParticleEmitterData(TeleportStation_PED1 : TeleportStation_PED0 ) {
  particles = "TeleportStation_PD1";
};

datablock ParticleData(TeleportStation_PD2 : TeleportStation_PD0 ) {
  colors[0] = "0.1 0.1 0.7 0.8";
  colors[1] = "0.1 0.1 0.7 0.4";
  colors[2] = "0.1 0.1 0.7 0.0";
};

datablock ParticleEmitterData(TeleportStation_PED2 : TeleportStation_PED0 ) {
  particles = "TeleportStation_PD2";
};
```

We only needed to change the particle colors and to use the correct particle
in our new emitters.

Testing the Emitters

We're not ready to use these emitters in our game, but we should test them.
Do the following.

1. Start up your Maze Runner prototype.

2. Load the "Maze Runner" mission.

3. Use the Creator to place a particle emitter (Mission Objects → Environment
   → ParticleEmitter).

4. Give the emitter (node) any name you like.

5. Use the `basePEND` ParticleEmitterNodeData datablock.

6. Select one of the three ParticleEmitterData datablocks we just examined
   (Figure 8.21).

ParticleEmitter Dialog Settings

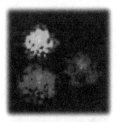

Resultant Emitters

Figure 8.21.
Testing the emitters.

8.9 fxShapeReplicator & fxFoliageReplicator

These two replicators are birds of a feather and are both created by Melvin May. Their purposes are multifold:

- allowing multiple objects to be placed automatically and randomly within specified bounds,
- allowing this to be done in such a way as to make the scene look more organic (i.e., not artificial), and
- reducing the network transmission cost of multiple related objects to that of a single object plus a few additional parameters.

Melvin May has managed to do this quite successfully, very much to the appreciation of Torque users. Furthermore, his fx objects are, for the most part, easy to understand and use.

Before we get into the usage of these two replicators, I'll give a succinct list of all parameters for both the fxShapeReplicator and the fxFoliageReplicator. To save space and due to the common nature of these replicators, I'll combine their parameters into one list, indicating when a parameter exists in the shape replicator but not the foliage replicator, or vice versa.

8.9.1 Replicator Features

The replicators have the following features:

- **Directed random placement.** Using a tricky inner- and outer-ellipse affordance, you can direct Torque to replicate a specific number of objects in random locations within a clearly defined area.
- **Multiple toggleable placement restrictions.** Because random placement wouldn't be any good if you couldn't specify rules for where to place and not to place, the replicator mission objects both have a slew of toggleable tests for placing objects.
- **Dimension and orientation controls.** In order to make a scene more organic, you can provide metrics that will allow objects to be randomly sized and oriented within set bounds.
- **Advanced culling.** The foliage replicator provides the ability to tune the culling algorithm. The culling algorithm is responsible for choosing when to render objects and directly affects frame rate. The ability to fine tune this is a real plus.
- **Animation and lighting.** Foliage can be both animated and lit (or self-lit). You have direct control over how this is done.

8.9.2 Placing Replicators

Replicators are placed much like any other item in the world. You just drag them and drop them where you wish them to be. The location of the replicator

Position	Can Place Here?
Inside area defined by `InnerRadiusX` and `InnerRadiusY`?	No
Inside area defined by `OuterRadiusX` and `OuterRadiusY`, **and** outside area defined by `InnerRadiusX` and `InnerRadiusY`?	Yes
Outside area defined by `OuterRadiusX` and `OuterRadiusY`?	No

Table 8.23.

Replicator placement rules.

can be the center of a placement target. The size and shape of this target are controlled by the inner and outer radius parameters. These parameters can be used to create two ellipsoidal areas. If we ignore restrictions for a moment, placement rules simply become those shown in Table 8.23.

8.9.3 Replicator Visual Feedback

Melvin May has supplied a nice visual feedback mechanism for seeing where the shapes will and will not be placed.

Examining the image in Figure 8.22, we can see two ellipses that were created with the following settings.

- `InnerRadiusX == 5, OuterRadiusX == 25`
- `InnerRadiusY == 15, OuterRadiusY == 20`

If you look closely, you will see that objects are randomly placed in the area outside inner ellipse and inside outer ellipse.

8.9.4 Seeds

A very important aspect of replicators is that they will produce the same result each time they are used as long as they are given the same `Seed`. The `Seed` is used as an input to a random number generator. This generator is used to produce and place all objects associated with the replicator.

8.9.5 Replicant Count

You may select how many objects you wish to replicate using either the `ShapeCount` or the `FoliageCount` parameter, depending upon which replicator you are using. It is important to understand that this is a theoretical maximum, not the guaranteed number of objects you will get.

8.9.6 Placement Restrictions (Restraints)

Besides the ellipses and the position, what else controls placement? There is a nice set of "knobs" with which we can tune placement rules. These are called restrictions or restraints in the foliage and shape replicators, respectively. Their names are pretty self-explanatory, but just in case, I'll explicitly spell out their use in Table 8.24 and show an example in Figure 8.23.

Figure 8.22.

Visual feedback of replicator.

Table 8.24.

Restrictions and restraints.

Restriction / Restraint	Result
AllowOnTerrain	If this is set to `true`, objects can be placed on terrain if present.
AllowOnInteriors	If this is set to `true`, objects can be placed on interiors (buildings, etc) if present.
AllowOnStatics	If this is set to `true`, objects can be placed on other shapes if present. This means that if you are using the fxShapeReplicator, it is possible to have objects get stacked on top of each other by a replicator. See Figure 8.23.
AllowedTerrainSlope	When objects are placed on terrain, they will not be placed on areas with a slope greater than or equal to this value.

AllowOnWater	AllowWaterSurface	AllowOnTerrain	Result
false	–	–	Objects cannot be placed in areas with water.
true	true	–	Objects can be placed on surface of water.
true	false	true	Objects can be placed on terrain below water.

Figure 8.23.

Stacked shapes
(`AllowOnStatics ==`
`true`).

In addition to the restraints listed in Table 8.24, fxShape-Replicators offer three additional parameters. `AlignToTerrain` causes shapes that are placed on terrain to align to the terrain's up vector. Furthermore, you can adjust how this alignment occurs by adjusting the parameter `TerrainAlignment`, which is a 3-value vector. Lastly, you can enable or disable shape collision boxes by setting `Interactions` to `true` or `false`, respectively.

Interactions Must Be True for Collisions

We just covered this, but I must restate it nonetheless. If you have the `Interactions` field set to `false`, collisions for fxShapes are turned *off*. A lot of new users have this problem and complain about it vociferously in the forums. I'm here to save you the embarrassment of being told, "Set the `Interactions` field to `true`. Duh." Hey, nobody is perfect.

8.9.7 Retries

Well, with all these rules determining whether an object can be placed, you must wonder what the replicator does if it finds it can't place an object. Well, just like you or me, it tries again. You can control the number of attempts the replicator will make per object with the `FoliageRetries` or `ShapeRetries` parameter. Why not just try until an object can be successfully placed, you ask? Consider the case in which there is no legal place left to put an object. In this case, without a retry limit, the replicator would attempt to place objects forever.

8.9.8 Foliage Dimensions

We've finished talking about the common attributes between the fxFoliage-Replicator and the fxShapeReplicator. Now let's jump into some of the additional features offered by the fxFoliageReplicator. Because we're going to be using the same image over and over to simulate some kind of foliage feature, we'd like an inexpensive way to make these images seem different. The dimension parameters give us this. For example, let's say we choose the following settings.

```
FixSizeToMax == false      MinWidth == 0.5     MaxWidth == 1.5
FixAspectRatio == false    MinHeight == 0.5    MaxHeight = 2.0
RandomFlip == true
```

What we would get are billboards that are randomly between 0.5 and 1.5 times their default width and 0.5 and 2.0 times their default height. Additionally, the image may be randomly flipped around its vertical axis (i.e., flipped horizontally). This flipping will be useful if we have a nonsymmetric image. So, what about that aspect ratio business? Well, if you are familiar with texture mapping, you will understand that without maintaining the proper aspect ratio, images may look stretched. The `FixAspectRatio` parameter forces the randomly selected height/width to be a fixed multiple of the original. Some example images in Figure 8.24 show what I'm talking about.

Figure 8.24.

Maintaining the aspect ratio.

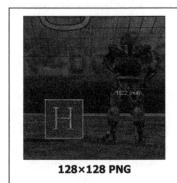  

| **128×128 PNG** | **Same PNG 2X Height**
FixAspectRatio == false | **Same PNG 2X Height**
FixAspectRatio == true |

Lastly, let's discuss `OffsetZ`. This is helpful to fix little issues you run into where the texture may be slightly embedded or slightly above a surface. If this happens, just increase or decrease `OffsetZ` slightly until the problem is fixed.

8.9.9   Shape Dimensions and Rotation

fxShapeReplicators allow you to adjust the dimension and rotation of shapes with the parameters in the Object Transforms group. You can allow random scaling by setting `ShapeScaleMin` and `ShapeScaleMax` accordingly. Additionally, you can allow for random rotation by setting `ShapeRotationMin` and `ShapeRotationMax` to nonzero values. Values are chosen between the minimum and the maximum on a per-axis basis. Finally, `OffsetZ` is offered under the group for fxShapeReplicators and has the same purpose as noted above.

8.9.10   Foliage Culling

Of all the attributes in the fxFoliageReplicator, the culling parameters were the least intuitive to me. So, before we jump into them, perhaps a quick description of view culling is in order.

View Culling

If you think about it for a moment, it will be apparent that it would be highly inefficient to render all objects in a mission, when only a small fraction of them are in a position to be visible. In reality, the objects in front of the camera are the only objects that we really need to render. This set of objects is called the potentially visible set (PVS). There are many ways to build a PVS. In the case of fxFoliageReplicators, when the `useCulling` parameter is `false`, each billboard is individually tested for visibility. In the case of a small set of billboards, this is probably the most efficient way to cull. However, once you have a large number of objects, this method quickly begins to consume too much CPU time.

Quadculling

At this point, you should consider turning on culling by setting `useCulling` to `true`. Now, culling is tested against a set of quads instead of individual billboards. A quad is a rectangular area (usually a square) with a fixed dimension. In the case of quadculling, a specified area is subdivided into multiple quads. Each object that is within an area defined by a quad is algorithmically associated with that quad. Objects that cross borders between quads are assigned to each quad they touch. Finally, if a quad is deemed to be visible,

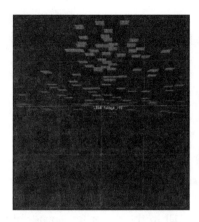 

Figure 8.25.
Visible feedback for culling.

all objects associated with that quad are marked as visible and subsequently rendered. The images in Figure 8.25 are taken from an in-game shot to demonstrate what the visible feedback for quadculling looks like. They demonstrate the discussion thus far.

Configuring (Quad) Culling

I'm sure that this is all just fascinating, but it still leaves us with the dilemma of how to choose whether to cull, and then if we choose to cull, how to set up our culling. Unfortunately, the number of factors involved turns this more into an art than a science, and the final test is always going to be frame rate. However, I'll supply some rules of thumb to help you out in your choice.

To Cull or Not to Cull

- Do not use culling for small sets (1–100) of billboards.
- Generally, it is better to use culling if the total billboards number at least two to three times the number of quads (accounts for overhead associated with algorithm).
- For a large number of objects (hundreds to thousands) spread over a large area (one quarter of map or more), it is best to use culling.
- Culling will not help much if your objects are not evenly distributed between the quads.

Selecting a `CullResolution`

- Select your `CullResolution` such that the number of objects comes out to at least two to three times the number of quads.
- Select your `CullResolution` such that it can evenly divide `OuterRadiusX` and `OuterRadiusY`. You may need to adjust these slightly to assist this process. Powers of two are nicest, if possible.

Testing Efficiency of Culling

As noted above, the best way to test the efficiency of your culling is to check your average frame rate. An easy (if possibly slightly inaccurate) way of doing this is the following.

1. Get out of Mission Editor Mode.
2. Start the console (~).
3. Type: `metrics(fps);`.
4. Exit the console (~).
5. Walk/fly around your scene and observe your frame rate. Look for hot spots where it dips.

The `metrics(fps);` command will create a GUI in the upper left corner of the screen, showing frame rate and mspf (milliseconds per frame). This GUI will be shut off when you start the Mission Editor and does not render properly while it is running.

Additionally, after hitting Apply (when setting your culling parameters), you can get additional data from the console (~). Each time you hit Apply, something like the following is printed in the console.

```
fxFoliageReplicator - Lev: 3 PotNodes: 85 Used: 58
                      Objs: 656 Time: 0.0016s
fxFoliageReplicator - Approx 0.06Mb allocated.
```

From this, we can see that the culling level is 3, which means it is a $2^3 \times 2^3$ (8×8) set of quads. The quads are approximately 58/85, or 68 percent, utilized (i.e., billboards are in 68 percent of the testable nodes). There are a total of 656 objects (500 billboards and 156 phantom objects due to retries). It takes about 16 milliseconds to build and render the fxObject. And finally, the entire fxObject takes up about 0.06 MB.

Other Culling Features

In addition to quadculling, there are some other features in the culling parameters section, specifically the view, fade, and alpha parameters. These parameters are not affected by the `useCull` parameter and are always on.

`ViewDistance` and `FadeInRegion` work together to determine when an object begins to fade into view and when it is fully faded in. These two parameters form concentric spheres around the camera, where `ViewDistance` defines the radius of the inner sphere and `FadeInRegion + ViewDistance` defines the radius of the outer sphere. When an object is at the perimeter of the outer sphere, it will begin to become visible, fading completely in at the perimeter of the inner sphere. If you wish your objects to stop rendering at an alpha greater than 0.0, you can cause this to happen by setting `AlphaCutoff` to the desired alpha, between 0.0 and 1.0. See Table 8.25 and Figure 8.26.

ViewClosest and FadeOutRegion also work together, but their effect is the opposite of ViewDistance and FadeInRegion. Conversely, these two parameters are used to determine when an object begins to fade out of view and then become fully transparent or not rendered. Again, these two parameters form concentric spheres around the camera, where ViewClosest defines the radius of the inner sphere and FadeOutRegion + ViewClosest defines the radius of the outer sphere. When an object is at the perimeter of the outer sphere it will begin to fade, fading completely out at the perimeter of the inner sphere. See Table 8.26 and Figure 8.27.

Billboard's Distance to Camera	Render?
Distance > ViewDistance + FadeInRegion	no
ViewDistance < Distance < ViewDistance + FadeInRegion	yes (if alpha > AlphaCutoff)
ViewDistance < Distance	yes

Table 8.25.

Using ViewDistance and FadeInRegion.

Figure 8.26.

ViewDistance and FadeInRegion.

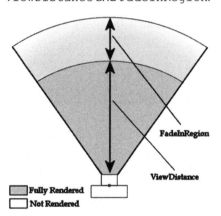

Figure 8.27.

ViewClosest and FadeOutRegion.

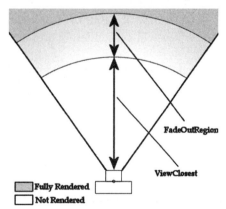

Billboard's Distance to Camera	Render?
Distance > ViewClosest + FadeOutRegion	yes
ViewClosest < Distance < ViewClosest + FadeOutRegion	yes (if alpha > AlphaCutoff)
ViewClosest < Distance	no

Table 8.26.

Using ViewClosest and FadeOutRegion.

You may wonder why you would want to do this. Consider the case where you are in a vehicle. Fading out will keep objects from suddenly being inside the vehicle.

Last, I'll mention `GroundAlpha`. This parameter can be used to force the bottom of billboards to have a lower alpha value. This can be used to moderate the harsh intersection between billboards and the ground, giving the transition a cleaner look. Just set it to a value lower than 1.0 to see its effect. Adjust it until you are pleased with the end result.

8.9.11 Foliage Animation

Foliage animation is a feature that allows us to make a more interesting and convincing scene. Consider the case where your foliage is long grass and fronds. Wouldn't it be more realistic if the grass and fronds blew in the wind? Yes, of course it would be, but how do we achieve this look? With foliage animation, of course!

Setting `SwayOn` to `true` will enable the animation. You may cause your billboards to sway side-to-side or and front-to-back using the `SwayMagSide` and `SwayMagFront` parameters, respectively. Furthermore, you can add a little spice to the swaying by allowing the sway times to vary between `MinSwayTime` and `MaxSwayTime`. Last, you may choose to enable `SwaySync`, where all objects will sway together in the same way, or you may disable it and all objects will sway on their own pattern.

One word of caution. If billboards sway so much that they touch each other, you will get rendering artifacts.

8.9.12 Foliage Lighting

Foliage lighting is the last parameter group we will discuss. It is another group that is used to make the scene look more interesting. With these parameters, you may enable self-lighting (`LightOn`). Furthermore, if you set `LightSync` to `false` and give different values for `MinLuminance` and `MaxLuminance`, each billboard will be self-lit with its own randomly selected level of light.

Please note that this lighting can be animated. If all of the above lighting parameters are set as noted and then you set `lightTime` to a nonzero value, each billboard's lighting will vary over time. `lightTime` is the time for a fade in one direction. So, to fade from `MaxLuminance` to `MinLuminance` back to `MaxLuminance` will require (`lightTime` * 2) seconds.

8.10 fxSunlight

As previously mentioned, the Sun object controls scene lighting and fxSunlight provides the ability to have a visible sun(s) in the sky. Upon first inspection, this mission object may seem a bit daunting, with its myriad parameters (lerps, animations, etc), but it is really quite easy to use. You've got to hand it to Melvin May, though. He hardly makes a resource without a "few" options.

8.10.1 fxSunlight Features

fxSunlight has the following features.

- **Local flare.** A bitmap representing the lens flare of a camera.
- **Remote flare.** A bitmap representing the sun itself.
- **Position/orientation parameters.** To make life easy, the fxSunlight parameters that control its position are similarly named to those found in the Sun mission object: namely, `azimuth` and `altitude`.
- **Animations.** Just about every characteristic of the fxSunlight object can be animated. Furthermore, the animation system is a very flexible key-based animation system.

8.10.2 Adding a New fxSunlight

1. Start the Creator.
2. Find and click Mission Objects → environment → fxSunlight.
3. Enter a name for this Sun in the pop-up box. (e.g., "Smiley").
4. Click OK.

At this point, if you look around, you should see the default fxSunlight. Now, do the following.

5. Switch to the Inspector.
6. Locate your new sun ("Smiley").
7. Select it.

8.10.3 Changing the Sun Images

fxSunlight has two texture parameters.

- `Media` → `LocalFlareBitmap`
  - This texture represents a lens-flare effect.
  - If you do not wish to have this effect, just clear this parameter.
  - This texture will render if it is in line of sight. If it is blocked by terrain or an object, it stops rendering.
  - It is best to use a texture with an alpha layer.
- `Media` → `RemoteFlareBitmap`
  - This texture represents the sun itself.
  - It, too, can be disabled, just by clearing this parameter.

327

- Unlike the local flare, this texture renders all the time, although the terrain and objects can occlude it.
- Again, it is best to use a texture with an alpha layer.

Note that you should make both textures the same way; that is, if one has an alpha layer, the second one should too.

8.10.4 Positioning the Sun (Render Position)

Unlike most mission objects, the standard position, rotation, and scale are meaningless and do not control where the fxSunlight object is rendered. However, there is a marker at `Transform` → `position`. I would just select a value for this such that the marker does not get in your way while editing.

Render position, when it is not being animated, is based on the same two concepts as those used for the Sun object, azimuth and elevation. If you do not understand these concepts, I suggest you quickly reread the Sun object description in Section 8.5.

- `SunOrbit` → `SunAzimuth`
  - This controls the horizontal angle of the fxSunlight effect's bearing about the *z*-axis.
  - Legal values: [0, 360).
  - Make this the same as Sun → `Misc` → `azimuth`.
- `SunOrbit` → `SunElevation`
  - In simple terms, this controls the elevation, but in reality, this is a polar angle. Again, if you don't understand this, see the Sun object description in Section 8.5.
  - Legal values: [–90, 90].
  - Make this the same as Sun → `Misc` → `elevation`.

8.10.5 Changing Lens Flare Effects

You can modify various effects, such as the following.

- `LensFlare` → `FlareTP`. If this is not checked, the lens flare will not render in 3rd POV.
- `LensFlare` → `Colour` (**r g b i**)
  - If you find a white lens flare boring, you can give it a different fixed color with this parameter.
  - Each individual value can be between 0.0 and 1.0.
  - Intensity has no effect.

- LensFlare → Brightness
  - You can set a fixed brightness with this parameter.
  - Legal values: [0.0, 1.0].
- LensFlare → FlareSize
  - This parameter can be used to scale the flare size to your preference.
  - This modifies the size of the sun, too.
  - Legal values: (0.0, inf).
- LensFlare → FadeTime
  - This parameter determines how long it takes the lens flare to fade away when it is occluded. Remember, occlusion turns it off.
  - Legal values: [0.0, inf).
- LensFlare → BlendMode. Understand that the flare is rendered, meaning it needs to be blended with the prior contents of the frame buffer. To accommodate various effects, fxSunlight supports three blending modes [0 .. 2].
  - **0.** glBlendFunc(GL_SRC_ALPHA, GL_ONE)
    Flare < r g b a > replaces frame buffer < r g b a >.
  - **1.** glBlendFunc(GL_SRC_ALPHA, GL_ONE_MINUS_SRC_ALPHA)
    Flare < r g b a > is linearly blended with the frame buffer < r g b a >.
  - **2.** glBlendFunc(GL_ONE, GL_ONE)
    Flare < r g b a > is added to frame buffer < r g b a >.

If you stopped right now, you would know 90 percent of what you need to know about the fxSunlight object. However, if you want to do some really cool things, like animate the color, brightness, and size, or if you want it to rotate and to move around over time, then continue reading.

8.10.6 Animating the Sun and Lens Flare

Now that we have an fxSunlight object set up, we can make it more interesting by animating some of the sun and lens flare effects. However, before we take a brief tour of the fxSunlight animations, let's discuss some common animation parameters.

Animation Overview

The fxSunlight animations are all similar in nature. So, we'll discuss how they work in general and then limit our discussion to specifics for each in the following pages.

Animations provide the parameters in Table 8.27. Tables 8.28–8.33 list the specific parameters for color, brightness, rotation, size, azimuth, and elevation, respectively.

Table 8.27.

Animation parameters.

Generic Parameter	Purpose
Enable Option	The names of these fields vary, but they all have the same purpose. They are Boolean values enabling or disabling animation for this fxSunlight feature.
LERP Enable	The LERP enables are Boolean values, enabling linearly interpolated (smooth) vs. noninterpolated (stepped) transitions.
Single Key Enable	Only color animation supports this feature. If this Boolean field is set to `true`, the colour animation will use its corresponding `RedKey` for all colour animations.
Min and Max Values (Extents)	These values define the outer limits of the animation range for this particular feature. Their types are feature-specific.
Key String(s)	Each animation has at least one key string, and some may have more. These keys are used for determining how the animation transitions occur. Key strings contain the letters *a* through *z*, where *a* is the beginning of a sequence and *z* is the end.
Animation Time	This floating-point value is used to define how long the animation takes to play in seconds and fractions of a second. This time is the round-trip time, i.e., Begin → End → Begin.

Table 8.28.

Color animation.

Generic Parameter	Specific Parameter
Enable Option	`AnimColour`
LERP Enable	`LerpColour`
Single Key Enable	`SingleColourKeys`
Min and Max Values (Extents)	`MinColour, MaxColour` (four-element floating-point vector)
Key String(s)	`RedKeys, BlueKeys, GreenKeys`
Animation Time	`ColourTime`

Table 8.29.

Brightness animation.

Generic Parameter	Specific Parameter
Enable Option	`AnimBrightness`
LERP Enable	`LerpBrightness`
Min and Max Values (Extents)	`MinBrightness, MaxBrightness` (floating-point)
Key String(s)	`BrightnessKeys`
Animation Time	`BrightnessTime`

Generic Parameter	Specific Parameter
Enable Option	`AnimRotation`
LERP Enable	`LerpRotation`
Min and Max Values (Extents)	`MinRotation, MaxRotation` (floating-point)
Key String(s)	`RotationKeys`
Animation Time	`RotationTime`

Table 8.30.
Rotation animation.

Generic Parameter	Specific Parameter
Enable Option	`AnimSize`
LERP Enable	`LerpSize`
Min and Max Values (Extents)	`MinSize, MaxSize` (floating-point)
Key String(s)	`SizeKeys`
Animation Time	`SizeTime`

Table 8.31.
Size animation.

Generic Parameter	Specific Parameter
Enable Option	`AnimAzimuth`
LERP Enable	`LerpAzimuth`
Min and Max Values (Extents)	`MinAzimuth, MaxAzimuth` (floating-point)
Key String(s)	`AzimuthKeys`
Animation Time	`AzimuthTime`

Table 8.32.
Azimuth animation.

Generic Parameter	Specific Parameter
Enable Option	`AnimElevation`
LERP Enable	`LerpElevation`
Min and Max Values (Extents)	`MinElevation, MaxElevation` (floating-point)
Key String(s)	`ElevationKeys`
Animation Time	`ElevationTime`

Table 8.33.
Elevation animation.

8.10.7 Maze Runner Lesson #13 (10 Percent Step)—Celestial Bodies

If you are building the Maze Runner game while you read this guide, we are now going to create some celestial bodies to go with our game. I have to apologize, but the celestial bodies we will implement are just too darn big (in terms of code) to show in the book. Instead, I will summarize their behaviors here and allow you to look at the scripts yourself.

Loading the Celestial Bodies

The celestial bodies example as been created for you. To add it to the Maze Runner mission, follow these steps:

1. Open the file "\MazeRunner\prototype\data\missions\mazerunner.mis".
2. Open the file "\MazeRunner\Lesson_013\CelestialBodies.cs" and copy the contents into your copy buffer (like you are doing a copy-paste operation).
3. Paste the data you just copied into the "mazerunner.mis" file before the following lines:

```
};
//--- OBJECT WRITE END ---
```

Now, you can restart your Maze Runner prototype, load the Maze Runner mission, and you should see three celestial bodies in the sky.

Dying Star

The first celestial body is the "Dying Star." This celestial body is designed to represent a sun in our game-world solar system. This sun is approaching the end of its life and has shifted from yellow to red. To create the effect of a sun with moving sunspots, I have animated the brightness, the coloration, the size, and the rotation. Together with the image we are using for the sun, it may give the illusion of an active sun surface.

Far Planet

The next celestial body is the "Far Planet." This celestial body is designed to represent a distant planet in our game-world solar system. It is stationary relative to the planet we are on.

Near Moon

The last celestial body is the "Near Moon." This celestial body is designed to represent a moon rotating about our planet. Its azimuth changes slowly over time; during this transition, it rises and falls in the sky.

8.11 Physical Zones (P-zones)

Physical zones are one of those simple, "Gee whiz, ain't that cool" kinds of constructs. In fact, of all the standard Torque mission objects, these are probably my favorite. Physical Zones, or p-zones for short, allow you to define areas in your game with modified gravity and/or velocity modifiers and/or an applied force. First, we will cover the very few parameters p-zones have, and then we'll leap right in.

8.11.1 `velocityMod`

The `velocityMod` attribute does pretty much what it sounds like it will do. Let's say we have a p-zone with a `velocityMod` of 2. If the player enters the

p-zone with a velocity of 10.0 world units per second, that player will leave the zone with a velocity of 20.0 world units per second. Actually, the velocity modification is instantaneous, occurring directly after entering the p-zone (Figure 8.28). It should be noted that there are some

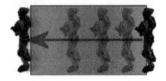

Figure 8.28.

Example of `velocityMod`.

issues with extraordinarily high `velocityMod` values. If the multiplier is too high, the engine can freeze for long periods or even crash. So, my suggestion is to keep the values low while you experiment. The upper bounds of [-40.0, 40.0] are really too high for most practical uses.

8.11.2 `gravityMod`

The `gravityMod` attribute specifies a local (area inside p-zone) gravity multiplier. In other words, if `gravityMod` is –2 and the game gravity is set to 1.0, then when the player enters the p-zone, the player will float upward (Figure 8.29). If the player has enough forward velocity upon entering the p-zone, the player will end up "skipping" across the p-zone until the player falls off the end or encounters an obstacle. Be careful with 0 or negative gravity zones. If the player gets stuck with his feet off the ground, he will be unable to move. Again, high values can cause problems for the engine. Caution is the word.

Figure 8.29.

Example of `gravityMod`.

8.11.3 appliedForce

Finally, we have the `appliedForce` vector. This attribute allows you to create an area where an invisible force will be applied to the character. This force can point in an arbitrary direction with a variable strength (Figure 8.30).

Table 8.34 shows values and their effects on the character while on a flat surface.

Table 8.34

Effects of `appliedForce` values.

0–99	100–399	400–1999	5000	40000
Practically no movement.	Sorta slides along.	Forced walk	Forced run	Can you say cannon?

Figure 8.30.

Example of `appliedForce`.

8.11.4 Maze Runner Lesson #14 (90 Percent Step)—Teleport Stopper

When the player runs into a teleport station, we'd like the avatar to be stopped. To do this, we can use a p-zone set up as follows.

```
%pzone = new PhysicalZone() {
  position = vectorAdd( "1 -1 0" , %Obj.getPosition() );
  rotation = "1 0 0 0";
  scale = "2 2 4";
  velocityMod = "0";
  gravityMod = "1";
  appliedForce = "0 0 0";
  polyhedron = "0 0 0 1 0 0 0 -1 0 0 0 1";
};
```

As can be seen, this code is meant to be script-driven; that is, we'll be substituting values in for `position` when we drop the object into the world.

The key things to notice are the following.

1. The `position` is offset by a vector (we haven't discussed `vectorAdd()` yet, but it adds two vectors and returns the result). The reason for this is that the polygon used to define the `polyhedron` field is offset. Its corner is at the origin, and therefore the cube is not centered. This can be corrected either by changing the `polyhedron` values or by offsetting while placing. I chose the latter.

2. `velocityMod` is set to zero. This means that shapes entering the p-zone should stop moving.

That is pretty much all for now. Later (Lesson #15, "Teleport Triggers"), we'll use this code in our teleporter-building scripts.

8.12 fxLight

This is another one of those fun mission objects provided by Melvin May. It is similar to the fxSunlight object, but instead of representing a sun, it is used to represent in-game lights. Unlike fxSunlight, this object casts light in the scene. It renders a representation of the light-source flare and casts light on terrain and other objects.

One major difference between fxLight and fxSunlight is that the fxLight object requires a datablock.

8.12.1 fxLight New Features

fxLight has the following features.

- **Offset.** fxLight objects can animate their position along a vector. This vector is relative to the fxLight's placement position.
- **Radius.** fxLight objects light the area around them in a sphere. The radius parameters control the size of this sphere.
- **Size.** fxLight objects, like fxSunlight objects, have a flare. However, because the distance of fxLights is near, versus the nearly infinite distance of fxSunlight objects, it is more realistic for their flare sizes to vary based on distance. The size fields enable this effect.

8.12.2 fxLight Sample

The sample below can be used to produce a simple light that varies between dark purple and light purple over a three-second period. The light from this object will extend up to five world units from the center. To mark the location of the light center, the flare is enabled and uses the file "corona.png" found with the GPGT Lesson Kit (Figure 8.31).

```
datablock fxLightData(TestfxLight0) {
  FlareOn = true;
  FlareBitmap = "~/data/GPGTBase/particletextures/corona";
  LightRadius = "5";
  AnimColour = true;
  MinColour = "0.25 0.0 0.25";
  MaxColour = "1.0 0.5 1.0";
  ColourTime = 3.0;
};
```

Figure 8.31.
Flare texture "corona.png."

8.13 Paths and Markers

Path mission objects are used to constrain the motion of objects, such as AI players, cameras, and shapes. They may contain a limited number of markers (more on this below). As their name would imply, markers mark a point on a path. Additionally, they supply some information that may or may not be used by objects that follow the path.

8.13.1 Path Object

The Path object is a simple container, derived from the SimGroup class. The only new features added to Path, which are accessible from script, are the `isLooping` field and the `getPathID()` method.

isLooping

This field is an indicator used by PathCamera objects to determine if a path is a closed loop (`isLooping` = `true`) or open (`isLooping` = `false`). This affects the way the PathCamera's internal algorithms consume (follow) the path.

getPathID()

In TGE, interiors (buildings, etc.) can be created with paths embedded in them. These special interiors (pathedInterior) need a means of tracking their paths. Thus, beyond having a unique sim ID, a path may have a path ID. Normal paths, those we put in the world, do not have this.

Limited Number Of Markers?

I noted above that there may be a limit on the number of markers a path can contain. This is not a limit imposed by the path but by the objects that use the path. Due to they way these objects transmit their data across the network (between server and client), paths containing 40 or more markers may cause issues—specifically an overrun in the number of bits a packet may contain. I only mention this here so those who are experimenting with pathedCameras, or the PathShape GG resource (qid = 4849) be aware that you may hit a snag using 40 or more markers in any one path.

Beyond this, you should feel free to use as many markers as you want.

8.13.2 Marker Object

The Marker object is the little beastie that does most of the work defining how our paths will behave. The fields of a marker define the following.

- `position`. Position of this marker.

- `rotation`. Rotation of this marker.
- `scale`. Not used.
- `seqNum`. Sequence in path this marker represents. Valid sequence numbers are 0 .. NumMarkers – 1.
- `type` (Normal, Position Only, Kink)

Figure 8.32.

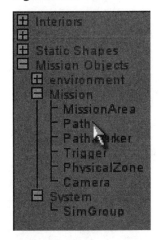

  - Normal. The object hits this point with both position and rotation.
  - Position. The object only uses the position information during interpolation and retains its current rotation.
  - Kink. This point in the path is discontinuous.
- `msToNext`. Time to next point in path.
- `SmoothingType`
  - Linear. Changes in path direction are abrupt (straight line).
  - Spline. Changes in path direction are smooth (curved).
- Position of next "target" on path. This is determined by the position of the marker, and its `seqNum` (sequence number).
  - `seqNum`. These values must start at 0 and continue to NumMarkers – 1.

Wow! All that sounds pretty techy and cool. Unfortunately, most of this information is just a hint. The camera is the only object that cares about all those parameters. If you want to have an AI character care about how smooth a path is, you'll have to write the appropriate scripts and examine the contents of these fields yourself. For most simplistic pathing purposes (an AI player following a path, or a shape following a path), a SimGroup of markers will be sufficient. You need not specify the remaining information, unless you actually care to use it in your scripts.

Figure 8.33.

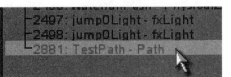

Figure 8.34.

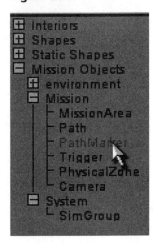

Proper Creation of Path

We're not going to be doing any work with paths in this book since paths are mainly used for camera pathing and AI pathing, which we don't discuss here. However, we'll talk briefly about placing a path.

Placing a path might seem a bit confusing at first, but just follow these simple steps.

1. Add a Path object. When you add a path object, it will show up in the Inspector tree, but not in the world. Don't worry; it's just a container (Figure 8.32).
2. Select our new path marker as the instant group (Figure 8.33).
3. Add as many path markers as you need (Figure 8.34).

Game Elements

Figure 8.35.

Path with four nodes.

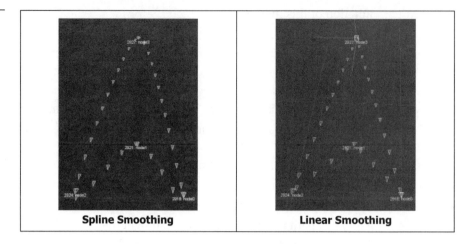

| Spline Smoothing | Linear Smoothing |

In Figure 8.35, I added four nodes. The first image shows the path with all nodes using the spline smoothing type. The second shows the same path using linear smoothing type. Notice (in the second image) how the turn points are sharp and the lines between nodes are straight.

8.14 Triggers

TGE Trigger objects are rectangular regions of space that react to the presence of other objects within that space. In versions prior to 1.4, only players and vehicles tripped a trigger. Now, items do also.

Triggers track three basic events:

- **Enter.** Something entered the trigger.
- **Exit.** Something exited the trigger.
- **Inside.** Something is inside the trigger region.

8.14.1 Placing a Trigger

Figure 8.36.

Object builder dialog.

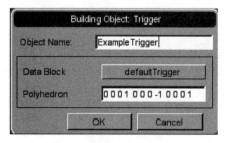

To place a trigger, we simply open the mission we want to contain this trigger, move to the right location, and start the Creator. Then, find the trigger object under Mission Objects → Mission → Trigger and select it. The object builder dialog will pop up and offer us some choices (Figure 8.36).

I usually just give it a name and press OK, but if you are using a custom datablock or if you wish to specify the Polyhedron dimensions numerically, this is your opportunity. I will normally resize, rotate, and translate the trigger manually.

8.14.2 Trigger Scripting

As noted above, the behavior of triggers is controlled by scripts. The triggers themselves require a datablock to be built, and subsequently, if we want to interact with them, we must provide callbacks.

Trigger Datablocks

The trigger datablock specifies exactly one field: `tickPeriodMS`. This parameter tells the trigger how many times to wake up and check for objects inside the trigger region.

```
datablock TriggerData( defaultTrigger ) {
  tickPeriodMS = 100; // Wake up ~ten times per second
};
```

Trigger Callbacks

Once we've created our datablock, we need to specify what the trigger does when triggered. As we discussed above, a trigger has three basic triggering actions.

- **Enter.** Something entered the trigger. When this happens, the trigger's `onEnterTrigger()` callback is called.

  ```
  function TriggerData::onEnterTrigger( %TriggerDB ,
      %Trigger , %EnterObj ) {
    // Do something
  };
  ```

- **Exit.** Something exited the trigger. When this happens, the trigger's `onLeaveTrigger()` callback is called

  ```
  function TriggerData::onLeaveTrigger( %TriggerDB ,
      %Trigger , %LeaveObj ) {
    // Do something
  };
  ```

- **Inside.** Something is inside the trigger region. Every `tickPeriodMS`, the trigger will wake up and check to see if there is something in this region. If something is inside the trigger, the `onTickTrigger()` callback is called.

Game Elements

```
function TriggerData::onTickTrigger( %TriggerDB ,
      %Trigger , %InsideObj ) {
  // Do something
};
```

Group Triggers

Group triggering is a method whereby we associate objects with a trigger and these objects are triggered when the trigger is activated (triggered). For this to work, two conditions must be satisfied.

Figure 8.37.

Trigger and shapes stored in same SimGroup.

1. Any objects to be group triggered and the trigger that triggers them must be contained within the same SimGroup/SimSet; i.e., if we looked at the Inspector, our object tree would look something like Figure 8.37.

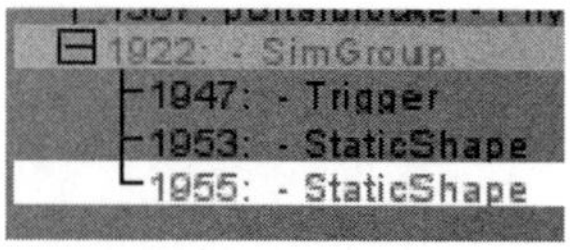

2. Each object that is to be triggered must specify an `onTrigger()` and/or an `onTriggerTick()` callback.

Figure 8.37.

Trigger and shapes stored In same SimGroup.

```
function ShapeBaseData::onTrigger( %DB , %Obj ,
      %TriggerState ) {
  // Do something
};
function ShapeBaseData::onTriggerTick( %DB , %Obj ) {
  // Do something
};
```

Now, each object in the SimGroup/SimSet will get an `onTrigger()` event when a player or vehicle enters or exits the trigger and an `onTriggerTick()` event every `tickPeriodMS` while a player or vehicle is inside the trigger.

8.14.3 Maze Runner Lesson #15 (90 Percent Step)—Teleport Triggers

In this lesson, we will examine the scripts needed to teleport the player from one teleport station to another. We will also look at the code that combines the prior parts of the teleport trigger components.

Trigger Datablocks

We could in theory use the DefaultTrigger datablock that comes with the kit, but it would be better to define a new one so we can guarantee that we have a unique namespace with which to scope our methods and callbacks. So, we will define our datablock as follows.

```
datablock TriggerData(TeleportTrigger) {
  tickPeriodMS = 100;
};
```

Teleport Scripts

Later, when we are writing our level-building scripts (Lesson #17 (Section 9.5.10)), it will be nice if we already have a method for attaching the particle effects and the physical zone to our teleporter triggers. With a little preplanning, this won't be that hard to do.

Teleport Trigger Planning

We haven't discussed it much yet, but the user (and we) will be able to define new levels by creating simple text files. These files will have "maps" of the level in them made up of various numbers and letters, representing the positions of level pieces like blocks, coins, and teleporters.

Knowing that our teleporters will be associated with letters in this file, we can plan on the teleporter trigger being a sort of parent. We will read the level file, create a trigger where it tells us to, and store information in the trigger that tells the trigger which of the three types of teleporters it is. Recall (assuming you jumped ahead to Chapter 14) that there are three types of teleporters (all of them function the same, but this allows us to have distinct sets that are connected to each other).

So, let's just assume that the letters used to represent teleporters are going to be x, y, and z. Furthermore, let's assume that the trigger is created first and then the type is stored in a field named `type`. Lastly, we will assume that the level loader will then call our teleport-builder script to add a particle emitter node and a p-zone in the same position as the trigger.

Teleport Trigger Implementation

All of that planning and assuming gets us some code like the following.

```
function Trigger::AttachEffect( %Obj ) {
  echo("\c5 Added Teleport Trigger");

  %emitter[X] = "TeleportStation_PED0";
  %emitter[Y] = "TeleportStation_PED1";
  %emitter[Z] = "TeleportStation_PED2";

  %effect = new ParticleEmitterNode() {
    position = vectorSub(%Obj.getWorldBoxCenter(), "0 0 2");
    rotation = "1 0 0 0";
    scale = "1 1 1";
    dataBlock = "basePEND";
    emitter = %emitter[%Obj.type];
    //emitter = "TeleportStation_PED0";
    velocity = "1";
  };
```

341

```
%Obj.myEffect = %effect;

%Pzone = new PhysicalZone() {
  position = vectorAdd( "1 -1 0" , %Obj.getPosition() );
  rotation = "1 0 0 0";
  scale = "2 2 4";
  velocityMod = "0";
  gravityMod = "1";
  appliedForce = "0 0 0";
  polyhedron = "0.0000000 0.0000000 0.0000000 1.0000000
                0.0000000 0.0000000 0.0000000 -1.0000000
                0.0000000 0.0000000 0.0000000 1.0000000";
};
%Obj.myPzone = %Pzone;
}
```

Basically, this function creates an array of particle emitter datablock names indexed by *x*, *y*, and *z*. Then, it creates a particle emitter in the position of the trigger (ID passed as argument to this function) and looks at the stored type to dereference the datablock array, getting the correct datablock name to match the type.

Next, the function creates a p-zone (remembering to offset it a little) in the same position as the trigger.

After this function is finished executing, there will be a trigger, a particle emitter node, and a p-zone all in the same location. *Voilà!* A teleporter station.

So, how do we make the teleporter "go"? Let's do that next.

Trigger Callbacks

To make the teleporters do work for us, we need to implement the `onEnterTrigger()` and `onLeaveTrigger()` callbacks.

Instead of showing you the code (which you can just load and examine), I will present the methodology used to teleport correctly.

onEnterTrigger()

This callback has the lion's share of the work. Initially, all triggers will start off active. When the avatar runs into a teleporter trigger, that trigger executes the following steps.

1. Check to see if it is disabled. If so, the callback aborts.
2. Enable the p-zone it owns (to be sure the avatar gets stopped).
3. Check for the existence of other triggers. When we create triggers in our level-building scripts, all triggers are added to one of three trigger groups

based on their type. Then, if we recall that all SimObject children can deter-mine what group (if any) they are stored in, it will become clear that each trigger can get the group it belongs in and choose a trigger from that group until it finds one that is not itself.

4. Disable the p-zone on the target trigger (so player is not stopped on exiting that trigger).

5. Disable the target trigger (to prevent teleport loops).

6. Do some fading effects and schedule a `setTransform()` call, moving the avatar to the location of the target trigger.

Once the avatar arrives at the target trigger, it has to leave that trigger to reactivate it. Also note that the `setTransform()` call moves the avatar and causes the current trigger to call its own `onLeaveTrigger()` callback, thus reactivating it.

onLeaveTrigger()

This callback has very little to do. Basically, when the avatar leaves the trigger area, the trigger will be told to re-enable the trigger and to `reactivate()` the p-zone.

Tricky Bits

While examining the scripts, you may notice a couple of bits of code that we have not yet discussed. The first of these is a call to `getRandomObject()`. It is being called on a SimGroup. This is a method I have provided in the included "systems" script files (loaded when we set up our environment). This method simply iterates over a SimSet (or child) and randomly selects an entry from the set, returning the ID of the selection.

```
... %Trigger.getGroup().getRandomObject() ...
```

The second bit involves the use of the function `getWords()`. In this line of code, we're replacing the position part of the player's transform with a new position while retaining the player's orientation information. This is done by getting the "words" representing the orientation. As you will learn later, a word is any string, and words are separated by spaces. Thus, we can look at the transform as a string containing seven words. Using `getWords()`, we sim-ply get the top four words and then paste them onto a new position matrix, making a new transform.

```
%newTransform = %newPos SPC getWords( %oldTransform, 3 , 6);
```

Game Elements

Trigger Cleanup

It is also worth mentioning that, when the trigger is destroyed, it will call its `onRemove()` callback, which will delete the effects attached to this trigger. Nice and clean.

```
function TeleportTrigger::onRemove( %DB, %Obj ) {
  if( isObject( %Obj.myEffect ) )
  %Obj.myEffect.delete();

  if( isObject( %Obj.myP-zone ) )
  %Obj.myPzone.delete();
}
```

8.15 Mission Objects Summary

In this mega-chapter, we have completely examined 14 major mission-placeable objects.

- **Terrains.** We learned about how the terrain is a 2 kiloworld unit × 2 kilo-world unit square that tiles infinitely in the world plane.
- **Water Blocks.** We learned how to represent liquid bodies using this object and how to interpret the myriad features and special effects it provides.
- **Sky.** We learned how this object is responsible for the sky box, clouds, general fog, up to three fog bands, and general visible distance limits.
- **Sun.** We learned that this object controls the scene lighting. We learned to control the source of the scene lighting through `azimuth` and `elevation` and the coloration and intensity of scene lighting through the `color` and `ambient` fields.
- **Precipitation.** We learned to create a "rain box" that can be used for a whole lot more than just rain.
- **Lightning.** We learned about both generated lightning and textured lightning.
- **Audio Emitters.** This meaty topic took a while to cover, but we came to understand that the versatile audio emitter object can be placed in the scene to produce 2D and 3D sounds. We learned all about general gain equations, looping and loop gaps, the 3D sounds zones (inner cone, outer cone, and outside volume), 3D gain distances (reference distance and max distance), and how to interpret the visual feedback this object provides while in debug mode.
- **Particle Emitters.** Following one meaty topic with another, we jumped into a discussion of the particle system and learned to differentiate a Particle-EmitterNodeData (PEND) from a ParticleEmitterData (PED) from a Particle-Data (PD), as well as about the features each of these classes provide.

- **fxShapeReplicators and fxFoliageReplicators**. We had fun discussing placement rules, the concepts of seeds and counts, how to select restrictions and restraints, how to enable or disable shape interactions, and how to set up the best culling for our needs.

- **fxSunlight**. We learned that this object provides the ability to render celestial bodies and supports a humongous set of features.

- **Physical Zones**. We saw that a lot of fun can be had combining the `velocityMod`, `gravityMod`, and `appliedForce` fields of these objects.

- **fxLight**. We covered this dynamic light object briefly.

- **Paths and Markers**. Here we examined how to create proper paths with these two classes and what their individual features mean and do.

- **Triggers**. Lastly, we discussed one of the most important mission objects, the trigger, which enables a wide variety of interactions with its individual and group triggering features.

Chapter 9
Game Setup Scripting

There are several scripting tasks that we will deal with in just about every game we make. This chapter gives an overview of the tasks related to setting up and maintaining a game. It will familiarize you with the fundamental Sim scripting classes and then examine I/O scripting. The following specific topics are covered in this chapter.

- **SimSet and SimGroup**. These are two container classes acting as base classes to the GuiControls and to the ScriptObject and ScriptGroup classes, respectively.

- **ScriptObject and ScriptGroup**. These two classes are used to create scripted classes. These special classes give us the ability to associate fields and methods with scripted classes, thus allowing us to neatly compartmentalize our scripts.

- **Device Inputs and Action Maps**. We will discuss how to build and use action maps to capture and redirect device inputs.

- **File I/O**. Here we will review the use of the file I/O classes.

- **Compiling and Executing Files**. At some time, we'll want to compile and execute scripts from files, so we'll talk about this briefly.

9.1 SimSet

SimSet is the root class in a hierarchy of SimObject containers. It is responsible for providing the base functionality and structure for all subsequent SimObject containers. It (and its children) should be treated as a traditional queue.

A SimSet is designed to hold a list of handles to SimObjects (or children of SimObjects). The SimObject is a fundamental class upon which all other objects that we will deal with are based.

Any one SimSet may contain only one instance of a handle to an existing SimObject, but a SimObject may be tracked by any number of SimSets; that is, no matter how many times we add() a handle to a SimSet, it is only stored there once, but we can add the handle to as many SimSets as we like.

```
//ts04(a);
%SO = new SimObject();
%Set0 = new SimSet();
%Set1 = new SimSet();
```

> Remember, when you see a code snippet with a statement like: \\ts04(a);, this means you can run the GPGT Lesson Kit, start either of the included missions, and then in the console (~) you may type: \\ts04(a); to run the sample.

Game Elements

```
%Set0.add( %S0);
%Set0.add( %S0);
echo( "Set 0 contains ", %Set0.getCount() , " objects." );
%Set1.add( %S0 );
%Set1.add( %Set0 );
echo( "Set 1 contains ", %Set1.getCount() , " objects." );
```

The above code produces the following output.

```
Set 0 contains 1 objects.
Set 1 contains 2 objects.
```

SimSet containers do not assume responsibility for their contents; that is, if we delete a SimSet, the handles and therefore the objects they represent are **not** deleted. However, when an object is deleted, it is automatically removed from all SimSets.

```
//ts04(b);
%Set1.delete(); // Self delete
echo( "Set 0 contains ", %Set0.getCount() , " objects." );
```

Set1 is now deleted, but S0 and Set0 still exist, so the above code produces the following output.

```
Set 0 contains 1 objects.
```

Because SimSets behave like queues, they have a front and a back. Objects added to a queue are added to the *back* of the queue. Furthermore, the front of the queue is index 0, and the back of the queue is index getCount() – 1.

```
//ts04(c);
%S1 = new SimObject();
%S2 = new SimObject();
%Set2 = new SimSet();
%Set2.add( %S1 );
%Set2.add( %S2 );
echo( "The ID of S1 is: ", %S1.getID() );
echo( "The ID of S2 is: ", %S2.getID() );
echo( "Object at front of Set 2 is ", %Set2.getObject(0) );
echo( "Object at back of Set 2 is ", %Set2.getObject(1) );
```

The above code produces the following output (IDs may vary).

```
The ID of S1 is: 2391
The ID of S2 is: 2392
Object at front of Set 2 is 2391
Object at back of Set 2 is 2392
```

We can manipulate the position of objects directly as long as we have a handle to the SimSet and the object.

```
//ts04(d);
echo( "The ID of S1 is: ", %S1.getID() );
echo( "The ID of S2 is: ", %S2.getID() );
%Set2.bringToFront( %S2 );
echo( "Object at front of Set 2 is ", %Set2.getObject(0) );
echo( "Object at back of Set 2 is ", %Set2.getObject(1) );
%Set2.pushToBack( %S2 );
echo( "Object at front of Set 2 is ", %Set2.getObject(0) );
echo( "Object at back of Set 2 is ", %Set2.getObject(1) );
```

The above code produces the following output (IDs may vary).

```
The ID of S1 is: 2409
The ID of S2 is: 2410
Object at front of Set 2 is 2410
Object at back of Set 2 is 2409
Object at front of Set 2 is 2409
Object at back of Set 2 is 2410
```

We can remove objects from our list at any time. This does not delete them.

```
//ts04(e);
%Set0.remove( %S0 ); // Take %S0 our of SimSet 1
echo( "Set 0 contains ", %Set0.getCount() , " objects." );
```

The above code produces the following output.

```
Set 0 contains 0 objects.
```

We can also empty a SimSet in one fell swoop.

```
//ts04(f);
echo( "Set 2 contains ", %Set2.getCount() , " objects." );
```

```
%Set2.clear(); // Remove all objects from SimSet 2
echo( "Set 2 contains ", %Set2.getCount() , " objects." );
```

The above code produces the following output.

```
Set 2 contains 2 objects.
Set 2 contains 0 objects.
```

Lastly, for debug purposes, a function is provided to dump the contents of a SimSet to the console:

```
//ts04(g);
%S3 = new SimObject();
%S4 = new SimObject();
echo( "The ID of S3 is: ", %S3.getID() );
echo( "The ID of S4 is: ", %S4.getID() );
%Set3 = new SimSet();
%Set3.add( %S3 );
%Set3.add( %S4 );
%Set3.listObjects();
```

The above code produces this output (object IDs may be different):

```
The ID of S3 is: 2418
The ID of S4 is: 2419
  2418: SimObject
  2419: SimObject
```

A SimSet cannot hold a reference to itself. The reason for that is explained in the next section.

9.2 SimGroup

A SimGroup is similar to a SimSet with a few exceptions. Any one SimObject may only be tracked in one SimGroup at a time. It can simultaneously be in any number of SimSets, but if we add a SimObject to a SimGroup when it is already present in another SimGroup, the reference to the SimObject will be removed from the prior SimGroup automatically.

```
//ts05(a);
%S0 = new SimObject();
%Group0 = new SimGroup();
%Group1 = new SimGroup();
%Set0 = new SimSet();
```

```
%Set0.add( %S0);
%Group0.add( %S0);
echo( "Set 0 contains ", %Set0.getCount() , " objects." );
echo( "Group 0 contains ", %Group0.getCount() , " objects." );
echo( "Group 1 contains ", %Group1.getCount() , " objects." );
%Group1.add( %S0 );
echo( "Set 0 contains ", %Set0.getCount() , " objects." );
echo( "Group 0 contains ", %Group0.getCount() , " objects." );
echo( "Group 1 contains ", %Group1.getCount() , " objects." );
```

S0 can only be in one SimGroup at a time, but it can be in both a SimSet and a SimGroup at the same time, as the following output shows.

```
Set 0 contains 1 objects.
Group 0 contains 1 objects.
Group 1 contains 0 objects.
Set 0 contains 1 objects.
Group 0 contains 0 objects.
Group 1 contains 1 objects.
```

Second, and of great importance, if we delete a SimGroup, this causes the automatic deletion of all objects in the SimGroup. This is the reason SimSets may not reference themselves (SimGroup is a child of SimSet).

//ts05(b);
```
echo( "Set 0 contains ", %Set0.getCount() , " objects." );
%Group1.delete();
        // Self deletes, and automatically deletes %S0
echo( "Set 0 contains ", %Set0.getCount() , " objects." );
```

By deleting Group1, which contained S0, we have also deleted S0, thus removing it from Set0, as can be shown by the following output.

```
Set 0 contains 1 objects.
Set 0 contains 0 objects.
```

9.3 ScriptObjects and ScriptGroups

When I first ran across these two classes, I was a bit puzzled and didn't see the value of having a class dedicated to scripting. I mean, hey, we have variables and functions. We've got packages. What else do we need? Then, little by little, I experimented and soon found that these two classes are practically indispensable.

9.3.1 ScriptObject

The ScriptObject is a noncontainer class provided to allow the creation of TorqueScript-only classes. It is derived from the SimObject (not SimSet) class. This class provides the ability to group data fields and to associate the class with one or more namespaces. The general syntax of a ScriptObject is as follows.

```
// In TorqueScript
%handle = new ScriptObject( [ Name ] ) {
  [class = AClassName;]
  [superClass = AnotherClassName;]

  [dynamic_field0 = InitialValue0;]
  ...
  [dynamic_fieldN = InitialValueN;]
};
```

This syntax is simpler than it looks. Let's break it down in Table 9.1.

Table 9.1

ScriptObject syntax.

Syntax Element	Description
`%handle`	The variable where the object's handle will be stored.
`Name` (optional)	Any expression evaluating to a string, which will be used as the object's name.
`class` (optional)	A special field that tells the Torque engine to insert `AClassName` into the namespace calling sequence for this object between `Name` and `ScriptObject`.
`superClass` (optional)	A special field that tells the Torque engine to insert `AnotherClassName` into the namespace calling sequence for this object between `Name` and `ScriptObject`.
`dynamic_fieldN` (optional)	As with any other object created in script, you may add as many dynamic fields as you wish.

Note that, if you use both `class` and `superClass`, the object's calling sequence will be the following.

Name → AClassName → AnotherClassName → ScriptObject → SimObject

9.3.2 ScriptGroup

The ScriptGroup class is a container class that provides all the same features as a ScriptObject with one minor difference—it is derived from SimGroup instead of SimObject. Thus, objects created from this class have all the behaviors of a ScriptObject while also having the behaviors of a SimGroup container.

The namespace chain for this object looks like the following.

Name → AClassName → AnotherClassName → ScriptGroup → SimGroup → SimObject

It's an Object

Instances of ScriptObject and ScriptGroup classes are objects. This means they can have fields associated with them.

```
%obj = new ScriptObject( Square ) {
  width = 10.0;
  height = 5.0;
};
```

Now, we can write little functions to manipulate them.

//ts06();

```
function printAreaOfSquare ( %Square ) {
  echo("The area of this square is: ", %Square.width * %Square.height);
}
```

To run this, we would have to type `printAreaOfSquare( %obj );`, producing:

```
The area of this square is: 50
```

They Support Namespaces

In truth, it wouldn't be great if we had to write a named function for each case we wanted to handle; better would be to use namespaces and overload a single method name.

Because ScriptObjects and ScriptGroups support namespaces, we can do the following.

//ts07();

```
%obj0 = new ScriptObject( Square ) {
  width = 10.0;
  height = 5.0;
};

%obj1 = new ScriptObject( Circle ) {
  radius = 10.0;
};
```

353

```
function Square::printArea( %this ) {
  echo("The area of this square is: ",
      %this.width * %this.height);
}
function Circle::printArea( %this ) {
  echo("The area of this circle is: ",
      %this.radius * %this.radius * 3.1415927 );
}
Square.printArea();
%obj1.printArea();
```

The above code would give us the following output.

```
The area of this square is: 50
The area of this circle is: 314.16
```

This is better, but now it seems we have to name all of our circles "Circle" if we want this to work. That kind of kills the ability to use names in addition to IDs to reference objects. Fortunately, there are two key words that we can use to add generic namespaces to the objects we create—class and superClass.

//ts08();

```
%obj = new ScriptObject( Square0 ) {
  class = "Square";
  width = 10.0;
  height = 5.0;
};

%obj = new ScriptObject( Square1 ) {
  class = "Square";
  width = 10.0;
  height = 50.0;
};

Square0.printArea();
Square1.printArea();
```

The above code would give us the following output.

```
The area of this square is: 50
The area of this square is: 500
```

So, `class` seems pretty useful, but what is this `superClass` business? It allows us to use yet another class name in the chain, below the one added by the `class` keyword.

```
//ts09();

function Doberman::printMessage( %this ) {
  echo("A ", %this.getName(), " is a ...");
  Parent::printMesage( %this );
}

function Canine::printMessage( %this ) {
  echo("... ", %this.class, " which is a ...");
  Parent::printMesage( %this );
}

function Animal::printMessage( %this ) {
  echo("... ", %this.superClass, ".");
}

%obj = new ScriptObject( Doberman ) {
  class = "Canine";
  superClass = "Animal";
};

%obj.printMessage();
```

The code above produces the following interesting output.

```
A Doberman is a ...
... Canine which is a ...
... Animal.
```

Callbacks, Too?

ScriptObjects and ScriptGroups support the `::onAdd()` and `::onRemove()` callbacks. This means that we can have them do initialization and cleanup work when we create/delete them, just like when we create other mission objects.

If this is not very clear, please continue reading. In Section 10.4, I will give an overview of the callback concept and discuss a few important standard callbacks.

Not Networked

Just like dynamic fields, neither ScriptObject nor ScriptGroup are networked; that is, instances of these classes created by the server will be visible only to the server (except for the single-player and listen-server cases (see Section 2.1.15), where the client is local).

If you want information shared with the clients from either of these classes, you will have to write networking scripts to do so.

9.4 Device Inputs and Action Maps

When we speak of inputs in the context of TGE, we are talking about user inputs from keyboards, mice, joysticks, and other devices. Although other types of inputs are possible, the only ones we are interested in are those that are used to control gameplay. That said, inputs flow into and through TGE as follows (Figure 9.1).

1. The OS processes inputs and passes them to the TGE platform layer.
2. The TGE Platform identifies and categorizes the inputs and passes them on to the game.
3. The game processes the input if it can or ignores it if there is no defined action for the input.

The game input processing is the part we are interested in. As can be seen from Figure 9.1, the input is processed within the game as follows.

1. The GlobalActionMap gets first dibs on the inputs. If it has no mapping for the input, the input is passed on to the GUI, more specifically the Canvas.
2. The Canvas attempts to process the input, but passes the input on if it has no GUI controls programmed to use it.
3. The input is passed to any active action maps for processing. If none of the currently stacked action maps is coded to use the input, the input is dropped.

Figure 9.1

Flow of inputs for TGE.

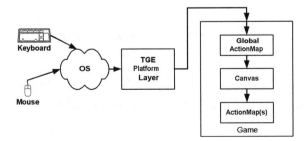

ActionMap is a special class designed to capture and redirect inputs. There are two kinds of ActionMap: the GlobalActionMap and the normal ActionMap. The main differences between these are as follows.

- **GlobalActionMap.** This is the daddy of input processors and supersedes all other processing methods. This action map should not be popped from the processing stack.
- **ActionMap.** This is a generic action map. It takes lower priority than all other processing methods. These action maps can be pushed and popped from the processing stack as the game's requirements change.

9.4.1 Defining Action Maps

To create a new (blank) action map, we use the following syntax (explained in Table 9.2).

```
new ActionMap( ActionMapName );
```

Syntax Element	Description
new	A keyword instructing TGE to create a new instance of the following console class. Returns a handle to the new ActionMap.
ActionMap	Console class name for action maps.
ActionMapName	The name for the new action map.

Table 9.2.

Creating a new action map.

Binding Inputs to Actions

Subsequent to creating a blank action map, we must bind inputs to actions (or responses). This binding associates a specific input with a specific function or scripted response.

To add new mappings, use one of the following two functions.

```
ActionMapName.bind( device , action , [ modifier spec , ... ] , command );
```

This first binding method, bind, is used to bind a single command to an action (Table 9.3). It has the further ability to modify the behavior of pointing devices via special modifiers. The command (a function) bound to this action will be automatically passed a value (as the first and only argument to the function) corresponding to whether the device is in the on or off (pressed or released) state. A function that is used for binding should have the following form.

Game Elements

```
// Assume this is bound to a mouse button
function aBindFunction( %val ) {
  if( %val )   {
    echo("Mouse button was pressed.");
  }
  else {
    echo("Mouse button was released.");
  }
}
```

The second binding function is the following.

```
ActionMapName.bindCmd( device, action, makeCmd, breakCmd );
```

This second binding method, `bindCmd`, will bind one function to the on (break) event and one function to the off (break) event (Table 9.4). Both functions are optional, but at least one should be specified. A function used for this kind of binding takes no arguments at all.

Tables 9.5–9.7 are provided for your reference and describe the most commonly used devices, actions, and modifiers. For a full listing, please see the appendices.

Table 9.3.

Adding new mappings using `bind`.

Syntax Element	Description
ActionMapName	Previously defined action map.
bind	Console method used to add a new action for the specified key.
device	Device name (see Table 9.5).
action	Device action (see Table 9.6).
modifier spec	Special modifiers (see Table 9.7).
command	Command to execute when this binding triggers.

Table 9.4.

Adding new mappings using `bindCmd`.

Syntax Element	Description
ActionMapName	Previously defined action map
bindCmd	Console method used to add a new action for the specified key.
device	Device name (see Table 9.5).
action	Device action (see Table 9.6).
makeCmd	Command to execute on key press.
breakCmd	Command to execute on key release.

Device	Description
keyboard*N*	This is the *N*th keyboard hooked up to the system. For the first keyboard, either `keyboard` or `keyboard0` is acceptable.
mouse*N*	This is the *N*th mouse hooked up to the system. For the first mouse, either `mouse` or `mouse0` is acceptable.
joystick*N*	This is the *N*th joystick or gamepad hooked up to the system.
unknown*N*	This is the *N*th unknown device hooked up to the system. In other words, some device has been sampled, but TGE doesn't know what it is.

Table 9.5.

Devices.

Action	Description
button0, button1, . . . , button31	This is a mouse, joystick, or gamepad button press. For the mouse, buttons 0, 1, and 2 are left, right, and middle buttons, respectively. See the appendix for other button mappings.
a..z A..Z 0..9 F1..F12 etc.	These are keyboard inputs. Because this list is so long and in order to accommodate possible variances for special keyboards and other devices, a GUI has been provided with the GPGT Lesson Kit that displays the current action, be it keyboard, mouse, joystick/gamepad, or other device. Simply start the GPGT Lesson Kit and click GUIsSampler → guiInputCtrl. Follow the instructions provided in the sample.
shift ctrl alt	These are modifiers and are not used standalone, but they are included in the action string; for example, `shift p` is the **SHIFT** key and the **P** key pressed at the same time.
lshift, rshift, lctrl, rctrl, lalt, ralt	These are special modifier actions.

Table 9.6.

Actions.

Action Modifiers	Description
D %x %y	Has dead zone. This is used to add a dead zone for the mouse. Motions in this zone will not be recorded. This can be used to remove the jitter caused by a "nervous hand."
S %s	Has scale. This is used to scale the mouse motion (by a multiple).
I	Inverted. This is used to invert the mouse.
R %s	Has scale. Same as `S`.

Table 9.7.

Special modifiers used to modify mouse inputs.

Bind Samples

Before going any further, let's look at a few binding examples and break them down.

```
moveMap.bind(keyboard , "alt c" , toggleCamera);
```

In the above binding, we have bound the `toggleCamera()` function to the `alt c` event. As soon as the **ALT** and **C** keys are pressed (together), `toggleCamera()` will be executed on that client. When the `toggleCamera()` method is called, the engine will pass a 1 or a 0 as the first argument to the function. A 1 represents a make (key-press) event, while the 0 represents a break (key-release) event. So, remember that the function will be called twice per key press, not once.

```
moveMap.bindCmd(keyboard , "n" ,
    "NetGraph::toggleNetGraph();" , "");
```

In the above binding, we have bound the `NetGraph::toggleNetGraph()` method to the `n` make event. As soon as the **N** key is depressed, `NetGraph::toggleNetGraph()` will be executed on that client. Nothing is scheduled to occur on the key-break (release) event.

```
moveMap.bindCmd(keyboard , "n" , "" ,
    "NetGraph::toggleNetGraph();");
```

In the above binding, we have bound the `NetGraph::toggleNet-Graph()` method to the `n` break event. As soon as the **N** key is released, `NetGraph::toggleNetGraph()` will be executed on that client. Nothing is scheduled to occur on the make (key-press) event.

Multiple Binds

It should be noted that binding more than one key to the same action (using the same action map) is not allowed. TGE will do its best to preempt this kind of assignment. Normally, if one attempts to bind two inputs to the same response, the second binding will silently fail. However, this behavior is not consistent. So, it is best to be aware of this and to check your action maps for duplicate assignments.

To be clear, the following is a multiple bind.

```
moveMap.bindCmd(keyboard , "n" , "" ,
    "NetGraph::toggleNetGraph();");
moveMap.bindCmd(keyboard , "m" , "" ,
    "NetGraph::toggleNetGraph();");
```

This will only bind the `toggleNetGraph` function to the **N** key.

Overriding Binds

Overriding binds is a different story. You may override a bind at any time you wish. Simply specify the bind with a new set of functions.

```
moveMap.bindCmd(keyboard , "n" , "" ,
    "NetGraph::toggleNetGraph();");
moveMap.bindCmd(keyboard , "n" , "" , "nukeEM();");
```

The above example rebinds the **N** key. It will now call the function `nukeEm()` on a break (key-release) event.

Unbinding

There will be cases where we want to undo a binding. To do this, we use the following syntax (explained in Table 9.8).

```
ActionMapName.unbind( device, action );
moveMap.unbind( keyboard , "n" );
```

Saving Binds

We will also find it useful to save our binds on occasion. The ActionMap class provides this ability as follows (Table 9.9).

```
ActionMapName.save( [ filename ] , [ append ] );
moveMap.save( "~/client/myActionmaps/movemap.cs" , false );
```

Syntax Element	Description
ActionMapName	Previously defined action map.
unbind	Console method used to remove an action from an action map.
device	Device name (see Table 9.5).
action	Device action (see Table 9.6).

Table 9.8.
Undoing a binding.

Syntax Element	Description
ActionMapName	Previously defined action map.
save	Console method used to save/dump an action from an action map.
filename (optional)	A valid filename to dump the action map to. If no filename is specified, the action map is dumped to the console.
append (optional)	A Boolean value specifying whether to append to the file or overwrite it. The default (false) is to overwrite.

Table 9.9.
Saving binds.

Table 9.10.

Activating a nonglobal action map.

Syntax Element	Description
ActionMapName	Previously defined and bound action map.
push	Console method used to activate the action map and place it on the top of the nonglobal action map stack.

Table 9.11.

Deactivating a nonglobal action map.

Syntax Element	Description
ActionMapName	Previously defined, bound, and activated action map.
pop	Console method used to deactivate an action map and remove it from nonglobal action map stack.

Activating Action Maps

Once an action map has been created and the bindings have been assigned, it must be activated in order to be used. To activate a nonglobal action map, we use the following syntax (Table 9.10).

```
ActionMapName.push();
```

Subsequently, an active nonglobal action map can be deactivated using the following syntax (explained in Table 9.11).

```
ActionMapName.pop();
```

Please note that popping only removes the specified action map from the nonglobal action map stack. All other action maps stay in place.

Deactivating the GlobalActionMap

It should also be noted that the GlobalActionMap does support both the push() and the pop() console methods. However, it is not suggested that you use these methods on the GlobalActionMap. That said, you may use the pop() console method to temporarily disable the GlobalActionMap and the push() console method to reactivate it at a later time.

Nonglobal Action Map Stack

We have alluded to the concept of stacking but have not clearly stated what this means in the context of action maps.

The concept of stacking only applies to normal action maps as no stacking order will allow them to take precedence over either the GlobalAction-Map or the Canvas. An action map is placed on the top of a virtual stack of nonglobal action maps when it is activated (pushed). Action maps higher in the nonglobal action map stack will be first to process any inputs which have made it past the Canvas. Therefore, if an action map redefines a binding defined by an action map lower in the stack, the binding of the higher action map will take precedence. Stacking action maps is a nice way of compositing action bindings based on current context.

9.4.2 Maze Runner Lesson #16 (90 Percent Step)— MoveMap

In this short lesson, we will examine the action map that is included with the prototype content and discuss some small changes to it and other scripts that will ensure the behavior we are expecting from our game.

Required Behavior

In our game, we want the following key mappings.

W	Move forward.
A	Move left.
S	Move backward.
D	Move right.
SPACEBAR	Jump.
Mouse Move	Camera yaw and pitch.
TAB	Switch 1st and 3rd POV.

We would specifically like to disable (eventually) the following key mapping.

ALT + C	Free camera mode.

We don't want people using free-camera mode to cheat and find coins without risking their avatar's life.

> The MoveMap defined in the prototype content used for MazeRunner is standard and matches the one provided with all TGE samples, including the free Demo and the FPS starter kit that comes with the full SDK.

MoveMap

The prototype content we copied into our "\MazeRunner" directory contains two files that define an action map already implementing the above mappings as well as many others. The name of this action map is MoveMap.

One of the things that new users find confusing is the fact that MoveMap is created in two places. It is created in the file "\MazeRunner\prototype\client\scripts\default.bind.cs" and in the file "\MazeRunner\prototype\client\config.cs".

So, where do we go if we want to modify this action map? Well, if we look in the function `initClient()` in the file "\MazeRunner\prototype\client\init.cs", we will see the following code.

```
// Default player key bindings
exec("./scripts/default.bind.cs");
exec("./config.cs");
```

The first file, "default.bind.cs", is the correct location to define new bindings for the moveMap action map. However, if you do decide to modify or add bindings, be sure to delete the "config.cs" file first. Otherwise, it will wipe out the changes you made in "default.bind.cs". The "config.cs" file is automatically stored by the scripts that come with the prototype and is meant to reflect any changes we might make using the options dialog. However, adding new bindings and/or functions needs to be done by hand, so remember to always stop the engine, delete the "config.cs" file, and (only) then add your new bindings to "default.bind.cs".

Making Our Changes

In our game, we are happy with the current mappings, except that we wish to eventually disable free-camera mode. So, when we want to do this, simply remove the following line from "default.bind.cs".

moveMap.bind(keyboard, "alt c", toggleCamera);

For now, I suggest leaving this in, but when we get ready to release our game to the public, this line needs to be removed. Additionally, we might want to remove the following code from "default.bind.cs".

```
function toggleCamera(%val) {
  if (%val)
    commandToServer('ToggleCamera');
}
```

If you are having trouble finding newly added files, you may at any time do the following to refresh the file manager.

```
$oldModPath =
getModPaths();

setModpaths("");

setModpaths(
$oldModPath);
```

9.5 File I/O

Torque has a file manager that maintains a working list of all the files found in the game directory and all subdirectories. This list is created on start-up. Additionally, TGE 1.4 is capable of finding files added to one of the mod paths after the game has started.

9.5.1 Locating Files

In order to locate files listed by the file manager, we use two functions provided by TGE: findFirstFile() and findNextFile(). These functions are meant to be used together.

> When using the file finding functions, remember that file names consist of a path, a name, and an extension. You must add the appropriate wildcards when searching for files down a path.
>
> ```
> echo( findFirstFile( "*/specialPrefix_*.cs" ) );
> ```

findFirstFile()

This function will locate the first instance of a specified file or filename pattern in the file manager's list. It then marks the location of this file in the list and returns the filename. The pattern supplied to this function may contain wildcards.

```
findFirstFile( pattern );
```

Try the following example.

```
//ts11();
echo( findFirstFile( "*.cs" ) );
```

Please note that subsequent calls will return the same value. It is important to understand that each time this function is used, it sets the location of `firstMatch`. Thus, having two functions calling this function in an overlapping fashion will have undesirable results.

findNextFile()

Having found the first instance of a filename or filename pattern, we may wish to find subsequent instances. This function does that for us. It will return one new match each time we call it until it finds no more matches, at which time it will return the null string ("").

```
findNextFile( pattern );
```

Try the following example.

```
//ts12();
echo( findNextFile( "*.cs" ) );
```

If we specify a pattern that does not match that of our call to `findFirst-File()`, results will be indeterminate.

The following function lists all files found matching a specified pattern.

```
//ts13();
function listAllFiles( %pattern ) {
  %filename = findFirstFile( %pattern );
  while("" !$= %filename ) {
    echo(%filename);
    %filename = findNextFile(%pattern );
  }
}
listAllFiles("*gui*");
```

9.5.2 Wildcards

It was mentioned above that we can use wildcards in our file patterns. Table 9.12 shows the wildcards that TGE supports.

Table 9.12.

Wildcards supported by TGE.

Wildcard	Meaning	Sample
*	The standard "matches all" wildcard.	"*.cs"
~	This equates to the mod directory. For example, when using the GPGT Lesson Kit, "~/*.cs" is the same as "gpgt/*.cs".	"~/main.cs"
.	This file location relative wildcard can be interpreted as "current directory of this file," i.e., this equates to the current directory of the script file it is used in.	"./test.cs"

9.5.3 Counting Files

We can count the number of files matching a specified pattern using the following function.

```
getFileCount( pattern );
```

9.5.4 Calculating File CRC

A CRC (cyclic redundancy code) is a useful thing to have if you need to ensure that users are using the correct version of a file prior to starting the game. Thus, TGE provides a function for calculating the CRC of a file:

```
getFileCRC( filename );
```

In a multiplayer scenario, the server and the client can compare CRCs, and if a client has a file with the same name but a different CRC, then that client's file is either corrupted, modified, or of a different version than that found on the server.

9.5.5 Filename Expansion

Frequently, it is useful to skip a lookup on a file and do a direct expansion of the file from a filename using wildcards. This can be accomplished with the following function.

```
expandFileName( filename );
```

The Slash (/) versus the Dot (.) versus the Tilde (~)

There are three special file path prefixes used in TorqueScript. The first of these is the the slash (/), the second is the dot (.), and the third is the tilde (~).

A slash as the first part of a path tells the engine to start searching in the root directory. The root directory for a TGE game is the directory in which the first "main.cs" file is found.

A dot means to start looking in the current directory. That is, look in the directory where the file that contains this script was found.

A tilde means to look in the mod paths. In our scripts, we can build up the mod path by calling setModPath() and passing a path or semicolon-specified paths. All mod paths are children of root.

9.5.6 Filename Subelements

The file finding/expanding functions return strings that may contain a path, a file prefix, and a file suffix. It is often necessary to examine just one of these filename subelements. Fortunately, the authors of Torque foresaw this need.

Extracting File Path

To extract a file path from a filename, use the following method.

```
filePath( filename );
```

If the filename contains no path or is not valid, this function will return a null string.

Extracting File Name

A file "name" is considered to be everything but the path; i.e., the prefix + suffix. To extract a file name from a filename, use the following method.

```
fileName( filename );
```

This will remove the path, if one exists, and return the remainder of the string.

> Filename expansion is context-based. So, do not make the mistake of trying to use this function from the console. For this function and other functions like it to work, the function requires context. A file provides context to the console while it is parsing that file, but when we open the console and type commands in the command line, we are working in a context-less environment. Thus, this function cannot expand a filename to match the context.

Extracting Prefix

The prefix of a filename is the last part of a file's name, before the dot (.). For example, the prefix of the filename "test.png" would be "test". File paths are not part of a file's prefix. To extract a file prefix from a filename, use the following method.

```
fileBase( filename );
```

Extracting Suffix

The suffix of a filename is the last part of a file's name, including and after the dot (.). For example the suffix of the filename "test.png" would be ".png". To extract a file suffix from a filename, use the following method.

```
fileExt( filename );
```

9.5.7 Before Reading or Writing

We're almost ready to start discussing the actual reading and writing of files, but before we do, let's discuss two more functions.

Is It a Valid File?

Before attempting to read or write a file, we should always verify that it exists or is valid. TGE provides the following Boolean-returning function for this purpose.

```
isFile( filename );
```

This function will return `true` if the file is a valid member of the file manager's list and `false` otherwise. Of course, writing to a file that does not exist will create that file, including any subdirectories that may be required as part of the filename's full path.

Can I Write to It?

If we want to write to a file, we'd better check that it is writeable.

```
isWriteableFileName( filename );
```

Please note that this will return `false` if the file does not exist; thus, for writes, we can be lazy and just check this, skipping the `isFile()` check.

9.5.8 Reading Files

So, we've talked about how to find our files and get some information about them, but how do we read them? TGE provides a class called FileObject. We can use this class in our scripts to both read and write files.

In order to read a file, we must do the following.

1. Open the file for reading.

2. Read a line from the file.

3. Repeat step 2 until we reach the end of the file or have completed our task.

4. Close the file.

The following function was extracted from a post and modified slightly.

```
//ts14();
function readFile( %filename ){
  %file = new FileObject();
  if(%file.openForRead(%filename)) {
    while(!%file.isEOF()) {
    %input = %file.readLine();
    echo(%input);
    }
  } else {
    %file.delete();
    return false;
    }
  %file.close();
  %file.delete();
  return true;
}
readFile( expandFilename( "~/prefs.cs" ) );
```

In this example, we create a new instance of a FileObject and then use it to open and to read the file. When we are done, we use it to close the file, and then we delete the object. The key methods used are the following.

- `openForRead( fileName )`. This method will attempt to open the files specified by the string *fileName* for reading. If it is not successful, it will return `false`.

- `readLine()`. This methods returns the next full line (terminated by a new line) in the file. If no lines remain, a null string will be returned.

- `isEOF()`. This method checks to see if the end of the file has been reached and returns `true` if it has.

- `close()`. This method closes the file. *Do not forget to do this.*

That is pretty much it. Very simple.

9.5.9 Writing Files

Writing files is only slightly more complicated than reading them. Before we write to a file, we must answer one very important question: do we want to overwrite the file or append it?

Overwriting Files

To overwrite a file, we do the following.

1. Open the file for writing.
2. Write to it.
3. Repeat step 2 until we are done.
4. Close the file.

```
function writeFile( %filename , %data ) {
  %file = new FileObject();
  if(! %file.openforWrite( %filename ) ) {
    %file.delete();
    return false;
  }
  %file.writeLine( %data );
  %file.close();
  %file.delete();
  return true;
}
```

In this example, we create a new instance of a FileObject and then use it to open and to write the file. When we are done, we use it to close the file, and then we delete the object.

The key methods used are the following.

- `openForWrite( `*fileName*` )`. This method will attempt to open the file specified by the string *fileName* for writing. If the specified file does not exist, it is created, *but not yet added to the file manager list*. If the file already exists, it is cleared, and we start writing at the front of the file. If the open fails, this method will return `false`.
- `writeLine()`. This method writes a string to the file and appends a new-line character.
- `close()`. This method closes the file, just as it did for reading, but with one exception. If we opened a new file, at this time the filename is added to the file manager's list. Only now can we read it.

Appending to Files

To append to an existing file, we do the following.

1. Open the file for appending.
2. Write to it.
3. Repeat step 2 until we are done.
4. Close the file.

```
function appendToFile( %filename , %data ) {
  %file = new FileObject();
  if(! %file.openforAppend( %filename ) ) {
    %file.delete();
    return false;
  }
  %file.writeLine( %data );
  %file.close();
  %file.delete();
  return true;
}
```

In this example, we create a new instance of a FileObject and then use it to open and to append to a file. When we are done, we use it to close the file, and then we delete the object.

The key methods used are the following.

- `openForAppend( fileName )`. This method will attempt to open the file specified by the string *fileName* for appending. If the specified file does not exist, it is created *but not yet added to the file manager list*. If the file already exists, it is opened, and we start writing at the end of the file. If the open fails, this method will return `false`.

- `writeLine()`. This method writes a string to the file and appends a new-line character.

- `close()`. This method closes the file, just as it did for reading, but with one exception. If we opened a new file, at this time, the filename is added to the file manager's list. Only now can we read it.

9.5.10 Maze Runner Lesson #17 (90 Percent Step)—Level Loader

In this lesson, we will discuss the level-loader code. We will not be listing all of the code here, as it is rather lengthy. Instead, we will describe how it works and how the code is structured.

Please note that the level loader is responsible for loading and starting all elements of the level. This includes the fireball-shooting block, which we have not completely covered yet. Specifically, we have not discussed the fireballs themselves, nor have we spoken of the code that fires them. If you wish, you may skip ahead to Lesson #20 (Section 11.4.3) to see how they work. Not doing so will not affect the current lesson, but until we complete that lesson, the level loader won't start the fireball blocks correctly.

Copy Required Files

From the accompanying disk, please copy the file "\MazeRunner\Lesson_017\ levelloader.cs" into "\MazeRunner\prototype\server\scripts\MazeRunner".

Now, edit the function `onServerCreated()` in the file "\MazeRunner\ prototype\server\game.cs" to look like the following (bold lines are new or modified).

```
exec("./MazeRunner/teleporters.cs"); // MazeRunner
exec("./MazeRunner/levelloader.cs"); // MazeRunner
```

Levels versus Layers

In the following description, we will be using the words *level* and *layer*. A level is comprised of one or more layers of game elements. A level may have any number of layers.

Level Files

The premise of this level loader is quite simple. Our goal is to load a single mission and then, at any time we wish, load the components that make up a level. By using a level map and a level loader, we may define as many levels as we want without needing to hand-create an entire mission and then load the mission (which is generally slower than placing items by script for single-player games).

The first thing we need to do is define the parts of a level file.

Level File Format

We want to be able to make levels with multiple elements and multiple layers. To do this, the level file cannot be constrained to a fixed length. Instead, it must be dynamic.

After some thought, I came up with the syntax for this file shown in Table 9.13.

That is it for the syntax. Now, let's designate what letters mean in the actual layer definitions (those 16 lines).

Line/Element	Meaning
Line 0	This line is used to store the numeric ID of the level that follows this one.
LAYER_UP	This will increment the current elevation at which blocks and other elements are being placed by 4 world units.
LAYER_DOWN	This will decrement the current elevation at which blocks and other elements are being placed by 4 world units.
LAYER_DEFINE	This indicates to the level loader that the next line in the file will specify a layer type.
BLOCKS	This indicates to the level loader that the next 16 lines will contain a map that designates where blocks are placed.
OBSTACLES	This indicates to the level loader that the next 16 lines will contain a map that designates where obstacles (teleport stations and fireball blocks) are placed.
PICKUPS	This indicates to the level loader that the next 16 lines will contain a map that designates where pickups (coins) are placed.
PLAYERDROPS	This indicates to the level loader that the next 16 lines will contain a map that designates where the player will be dropped at the beginning of the mission.

Table 9.13.

Level-file elements.

Tokens

Each layer definition is composed of 16 lines of 16 characters, meaning that each layer definition may have up to 256 elements in it. Because we have a multitude of things to place (and because we want to leave room for expansion), we will be reusing letters (tokens) between layer types. Table 9.14 lists what individual tokens mean in the various layer contexts.

Layer Type	Token	Meaning
BLOCKS	A-J	These designate one of the level blocks we discussed in Lesson #5 (Section 6.5.6).
	0-9	These are the fade blocks. The number specifies the number of seconds until the block fades. We will discuss how this fading works in Lesson #18 (Section 10.3.7).
OBSTACLES	X, Y, Z	One of these will produce a teleport station.
	0-9	These are the fireball blocks, where each number is a block firing in a specified direction. For example: 0—North, 1—NorthEast, ..., 7—East , 8—NorthEast, and 9 is random.
PICKUPS	C	A coin.
PLAYERDROPS	P	A player drop point. The player is dropped at the first point found.

Table 9.14.

Definitions of tokens.

Level-Loader Mechanics

The mechanics of the loader are pretty straightforward. It will consume whatever file it has been told to load until it has placed all of the contents or until it hits some kind of error in the level file.

Level-Loader Definition

So, we have some rules upon which to base our level building, and thus we have rules upon which to base the design of the loader. Furthermore, we know the loader must read the file until it is consumed, regardless of how many layers are defined in the file. Let's get started.

Go ahead and load up the "levelloader.cs" file in your favorite browser and then follow along as we discuss it here.

Elevations and Level Increments

The first thing we do in our loader is define some global variables for tracking.

- $BaseElevation. Beginning elevation for every new level (not layer).
- $LevelIncrement. Level up/down step size.
- $CurrentElevation. Current elevation we are building at (current layer).

Classifying Tokens

We are dealing with a lot of different tokens. We will need to categorize these tokens into groups to minimize our code size. Because we don't want to waste time doing multiple comparisons to determine if any one token is a teleporter, a fireball block, etc., we need a way to reduce the effort required to categorize tokens. The trick is to create an array where the index of the array is the expected token and the value in the array gives us the information we need. For example:

```
$BLOCKCLASS[A]  =  NORMAL;
$BLOCKCLASS[B]  =  NORMAL;
$BLOCKCLASS[C]  =  NORMAL;
// ...
$BLOCKCLASS[0]  =  FADE;
$BLOCKCLASS[1]  =  FADE;
$BLOCKCLASS[2]  =  FADE;
// ...
```

In the above code, we're saying that any token A..C will correspond to a normal block while 0..2 will be a fade block.

So, we don't want to write the code like the following.

```
if( ( %token $= A ) || ( %token $= B ) || ( %token $= C ) ) {
    // Normal Block Code Here
```

```
}
else if ( ( %token $= 0 ) || ( %token $= 1 ) || ( %token $= 2 ) ) {
  // Fade Block Code Here
}
```

Instead, we can write it like the following.

```
switch$( $BLOCKCLASS[%token] ) {
case NORMAL:
  // Normal Block Code Here
case FADE:
  // Fade Block Code Here
}
```

As you can see, this code is not only more elegant but also significantly faster than the multiple comparison case before (and that was with only 6 of the 20 possible block cases shown).

buildLevel()

We've prepared the globals and helper variables we'll need; now let's write the loader function.

The buildLevel() function takes a single argument containing the numeric ID of the level to load. The function assumes that all level files are stored in the directory "\MazeRunner\prototype\data\Missions\LevelMaps". Given the number 0, the loader will attempt to open a file named "\MazeRunner\prototype\data\Missions\LevelMaps\levelNum0.txt". If the level loader successfully opens this file, the first thing it will do is read the first line, which contains the numeric ID of the level that follows this one. If no next level is defined, the loader fails out.

So far, nothing mysterious has been done, but the next bit of code may seem strange. For several lines, you will see bits of code like the following.

```
if( isObject( gameLevelGroup ) )
  gameLevelGroup.delete();
MissionCleanup.add( new SimGroup( gameLevelGroup ) );

gameLevelGroup.add( new SimGroup( mazeBlocksGroup ) );
gameLevelGroup.add( new SimGroup( fadeGroup ) );
gameLevelGroup.add( new SimGroup( FireBallMarkersGroup ) );
gameLevelGroup.add( new SimGroup( TeleportStationGroupX ) );
gameLevelGroup.add( new SimGroup( TeleportStationGroupY ) );
gameLevelGroup.add( new SimGroup( TeleportStationGroupZ ) );
gameLevelGroup.add( new SimGroup( TeleportStationEffectsGroup ) );
gameLevelGroup.add( new SimGroup( CoinsGroup ) );
```

Remember that we are building our levels dynamically. As part of this effort, we are destroying the prior level if it exists. Also, to make our lives simple, we will be tracking all of our objects in named SimGroups. This is ideal because much of the processing our game does is of an iterative nature, and it is easy to iterate over a SimGroup.

So, the above statement and the remainder like it in the function are merely removing the last level's SimGroups (if they exist) and then creating the following named SimGroups.

- **gameLevelGroup.** This is the big daddy of all level SimGroups. It will contain all of our subsequent SimGroups for this level. Thus, deleting just this group kills all the child groups and their contents.

- **mazeBlocksGroup.** All normal blocks are stored in this group.

- **fadeGroup.** All fadable blocks are stored here. Later, we will iterate over this group to maintain the fadeblocks' behaviors.

- **fireBallMarkersGroup.** All fireball blocks are stored here. Like the fadeGroup, we iterate over this group to keep the fireball blocks firing.

- **TeleportStationX..TeleportStationZ.** These three sets are used to store the three types of teleporter. Teleport stations stored in the same group will target each other.

- **TeleportStationEffectsGroup.** Although we have an onRemove() method that deletes the p-zone and particle emitter node attached to a trigger when the trigger is deleted, I prefer to store the IDs of these effects in a SimGroup, too. That way, there is no question that they will get deleted on level load (or on mission exit).

- **CoinsGroup.** This last group stores all coins (that have not been picked up). We will use this later to determine when the level is complete and it is time to load the next one.

Next, we will see the beginning of the level-loader's main processing loop.

```
while(!%file.isEOF() ) {
```

From this point on, the level loader will read in lines from the file until the file is empty or an error occurs.

Upon first entering this loop, the function reads a line and checks to see what task it represents: LAYER_UP, LAYER_DOWN, or LAYER_DEFINE. For a LAYER_UP or a LAYER_DOWN, we increment/decrement and then go back to the top of the loop (by using continue) to get the next task. If the task does not match any known task type, the function aborts.

Eventually, the task we get will be a LAYER_DEFINE. This tells the loader that the next line will be a LAYER_TYPE. So, the level loader reads the next line and decides which layer type it is: BLOCKS, OBSTACLES, PICKUPS, or PLAYERDROPS. If it is none of these, the function fails out.

Assuming the function read a valid layer type, it will use another of those system scripts supplied with the kit and load the next 16 lines into an arrayObject (a scripted class I created so that we may create arrays that can be passed between functions and methods).

After reading in the next 16 lines (into our arrayObject), the level loader will then pass this array to a specialized function that does the layout for that level type.

- **layOutBlocks()**. This lays out normal blocks and fade blocks.
- **layOutObstacles()**. This lays out fireball blocks and teleport stations.
- **layOutPickups()**. This lays out coins.
- **playerDrop()**. This will drop the player into the level at a specified point.

After the current layout pass, the loader goes back to the top of the file-reading loop and continues until the end of the file (or error).

Eventually, the file will be empty, and we will drop out of the loop. At this point in the code, you will see a function (in two places) that may not yet be familiar to you.

```
if( fadeGroup.getCount() )
    fadeGroup.schedule( 5000 , fadePass );

if( FireBallMarkersGroup.getCount() )
    FireBallMarkersGroup.schedule( 5000 , firePass );
```

In both of the above statements, the script is telling the engine to schedule an event to occur in 5000 milliseconds. The first event is the calling of the method fadePass(). It will be called as follows.

```
fadeGroup.fadePass();
```

The second event is the calling of the method firePass(). It will be called as follows.

```
FireBallMarkersGroup.firePass();
```

Each of these statements will cause a special function (not yet covered) to iterate over the specified SimGroup and to "do something" to each entry. We will cover this in Lesson #18 (Section 10.3.7).

`layOutBlocks()`

We will talk about the first of the four layout functions, and then I will leave you to examine the other three on your own.

This function has the responsibility for creating content in the world based on the values in the arrayObject it has been passed.

To do its jobs, the function uses a nested loop and reads every token of every line and parses these tokens by category (using the trick we discussed at the beginning of this lesson) and then by specific type.

It is assumed that every token represents a world space of "4 4 4". Thus, the current position is incremented by "4 4 0" to keep us on the current layer.

When a token is found that matches a known category, an object in that category is created. Being smart, we named our files and datablocks in such a way that we can merely append the token to a generic version of the file-name or datablock name when loading a file or building an object from a datablock.

Once this function has consumed all of the lines in the arrayObject, it deletes the object.

Temporary Spawn Point

One side effect of destroying a level is that the player will fall into the lava because there is no place to stand. So, to solve this problem, while the level loads, we should create a place for the player to stand temporarily. This can be accomplished by editing the file

"\MazeRunner\prototype\data\Missions\mazerunner.mis"

and adding the following to the end of the mission file (bold lines are new).

```
new TSStatic() {
  position = "0 0 295";
  rotation = "1 0 0 0";
  scale = "1 1 1";
  shapeName = "~/data/MazeRunner/Shapes/MazeBlock/blockA.dts";
  };
};
//--- OBJECT WRITE END ---
```

Additionally, to get the spawn to work properly, we need to move the spawn point. So, in the same file, locate our spawn point and change the position to the following.

```
new SimGroup(PlayerDropPoints) {
  new SpawnSphere() {
  position = "0 0 300";
  rotation = "1 0 0 0";
  scale = "1 1 1";
  dataBlock = "SpawnSphereMarker";
  radius = "1";
  sphereWeight = "100";
  indoorWeight = "100";
  outdoorWeight = "100";
    locked = "False";
    lockCount = "0";
    homingCount = "0";
  };
};
```

Now, when we start the mission, the player will be high above the cauldron, and on subsequent loads the avatar will be moved here temporarily.

Testing the Level Loader

At this point, you should be able to test the level loader. Simply start the GPGT Lesson Kit, open the "Maze Runner" mission, open the console, and type `buildLevel( 0 );`. Your player should be moved to the extra block we just inserted for a few seconds, and then it should drop onto a new level.

9.6 Compiling and Executing Files

Any file containing a valid script can be compiled and/or executed. We have the freedom to only compile a file, but executing a file implies that it will be compiled if we have not already done so.

9.6.1 Compiling

We can compile a file without reloading it. This way we don't override functionality accidentally or in some other way corrupt our environment. A successful recompile produces a new file with the same name plus the extension ".dso" appended.

In order to compile a file, we use the following syntax (Table 9.15).

```
compile( filename );
```

Please note that `compile()` will always return 1 if the file is of nonzero length and it exists. Thus, at this time, the return value is not very useful.

Table 9.15.

Compiling a file.

Syntax Element	Description
compile	This is the function name.
filename	This is a string containing a complete or partial path and the name of the file to be compiled. compile() can expand relative paths.

9.6.2 Executing

As was noted above, executing a file implies that we will recompile it (if necessary) and then reload it. Reloading basically runs the contents of the file, replaces any redefined functions with the new ones, and creates any datablocks defined in the file. The following syntax is described in Table 9.16.

```
exec( filename [ , noCalls [ , journalScript ] ] );
```

Please note that it is illegal to exec() zero-length (empty) files. So, if you need one as a placeholder, put the following statement in the file.

```
return;
```

Table 9.16.

Executing a file.

Syntax Element	Description
exec	This is the function name.
filename	This is a string containing a complete or partial path and the name of the file to be compiled. exec() can expand relative paths.
noCalls	If this Boolean value is true, it instructs the engine not to execute any code found in the file. Only packages and functions are reloaded. All functional code is skipped.
journalScript	Boolean value specifying whether this is a journal file or not.

9.7 Game Setup Scripting Summary

In this chapter, we learned about some of the classes and features that Torque provides for setting up and maintaining a game.

We learned about the SimSet and SimGroup containers.

We then discussed how to create scripted objects using the ScriptObject and ScriptGroup classes. We also learned how these special classes provide namespace scoping and callbacks.

We learned about action maps and how to connect user inputs to game actions and reactions.

Next, we discussed how the file subsystem operates (from the scripted viewpoint) as well as how to locate files and to parse the components of a file path and filename. We closed by learning how to read from, create, and write to new files, as well as how to append to existing files.

Last, we discussed how to compile and execute script files.

Chapter 10
Gameplay Scripting

This chapter gives an overview of the scripting tasks that are related to implementing gameplay. It will familiarize you with the following specific topics.

- **Callbacks.** We need to understand what they are and what a small set of them do in order to discuss some larger topics later.
- **Event scheduling.** As an event-driven simulation, our games often require events to occur at some time in the future. The event-scheduling features of TGE make this possible.
- **Manipulating strings.** TorqueScript deals with all data as strings (before these strings are converted to their proper types). Here, we talk about the many ways we can manipulate this string data.
- **Scripted math.** Another big part of making games is math. We'll take a little time to review the math features available via scripting.
- **Dynamic scripting.** We'll discuss how to write dynamic code; that is, we'll talk about how to assemble and execute scripts at run-time.
- **Basic client-server communication.** We'll briefly discuss how basic client-server communications are achieved.

10.4 Callbacks

For the purpose of this guide, a callback is any console method that is automatically (or directly) called by the engine (or scripts) in response to some event. These callbacks are part of what drives a game; that is, game events are processed by the engine, firing callbacks, which subsequently trigger chains of scripted events.

Having defined what a callback is, we are not going to carry on about why we have them or how they work. Instead, we will discuss a few significant callbacks and then move on. There is also an appendix that documents all of the default TGE callbacks (see Appendix A).

10.1.1 onAdd() and onRemove()

For now, you need only be familiar with eight callbacks. The first two of these callbacks are the `onAdd()` and the `onRemove()` callbacks.

The `onAdd()` callback is called just after an object is instantiated. The `onRemove()` callback is called just prior to the object being deleted.

The calling sequence may still be a bit foggy, so see the following code.

```
//ts10();

function myTestDatablock::onAdd( %theDB, %theObj ) {
  echo("A new object: \cp\c2", %theObj.getName(),
    "\c0 was created with the datablock: \c2",
%theDB.getName() ) ;
}
function myTestDatablock::onRemove( %theDB, %theObj ) {
  echo("Deleting: \cp\c2", %theObj.getName(),
    "\c0 created with the datablock: \cp\c2",
%theDB.getName() ) ;
}
datablock StaticShapeData( myTestDatablock ) {
  category = "LessonShapes";
};
%obj = new StaticShape( testObject ) {
  datablock = "myTestDatablock";
};
%obj.delete();
```

Running this sample produces the following output.

```
A new object: testObject was created with the datablock:
    myTestDatablock
Deleting: testObject created with the datablock:
    myTestDatablock
```

So, what happened? The (nearly) exact sequence is as follows.

1. An instance of StaticShape is created using the myTestDatablock datablock and named testObject.

2. onAdd() is automatically called with two arguments, the ID of myTest-Datablock and the ID of the newly created StaticShape.

3. The method delete() is called on the instance of StaticShape named testObject.

4. Before the deletion occurs, the onRemove() callback is automatically called with two arguments, the ID of myTestDatablock and the ID of the to-be-deleted StaticShape.

This was mentioned before, but it is very important to remember that both the datablock ID and the object ID are passed automatically to callbacks when they are called by the engine, but if you call them manually, you may be responsible for passing one or both of these values yourself. Reread the sections on objects and datablocks in Chapter 4, "Introduction to Torque Script," if this is fuzzy.

10.1.2 `onCollision()`

The next callback you need to know about is the `onCollision()` callback. This callback is called whenever a collision between objects is registered by the engine. The `onCollision()` callback takes several arguments, and an instance of this callback could be defined as follows.

```
function PlayerData::onCollision( %colliderDB ,
                                  %colliderObj ,
                                  %collidedObj ,
                                  %vec ,
                                  %speed ) {
  //...
}
```

Describing the exact details of how and when this callback is called is beyond the scope of this volume. For now we'll just restate that it is called when there is a collision, and then we'll describe the arguments in Table 10.1.

Argument	Description
`%colliderDB`	This argument contains the datablock ID of the object that did the colliding.
`%colliderObj`	This argument contains the ID of the object that did the colliding.
`%collidedObj`	This argument contains the ID of the object that was collided with.
`%vec`	This argument contains a three-element floating point vector describing the direction and magnitude of the collision.
`%speed`	This last argument is provided to ease our coding work. It contains the magnitude of the prior vector, i.e., the velocity (or speed) of the collision.

Table 10.1.

Arguments for `onCollision()`.

10.1.3 `onWake()` and `onSleep()`

These two callbacks are associated with GUI controls. The `onWake()` callback is called when a GUI control or its parent is made the current content of the canvas. The `onSleep()` callback is called when the GUI control or its parent is removed from the canvas. Alternately for dialogs, `onWake()` is called when the dialog is pushed, and `onSleep()` is called when the dialog is popped. This may not mean a great deal to you yet, but it will make more sense when we get to Chapter 12, "Standard TGE GUI Controls."

10.1.4 `create()`

There are some who would argue that this is not a callback, and I would almost be willing to concede that point, except that this method is called as the result of a scripted action. That script is part of the standard TGE release. It is the World Editor scripts that call the `create()` method automatically when we attempt to create a new instance of a class in the world.

Some folks may argue with me yet, because this "callback" is scoped to object class names, not to datablocks.

This is not a valid argument, however. Yes, almost all callbacks are scoped to datablocks, but there are some callbacks that are scoped to object instances instead. This is one of those exceptions to the rule.

I repeat: this special method is needed for any GameBase child if we wish to be able to add an instance of it from the World Editor Creator. The GPGT Lesson Kit fully defines all the `create()` methods. If you would like to see how they are written, do a search for the string "`::create`".

10.1.5 `onEnterTrigger()` and `onLeaveTrigger()`

We already discussed these callbacks in Chapter 8, "Mission Objects," but just to refresh your memory:

- `onEnterTrigger()` is called when a shape enters the bounds of a trigger, and
- `onLeaveTrigger()` is called when a shape leaves the bounds of a trigger.

In Chapter 8, we did discuss other callbacks associated with the trigger, but we won't be using them in the prototype for our game.

10.2 Event Scheduling

We have discussed callbacks, and thus we understand the concept of a method being called due to an engine event, such as a collision, an object creation or deletion, etc. However, what if we want to create our own event sequences? Is there a way to do this? Yes; read on.

10.2.1 Motivation and Concepts

There will be times when we would like to schedule "something" to happen at a future time. Furthermore, we might only want this something to occur if a specific object exists. We might also want this something to execute standalone like a function, or on an object (like a callback). Thinking ahead, we might also want to be able to check if the event has executed or if it is still pending. Knowing that it is pending, we may choose to cancel an event(s) we previously issued. All of this we can do.

10.2.2 Scheduling Our Own Events

TGE provides both a function `schedule()` and a method `schedule()` for scheduling events, allowing us to schedule standalone events (using the function) or events that execute on an object (using the method).

The `schedule()` Function

This form of `schedule()` is used to call a function at some future time. It has the following syntax (Table 10.2).

```
%eventID = schedule( timeInMS , objID || 0 , functionName,
                     arg0, ... , argN );
```

Syntax Element	Description
eventID	Upon successfully scheduling an event, the `schedule()` function returns a unique ID for the event.
timeInMS	Time in milliseconds until this event will be executed.
objID	For this argument, we can supply a handle to an object or we can pass 0. If an object handle is passed and the object associated with the handle is deleted prior to `timeInMS`, the event will automatically be canceled.
functionName	This is the unadorned name of the function to execute, e.g. "echo"
arg0, ... , argN	Optionally, we may supply extra arguments to the event. These arguments may be constants or strings.

Table 10.2.

The `schedule()` method.

We use this function as follows.

```
//ts15();
schedule( 1000 , 0 , echo, "Hello world!" );
```

After 1 second passes ...

```
Hello World!
```

Alternately, we could attach our event to an object.

Game Elements

```
//ts16();
%obj = new ScriptObject( test );
schedule( 1000 , %obj , echo, "Hello world!" );
%obj.delete();
```

After 1 second passes... nothing happens, because the delete canceled the event.

The schedule() Method

This form of schedule() is used to call a function at some future time. It has the following syntax (Table 10.3).

```
%eventID = objID.schedule( timeInMS , functionName,
                                      arg0, ... , argN );
```

Syntax Element	Description
eventID	Upon successfully scheduling an event, the schedule() method returns a unique ID for the event.
objID	Because this version of schedule() is a console method, it must be executed on a object, thus we use any acceptable form of an object handle.
timeInMS	Time in milliseconds until this event will be executed.
functionName	This is the unadorned name of the function to execute, e.g. "echo".
arg0, ... , argN	Optionally, we may supply extra arguments to the event. These arguments may be constants or strings.

We use this function as follows.

```
//ts17();

%obj = new ScriptObject(test);

function test::doit( %this , %val ) {
  echo(%this.getName(), " says ", %val );
}

%obj.schedule( 1000 , doit , "Hello world!" );
```

After 1 second passes, we see the following.

```
test says Hello World!
```

As with the function version, which watches an object handle, if we were to delete the object, the event would be canceled.

```
//ts18();
```

```
%obj = new ScriptObject( test );
%obj.schedule( 1000 , doit , "Hello world!" );
%obj.delete();
```

After 1 second passes… once again nothing happens because the delete canceled the event.

10.2.3 Checking For and Cancelling Pending Events

So far, we know how to schedule an event, but it can often happen that we need to check if an event has executed prior to doing something new. Or, if the event is pending, we may need to cancel it.

isEventPending()

TGE provides a function to check for pending events. This function checks to see if an event is still queued in the event queue. It returns `true` if the event is found and `false` if not. The syntax is as follows (Table 10.4).

```
%pending = isEventPending( eventID );
```

Syntax Element	Description
%pending	As noted, this method returns a Boolean value indicating `true` (the event is pending) or `false` (the event is not pending).
eventID	This is an ID previously returned from either the `schedule()` function or method.

Table 10.4.
Checking for pending events.

Event Times

If an event is in fact still pending, we can gather additional data about it, including the time since it started (in milliseconds).

```
%sinceStartedMS = getTimeSinceStart( eventID );
```

We can also find out the time left until it executes (in milliseconds).

```
%remainingMS = getEventTimeLeft( eventID );
```

And we can find out the total duration for the schedule.

```
%durationMS = getScheduleDuration( eventID );
```

The syntax element `eventID` is an ID previously returned from either the `schedule()` function or method.

cancel()

Events dependent on an object are automatically canceled if the object is deleted; thus, if we know our event is tied to an object, we can just delete the object. However, this may not always be suitable, and in fact often it is not. Thus, TGE provides a `cancel()` function with the following syntax:

```
cancel( eventID );
```

The syntax element `eventID` is an ID previously returned from either the `schedule()` function or method.

10.2.4 Event Scheduling and Accuracy

It is important to step back for a moment and ask the following question: "Just how accurate is my event timing going to be, and do I care?" Regardless of when an event is scheduled, it will not be executed until there is a tick. Additionally, there are other factors that can affect timing, including engine internals, network latency, etc. So the answer for the first part of the question would be, "Not entirely accurate." In fact, you may experience a small amount of drift (positive or negative) in the actual time before an event occurs. This is significant for very short-order events (less than 32 milliseconds), and very long-order events that are cascaded (i.e., event A schedules event B, ...). Thus, you must consider the second part of the question carefully. Overall, the accuracy of the event-scheduling system is usually sufficient to handle most of our needs, but you will sometimes find it is not. At that point, you may need to write engine code instead of relying on event-driven scripts.

The following code demonstrates the timing variances that can occur for scheduled events.

```
function accuracyCheck( %scheduledTime, %time , %repeats ) {
  %actualTime = getRealTime() - %scheduledTime;

  echo("Requested Execution Time: " , %time ,
      " :: Actual Execution Time: " , %actualTime ,
      " :: Difference (ms): " , %actualTime - %time);
```

```
  if( %repeats) {
    %repeats = %repeats - 1;
    testscheduleAccuracy ( %time ,%repeats);
  }
}

function testScheduleAccuracy( %time , %repeats ) {
  schedule( %time , 0 , accuracyCheck , getRealTime() , %time , %repeats );
}
```

Here is some sample output from a call to testScheduleAccuracy().

//ts19();
testScheduleAccuracy(1 , 10);
```
Requested Execution Time: 1 :: Actual Execution Time: -3
   :: Difference (ms): -4
Requested Execution Time: 1 :: Actual Execution Time: -3
   :: Difference (ms): -4
Requested Execution Time: 1 :: Actual Execution Time: -3
   :: Difference (ms): -4
Requested Execution Time: 1 :: Actual Execution Time: -3
   :: Difference (ms): -4
Requested Execution Time: 1 :: Actual Execution Time: -3
   :: Difference (ms): -4
Requested Execution Time: 1 :: Actual Execution Time: -3
   :: Difference (ms): -4
Requested Execution Time: 1 :: Actual Execution Time: 13
   :: Difference (ms): 12
Requested Execution Time: 1 :: Actual Execution Time: 13
   :: Difference (ms): 12
Requested Execution Time: 1 :: Actual Execution Time: 13
   :: Difference (ms): 12
Requested Execution Time: 1 :: Actual Execution Time: 13
   :: Difference (ms): 12
Requested Execution Time: 1 :: Actual Execution Time: 13
   :: Difference (ms): 12
```

Rerun this a few times. Your results should vary.

Repeating an Event

It may not be obvious at first, but if you want to create an event that repeats, you must reschedule that event. The simplest way to do this is by putting a call to schedule() in the function that you are scheduling, or in a function that the scheduled function calls. Here is a simple example.

```
function repeatForever( ) {
  // do something
  schedule( 1000, 0 , repeatForever ) ;
}
```

It is generally safer to tie scheduled events to the existence of an object. Otherwise, it is easy to get runaway schedules occurring in the background. Over time, these may eat a lot of CPU time.

In this example, we could either schedule `repeatForever()` or call it directly, and it would continue to be rescheduled every 1000 milliseconds until the engine stopped.

10.3 Manipulating Strings

As noted in Chapter 4, "Introduction to TorqueScript," all operands in Torque-Script are treated as strings. Therefore, it would be good for us if there were facilities for parsing and otherwise manipulating these strings.

TGE provides a good-sized list of console functions dedicated to string manipulations ranging from the mundane to the complex. I'll list them all here and demonstrate the more tricky functions/concepts.

10.3.1 Words

In TorqueScript, every whitespace-separated element in a string is called a *word*. For example, in the string "Torque Is Cool", we have three words: word 0 is "Torque", word 1 is "Is", and word 2 is "Cool". Table 10.5 shows the functions for manipulating words.

Table 10.5.

Manipulating words.

Function	Description
firstWord(text)	Returns first word in string `text`.
getWord(text , index)	Returns word at `index` in string `text`. `index` 0 is first word and so on.
getWordCount(text)	Returns count of all words in string `text`.
getWords(text , index [, endindex])	Returns all words in string text between `index` and (optional) `endindex`. If `endindex` is not supplied, end of string is assumed.
removeWord(text , index)	Removes the word at `index` in string `text`. Also removes the whitespace following the word located at `index`.
restWords(text)	Returns all words in string `text` excluding first word.
setWord(text , index , replace)	Replaces the word in string `text` at `index` with the string in `replace`.

```
//ts20();
%test = "Torque cool!";
echo( %test , " has " , getWordCount( %test ) , " words." );
%test = setWord( %test , 0 , "Torque is is" );
echo( %test , " has " , getWordCount( %test ) , " words." );
%test = removeWord( %test, 1 );
echo( %test , " has " , getWordCount( %test ) , " words." );
while ( "" !$= %test ) {
  echo( firstWord( %test ) );
  %test = restWords( %test ) ;
}
```

10.3.2 Tokens

Frequently when we parse files, we will read in strings that are actually a series of tokens separated by some delimiter. Some common delimiters are:

$$" ; : , | " .$$

TGE supplies a single function that can be used to pull these tokens out of a string in an iterative fashion. The way this function works seems a little mysterious at first, but is actually pretty straightforward. So, let's define it, then use it (Table 10.6).

Function	Description
nextToken (str , tokenVar , delim)	This function returns a truncated version of the passed-in string str, where the part that has been truncated is equal to the first token along with the first instance of delim. Furthermore, the function places the removed token into the named variable tokenVar. Note that tokenVar does not include the delimiter.

Table 10.6.

Pulling out tokens using delimiters.

```
//ts21();
function printTokens( %tokenString ) {
  %tmpTokens = %tokenString;
  while( "" !$= %tmpTokens ) {
    %tmpTokens = nextToken( %tmpTokens , "myToken" , ";" );
    echo( %myToken );
  }
}
printTokens( "This;is;a;sample;string;of;tokens;." );
```

In this example, we've take a string of tokens separated by semicolons and iteratively stripped them out of the string from left to right. The nextToken()

method places each token in a variable, which we specify, named `%myToken`. After stripping out a token, the remainder of the string is returned by the method. Because we're actually manipulating the string as part of our processing loop, it is a good idea to work with a copy of the string.

There is one more thing you need to know. We actually named the temporary token variable "myToken", and TGE was smart enough to know that that means `%myToken`. However, TGE did this because `nextToken()` was called from within a function. If you use `nextToken()` in a file that is being executed outside the scope of a function, or if you use it directly in the console, "myToken" will become the global variable `$myToken`. Pretty smart, eh?

10.3.3 Records

So far, we have words and tokens. The next data-organizing methodology to understand is records. A *record* is nothing more than a string that ends in a newline character. Thus, if we have a string containing elements separated by newlines, each element is considered to be a record. Records can have multiple words and/or tokens. In fact, this is really a kind of special case where the delimiter in our token string can only be the newline character "\n" (same as the operator "NL"). Table 10.7 explains the functions used with records.

Table 10.7.

Working with records.

Function	Description
getRecord(text , index)	Returns the record in string `text` at `index`.
getRecordCount(text)	Returns the number of records in string `text`.
getRecords(text , index [, endIndex])	Returns the records in string `text` between `index` and `endIndex` (or end of string if `endIndex` is not specified).
removeRecord(text , index)	Removes the record in string `text` located at `index`. Also removes newline character following the record located at `index`.
setRecord(text , index , replace)	Replaces the record in string `text` at `index` with the string `replace`.

```
//ts33();
function testRecords( %recordString ) {
  %tmpRecord = %recordString;
  echo( %tmpRecord, "\n" );
  for( %count = 0; %count < getRecordCount( %tmpRecord );
        %count++ ) {
```

```
  %theRecord = getRecord( %tmpRecord , %count );
  echo( "Current record: ", %theRecord );

  if ( %theRecord $= "test" ) {
    echo("\c3Replacing records...");
    %tmpRecord = setRecord( %tmpRecord , %count ,
          %theRecord NL "of" NL "records." );
  }
}

while ( getRecordCount( %tmpRecord ) ) {
  %concatRecordString = %concatRecordString SPC
        getRecord( %tmpRecord , 0 );
  %tmpRecord = removeRecord( %tmpRecord , 0 );
}
echo( "\n", %concatRecordString );
}
testRecords( "This" NL "is" NL "a" NL "test" );
```

10.3.4 Fields

The final data-organizing methodology to understand is fields. A field is nothing more than a string that ends in a newline character or a TAB character. Table 10.8 explains the functions used with fields.

Function	Description
getField(text , index)	Returns the field in string text at index.
getFieldCount(text)	Returns the number of fields in string text.
getFields(text , index [, endIndex])	Returns the fields in string text between index and endIndex (or end of string if endIndex is not specified).
removeField(text , index)	Removes the field in string text located at index. Also removes newline character or TAB character following the field located at index.
setField(text , index , replace)	Replaces the field in string text at index with the string replace.

Table 10.8.
Working with fields.

It would be wasteful to show the whole sample routine, so an abbreviated version is shown below. It is nearly identical to the above records test with the few exceptions shown.

Game Elements

```
//ts34();

function testFields( %fieldString ) {
// ... Same as testRecords() except using field functions ...
  echo("\c3Replacing fields...");
  %tmpField = setField ( %tmpField , %count , %theField
                          NL "of" TAB "fields." );
// ... Same as testRecords() except using field functions ...
}
testFields( "This" TAB "is" NL "a" TAB "test" );
```

10.3.5 Conversion

Table 10.9.

Converting characters.

Function	Description
strlwr(string)	Converts all alpha characters in string to lowercase.
strupr(string)	Converts all alpha characters in string to uppercase.

Alphabetic characters in a string can be converted from uppercase to lowercase and vice versa (Table 10.9).

```
//ts35();
echo( strlwr("YEAH these ARE") SPC strupr("pretty OBVIOUS.") );
```

10.3.6 Metrics

The function strlen(string) returns the length of a string.

10.3.7 Searching and Replacing

TGE provides a few standard ways of searching for strings and characters within strings. These searches are all case sensitive.

Table 10.10.

Searching for strings and characters.

Function	Description
getSubStr(string , start , numChars)	Returns a string composed of all the characters in string beginning at start and continuing for numChars or until the end of the string, whichever comes first.
strchr(string , char)	Returns a string composed of all the characters in string beginning at the first instance of char and continuing until the end of the string. Returns null string if char not found (case sensitive).

Function	Description
strpos(source , target [, offset])	Returns the location of the first instance of string `target` in string `source`. Optionally, a starting `offset` may be provided, telling the function to ignore all characters before that point. If no match is found, −1 is returned.
strreplace(string , from , to)	Replaces all occurrences of the string `from` with the string `to` in `string` and returns this new string (case sensitive).
strstr(string , substr)	Returns position of first occurrence of `substr` in `string`. Returns −1 if not found.

Table 10.10 (continued).

```
//ts36();

%testString = "TGE is cool. TGE is fun. TGE Rocks. Use TGE to make a game!";

echo( %testString, "\n" );

// Get string length
%len = strlen(%testString);
echo( "\c3This string is ", %len , " characters long.", "\n" );

// Count instances of TGE
%lastTGE = -1;
while( %foundAt >= 0 ) {
   %foundAt = strpos( %testString , "TGE" , %lastTGE + 1 );
   if ( %foundAt > -1 ) {
      %lastTGE = %foundAt;
      %count++;
   }
}
echo( "\c3It contains ", %count, " instances of the substring TGE.", "\n" );

// Replace all instances of TGE
echo( "\c3Replacing all instances of TGE...", "\n" );
%testString2 = strReplace( %testString , "TGE", "Torque Game Engine" );
echo( %testString2, "\n" );

// Only replace last instance of TGE
echo( "\c3Replacing last instance of TGE...", "\n" );
%testString3 = getSubStr( %testString , 0 , %lastTGE ) "the Torque Game Engine" @
      getSubStr( %testString , %lastTGE + 3 , %len );
```

```
echo( %testString3, "\n" );

// Modify and print the last sentence.
echo( "\c3Modifying and printing last sentence only...", "\n" );
%testString4 = strchr( %testString , "U" ) ;
%testString4 = strReplace( %testString4 , "a game" ,
        "\cp\c3games\co that Rock" );
echo( %testString4, "\n" );
```

10.3.8 Comparisons

We have a means of comparing arithmetic values (1, 2, 3, ...), and we have the string comparison operator $=, but there are no string operators corresponding to the arithmetic operators > and <. Thus, TGE provides two functions to accomplish this work. The first is case sensitive, while the second is not (see Table 10.11).

Table 10.11.

Making lexicographic comparisons.

Function	Description
strcmp(string1 , string2)	Does case-sensitive lexicographic comparison of string1 and string2. Returns the following. −1 if string1 comes before string2 in alphabetical order. 0 if string1 is equivalent to string2. 1 if string1 comes after string2 in alphabetical order.
stricmp(string1 , string2)	Does case-*insensitive* lexicographic comparison of string1 and string2. Returns the following. −1 if string1 comes before string2 in alphabetical order. 0 if string1 is equivalent to string2. 1 if string1 comes after string2 in alphabetical order.

```
//ts37();

echo("\c3Lexicographic comparisons are not the same as
    arithmetic comparisons...");
echo("100 - 10 == 90, but strcmp( \"100\" , \"10\" ) == " ,
    strcmp( "100" , "10" ) );
echo("\n", "\c3Don\'t forget about case-sensitivity...");
echo("strcmp( \"ABC\" , \"abc\" ) == " , strcmp( "ABC" ,
    "abc" ) , ", but " );
echo("stricmp( \"ABC\" , \"abc\" ) == " , stricmp( "ABC" ,
    "abc" ) );
```

10.3.9 Trimming and Stripping

It will often be necessary to clean up strings before displaying or storing them. To enable this task, TGE supplies some standard utility functions (Table 10.12).

Function	Description
ltrim(string)	Returns string with all leading whitespace removed.
rtrim(string)	Returns string with all trailing whitespace removed.
stripChars(string , chars)	Returns string with all characters in string chars removed.
stripMLControlChars(string)	Returns string with all TorqueML characters removed.
stripTrailingSpaces(string)	Returns string with all trailing spaces and underscores removed.
trim(string)	Returns string with both trailing and leading whitespace removed.

Table 10.12.

Cleaning up strings.

```
//ts38();
%toClean = "<tab:60> I'm,<spush><font: arial: 8> " @
          "all, clean,____ <spop>";
echo("\c3Cleaning up an ugly string...");
echo(%toClean);

echo("\n", "\c3Remove Mark-up language...");
%toClean = stripMLControlChars( %toClean );
echo(%toClean);

echo("\n", "\c3Remove leading and trailing spaces...");
%toClean = trim( %toClean );
echo(%toClean);

echo("\n", "\c3Remove commas...");
%toClean = stripChars( %toClean , ",");
echo(%toClean);

echo("\n", "\c3Get rid of underscores...");
%toClean = stripTrailingSpaces( %toClean );
echo(%toClean);
```

10.4 Scripted Math

TGE provides a rich set of console math functions. The majority of these functions are centered around 3D mathematics, but there are a few other categories as well. All of these functions are documented in the "Console Functions" appendix. However, we will take a brief tour of these functions so you know what is available to you.

10.4.1 Floating-Point Arithmetic

All the arithmetic functions take floating-point values and return floating-point results, but they can be used for integer mathematics, too (Table 10.13).

```
//ts39();

echo( "|-5| == ", mAbs( -5 ), "\n" );
echo( "Next greatest integer from 4.3 == ", mCeil( 4.3 ),
    "\n" );
echo( "Next smallest integer from 4.3 == ", mFloor( 4.3 ),
    "\n" );
echo( "2 raised to the power of 3.14159 == ", mPow( 2 ,
    3.14159 ), "\n" );
echo( "Square root of 2 == ", mSqrt( 2 ), "\n" );
```

10.4.2 Trigonometric Functions

We use trigonometric functions frequently to solve problems in the realm of 3D games; thus, TGE has provided a complete set of these functions to be used in TorqueScript (Table 10.14).

10.4.3 Vectors

In addition to trigonometric calculations, we will frequently be calculating vector results to move game objects, check for intersections, and various other tasks. A good set of vector functions simplifies this work (Table 10.15).

10.4.4 Matrices

Hopefully, you won't find yourself needing to do too many matrix calculations, but if you do, TGE provides some functions (Table 10.16).

Most of these have obvious uses, but `MatrixMulPoint()` may seem a bit mysterious. This can be used to translate a point by a transform. Having this operation available makes it possible to check for collision between an object's scaled objectBox and other objects like the terrain. In fact, this exact problem was solved in *Tribes 2* using `MatrixMulPoint()`. The gist of the solution went something like the following.

```
// Pseudocode for scaled objectBox vs. terrain penetration
// 1. Obtain objectBox for shape and scale both vectors
// appropriately to match object's scale.
%objBox = %obj.getObjectBox();
// ... do scaling here ...

// 2. Create array of eight points containing untranslated
// position of objectBox bounds.
%transform = %obj.getTransform();

// 3. Acquire object's transform. Iterate over array and use
// 'MatrixMulPoint()' to calculate translated position of vertices.
for(%count = 0; %count < 8; %count++) {
   %newBoundPos[%count] = matrixMulPoint( %transform,
                                       %oldBoundPos[%count] );
}

// 4. Iterate over new bounds points using rayCast to check
// for collision between bounds and terrain.
%collision = 0;
for(%count = 0; %count < 7; %count ++) {
   %obj = containerRayCast(
      %oldBoundPos[%count] ,
      %newBoundPos[%count] ,
      $TypeMasks::TerrainObjectType ,
      0 );
   %collision |= %obj;
}

// 5. If %collision is not zero, a collision occurred.
if (%collision)
   echo ( "Oops, got a collision!" );
```

10.4.5 Quadratics and Cubics

If you're not a mathematician, these functions may sound a bit spooky, but if you dredge up your old algebra and calculus notes, you'll recall that they are simply the following.

- **Quadratic.** Second-order polynomial of the form: $ax^2 + bx + c = 0$. Warning: This function produces the inverse of the solution (see example below).
- **Cubic.** Third-order polynomial of the form: $ax^3 + bx^2 + cx + d = 0$. This function works as expected.

Table 10.13.
Arithmetic functions.

Function	Description
mAbs(operand)	Returns the absolute (nonnegative) value of operand.
mCeil(operand)	Returns the next greatest integer (as a float) starting at operand and rounding up: mCeil(4.5) returns 5.0.
mFloor(operand)	Returns the next smallest integer (as a float) starting at operand and rounding down: mFloor(4.5) returns 4.0.
mLog(operand)	Returns the natural log of operand.
mPow(operandA , operandB)	Returns the value operandA ^ operandB; i.e., operandA raised to the power of operandB.
mSqrt(operand)	Returns the square root of operand.

Table 10.14.
Trigonometric functions.

Function	Description
mAcos(operand)	Returns the inverse cosine of operand.
mAsin(operand)	Returns the inverse sine of operand.
mAtan(operand)	Returns the inverse tangent of operand.
mCos(operand)	Returns the cosine of operand.
mDegToRad(operand)	Converts operand from degrees to radians.
mRadToDeg(operand)	Converts operand from radians to degrees.
mSin(operand)	Returns the sine of operand.
mTan(operand)	Returns the tangent of operand.

Table 10.15.
Vector functions.

Function	Description
VectorAdd(vect1 , vect2)	Adds vect1 and vect2.
VectorCross(vect1 , vect2)	Calculates cross product of vect1 and vect2.
VectorDist(vect1 , vect2)	Calculates distance between points specified by vect1 and vect2.
VectorDot(vect1 , vect2)	Returns scalar dot product of vect1 and vect2.
VectorLen(vect)	Returns length of vector vect.
VectorNormalize(vect)	Returns unit-length version of vect.
VectorOrthoBasis("x y z angle")	Returns a 3×3 matrix containing the orthogonal basis of the vector described by the axis-angle representation <x y z> angle.
VectorScale(vect , scalar)	Scales the vector vect by the amount scalar.
VectorSub(vect1 , vect2)	Subtracts vect2 from vect1.

Function	Description
MatrixCreate(Pos , Rot)	Creates a 3 × 3 matrix from the three-element floating-point position vector Pos and the four-element floating-point axis-angle vector Rot.
MatrixCreateFromEuler ("Ax Ay Az")	Creates a matrix from the Euler angles "Ax Ay Az".
MatrixMulPoint(transform , point)	Multiplies the three-element floating-point point vector by the standard seven-element floating-point transform.
MatrixMultiply(Left , Right)	Multiplies the 3 × 3 matrices Left and Right.

Table 10.16.

Matrix functions.

Function	Description
mSolveQuadratic(a , b , c)	Solve for x0, x1 in second-order polynomial equation with factors a, b, c. **Warning: x0 and x1 are inverted.**
mSolveCubic(a , b , c , d)	Solve for x0, x1, x2 in third-order polynomial equation with factors a, b, c, d.

Table 10.17.

Quadratic and cubic functions.

The functions in Table 10.17 return a vector of values in the form "sol x0 x1 ... xn", where sol is the number of solutions and x0 ... xn are the values of those solutions.

The number of solutions, sol, should be 2 for a quadratic and 3 for a cubic or else the calculation has failed. A failure will occur (sol == 0) if there is no solution to the equation you are trying to solve. This always means that you have entered factors for an equation of the form $ax^2 + bx + c \neq 0$ or $ax^3 + bx^2 + cx + d! \neq 0$. These functions can only solve for equations that result in 0. x0 and x1 are the factored values for x. See the examples below for clarification.

```
// All samples below drawn from 1728 Software Systems
// Sample Calculations: http://www.1728.com/.
// Cool calculators and converters; check it out.

// Quadratic Test -
// (x + 2)(x + 3) = 0 => x^2 + 5x + 6 = 0
echo( "Solutions: ", mSolveQuadratic( 1 , 5 , 6 ) );
// Produces: 2 2 3 meaning there are two solutions,
// 2 and 3, but it is easy to see that we should have
// received 2 -2 -3. Be aware of this bug.
```

Game Elements

```
echo ( "X == " , mSolveQuadratic( 2 , 10 , -100 ) );

// Cubic Test:
// (x - 4) (x + 3) (x - 1) = 0 => 2x^3 - 4x^2 - 22x + 24 = 0
echo ( "Solutions: ", mSolveCubic( 2 , -4 , -22 , 24 ) );
// Produces: 3 -3 1 4 which matches the factored solution
// to the cubic above.
```

10.4.6 Miscellaneous

Centroids

A concept we deal with frequently is that of the center, or centroid, of an object or a space. It will often occur that we know the bounds of a space and want the exact center of that space. The method `getBoxCenter( Box )` does that for us. It takes a single string containing two three-element floating-point vectors representing the outer bounds of a (possibly irregular) rectangular solid region and returns a three-element floating-point vector representing the center of that rectangular solid.

```
//ts22();
```

```
%cube = "-1.0 -1.0 -1.0 1.0 1.0 1.0";
echo( getBoxCenter( %cube ) );
```

Random Numbers

You will, almost invariably, need random numbers at some time in the design of your game. Knowing this, the authors of TGE have provided some methods to produce them.

Initializing the Random Number Generator

You don't necessarily need to initialize the random number generator, but if you want to be able to repeat your random results (e.g. you're doing some debugging and want the same random sequence every time), simply set the seed to the same value before starting the sequence (Table 10.18).

You can also retrieve the seed value, prior to your sequence, in case you need to plug it in later.

Getting Random Values

There is only one function supplied for getting random values, but it can be called in a variety of ways (Table 10.19).

Function	Description
setRandomSeed(seed)	Sets random seed to seed.
getRandomSeed()	Returns current seed.

Table 10.18.

Initializing the random number generator.

Function	Description
getRandom( )	Returns a random value in the range [0.0 , 1.0].
getRandom(max)	Returns a random value in the range [0.0 , max].
getRandom(min , max)	Returns a random value in the range [min , max].

Table 10.19.

Getting random numbers.

```
//ts23();

%seed = getRandomSeed();
for ( %count = 0 ; %count < 100 ; %count++ ) {
  %x[%count] = getRandom( %count );
}

setRandomSeed( %seed );
for ( %count = 0 ; %count < 100 ; %count++ ) {
  %y[%count] = getRandom( %count );
}

%mismatches = 0;

for ( %count = 0 ; %count < 100 ; %count++ ) {
  if( %x[%count] != %y[%count] ) {
    error( "Failed to reproduce same sequence of random numbers!" );
    error("Seed:" SPC %seed );
    error("Count:" SPC %count );
    error(%x[%count] SPC "!=" SPC %y[%count] );
    %mismatches++;
  }
}
echo("There were ", %mismatches, " mismatches.");
```

Floating-Point Manipulation

On occasion, when you're doing a floating-point calculation, it would be nice if you could force the result to have a fixed number of decimal places. TGE provides the function mFloatLength(operand, numDecimals) that forces a floating-point value to have a specified number of decimal places.

Furthermore, TGE will round the last place up if the actual value extends beyond the specified range and if the next decimal place is greater than or equal to 5.

```
//ts24();
echo( mFloatLength( 1.196 , 2 ) );
echo( mFloatLength( 1.196 , 10 ) );
```

10.4.7 Maze Runner Lesson #18 (90 Percent Step)—Game Events

In this lesson, we will examine the scripts used to fade blocks in and out, and we will examine the functions used to shoot fireballs on a regular basis. Now that we have covered callbacks, scheduling, string manipulation, and scripted math, we should be ready to examine how these gameplay scripts work.

Please note: This lesson depends on Lesson #4 (Section 6.4.4).

Fade Blocks

There are three blocks of code we are interested in for the fade blocks. The first of these is in the file "\MazeRunner\starter.fps\server\scripts\ MazeRunner\levelloader.cs".

At the end of the function `BuildLevel()`, there is a little snippet of code that checks to see if there are any fade blocks in the fadeGroup SimGroup. If there are, the loader schedules a `fadePass()` in 5000 milliseconds.

```
if( fadeGroup.getCount() )
   fadeGroup.schedule( 5000 , fadePass );
```

`fadePass()`

This function has the task of coming back every `$stepTime` (1000) milliseconds and updating all of the fade blocks. The motivation for updating all the blocks simultaneously is that it gives us greater control over the behavior of the blocks than if each block scheduled its own maintenance. Also, by maintaining a single entry and exit point, we only use one schedule, thus reducing overhead.

```
function SimSet::fadePass( %theSet ) {
   %theSet.forEach( fadeStep , true );
   %theSet.schedule( $stepTime , fadePass );
}
```

As can be seen, this function merely iterates over the blocks in the set and runs `fadeStep()` on each of them.

In the code on this page, you will see a call to `forEach()`. This is not a standard function, but rather one of several utility functions that has been provided with the GPGT Lesson Kit as well as separately on the accompanying disk. Please see Appendix A.7, "Scripted Systems Quick Reference," under "GPGT Utilities" to learn more about this utility method and the others that have been supplied with this book.

`fadeStep()`

This function has the responsibility for advancing the fade status of an individual fade block by one time period. A fade block can be in one of three states.

- **waitToFadeOut.** The block is waiting to begin a fade.
- **waitToFadeIn.** The block is faded out and waiting to begin fading in.
- **wait.** The block is in a dead cycle waiting for all other blocks to complete the current fade cycle.

A fade cycle is always 10 seconds long (as implemented in "fadeblocks.cs"). During a single fade cycle, every single fade block will fade out, fade in, and wait for its peers to finish their fade cycle.

By using this method instead of allowing blocks to fade in, fade out, fade in, ad infinitum, without synchronizing, we avoid chaos. The game would be no fun if the blocks faded in and out chaotically. But, because we can rely on a cycle always taking 10 seconds and then repeating itself, the player can plan ahead after observing a cycle or two.

Enough talking. Let's look at the code.

```
function StaticShape::fadeStep( %theBlock ) {
  %theBlock.timer = %theBlock.timer - $stepTime;

  // Check for flip-time
  if( %theBlock.timer <= 0 ) {
    switch$(%theBlock.action) {
      case "waitToFadeOut":
      %theBlock.timer = $basePauseTime;
      %theBlock.startFade( $fadeTime , 0 , true );
      %theBlock.schedule( $fadeTime , setHidden , true );
      %theBlock.action = "waitToFadeIn";

      case "waitToFadeIn":
      %theBlock.timer = $basePauseTime;
      %theBlock.setHidden( false );
      %theBlock.startFade( $fadeTime , 0 , false );
      %theBlock.action = "wait";

      case "wait":
      %theBlock.timer = %Obj.maxTime;
      %theBlock.action = "waitToFadeOut";
    }
  }
}
```

As we can see, individual blocks have an internal timer containing some pre-defined value. When that timer gets down to (or below) zero, it is time to change the block's state and do some work.

Initially, all blocks will have the following values.

- **timer.** This value will be between 1000 and 10,000 milliseconds.
- **maxTime.** This value will be the same as timer. The value in this field is never changed after the block is implemented.
- **action.** All blocks start out executing the action waitToFadeOut.

Now, if we restrict our discussion to just one block and assume that the block has a timer and maxTime of 1000 milliseconds, over time, we will see the behavior described in Table 10.19.

Table 10.19.

Fade behavior of one block.

Time (ms)	Action(s)
0	• timer = timer − 1000 (0 <= 0 continue executing) **(block is visible)**. • action == waitToFadeOut. • Block starts to fade out. • Block schedules a hide. • action = waitToFadeIn. • timer = 10000.
1000	• timer = timer − 1000 (9000 > 0 skip) (block is invisible).
2000	• timer = timer − 1000 (8000 > 0 skip) (block is invisible).
3000	• timer = timer − 1000 (7000 > 0 skip) (block is invisible).
4000	• timer = timer − 1000 (6000 > 0 skip) (block is invisible).
5000	• timer = timer − 1000 (5000 > 0 skip) (block is invisible).
6000	• timer = timer − 1000 (4000 > 0 skip) (block is invisible).
7000	• timer = timer − 1000 (3000 > 0 skip) (block is invisible).
8000	• timer = timer − 1000 (2000 > 0 skip) (block is invisible).
9000	• timer = timer − 1000 (1000 > 0 skip) (block is invisible).
10000	• timer = timer − 1000 (0 <= 0 continue executing) **(block is invisible)**. • action == waitToFadeIn. • Block unhides. • Block starts to fade in. • action = wait. • timer = 1000.
11000	• timer = timer − 1000 (0 <= 0 continue executing) **(block is visible)**. • action == wait. • timer = 1000.
...	Sequence repeats.

The important thing to note about this behavior is that the fade blocks support up to ten blocks with incrementing (by 1000 milliseconds) fade times to be placed in order. Subsequently, these blocks will fade out in order. Then, one second after the last block fades out, the first block will start to fade back in. Thus, the fade in and out is deterministic and cyclic, allowing a player to observe a pattern and to memorize it.

Fireballs

There are three blocks of code we are interested in for the fireball blocks. The first of these is in the file "\MazeRunner\starter.fps\server\scripts\Maze-Runner\levelloader.cs".

At the end of the function `BuildLevel()`, there is a little snippet of code that checks to see if there are any fireball blocks in the FireBallMarkers-Group SimGroup. If there are, the loader schedules a `firePass()` in 1500 milliseconds.

```
if( FireBallMarkersGroup.getCount() )
  FireBallMarkersGroup.schedule( 1500 , firePass );
```

firePass()

This function has the task of coming back every `$stepTime` (1000) milliseconds and checking each fireball block to see if that fireball block should fire a new fireball. Again, controlling fireballs this way (as with fade blocks) allows us to use a single `schedule()` event to handle all of our fireball blocks. This is easy to understand and efficient.

```
function SimSet::firePass( %theSet ) {
  %theSet.forEach( doFire , true );
  %theSet.schedule( $fireTime , doFire );
}
```

doFire()

Again, we have created a function that will operate on individual blocks to enact each block's action if it is time to do so. Here is a summarized listing of the function.

```
function StaticShape::doFire( %marker ) {
  if( isObject( %marker.bullet ) ) return;

  // Handle random fire marker case
  %firePath = ( %marker.type == 9 ) ? getRandom( 0 , 9 ) :
    %marker.type ;
```

```
switch( %firePath ) {
//
// NORTH
//
case 0:
  %marker.shootFireBall( FireBallProjectile , "0 1 0" , 20 );

// ... similar code for case 1 .. 7

//
// DOWN
//
case 8:
  %marker.shootFireBall( FireBallProjectile , "0 0 -1" , 20 );
}
}
```

We have not examined the shootFireBall() method, but when this method executes, it will create a projectile and store the ID of that projectile in the block's bullet field. When a projectile strikes an object, the projectile will explode and then self-delete.

So, our doFire() method first checks to see if this block has a bullet by seeing if the value in the bullet field is still an object. If it is, then we do not yet need to fire another bullet, and the method exits.

If there is no current bullet, the method will next check to see if this is a random block. In the case that this block shoots in a random direction, it will get a random value between 0 and 8 and then continue.

Having selected a firing direction (or going with the fixed direction) we now enter a long case statement that shoots a new fireball by calling shootFireBall() and passing in the following information (in this order).

- **Projectile datablock.** This is the projectile to shoot.
- **Direction.** This is the direction to shoot in.
- **Velocity.** This is the velocity we want the fireball to move with.

Please note, we will examine the method shootFireball() in Lesson #20 (Section 11.4.3).

10.5 Dynamic Scripting

This topic isn't a real mind blower, but it is something to remember that you have in your arsenal of TorqueScript options.

First, remember that we are working *within* an interpreter. Furthermore, you should understand that code is evaluated during execution—not beforehand like in C or Java. This means that we can use certain parts of TorqueScript's syntax to build up powerful and flexible scripts that morph over time.

I call this *dynamic scripting*.

10.5.1 Square Brackets [ ]

In Chapter 4, "Introduction to TorqueScript," we discussed the fact that Torque uses [] to build up strings as follows.

```
//ts25();

%var[0] = 10;
echo(%var[0]);

// same as
echo(%var0);
```

The interpreter evaluates statements with square brackets, removing the brackets and replacing our original string with a more compact form. In essence, the square brackets are concatenation operators. Using them, we can concatenate two (or more) strings on the fly, building up a new variable name. Recall that, in the case of multi-dimensional arrays, not only are the elements inbetween the brackets concatenated, but all commas (,) are replaced with underscores (_). Consider the following code snippets.

```
$a=1;
$b=m;
$c=n;
$x[$a,$b,$c] = 10;
echo( $x1_m_n ); // Prints 10
```

In this example, we constructed a new name from the composite of the contents of several variables. Notice that the engine inserts "_" for the comma (,) separators.

Next, let's try including the dot (.) operator.

```
$x.[$a,$b,$c] = 10; // Gives syntax error
```

In this example, we try to combine both the dot (.) operator and square brackets, but TGE does not allow square brackets to follow a dot (.) directly.

Let's get a bit more creative.

Game Elements

```
$x._[$a,$b,$c] = 10;      // works, but gets 'lost' somehow
echo( $x._[$a,$b,$c] );   // hmmm... nothing
echo( $x._l_m_n );        // darn! nothing again
```

OK, that looked like it should work, but when we tried to print our values using the *exact* copy and what should have been an equivalent, neither worked. Why? Well, the dot operator only works on objects. We fooled TGE into thinking we had an object, but when it did not find an ID in $x, the remainder of the operation went into the wastebasket.

Fine, so let's try this with an object.

```
$x = new simObject();
$x._[$a,$b,$c] = 10;      // works and is retained
echo( $x._[$a,$b,$c] );   // Yeah!
echo($x._l_m_n);          // Sweet!
```

Excellent. Now, we know some ways of creating compound names dynamically on both variables and objects. So, how do we put this to use?

10.5.2 Precedence Operators ( )

Square brackets alone can't do it all. Sometimes, we need to use the precedence operators to force the engine to build our variables first. In particular, we are not allowed to follow a closing square bracket with an open curly bracket. Consider the following code.

```
//ts27();
%anObject = "ScriptObject";
%obj = new %anObject();
if( isObject( %obj ) )
  echo("It is an object. Congratulations!");
else
  echo("It is NOT an object. Try again...");
```

This just won't work. The interpreter doesn't know that it needs to expand the contents of %anObject first. So what about the following?

```
//ts28();
%anObject = "ScriptObject";
%obj = new [%anObject]();
if( isObject( %obj ) )
  echo("It is an object. Congratulations!");
```

```
else
   echo("It is NOT an object. Try again...");
```

This doesn't work either. It violates the syntax rules for the interpreter. The actual solution is to use the precedence operators.

```
//ts29();
%anObject = "ScriptObject";
%obj = new (%anObject)();
if( isObject( %obj ) )
   echo("It is an object. Congratulations!");
else
   echo("It is NOT an object. Try again...");
```

Another useful example occurs when we want to dynamically build an object's name. For example if we had three GUI controls named `tile_top`, `tile_middle`, and `tile_bottom`, we could access fields or methods of these controls as follows.

```
%name[2] = "top";
%name[1] = "middle";
%name[0] = "bottom";
for( %count = 0; %count < 3; %count ++ ) {
   %id = ( tile @ "_" @ %name[%count] ).getID();
   echo("Tile ", %name[%count], " has ID ", %id );
}
```

10.5.3 `eval()`

We still haven't dealt with creating function names on the fly. You may recall in our discussion of ScriptObjects (Section 9.3.2) when I said it is nice to be able to use regularly formatted (versus specialized) names for our functions; i.e., it's better to always call `printArea()` vs. `printCircleArea()`, `printSquareArea()`, etc. The reason we like this is because it reasonably leads us in the direction of building our function names on the fly from known, regular parts.

So, to solve the final part of this puzzle, we need to use a special function provided by TGE: `eval()`. The function `eval( scriptString )` will execute any valid script contained in the string `scriptString`.

This function will execute a string as if it were a script. With the use of TorqueScript's various string-building tools, we can build any function name, variable name, or string of script we please. Then we simply `eval()` it.

Game Elements

```
//ts30();

%test = 10;
%printTest = "echo(\"" @ %test @ "\");";
echo("eval(", %printTest, ") produces -->" );
eval( %printTest );
```

eval() can be used to create and modify both local and global variables:

```
//ts31();

%makeVarTest = "%newVar = 100;";
echo("evaluating script --> ", %makeVarTest );
eval( %makeVarTest );
echo("%newVar == ", %newVar );
```

10.5.4 call()

There is one more way of executing functions dynamically in script. *This only supports function-style calling, not method-style calling.* It isn't as much fun as eval(), but it is very straightforward and useful in a great number of cases. TGE provides a function named call(). call (funcname, [arg0, ..., argN]) executes the function named in the string funcName and passes the function any arguments provided in arg0, ..., argN.

```
//ts32();

%tmpVal = 100;
call( "echo" , "$", %tmpVal , " for TGE is a good price,
     Yes?" );
```

10.6 Basic Client-Server Communications

Although you can, in practice, ignore the client-server divide in the design of a single-player game, if you do and if you try to take that game to a multiplayer environment, you may find yourself reworking great gobs of code.

For example, it is easy in a single-player game to write scripts called by the action maps that manipulate server objects and variables. In the following example, we use the key stroke **CTRL + W** to make the current player play a hand-waving animation. All of this "bad" code might be placed in the "default.bind.cs" file.

```
// Bad Implementation of a Wave!!!
moveMap.bind(keyboard, "ctrl w", celebrationWave);
// ...
function celebrationWave(%val) {
  if(%val)
    $Game::Player.setActionThread("celWave");
}
```

So, why is the above code bad? Let's break it down.

- The code uses a variable $Game::Player which we are assuming has the server ID of the player in it. This has the following problems.

  - Action maps are in the client space, so no server variables should be visible, or at least should not be touched, in this scope.

  - The implication of this variable is that there is only one player, which breaks down as soon as there is another player in the game.

- There is a function celebrationWave() associated with **CTRL + W**. In and of itself, this is correct. The problem is that this function directly modifies a server object. This is wrong for the same reasons as listed above.

So, how do we solve this? Well, before we solve this specific problem, let's first talk in general about how client-server communications work.

Client ➜ Server Commands

Clients communicate with the server by requesting that the server execute a named command. The syntax of this request is as follows.

```
commandToServer( commandTag [ , arg0, ... , argN ] );
```

Calling this command (on the client) tells TGE to request that the server execute a console function with the name serverCmd + commandTag, using the arguments (if any) that were passed to commandToServer(). Regarding the commandTag, this can be a string ("xyz") or a tag ('xyz'), but tags are generally preferred.

A concrete example of this would look like the following.

```
// This method would be defined in one of the script
// files that is loaded by the server:
function Player::Doit() {
  // do something
}
```

> Tags are a feature that Torque uses to save networking bandwidth. Basically, a tagged string is stored locally (by the first sender) and given a unique numeric ID. Then, the first time the sender transmits this string to a new receiver, it informs the receiver that the string is a tagged string and tells the receiver what that tag ID is. Subsequently, when the sender wants the same receiver to use this 'tagged' string, it only needs to inform the receiver that it is sending a tag and then transmit the tag ID. In general, tags are much shorter than the strings they identify. Thus, using tags for often transmitted strings can produce significant benefits in terms of networking bandwidth savings.

```
// This method (likely in a separate file) would also be
// defined in one of the script files that is loaded by
// the server:
function serverCmdDoit( %client ) {
  %client.player.Doit();
}


// This command would be executed in function or method
// defined in a script file loaded by the client:
commandToServer( 'Doit' );
```

When commandToServer('Doit'); is called, TGE will instruct the server to call serverCmdDoit() and will pass in the ID of the calling client.

I repeat: *the engine automatically passes in the ID of the calling client. Therefore, all server commands (serverCmd*) must take the client ID as their first argument.*

Subsequently, the server will execute the function, and the player method doit() will be executed for the player associated with that client.

Please understand that the implication is that the player ID is stored in a field named player in the client connection object (%client.player). We do this in the "game.cs" file (take a look).

Server ➜ Client Commands

The server uses a similar method for executing commands on the client. The syntax of this request is as follows.

```
commandToClient( clientID, commandTag [ , arg0, ... , argN ] );
```

Calling this command (on the server) tells TGE to request that the numbered client execute a console function with the name clientCmd + commandTag, using the arguments (if any) that were passed to commandToClient(). Regarding the commandTag, this can be a string ("xyz") or a tag ('xyz'), but tags are generally preferred.

A concrete example of using commandToClient() would look like the following.

```
// This method would be defined in one of the script files
// that is loaded by the client:
function PlayGUI::DoSomething( %ID, %x, %y ) {
  // do something
}
```

```
// This method (likely in a separate file) would also be
// defined in one of the script files that is loaded by
// the client:
function clientCmdTellPlayGUIDoSomething( %x, %y ) {
  PlayGUI.DoSomething( %x , %y);
}


// This sample executes the same function on all clients
// connected to the server:
for( %clientIndex = 0; %clientIndex <
      ClientGroup.getCount(); %clientIndex++ ) {
  %someClient = ClientGroup.getObject(%clientIndex);
  commandToClient( %someClient , 'TellPlayGUIDoSomething'
                  %x , %y);
}
```

The above example iterates over each client (from the server side) and tells the client to do something with its PlayGUI at the coordinates *x, y*. In turn, each client executes the method `PlayGUI.DoSomething()` with those coordinates.

10.6.3 The Takeaway

So, we talked briefly about client-server communication here, but what should you take away from our discussion? Mainly, if you are going be using keystrokes (via action maps) to execute server commands or manipulate server variables, be sure to use the presented methodology. This way, if you decide to make your singleplayer game a multiplayer game in the future, you won't have to go back and fix all of the cases where you violated the client-server divide.

10.6.4 Waving Sample Solution

Below is the solution to our original "waving" problem from above.

```
// Server-Side Functions:
function serverCmdPlayCel(%client,%anim) {
  if (isObject(%client.player))
    %client.player.playCelAnimation(%anim);
}

function Player::playCelAnimation(%this,%anim) {
  if (%this.getState() !$= "Dead")
    %this.setActionThread("cel"@%anim);
}
```

```
// Client-Side Functions:
function celebrationWave(%val) {
  if(%val)
    commandToServer('playCel', "wave");
}

// MoveMap (client-side) Mapping
moveMap.bind(keyboard, "ctrl w", celebrationWave);
```

10.7 Summary

In this chapter, we discussed the features and classes that Torque provides for enabling gameplay and interaction from scripts.

We introduced the idea of callbacks and discussed the most significant (in the context of this guide) callbacks, including when they are called and how they are used.

We next learned about the very important feature of event scheduling. We came to understand that we can schedule functions to execute, and console methods to execute upon specific instances of objects. We learned how to track the progress of an event, how to cancel it, and how to repeat it.

Next, we talked about string manipulation and filled our heads with the concepts of words, records, fields, tokens, etc. Furthermore, we explored the purpose and usage of each of these concepts and the functions that Torque supplies to work with them.

Math is a big part of game writing, and so we discussed scripted math in great depth, discussing all of the most basic and most advanced math features and functions supplied by Torque and available in TorqueScript.

Our second-to-last discussion in this chapter explored the edges of scripting and taught us about some tricks and techniques that, if used properly, can create evolutionary and highly functional scripts.

Lastly, we dipped into the client-server aspect of the Torque Game Engine. We learned some dos and don'ts when it comes to trading data between client and server. Then, we learned how to send commands from clients to the server and from the server to clients.

Chapter 11
Special Effects

Special effects, in the context of this chapter, are those effects that are for the most part visual. We're talking about such things as explosions, debris, particle emitters, splashes, etc. Because each of these objects is unique in some sense, yet similar to each other or used by other effects classes, I thought it best to gather them here. So, there is some logic, even if you do consider it madness to refer to projectiles as special effects.

Please note that there is no direct path to discussing these due to their interconnectedness (try drawing the relationship tree some time); thus, this chapter will be alphabetically organized.

11.1 Debris

Debris objects are used to represent the refuse left behind by an exploding or destroyed object. However, this object is versatile enough to be used for various purposes, including a rockfall that blocks the road, the remains of a fallen building, etc.

11.1.1 Debris and DebrisData Features

Debris and DebrisData have the following features.

- **Rendering**
  - 2D debris (particle)
  - 3D debris (shape)
- **Physics**
  - Bouncing
  - Sliding
  - Falling
  - Velocity limiters
  - Spinning
  - Limited lifetimes
- **Behavior modifiers**
  - Subexplosions
  - Bounce off water
  - Replace debris with StaticShape

Game Elements

- Modify resting orientation
- Particle emission
- Fading away

11.1.2 Rendering

Debris can be rendered as a 2D or 3D object, depending on our needs.

2D Debris (Particle)

If we are viewing debris from a distance, it will probably be sufficient to use a billboard instead of a shape, which has a higher rendering penalty. In order to create debris using just a billboard (a single texture), we specify our datablock as follows.

```
datablock DebrisData( 2D_Debris ) {
  render2D = true;
  texture = "path to texture file";
  // ...
};
```

3D Debris (Shape)

Of course, if 2D would always cut it, we wouldn't be using a 3D engine, would we? So, for those cases in which an object is needed, we specify a 3D debris datablock as follows.

```
datablock DebrisData( 3D_Debris ) {
  render2D = false;
  shapeFile = "path to DTS file";
  // ...
};
```

11.1.3 Physical Properties

Debris can exhibit various random physical properties to give its behavior realism or a required effect.

Starting Radius

One of the first questions to answer is, "How far from the explosion point will the debris start?" As you will see in Section 11.3, most explosions take place in the centroid of the shape, and for big shapes, it might be expected that the debris starts some distance away from that point. By default, our debris will start 0.2 world units from this point, but the distance can be greater if necessary.

```
datablock DebrisData( startingRadiusDebris ) {
  // ...
  useRadiusMass = true; // Use defined radius if > 0.2 world units
  baseRadius = 4.0; // Start 4.0 world units from centroid
  // ...
};
```

Bouncing

It may make sense for the debris from an explosion to bounce a few times. To accomplish this, we need to set a few parameters in our datablock.

```
datablock DebrisData( bouncyDebris ) {
  // ...
  elasticity = 0.5; // A little bouncy, but not super-bouncy
  numBounces = 5;   // Bounce between: 3 and 7 times
  bounceVariance = 2; // ( numBounces +/- bounceVariance )
  // ...
};
```

Note that elasticity can only be between 0.0 and 0.99. In addition to bouncing off of solid objects, we can cause debris to bounce off of water. Here, we are telling the engine to add the water type to our collision list.

```
datablock DebrisData( bounceOffWaterDebris ) {
  // ...
  ignoreWater = false; // Bounce when we hit water too
  // ...
};
```

Sliding

It might also be useful for our debris to slide a bit or, alternatively, to arrest quickly.

```
datablock DebrisData( slidingDebris ) {
  // ...
  friction = 0.1; // Slide for a long while before arresting
  // ...
};
```

```
datablock DebrisData( quickArrestDebris ) {
  // ...
  friction = 1.0; // Stop sliding quickly
  // ...
};
```

Velocity and Falling

Now having solved where the debris will start and how it will behave when it first hits something, we need to give it some oomph! We need to determine at what rate it is initially moving and decide how gravity will affect it.

```
datablock DebrisData( highSpeedDebris ) {
  // ...
  velocity = 20.0; // Debris starting velocity of:
                   // 19.5 - 20.5 world units/second
  velocityVariance = 0.5; // velocity +/- velocityVariance
  terminalVelocity = 30.0 // maximum velocity of
                          // 30 world units/second
  // ...
};
```

The above datablock will produce a quickly moving debris effect, whereas the one below will create a slowly moving effect. Additionally, we've set the gravModifier to a negative value, meaning that the debris will float up instead of falling down.

```
datablock DebrisData( lowSpeedFloatUpDebris ) {
  // ...
  velocity = 2.0;   // Debris starts with velocity of:
                    // 1.5 - 2.5 world units/second
  velocityVariance = 0.5; // velocity +/- velocityVariance
  gravModifier = -1.0; // Debris floats UP
  terminalVelocity = 3.0; // Prevent debris from
                          // accelerating past 3
                          // world units/second
  // ...
};
```

Spinning

Debris that maintains the same orientation would be a bit boring, so TGE provides a means of spinning the debris. The spin magnitude can be limited to a specific range of degrees per second, and TGE will randomly select a value in this range.

```
datablock DebrisData( slowSpinDebris ) {
  // ...
  minSpinSpeed = -60;
  maxSpinSpeed = 60;
  // ...
};
```

Lifetime

Well, we've gotten to the end of the physical properties list. Now, we have one more decision to make. How long will this debris last? In total, TGE will not allow debris to exist longer than 1000 seconds, but that should be sufficient for most needs.

```
datablock DebrisData( twoMinuteDebris ) {
  // ...
  lifetime = 240.0; // This debris lasts exactly two minutes
  lifetimeVariance = 0.0; // lifetime +/- lifetimeVariance
  // ...
};
```

11.1.4 Additional Behaviors

Beyond the physical properties, there are a few things we can modify to make our debris really work for us. We can instruct debris to exhibit several behaviors during its lifetime, on last bounce, or at the end of its life.

Explosions

We can cause debris to explode when it achieves `maxBounce`. And yes, this explosion can make more debris; just be sure not to use the same datablock or you could cause a cyclic explosion that will eventually crash the engine.

```
datablock DebrisData( explodingDebris ) {
  // ...
  explodeOnMaxBounce = true; // Blow up on last bounce
  explosion = "an explosion datablock";
  // ...
};
```

Replace Debris with StaticShape

Sometimes we don't want our debris to disappear. Perhaps, for our gameplay, we need this debris to build up and remain for the remainder of the mission. Well, this can easily be accomplished.

```
datablock DebrisData( staticDebris ) {
  // ...
  staticOnMaxBounce = true; // Do not delete this shape
  // ...
};
```

Because there are several endings for any particular debris, combining other endings with this one, such as explode or fade, may not give you the results you are looking for. Also, accumulating too much debris can kill your frame rates, so you may want to limit debris in some way.

Fixing Orientation

In addition to causing debris to remain in the world, either permanently as a static or by giving it a long lifetime, we may wish for it to be oriented to the surface below it when it comes to rest. Thus, there is a way to tell the engine to correct the orientation of our debris when it achieves maxBounce.

```
datablock DebrisData( reOrientedDebris ) {
  // ...
  snapOnMaxBounce = true; // Snap to surface below me
  // ...
};
```

Fireballs, Particle Trails, Etc.

Having just survived an explosion, the fundamental components of this destroyed shape (the debris) may be on fire and/or trailing smoke or dust. We need a way to simulate this. Fortunately, each debris can have up to two particle emitters attached to it. Thus, if we so choose, we can specify two PEDs.

```
datablock DebrisData( flamingDebris ) {
  // ...
  emitters[0] = "FireBall"; // A PED simulating a fireball.
  emitters[1] = "SmokeTrail"; // A PED simulating smoke.
  // ...
};
```

Fading Away

Perhaps appropriately, the last effect we can control for debris is fade. Specifically, if we so choose, we can specify that debris will fade out of sight over the last second of its lifetime.

```
datablock DebrisData( fadeoutDebris ) {
  // ...
  fade = true; // Fade out in last second of lifetime.
  // ...
};
```

```
datablock DebrisData( poppingDebris ) {
  // ...
  fade = false; // Don't fade, just pop out of existence
                // suddenly
  // ...
};
```

11.1.5 Using Debris

Debris is used by a number of classes and can also be used standalone; i.e., it is possible to create a standalone debris object.

Used-by Classes

Debris is used by the following classes.

- **ShapeBaseData.** Created when shape transitions to "Destroyed."
- **ShapeBaseImageData.** Used to represent ejected shell casings.
- **ExplosionData.** Used to represent explosion debris.

Standalone

To create a standalone instance of debris is as easy as the following.

```
datablock DebrisData( standaloneDebris ) {
  // Fill in parameters to suit your needs.
};

%myDebris = new Debris() {
  datablock = standaloneDebris;
  position = "a position vector";
};
```

Alternatively, if you don't wish to specify position and you would like to give this debris an initial velocity (prior to internally applied velocities), you could use the following code.

```
%myDebris = new Debris() {
  datablock = standaloneDebris;
};

%myDebris.init( "a position vector" , "a velocity vector" );
```

11.2 Decals

Decals in the context of TGE are temporarily rendered textures that are applied to objects to represent things like footprints, bullet holes, other types of damage, etc. Most properties of decals are controlled by the objects that use them, but there are a few things we can control.

11.2.1 DecalManager and DecalData Features

DecalManager and DecalData have the following features.

- **Variable timeout**
- **Total decal caps**
- **Global enable**

11.2.2 Decal Properties

For the decals themselves, we can only specify a minimal set of information via the datablock. Specifically, we can specify the size of the decal and the texture it uses.

```
datablock DecalData ( sampleDecal ) {
  sizeX = 0.25 ; // 1/4 world unit 'wide'
  sizeY = 0.50 ; // 1/2 world unit 'tall'
  textureName = "Path to texture file";
};
```

That is about it. Table 11.1 shows a few other global parameters that are used by the decal manager.

Table 11.1.

Variables used by DecalManager.

Variable Name	Description	Sample or Range
`$pref::Decal::decalTimeout`	This is the time a decal lives before self-deleting. It is specified in milliseconds.	[0 , inf) (default is 5 seconds)
`$pref::Decal::maxNumDecals`	This is the limit on how many decals may exist at any one time. Once this limit is passed, old decals are immediately deleted to allow for new decals.	256 (default)
`$pref::decalsOn`	This is a global toggle to enable/disable decals.	[true , false] (true by default)

11.2.3 Using Decals

Decals are used by two classes, ProjectileData and PlayerData. They cannot be created standalone.

Used-by Classes

Decals are used by the following classes.

- **ProjectileData.** Used to specify a 'bullet' mark on collision.
- **PlayerData.** Used for footprint(s).

See Section 7.3.2, "Player Special Effects," for an example of decals in use.

11.3 Explosions

The concept of explosions hardly needs to be introduced, but a review of the myriad features TGE provides to implement them would be worthwhile. Explosions can be thought of as a composite object and include the following subcomponents: particles, shapes, debris, and lighting.

Additionally, the following may be associated with an explosion.

- **Camera shake.** A nearby explosion can be programmed to shake the client's camera.
- **Sound.** A sound can be associated with each explosion.
- **More explosions.** Explosions can spawn subexplosions.

11.3.1 Building up an Explosion

General Control

Ignoring all the components and focusing on the explosion as if it were a single entity, we can control the following elements.

Post-Creation Play Start Time

```
datablock ExplosionData( delayedFuseExplosion ) {
  // ...
  delayMS = 4000;      // Play explosion between 3 and 5
                       // seconds after
  delayVariance = 1000; // creation. delayMS +/-
                       // delayVariance
  // ...
};
```

In effect, we can delay the beginning of an explosion for a maximum of about 65.5 seconds (65,536, or 2^{16}, milliseconds) after the actual explosion object has been created. The question that arises is, "Why do this?"

To answer that question, we first have to explain how explosions play out. The gross steps an explosion takes are the following.

1. Object created.
2. Explosion event starts.
3. Subexplosion objects created.
4. Main explosion event plays.
5. Explosion ends.

The key thing to notice is that subexplosions are spawned at the same time the main explosion starts to play. So, if we did not have this delay mechanism, all of our explosions would overlap, and that would not be much fun.

Explosion End Time and Play Speed

In addition to specifying a starting time, we can specify how long the event lasts. TGE provides a knob for "scaling" the event.

```
datablock ExplosionData( longExplosion ) {
  // ...
  lifetimeMS = 20000; // Play explosion for 19 to 21 seconds.
  lifetimeVariance = 1000; // lifetimeMS +/- lifetimeVariance
  // ...
};
```

So, what about this scaling business? What use is it if we can control the lifetime? Well, besides being nice for quick tuning, it is also nice to adjust an inherited explosion where the only thing we want to change is the rate it plays at.

```
datablock ExplosionData( halfAsLongExplosion :
                         longExplosion ) {
  // ...
  playSpeed = 2.0; // Voila, scaled to play twice as fast!
  // ...
};
```

Initial and Subsequent Scaling

Not all explosions are made equal, and over time, the size of an explosion normally evolves. Thus, TGE provides two sets of features. One is for initial scaling.

```
datablock ExplosionData( humongousExplosion ) {
  // ...
```

```
explosionScale = 5.0; // Explosion fills a 5-world units cube
// ...
};
```

A second feature is for scaling over time. By the way, if you have already looked at the particle emitters description in Chapter 8, "Mission Objects," the following should look familiar.

```
datablock ExplosionData( resizingExplosion ) {
    // ...
    explosionScale = 5.0;
    sizes[0] = "1.0 1.0 1.0";
    sizes[1] = "1.0 1.0 1.5";
    sizes[2] = "1.0 1.0 2.0";
    sizes[3] = "0.1 0.1 0.1";
    times[0] = 0.0;
    times[1] = 0.33;
    times[2] = 0.66;
    times[3] = 1.0
    // ...
};
```

The above explosion starts out filling a 5-world units cube. It smoothly increases in height until it hits 10 world units (5.0 x 2.0 world units) at two-thirds of the way through its lifetime. Scaling then reverses direction and in the remaining third of its life it shrinks to a 0.5-world units cube. Poof!

Facing

Depending on the effect we are trying to achieve, an explosion should or should not rotate to face the viewer. Please note that this rotation is the entire explosion object and not related to the settings applied to the particles.

```
datablock ExplosionData( faceMeWhenYouExplode ) {
    // ...
    faceViewer = true; // This explosion rotates to face the camera
    // ...
};
```

Initial Offset

The last of the basic explosion control mechanisms controls the initial position of the explosion center. Because it would be boring to have subexplosions always forming in the same location, TGE provides a feature wherein we can

Game Elements

specify an offset, which is then multiplied by a unit-length vector with a random facing. The tip of the resultant vector will be the explosion's center.

```
datablock ExplosionData( formWithinTwoMeterRadiusExplosion
) {
  // ...
  offset = 2.0;      // Explosion will form at a random point
                     // two world units from creation position
  // ...
};
```

11.3.2 Particles

Now that we've got the basic parameters of our explosion set, we need to choose our particles. TGE explosions support up to five independent particle emitters. Furthermore, one of these emitters is standalone and four are played together. The single emitter is not treated the same as the four other emitters.

Standalone Emitter

The standalone emitter has two knobs not available for the other four generic emitters. We can control the radius within which this emitter forms from the explosion center, which is similar to the offset principle for the emitter itself. Also, we can select a particle density for this emitter in addition to the controls provided by the emitter definition itself.

```
datablock ExplosionData( uniEmitterExplosion ) {
  // ...
  particleEmitter = "Some PED";
  particleDensity = 0.6;
  particleRadius = 1.2;
  // ...
};
```

The above explosion uses some particle emitter to randomly produce particles whose origin is somewhere within a sphere having a radius of 1.2 world units. This emitter will move continuously over the life of the explosion and has a density of 60 percent.

Those Other Emitters

The other emitters can optionally be used to specify up to four additional emitters whose position is the center of our explosion.

```
datablock ExplosionData( fourEmitterExplosion ) {
  // ...
  emitter[0] = "Some PED 0";
  emitter[1] = "Some PED 1";
  emitter[2] = "Some PED 2";
  emitter[3] = "Some PED 3";
  // ...
};
```

11.3.3 Explosion Shape

Alternately, or in addition to particles, we may choose to represent our explosion with a mesh. Furthermore, this shape can be animated. If we so choose, we can create an animation named ambient, which TGE will automatically start when the explosion starts.

```
datablock ExplosionData( shapeExplosion ) {
  // ...
  explosionShape = "Path to a DTS file";
  // ...
};
```

11.3.4 Debris

Now that we know what our explosion is composed of, we can choose to add some debris to liven things up. Our debris is emitted in much the same fashion as particles from a particle emitter. Therefore, these parameters should mostly look familiar.

```
datablock ExplosionData( explosionWithDebris ) {
  // ...
  debris = "Some Debris datablock name";
  debrisNum = 1000;  // Between 800 and 1200 debris ejected
  debrisNumVariance = 200;  // debrisNum +/- debrisNumVariance
  debrisThetaMin = 0.0;  // Straight up, to
  debrisThetaMax = 180.0;  // Straight down
  debrisPhiMin = 0.0;  // Straight down Y, to
  debrisPhiMax = 360.0;  // All the way around (full rotation)
  debrisVelocity  = 20.0;  // Eject @ between 20 and 30 world units/second
  debrisVelocityVariance = 10.0;  // debrisVelocity +/- debrisVelocityVariance
  // ...
};
```

Actually, these controls are a little nicer than particle controls in a way because both phi (left-right) and theta (up-down) can be varied within a range, and the randomness is free.

11.3.5 Lighting Effects

So, what if we want our explosion to emit light? Can we do it? Heck yes. In fact, we can emit a light that changes both color and radius over the lifetime of the explosion.

```
datablock ExplosionData( lightedExplosion ) {
  // ...
  lightStartColor = "1.0 1.0 0.8"; // Start off light yellow
  lightEndColor = "0.6 0.0 0.0"; // End a deep maroon
  lightStartRadius = 5.0; // Start with a 5-world units radius
  lightEndRadius = 15.0 // End with a 15-world units radius
  // ...
};
```

11.3.6 Camera Shake

Finally, we've completed the list of things we'll be seeing. Now let's look into a physical effect. Normally, if a viewer is near enough to an explosion and there is enough energy involved, you would expect the view to shake for a bit as a result. TGE allows us to do this, too.

```
datablock ExplosionData( rockMeExplosion ) {
  // ...
  shakeCamera = true;
  camShakeRadius = 20.0;
  camShakeAmp = "1.0 1.0 1.5";
  camShakeFreq = "8.0 10.0 8.0"
  camShakeFalloff = 2.0;
  camShakeDuration = 3.5;
  // ...
};
```

The above explosion will cause all cameras within a radius of 20 world units to shake. The amplitude of this shaking will be moderate, though slightly stronger in the up-down direction. The oscillation for the shaking will be somewhat weak to normal in the y (front-back) direction. What this means is the shaking is stronger up-down but happens faster back-and-forth. Yes, it is weird, but it's an example! Finally, the strength of the shaking will fall off to half its strength at the outer limits and then fall off to zero abruptly. This

shaking will last for about 3.5 seconds from the start of the explosion. Boom!
Rumble... rumble....

11.3.7 Sound

I know, you may be thinking, "What good is an explosion without sound?"
Good, but not great by any means. Fortunately, we won't have to find out. We
can specify a sound to accompany our explosion. This sound should probably
be a 3D sound, but 2D works for some cases, too.

```
datablock ExplosionData( soundMeExplosion ) {
  // ...
  soundProfile = "A sound profile name";
  // ...
};
```

11.3.8 Subexplosions

That's it, right? I'm thinking, "Why have one of a good thing when you can
have more than one?" And so were those canny GarageGames programmers.
Each explosion can spawn up to five more subexplosions, which can each
spawn five more, and so on. Well, don't get carried away, OK?

```
datablock ExplosionData( MamaExplosion ) {
  // ...
  subExplosion[0] = "BabyExplosion0"; // An explosion datablock name
  subExplosion[1] = "BabyExplosion1"; // An explosion datablock name
  subExplosion[2] = "BabyExplosion2"; // An explosion datablock name
  subExplosion[3] = "BabyExplosion3"; // An explosion datablock name
  subExplosion[4] = "BabyExplosion4"; // An explosion datablock name
  // ...
};
```

11.3.9 Thinking about Damage

It would be a very strange explosion that did not have some kind of effect, be
it damage or something else. Therefore, TGE supplies a nice console function
to calculate how much an object is affected by the explosion. The name is a
bit misleading, but basically, the function returns a value telling us how covered by the explosion this shape is. A requirement for this to work is that we
specify which shapes can be affected.

```
%boom = new Explosion() {
  // ...
};
```

```
// Check to see if player got hit
%coverage = calcExplosionCoverage( %boom.getPosition() ,
        %player,
        $TypeMasks::PlayerObjectType );
if ( %coverage > 0.0 ) echo("Ouch! ouch! ouch!");
```

11.3.10 Using Explosions

Explosions are spawned in a number of ways and by a number of classes. Nicely, they can be made standalone, too.

Used-By Classes

Explosions are used by the following classes.

- **ShapeBaseData.** Created when shape transitions to "Destroyed."
- **SplashData.** Created on precipitation impact.
- **ProjectileData.** Yeah, it's pretty obvious. Sure, an explosion would be good for this.
- **DebrisData.** Gee. Explosions spawn debris; debris can spawn explosions. It's a vicious circle.
- **ExplosionData.** Woohoo! Let's blow it up reeeaaal gooood.

Standalone

To create a standalone instance of an explosion is as easy as the following.

```
datablock ExplosionData( MyExplosion ) {
  // Fill in paramters to suit your needs.
};

%myDebris = new Explosion() {
  dataBlock = MyExplosion;
  position = "a position vector";
};
```

11.3.11 Maze Runner Lesson #19 (10 Percent Step)—FireBall Explosion

In this lesson, we will examine three datablocks that are supplied with the MazeRunner prototype code. These datablocks are used to implement the explosion that occurs when a projectile (see Lesson #20) explodes.

If you look in file "\MazeRunner\prototype\server\scripts\MazeRunner\FireBall.cs", you will find the following three datablocks.

- **FireBallExplosionParticle.** This datablock defines the particles that are used in the explosion.
- **FireBallExplosionEmitter.** This datablock defines the pattern for the explosion emission.
- **FireBallExplosion.** This datablock defines the way in which the emitter is played and the effects that the explosion has on the surroundings.

FireBallExplosionParticle

Let's look at the code for this emitter.

```
datablock ParticleData(FireBallExplosionParticle : baseSmokePD0 ) {
    lifetimeMS = 750;
    lifetimeVarianceMS = 200;
    colors[0] = "1 0.2 0.2 1.0";
    colors[1] = "1.0 0.6 0.2 0.0";
    sizes[0] = 1.5;
    sizes[1] = 3.5;
};
```

We will first notice that it is inheriting from datablock baseSmokePD0. This is very important for the following reasons.

1. A large variety of effects can be created using a small set of particle textures.
2. The GPGT Lesson Kit comes with a variety of predefined particle datablocks as well as emitters. You should use these as the base (through inheritance or good old cut-copy-paste) for your own particle effects and tweak just the parts that you need.
3. A large variety of effects can be created using a small set of particle textures. Yes, I just said this, but I want to drive the point home. You don't need to go crazy and create a ton of textures. Instead, tweak the datablock fields, and you will be surprised at the number of effects you can achieve.

In this case, we are inheriting a basic smoke particle and then adjusting the fields in Table 11.2.

Fields	Purpose of Change
lifeTimeMS lifeTimeVarianceMS	The base particle has a rather long life, but we want our explosion particles to live for a shorter time.
colors[0] colors[1]	We're trying to get a reddish explosion that fades to a dark orange.
sizes[0] sizes[1]	The particle should start off fairly big and rapidly grow to a little more than double its original size.

Table 11.2.
Fields being adjusted.

FireBallExplosionEmitter

Next, we must define an emitter. In this case, our emitter is new and does not inherit from a base emitter.

```
datablock ParticleEmitterData(FireBallExplosionEmitter) {
  ejectionPeriodMS = 7;
  periodVarianceMS = 0;
  ejectionVelocity = 1;
  velocityVariance = 1;
  ejectionOffset = 0;
  thetaMin = 0;
  thetaMax = 60;
  phiReferenceVel = 0;
  phiVariance = 360;
  overrideAdvances = false;
  particles = "FireBallExplosionParticle";
};
```

The above datablock will produce an emitter that will create a large number of particles in a short period. These particles will be ejected at between 1 and 2 world units per second with no offset. The direction of the emitter will vary from straight up to just above horizontal. Additionally, particles will be ejected in a complete circle about the up vector at the point of explosion. Lastly, this emitter uses the particle we just defined.

FireBallExplosion

This last datablock uses the prior two to define the actual explosion.

```
datablock ExplosionData(FireBallExplosion) {
  lifeTimeMS = 2000;
  particleEmitter = FireBallExplosionEmitter;
  particleDensity = 50;
  particleRadius = 0.2;
  faceViewer = true;

  // Dynamic light
  lightStartRadius = 0;
  lightEndRadius = 6;
  lightStartColor = "1 0.2 1";
  lightEndColor = "1 0.6 0.2";
};
```

This explosion will live for 2 seconds, emitting particles the entire time. It uses the emitter we just defined and limits the number of simultaneous particles to just 50 at any one time. It varies the point of ejection randomly by up to 0.2 world units about the point of explosion. The particles are made to face the viewer at all times, thus making sure that the clouds of particles are always nice and uniform. The explosion will produce light in a radius of 6 world units that starts off reddish and ends a dark orange. Please note that, because the blocks are self-illuminating, this effect will not be very visible. You may wish to re-export the blocks without self-illumination enabled to see if the effect is more pleasing this way.

11.4 Projectiles

Although the concept of a particle has a very strong tie to weapons, in truth, these objects do not have to be associated with any weapon. Their real value is that they represent an object that can be put into motion and will eventually collide with another object and do something. Yes, it's vague, but that is the point. Projectiles are a versatile object and can be used for many kinds of interactions, not *just* to represent arrows, bullets, and balls of plasma.

11.4.1 Designing a Projectile

The Beginning

As noted above, a projectile is an object "in" the world. It has a starting position, an ending position, and may interact with objects between those two points. Our first focus is on understanding how to get this particle into the world at its starting point.

```
%bullet = new Projectile() {
   dataBlock = %projectile;
   initialVelocity = %muzzleVelocity;
   initialPosition = %ownerObj.getMuzzlePoint(%mountSlot);
   sourceObject = %ownerObj;
   sourceSlot = %mountSlot;
};
```

This sample is a snippet of code taken from some example code that comes with the GPGT Lesson Kit. As can be seen, it is completed parameterized. The important things to note are the following.

- **dataBlock.** Initialized with some known datablock definition. Quite standard.
- **initialVelocity.** The projectile is told its initial velocity *on creation*. The implication here is that we can choose any velocity and direction for

this projectile that we want, when we create it. It isn't magically determined by some engine code related to weapons or some such.

- **initialPosition.** Normally, we specify a position for objects when we create them, but a new field was added to reduce interdependency, and thus we have initialPosition. This is where our bullet starts, and it, too, can be anywhere we want it to be.
- **sourceObject.** As a rule, this should be the player or other entity that is responsible for the creation of this projectile. The main purpose of this field is to give a rendering priority hint to the engine. If the projectile "belongs" to the client's camera, it will get processing priority there. If there is no source object (i.e., this is created standalone), set this to 0.
- **sourceSlot.** This should match the slot the firing weapon is mounted to. If this projectile is not associated with a weapon/slot, it should be set to −1.

That is it. We've created a projectile and set it on its way. Not very hard and not really interesting. As is often the case, the interesting stuff is embedded in the object's datablock.

The Datablock

Projectiles are fairly flexible, exhibiting a significant set of traits, all of which are configured via the datablock.

Projectile Representation

It is not strictly required, but if we want, the projectile can have an associated shape.

```
datablock ProjectileData ( HumongoProjectile ) {
  projectileShapeName =   "Some DTS file";
  scale                   "20.0 20.0 20.0";
  // ...
};
```

In this datablock, we have specified some mesh to represent the projectile and have scaled it 20 times in each dimension.

Shape Animations

If we have chosen to use a shape, we can additionally supply two animations named activate and maintain. The activate thread will play immediately after the shape is created. We can specify this to be a cyclic or a noncyclic animation. If the activate thread is noncyclic, and if we have specified a `maintain` thread, the `maintain` thread will begin playing as soon as the `activate` thread finishes. The `maintain` thread can also be cyclic or noncyclic.

Ballistics and Gravity

A projectile may choose to ignore gravity and to follow a nonballistic trajectory, or to add some challenge to aiming, we can play with the way gravity affects our ballistic projectile.

```
datablock ProjectileData( NonBallisticProjectile ) {
  // ...
  isBallistic = false; // Not affected by gravity
  // ...
};

dataBlock ProjectileData( steepArcProjectile ) {
  // ...
  isBallistic = true; // Is affected by gravity, and ...
  gravityMod = 3.5; // gravity affects this 3.5x more than normal objects
  // ...
};
```

Bouncing Around and Arming Delays

It may not always be appropriate for a projectile to do damage right away. It might be nice to create a weapon that can bounce its projectiles off of obstacles for a certain amount of time prior to doing damage. We can accomplish this by making the projectile bouncy and by delaying its activation.

```
dataBlock ProjectileData( delayedBouncingProjectile ) {
  // ...
  armingDelay = 16;        // Delay arming for ~1/2 second (16 ticks)
  bounceElasticity = 1.0; // I'm pretty bouncy
  bounceFriction = 0.5;   // Reduce projectile velocity by this factor and
                          // a multiple of the tangent to impact.
  isBallistic = true;     // Only ballistic projectiles can bounce.
  // ...
};
```

If a projectile is not yet armed, it will only bounce if it is ballistic. Nonballistic projectiles penetrate, instead.

Particles

Projectiles have the ability to attach up to two emitters to them. However, these emitters play at different times. The rules for their activation are simple. The emitter specified by `particleEmitter` always plays when the projectile is not underwater. The emitter specified by `particleWaterEmitter` plays when the projectile is underwater. Neither plays when the projectile is entering or leaving the water. That is a job for the splash object. Having clarified that, the following is how we specify them.

```
datablock ProjectileData( DualEmitterProjectile ) {
  // ...
  particleEmitter  = "Some PED for above water ONLY";
  particleWaterEmitter = "Some PED for below water ONLY";
  // ...
};
```

Lit Projectiles

Our projectile can emit a light for the duration of its life. Additionally, we can specify whether the light should be emitted when the projectile is under water and what the color should be for each case (below water or above water). Both cases share the same light radius.

```
datablock ProjectileData( LitProjectile ) {
  // ...
  hasLight = true;
  lightColor = "0.8 0.8 1.0";
  hasWaterLight = true;
  waterLightColor = "0.8 0.8 1.0";
  lightRadius = 4.5;
  // ...
};
```

Explosions

Many times, we will want some kind of explosion effect when our projectile is armed and strikes something. Explosions will not happen until the particle is armed. As with particles and light, we have the ability to specify above- and below-water behaviors. However, the relationship for these two explosions are a little different than the prior two effects. Table 11.3 is supplied to clarify which explosion we get based on what explosions are specified and if the projectile is currently underwater or not.

Explosion Specified	Water Explosion Specified	Under Water?	Playing Emitter
N	Y	N	- none -
N	Y	Y	waterExplosion
Y	N	N	explosion
Y	N	Y	explosion
Y	Y	N	explosion
Y	Y	Y	waterExplosion

Table 11.3.

Explosions above and below water.

Specifying our explosion datablocks works as follows.

```
datablock ProjectileData( NormalExplodingProjectile ) {
  // ...
  explosion = "An Explosion Datablock";
  waterExplosion = "An Explosion Datablock";
  // ...
};
```

Splashes

It was mentioned above that a projectile entering or leaving the water will try to render a splash, and this is true, as long as one is specified.

```
datablock ProjectileData( SplashOnWaterStrikeProjectile ) {
  // ...
  splash = "A Splash Datablock";
  // ...
};
```

Bullet Holes

It may be the case that we would like the projectile to leave a mark when it explodes. Currently, TGE allows us to make these marks using decals, but only for explosions that happen on interiors or the terrain. Because TGE shapes use simplified collision-detection meshes, it isn't very easy to apply decals to shapes. It can be done but will require some coding.

As a bonus, TGE allows us to specify up to six different decals, one of which will randomly be applied to the interior or terrain when the projectile explodes.

```
datablock ProjectileData( MultiDecalProjectile ) {
  // ...
  decals[0] = "Decal Datablock 0";
  decals[1] = "Decal Datablock 1";
  decals[2] = "Decal Datablock 2";
  decals[3] = "Decal Datablock 3";
  decals[4] = "Decal Datablock 4";
  decals[5] = "Decal Datablock 5";
  // ...
};
```

Sound

Although some projectiles are noiseless, it is often nice to have a sound associated with our projectile. Furthermore, if the sound is 3D and the projectile is not too fast, we can get a nice "just missed" effect with a good sound system. Simply specify an audio profile to use, and the projectile will play the sound starting when the projectile is created and ending when the projectile explodes or fades away.

```
datablock ProjectileData( NoisyProjectile ) {
  // ...
  sound = "An Audio Profile";
  // ...
};
```

Lifetime and Fading Away

Consider what would happen if all misses kept traveling forever and never got removed. Eventually, the game could have tens of thousands of objects consuming CPU time. Thus, TGE imposes a maximum life for each projectile of 128 seconds (just over two minutes). The lifetime of a projectile is in ticks (1/32 of one second). Here is a particle that will live for one minute.

```
datablock ProjectileData( OneMinuteProjectile ) {
  // ...
  lifetime = 32 * 60; // Live for one minute
  // ...
};
```

Also, because slow-moving projectiles should not just pop out of existence, TGE has a feature that allows us to start fading the particle out of sight after a number of ticks.

```
datablock ProjectileData( SlowFadeProjectile ) {
  // ...
  lifeTime = 32 * 5;      // Lives for 5 seconds
  fadeDelay = 32 * 1;     // Starts fading at 1 second (i.e. 4 second fade)
  // ...
};
```

Inherited and Muzzle Velocities

Recall when I said we (our scripts) are responsible for imparting actual velocities to the projectile? Well, the smart GarageGames programmers provided a
couple of standard fields that we can use in our scripts. To specify the projectile's initial (muzzle) velocity, use the following.

```
datablock ProjectileData( SupaFastProjectile ) {
  // ...
  // Tell scripts to set velocity @ 8000 world units/second !!!
  muzzleVelocity = 8000.0;
  // ...
};
```

To specify the velocity that the projectile should inherit from any object it is
attached to, use the following.

```
datablock ProjectileData( FallBehindProjectile ) {
  // ...
  velInheritFactor = 0.5; // Only inherit half of velocity
  // ...
};
```

11.4.2 Using Projectiles

Only one class has a field for projectiles, and that is only so that TGE can
optimize for state-machine transitions. That class is the ShapeBaseImageData
class. You don't need to specify a projectile, but if you are using one, it is a good
idea, as this will help avoid rendering hiccups while the weapon is fired.

Standalone

Because projectiles are always created by scripts, it is our responsibility to
initialize all pertinent parameters for them. If you find this confusing, you
should refer to the code for the GPGT Lesson Kit's Projectiles Lesson. Because
I know you're just dying to see some code, here is a truncated version of the
code from the GPGT Lesson Kit for a standard projectile weapon (this code
was derived from the standard TGE SDK crossbow script).

```
function EGWeaponImage::onFire( %imageDB , %ownerObj ,
                                %mountSlot ) {
  %projectile = %imageDB.projectile;

  // Determine initial projectile velocity based on the
  // gun's muzzle point and the object's current velocity
  %muzzleVector = %ownerObj.getMuzzleVector(%mountSlot);
  %objectVelocity = %ownerObj.getVelocity();
  %muzzleVelocity = VectorAdd(
    VectorScale(%muzzleVector, %projectile.muzzleVelocity),
    VectorScale(%objectVelocity, %projectile.velInheritFactor));

  // Create the projectile object
  %bullet = new Projectile() {
    dataBlock = %projectile;
    initialVelocity = %muzzleVelocity;
    initialPosition = %ownerObj.getMuzzlePoint(%mountSlot);
    sourceObject = %ownerObj;
    sourceSlot = %mountSlot;
    client = %ownerObj.client;
  };

  MissionCleanup.add(%bullet);
  return %bullet;
}
```

11.4.3 Maze Runner Lesson #20 (90 Percent Step)—The FireBall

In this lesson, we will examine three of the six datablocks that are supplied with the MazeRunner prototype. These datablocks are used to implement the projectile representing the fireball.

If you look in the file "\MazeRunner\prototype\server\scripts\MazeRunner\FireBall.cs", you will find three datablocks.

- **FireBallParticle.** This datablock defines the particles that are used for the projectile's trail.

- **FireBallEmitter.** This datablock defines the pattern for the trail.

- **FireBallProjectile.** This datablock defines the projectile itself and uses the above two datablocks as well as the three we discussed in Lesson #19 (Section 11.3.11) (FireBallExplosionParticle, FireBallExplosionEmitter, and FireBallExplosion), which are used for the explosion.

FireBallParticle

Again, we have chosen to implement our particle datablock by using inheritance, but this time many parameters have been modified.

```
datablock ParticleData(FireBallParticle : baseSmokePD0 ) {
  dragCoeffiecient = 0.0;
  gravityCoefficient = 0.0;
  inheritedVelFactor = 0.0;

  lifetimeMS = 350;
  lifetimeVarianceMS = 50;

  spinRandomMin = -30.0;
  spinRandomMax = 30.0;

  colors[0] = "1 0.7 0.7 1.0";
  colors[1] = "1 0.7 0.7 1.0";
  colors[2] = "1 0.7 0.7 0";
  sizes[0] = 0.5;
  sizes[1] = 0.7;
  sizes[2] = 1.0;
  times[0] = 0.0;
  times[1] = 0.3;
  times[2] = 1.0;
};
```

The particles this produces will not be affected by drag or by gravity, nor will they inherit any velocity from the emitter. This means that they will just hang in the air where they are produced. They have a pretty long lifetime, between 300 and 400 milliseconds. As they hang in the air, they will spin back and forth between minus 30 and 30 degrees. Lastly, the smoke will start as medium sized off-white puffs and end as large gauzy white puffs.

FireBallEmitter

The emitter datablock is fairly short because it doesn't have a lot to do for smoke trails.

```
datablock ParticleEmitterData(FireBallEmitter) {
  ejectionPeriodMS = 20;
  periodVarianceMS = 5;
  ejectionVelocity = 0.25;
  velocityVariance = 0.10;
  thetaMin = 0.0;
```

```
    thetaMax = 180.0;
    particles = FireBallParticle;
};
```

This emitter will produce a new particle every 15 to 25 milliseconds, meaning that the trail may be a little spotty (the projectile is moving at 20 world units per second if you will recall from Lesson #18 (Section 10.3.7)).

The particles themselves have very little velocity when ejected, and they are all ejected between straight up and straight down (we could make this range smaller to create a more narrow trail).

Lastly, the emitter uses the particle datablock we just discussed.

FireBallProjectile

This datablock brings all of the work in the prior lesson and this one together to create the fireball.

```
datablock ProjectileData(FireBallProjectile) {
  projectileShapeName =
    "~/data/MazeRunner/Shapes/Projectiles/projectile.dts";
  explosion = FireBallExplosion;
  particleEmitter = FireBallEmitter;
  armingDelay = 0;
  lifetime = 5000;
  fadeDelay = 4800;
  isBallistic = false;
};
```

This particle uses a mesh that is provided with the GPGT Lesson Kit. It is nothing more than a very small elongated pyramid with a simple texture applied (Figure 11.1). It uses the explosion datablock and the (smoke trail) emitter defined above.

There is no arming delay, so the projectile will explode as soon as it strikes an object.

Figure 11.1.

Fireball projectile.

The projectile will live for 5 seconds and begin to fade at 4.8 seconds. At the end of its lifetime, it will automatically be deleted if it has not already impacted upon something.

It is nonballisitic and will travel in a straight line along the path on which it is fired.

shootFireBall()

We deferred our discussion of the fireball-shooting method until this chapter
so we would have the proper context. The main thing to understand is that,
when we create a projectile and put it into the world, it starts with an instantaneous velocity and direction (as specified at creation time).

```
function StaticShape::shootFireBall( %marker, %projectile ,
                                     %pointingVector , %velocity) {
  %bullet = new Projectile() {
    dataBlock = %projectile;

    initialVelocity = vectorScale( vectorNormalize(%pointingVector) ,
                            %velocity );
    initialPosition = %marker.getWorldBoxCenter();

    sourceObject = -1;
    sourceSlot = -1;
    theMarker = %marker;
  };

  %marker.bullet = %bullet;
  MissionCleanup.add(%bullet);
}
```

The most important things to see in the above code are the following.

1. The initial velocity is a combination of a direction and a magnitude.
2. The projectile can have any initialPosition, and we are choosing the
   centroid of the fireball block. This is important, because it demonstrates
   that collision detection only occurs for penetrations of a collision mesh, not
   for objects or rays leaving the mesh, as is the case with this projectile.

11.5 Sounds

TGE supports both 2D and 3D sounds. Standard TGE uses OpenAL for sound
support, but resources have been written on how to use other libraries like
FMOD. Sound is an area in TGE that, at first, may seem difficult, but in the
end turns out to be simple and well organized. All TGE sound is supported
via three mechanisms.

- Audio descriptions (ADs)
- Audio profiles (APs)
- Console functions

Game Elements

Additionally, there are two defunct features (which could be made to work with some love).

- AudioSampleEnvironment
- AudioEnvironment

11.5.1 Sound Dimension

For simplicity, sounds are often described as being either 2D or 3D. Now, both 2D and 3D sounds are 3D in the sense that, when they are played, the user's gaming setup will attenuate and otherwise modify them. The actual distinction being made here is how the sounds will be calculated and treated prior to being sent to the speaker(s).

2D Sounds

These are sounds that have no apparent source. Their gain is not attenuated by position or orientation. Some sounds with this dimension are:

- menu and interface feedback sounds,
- intro music,
- background music, and
- global environmental sounds (wind, thunder, rain, etc.).

3D Sounds

These are sounds with a specific source. Therefore, their gain is attenuated by position or orientation as related to the listener. Furthermore, if advanced features are enabled, 3D sounds can be attenuated and modified by the environment, occlusion, etc. A small sampling of sounds with this dimension are:

- player footfalls,
- vehicle noises,
- weapon noises, and
- local environmental sounds (waterfalls, rivers, surf, birds in a stand of trees, etc.)

11.5.2 AudioDescription and AudioProfile

Throughout the scripts, you will find datablock fields and other bits of code that take either an AudioProfile and/or an AudioDescription. The purpose of each of these is to encapsulate sound-specific data so it doesn't have to be explicitly stated later. In other words, by using the AP/AD (AudioProfile/ AudioDescription) mechanism, we simplify our life just like when we use datablocks.

AudioDescription

The job of the AudioDescription datablock is to define how a sound plays. It answers the following questions.

- Is the sound 2D (it doesn't attenuate), or is it 3D?
- If the sound is 3D, what kind of sound cones does it have? (See Section 8.7, "Audio Emitters.")
- Does the sound loop?
- If it loops, how many times does it loop and at what intervals does it repeat?
- What is the maximum gain for this sound?
- What channel does it play on?

AudioProfile

The job of the AudioProfile datablock is to define what sound is played. It answers the following questions.

- What sound (file) is used for this sound?
- Should this sound be preloaded? Preloading is useful for sounds that would take a long time to load from disk or otherwise might cause a discernible listening gap if not already in memory.
- What AudioDescription does this sound use?

11.5.3 Sound Channels

All TGE demos and kits come with certain sound channels dedicated to certain tasks. It is best and easiest to not change the ones that exist, but instead to add a new channel if needed. The TGE channels are as follows.

- `$DefaultAudioType`. Channel 0.
- `$GuiAudioType`. Channel 1 (dedicated to GUI sounds).
- `$SimAudioType`. Channel 2.

11.5.4 Using Sound

Because the AudioEmitter mission object uses all the same concepts, we will not be reviewing the parameters for either ADs or APs in depth. Instead, a summary is provided in the appendix, and if this is insufficient, a review of Section 8.7, "Audio Emitters," should clarify things. For now we'll restrict ourselves to discussing standalone usage.

TGE provides a complete set of OpenAL functions for playing and manipulating our sounds.

11.5.5 new versus datablock for Profiles/Descriptions

Sometimes, when looking at the examples, you will see audio profiles and descriptions created using the `new` keyword, and other times using the `datablock` keyword. This may seem arbitrary at first, but it is not.

An AudioProfile or an AudioDescription object created with the `new` keyword is nonnetworkable. In other words, these objects cannot be used to play sounds on remote clients.

An AudioProfile or an AudioDescription object created with the `datablock` keyword is networkable. In other words, the server can play sounds using these on remote clients.

Our focus in this guide is on the single-player usage of Torque, but because the `new` vs. `datablock` distinction is important to understand early, we will take the time now to look at some examples. In fact, why don't we use a lesson to clear up any confusion on the distinction between `new` versus *datablock*.

11.5.6 Maze Runner Lesson #21 (10 Percent Step)—Game Sounds

In this lesson, we will examine the different methods available to create AudioDescription and AudioProfile objects. This work will subsequently be used in Section 14.7, "Finishing the Prototype," to add sound to our game interfaces and game world.

For our game, we will need AudioDescriptions and AudioProfiles to play the following sounds.

- **Splash screen music**. We'd like to add some music to our splash screen when it is shown. This is a nonnetworked nonlooping 2D sound.

- **Button-over and button press sounds for main menu**. We want our buttons to provide feedback when the mouse hovers over them and when we click on them. These are both nonnetworked nonlooping 2D sounds.

- **In-game music**. We'd like some background music while playing our game, preferably an ambient loop of some sort. This is a nonnetworked looping 2D sound.

- **Fireball firing and explosion sound**. It doesn't make much sense for our fireball blocks to shoot a fireball silently, and the explosion when the fireball collides with something should not be silent, either. These are both networked nonlooping 3D sounds.

The Audio Descriptions

In order to create audio profiles, we need to create audio descriptions first. Why? Because, the AudioProfile object uses the AudioDescription object.

In our list (above), we have three nonnetworked nonlooping 2D sounds, one nonnetworked looping 2D sound, and two networked nonlooping 3D sounds. In total, this equates to a requirement for three different audio descriptions.

Nonnetworked Nonlooping 2D Audio Description

```
new AudioDescription( MazeRunnerNonLooping2DADObj ) {
   volume    = 1.0;
   isLooping = false;
   is3D      = false;
   type      = $GuiAudioType;
};
```

Using the new keyword, we have created an instance of AudioDescription descriptively named MazeRunnerNonLooping2DADObj. An audio profile using this description has the following attributes.

- Is nonnetworked. It is a normal object, not a datablock.
- Plays at full volume for the channel the sound is using.
- Is nonlooping.
- Is not 3D.
- Is assigned to the $GUIAudioType channel and will thus be attenuated by changes to that channel.

Nonnetworked Looping 2D Audio Description

```
new AudioDescription( MazeRunnerLooping2DADObj ) {
   volume    = 1.0;
   isLooping = true;
   loopCount = -1;
   is3D      = false;
   type      = $GuiAudioType;
};
```

Using the new keyword, we have created an instance of AudioDescription descriptively named MazeRunnerLooping2DADObj. An audio profile using this description has the following attributes.

- Is nonnetworked. It is a normal object, not a datablock.
- Plays at full volume for the channel the sound is using.
- Is looping.
- Loops infinitely (we assigned −1 to loopCount, but we could have left it unspecified, as well, since the default value is −1).
- Is not 3D.
- Is assigned to the $GUIAudioType channel and will thus be attenuated by changes to that channel.

451

Networked Nonlooping 3D Audio Description

```
datablock AudioDescription( MazeRunnerNonLooping3DADDB ) {
  volume       = 1.0;
  isLooping     = false;
  is3D        = true;
  ReferenceDistance = 2.0;
  MaxDistance   = 20.0;
  type        = $SimAudioType;
};
```

Using the *datablock* keyword, we have created an instance of AudioDescription descriptively named `MazeRunnerNonLooping3DADDB`. An audio profile using this description has the following attributes.

- Is networked. It is a datablock.
- Plays at full volume for the channel the sound is using.
- Is nonlooping.
- Is 3D.
- Plays at max volume between 0 and 2 world units and attenuates to nearly zero at a distance of 20 world units from the source position of the 3D sound.
- Is assigned to the `$SimAudioType` channel and will thus be attenuated by changes to that channel.

The Audio Profiles

Now that we have our three audio descriptions, we can create our audio profiles. In this case, we need one each for the sounds, but since several of these sounds, are similar execept for the sound file played, we will only examine one from each category.

The Nonlooping GUI Sounds (Splash Screen and Buttons)

```
new AudioProfile(MazeRunnerGGSplashScreen) {
  filename  = "~/data/GPGTBase/sound/gui/GGstartup.ogg";
  description = MazeRunnerNonLooping2DADObj;
};
```

Using the `new` keyword, we have created an instance of AudioProfile named `MazeRunnerGGSplashScreen`. This audio profile will be used when the GarageGames splash screen is shown and has the following attributes.

- It plays the GarageGames startup sound from the demo kit. (This sound file was renamed to GGStartup.ogg from startup.ogg and included with GPGT base data for your use).

- It uses our nonlooping 2D AudioDescription object `MazeRunnerNon-Looping2DADObj`.

The Looping GUI Sound (In-Game Music)

```
new AudioProfile(MazeRunnerLevelLoop) {
    filename    = "~/data/GPGTBase/sound/gui/levelLoop.ogg";
    description = MazeRunnerLooping2DADObj;
};
```

Using the `new` keyword, we have created an instance of AudioProfile descriptively named `MazeRunnerLevelLoop`. This audio profile will be used for in-game music and has the following attributes.

- It plays a short ambient loop provided on the accompanying disk.
- It uses our looping 2D AudioDescription object `MazeRunnerLooping2DADObj`.

The Networked Sounds (Fireball Firing and Explosion)

```
datablock AudioProfile(MazeRunnerFireballExplosionSound) {
    filename = "~/data/GPGTBase/sound/GenericExplosionSound.ogg";
    description = MazeRunnerNonLooping3DADDB;
};
```

Using the `datablock` keyword, we have created an instance of AudioProfile descriptively named `MazeRunnerFireballExplosionSound`. This audio profile will be used for the sound effect attached to a fireball explosion and has the following attributes.

- It plays a generic explosion sound that is included on the accompanying disk for your use. This sound is derived from the file "Crossbow_explosion.ogg" found in the TGE Demo.
- It uses our nonlooping 3D AudioDescription datablock `MazeRunnerNon-Looping3DADDB`.

Using The Audio Profiles

All of the above audio descriptions and audio profiles are provided on the accompanying disk. We will be using them later when we follow the instructions in Section 14.7, "Finishing the Prototype." However, the question of use should at least be addressed. How does one use these new sounds?

The sounds we created are used in three ways.

1. **Attached to a GUI control.** The button-over and button-press sounds above will be used by a GUI button control. As you will see in Chapter 12, this attachment is achieved using GUI profiles.

Game Elements

2. **Attached to a special effect.** Our explosion sound is used by the explosion object. As we saw in Section 11.3, "Explosions," we can assign an AudioProfile datablock to the ExplosionData `soundProfile` field. When an explosion is created with this datablock, it will automatically play the sound specified by our AudioProfile datablock.

```
datablock ExplosionData( FireballExplosion ) {
  // ...
  soundProfile = MazeRunnerFireballExplosionSound;
  // ...
};
```

3. **Played manually.** Lastly, we can play sounds manually. We simply call `alxPlay()` and pass it the name or ID of a nonnetworked 2D sound AudioProfile.

```
// Play the GG Splash Screen Sound
alxPlay( MazeRunnerGGSplashScreen );
```

11.6 Special Effects Summary

This short chapter was dedicated to discussing a set of classes that have no true home but by their nature define or enable a variety of special effects. These classes included the following.

- **Debris.** The detritus left over by an explosion.
- **Decals.** Textures applied to surfaces to give the impression of bullet holes, scorch marks, footprints, etc.
- **Explosions.** A special effect dedicated to pyrotechnic displays and interactions with the camera that provide a convincing effect.
- **Projectiles.** A shape not only used to represent the output of weapons, but that can be used for a variety of other effects.
- **Sounds.** AudioProfiles and AudioDescriptions, used for networked vs. nonnetworked sound.

In each discussion, we summarized the features provided by the individual class, how to use the class alone if possible, and how the class interacts with other TGE special effects or other classes.

Chapter 12
Standard TGE GUI Controls

12.1 Standard GUIs

In this chapter, we will take a look at what is required to make use of several standard TGE GUI controls. We will not discuss the usage of every GUI control provided in TGE but will instead restrict ourselves to discussing the commonly used ones. Specifically, we will discuss the following controls.

- Windows, containers, and panes
  - GuiControl
  - GuiFrameSetCtrl
  - GuiScrollCtrl
  - GuiStackControl
  - GuiPaneControl
  - GuiTabBookCtrl
  - GuiTabPageCtrl
  - GuiWindowCtrl
- Backgrounds and borders
  - GuiBitmapBorderCtrl
  - GuiBitmapCtrl
  - GuiChunkedBitmapCtrl
  - GuiFadeInBitmapCtrl
- Text
  - GuiMessageVectorCtrl
  - GuiMLTextCtrl
  - GuiMLTextEditCtrl
  - GuiTextCtrl
  - GuiTextEditCtrl
  - GuiTextListCtrl
- Buttons
  - GuiButtonBaseCtrl
  - GuiBitmapButtonCtrl
  - GuiButtonCtrl
  - GuiCheckBoxCtrl
  - GuiRadioCtrl
- Menus
  - GuiMenuBar
  - GuiPopupMenuCtrl
- Sliders and Scales
  - GuiFilterCtrl
  - GuiSliderCtrl
  - GuiTextEditSliderCtrl
- Miscellaneous
  - GuiCursor
  - GuiDirectoryFileListCtrl
  - GuiDirectoryTreeCtrl
  - GuiInputCtrl
  - GuiMouseEventCtrl
  - GuiTreeViewCtrl

However, before we leap into the examples, let's take some time to familiarize ourselves with some GUI basics.

12.1.1 Interfaces versus GUIs

For the sake of clarity, I will be using four terms while discussing GUIs. The first term is *interface*. When I use the term interface, I mean an entire game interface, such as a main menu, a help dialog, etc. *An interface is composed of one or more GUI elements.* The other three terms I will use are *GUI, control,* and *GUI element(s)*. I will use each of these interchangeably to keep the discussion from being too dry. Each of these terms refer to *any single GUI class* which may or may not contain other controls. For example, a GuiBitmap, a GuiButtonCtrl, and a GuiScrollCtrl are all GUI elements, whereas an interface might be composed of all three of these, plus additional GUI elements.

12.1.2 The Canvas

Since days of old, when working with user interfaces, it has been common to refer to the base interface's layer as the *canvas*. All GUI controls are stacked (placed in) the canvas. Torque supports a single canvas named, intuitively, Canvas. The canvas can display two generalized categories of interfaces:

1. Dialogs.
2. Everything else.

In most respects, a dialog is not different from other controls, but it is treated differently. We will discuss the why and the how of this shortly.

Current Canvas Content

All nondialog interfaces are only displayed if they are the current content of the canvas. Furthermore, the canvas only has one content at a time. In order to set an interface as the contents of the canvas, we write a statement like the following.

```
Canvas.setContent( myCoolInterface );
```

In this example, we are making an interface named myCoolInterface the new (and thus the current) content of the canvas. This unloads the current content and replaces it with myCoolInterface.

Dialogues and Layers

Most of the time, exchanging the current canvas content is what we want. However, occasionally, we would like to retain the current canvas content while we temporarily display another interface over the current one. What we're talking about is a dialog. In order to display a dialog, we do the following.

```
Canvas.pushDialog( myCoolDialog , 1 );
```

In this example, we are pushing an interface named myCoolDialog onto Layer 1 of the canvas. The current content of the canvas is retained, as well as any interfaces already pushed onto any canvas layers. This method allows us to have as many interfaces open as we need. Note that, if no layer is provided as the second argument to pushDialog(), the dialog is pushed onto the default layer, Layer 0.

Later, we can pop a dialog in three ways.

```
Canvas.popDialog( );
// or
Canvas.popDialog( myCoolDialog );
// or
Canvas.popDialog( 1 );
```

The first popDialog() will pop the last interface that was pushed, which in this case would be myCoolDialog. The second popDialog() will do a lookup on myCoolDialog and pop it if it is found. The third and last popDialog() will pop all interfaces in Layer 1. I repeat, *all* interfaces in Layer 1. This is a nice way to pop multiple stacked dialogs at the same time.

> Replacing the current content of the canvas does not affect dialogs. Dialogs are content that float over the canvas's current contents.

Canvas Extent vs. Screen Size

The canvas is in effect a boundless entity that extends beyond the visible screen. The "0 0" coordinate of the canvas is merely a reflection of the "starting" position of the screen (upper-left corner), and the extent is a reflection of the width and height of the screen. It is completely legal to position GUI elements outside the visible bounds of the screen. In fact, this is true of all controls, not just for the canvas. All controls will clip the parts of their children that are outside the control's own visible bounds.

12.1.3 The Structure of a .gui File

Each interface that we make the content of the canvas and each interface that we push onto the canvas is a separate entity. For instance, we may have any of the following interfaces: splash screen, main menu, credits, settings dialog(s), help dialog(s), play GUI, etc. Each of these interfaces exists individually as a hierarchy of GUI controls, stored in a separate .gui file. The .gui files can be created by hand, by script, or with the GUI editor. The Torque standard is to have one interface definition per .gui file, and the general organization of such a file is as follows.

1. An optional block of code.

2. The definition of the interface between two comment lines.

```
//--- OBJECT WRITE BEGIN ---
//--- OBJECT WRITE END ---
```

3. A second optional block of code.

   A GUI file with just the sections delimited would look like this:

```
// Optional code block #1
//--- OBJECT WRITE BEGIN ---
// Interface definition
//--- OBJECT WRITE END ---
// Optional code block #2
```

The lines in bold are optional.

Optional Code Block #1

This optional block of code can be added by hand *after* generating and saving an interface file, using the GUI editor. Normal bits of code that go here are:

- GUI profile(s) used in subsequent GUI definitions,
- `onAdd()` callback definitions for subsequent GUI elements, and
- miscellaneous code and global variables.

Interface Definition

This required block is generated by the GUI editor or by hand. If generated by the GUI editor, it will be delimited by two (optional) comment lines and look something like the following.

```
//--- OBJECT WRITE BEGIN ---
new GuiChunkedBitmapCtrl( parentGUI ) {
  horizSizing = "width";
  vertSizing = "height";
  position = "0 0";
  extent = "640 480";

  new GuiControl( childGUI ) {
    // ...

    new GuiTextCtrl( grandChildGUI ) {
      // ...
    };
```

```
   // ...

  };
  // ...
};
//--- OBJECT WRITE END ---
```

The comment lines (highlighted) allow the GUI editor to find the interface definition and preserve the optional codeblocks surrounding it in the case that we later reload our GUI with the editor and edit it. *Yes, both code blocks will be preserved.*

If we look at the above example skeleton, we will see that there is one `parentGUI` (named this way for the sake of the example) which can then have child GUIs, grandchild GUIs, etc., inside it. We'll talk more about the design of the GUI definition shortly, but let's first address the second code block.

Optional Code Block #2

We can optionally-hand edit the file and add a second block of code after the interface definition. Normal bits of code that go here are:

- `onWake()`, `onSleep()`, and `onRemove()` callback definitions as well as any other callbacks that might be associated with the prior GUI elements, and

- miscellaneous code.

OK, we're doing well. We know a little bit about the canvas, and we understand the structure of a .gui file. Now, let's talk about the general structure of an interface.

General Design of Interfaces

When building an interface, I suggest using the following steps.

1. Select a control to be the base container for this interface. Good choices are GuiControl, GuiBitmapCtrl, or GuiChunkedBitmapCtrl (among others).

2. Position the base GUI at "0 0" and make the extent equal to that of the canvas.

3. Use a `horizSizing` of "width" and a `vertSizing` of "height". This last step is very important because we want our base GUI to cover the entire visible screen. The extent is not so important as the `horizSizing` and the `vertSizing`. (The GUI editor will automatically do this and the prior step for you when you create a new interface: File → New GUI).

4. Now, add all other GUI elements you wish to have into your selected base GUI.

Game Elements

```
new GuiChunkedBitmapCtrl(MyCoolInterface) {
  // ...
  horizSizing = "width";
  vertSizing = "height";
  position = "0 0";
  extent = "640 480";
  // ...

  new GuiWindowCtrl() {
    // ...
  };

  // ...

  new GuiWindowCtrl() {
    // ...
  };
};
```

Well, we've gone on for a bit now, and I haven't told you what makes a nondialog different from a dialog. The short answer is nothing. Yes, that's right. In theory, there is no difference between a nondialog and a dialog except the way we choose to display them. In practice, however, there is usually one more important difference—how they capture inputs. To understand this, we need to explore how GUIs capture inputs in general.

In order to understand how inputs are captured by GUI elements, we need to explore the following concepts: layers, first responders, focus, and modality.

How a GUI Captures Inputs

Layers

Unfortunately, the term *layers* has been and is used regarding dialogs. We are not currently discussing dialog layers. Instead, we are discussing the more general concept of layering.

The canvas can be considered to be the *bottom layer* of the control stack. Each visible control is stacked onto this canvas, making a "layer." Those controls on the bottom are rendered first, and those on the top are rendered last. Thus, at the end of any rendering cycle, the topmost GUI controls will have rendered over all other elements below them, properly occluding and masking them.

Now, recall our discussion from Section 9.5 regarding I/O processing order. Input events are passed from the operating system to the Torque platform code layer, which then passes the inputs to:

1. the GlobalActionMap, then to

2. the Canvas, then to

3. any active (nonglobal) ActionMaps.

Imagine that the the mouse input events (the ones *not* captured by the GlobalAc-tionMap) are like marbles falling onto our interface. Each marble will fall from the location of the cursor and hit the first GUI it encounters. This is the first GUI that will be given an opportunity to capture and to use the mouse event.

If a control does nothing with the event, it can either allow the marble to "fall through" until a GUI lower in the stack finally uses the event, or the event can immediately be sent to the ActionMap stack.

For a modeless control (we will define modality below), the event con-tinues to fall through. For a modal control, the uncaptured event is passed directly to the ActionMap stack. Notice that I did not say modal interface.

Generally, you can consider an interface to be modal if any GUI in the interface is modal, but in practice the best way to do this is to make the base layer of the interface modal and to allow all the higher layers to behave nor-mally (i.e., be modeless).

Keyboard events are a little more tricky. Because there is no parallel to the "mouse pointer location" idea, we need to discuss a new concept.

First Responders

Because a keystroke comes from no specific physical location, there needs to be a mechanism that tells TGE which GUI to send the keystroke to. This concept is called *first responder*.

Some controls will automatically become first responder, but sometimes a control needs a little help (or discouragement). For example, in the case where there are two controls that are on the same layer and both want to be the first responder, the question arises, "Which of these will be first responder?"

The first responder will be:

1. the control that was first responder on the last processing pass, or

2. the control that is made first responder by the method `makeFirst-Responder()`, or

3. the control that is made first responder as the result of a mouse-click or **TAB** transition.

Note that some controls will take back the first-responder role even when another control has been clicked.

> If you are using version 1.4 or later of the engine, this discussion does not apply. The concept of first responder has been deprecated in lieu of a more standard focus-based system. So, if you are not using version 1.3 or prior, skip ahead to "Focus."

Focus

A GUI can have what is called *focus*. This term implies that the control is visible and active. However, the main thing to know about focus is that the

Game Elements

control that has focus and is first responder will be the one to receive keyboard inputs.

Mouse movements and clicks can change the current focus, so how do we force a GUI to retain focus regardless of the mouse position/action?

Modality

The fourth and final concept we need to wrangle with is modality. Modality is usually discussed in the same breath as dialogs, but it is a term that can be applied to any control. Namely, a control can be modeless, or it can be modal. Furthermore, a modeless GUI does not attempt to hold onto the focus. It will freely give up the focus to whatever other GUI wishes to take it. The modal GUI is less friendly, however, and once it has the focus, it does not relinquish it until its purpose is served and it chooses to release focus. All controls are modeless by default, although some do actively seek to attain first-responder status (GuiTextEditCtrl, for one), which is not the same as being modal.

We can retain focus either by:

1. making our GUI modal (not very friendly and not suggested unless truly necessary),

2. covering all other GUIs such that they do not have the possibility of getting focus (we can easily do this by placing the GUI control that we want to have the focus in a GUI control that covers the entire canvas), or

3. forcing first-responder status by using the `makeFirstResponder()` method call.

Please note that sometimes you need to make a control be first responder, and sometimes you need to force a control to not be first responder.

Wow! We have come a long way. We now have at least a passing understanding of some GUI concepts. Still, we have a way to go before discussing individual GUI elements. Now, let's talk about some more advanced topics.

> If you are using version 1.4 or later of the engine, this discussion does not apply. The concept of modality has been deprecated in lieu of a more standard focus-based system. So, if you are not using version 1.3 or prior, skip this.

12.2 GUI Profiles

Similar to the concept of datablocks for shapes, we have GUI control profiles (GuiControlProfile) for GUIs. These are *unique* objects that are instantiated on the client and used repeatedly in the creation, initialization, and use of GUIs. They save us having to constantly redefine common attributes on a GUI-by-GUI basis. Like datablocks, they provide a single location from which to draw common attributes, but this space is not static (like a datablock).

The syntax for a GuiControlProfile is as follows.

```
new GuiControlProfile ( GuiProfileName [ : parentProfile ] ) {
  field_0 = value;
...
  field_N = value;
...
  [dynamic_field_N = value;]
};
```

Like datablocks, each GuiControlProfile is expected to be unique; thus, creating a second profile with the same name as a prior one will in effect override it. However, to be safe, always delete a profile if you are going to redefine it. Also, do not delete a profile that is currently in use, or you will crash the engine.

Like datablocks, we can inherit (copy) from a previously defined profile if we so choose.

Not all fields that can be defined in a GuiControlProfile are used by every GUI control, nor are they all used in the same way. We are, of course, free to add our own dynamic fields to any profile at any time.

12.2.1 Visual Attributes of GUI Control Profiles

As you would expect, the majority of the fields in GUI control profiles are for enabling and/or modifying visual aspects of a GUI. It should be said once more that not all of these values are treated equally between GUIs, and experimentation will be necessary for controls not documented here. However, after reading the remainder of this chapter, you should have a reasonable idea of what to expect when you use these fields.

Bitmap

There are several controls that use a bitmap. Thus, it makes sense that the bitmap should be specified here. This simplifies GUI creation and easily allows us to have controls in different places all using the same graphics file.

Unlike bitmaps used elsewhere in Torque, GUI bitmaps *may have any reasonable dimension* and need not be sized as a power of two.

```
new GuiControlProfile ( usesABitmapProfile ) {
  // No need to specify suffix
  bitmap = "./some_path/somebitmapname";
};
```

Game Elements

Borders

All controls can have a border. The border parameters in a GuiControlProfile
are as follows.

- **border.** This integer value specifies the control-specific border type, of
  which there are up to five possibilities:
  - 0—disabled, and
  - 1, 2, 3, 4—control-specific implementation.
- **borderColor.** A three-value integer vector containing the RGB colors for
  a normal border.
- **borderColorHL.** A three-value integer vector containing the RGB colors
  for an "is highlighted" border.
- **borderColorNA.** A three-value integer vector containing the RGB colors
  for a "not active" border.
- **borderThickness.** This integer field determines the thickness of a border
  in pixels.

```
new GuiControlProfile ( aintGotNoBorderProfile ) {
   // Never rely on defaults, turn it off yourself!
   border = false;
};

new GuiControlProfile ( pencilThinBorderProfile ) {
   border = true;
   borderColor   = "0 0 0";
   borderColorHL = "0 0 0";
   borderColorNA = "0 0 0";
   borderThicknes = 1;
};

new GuiControlProfile ( rainbowBorderProfile ) {
   border = true;
   borderColor   = "255 0 0";
   borderColorHL = "0 255 0";
   borderColorNA = "0 0 255";
   borderThicknes = 2;
};
```

Cursors

What is a cursor, you ask? What we're talking about here is that little blinky
thing that shows up in text boxes and the like. We can colorize it with the
cursorColor field.

```
new GuiControlProfile ( angryRedBlinkyThingProfile ) {
  cursorColor = "153 0 0";
};
```

Background/Fill Colors and Opacity

If we're not using a bitmap as our background, we will need to decide what color it should be. Thus, TGE has provided the following fields.

- **fillColor.** This contains the four-element integer vector containing the RGBA values for a control's background.

- **fillColorHL.** This contains the four-element integer vector containing the RGBA values for a control's background when it is highlighted.

- **fillColorNA.** This contains the four-element integer vector containing the RGBA values for a control's background when it is inactive.

> You may completely disable backfill by setting the opaque field to false. If this field is set to true, then the backfill will be rendered with the specified translucency.

Notice that the background color vectors have four elements, not three. This means you can define an alpha channel and make an element translucent or even transparent.

```
new GuiControlProfile ( aTranslucentPurplishWindowProfile ) {
  opaque = false;                      // Enable translucency/transparency
  fillColor = "153 102 255 128";    // 50% translucent
  fillColorHL = "153 102 255 200";  // 22% translucent
  fillColorNA = "153 102 255 64";   // 75% translucent (almost transparent)
};
```

Fonts

Images can do a lot for transmitting ideas, but we will often have to break down and actually write something. That is, we'll have to use words to make ourselves clear. Because nobody likes to be boring, it makes sense to have some way to make our text a little more interesting than the default Arial font. TGE supplies myriad fields to enable text coloring. Please be aware that some of these field names are aliased, so the last definition is the definition that will be used for both (Table 12.1).

For convenience, I have included the color codes in Table 12.1. Why? Well, if you recall from earlier when we discussed the console in TorqueScript, I mentioned that you can use escape sequences to color text. This colorization applies to the console and many of the text controls.

So we've learned to colorize our text, but can we select a typeface and point size, too? You bet! We can select our font typeface with the fontType field and determine the point size of the font with the fontSize field.

Table 12.1.

Fields for text coloring.

field	alias	Color Code	Purpose
colors[0]	fontColor	\c0	Three-element integer vector defining default text color.
colors[1]	fontColorHL	\c1	Three-element integer vector defining highlighted text color.
colors[2]	fontColorNA	\c2	Three-element integer vector defining inactive text color.
colors[3]	fontColorSEL	\c3	Three-element integer vector defining selected text color.
colors[4]	fontColorLink	\c4	Three-element integer vector defining hyperlink text color.
colors[5]	fontColorLinkHL	\c5	Three-element integer vector defining selected hyperlink text color.
colors[6]	--	\c6	Three-element integer vector defining user-defined text color.
colors[7]	--	\c7	Three-element integer vector defining user-defined text color.
colors[8]	--	\c8	Three-element integer vector defining user-defined text color.
colors[9]	--	\c9	Three-element integer vector defining user-defined text color.

If you are working with a version of TGE prior to 1.4, the UFT extension is GFT, instead. Also, versions prior to 1.4 do not support Unicode. In either case, you may install custom fonts in your game by doing the following.

1. Be sure the font is installed on your system.

2. Create a GuiControlProfile specifying the font you want to use at the type size you want to use it.

3. Create a control using this profile.

4. Run your game.

At this point, if the font shows up, you are done. Now, just be sure not to delete the UFT/GFT file, and you can use this font on any system, even if the user doesn't have it installed. TGE will use the generated one.

fontType (An Aside)

I know that when I first picked up TGE, it was not at all clear what my choices were for fonts. I poked around for a bit and found some files with a GFT suffix (see " ~ \common\ui\cache\"). The strange thing was that, when I ran TGE on different platforms, I found different files in this directory.

Huh? Well, a little more research and reading showed that the GFT files are a side effect of a successful font build; i.e, as I specified new fonts, if the build was successful, I would find a new GFT file with a matching name.

Because I know it is nice to have a reference, I have supplied a list of commonly installed fonts. Select a font from the following list of 47 common fonts and try it.

Arial	Georgia Bold Italic	Tahoma
Arial Black	Georgia Italic	Tahoma Bold
Arial Bold	Impact	Times New Roman
Arial Bold Italic	Impact Italic	Times New Roman Bold
Arial Italic	Lucida Console	Times New Roman Bold Italic
Comic Sans MS	Lucida Sans Unicode	Times New Roman Italic
Comic Sans MS Bold	Microsoft Sans Serif	Trebuchet MS
Courier	Modern	Trebuchet MS Bold
Courier New	Palatino Linotype	Trebuchet MS Bold Italic
Courier New Bold	Palatino Linotype Bold	Trebuchet MS Italic
Courier New Bold Italic	Palatino Linotype Bold Italic	Tunga
Courier New Italic	Palatino Linotype Italic	Verdana
Franklin Gothic Medium	Roman	Verdana Bold
Gautami	Script	Verdana Bold Italic
Georgia	Small Fonts	Verdana Italic
Georgia Bold		

For example, let's try one of my favorites, Tahoma Bold, at 10 points.

```
new GuiControlProfile ( sweetTahomaBoldProfile ) {
  fontType = "Tahoma Bold";
  fontSize = 10;
}
```

If this works, the first time we try to use this profile, a new UFT file named "Tahoma Bold_10.uft", will appear in our font cache directory. If the font failed to get constructed, TGE will try to use Arial instead.

You know, Tahoma Bold isn't really all that legible on the screen at only 10 points. In fact, it may not be legible at all on a Macintosh, which brings up the concept of target platforms and their variances.

Platform Variances

The folks who designed TGE had it all together the day they designed the text-formatting features. Someone realized that different platforms have different standard screens with different aspect ratios and different "expected" fonts. Thus, a way was needed to target profiles to platforms. That targeting is provided with the `$platform` variable. This global variable is set by the engine if it can determine the current platform type. It can take the following values.

- `macos`. It's a Macintosh, or at least it's running OSX or OS9.
- `windows`. Some version of Windows.

- `X86UNIX`. Unix.
- `Linux`. Linux.
- `OpenBSD`. OpenBSD.
- `Unknown`. This means that TGE could not identify the OS.

Honestly, I'm sure that the `$platform` variable wasn't created with *only fonts* in mind. In fact, the only time we really care about this for fonts is when we're dealing with the Macintosh. Those guys just have to be different; or perhaps it's the PC guys who are different? Whatever the case, fonts on the Mac are quite different from those on PCs, due to several factors, which include strange aspect ratios and, more importantly, expectations. OSX (and OS9 before it) uses a different font set from those found under Windows.

So, how do we make our fonts Mac and PC friendly? Like this.

```
new GuiControlProfile ( makeAMACGuyHappyProfile ) {
  fontType = ($platform $= "macos") ? "Courier New" :
      "Lucida Console";
  fontSize = ($platform $= "macos") ? 14 : 12;
};
```

Font Not Found?

In case you missed it above, if TGE cannot build your font, it will subsitute Arial at the point size you selected. Failing that, the engine will fail out, complaining about Arial fonts needing to be on the system. Sheesh! Really though, I've never seen it happen yet.

Unicode

Versions 1.4 and later support Unicode fonts, as well. Unicode is a method of encoding keyboard keys to corresponding numeric values. ASCII is the old-fashioned way of doing this, but with the world rapidly growing smaller and with a number of non–Latin-based alphabets being used on keyboards today, a new encoding was and is required. Thus Unicode was born.

In short, if you want to penetrate a foreign market, one of the things you must be able to do is match that market's keyboard scheme. TGE is ready.

Text Formatting

We're doing pretty well so far. We've done a lot to get our GUIs looking nice and our fonts looking interesting. However, what happens if we try to use some text and it doesn't align nicely in the control. Using spaces to justify/space our text isn't a very appealing solution. Does TGE help us out? Yes, it does. There are two fields that deal with how text is formatted.

The first is the `justify` field, which can take the following values:

- `left`—left justified,
- `right`—right justified, and
- `center`—centered.

Then, for those cases where it isn't the justification we care about so much as the fact that the text rides too close to the edge, we can adjust our offset with the `textOffset` field, which takes a two-element vector defining the *x-y* offset of the upper-left corner of the first text character in pixels.

```
new GuiControlProfile ( centerMyTextProfile ) {
  justify = center;
};


new GuiControlProfile ( slightOffsetTextProfile ) {
  // Offset 4 pixels from left and 6 pixels from top
  textOffset = "4 6";
};
```

We've talked about how GUI control profiles contribute to the look of a GUI; now let's talk about how they affect behavior.

Autosizing

There are a few controls that may need to resize either their heights or widths to fit their parent control. Among these are the GUITextCtrl, GuiTextList-Ctrl, and GuiMLTextEditCtrl. To declare this functionality, TGE provides two Boolean fields.

- **autoSizeHeight.** Allows the control to resize its height to accommodate multi-line/row contents.
- **autoSizeWidth.** Allows the control to resize its height to accommodate multi-character/column contents.

Key and Mouse Attributes

There are a few key and mouse attributes that I should at least touch upon.

- **mouseOverSelected.** If this is set to `true`, the control will be selected when the mouse hovers over it.
- **returnTab.** If this is specified, the control will generate a tab event when it is in focus and the **ENTER** key is pressed.
- **canKeyFocus.** If `true`, this control can be given keyboard focus.

> Just setting these values to `true` does not guarantee the behavior. These fields only work if the control can behave in this way. For example, setting these on a label (GuiTextCtrl) would do nothing, but setting them on a text edit control (GuiTextEditCtrl) would work.

Game Elements

Modality

Again, if you are using version 1.4 or later, this concept is deprecated. The following only applies to versions 1.3 and prior.

We discussed modality above. Here is where we learn how to enable it. Simply set the Boolean field `modal` to `true`, and your control should be modal. My suggestion is that most controls have this set to `false` unless it really makes sense to *force* the user to deal with a GUI explicitly and first.

Input Restrictions

Besides the often onerous restriction of a modal GUI, what other restrictions are there? Well, just one. We can restrict text-entry fields to allow only numeric input by setting the Boolean field `numbersOnly` to `true`.

Audio Attributes

Because it would be a real bummer to have to define the sound for each and every button, TGE supplies two fields to do so in a GUI control profile instead.

- **soundButtonOver.** Play the sound represented by this AudioProfile when the mouse moves over this button.
- **soundButtonDown.** Play the sound represented by this AudioProfile when the button is pressed.

12.3 GuiControl—the Root GUI Class

GuiControl is the root class to all GUI controls and thus provides many fields and console methods. When it is used at all, it is normally used as a container for other controls, as it has very few rendering features and does nothing with inputs.

12.3.1 Profiles

Nearly all controls require a profile. Furthermore, every time a control wakes up, it looks for its profile. If for some reason no profile is specified, the control will do its best to find one, using the following rules.

1. Use the profile specified by the user unless it is equal to the null string, `""`.
2. Try to find a profile whose name is the first part of the control class name + the word profile (e.g., GuiButtonCtrl would look for GuiButtonProfile).
3. Use GuiDefaultProfile (a profile with this name must always be created, and always before other profiles are created).

Interestingly, profiles can be changed at any time. Also, the contents of a profile (i.e., the fields) can be modified from script.

In order to set the original profile, assign a value to the profile field. This value can be the null string. If it is, the engine will search for a profile and replace the null string with the name of the first matching profile found.

To change a profile after a control is created, call the `setProfile()` console method. The control's `profile` field can generally be updated using direct assignment, but caution and plenty of verification are in order if you intend to use this method.

```
// Creation ...
new GuiControl( myTestControl ) {
  profile = someProfile;
};

// Changing by console method
myTestControl.setProfile( someOtherProfile );

// Changing by assignment ( not suggested )
myTestControl.profile = someOtherProfile;
```

12.3.2 Extents and Position

All controls have two extents, `extent` and `minExtent`. The former is a two-element integer vector defining the control's initial width and height. The latter (not actually used in all controls) is also a two-element integer vector that specifies the minimum width and height dimensions the control can assume. If we did not have `minExtent`, a control could be scaled down to a point where it was too small to use or view, either because the parent was resized, or because we resized the control ourselves using the mouse. `minExtent` prevents either of these cases.

`position`, also a two-element integer vector, is the initial *x* and *y* coordinate of the upper-left corner of the control.

```
new GuiControl( myTestControl2 ) {
  position = "10 20";     // start at < 10 , 20 >
  extent= "100 200";      // Start 100 pixels wide, 200 pixels high
  minExtent = "80 80";    // Do not allow to shrink below 80x80 pixels
};
```

12.3.3 Position and Sizing

Because the canvas may have various dimensions (as a result of user-selected resolution changes and/or GUI editor resizing), several ways are supplied to modify/maintain the sizing of a control. There are two fields, `horizSizing` and `vertSizing`. The settings and behavior of both of these fields are

Game Elements

thoroughly covered in Section 3.14, "The GUI Editor." Please refer there for how these two fields interact and control the sizing of a control.

To retrieve the current position of the control, we can use the `getPosition()` method, which returns a two-element integer vector containing the current position of the control's upper-left corner. Then, to modify the position and/or the size of this control, we can use the `resize()` method.

```
// Move this control down 10, left 10, and resize it to
// "100 100"
$position = $test.getPosition();
$newX = getWord( $position , 0) + 10;
$newY = getWord( $position , 1) + 10;
$test.resize( $newX , $newY , 100 , 100 );
```

12.3.4 Initial Visibility

If we so choose, we can cause a control to start off invisible (not rendered). Just set the Boolean field `visible` to `false`. By default, it is set to `true`.

12.3.5 Accelerators

Often, it is nice to be able to activate a control via some combination of key presses. To facilitate this, TGE GUIs support accelerators. By setting the `accelerator` field to some combination of modifier(s) + key, we can enable access to buttons and many other controls from the keyboard.

```
new GuiButtonCtrl( myAcceleratedTestButton ) {
  // Ctrl+Alt+X activates this button
  accelerator = "Ctrl Alt X";
};
```

Modifiers

Modifiers can be **CTRL**, **SHIFT**, or **ALT**.

Keys

Keys include the following: F1, F2, F3, F4, F5, F6, F7, F8, F9, F10, F11, F12, A, B, C, D, E, F, G, H, I, J, K, L, M, N, O, P, Q, R, S, T, U, V, W, X, Y, Z.

12.3.6 Commands and $thisControl

Many controls will wish to execute a command when activated, and a smaller set may need an alternate (secondary) command for other events. These commands can be small scripts or just calls to functions. They are declared as follows.

```
new GuiButtonCtrl( myTestButton ) {
  command = "doSomething();";
  altCommand = "doSomethingElse();";
};
```

Be aware that any control that executes a `command` will first set the global variable `$thisControl` to the ID of the calling control. For example, when a button is clicked, it will do the following.

1. Set `$thisControl` to the ID of the button.
2. Execute the script specified by `command`.

Only the following controls use `altCommand`.

- GuiSliderCtrl
- GuiTextCtrl
- GuiTextEditCtrl
- GuiTreeviewCtrl

12.3.7 Variables

Interestingly, each control can have a variable associated with it. How it uses this variable is up to the control, but normally the variable contains the current value of this control.

```
$test = new GuiButtonCtrl( testButton ) {
  variable = "testButtonValue";
};

// Access this variable like this:
echo("testButtonValue == ", $testButtonValue );
```

12.3.8 Becoming First Responder

There will be times when we want a control to capture keyboard inputs. To have a control start catching the input, we must call the `makeFirstResponder()` method with a Boolean value of `true`. To make it stop, simply call this method with a value of `false`. Also, don't forget that this concept only applies to version of TGE prior to 1.4.

```
// Capture keyboard inputs
testButton.makeFirstResponder( true );
```

Game Elements

12.3.9 Current and Subsequent Visibility

We know how to tell the control whether it should start off visible, but what if we want to change this? Use the setVisible() method and pass it either true or false based on our needs.

```
testButton.setVisible( false ); // Hide the button
```

We can also check for visibility with the isVisible() method.

```
echo("This button is", (testButton.isVisible() ? " " :
    " not "), "visible");
```

12.3.10 Awake and Active?

A control can be awake or asleep, active or inactive. These modes can be interpreted as follows.

- **(isAwake()** == true). Self or parent is current content of canvas or canvas layer.
- **(isAwake()** == false). Self or parent is not current content of canvas or canvas layer.
- **(isActive()** == true). Currently enabled.
- **(isActive()** == false). Currently disabled.

In addition to checking the status of active, we can set it with the setActive() method.

```
testButton.setActive( false ); // Disable this button
```

12.4 GUI Console Methods, Callbacks, and Scoping

GUIs and GuiControlProfiles, like all TGE objects, support console methods and callbacks.

12.4.1 Console Methods for GuiControl and Children

You may not find much use for this, but just in case, I want you to know that you can in fact define console methods on GuiControleProfile objects. However, you can only define console methods for GuiControlProfile objects in either the namespace GuiControlProfile:

```
$profileA = new GUIControlProfile( testProfileA ) {
  \\...
};

function GUIControlProfile::testit( %this ) {
  echo("GUIControlProfile::testit(",%this, ")");
}

$profileA.testit();
```

or in the SimObject namespace (GuiControlProfile's parent is SimObject):

```
function simObject::testit2( %this ) {
  echo("simObject::testit(2",%this,")");
}

$profileA.testit2();
```

The class, className, and superClass keywords are not recognized and cannot be used to extend the namespace of GuiControlProfile objects.

12.4.2 Console Methods for GuiControlProfile and Children

More useful to us than console methods for GuiControlProfile are console methods for GuiControl and all its children. GUIs have a lot of callbacks and you'll find it very useful to be able to scope console methods to specific object instances. Fortunately, the normal scoping rules and methods apply to GUI controls. In other words, we can scope methods to GuiControl and its parent classes, *and* we can scope to the object's name.

```
new GuiBitmapButtonCtrl(LessonsButton) {
  // ...
};

function LessonsButton::test(%this) {
  echo( "LessonsButton::test(" @ %this @ ")" );
}
```

Thus, typing

```
LessonsButton.test();
```

will print the following in the console.

```
LessonsButton::test(LessonsButton)
```

If you need a review of the scoping rules, go back to Chapter 4, "Introduction to TorqueScript." If you want to know what the callbacks are for different GUI controls, take a peek at Appendix A.4, "GUI Controls Quick Reference." I'll be giving some code samples below to handle certain useful GUI callbacks.

12.5 GUI Skinning

Several controls offer the additional ability to "skin." In effect, we can create a graphic image or array of images that will then be used to cover the control. This offers us a simple means of giving our game GUIs their own flavor. However, this power does come at a price. Specifically, we need to understand how this skinning graphic is laid out and how we create it. Don't worry; it's not that hard.

12.5.1 Bitmap Arrays

Almost every skin we will use is a single graphic file that has been laid out in some sort of an array (skin elements organized in rows and columns). The purpose of the rows and columns is determined on a per-control basis, but all of these arrays follow the same rules.

General Rules

These are the general rules to be followed.

- The format of the graphic file must be nonlossy and support an alpha channel (in theory you can do some controls with a 24-bit BMP (no alpha-channel) or a JPG (lossy), but it is likely this won't work well). PNG is the preferred format.
- The graphic file *does not* need to be sized as a power of two. Any (reasonable) ratio will do.
- All elements must be separated by one pixel at their nearest point.
- The first pixel row of the graphic contains no elements, just a single color. This color becomes the "array-divider color." The array-divider color is used by Torque to identify rows and columns.
- All arrays of subelements are arranged left-to-right and top-to-bottom; i.e, if there is some element numbering implied, the upper-left element is zero and the lower-right element is $N - 1$, where N is the total number of elements.

Column Rules

These are the rules to be followed for columns.

- The first column of elements must align with the left edge of the array.
- Elements in a column (excluding the first column) do not need to left-align with those elements in the rows above or below them.

Row Rules

These are the rules to be followed for rows.

- The first row of elements starts one pixel from the top of the graphic.
- All elements in a row must top-align with all other elements in that row.
- All elements in a row must be one pixel apart at their nearest point in the row; i.e., shapes may be irregular, but the extents of elements must be one pixel apart.
- The rightmost element in a row does not need to align to the edge of the graphic; i.e., there can be empty space on the right of a row.
- The bottommost row does not need to align with the bottom of the graphic. Again, there can be buffer space.

Now, it may seem like this is a lot to remember, but it really isn't that bad, and you'll have examples to follow. Figure 12.1 shows a simple example and a more complicated one.

Most of the difficulty in creating a skin comes from following the prior rules and in knowing the layout requirements for the current control. I will give a layout for each skinnable control below so you know what you're looking at when you make your own, but here I'd like to stress some points that will make your life easier.

- Always use PNG files if you can. These support alpha channels, are reasonably sized, and you *don't have to worry about artifacts*.
- Make the subelements separately, then assemble the array as layers. It will be *much* harder to make your elements if you try to make them all in one graphic layer.
- Make the subelements at the maximum resolution you expect them to be displayed, unless they require a specific sizing (the bitmaps for GuiBitmap-BorderCtrl and GuiWindowCtrl are sensitive to scaling).
- Use pure red (255 0 0) as your array-divider color *if you can*, or use another color that is not present in the element. You can use a tool to analyze the color mix of your subelements. Then, just pick a color that is not in the controls already. This is not a strict rule, but it makes designing skins easier if you follow it.

Figure 12.1.

Examples of bitmap arrays.

a. Check box array (so simple…).

b. Scroll array (Ewww…).

- Do not use transparency as your array-divider color unless you absolutely have to. No bitmap arrays require this.
- Never use translucency (alpha lower than 1.0 and higher than 0.0) as your array-divider color, period. I mean it.
- More? Sure, but I'm sure that many people reading this are more artistically inclined than I am, so I'll stop here.

12.5.3 Enabling Skinning

In order to enable skinning for controls, we use two fields in the GuiControl-Profile.

- `hasBitmapArray` (deprecated in version 1.4 +). Boolean value enabling skinning.
- `bitmap`. Path to the bitmap skin to use to theme this control.

```
new GuiControlProfile ( usesBitmapArray ) {
    hasBitmapArray = true;
    bitmap = "path to bitmap array file";
};
```

> Many controls require the presence of a bitmap in their profile. If you use a profile that does not have a bitmap for a control that requires one, the engine will not render the control. Be sure to include bitmaps in control profiles that require them. You were warned.

Now, finally, let's talk about the specific GUI controls.

12.6 Container Controls

This first category of controls contains the standard container-type controls. Don't forget, though, that all controls can act as containers to other controls.

12.6.1 GuiFrameSetCtrl

This control is used to automatically or manually frame any number of child controls, in regular row-column format.

The first time you try to use it, it may seem a little odd, but once you understand the rules by which it operates, you'll be using it for all kinds of tasks.

Setting Up Rows and Columns

To use this control, simply place it and give it an initial extent. Then, to divide the control into rows and columns, simply specify the starting position of each column in the `columns` field and each row in the `rows` field. For example, we could make a 3 × 3 matrix of cells where each cell is 100 by 100 pixels, by using the field settings shown in Table 12.2.

Now, we need to add some children.

Table 12.2.

Setting up rows and columns.

Field	Value(s)
position	"100 100"
extent	"300 300"
columns	"0 100 200"
rows	"0 100 200"

Inserting Controls

In this example, we'll just use nine buttons. To add these buttons, simply select your new GuiFrameSetCtrl and add nine GuiButtonCtrl controls as children. If you pay attention, you will see that the controls are added left-to-right and top-to-bottom; that is, the buttons are (automatically) added in the following order:

- button 0 → < Column 0 , Row 0 >
- button 1 → < Column 1 , Row 0 >
- button 2 → < Column 2 , Row 0 >
- button 3 → < Column 0 , Row 1 >
- ...
- button 8 → < Column 2 , Row 2 >

So, what happens if we remove a control?

Removing Controls

If we remove a child control, all of the children will shift as required to fill the empty slot. Furthermore, newly added controls will go at the end of the list. Just keep this in mind if you are making and destroying these controls dynamically.

How Borders Work

This control will allow you to specify dragable borders between the rows and column. In order to do this, specify these fields shown in Table 12.3.

Field	Meaning
borderWidth	Width of borders in pixels.
borderColor	Color and opacity of borders.
borderEnable	Enable border color rendering. Can be "alwaysOn", "alwaysOff", or "dynamic".
borderMoveable	Enable border dragging. Can be "alwaysOn", "alwaysOff", or "dynamic".

Table 12.3.
Using borders.

Please note that, if you disable border color rendering, dragging the border will also be disabled.

Fudge?

There is an odd field named fudgeFactor. When set to a positive number, this value is subtracted from every border, making them each that many pixels shorter on each end. This does not affect the ability to grab a border.

Autobalancing

So, what if we would rather maintain balanced cells? We can enable the autobalancing feature by setting `autobalance` to `true`. Now, the control will automatically attempt to make all of the cells the same size the next time it wakes up.

Scripting the GuiFrameSetCtrl

It is possible to manipulate this control from script. Table 12.4 shows all the things we are allowed to do to this control from within a script.

Table 12.4.

Manipulating the GuiFrameSetCtrl.

Method	Purpose
addColumn()	Add a new column to the control. All contents will shift.
removeColumn()	Remove a column from the right side of the control. Contents will shift but will **not** be deleted.
addRow()	Add a new row to the control. All contents will shift.
removeRow()	Remove a row from the bottom of the control. Contents will shift but will **not** be deleted.
getColumnCount()	Return the current number of columns in the frame.
getRowCount()	Return the current number of rows in the frame.
getRowOffset(row)	Return the beginning pixel offset for `row`.
getColumnOffset(column)	Return the beginning pixel offset for `column`.
setRowOffset(row , offset)	Set the beginning pixel `offset` for `row`.
setColumnOffset(column , offset)	Set the beginning pixel `offset` for `column`.

In order to create empty blocks in a GuiFrameSet, simply add a GuiControl as an element for each cell you wish to be blank.

12.6.2 GuiScrollCtrl

This control is used to contain a resizeable control. These resizeable controls are made children of the GuiScrollCtrl, which then allows the user to use scroll bars to move to a specific location within the child control.

GuiScrollCtrl can be programmed to supply a vertical and/or a horizontal scroll bar. These scroll bars will be enabled (based on field settings) always, never, or when the child content expands beyond the vertical or horizontal bounds of the view area.

This control also provides a configurable margin and control over the thumb affordance (the little slidey thing on the scroll bars).

Lastly, from script we can force the control to scroll to the top or bottom of the child.

Configuring GuiScrollCtrl

As noted above, this control provides a few configuration options.

Scroll Bars

We can control when or if either the vertical and/or horizontal scroll bars will be rendered by using the `hScrollBar` and `vScrollBar` fields. These fields can be given the following values.

- **alwaysOn.** Scrollbar always renders.
- **alwaysOff.** Scrollbar never renders.
- **dynamic.** Scrollbar renders based on size of child.

Additionally, if we've chosen to render the scroll bars, we can select either scaling or nonscaling thumbs. The thumb is the little box on the scroll bar that allows us to scroll by dragging. Normally, this thumb scales relative to how "full" the scroll dimension (vertical or horizontal) is. However, for really big children or really small scrolls, this behavior can cause the thumb to scale to a very tiny size, making it difficult to grab with the mouse. Thus, we can force the thumbs to maintain a fixed size, using the `constantThumbHeight` field.

```
new GuiScrollCtrl() {
   hScrollBar = "dynamic";        // Render horizontal scrollbar as needed
   vScrollBar = "alwaysOn";       // Always render vertical scrollbar
   constantThumbHeight = false;   // Scale thumb dynamically
};
```

Margins

We can make minor adjustments to the margins of a scroll area; that is, we can set a fixed margin that will cause the child to fit within a box defined by the `childMargin` field. This field takes a two-element integer vector. The first value in the vector is the left-right margin, and the second value is the top-bottom margin. Both margins are in pixels. The GuiScrollCtrl already provides a margin for its children, but this allows us to further expand that margin, to account for various cases where the content may be occluded by a parent of the GuiScrollCtrl.

```
new GuiScrollCtrl() {
   childMargin = "10 10";
};
```

Ignoring First Responder

We can control whether this control will be allowed to become first responder. The setting of first responder state is still controlled by the GuiControl method

Game Elements

makeFirstResponder(), but we can force this GUI to ignore this request by setting the willFirstRespond field to false. Also, don't forget that this concept only applies to versions of TGE prior to 1.4.

```
new GuiScrollCtrl() {
  // Do not become firstResponder...ever
  willFirstRespond = false;
};
```

Scripting GuiScrollCtrl

GuiScrollCtrl provides two console methods that allow us to scroll the contents from script.

- scrollToBottom(). Scroll all the way to the bottom of the child.
- scrollToTop(). Scroll all the way to the top of the child.

No scripting control is provided for horizontal scrolling.

GuiScrollCtrl Skin

This control has what is probably the most complicated (looking) skin. The bitmap array is organized as shown in Table 12.5.

12.6.3 GuiStackControl

This very simple container is used to hold any other control in a fixed-width stack. To use this control, simply place it and then start adding other controls to it as children. These controls will stack up on each other. You may control the direction of this stacking by setting the stackFromBottom field to true or false. If it is true, the controls will stack bottom to top; otherwise, they will stack from top to bottom (the default). The control can be resized horizontally but not vertically.

If it isn't clear, the purpose of this control is to allow us to dynamically place other controls and to be guaranteed that they will all take on the same width and that they will stack perfectly against their mates. See the images in Figure 12.2 for clarification.

Please note that, if you do not want the controls to be right next to each other, you may add some space by setting the padding field to a positive value.

12.6.4 GuiPaneControl

Here is another simple but useful container control. This control is designed to provide us with a simple dropdown area that can contain any other control(s). The user can simply hide/show the pane by clicking on the caption bar at the

Table 12.5.

Bitmap array for GuiScrollCtrl skin.

Sample Array Image	Column 0	Column 1	Column 2
	Up-Scroll Normal	Up-Scroll Depressed	Up-Scroll Inactive
	Down-Scroll Normal	Down-Scroll Depressed	Down-Scroll Inactive
	Top of Vertical Thumb Normal	Top of Vertical Thumb Depressed	Top of Vertical Thumb Inactive
	Middle of Vertical Thumb Normal	Middle of Vertical Thumb Depressed	Middle of Vertical Thumb Inactive
	Bottom of Vertical Thumb Normal	Bottom of Vertical Thumb Depressed	Bottom of Vertical Thumb Inactive
	Vertical Bar Normal	Vertical Bar Depressed	Vertical Bar Inactive
	Right-Scroll Normal	Right-Scroll Depressed	Right-Scroll Inactive
	Left-Scroll Normal	Left-Scroll Depressed	Left-Scroll Inactive
	Left of Horizontal Thumb Normal	Left of Horizontal Thumb Depressed	Left of Horizontal Thumb Inactive
	Middle of Horizontal Thumb Normal	Middle of Horizontal Thumb Depressed	Middle of Horizontal Thumb Inactive
	Right of Horizontal Thumb Normal	Right of Horizontal Thumb Depressed	Right of Horizontal Thumb Inactive
	Horizontal Bar Normal	Horizontal Bar Depressed	Horizontal Bar Inactive
	Lower-Right Affordance Normal	Lower-Right Affordance Depressed	Lower-Right Affordance Inactive

Figure 12.2.

Using GuiStackControl.

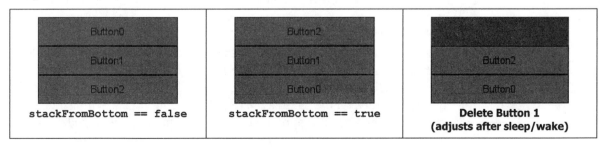

| `stackFromBottom == false` | `stackFromBottom == true` | **Delete Button 1 (adjusts after sleep/wake)** |

Figure 12.3.

Console script error pane.

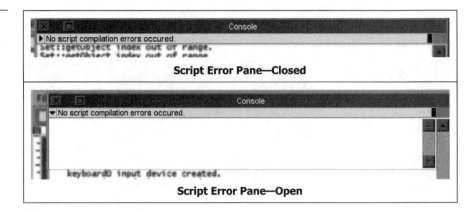

top. An example of this control that you should be familiar with is the console script error pane (see Figure 12.3).

Please note that normally this control will be populated with a single scroll control, which will then contain a self-expanding control like GuiMLTextCtrl or GuiTextListCtrl.

GuiPaneControl Skin

This control uses a very simple skin which is ordered as shown in Table 12.6.

Table 12.6.

Bitmap array of GuiPaneControl skin.

Sample Array Image	Column 0	Column 1	Column 2
	Pane Open Button	--	--
	Pane Close Button	--	--
	Caption Bar Begin	Caption Bar	Caption Bar End + Pane Toggle Button

Please note that you may make all of these buttons and bars the same if you like. In the end, clicking anywhere on the bar will open or close it. The variances in the bar graphic merely supply a recognizable affordance.

> This control will decide how tall to make the caption bar based on the height of the first row in the skin bitmap. So, if you need the caption bar to be taller or shorter, adjust the skin.

Caption Text

The caption bar may display a short (255 or fewer characters) text string. Furthermore, this text may be rendered in front of or behind the caption bar.

To specify the text, set the `caption` field to the text you want. To specify the render order, set the `barBehindText` to `true` or `false`. Setting it to `true` will render the text in front of the bar; setting it to `false` will render the bar in front of the text (Figure 12.4).

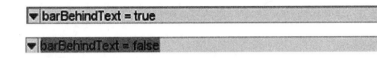

Figure 12.4.
Caption bar.

Disabling Collapses

Although the control is really meant to be opened and closed, we may tell the control that it cannot be collapsed. Simply set the `collapsable` field to `false`.

Please note that, if the control is collapsed when we set this field, it will not open when the caption is clicked. So, in effect, setting this field to `false` locks the pane.

Scripting the Control

There isn't much we can script on this control, but it is possible to toggle the pane open and closed using the method `setCollapsed( collapse )`, which will collapse if `collapse` is `true`, otherwise it will be open. Be aware that, if the pane collapsing is disabled, this method will do nothing.

12.6.5 GuiTabBookCtrl and GuiTabPageCtrl

A tab book is something that many of us have come to take for granted. It is a control that contains an unspecified number of tabbed panes. By clicking on any of the tabs, the pane that is associated with the tab is brought to the front and made visible. It's like an index file, except it is completely 2D (Figure 12.5).

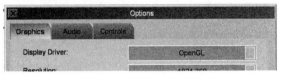

Figure 12.5
Tabbed panes.

Configuring GuiTabBookCtrl

To use this control, we must first place it and size it to our liking. Once that is done, we need to decide where the tabs should be as well as how large they should be. Right now, tabs can be on top or on the bottom of the tab pages and can be any size we wish. In the future, the engine may also support tabs on the right and left.

To specify the tab positions and sizes, set the fields as shown in Table 12.7.

Field	Description
tabPosition	May be "Top" or "Bottom".
tabHeight	Height of tabs in pixels.
tabWidth	Width of tabs in pixels.

Table 12.7
Setting tab positions and sizes.

Wow, that was pretty simple! Now, let's add some tab pages.

Adding Tab Pages

The first thing you must know about adding content to a tab book is that the GuiTabBookCtrl may only contain GuiTabPageCtrl controls. If you try to place any other kind of control in a tab book, the new control will either drop into the first tab page the engine finds (owned by this book), or the control will drop onto the book's parent.

To add pages (and therefore tabs), simply select the book we just created as the instant group and start adding GuiTabPageCtrl controls until you have enough pages.

We can add text to a page's tab by setting the text field of the GuiTab-PageCtrl we just added.

After we add our pages, we will need to put content in the pages.

Editing Tab Pages

Editing pages is a breeze. Simply click on the tab for the page you wish to modify and start dropping controls into the page. We can tab through pages while in the editor, making it exceptionally easy to modify our tab book.

Dynamic Page Creation/Destruction

We can add and remove pages from our tab books from script by calling the two methods in Table 12.8.

Table 12.8.

Adding and removing pages.

Method	Description
addpage ([pageName])	Add a new page to the GuiTabBookCtrl and return the ID of the GuiTabPageCtrl that was added. You may optionally specify the text for the page's tab by passing a value in pageName.
removePage (index)	Remove the page at index (left to right) position.

More Scripting

Aside from dynamically adding and removing pages, we can also specify two callbacks for a GuiTabBookCtrl (Table 12.9).

Table 12.9.

Two callbacks for GuiTabBookCtrl.

Callback	Description
onClearSelected()	Called when right mouse is clicked in a page and the mouse is over a valid control (besides the page itself).
onTabSelected(tabText)	This callback is called when a tab is clicked and prior to the page associated with that tab being (re-)displayed. It is passed the text in the page's tab.

12.6.6 GuiWindowCtrl

This control provides the familiar window metaphor. This is a completely skinnable control. By default, TGE comes with the graphics required to skin this as a standard Windows- or OSX-style window (Figure 12.6). These windows provide standard window behaviors through the following fields.

Figure 12.6.
Window skins.

a. Windows theme.

b. OSX theme.

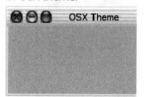

- `canClose`. Boolean value enabling close icon and ability to close window.
- `canMaximize`. Boolean value enabling maximize icon and ability to maximize window.
- `canMinimize`. Boolean value enabling minimize icon and ability to minimize window.
- `canMove`. Boolean value enabling dragging. If true, the window can be dragged by the upper bar.
- `closeCommand`. This script is executed when the window is closed.
- `minSize`. A two-integer vector describing the minimum size this window can take when drag-resized. This does not affect minimized size, which is always just the drag-bar and buttons.
- `resizeHeight`. Boolean value enabling height drag-resizing, i.e., the window can be height-resized by dragging a corner or edge.
- `resizeWidth`. Boolean value enabling width drag-resizing, i.e., the window can be width-resized by dragging a corner or edge.

```
new GuiWindowCtrl() {
  //...
  resizeWidth = "1";
  resizeHeight = "1";
  canMove = "1";
  canClose = "1";
  canMinimize = "1";
  canMaximize = "1";
  minSize = "50 50";
};
```

The sample GuiWindowCtrl definition above creates an unnamed window that can be resized in both height and width, and can be moved, closed, minimized, and maximized. It also has a minimum drag size of 50 × 50 pixels.

GuiWindowCtrl Skin

As noted above, this is a fully skinnable control. This skinning is controlled by two GuiControlProfile fields and a bitmap.

- **hasBitmapArray.** Boolean value enabling skinning.
- **bitmap.** Path to the bitmap skin.

Table 12.10.

Bitmap array for GuiWindowCtrl skin.

Sample Array Image	Column 0	Column 1	Column 2	Column 3	Column 4
	Close Button Normal	Close Button Depressed	Close Button Inactive	—	—
	Maximize Button Normal	Maximize Button Depressed	Maximize Button Inactive	—	—
	Revert Button Normal	Revert Button Depressed	Revert Button Inactive	—	—
	Minimize Button Normal	Minimize Button Depressed	Minimize Button Inactive	—	—
	Title Bar Left Edge	Title Bar Right Edge	Title Bar Middle	—	—
	Title Bar Left Edge Inactive	Title Bar Right Edge Inactive	Title Bar Middle Inactive	—	—
	Left Edge	Right Edge	Lower Left Corner	Bottom Edge	Lower Right Corner

The bitmap array is organized as shown in Table 12.10.

Making Your Own GuiWindowCtrl Skin

Sometimes it isn't enough just to see a finished example, so let's make a simple window skin together and then improve on it a bit.

As a rule, I like to start simple then work my way up. Thus, we will make a simple GuiWindowCtrl bitmap array together.

Setting up.

1. Open your graphics program of choice.
2. Create a blank 300 × 300 image with a red (255 0 0) background.
3. Enable a viewable grid and adjust it to 1 × 1 pixels.
4. Zoom in on the upper-left corner of your image until the grid is at one-pixel scale.

Button blanks.

1. Select a foreground color of (64 64 64).

2. Create a new transparent layer and rename it "Button Blanks."

3. In this new layer, using a rectangular selection tool starting at X:0 Y:1, select a 17 × 14 pixel area.

4. Flood fill the selection.

5. Copy the selection and paste it to this layer as a new selection, placing it at X:10 Y:1.

6. Paste another selection in this row, maintaining the one-pixel distance.

7. Make three more rows, and you should have an image like the one in Figure 12.7.

Upper bars normal.

1. Create a new transparent layer and name it "Top Bar Normal."

2. Select a new fill color of (128 128 128).

3. Create two 5 × 23 rectangles and one 38 × 23 rectangle, again maintaining one pixel between this new row and those above, as well as one pixel between each element in the row (Figure 12.8).

Upper bars inactive.

1. Create a new transparent layer.

2. Copy the bars we just made (Figure 12.8) and paste them into our new layer.

Edges and bottom.

1. Create a last layer and name it "Edges + Bottom."

2. Create the following parts: 3 × 9, 3 × 9, 3 × 3, 7 × 3, and a last 3 × 3.

3. Our final image should look like Figure 12.9.

That is it! We now have a very simple GuiWindowCtrl bitmap array. Go ahead and save it, duplicate it, and then save the duplicate as a PNG. Use this PNG in a test window, and it should look like Figure 12.10.

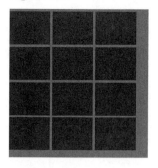
Figure 12.7

Figure 12.8

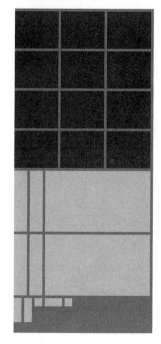
Figure 12.9

Figure 12.10

Our new GuiWindowCtrl skin in use.

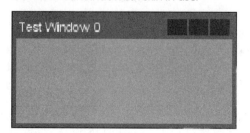

12.7 Backgrounds and Borders

The controls in this category are normally used as backgrounds to other controls, but they are quite versatile and can be used for a number of more advanced effects. I'll give you a hint. Think in terms of layers and what you could do by enabling and disabling these layers. Combine this with the concept of masking and, well ...

12.7.1 GuiBitmapCtrl

This control is used to display any reasonably sized image. In TGE versions prior to 1.3, this control could only accept a bitmap with a maximum size of 256 × 256 pixels. For larger images, the GuiChunkedBitmapCtrl was used. This limitation is no longer in place.

The Bitmap

The initial bitmap is specified as a field in the control.

```
new GuiBitmapCtrl( myTestBitmap ) {
  bitmap = "./someImage";
}
```

Subsequently, this can be changed using the setBitmap() method and a complete path to a new image.

```
myTestBitmap.setBitmap( expandFilename("./someImage2.png") );
```

In the above example, it is implied that there is an image file with the name "someImage2.png" in the same directory as the script.

Wrapping and Offset

When creating a GuiBitmapCtrl, we can specify the wrap field as either true or false. If wrap is set to false and the image is larger than the GuiBitmapCtrl extent, the image will be scaled down. Vice versa, if the extent is larger than the image, it will be scaled up. However, if wrap is true, no scaling will occur. The image may be clipped or repeated based on size versus extent.

In addition to wrapping, we can offset an image using the setValue() method.

```
function TestBitmap2::scrollMe( %this ) {
  if(! %this.isScrolling ) return;
  %this.curX += 2;
```

```
%this.curY += 2;

if( %this.curX >= 256) {
  %this.curX = 0;
  %this.curY = 0;
}

%this.setValue( %this.curX , %this.curY );
%this.schedule( 32 , scrollMe );
}
```

The code above comes right from the GPGT Lesson Kit. It is used to scroll the
sample image. Note that positive values cause the image to be offset up and
left, whereas negative values cause it to be offset down and right. All values
are in pixels.

12.7.2 GuiChunkedBitmapCtrl

This control is the big brother to GuiBitmapCtrl and serves basically the same
purpose. It was used in days of old to render images larger than 256 × 256.
It did this by cutting up the image and storing it appropriately on the video
card/memory. Today's hardware has made this control pretty much obsolete,
but there are a few variances in its behavior, so we'll discuss it briefly.

The Bitmap

As with GuiBitmapCtrl, the initial bitmap is specified using the `bitmap` field.
Also like GuiBitmapCtrl, this control does support changing the bitmap after
creation using the `setBitmap()` method.

Tiling

Whereas GuiBitmapCtrl had a wrapping functionality, GuiChunkedBitmapCtrl
has tiling. Tiling is controlled by the Boolean `tile` field and behaves pretty
much the same as wrapping, but not quite as reliably.

The `useVariable`

A significant difference between GuiBitmapCtrl and GuiChunkedBitmapCtrl
is the `useVariable` field. If this field is set to `true`, we can specify a variable name in the bitmap string instead of a path. Then, when this control is
rendered, it will look at the contents of the named variable for the path to its
image file. This field is only checked when the `onWake()` callback is called.
So, you may only change a bitmap using this field between wakes.

Game Elements

In the following example, we've chosen to use a named variable to specify our path instead of doing so directly.

```
new GuiChunkedBitmapCtrl() {
  // ...
  useVariable = true;
  variable = "MyBitmap";
  bitmap = "";
};
```

Of course, for this to work, we must have defined $MyBitmap.

```
$MyBitmap = expandFileName( ".\some\path\to\some\image" );
```

12.7.3 GuiBitmapBorderCtrl

This skinnable control is used to adorn other controls with a frame (or border).

GuiBitmapBorderCtrl Skin

The bitmap array for this control is organized as shown in in Figure 12.11.

Figure 12.11.

Bitmap array for GuiBitmapBorderCtrl skin.

Column 0	Column 1	Column 2	Column 3	Column 4
Upper-left border	Upper-right border	Top border	--	
Left border	Right Border	Lower-left border	Lower border	Lower-right border

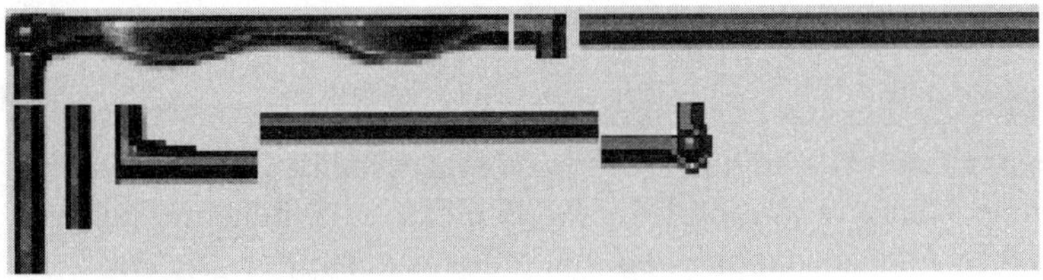

Making Your Own GUIBitmapBorderCtrl Skin

Learning to make skins for the border control is a step-by-step process. In this section, I will provide you with the basic steps needed to make a plain border. Once you have mastered this process, you should feel free to create more advanced borders using the same rules.

Setting up.

1. Open your graphics program of choice.

2. Create a blank 300 × 300 image with a red (255 0 0) background.

3. Enable a viewable grid and adjust it to 1 × 1 pixels.

4. Zoom in on the upper-left corner of your image until the grid is at one-pixel scale.

Top of bitmap border.

1. Create the three components of the upper bar: upper-left, lower-right, and middle. In this example, they are purple, blue, and cyan, respectively (Figure 12.12).

Sides and bottom.

1. Create the two sides and the bottom components: left, right, lower-left, bottom, and lower-right. In this example, they are green, yellow, pink, pale-yellow, and red-brown, respectively (Figure 12.12).

End result.

1. Our end result would look something like the image in Figure 12.13.

Figure 12.12

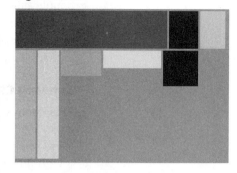

Figure 12.13

12.7.4 GuiFadeInBitmapCtrl

This control is used to display an image by fading it in, waiting, and then fading it out over specified times. There is no good way to make this cycle repeat. In fact, the only way to cause the fading cycle to start over is to put the control to sleep and then wake it up again.

Setting Up the Fade

Setting up the GuiFadeInBitmapCtrl is relatively simple. There are three fields that specify the fade timing.

```
new GuiFadeInBitmapCtrl( myFadeInBitmap ) {
   fadeInTime = 1000; // Fade in over one second
   waitTime = 2000; // Stay visible (without fading) for two seconds
   fadeOutTime = 500; // Fade out over a half-second
};
```

The mechanics of this control are quite simple. Upon waking, the control will start to fade in a bitmap over a period of time `fadeInTime`. Once the fade in is complete, the image will stay faded in for `waitTime`. Finally, the image will fade out for `fadeOutTime`.

When the whole process is complete, the engine will set the field `done` to `true`. Please remember that the engine never sets this to `false`. So, if you are relying on this value, be sure to clear it when you put the control to sleep and be double sure that it is saved as false or set to false in the onAdd() method.

Interestingly, fadeInTime and waitTime can both be set to zero, but setting fadeOutTime to zero will cause the bitmap to display forever at full alpha, i.e., it won't fade out.

Sensing Clicks

This control is often used to display a splash image when starting a game or as an interlude between missions, etc. Users will frequently want to bypass these screens (once they've seen them enough times to stop being impressed with the artwork).

As a game player, you probably will recall that the most frequently used way to bypass these screens is either an **ESC** key press, a **SPACEBAR** key press, or a left mouse click.

TGE has supplied the ability to sense a left mouse click via the click() callback. If the user presses the left mouse button while the cursor is over this control, the click() method will fire (if specified). If you want the other mentioned inputs to be sensed, you'll need to use a GuiInputCtrl (see Section 12.12.3).

```
function myFadeInBitmap::click( %this ) {
  echo("myFadeInBitmap::click() => User clicked the left
      mouse button.");
};
```

To stop this control from being displayed, simply remove it from the canvas.

If you wish to capture key presses on a GUIFadeInBitmapCtrl GUI or any other GUI that does not normally catch them, simply add a 1 × 1 button positioned at <0 0>, set the accelerator field of the button to the key you want to catch, and use the command field to execute the task you need. Repeat this for every key you need to catch. This is a lot better than using an ActionMap for these special cases.

12.8 Text Controls

This section discusses the various controls whose purpose it is to store, display, or take as input, text values.

12.8.1 GuiMessageVectorCtrl

This control is normally used to build a chat HUD, but it can be used for a number of other purposes as well. In order to use this control, a Message-Vector object must also be used (see "The MessageVector" below).

Since the actual data to be displayed is stored in the MessageVector and not this control, we can remove and add GuiMessageVectorCtrl controls at will and not corrupt message data.

This control is capable of displaying colorized text.

Child Only

This control is not allowed to exist standalone. It must instead be made a child of a control that allows for expansion of the child. Thus, if you wish to use it, you must make this control the child of a GuiScrollCtrl. If you do not do this, you'll crash the engine when you try to attach the GuiMessageVectorCtrl to a nonempty MessageVector or when you attempt to add text to a MessageVector that is already attached to it.

A suitable definition of a GuiMessageVectorCtrl would look something like the following.

```
new GuiScrollCtrl() {
  // ...
  new GuiMessageVectorCtrl(testMessageVectorCtrl) {
    // ...
  };
};
```

The MessageVector

So, what is this business about MessageVectors? Well, as noted above, the GuiMessageVectorCtrl only has one job. That job is to display the contents of a MessageVector. The MessageVector is a standalone class that can contain a variable amount of text. MessageVectors don't have any special fields, and thus creating one is as simple as the following.

```
$myMsgVector = new MessageVector();
```

Once the MessageVector has been created, text can be added to the front or to the back of what is basically a text queue, as follows.

```
$myMsgVector.pushFrontLine( "some string" ); // Put text at front of queue
$myMsgVector.pushBackLine( "some string" ); // Put text at back of queue
```

We can also insert text in the middle of the queue using the insertLine() method.

```
$myMsgVector.insertLine( 5 , "some text" );
```

Later, we can peek at a line of text in the MessageVector using the getLineText() method.

```
echo( "Line 10 => ", $myMsgVector.getLineText( 10 ) );
```

At any time, we can remove lines using the `popFrontLine()`, `popBack-Line()`, or `deleteLine()` methods.

```
$myMsgVector.popFrontLine();
$myMsgVector.popBackLine();
$myMsgVector.deleteLine( 5 );
```

Interestingly, we can also save the contents of a MessageVector to a file.

```
$myMsgVector.dump( "~/chat.log" , "My Chat Log" );
```

The above example would create a file named "chat.log" in the current mod directory, make the first line of this file equal to "`My Chat Log`", and then dump the contents of `$myMsgVector` to the file. The file is automatically closed at the end of the dump.

MessageVector and Tags

MessageVectors support one more interesting feature—tags. When we add lines of text to a MessageVector, we are allowed to supply a unique integer value (greater than 0) as a tag. Later, we can use these tags to do searches.

For a complete treatment of MessageVector syntax, please see Appendix A.4, "GUI Controls Quick Reference."

Attaching a MessageVector

OK, so far we've talked a lot about the place we store our text (the Message-Vector), but not the control that displays the text (the GuiMessageVectorCtrl). To display the text from a MessageVector, we simply attach it to any currently active GuiMessageVectorCtrl.

```
testMessageVectorCtrl.attach( $myMsgVector );
```

In the above example, we are attaching our previously defined MessageVector `$myMsgVector` to the GuiMessageVectorCtrl we declared at the start of this discussion (testMessageVectorCtrl).

That's it! If we've done everything correctly, the text will now be displayed in our chat HUD (or whatever it is being used as).

At a later time, we can disconnect the MessageVector using the `detach()` method.

```
testMessageVectorCtrl.detach();
```

Note that multiple detaches are allowed, but if a GuiMessageVectorCtrl is not attached to a MessageVector, it will print a warning when the `detach()` method is called.

Also note that a single MessageVector can be attached to multiple GuiMessageVectorCtrl controls.

12.8.2 GuiMLTextCtrl

This control is a markup-language–supporting text control (ML = markup language). In addition to printing multi-line text, this control will accept TGE Markup Language (TorqueML) formatted text, allowing us to make changes to the font, font weight, color, etc. A complete listing of the TorqueML tokens and the syntax for using them is supplied in Appendix A.4, "GUI Controls Quick Reference." This control also supports `onURL()` and `onResize()` callbacks. To use one of these controls, do the following.

1. Open the GUI that will contain our new GuiMLTextCtrl using the GUI editor.
2. Select appropriate control as "add-parent" for the GuiMLTextCtrl (can be embedded in any control).
3. Add GuiMLTextCtrl.
4. Position, size, and configure GuiMLTextCtrl.
5. Add your text.
6. Reflow the GuiMLTextCtrl.

Configuring GuiMLTextCtrl

The GuiMLTextCtrl only has a few new fields.

- **allowColorChars.** This enables colors defined in the selected profile to take effect. I suggest setting this to `false` and using TorqueML instead.
- **deniedSound.** This is a reference to an audio profile that should be played when an attempt is made to place more text than `maxChars` in this control.
- **lineSpacing.** An integer value specifying the number of pixels between lines.
- **maxChars.** This integer value can be used to place a cap on the number of characters this control will display. All characters are counted, including formatting characters. Set this to –1 for no limit.
- **text.** This string is the initial contents of the control. This is most useful for making ML labels. Note that the GUI editor will clip this at 255 characters, so it is usually best to use the `setText()` method instead of static assignment.

497

Scripting GuiMLTextCtrl

This control can be scripted in the following ways.

Adding, Setting, and Clearing Text

There are two means of adding text to this control.

```
// Add text without reformatting
%control.addText( "Add this text", false );

%control.setText( "Make the text equal to this" );
```

The first method adds text to the end of the control without optionally reformatting the displayed text. The second method sets all text in the control to the passed content. This method can also be used to clear the control. Simply pass a null string, "".

Formatting and Reflowing

As noted, when adding text we have the option of causing the control to reformat. This basically causes the control to reevaluate the contents and to be sure that everything is displayed correctly. However, forcing a reformat every time we add a line of text might be wasteful if we are adding many lines at once. Thus, we can wait until we are done and then reflow the control at the end.

```
%control.forceReflow();
```

This will reformat the control just once. It is worth mentioning that, if you add text and don't reformat or reflow, the text will not be displayed.

Scrolling and Tags

If we have embedded our GuiMLTextCtrl in a GuiScrollCtrl, we can force the contents to scroll to the top.

```
%control.scrollToTop();
```

We can also force the contents to scroll to an embedded tag.

```
%control.scrollToTag( 10 ); // Scroll to tag ID #10
```

Tags are special (nonprinting) TorqueML content that can be embedded in our text. This is useful for making context-sensitive help pages.

TorqueML

The TGE Markup Language, TorqueML, is pretty extensive and can do many of the things that HTML can do. A complete listing of the TorqueML tags is provided in Appendix A.4, "GUI Controls Quick Reference," but I'll cover a few concepts and highlights here to help speed you on your way.

Syntax Closure

Unlike modern HTML, TorqueML does not require closure for most of its formatting characters. In other words, once an effect is applied, it stays in effect. The exceptions to this are clipping and hyperlinks, both of which have a closure tag.

Attribute Stacking

Instead of the standard closure mechanisms, TorqueML supplies the concept of an attribute stack. Thus, we can push the current formatting attributes to the attribute stack, apply some changes, print some text, and then pop our old formatting attributes back off the stack.

```
<font:arial:10>
This text is in Arial-10.
<spush>
<font:arial:14>
This text is in Arial-14.
<spop>
This text is in Arial-10.
```

Tables and Tabs

TorqueML doesn't really support tables, but it does support a formatting feature that allows us to easily columnize our text in a table-like format. For example, to make a two-column table, do the following.

```
<tab:60>
Torque    Rocks<br>
GPGT      Makes Learning Easier<br>
This line will be too      long<br>
```

This statement has told TGE to make the first column 60 pixels wide. Subsequently, the first TAB in every line will cause the text following the TAB to move over to pixel 61. Thus, our sample would print out something like the following.

```
Torque          Rocks
GPGT            Makes Learning Easier
This line will be toolong
```

As can be seen, the formatting is somewhat lacking. It would be better to make the first column of the third line clip instead.

Clipping

Fortunately for us, TorqueML supplies a method of clipping text to a specific pixel width.

```
<tab:60>
Torque   Rocks <br>
GPGT     Makes Learning Easier <br>
<clip:58>This line will be too</clip> long <br>
```

The first column on the third line has been instructed to clip its contents to 58 pixels. Now, when displayed, we get something like the following.

```
Torque         Rocks
GPGT           Makes Learning Easier
This line ...  long
```

This may seem a bit strange, but consider the case where you are printing data via a scripted formatting system. In cases like this, you have no good way to know in advance if the data will be too wide for your column, thus, you must clip it to maintain formatting.

Tags

We touched on tags above, but for completeness, we'll discuss them here. Tags are nonprinting TorqueML elements that are used to mark a line for later searching and locating. To add a tag, simply specify it as follows.

```
<tag:100>
```

Later, we can scroll to the line marked with this tag using the `scrollToTag()` method. It's that simple. The only rule to remember is that tags must be unique integer values greater than zero.

12.8.3 GuiMLTextEditCtrl

This control is a TorqueML-formatted text entry. Nearly all of its functionality derives from its parent GuiMLTextCtrl. Its purpose is to provide a "nicely formatted" text entry field. The simplest way to use this control is to pre-specify the font, margins, etc. in the `text` field. Subsequent text typed into the control will now follow these formatting rules.

```
new GuiMLTextEditCtrl ( TorqueMLFormattedTextEntry ) {
  text = "<font:Tahoma Bold:22 >";
};
```

Text that is typed into our example control (above) will now be formatted as Tahoma Bold at 22 points.

Escaping

This control provides a special field named `escapeCommand` where we can specify a command to execute when the **ESC** key is pressed while this control is in focus.

```
new GuiMLTextEditCtrl ( TorqueMLFormattedTextEntry ) {
  escapeCommand = "doit();"; // Run doit() when ESC is pressed
};
```

12.8.4 GuiTextCtrl

This is a label, plain and simple. It displays a fixed (256 characters or fewer) amount of text on one line. It can be updated dynamically from script if needed, but beyond that it isn't very flexible.

```
new GuiTextCtrl( ourLabel ) {
  maxLength = 12;
  text= "Torque Rocks!";
};
```

When displayed, the above example will print "Torque Rocks", without the exclamation point because we have limited the text length to 12 characters.

Changing Labels

Subsequently, we can update the contents of the control using the `setText()` method.

```
ourLabel.setText("Torque is Cool");
```

Again, our text will be clipped because the text we have specified is too long.

`altCommand`

Interestingly, this control provides an `altCommand` action. That is, if the field `altCommand` is specified, the function specified there will be called when this control is active and the **ENTER** key is pressed. This only applies to the children of GuiTextCtrl, which we will talk about next.

12.8.5 GuiTextEditCtrl

This is a simple single-line text entry control. It is a child of GuiTextCtrl and is thus limited to a maximum of 256 characters and can be limited with the same mechanisms provided by its parent. This control can also recall prior entries (a history) and allows them to be recalled via the up and down arrows on the keyboard.

escapeCommand and altCommand

Remember that GuiTextCtrl allowed us to specify an `altCommand`? Well, as the child of that control, GuiTextEditCtrl will evaluate the script specified in `altCommand` when the **ENTER** key is pressed. Additionally, we can specify a script for the **ESC** key in the suitably named field `escapeCommand`.

Passwords

If we are using this text entry as a password field, we can tell TGE to print asterisks instead of characters as the user types by setting the `password` field to `true`.

Numeric Only

Recall that we can set the profile field `numbersOnly` to `true`. Doing so causes this control to only accept numeric inputs.

I'm Full!

Because this control has a limit on the amount of data it can accept, we need a way to provide feedback to the user when they attempt to exceed that limit. This can be done by specifying an audio profile for the `deniedSound` field. Then, when the size limit is reached and an attempt is made to add more characters, the `deniedSound` will play.

Your History?

This control has the nice feature of retaining a history of prior values. They can be recalled using the up and down arrow keys. We, as the designers, can specify a limit on the number of history lines by setting the field `historySize` to any integer value of zero or greater, zero being no history.

Tab Completion

In addition to the commands fired by **ENTER** and **ESC**, we can specify that the **TAB** key will fire a callback. To do this, set the field `tabComplete` to `true` and provide a callback definition.

```
function GuiTextEditCtrl::onTabComplete( %this ) {
  // Do something
}
```

Validation

As if all the scripts that get called were not enough, we can specify one more. If we specify a script or function name in the `validate` field, it will be called every time this control loses focus.

Moving the Cursor

Lastly, it will occasionally be useful to either know or set the position of the cursor in the control. Thus, two functions are provided for this purpose.

```
%control.getCursorPos()
```

```
%control.setCursorPos( 20 ); // Move cursor after character 20
```

12.8.6 GuiTextListCtrl

This control is a multiline list of selectable entries. Alone, it can be used to display data, but in concert with other controls (buttons), it can be used as a selection control. Furthermore, this can be made the child of a GuiScrollCtrl to allow for long lists.

Configuring GuiTextListCtrl

This child of GuiTextCtrl adds three new fields.

- **clipColumnText.** If we are implementing columns, setting this field to `true` tells TGE to clip the contents of a column if it is too wide.
- **columns.** Again, if we are implementing columns, we must specify a list of integer widths for each column using this multi-entry integer vector.
- **fitParentWidth.** When this field is set to `true`, the GuiTextListCtrl will expand to fit the width of the parent and no further. This means that, if the control is embedded in a GuiScrollCtrl, its horizontal bar will not be activated. In short, if our text is wider than the scroll area, it will be clipped. If we don't want our rows to be clipped, we need to set this field to `false`.

Now the GuiTextListCtrl will expand to the size of the widest line of text, possibly activating a parent scroll control's horizontal scroll bar.

Rows and Columns

If we so choose, we can cause text to be formatted into columns. Columns are separated by the TAB character.

So, if we have specified a value "50 100 150" in the `columns` field, we could add some text to our control and expect that the first column should start at pixel offset 50, the second (TAB-separated) column should start at pixel 100, and the third column should start at pixel 150.

Don't be confused by the slight variance between this behavior and that of GuiMLTextCtrl. For GuiMLTextCtrl, the first value specifies the start location of the second column. For this control, it specifies the location of the first column.

Scripting GuiTextListCtrl

This control can be scripted in the following ways.

Adding Rows

Text can be added to the GuiTextListCtrl using the `addRow()` method.

```
%control.addRow( 0 , "Some text", 1 );
```

This example specified that we want the string "Some text" to be added at row 1 and given an ID of 0. The row argument is optional, and if not specified, new text is added to the end of the list. However, we always need to specify an ID, but these IDs do not need to be unique and can be zero if you don't intend to use them for any purpose.

Changing and Removing Rows

It is possible to change the text in an entry at a later time, but to do so, we must have specified a unique ID for the row. Then we can do the following.

```
%control.setRowByID( 0 , "Some new text" );
```

Here, we have changed the text in the row with ID 0 to "Some new text". If multiple rows have the same ID, the first row with this ID will be the one changed.

We can also remove a row if we choose. In the case below, we will remove a numbered row (2). Please remember that row numbering starts at 0.

```
%control.removeRow( 2 ); // Removes row 2
```

If we have specified a unique ID for a row, we can use that ID to find and remove the row.

```
%control.removeRowByID( 3 );
```

Again, if multiple rows have the same ID, the first row with this ID is the one affected.

Clearing the List

We can clear a list at any time as follows.

```
%control.clear();
```

Getting Row Attributes

As most of the time we are accessing rows for selection purposes, there are myriad methods for getting row attributes. We can get the first row number with a specified ID.

```
%control.getRowNumByID( 2 ); // Return number of row with ID 2
```

We can get the ID of a specific row.

```
%control.getRowID( 4 ); // Get ID of row 4
```

We can get the text in a row.

```
%control.getRowText( 15 ); // Get text in row 15
```

We can get the text in the first row with a specific ID.

```
%control.getRowTextByID( 12 ); // Get text of first row with ID 12
```

Finally, we can get the ID of the currently selected row.

```
%control.getSelectedID();
```

If no row is selected, the above call will return −1.

Row Count

We can count how many rows there are with the rowCount() method.

```
echo("This GUITextListCtrl has" SPC %control.rowCount() SPC "rows.");
```

Navigating

Thus far, we've worried about the contents of rows, but how do we navigate our list? First, we can search for a row with a specific text value, like this.

```
%control.findTextIndex( "this text" );
```

The above code will return the first row encountered that has the exact string "this text". If no match is found, the method returns –1.

As the user is expected to select an entry from this list, we might also be expected to be able to find it. If a row is selected, we can retrieve its ID using the `getSelectedID()` method. Sometimes, though, we would like to force an entry to be selected. We can do this in two ways, either by ID or directly by row number.

```
%control.setSelectedByID( 43 ); // Select first row with ID 43

%control.setSelectedRow( 14 ); // Select row 14
```

In either of these cases, if the ID or the row does not exist, no row will be selected.

Scrolling

Sometimes when we are selecting a default row, that row may not be guaranteed to be in the visible set of rows (i.e., it is off screen in the scroll list). We can force this line to show itself as follows.

```
%control.scrollVisible( 10 ); // Make sure row 10 is visible
```

There is no guarantee on the exact location of the line on our screen, but it will be visible.

(De-)Activating Rows

It will on occasion be necessary to (de-)activate a row, say an option is (not) meaningful or available in the current context. Thus, we can toggle whether a row is active.

```
%control.setRowActive( 10 , false ); // Deactivate row 10
```

We can check to see if a row is active, too.

```
if ( %control.isRowActive( 10 ) ) {
  echo("Row 10 is active!");
```

```
} else {
  echo("Row 10 is not active!");
}
```

We would, of course, expect the above code to print: `Row 10 is not active!`

Active rows are still rendered and still selectable. The ability to mark rows as in/active is provided to allow us to modify our script behaviors based on the settings of a particular line.

Sorting

Last to mention but not least in importance is the fact that we can sort our lists. This comes in handy for those of use who are too lazy to be sure entries are in the right order or in cases where it is out of our hands. We can sort alphabetically on a specific column or numerically (again, by column).

```
%control.sort( 2 , true ); // Increasing sort on column 2

%control.sortByNumerical( 0 , false ); // Decreasing numeric sort on column 0
```

12.9 Buttons

This section describes the controls used for buttons.

12.9.1 GuiButtonBaseCtrl

This is the base class to all other buttons and should *not* be used to make buttons. Its only job is to provide common fields and methods for the GuiBitmap-ButtonCtrl, GuiButtonCtrl, GuiCheckBoxCtrl, and GuiRadioCtrl controls.

This control supports three styles of buttons (selected through the `buttonType` field).

- **Push buttons (`buttonType == PushButton`).** This is your standard button. It depresses when clicked and goes back to its normal state when the mouse is moved or the mouse button is released.

- **Toggle buttons (`buttonType == ToggleButton`).** This is like a push button except that it retains the current state when the mouse button is released.

- **Radio buttons (`buttonType == RadioButton`).** This is like a toggle button, but this button is also grouped with other buttons. Within the group, only one button may be "on," while all others are "off." Selecting a new button as the "on" button changes all other buttons in the group to "off."

All buttons are allowed to have some text in them. This text is set in the button's `text` field. Not all button types will display the text; GuiBitmap-Button specifically does not, although, in the case of a GuiBitmapButton, if the graphic is not available, a default button will be displayed instead and it will display the text. This is a nice debug/design feature.

Game Elements

Grouping Radio Buttons

So, we can group radio buttons, but how do we do it? First, all radio buttons that are going to be grouped need to be at the same level; that is, they should have the same parent. Second, to group them, set every grouped radio button's groupNum field to the same nonnegative value. It is perfectly acceptable for different groups with different parents to have the same groupNum. However, only radio buttons with the same parent and the same groupNum will communicate with each other and act like a radio-button group. All other radio buttons will be treated separately.

Note that, by default, all radio buttons in a group start off unselected, so you may wish to preselect a button when the interface first wakes up. See below for how this can be done.

Getting and Setting Button Data

Now that we have our buttons, we need some ways to get and set their values. It may sometimes be desirable to be able to check the text value of a button or to change it. For these purposes, there are two methods.

```
$buttonText = %button.getText();

%button.setText( "New button text" );
```

As mentioned in "Grouping Radio Buttons" above, we may at some time wish to select a button from script. To do this, simply use the performClick() method.

```
%button.performClick(); // Send click event to this button
```

Button Scripts

Lastly, how do we program the button to do something when clicked? Recall that all children of GuiControl provide a field named command. In this case, command should be a small script or a function call of some sort. This command will be called when the user clicks the button and releases the mouse button, not before.

12.9.2 GuiBitmapButtonCtrl

This control is a skinnable button. Unlike other skinned controls, this control takes a maximum of four normal (nonarray) graphics. Graphics files for this control use the following naming convention.

```
prefix_tag.suffix
```

- **prefix.** Any name for the image file.

- **_tag.** One each of the following (based on button state).
  - **_n.** Normal.
  - **_h.** Highlighted.
  - **_d.** Depressed.
  - **_i.** Inactive.
- **suffix.** png, jpg, bmp, etc.

For example, we could provide the four images in Figure 12.14.

gglogo_n.png (normal)	gglogo_h.png (highligted)	gglogo_d.png (depressed)	gglogo_i.png (inactive)

Figure 12.14.

Using GuiBitmapButtonCtrl.

To use these images, we set the `bitmap` field to "path + prefix". In other words, we specify the relative or absolute path and the prefix of the filename. The control is smart enough to load all four images based on this information. Specifically, `bitmap` would be set to "./gglogo".

If an image file is not provided for one or more of the states highlighted, depressed, or invalid, the normal image will be substituted. Sensibly, *the normal image is always required*.

A nice shortcut for setting up these buttons is to set the extent to "0 0" in the GUI inspector and then to press Apply. This will cause the GUI to expand to the size of the image file. Nice, eh?

Interestingly, the four different images need not be the same size; however, results may vary based on what choices you make here.

We can change the bitmap at a later time using the `setBitmap()` method.

```
myButton.setBitmap("full path + prefix");
```

12.9.3 GuiButtonCtrl

This is a standard button. It defaults to a `buttonType` of `PushButton`. All functionality comes from its parent, GuiBaseButtonCtrl.

12.9.4 GuiCheckBoxCtrl

This skinnable control displays the perennial checkbox. By default, this control toggles between on and off.

Game Elements

Table 12.11.

Sample image of checkboxes.

Sample Array Image	Row	Column 0
	0	Unchecked Normal
	1	Checked Normal
	2	Unchecked Inactive
	3	Checked Inactive

Table 12.12.

Sample image of radio buttons.

Sample Array Image	Row	Column 0
	0	Unchecked Normal
	1	Checked Normal
	2	Unchecked Inactive
	3	Checked Inactive

Skinning

- Define a profile with the following settings.

```
new GuiControlProfile ( aProfileName ) {
  // ...
  hasBitmapArray = true;
  bitmap = "path to bitmap array graphic";
};
```

- Provide an image file with the structure in Table 12.11.

12.9.5 GuiRadioCtrl

This is a skinnable radio-button control. It is used when a group of buttons must have only one button set at any one time.

Skinning

- Define a profile with the following settings.

```
new GuiControlProfile ( aProfileName ) {
  // ...
  hasBitmapArray = true;
  bitmap = "path to bitmap array graphic";
};
```

- Provide an image file with the structure in Table 12.12.

In order for the radio control to behave properly, the buttons all need to have the same parent and groupNum. In the following example, either "Radio 0" or "Radio 1" can be selected, but not both.

```
new guiControl() {
  new GuiRadioCtrl() {
    profile = "GuiRadioProfile";
    //..
    text = "Radio 0";
    groupNum = "1";
    buttonType = "RadioButton";
  };
  new GuiRadioCtrl() {
    profile = "GuiRadioProfile";
    //..
    text = "Radio 1";
    groupNum = "1";
    buttonType = "RadioButton";
  };
};
```

12.10 Menus

This section describes the controls used for menus.

12.10.1 GuiMenuBar

This semi-skinnable control displays the familiar menu-bar metaphor. By semi-skinnable, I mean that graphic icons can be embedded in menu items, but the bar and the dropdowns themselves are not skinned.

Creating a GuiMenuBar

GuiMenuBar does not provide any new fields. Also, a GuiMenuBar is normally placed at the top of its parent, but in theory it can be placed in any position. A simple definition would look something like the following.

```
new GuiMenuBar( myMenuBar ) {
  position = "0 0";
  horizSizing = "width";
  vertSizing = "bottom";
  // ...
};
```

Menu Item Icon Arrays

* Define a profile with the following settings:

```
new GuiControlProfile ( aProfileName ) {
  // ...
```

511

```
    hasBitmapArray = true;
    bitmap= "path to bitmap array graphic";
};
```

- Provide an image file with the structure in Table 12.13.

Table 12.13.

Sample image of menu icons.

Sample Array Image	Row	Column 0 (normal)	Column 1 (selected)	Column 2 (inactive)
	0	Checked Mark	Not-Checked Mark	Inactive Checked Mark
	1	Optional Icon 0	Optional Icon 0	Optional Icon 0
		...	...	...
	N	Optional Icon N	Optional Icon N	Optional Icon N

In effect, a GuiMenuBar can have any number of icon rows, but the first (0) row is normally reserved for the "checked" icons. You can of course use any icon for "checking" that you wish, and you can use those icons elsewhere, too.

GuiMenuBar Guidelines/Rules

The following guidelines/rules apply when building menus.

1. Place and size the initial menu bar using the GUI editor.
2. Open the .gui file (or use a separate .cs) and write code to populate the menu.
3. Text values for menus and menu items should not start with a digit.
4. Menu items may optionally have accelerators.
5. Menus and menu items may be enabled and disabled from script.
6. Menu items may have separator lines (-) between them.
7. Text for menus and menu items can be dynamically changed from scripts.
8. Menu items can be hidden.
9. Menu items can have checkbox behavior and radio behaviors, including the display of a currently checked image in the menu.
10. Menus and menu items can be identified or referred to either by their text or ID.
11. Hierarchical (cascading) menus are not supported.
12. Menus do not support accelerators (only menu items support this).

Menus and Menu Items

GuiMenuBar supports only one level of menu; i.e., it does not support cascading menus, just dropdowns. The parent items in the main bar are referred to as menus, whereas the dropdowns are referred to as menu items. In order to use the GuiMenuBar, it must have menu items to select. To add menu items, we need menus. So, let's learn how to add menus first.

Adding, Removing, and Clearing Menus

The normal order of operations for adding menus to the GuiMenuBar is as follows.

```
// 1 - Clear all menus from menu bar
myMenuBar.clearMenus();

// 2 - Add a new menu
myMenuBar.addMenu( "Test0" , 0 ); // Add menu 'Test' as menu ID 0

//.. repeat step 2
```

Later, we can clear the menu again if we wish, destroying all contents, or we can remove just one menu.

```
myMenuBar.removeMenu( "Test0" ); // Can use name or ID of menu
```

Adding, Removing, and Clearing Menu Items

Now that we have menus in place, we can add our menu items.

```
// Add new menu items to "Test 0" menu
myMenuBar.addMenuItem( "Test0" , "SubMenu0", 0 );
myMenuBar.addMenuItem( 0 , "SubMenu1", 1 );
// ..
//.. repeat for other menus
```

In the above example, we have added two menu items to menu "Test0". When adding these menu items, we can refer to menu "Test0" by name or by its numeric ID (0, in this case). Be aware that each menu item has a per-menu unique ID, not a completely unique ID; that is, menu items in *different* menus may have the *same* IDs, but menu items in the same menu may not.

As with menus, we can both clear menu items (this removes all menu items from a single menu), or we can remove a specific menu item.

```
myMenuBar.clearMenuItems( "Test0" ); // Can use name or ID of menu

myMenuBar.removeMenuItem( "Test0" , "SubMenu0" ); // Can use names or IDs
```

Adding Bitmaps and Dividers

In addition to adding normal text to our menu items, we can add dividers.

```
// This adds a divider as item 2
myMenuBar.addMenuItem( "Test0" , "-", 2 );
```

We can also add bitmaps.

```
// Use row 4 bitmaps
myMenuBar.setMenuItemBitmap( "Test0", "SubMenu1" , 4 );
```

The above statement says to display one of the bitmaps found in row 4 of the bitmap array specified in this GuiMenuBar's profile. Rows start at 0 and have three columns—normal, selected, and inactive. Accordingly, menu-item states determine which bitmap in the row is used.

Bitmaps can be changed or removed at any time. To remove a bitmap, simply pass an index of –1 as the row number to the above method as follows.

```
// Remove bitmaps
myMenuBar.setMenuItemBitmap( "Test0", "SubMenu1" , -1 );
```

Accelerators and Check Groups

Like buttons, menu items can be accelerated. Also, if we want to add a radio-button list to a menu, we can. The addMenuItem() method comes with two optional arguments. Thus, to add an accelerated menu item, we would do the following.

```
// Add an accelerated menu item that will activate
// if CTRL + H are pressed
myMenuBar.addMenuItem( "Test0" , "Help", 3, "CTRL H" );
```

If we wanted to make items part of a radio group, we could do this:

```
// Make a three choice radio group
myMenuBar.addMenuItem( "Test1" , "Option 0", 0, "", 0 );
myMenuBar.addMenuItem( "Test1" , "Option 1", 1, "", 0 );
myMenuBar.addMenuItem( "Test1" , "Option 2", 2, "", 0 );
```

In the above example, we have three nonaccelerated items that are all part of the same check group, which is zero. Check groups must be unique within any menu but may be reused between different menus.

It is acceptable to use a check group of –1. This means that the checked item will behave like a checkbox instead of a radio control.

Hiding Menus and Menu Items

GuiMenuBar is designed with context sensitivity in mind. Thus, we may want to hide menus or to deactivate them based on our current context. A menu can be (de)activated as follows.

```
myMenuBar.setMenuEnable( "Test0", false ); // deactivate
```

This will make the menu unselectable. Also, the menu text will now display in the profile-specified inactive color (fontColorNA). If it is not enough to enable/disable the menu, we can also (un)hide it.

```
myMenuBar.setMenuVisible( "Test0", false ); // hide this menu
```

Similar features are provided for menu items.

```
// deactivate
myMenuBar.setMenuItemEnable( "Test0", "SubMenu1" , false );

// hide SubMenu1
myMenuBar.setMenuItemVisible( "Test0", "SubMenu1" , false );
```

Remember that, when a menu item is inactive, the inactive version of the bitmap will be displayed if a bitmap is used for this item.

Modifying Menu and Menu-Item Text

Also in line with context sensitivity is the idea of changing menu and menu-item text. This can be done as follows.

```
myMenuBar.setMenuText( "Test0", "TestMenu0" );

myMenuBar.setMenuItemText( "TestMenu0", "SubMenu0", "TestSubMenu0" );
```

Script Check Selection

We can force a checkable item to be (un)checked from script by using the setMenuItemChecked() method.

```
// check item 1
myMenuBar.setMenuItemChecked( "Test1", "Choice 1", true );
```

onMenuSelect()

When a menu is selected, the engine will first attempt to execute the callback onMenuSelect(). Then, it will open the dropdown menu containing the

515

menu's menu items. This ordering allows us to modify the menu's contents prior to its display. The onMenuSelect() callback is documented in Appendix A.4, "GUI Controls Quick Reference."

onMenuItemSelect()

Lastly, we need a callback to tell us when an menu item has been selected. It is the onMenuItemSelect() callback that does this for us. This callback is called after the menu item is selected and the mouse button is released. It, too, is documented in Appendix A.4, "GUI Controls Quick Reference."

12.10.2 GuiPopupMenuCtrl

This is a traditional pop-up menu. When a left mouse click is applied to this control, a list will pop up. This list will either be above or below the control depending on its placement, how many entries are in the list, and the nearness of the bottom of the screen (not parent). In the case that the list is taller than the height of the screen or maxPopupHeight, it will scroll automatically. Additionally, each text entry can be themed with a coloring scheme.

Creating a GuiPopupMenuCtrl

The GuiPopupMenuCtrl has only one new field. Its purpose is to control the height of the pop-up menu. With it, we tell the control the maximum number of entries it may display.

```
new GuiMenuBar( myPopupMenu ) {
  maxPopupHeight = 4; // Show only 4 entries at a time
  // ...
};
```

Scheming

No, this is not how we turn the pop-up menu into some kind of evil control with nefarious purposes. Instead, think in terms of font formatting. The GuiPopupMenuCtrl gives us the ability to create font-formatting schemes. We can scheme individual entries. With a scheme, we can specify the font colors for the standard states—enabled, selected, inactive.

```
myPopupMenu.addScheme( 1 , "0 0 0", "255 0 0", "64 64 64" );
```

Here, we have create a numbered scheme (1), with an enabled color of black, a selected color of red, and a disabled/inactive color of dark gray. Scheme 0 is reserved for the values provided in the profile.

Skinning

This control is partially skinnable and uses the same skin as the GuiScrollCtrl.

Adding Entries

Adding entries to the pop-up menu is simplicity itself. Below, we add two entries to our pop-up menu. The first uses the default scheme, and the second uses the scheme we created above.

```
myPopupMenu.add( "Entry 1", 0 , 0 ); // Entry Text, ID, Scheme
myPopupMenu.add( "Entry 2", 1 , 1 ); // Entry Text, ID, Scheme
```

Modifying Entries and Current Button Text

When a menu entry is selected, the text in that entry replaces whatever text was previously displayed on the pull-down menu button. Subsequently, we can modify this value using the setText() method.

```
myPopupMenu.setText( "New Text" ); // Display "New Text" on button.
```

Additionally, once we've selected an entry, we can change the text of that entry.

```
myPopupMenu.replaceText( "Yo" ); // Change selected entry text to "Yo"
```

Navigating

We will on occasion wish to navigate our pull-down menu from script. TGE provides the ability to find an entry by text:

```
myPopupMenu.findText( "Yo" ); // Return entry number of first "Yo"
```

text by ID:

```
// %entryText now contains "Entry 2"
%entryText = myPopupMenu.getTextByID( 1 );
```

ID of currently selected:

```
// Return ID of current selection (-1 for none)
myPopupMenu.getSelected();
```

and text of currently selected:

```
// Return text of current selection ("" for none)
myPopupMenu.getText();
```

Lastly, we can set the current selection from script.

```
myPopupMenu.setSelection( 1 ); // Select entry with ID 1
```

Starting Over

Although this control is not as configurable as a GuiMenuBar, it can be cleared using the `clear()` method. This will remove all entries *and* all schemes, allowing us to start from scratch.

Sorting

This control can be sorted alphabetically using the `sort()` method.

Callbacks

The order of calls may be a little tricky if you don't understand it. There are three entry points to the callback stream for this control.

1. If the user opens the menu and clicks on an entry, the order of events is as follows.
   - Menu closes on click (not button release).
   - If valid selection, `onSelect()` is called, else `onCancel()` is called.
   - If `command` field was specified, specified script is executed.
2. If a script chooses the selection via the `setSelection()` method:
   - if valid selection, `onSelect()` is called, else
   - `onCancel()` is called followed by `command` script if it was specified.
3. If a script forces the `onAction()` callback via the `forceOnAction()` method:
   - if `command` field was specified, specified script is executed.

```
myPopupMenu.forceOnAction();
```

12.11 Sliders and Scales

This section describes the controls used for sliders and scales.

12.11.1 GuiFilterCtrl

This odd control allows us to specify a multi-knotted spline-like GUI that can be used to create a vector of floating-point values (one per knot), where each value is between 0.0 and 1.0. The control can be used both as an input device and as a feedback device (we can set the position of each knot from script).

Creating a GuiFilterCtrl

When creating this control, we need to specify an initial number of knots (two at a minimum). We can also specify the initial values for these knots.

```
new GuiFilterCtrl( myFilter ) {
  controlPoints = 3;
  filter = "0.0 0.5 1.0"; // Initial positions left-to-right
  // ...
};
```

It is perfectly legal to change the number of control points a filter has at a later date by simple assignment.

```
myFilter.controlPoints = 4;
```

Using for Input

This control is normally used for input. The user can click on a point and drag it up or down. At any time, we can retrieve the current positions of the knots from script as follows.

```
myFilter.getValue();
```

The knot values are returned in a vector of space-separated floating-point values, where the first entry is knot 0 (left), and the last is entry is knot $N - 1$ (right), where N is the total number of knots.

Using for Output

This control can be updated from script and used as a feedback mechanism. The update is accomplished by passing a new vector of knot values to the control.

```
myFilter.setValue( " 0.25 0.33 0.66 1.0" );
```

If you intend to use a filter as an output-only control, you should fully cover the "face" of the filter with another control to block mouse inputs.

Identity Crisis!

OK, the control doesn't experience mental breakdowns, but we may want to "straighten" it out on occasion. By calling the `identity()` method, we can force the control to align its knots on a 45-degree line from 0.0 on the left to 1.0 on the right.

12.11.2 GuiSliderCtrl

This is a numeric slider control. It allows a value between a lower and upper range to be selected using a sliding interface.

Creating a GuiSliderCtrl

When creating this control, we need to specify an initial number of ticks, initial ranges, and the initial value.

```
new GuiSliderCtrl( mySlider ) {
    // 5 inner ticks and two outer ticks == 7 total ticks
    ticks = 5;

    // Range: [-1.0, 1.0] inclusive
    range = "-1.0 1.0";

    // Start at 0.0
    value = 0.0;
    // ...
};
```

Like the filter control, we can adjust these values later in script by simply assigning them:

```
mySlider.ticks = 3;
mySlider.range = "0.0 1.0";
mySlider.value = 0.25;
```

Getting Data

We can peek directly at the value, or we can call the method `getValue()`. The method is provided to enable consistent coding.

```
if( mySlider.value == mySlider.getValue() ) {
  echo("This is always true");
}
```

altCommand

This control executes the script specified with the `command` field when the slider is released, and if we specify a script in `altCommand`, that script is executed every sim tick while this control is "active" and selected.

12.11.3 GuiTextEditSliderCtrl

This is another floating-point slider control, but it uses up-down buttons instead of a left-right slider. This control is a bit more flexible in terms of its output, as it uses a standard-C printf-style formatting string.

Creating a GuiTextEditSliderCtrl

When creating this control, we need to specify an initial format, initial ranges, and the step increment:

```
new GuiTextEditSliderCtrl( mySlider ) {
  format = "%5.5f"; // Standard-C sprintf formatting is used
  range = "-5.0 20.0" // Range: [-5.0, 20.0] inclusive
  increment = 0.25;   // In-/De-crement in steps of 0.25
  // ...
};
```

This may be sounding repetitive by now, but these values can be changed by assignment at any time.

12.12 Miscellaneous Controls

This section describes various other controls you might wish to use.

12.12.1 GuiCursor

TGE allows us to define our own cursors, using a simple image file and some information defining the location of the cursor's hot spot. In order to use a custom cursor, tell the canvas to activate it using the `Canvas.setCursor()` method.

```
new GuiCursor(HOWCrosshair) {
  hotSpot = "30 30";
  bitmapName = "./cursorImages/HOWCrosshair";
};
```

12.12.2 GuiDirectoryTreeCtrl and GuiDirectoryFileListCtrl

Torque comes with two controls that are designed to be used in tandem but that can be used separately. I will be describing them together, but once we are done discussing them, you should not find it too challenging to separate them.

The first of these controls is GuiDirectoryTreeCtrl. It is used to display the folder structure of a specified directory and subdirectory in our game's "mod path" (directories that our game can see).

The second control is GuiDirectoryFileListCtrl. It is used to display a list of files. At first, this might seem redundant to the GuiTextListCtrl. However, the GuiDirectoryFileListCtrl is able to auto-populate once we specify a directory to look in, making it nicer to work with for this case.

Creating These Controls

Both of these controls must be created as children of their own GuiScrollCtrl. If we do not do this, the controls will not expand correctly and will generally look bad. Beyond that, there isn't much involved with setting up the default version of each control.

If you are customizing your controls, you are allowed to modify the skin texture for the GuiDirectoryTreeCtrl. So, let's talk about that next.

Skinning GuiDirectoryTreeCtrl

- Define a profile with the following settings.

```
new GuiControlProfile ( aProfileName ) {
  // ...
  hasBitmapArray = true;
  bitmap = "path to bitmap array graphic";
};
```

- Provide an image file with the structure in Table 12.14. I have shown the image map twice, both uncut (left) and cut (right). If you are modifying this to match your own art or theme, be very careful to maintain the pixel ratios of the original bitmap array.
- Provide an open-folder and a closed-folder icon. These icons must be located as follows:
  - Open-folder image ▣ must be named "/common/ui/folder.png".
  - Closed-folder image ▢ must be named "/common/ui/folder_closed.png".
- Provide a leaf-node icon image ▤ named "/common/ui/default.png".

Scripting GuiDirectoryTreeCtrl

This control is a child of the GuiTreeViewCtrl (see Section 12.12.15), so it inherits all of that control's functionality. Additionally, it adds two new methods and a callback (Table 12.15).

Uncut	Cut	Meaning
	⌐	Branch back.
	L	Branch to file/folder.
	⊢	Branch to folder.
	⊖-	Root branch close button (single-branch).
	⊖-	Root branch close button (multi-branch).
	⊖-	Final folder close button.
	⊖-	Middle branch close button.
	⊕-	Root branch open button (single-branch).
	⊕-	Root branch open button (multi-branch).
	⊕-	Bottom branch open button.
	⊕-	Middle branch open button.
	|	Down branch connector.
	◼	No branches button (empty tree).

Table 12.14.

Skin texture for directory tree.

Game Elements

Table 12.15.

Methods and callbacks for GuiDirectoryTreeCtrl.

Method	Description
setSelectedPath(path)	Set the path (which will be traversable) to path.
getSelectedPath( )	Return the path that is actually selected (if any).
Callback	**Description**
onSelectPath(path)	This is called when the users clicks on a directory in the tree and passes the full path to that directory.

Please be aware that, although the methods in Table 12.15 sound similar, one is being used to initialize the tree and the other is returning a selection (if any), which is not exactly the same.

Scripting GuiDirectoryFileListCtrl

This control is also a child of the GuiTextListCtrl, so it inherits all of that control's functionality. Additionally, it adds two new methods (Table 12.16).

Table 12.16.

Method for GuiDirectoryFileListCtrl.

Method	Description
setPath(path [, filter])	Display all files in the specified path optionally matching the specified filter.
getSelectedFile( )	Returns the currently selected file name, if any.

It is very important to remember that this control inherits the click behavior of its parent and thus will execute any script that has been specified in its command field when the user clicks on a valid line in the control.

Filtering

Filtering uses the same string-matching rules that we discussed earlier when we learned about Torque's string-manipulation functions in Chapter 10, "Gameplay Scripting." The important thing to remember is that filenames have the path stripped off before the comparison happens, so we can use the filter to exclude flat file names only. For example, to display all GUI files, our filter would be "*.gui".

12.12.3 GuiInputCtrl

This control is used to capture all input events. Input events in this case are such things as mouse clicks and/or keystrokes. For every input event, a single callback is fired.

Getting It All

Understand that, if you use this control any place in the current interface, it will capture *all* inputs, period. This control can be a rather nasty one, but it serves its purpose, and we can remove it when we don't need it any longer.

Creating

To create one of these, we could use this snippet:

```
new GuiInputCtrl(gsTestInputCtrl) {
  profile = "GuiInputCtrlProfile";
};
```

All Your Base Are Belong to Us

OK, I don't really mean all your base(s); I mean all your inputs. Once created, this control sinks all device inputs. For every input, the following callback is called.

```
onInputEvent( %this, %deviceString, %actionString, %makeOrBreak )
```

This callback takes the following arguments.

- **%deviceString.** A string specifying the device name: keyboard, mouse0, etc.
- **%actionString.** A string specifying the action: a, b, tab, button0, etc.
- **%makeOrBreak.** Only applies to release of special device buttons and modifier keys, `false` for all others.

Because it would be sheer madness to try to cover all the inputs and what they mean, a GuiInputCtrl sampler has been provided to allow you to see what the inputs are. You will find it in the GUI Sampler part of the kit. To see it, run the GPGT Lesson Kit and select GUIs Sampler → GuiInputCtrl.

12.12.4 GuiMouseEventCtrl

This control is used to capture a large variety of mouse inputs. The designers of TGE decided to limit each control to only capture and react to inputs that were normally pertinent to that control. However, they knew that special cases would arise in which the user might want to capture a large variety of inputs. Thus, the GuiMouseEventCtrl was born. It captures all of the following events.

Left Mouse Button Press	Left Mouse Release	Left Mouse Drag
Right Mouse Button Press	Right Mouse Release	Right Mouse Drag
Mouse Move	Mouse Enter	Mouse Exit

Game Elements

Additionally, it handles the following modifiers.

Left Shift	Right Shift	Either Shift
Left Control	Right Control	Either Control
Left Alt	Right Alt	Either Alt

Please note that a *drag* is mouse motion with a button pressed, *entering* means to enter the bounds of the control, and *exiting* means to leave the bounds of the control. Mouse *moving* is like dragging but without the button pressed.

Configuring

There isn't much involved in setting up one of these controls. Simply place it as a child of any other control and be sure it covers the hot area where you want events to be recorded. You can even make a GuiMouseEventCtrl a child of another GuiMouseEventCtrl if you need to.

GuiMouseEventCtrl Callbacks

To acquire information from this control, write a set of general callbacks scoped to GuiMouseEventCtrl or specific ones scoped to the name of your control with the following form.

```
function myMouseEventCtrl::EVENT_NAME( %theControl ,
                                       %modifiers ,
                                       %point ,
                                       %clicks ) {
  // ...
}
```

This callback will respond to an event EVENT_NAME and will receive

- any modifiers (**SHIFT**, **CTRL**, **ALT** keys that are pressed at time of the event),

- the location of the mouse relative to the <0, 0> in the canvas (not the GuiMouseEventCtrl control), and

- the number of clicks that were recorded within the last half-second (0—no clicks, 1—single click, 2—double click, etc.).

EVENT_NAME

The possibilities for EVENT_NAME are shown in Table 12.15.

EVENT_NAME	Captures
onMouseDown	Left mouse button pressed.
onMouseUp	Left mouse button released.
onRightMouseDown	Right mouse button pressed.
onRightMouseUp	Right mouse button released.
onMouseMove	Mouse moved while no button is pressed.
onMouseDrag	Mouse moved while left mouse button is pressed.
onRightMouseDragged	Mouse moved while right mouse button is pressed.
onMouseEnter	Mouse entered control region.
onMouseLeave	Mouse exited control region.

Table 12.15

GuiMouseEventCtrl callbacks.

%modifiers

The %modifiers argument is a bitmask that can be logically compared against the values in these global variables:

```
$EventModifier::LSHIFT    $EventModifier::RSHIFT
$EventModifier::SHIFT
$EventModifier::LCTRL     $EventModifier::RCTRL     $EventModifier::CTRL
$EventModifier::LALT      $EventModifier::RALT      $EventModifier::ALT
```

Note that the unadorned version of **SHIFT**, **CTRL**, and **ALT** will compare true if any key of this variety is pressed.

The code to check for a specific modifier or set of combined modifiers looks like the following.

```
if( %modifier & ( $EventModifier::LSHIFT | $EventModifier::ALT ) ==
    ( $EventModifier::LSHIFT | $EventModifier::ALT ) ) {
  echo( "The LEFT shift key is pressed and one of
      the ALT keys is pressed." );
}
```

%point

The first time you use this control, you may be disappointed to find that the click point that is passed into the callback is always relative to < 0,0 > in the canvas. Don't worry, though. If you need to calculate the position of the click relative to the upper-left corner of the control that captured it, simply use a script like the following.

```
function myMouseEventCtrl::onMouseDown( %theControl , %modifiers ,
                                  %point , %clicks ) {
```

```
%tmpControl = %theControl.getGroup();
%Offset = %point;
while( isObject( %tmpControl ) )
{
  %Offset = vectorSub( %Offset , %tmpControl.position );
  %tmpControl = %tmpControl.getGroup();
}
// ...
}
```

This code iterates upward through each parent until we get to the root control, and along each iteration it subtracts the position of that control relative to its parent from the original click point. By the end of this loop, the variable %Offset contains the position of the click relative to the $<0, 0>$ coordinates of the control myMouseEventCtrl.

`%clicks`

The last argument is the click count. When we click in this control, the control will increment an internal click counter to 1. Then, it will add any subsequent clicks to this counter for the next half-second. After that time, the counter goes back to 0, then 1, and accumulates for another period, ad infinitum. The purpose of this mechanism is to allow us to differentiate clicking styles—i.e., single click, double click, triple click, etc.

12.12.5 GuiTreeViewCtrl

This control is used to display a left-aligned tree. We are accustomed to seeing these used for displaying directories and data where there is some hierarchy and/or inheritance associated with the data.

Although this control can be used to make simple and elaborate trees (Figure 12.15), I will only be discussing how to make simple trees. Why? Because the elaborate tree mechanism was added to enable the creation of a more detailed Inspector tool. Therefore, the only icons available are those used by the Inspector.

I'll list the syntax for the elaborate tree, but you will have to dig into the engine if you want to try to use it for your projects. By that time, you would likely be expanding the icon list anyway, so further discussions between us on this topic would be a wash.

Creating a GuiTreeViewCtrl

To create a tree view, simply create a GuiScrollCtrl and then add an instance of GuiTreeViewCtrl as a child. The tree view relies on the scroll control to handle resizing and, as you might imagine, scrolling.

Figure 12.15.

Left-aligned tree views.

a. Simple tree.

b. Elaborate tree
(inspector-specific).

Configuring GuiTreeViewCtrl

Depending on how we want to use this tree, there is either very little to do or a great deal to do. We will start off talking about the basics and then move on to the harder stuff.

To set up the tree, we must specify a few fields. Those fields have the functions and effects shown in Table 12.16.

Field	Function/Effect
tabSize	This is the pixel size used to indent subtree items.
textOffset	This is the pixel offset between the end of the tree image and the text describing a level in the tree.
fullRowSelect	If this value is true, a row may be selected anywhere parallel to the item; otherwise, the user will be required to click directly on the text or icon to select it.
itemHeight	Not adjustable, but specifies the height of a line and is based on the tallest item in the line.
destroyTreeOnSleep	If set to true, the tree is reset every time it goes to sleep.
mouseDragging	You may ignore this field.
multipleSelections	Allows the user to highlight multiple entries in the tree.

Table 12.16.

Fields for setting up a tree view.

Skins and Icons for GuiTreeViewCtrl

This control uses the same bitmap array, folder open/closed icons, and leaf node icon as are used for the GuiDirectoryTreeCtrl (Section 12.12.2). Please refer to the skinning directions for that control to learn more about the basic skin and icons used here.

Elaborate Icons

This control may also display a limited set of predefined icons. Please note again that the purpose of this feature is to support the new Inspector, which has nice icons depicting various object types.

If you want to start digging and modifying this feature to use in your own creations, one of the first things you will have to do is build a library of icons.

A GuiTreeViewCtrl will try to build an icon library every time it wakes up by calling the callback onDefineIcons(). If you want to include icons in your tree, you should create the icons and store them in a fixed location. Then, use a callback to build the control's icons library as follows.

```
function GuiTreeeViewCtrl::onDefineIcons( %theControl ) {
 %icons = "path/icon_file_name0" @ ":" @
```

529

```
                    "path/icon_file_name1" @ ":" @
                    "path/icon_file_name2" @ ":" @
                    "path/icon_file_name3" @ ":" ;
    %theControl.buildIconTable( %icons );
}
```

Adding Items to a Tree

We may populate a tree in one of two ways. We can either manually add new items (lines of text) to a tree, or we can use the tree to open a SimSet. Let's discuss the manual method first.

To manually add an item to an existing tree, we simply write some code like the following

```
%myTree.insertItem( 0 , "Item Text" );
```

This statement will insert a new item into the tree and attach it to root (entry 0). This item will display the string "Item Text" in the tree.

Parent Indexes

When manually adding elements to a tree, each item added to the tree is assigned an index. Later, when we want to add a new item into the tree, we must remember this index and add our new element to the index. Please note that indexes are never reused for any individual tree.

For example, the following script will produce a tree like Figure 12.16.

Figure 12.16.

Newly inserted entries.

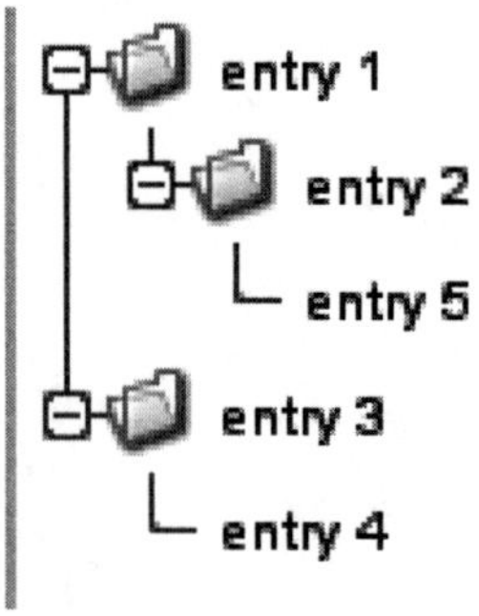

```
// Creates index 1 attached to root (0)
%myTree.insertItem( 0 , "entry 1" );

// Creates index 2 attached to 1
%myTree.insertItem( 1 , "entry 2" );

// Creates index 3 attached to root (0)
%myTree.insertItem( 0 , "entry 3" );

// Creates index 4 attached to 3
%myTree.insertItem( 3 , "entry 4" );

// Creates index 5 attached to 2
%myTree.insertItem( 2 , "entry 5" );
```

You should note that the insertItem() method returns the index for the element it just inserted, so you don't have to count or anything heinous like that. Instead, just save the return values if you need them at all.

Assigning a Value

It is possible to give each entry a value in addition to text. This value can later be retrieved and can be any valid string. To create an item with a value, do the following.

```
%myTree.insertItem( 0 , "entry 10", "oops" );
```

If we called this on the tree we just created, the tree would have a new folder with the text "entry 10", and it would have a value of "oops" stored at that entry (not visible). (See Figure 12.17.)

If we recall the above discussion of "Parent Indexes," it will also be clear that the ID of this item is 6, as in the sixth item we have added.

Figure 12.17.

Entry inserted at end of list.

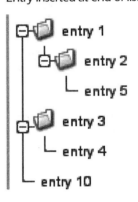

Inserting Icons

In order to use icons in your image (instead of the default folders), use the `insertItem()` method.

```
%myTree.insertItem( 0 , "some text", "Sun" );
```

This code will produce a tree entry with the "Sun" icon. The full syntax of `insertItem()` is as follows.

```
insertItem( parent_id , text [ , value , iconString ,
            normalImage , expandedImage ] );
```

Opening a SimSet

The second way to populate a tree is to have it open a SimSet. To do so, simply use the method described in Table 12.17.

Method	Description
`open( setID [ , editable ] )`	This will populate a tree with the contents of a SimSet identified by `setID`. This set will be traversed, and all sets within will be traversed, until all branches have been followed to a leaf. Optionally, we enable or lock the SimSet by passing `true` or `false` in the position of `editable`. If the set is locked, we won't be able to use tree methods to modify it.

Table 12.17.

Opening a SimSet.

A sample open looks like the following.

```
// Open a SimSet and lock it (not modifiable)
%myTree.open( %mySimSet , false );
```

Clearing Trees

We can empty a tree from script as follows.

```
%myTree.clear();
```

This will empty the tree of items, but it will not modify any SimSet that may have been loaded.

Counting Items

It is possible to count the number of items currently in a tree as follows.

```
echo ( "myTree has ", %myTree.countItems() , " items in it." );
```

For our current tree, the above code would produce the following.

```
myTree has 6 items in it.
```

Finding Items

Once we have a tree, we can search for items in the tree by name as follows.

```
%item = %myTree.findItemByName("entry 10"); // Returns 6
```

If this were called on the tree we created above, the variable `%item` would contain the value 6.

Querying Items Directly

Once we have an item ID, we can get information about the item's text and value as follows.

```
%text = %myTree.getItemText( %item ); // %item contains 6
%value = %myTree.getItemValue( %item ); // %item contains 6
echo( "Tree entry: ", %item , " has text label: " ,
      %text , ", value: ", %value );
```

Assuming we are writing these sample snippets in order, the above code will produce the following.

```
Tree entry: 6 has text label: entry 10, value: oops
```

Editing Items

It is possible to manipulate the contents of an item after we add it like this, resulting in the new tree shown in Figure 12.18.

```
%myTree.editItem( %item , "entry 6" , "fixed" );
```

Now, if we reran our prior query code, we would get the following.

```
Tree entry: 6 has text label: entry 6, value: fixed
```

Don't forget that, if we opened a SimSet in the locked state, this will not work—i.e., no changes will be allowed.

(De)selecting items

The user may select and deselect an item from the tree using a mouse, keyboard, or other device, but sometimes we will want to modify selection states from script.

To select an item in our list we do the following.

```
%myTree.addSelection( %item ); // "entry 6" now selected
```

Or we can set the selection/deselection status of an item as follows.

```
%myTree.selectItem( %item , false ); // "entry 6" is deselected
```

It should be noted that `addSelection()` does not return a value, but `selectItem()` will return `true` or `false` to indicate success or failure (bad item or unable to modify).

On the flip side, we can deselect the previously selected item (as we just did with `selectItem()`).

```
%myTree.clearSelection();
```

Or we can target a deselect.

```
// De-select "entry 6" (already not selected)
%myTree.removeSelection( %item );
```

Neither of these two methods returns a value.

Querying Selected Items

Once an item is selected, it is possible to query that item as follows.

```
%item = %myTree.getSelectedItem(); // Will be 0
```

Figure 12.18.

Editing an entry (item).

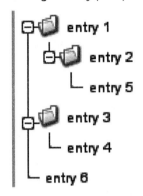

533

Game Elements

It should be noted that, in the case of multiple selections, this will only ever return the ID of the last selected item, and if no items are selected, it will return 0.

Expanding Items

Another manipulation that we might want to do from script is the expansion and collapse of the tree or a branch of the tree. This can be achieved as follows, producing the results shown in Figure 12.19.

```
%myTree.expandItem( 1 , false ); // Collapses branch 1
%myTree.expandItem( 3 , false ); // Collapses branch 3
%myTree.expandItem( 4 , true ); // Expands 3 and then 4
```

Figure 12.19.

Collapsing and expanding folders.

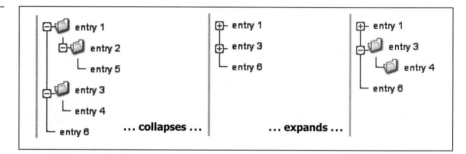

Removing Items

So, what about removing items? Easy. We can remove an item using its index.

```
%myTree.removeItem( 6 ); // Remove item that we labelled "entry 6"
```

Or we can remove the current selection.

```
%myTree.addSelection( 1 );
%myTree.deleteSelection();
```

In either of these cases, if we had instead opened a SimSet, and if we had locked it, no deletions would be allowed.

String Operations

There is a cool feature that is often used to create paths and other constructs:

```
%myString = %myTree.getTextRoot( 4 , "/" );
echo( %myString );
```

This code will produce the following output.

```
/entry 3/entry 4
```

Please note, the second argument in the above call to `getTextRoot()` is an optional delimiter and can be a string.

Tree Relationships

To round out the GuiTreeViewCtrl's set of methods is a short list of methods used for getting item IDs based on an item's position in the tree (Table 12.18).

Method	Description
getChild(item)	Returns the ID of the first child of this item, or 0 if item has no children.
getParent(item)	Returns the ID of the parent of this item, or 0 if item is root.
getNextSibling(item)	Returns the ID of next entry in same branch as item (below item), or 0 if no such entry exists.
getPrevSibling(item)	Returns the ID of prior entry in same branch as item (above item), or 0 if no such entry exists.

Table 12.18.

Getting item IDs.

GuiTreeViewCtrl Callbacks

No control would be complete without adding a few callbacks. GuiTreeViewCtrl is no exception and adds the callbacks shown in Table 12.19.

Callback	Called when...
onAddSelection(ID)	... a new item is added to a SimSet tree.
onDeleteSelection()	... an item is deleted.
onInspect(id)	Same as onSelect() except **only** called on leaf nodes.
onRemoveSelection(item)	... item is deselected.
onRightMouseDown(x , y , id)	... mouse is clicked over a SimSet object item. Passes in <x,y> position of click and object ID.
onRightMouseDown(x , y)	Same as above for non-SimSet trees.
onSelect(id)	... an item is selected in the tree. id will contain the node's text for a normal list, the field name for SimSets when the selection is not an object, and the ID of an object if the selection is an object.
onUnselect(id)	Reverse of onSelect().

Table 12.19.

Callbacks for GuiTreeViewCtrl.

12.13 Summary

In this chapter, we covered a massive load of TGE standard GUI topics. This chapter was structured to teach about GUIs in general and then to lead you through the various techniques for using the 35 most commonly needed and used controls (the canvas is a control, too). It is also structured to act as a reference. In addition, a complete appendix (Appendix A.4, "GUI Controls Quick Reference") is supplied that contains almost all of the information in this chapter (in a more succinct form) and completely documents all fields, methods, and callbacks (some of which are not mentioned at all in this chapter).

In the beginning, we discussed the fundamental concept of the canvas. We learned about the two categories of controls it contains: dialogs and everything else. We then learned the difference between the canvas's current content and the pushing and popping of dialogs which float above that content. We also learned that all interfaces are constructed by stacking controls on top of controls, and that stacked controls are the children of the parents they stack upon.

Our next topic was input capture. We explored the concept of mouse inputs to GUI layers using the falling marble analogy. Then we examined the first-responder concept, which is used in older versions of the engine (prior to version 1.4) to help sort out input rules between controls on the same level in a layer. Next, we looked at focus and came to understand that focus can be attained by clicking in a control or by tabbing to it from another control. Lastly, we looked at modality (also not used after version 1.3), which is used to force layers to take ownership, or conversely to allow it to be taken away.

Done with general topics (for now), we jumped into a discussion of the GUI profile. We came to understand that these are templates containing information about bitmaps, borders, fill details, fonts, text formatting, and input behavior, which are specified and then used by subsequent controls to define basic behavior and presentation.

Finally, we got to our first placeable control, the root class to all controls, GuiControl. We spent time examining its use of profiles. Then we looked at how to specify and modify extents, position, and sizing. Next we learned that any GuiControl or child can be visible or not visible. After that, we talked about the use of accelerators to tie controls to keyboard and other events. Then we examined the serious topic of `command` and `altCommand`, two fields that can contain scripts that will be executed at specific times based on the type of control they are specified for. We also examined the `$thiscontrol` variable, which is set prior to any and all callback/`command`/`altCommand` calls. Lastly, we talked about this control being awake, asleep, active, and inactive, as well as how this affects its and its children's behaviors.

Before continuing in our discussion on individual controls, we swung back and talked about a general topic: skinning. We learned that many controls can be skinned. This led to a discussion of bitmap arrays, the rules for organizing them, and a walk-through creating one.

For the remainder of the chapter, we blazed our way through control after control in the following categories.

- **Container controls.** Frames, scrolls, stacks, panes, tab books, and windows.
- **Backgrounds and borders.** Bitmap borders, bitmaps versus chunked bitmaps, and the fade-in bitmaps.
- **Text controls.** Message vectors, Torque Markup Language text displayers and edit areas, labels, single-line text edits, and the very useful text list control.
- **Buttons.** Skinned buttons, plain push buttons, and specialized skinned check boxes and radio buttons.
- **Menus.** Menu bars and pop-up menus.
- **Sliders and scales.** The specialized spline (filter) control, a horizontal slider, and a text slider.
- **The grab bag (miscellaneous controls).** Cursors, directory viewers, an input capturing control, a mouse capture control, and the generic tree viewer.

If you have examined the samples that come in the GPGT Lesson Kit GUIs Sampler (start the GPGT Lesson Kit and click the "GUIs Sampler" button to see these), you will be well on your way to making use of each of these controls to make your own interfaces. To help accelerate this learning, we will examine the creation of several interfaces as the topic of our next chapter.

Chapter 13
Game Interfaces

13.1 Game Interfaces

As we established earlier, all games have some minimum set of interfaces. In this chapter, we will design two sets of interfaces that we can later use when we make games. The purpose of these interfaces is twofold. First, they are learning aids. We will learn how to make simple interfaces, combining several basic GUI controls. Second, they can be used over and over for demo games and prototypes. In the future, we can skip right to working on game content without needing to deal with the mundane items like menus, splash screens, etc.

The interfaces we will be designing in this chapter are as follows.

- **Splash screens.** Splash screens are those GUIs that get displayed when the game starts or during interludes. Games may have multiple splash screens, each providing some information such as game title (screen), company logos, copyright information, etc. For this sample, there will be just one splash screen. It will be used to display a hypothetical company logo.

- **Menus.** As with splash screens, games may have many menus. We'll keep our lives simple and provide a single (main) menu.

- **Credits.** Because we don't want to forget to thank those who have helped us to create our wonderful game, we'll need a credits screen. This is like a splash screen except that it will list our credits information and is usually not displayed until the end of the game, or on demand from the main menu. We'll choose the latter.

At the end of this chapter, we will have made two versions of each of the above interfaces: one set in a "Toon" theme, which we will make together, and the second set in a "Tech" theme, which you should make to practice.

After we have created these basic GUIs, we will work together and make some common HUD interfaces, including the following.

- **Counters.** We will make some generic counters that can be used to track any numeric information in the game.

- **Vertical feedback bars.** We will make some generic vertical feedback bars that graphically display the values in the range 0.0 to 1.0.

- **Strip compass.** Although a good compass should be made in C++, we'll make one using just standard GUI controls and scripts to prove that you can in fact prototype just about anything in TorqueScript.

> All of the interfaces we will discuss in this chapter are provided in a completed and working state in the GPGT Lesson Kit. You may view any of them at any time by running the GPGT Lesson Kit, clicking the "Interface Sampler" button, and then clicking the button that has the name of the interface you wish to examine. Additionally, you may add new interfaces to this kit. Simply follow the direction supplied in Appendix B, "GPGT Lesson Kit Docs."

At any time, you may look at the finished product of all interfaces by running the GPGT Lesson Kit and clicking on "Game Interfaces" from the main menu.

Please note that it is best to create the following examples in order because I will only give detailed explanations the first time we see something new. Subsequently, I may gloss over the same topic. Therefore, unless you have seen the prior explanations, some discussions may be confusing.

13.1.1 Before We Start

Let's discuss our design method. You can make new interfaces in two basic ways.

1. You can use the GUI editor and create a new interface. If you're comfortable with this method, please feel free to use it. If you don't know how to do this, please go back and review Section 3.14, "The GUI Editor."

2. I prefer to make my interfaces from a blank template. That is, I'll take an interface I already have, copy the .gui file to a new directory, cut out the fat, and then make sure the new file gets loaded by the client. Once I've done this, I can just pick my new interface out of the named list of current interfaces and edit it.

In the following pages, we will be making these interfaces and HUDs using the second method. Unless otherwise specified, the starting .gui files will all contain the following code.

```
//--- OBJECT WRITE BEGIN ---
new GuiControl( useAUniqueNameHere ) {
   profile = "GuiDefaultProfile";
   horizSizing = "width";
   vertSizing = "height";
   position = "0 0";
   extent = "800 600";
   minExtent = "8 2";
   visible = "1";
};
//--- OBJECT WRITE END ---
```

For each GUI to be created, take the above code and do the following:

1. Create a directory somewhere under " ~ \client\ui\". For example, in the GPGT Lesson Kit, the *Splash (Toon)* interface is located under the directory " ~ \client\ui\200_GameGUIs\ggsSplashToon\".

2. Copy the above code into an appropriately named file. *Splash (Toon)* is in the file "ggsSplashToon.gui".

3. Make sure the file is executed from the `initClient()` function (usually) located in " ~ \client\init.cs".

Now, when we (re)start the GPGT Lesson Kit and start the GUI editor, we'll find our newly loaded interface in the existing interfaces list. If you don't find it, check the log for errors. I always mistype something; maybe you did, too.

13.2 Toon-Themed Interfaces

Our first set of GUIs will be designed using a sort of carefree cartoon theme. Yes, I know, the art in Figure 13.1 isn't that much like a cartoon, but please bear with me. The thing to concentrate on is consistency in our theme.

| Splash Screen | Main Menu | Credits Screen |

Figure 13.1.
Cartoon-themed screens.

13.2.1 Splash (Toon)

Our first interface is very simple. We can make a splash screen with just a few GUI controls. For this example, we just want our made-up company logo to be splashed for a few seconds, and then we want to automatically proceed to the main menu. The perfect GUI control for this kind of screen is a GuiFadeInBitmapCtrl. Let's look at how to create this interface.

The Splash Interface

- Make a graphics file in your favorite editor that looks something like Figure 13.2. The image should be the highest resolution you expect the user to play at, or perhaps one scale larger. Ours is a 1024 x 768 24-bit color image, saved as a JPEG file. Copy your file, or the one from the GPGT Lesson Kit, to the directory where your .gui file is.
- Start the GPGT Lesson Kit.

Figure 13.2.
Splash screen.

- Now, using the GUI editor, open the splash screen interface and add a GuiFadeinBitmapCtrl control with the following parameters.

```
new GuiFadeInBitmapCtrl( ggsSplashToonFadeinBitmap ) {
   profile = "GuiDefaultProfile";
   horizSizing = "width";
   vertSizing = "height";
   position = "0 0";
   extent = "800 600";
   minExtent = "8 2";
   visible = "1";
   bitmap = "./splash";
   wrap = "0";
   fadeinTime = "1000";
   waitTime = "2000";
   fadeoutTime = "1000";
   done = "0";
};
```

You'll want to use your own name for the GUI, but it does need a name because we're going to write some code for it. The important things to note are the following.

- `horizSizing` and `vertSizing` use "width" and "height", respectively. This GUI will always resize itself to the extents of its parent.
- `wrap` is set to `false`.
- The control will fade in over one second, wait for two seconds, and fade out over one second.

The Splash Interface Code

Now, we have to make some code to go with this interface. Why? For a few reasons.

1. We need to set the `done` parameter to `false` every time this interface is added, just to be safe. Otherwise, we could accidentally save the interface and it would later skip right to `done`.
2. Once the GUI is done fading out, it won't actually do anything else automatically. We need to check for the `done` state and move on to the main menu.
3. We want to allow the user to skip this screen by clicking the mouse, and this requires a little code.

Setting `done` to `false` is easy, but writing code to patrol for `done`—although simple—is not a one-liner. In these GUIs, we'll be using the event-manager code that is provided with the GPGT Lesson Kit, and separately on the CD ("Base\ Scripts\EGSystems"). If you're not familiar with it, the event manager is a set of scriptObject classes that manage various kinds of events and sequences. Appendix A.6, "Scripted Systems Quick Reference," outlines how this code works. In case this is your first time seeing it, I'll explain what the code does below.

onAdd() *and* onRemove()

It will be the job of onAdd() to set done to false and to create our task manager. onRemove() will be responsible for destroying the task manager when the GUI is removed.

```
function ggsSplashToonFadeinBitmap::onAdd( %this ) {
  %this.done = false;

  %this.taskMgr = newTaskManager();
  %this.taskMgr.setTarget(%this);

  %this.taskMgr.setDefaultTaskDelay(100);
  // add a repeating task to the task manager and start it running
  %this.taskMgr.addTask( "checkIsDone();", -1 );
}
```

This onAdd() console method does the following.

- It is scoped to our (named) GUI ggsSplashToonFadeinBitmap.
- It sets the done field to false.
- It creates a new task manager using the newTaskManager() helper function.
  - Because we want this task manager to call all functions it executes in the scope of this GUI ("ggsSplashToonFadeinBitmap"), we'll tell the task manager to target %this (the handle of our GUI).
  - Also, this task manager will loop continuously, and we want it to use a default value of 100 milliseconds for the loop.
  - Lastly, it adds one task (checkIsDone();) and tells the task manager that this task is always rescheduled (i.e., it repeats forever).

```
function ggsSplashToonFadeinBitmap::onRemove( %this ) {
  %this.taskMgr.stopSelfExecution();
  %this.taskMgr.clearTasks();
  %this.taskMgr.delete();
}
```

This onRemove() console method does the following.

- It is scoped to our (named) GUI ggsSplashToonFadeinBitmap.
- It assumes the task manager is running and stops it.

- It deletes all outstanding tasks in the task manager.
- It tells the task manager to delete itself (the prior two steps were included to show that they exist, but be aware that deleting a task manager will stop execution of outstanding tasks, and clear the task list automatically).

onWake() and onSleep()

Now that we're ready to go, the `onWake()` method will be responsible for starting the task manager polling, and `onSleep()` will be responsible for stopping it.

```
function ggsSplashToonFadeinBitmap::onWake( %this ) {
  // Need to clear this as it only gets set to true
  // by the control
  %this.done = false;

  %this.taskMgr.selfExecuteTasks( true );
}
```

This `onWake()` console method does the following.

- It is scoped to our (named) GUI ggsSplashToonFadeinBitmap.
- It sets `done` to `false` again. This is a bit of overkill, but it is the safest way to deal with this. Now, the GUI is guaranteed to replay every time it wakes.
- It tells the task manager to start polling (self-executing). The argument `true` is telling the task manager to ignore any times specified for tasks and to instead use the task manager's default value, which we earlier set to 100 milliseconds.

```
function ggsSplashToonFadeinBitmap::onSleep( %this ) {
  %this.taskMgr.stopSelfExecution();
}
```

This `onSleep()` console method does the following.

- It is scoped to our (named) GUI ggsSplashToonFadeinBitmap.
- It tells the task manager to stop.

click()

If you recall, we want the user to be able to click the mouse at any time to skip this splash screen. The GuiFadeinBitmapCtrl control provides a callback named `click()` that is called when the control is awake and the mouse is clicked. We'll create an instance of this scoped to our GUI and make it do some work.

```
function ggsSplashToonFadeinBitmap::click( %this ) {
  %this.done = true;
}
```

This `click()` callback does the following.

- It is scoped to our (named) GUI ggsSplashToonFadeinBitmap.
- It sets done to true (we let the `checkIsDone()` task do all the real work).

The `checkIsDone()` Task

OK, we're almost done. The last bit of code is the console method that is supposed to check for done. When done is true, the splash screen will load the main menu.

```
function ggsSplashToonFadeinBitmap::checkIsDone( %this ) {
  if( %this.done ) {
    %this.taskMgr.stopSelfExecution();
    Canvas.setContent(ggsMainMenuTech);
  }
}
```

This `checkIsDone()` console method does the following:

- It is scoped to our (named) GUI ggsSplashToonFadeinBitmap.
- It checks for done equals true, and if it is true,
  - it stops the task manager, and
  - it sets the canvas content to the main menu (which we haven't made yet).

13.2.2 Main Menu (Toon)

We now have one working interface. Now, let's make the main menu interface.

Before you start, make sure you've got a template .gui file (like we described at the beginning of this chapter) in a directory where your main menu will be located and be sure that it is getting executed.

For this interface, you should use a template like the following (use your own name for the GUI).

```
new GuiChunkedBitmapCtrl(ggsMainMenuToon) {
  profile = "GuiDefaultProfile";
  horizSizing = "width";
  vertSizing = "height";
  position = "0 0";
  extent = "800 600";
```

Game Elements

```
minExtent = "8 2";
visible = "1";
bitmap = "./back"; // This is the image we're about to make.
useVariable = "0";
tile = "0";
}
```

The Main Menu Interface

Figure 13.3.

Graphic for main menu.

Make up a graphics file in your favorite editor that looks something like that in Figure 13.3. The image should be the same as our splash interface with a few differences. First, there is no label on this one. Second, it is a grayscale image. Third, I've made it a bit dark so it provides good contrast for our buttons (Figure 13.4). Copy your file (named "back.jpg") or the one from the GPGT Lesson Kit to the directory where your .gui file is.

For this menu, we're going to have three buttons: Play, Credits, and Quit. For each of these buttons, let's make graphics.

The graphics are going to be used by a bitmap button, so when we make them, we'll want to make four versions of each. The versions will be for the four states: normal, highlighted, depressed, and inactive. For example, our four Play button images can be seen in Figure 13.4.

Figure 13.4.

Four Play button images.

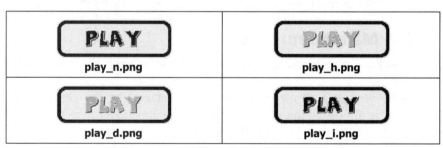

The images are all 24-bit PNG files measuring 640 × 480. Notice that "play_i.png" is the same as "play_n.png". We could in fact just create the normal, depressed, and highlighted versions of the button and not supply the inactive one since we don't need it. However, although the engine will automatically use the normal image for our missing inactive image if the need arises, it will print a warning message. I personally don't like warning messages, so I always supply a button for all four cases. We could just as easily use a 1 × 1 transparent PNG for the inactive button.

- Now, start the GPGT Lesson Kit.
- Using the GUI editor, open the main menu interface. At this point, your interface should look just like the first image we made ("back.jpg").
- Add three GuiBitmapButtonCtrl buttons to the GUI and arrange them so that they line up down the center. When you're done, the screen should look like Figure 13.5.

Figure 13.5.

Completed main menu.

The Main-Menu Interface Code

There is no separate code file for our main menu. All the code we need to write is embedded in the command field for each of the three buttons:

```
//Play Button =>
command = "quit();";

//Credits Button =>
command = "Canvas.setContent(ggsCreditsToon);";

//Quit Button =>
command = "quit();";
```

Currently, the Play button will quit (or in the case of the GPGT Lesson Kit version, it will go back to the "Game GUIs" menu). We'll change this to a play interface later when we finish our game.

The Credits button will load our credits interface as the contents of the canvas, and the Quit button quits.

13.2.3 Credits (Toon)

The next interface we'll make is the credits interface. This interface is quite similar to our main menu. In fact, it will use the very same template (obviously, in a new directory and with a new name). We use the very same JPEG image as we used for the main menu.

The credits interface is going to load and display the contents of a text file in an attractive manner. We're using an external source for the text content, because this makes it easy to edit and correct mistakes.

The Credits Interface

- Copy your template and the graphics file to a new directory and be sure that "init.cs" is executing them.

Game Elements

- Start the GPGT Lesson Kit.
- Using the GUI editor, open the credits interface. It should look just like our main menu did when we started working on it (see Figure 13.3).
- We're going to use a GuiMLTextCtrl to display our credits. To do this, we'll need a GuiScrollCtrl as the parent. So, using the GUI editor, add a GuiScrollCtrl to our credits interface and then make a GuiMLTextCtrl the child. When you're done, you should have something like the following.

```
new GuiScrollCtrl() {
  profile = "GuiScrollProfile";
  horizSizing = "center";
  vertSizing = "relative";
  position = "150 50";
  extent = "500 500";
  minExtent = "8 2";
  visible = "1";
  willFirstRespond = "1";
  hScrollBar = "alwaysOff";
  vScrollBar = "alwaysOff";
  constantThumbHeight = "0";
  childMargin = "4 4";
  new GuiMLTextCtrl(ggsCreditsToonMLText) {
    profile = "GuiDefaultProfile";
    horizSizing = "width";
    vertSizing = "bottom";
    position = "6 6";
    extent = "500 500";
    minExtent = "8 2";
    visible = "1";
    lineSpacing = "2";
    allowColorChars = "0";
    maxChars = "-1";
  };
};
```

You'll want to use your own name for the GuiMLTextCtrl, but it does need a name because we're going to write some code for it.

- Note that the GuiScrollCtrl uses the following settings.
  - It uses the default `profile`. We'll want to change this soon.
  - `horizSizing` and `vertSizing` of "center" and "relative" respectively. This means that the control will resize to take up all of the space of its parent from top to bottom and maintain an aspect ratio with its parent horizontally while staying centered.
  - The scroll bars are both turned off all the time.

- There is a small child margin.
- Note also that the GuiMLTextCtrl has the following settings.
  - It uses the default profile. We'll want to change this soon.
  - It resizes to fit the width and height of its parent.

Before we move on to the credits GUI code, let's do one more thing. We want the user to be able to press **ESC** in order to return to the main menu. The easiest way to do this is to create a button that uses the **ESC** key as an accelerator and then have it positioned off screen. This way, it won't render, but it will still respond to an **ESC** button press. The (abbreviated) code for this button would look like the following.

```
new GuiButtonCtrl() {
  // ...
  position = "-1 -1";
  extent = "1 1";
  command = "Canvas.setContent(ggsMainMenuToon);";
  accelerator = "escape";
};
```

Notice that the button is 1 × 1 pixel positioned at < –1, –1 >, thus putting it off screen. The command this button executes sets the main menu as the contents of the canvas.

Simply make this button a child of the credits interface, and it will work.

The Credits Interface Code

OK, at this point we have the GUI controls in place, but the GuiScrollCtrl and the GuiMLTextCtrl will be using default profiles. So, the current credits interface will look something like the image on the left in Figure 13.6, when we would rather it look more like the image on the right. To fix this problem, we'll need to write our own GuiControlProfile for the GuiScrollCtrl and for the GuiMLTextCtrl.

Figure 13.6.
Credits interface.

Custom Profiles

By default, the scroll profile uses either a Windows or OSX theme (based on your platform). Both themes use a completely white and opaque background and have a white border. Also, they both use a graphic for the scroll bars, arrow buttons, and the scroll thumb. Our needs are a little different, though. First, we want our background to be transparent (our image is dark enough to act as a background to our ML text). Second, we don't want to display any graphics.

We could make a completely new profile to meet our needs, but to make our lives easy, we'll make a profile that derives from the default GuiScrollProfile.

```
if(!isObject(gsToonCreditsScrollProfile))
  new GuiControlProfile ( gsToonCreditsScrollProfile :
                          GuiScrollProfile) {
    border = 0;
    opaque = false;
  };
```

This profile disables the border and sets the control to translucent (not opaque). The hidden benefit of inheriting from GuiControlProfile is that we can use its graphics array (which is required by the control), but since we're not rendering it, we don't really care what it is. That is, we don't have to create and specify a new bitmap array.

So, what about the GuiMLTextCtrl? We'll inherit again, but the only thing we need to change is the opacity of the control.

```
if(!isObject(gsToonCreditsMLTextProfile))
  new GuiControlProfile (gsToonCreditsMLTextProfile) {
    opaque = false;
  };
```

Great! Now we have the two profiles, but we need to decide where to put them. We could put them at the top of the .gui file, but I prefer to put my profiles in a separate .cs file. Then, I load the .gui file from the .cs file. This way, I can have profiles and console methods in one place and have that be separate from my interface definition. Please be sure that you load the .gui file *after* the profile definitions, or else the control will fail to be defined (they have to be defined to be used).

Filling the GuiMLTextCtrl

At this point, the only thing we have left to do is write some code to put text in the GuiMLTextCtrl, and then to write that text. To fill the GuiMLTextCtrl, we'll need two pieces of code. First, we'll need some code to read a file and dump the contents to the control.

```
// 1. Clear all content.
// 2. Open the file gsMLTextContent.txt (abort if not found)
// 3. Read the file and push the contents into this GuiMLTextCtrl

function gsToonCreditsMLTextProfile::reload( %this ) {
  %this.setValue(""); // Clear it
  %file = new FileObject();
  %fileName = expandFileName( "./gsMLTextContent.txt" );
  echo( "Attempt to open " , %fileName );
  %fileIsOpen = %file.openForRead( %fileName );
  echo( "Open for read " , (%fileIsOpen ? "succeeded" : "failed" ) );

  if( %fileIsOpen ) {
    while(!%file.isEOF()) {
      %currentLine = %file.readLine();
      echo(%currentLine);
      %this.addText( %currentLine, true );
    }
  }
  %this.forceReflow();

  %file.close();
  %file.delete();
}
```

This `gsToonCreditsMLTextProfile::reload()` console method does the following.

- It is scoped to our (named) ML text GUI gsToonCreditsMLTextProfile.
- It opens the file ".\gsMLTextContent.txt".
- It reads the file line by line until the end of the file and then closes it.
- It dumps every read line to the GuiMLTextCtrl using the `addText()` console method.
- After reading the contents of the file, it forces a reflow on the GuiMLTextCtrl.
- Lastly, it closes the file and deletes the file object.

In order to use our new file-reading code, we need to have the `onWake()` method call it.

```
function gsToonCreditsMLTextProfile::onWake( %this ) {
  %this.reload();
}
```

Finally, we make a new file named "./gsMLTextContent.txt" and put the following text in it:

```
<just:center>
<color:FFFFFF><spush><just:center>
<br><br>
<font:Comic Sans:40><color:b10028><shadowcolor:001a69>
      <shadow:1:1>My Big Game<spop><br><br>
<font:Palatino LinoType:36>Playground Productions <br><br>

<tab: 300, 300>
<just:left>
<spush><font:Arial Bold:18> Written by:
      Edward F. Maurina III
<color:b09100><shadowcolor:dddddd><shadow:1:1>
      Hall Of Worlds, LLC<br><br>
<spop>

<just:left>
<spush><font:Arial Bold:18> Brought to you by:
      GG Press (tm)
<color:b09100><shadowcolor:cccccc><shadow:1:1>
      Garage Games<br><br>
<spop>

<br><br><font:Arial Bold:16>
<spush>
<lmargin%:1>I just want to thank...<br><br>

<tab: 150, 300>
My Wife Teresa...<br><br>
The Staff at Garage Games, and...and...sniff<br><br>
You the customer...for making this possible... :)<br><br>

<br><br><br><br><br><br>

<spush><just:center>(Escape for Main Menu)<spop>
<spop>
```

We've gotten to the end of our Toon series. Now, you should do it all again, except use new graphics from the Tech series.

13.3 Tech-Themed Interfaces

If you're skipping ahead, please go back to the start of the Toon-themed series. If not, please take a look at the images in Figure 13.7. Now that you've seen the differences, please follow the steps outlined for the Toon series, but use new art for a sort of Tech theme (or choose your own theme). Please note that the Tech-themed menu adds a new button. You may add this if you wish, or add only the original three, skipping the Options button.

Splash Screen

Main Menu

Credits Screen

Figure 13.7.
Tech-themed screens.

Please feel free to use the images provided with the GPGT Lesson Kit. If you're copying my art, I expect that the second time through should only take about an hour or less to achieve. If you're making your own art, then most of your time will likely be spent making the art. That is, once you've got a working set of interfaces, it is quite easy to re-theme them: add a few extra touches here and there, and then you're done!

Now that you're feeling pretty good and you've become a bit of an expert at making GUIs, let's go make some HUDs.

13.4 Common HUDs

The last set of set of interfaces we will make in this book will be some common HUDs. The most common set of HUDs you'll find in video games are the following.

- **Counters.** Almost all video games use some kind of numeric feedback to give score, ammo count, health status, etc (see Figure 13.8a). Thus, we'll take the time to make a simple set of customizable counters that can handle up to nine digits.

- **Feedback bars.** If a game doesn't use numeric feedback, it will almost surely use some kind of graph instead (see Figure 13.8b). Often both are present. Thus, we'll make a vertical bar to supplement the horizontal bar that comes with TGE.

- **Strip compass.** OK, not all games have compasses, but I see requests for this kind of thing a lot, and the compasses that folks have submitted as resources are always popular. Problem is, all the compasses that folks have submitted are C++-based, and new users may not want to mess with the code. Thus, this strip compass is entirely TorqueScript based (see Figure 13.8c).

Figure 13.8.
Some common HUDS.

a. Counters.

b. Feedback bars.

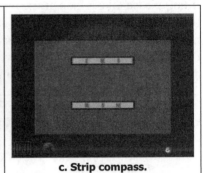

c. Strip compass.

13.4.1 Counter HUDs

A counter HUD should be flexible enough that the digits can be placed in any position, and also allow different styles of digits. We'll make a simple set of counters that use bitmap images for the digits. Additionally, we'll write scripts that handle up to nine digits (or actually a max count). This can be expanded if you need, but nine is usually enough. These counters will come with and without frames.

Counter HUD Images

Before we start, we'll need to make some graphics files for our counters. You can make your own graphics, or use the ones from the GPGT Lesson Kit.

- **Digits.** The GPGT Lesson Kit contains digital and comic-style digits in blue, green, and yellow. Additionally, gray digits are provided as templates so you can simply adjust the color and perhaps add other effects as you wish. All digits are 50 × 50 pixels.

0	1	2	3	4	5	6	7	8	9
0	1	2	3	4	5	6	7	8	9

- **Frames.** Optionally, you can create frames for the digits. The GPGT Lesson Kit includes several frame variations (corroded (not shown) and non-corroded).

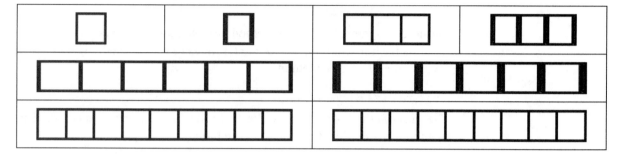

Counter HUD GUI Controls

Depending on how you choose to implement your counter, you'll have either two or three sets of GUI controls involved. All counters will have a GuiControl as a container for the digits, an optional GuiBitmapCtrl for the frame, and up to nine GuiBitmapCtrl controls for the digits (I count this as one set).

In order to build your HUD, follow these steps.

1. Add and position a GuiControl as a child of the interface that should contain this HUD.
2. Add the GuiBitmapCtrl controls that will be the digits as children of the GuiControl we just added.
3. Optionally, add the frame GuiBitmapControl as a child of the GuiControl.

These HUD controls need to have certain names.

1. The GuiControl container can have any name, but it needs some name for scoping our console methods.
2. The GuiBitmapCtrl digits need unique names of the form aDigit0, aDigit1, etc. Notice that they all have the same prefix but different numeric values.
3. The (optional) GuiBitmapCtrl for the frame does not need to be named.

Now that we've named the controls, we need to add some dynamic fields to the GuiControl container.

- **numDigits.** This should be between 1 and 9 (or greater if you modify the scripts to handle more digits).
- **digitTileName.** This should be the same as the prefix we used when naming the GuiBitmapCtrl controls used for the digits. In this example, the value would be "aDigit".
- **digitPath.** This field tells the scripts where to find the digit bitmap. This path can be relative or nonrelative and should be of the form ".\counters\ blueDigits\digi". Notice that there is no ending slash.

OK, now we're ready to write the scripts!

Game Elements

Count HUD Scripts

We need a minimum of three methods to use these counters: (1) a method to initialize the counter, (2) a `getCounterValue()` method, and (3) a `setCounterValue()` method.

initializeBitmaps()

The first method we need is the `initializeBitmaps()` method. This method is responsible for setting up the bitmaps.

```
function GuiControl::initializeBitmaps( %this ) {
  if( "" $= %this.digitPath ) return false;
  for( %count = 0; %count < 10 ; %count++ ) {
    %this.digitBitmap[%count] =
      expandFilename( %this.digitPath @ %count );
  }
}
```

This method basically expands the `digitPath` we supplied into a list of ten images, one per possible digit (0..9).

setCounterValue()

The main method we need is the `setCounterValue()` method. This method is responsible for actually displaying a numeric value.

```
function GuiControl::setCounterValue( %this , %newCount ) {
  // Check to be sure that the required fields have been set:
  //
  // numDigits - Number of digits in this counter
  // digitTileName - Prefix for tile names used in this
  //      counter (i.e. names of the controls)
  // digitPath - Path to tiles used in this counter
  //
  if( "" $= %this.numDigits ) return false;
  if( "" $= %this.digitTileName ) return false;
  if( "" $= %this.digitPath ) return false;

  // Store the currentCount
  %this.currentCount = %newCount;
  %newCountDigits = strlen( %newCount );

  if ( %newCountDigits > %this.numDigits ) { // Overflow
    for( %count = 0 ; %count < %this.numDigits ; %count++ ) {
      %tmpDigit[%count] = 9;
    }
  }
```

```
    else {
      // Pad with zeros so our 'newCount' string is exactly
      // %this.numDigits wide
      %tmpNewCount = "";
      for( %count = %this.numDigits - %newCountDigits ;
           %count > 0 ; %count-- ) {
        %tmpNewCount = %tmpNewCount @ "0";
      }

      %tmpNewCount = %tmpNewCount @ %NewCount;

      // Get digits in reverse order and store them
      for( %count = 0 ; %count < %this.numDigits ; %count++ ) {
        %tmpDigit[%count] = getSubStr( %tmpNewCount ,
                                %this.numDigits - 1 - %count , 1 );
      }
    }
  }
  // Change the bitmaps for each digit in the display
  for( %count = 0 ; %count < %this.numDigits ; %count++ ) {
    (%this.digitTileName @ %count).setBitmap(
      %this.digitBitmap[%tmpDigit[%count]] );
  }
  return true;
}
```

This method does the following.

- Checks that the required fields are present and ditches if they are not.

- Stores the new count value as the current count.

- Checks to see if the count that was passed is too large. If it is, all the digits are set to nine, and the counter ditches. This is an overflow case.

- If the basic checks are passed, the routine iterates over each count value and extracts the digit. Then it uses the extracted digit to assign a bitmap digit to the correct tile. By default, unset tiles are set to 0.

getCounterValue()

Because it is good to create symmetric functionality for game objects, we'll create a getCounterValue() method, too.

```
function guiControl::getCounterValue( %this ) {
  return %this.currentCount;
}
```

Game Elements

This function simply returns the `currentCount` value we stored in `setCounterValue()`.

As was previously mentioned, these scripts can be expanded to handle as many digits as you like. Also, as an exercise, you might try adding non-numeric handling code.

13.4.2 Vertical Feedback Bar HUDs

As mentioned above, an alternate to the digit counter is a feedback bar of some type. TGE comes with a horizontal bar, but I often wish to use a vertical (or other) style bar. TGE does come with a specialized vertical bar for the player's health/energy, but I prefer to use this scripted one. This HUD is used to represent a value between 0.0 and 1.0 in steps of 0.1. In this sample, the HUD is arranged as a vertical bar, but this code will handle having the indicator tiles in any configuration. However, helper code has been provided to make the design of a vertical bar easier. You'll have to write your own `resize()` method for other arrangements.

Vertical Feedback Bar HUD Images

The vertical feedback bar has one image: the frame for the HUD. Some sample frames are included in the GPGT Lesson Kit so you can use this right away. The templates for these frames are provided so you can modify them. The design of these vertical frames is important. If they are not designed properly, you will not be able to (successfully) use the provided `resize()` method. This method makes tile placement a cinch. So, let's discuss the design of this frame.

The provided frames all have the same properties (see Figure 13.9).

Figure 13.9.

Vertical feedback bar.

- There are eleven cells, and the top cell is a graphic indicating the type of indicator (damage or energy). You can put any graphic you like here by editing the provided templates. The bottom cells are for separating our feedback indicators.
- The top indicator cell starts at < 0, 50 >, and each cell after that is set at a delta of < 0, 45 > pixels.
- The complete image is 50 pixels wide and 500 pixels tall.

Overall, the frames included in the GPGT Lesson Kit have a kind of known symmetry and regularity; i.e., the cells that represent the indicators are not oddly shaped and do not exist at irregular spacings. We'll see why in a moment.

Vertical Feedback Bar HUD GUI Controls

As with the counters, the vertical feedback HUDs are composed of three sets of GUI controls. First, a GuiControl is used as the container for our HUD.

Second, a GuiBitmapCtrl is used as the frame for the HUD. Third, a set of GuiControl controls are used as the indicators. To make this last set of controls act as controls, we make custom profiles for them. We'll address this in the scripts section below. For now, let's assemble our HUD.

In order to build your HUD, follow these steps.

1. Add and position a GuiControl as a child of the interface that should contain this HUD.

2. Add the GuiControl controls that will be the indicators as children of the GuiControl we just added. Just make ten and place them at < 0, 0 > for now.

3. Add the frame GuiBitmapControl as a child of the GuiControl container.

4. Resize the container and the frame to have the same dimensions and be sure that the frame is above (in front of) the GuiControl indicators.

These HUD controls need to have certain names.

1. The GuiControl container can have any name, but it needs some name for scoping our console methods.

2. The GuiControl indicators need unique names of the form DamageBar0-**Indicator0**, DamageBar0**Indicator1**, etc. Notice that they all have the same prefix but different numeric values. The "Indicator" portion of the name is required.

3. The GuiBitmapCtrl for the frame needs to have a name of the form Damage-Bar0Indicator**Frame**. Notice that the prefix is the same as that for the indicators.

Now that we've named the controls, we need to add a dynamic field to the GuiControl container: `feedbackBarPrefix`. This should be a string containing the prefix you used for the indicators and frame. In this example, this field would contain `DamageBar0`.

OK, now we're ready to write the scripts!

Vertical Feedback Bar HUD Scripts

We have two kinds of scripting to do. First, we need to make some custom profiles for our GuiControl controls. Second, we have to make scripts update the bars. As an added bonus, we'll do an (optional) final script that will make positioning and creating these counters a cinch.

Custom Profiles

Our indicators are made from the GuiControl control. To make this work, we need a custom profile that will make these controls opaque with a predefined background color. Additionally, we may wish to make the container

GuiControl opaque with a different background color. These profiles will look like the following.

```
// A container profile
new GuiControlProfile (feedbackBarBackColorProfile0) {
   opaque = true;
   fillColor = "20 20 20 255";
};

// An indicator profile
new GuiControlProfile (feedbackBarIndicatorColorProfile0) {
   opaque = true;
   fillColor = "255 255 255 255";
};
```

The first profile is a gray color and used for the container. The second profile is a fully white color and used for the indicators. Please understand that, if it pleases you to do so, each indicator tile can have its own profile, and each can be a different color. Once you've created custom profiles, be sure they get loaded before the .gui file and then use them as the profile for your controls.

Feedback Scripts

The guts of this HUD are the scripts that update the display. I'm providing two methods, and as an exercise, you should modify them a bit and add a third. The two provided methods are setFeedbackGUIValue(), which sets the indicators based on a passed value, and flashIndicatorBar(), which is used to cause the changed indicator cells to flash (optionally, of course).

```
function GuiControl::setFeedbackGUIValue( %this , %value ) {
   // Check for the required indicator prefix field
   if("" $= %this.feedbackBarPrefix) return;

   // Generate an 'index' from %value
   if ("" $= %value) %value = 0;

   if(%value > 1.0)
      %value = 1;
   else if(%value < 0.0)
      %value = 0;
   else
      %value = %value;

   %this.curIndex = mFloor( 10 * %value );
```

```
for(%count = 1; %count <= 10; %count ++) {
  %toggleCheck =
    (%this.feedbackBarPrefix @ "Indicator" @ %count).isVisible();
    (%this.feedbackBarPrefix @ "Indicator" @ %count).setVisible(
      %this.curIndex >= %count );
  if( %toggleCheck !=
    (%this.feedbackBarPrefix @ "Indicator" @ %count).isVisible() ) {
    if( %this.flashTime > 0 ) {
      (%this.feedbackBarPrefix @ "Indicator" @
      %count).flashIndicatorBar( %this.flashTime );
    }
  }
}

%this.prevIndex = %this.curIndex;
%this.currentValue = %value;
}
```

This method does the following.

- Checks that the required field is present, and ditches if it is not.
- Checks that the count is between 0.0 and 1.0 and, if not, adjusts it so that it is.
- Because this method uses values between 0 and 10, it multiplies and further massages the value so that it meets our requirements.
- The method loops over each tile and decides whether it should be visible or not visible. If a tile is changed from visible to not visible, or vice versa, the flashIndicatorBar() method is called.
- The method finishes by saving the current index and actual values.

So, what about this flashing? It is a pretty common thing to have indicators flash when they change. So, as part of the fun, we're going to add this functionality.

```
function GuiControl::flashIndicatorBar( %this , %flashTime ) {
  %flashPeriod = %flashTime / 3;
  %isVisible = %this.isVisible();
  %this.schedule( %flashPeriod * 1 , "setVisible",
                  ! %isVisible );
  %this.schedule( %flashPeriod * 2 , "setVisible", %isVisible );
}
```

This method does the following.

- Divides the flash time into three parts.

- Toggles the indicator visibility.
- Schedules the indicator visibility to toggle again in one flash period, and then once more in two flash periods, for a total of three toggles.

Flashing is optional. I didn't mention it earlier, but if you want the indicator to flash when it changes, you'll need to add one more dynamic field to the frame: `flashTime`. This field should be the number of milliseconds you want the indicator to flash.

Design Helper Method

At this point, we've written all the required code. However, when designing this tutorial, I noticed that it was a real hassle to position the tiles. Thus, I've added another piece of code. This code is used to resize the frame and pre-position the indicator tiles. This version of the method only works for vertical bars.

```
function GuiControl::resizeVBAR( %this ) {
  // Check for the required indicator prefix field
  if("" $= %this.feedbackBarPrefix) return;
  if("" $= %this.originalframeDimensions) return;
  if("" $= %this.firstIndicatorY) return;
  if("" $= %this.IndicatorHeight) return;

  // Resize and reposition the frame first
  %ContainerWidth = getWord( %this.getExtent() , 0 );
  %ContainerHeight = getWord( %this.getExtent() , 1 );
  (%this.feedbackBarPrefix @ "Frame").resize(
      0 , 0 , %ContainerWidth , %ContainerHeight );

  // Resize and reposition the indicators
  %originalFrameWidth = getWord(
          %this.originalframeDimensions , 0 );
  %originalFrameHeight = getWord(
          %this.originalframeDimensions , 1 );
  %resizdFirstIndicatorY = (
          %this.firstIndicatorY / %originalFrameHeight)
          * %ContainerHeight;
  %indicatorHeightDelta = (
          %this.IndicatorHeight / %originalFrameHeight)
          * %ContainerHeight;
  %indicatorY = %resizdFirstIndicatorY;
  for(%count = 10; %count >= 1; %count --) {
  (%this.feedbackBarPrefix @ "Indicator" @ %count).
    resize( 0 , %indicatorY , %ContainerWidth ,
          %indicatorHeightDelta );
```

```
        %indicatorY = %indicatorY + %indicatorHeightDelta;
    }
}
```

This method relies on the presence of some new dynamic fields:

- **originalFrameDimensions.** This two-element integer vector contains the width and height of the original frame graphic. In the samples this is "50 500".
- **firstIndicatorY.** This is an integer value that denotes top-to-bottom *y*-offset of where the first indicator should be. In our sample, this is would be at pixel "50".
- **IndicatorHeight.** This is an integer value specifying the full-size height of each indicator cell.

Knowing what these value are, the method does the following.

- Checks that the required fields are present, and ditches if they are not.
- Calculates the new size of the container.
- Grabs the original frame width and height.
- Calculates the new resized height for the first cell.
- Repositions and resizes the frame.
- Calculates the delta height for each indicator cell.
- Loops over the indicator cells and repositions and resizes each.

Why is this even necessary? Well, as I mentioned, when you move the frame around and resize the elements, it becomes a real hassle to keep everything properly aligned. This is compounded by the fact that, when we open and close the editor to edit and test the GUI, the GUI controls are often resized and repositioned.

13.4.3 Strip Compass HUD

Our last HUD is a compass displayed as a strip. I call this a strip compass, but you can call it whatever you like. Basically, the challenge here is to make a 2D representation of what is fundamentally a 3D object, and to do so in script. This compass is designed to take a pointing vector and translate that to a compass direction. It is assumed that $+y$ is north and $+x$ is east (as is the case in the TGE world model).

Strip Compass HUD Images

The strip compass has two image files: (1) the frame and (2) the strip (Figure 13.10). As you can see, the frame is fairly simple. It has an outer strip, a center marker, and a screen. This screen is mostly translucent and the whole thing is designed to overlay the strip.

Figure 13.10.

A strip compass.

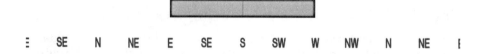

The strip may seem odd at first. It seems to be a lot larger than what it needs to be. In fact, because we want to make it possible to display any point on the compass by shifting our strip leftward, it needs to be wide enough and contain enough elements to show all compass points along its leftward travel. This means we need twelve points on the compass, versus the standard eight. Four are repeated.

The provided strip is 1200 pixels wide and 50 pixels tall. The frame is 400 pixels wide and 50 pixels tall.

Strip Compass HUD GUI Controls

The strip compass has three GUI controls that are used to represent it: (1) a GuiControl used as a container, (2) a GuiBitmapCtrl used as the strip, and (3) a GuiBitmapCtrl used as the frame.

When we place our controls, they are placed as follows.

1. The container control is placed as a child of some GUI (i.e., whatever interface contains the compass). The dimensions of this control are "400 50". This control should be named.

2. The strip is placed as a child of the container at "0 0". The dimensions of this control are "1200 50". This control *must* be named.

3. The frame is placed as a child of the container (covering the strip) at "0 0". The dimensions of this control are "400 50".

For scripting purpose, the container control needs two dynamic fields.

- **stripName.** This field contains the name of our strip control.

- **stripWidth.** This field contains the pixel width of the original graphics file used for the strip.

Please note that if you require the strip and frame to be of a different dimension, you may resize them prior to saving your work, but—and this is a big but—please be sure that you maintain the same ratio between the frame width and the strip width. In addition, be sure that the stripWidth dynamic field matches the width you've chosen for the control; i.e., if you choose to shrink the control by half, the dimensions and fields would be as follows.

- `Container = "200 25"`
- `Strip = "600 25"`
- `Frame = "200 25"`
- `container.StripWidth` (dynamic field) = 600

Strip Compass HUD Scripts

If you don't have a good grasp of 3D graphics mathematics, you should probably stop at this point and go bone up by reading the appendix in Akenine-Möller and Haines's *Real-Time Rendering, Second Edition* (A K Peters, Ltd., 2002) or whatever book(s) you use as reference. Once you are properly girded, carry on.

It is a well-known fact that we can convert a two-dimensional vector (i.e., in a plane) into a 360-degree angular value theta, where theta is the rotation about a vector perpendicular to the plane and represents the rotation from some arbitrary location. In other words, we're going to use the dot-product and some things we know about the TGE world to calculate an angle.

```
function GuiControl::updateCompass( %this , %facingVector) {
  // Check for the required fields stripName and stripWidth.
  if ( "" $= %this.stripName ) return;
  if ( "" $= %this.stripWidth ) return;
  // Normalize the facing vector (just in case)
  %facingVector = vectorNormalize( %facingVector );

  // We can use the dot product and some tricks to figure out
  // what part of how we should position our strip to properly
  // indicate our facing direction.
  %leftFacing = ( vectorDot( "1 0 0" , %facingVector ) < 0) ? true : false;

  // remember 0 1 0 is forward, and that we can get the angle
  // between X and Y in radians using the DOT product:
  %forwardTheta = vectorDot( "0 1 0" , %facingVector );

  // Now, knowing our facing and theta, we can calculate
  // our right-hand rotation about Z in degrees:
  if( %leftFacing ) {
    %rotationDegrees = 360 - ( mACos( %forwardTheta ) *
                              180.0 / 3.1415927);
  }
  else {
    %rotationDegrees = mACos( %forwardTheta ) *
                              180.0 / 3.1415927;
  }
```

```
// We've created a strip that is three times as wide as
// the frame, giving it 12 compass points vs. the normal 8.
//
// If we calculate our rotation as a percentage, account
// the ratio 8/12, and scale based on our current extent
// vs. the pre-scaled width of the image, we can
// calculate the exact position to place the strip at:
%curPosY = getWord( %this.stripName.getPosition() , 1 );
%curExtX = getWord( %this.stripName.getExtent() , 0 );
%curExtY = getWord( %this.stripName.getExtent() , 1 );

%percentageRot = %rotationDegrees / 360.0;
%extentRatio = %curExtX / %this.stripWidth;

// recall this is a left-shift
%newPosX = -1 * (8 / 12 * %percentageRot * %extentRatio
                 * %this.stripWidth);
%this.stripName.resize( %newPosX, %curPosY, %curExtX,
                        %curExtY );
}
```

This method does the following.

- Checks that the required fields are present, and ditches if they are not.
- Normalizes the facing vector to make it nicer to work with.
- Checks to see if we are left- or right-facing. The dot-product only provides the angle between two vectors, up to 180 degrees. Thus, we need to determine which half of the circle this is to get the whole picture.
- Calculates the right-hand rotation about a vector "0 0 1", which is the TGE world up vector.
- Calculates the linear offset for the strip based on some known quantities, including the current angle of rotation, strip width, and the ratio of the normal points (8) to actual points (12) on the strip.
- Repositions and resizes the strip.

13.5 Summary

In this chapter, we examined several GUI controls working in tandem to produce new and useful results.

We discussed the following standard interfaces.

- **Splash screens.** This is a basic screen, of which most games have at least one and often several. They are used to display many different kinds of information, including the game title, company logos, and even interlevel art.

- **Main menus.** This interface really needs no introduction, but we did learn about how to implement it and then to hook other interfaces to it.
- **Credits screens.** This is another common interface, used to thank the folks who worked hard on your game, to provide additional information, etc.

As part of the above effort, we produced two variations of each interface (Toon and Tech themes) for a grand total of six interfaces.

Having completed the more serious discussion, we then launched into a discussion of HUDs and learned how to make the following three useful HUDs.

- **Counters.** The counter HUD is seen in almost every game in some form or another, making it worthwhile to explore one means of creating one.
- **Vertical feedback bars.** Another prevalent HUD is the feedback bar. Since Torque already supports a horizontal bar, we worked together to create a vertical version using only scripts and GUI controls.
- **Strip compasses.** Lastly, to show that C++ is nice but not necessary for creating HUDs with complicated behaviors, we made a strip compass. This HUD represents a 3D compass that rotates. We produced the same effect in 2D using a little bit of math knowledge and the powerful and useful TorqueScript language.

Making the Game

Chapter 14
Putting It All Together

14.1 Maze Runner: A Simple Single-Player Game

Maze Runner is a simple platform game brought into the 3D realm. It isn't based on a specific game, but it is inspired by games I have played. My purpose for this game was not to create a new blockbuster but rather to provide an easy-to-understand game idea upon which we could hang examples as we worked through the guide.

A 60-second summary of this game would read something like the following.

In this game, you run around a maze and pick up coins. Your goal is to pick up all the coins while avoiding various obstacles. Mazes will vary in size and in scope. They may run along one level, or have multiple levels. Along the way, as you hunt for all of the coins, you will need to avoid disappearing bridges that may drop you to a lower level or into a fiery cauldron below. You will be blocked by fireballs and impassable chasms. To get around these obstacles, you will have to use your ingenuity and the occasional teleport station. Timing, awareness of your surroundings, agility, and a little luck are all required for winning. You will start with three lives and gain a new life for each level you complete. To continue the game, pick up all of the coins and move on to the next level. Get the highest score and win the admiration of your peers! Good luck.

14.2 Game Elements

Let's stop for a moment and define the term *game element*. This is a term that I am using to describe any and all of the pieces that are used to create a game. For example, all of the following listed items are game elements:

- **The game view.** This general term incorporates point of view, field of view, and other view-related concepts and describes the end view of our game. We discuss this in Chapter 7, "Gameplay Classes."

- **Interfaces and HUDs.** However much we might wish to ignore it, all games require some GUI work and will have a variety of interfaces (splash screens, main menus, play GUIs, etc.) and some HUDs (counters, indicator bars, etc.).

- **Players and opponents.** Although we could certainly have a game with no directly identifiable players or opponents, 3D games generally do have at least one model representing the player and other models opposing this player in some fashion.

- **Weapons.** This seems pretty straightforward, but what I really mean here is weapons *and weapon analogues*. The analogue, in this case, is something that functions like a weapon but may not necessarily do damage.

- **The world.** This is a rather large game element and is in fact composed of a multitude of subelements, including terrain, water, the sky, environmental objects (trees, rocks, grass, etc.), environmental effects (rain, wind, lightning, the sun(s) and planets, etc.), structures (buildings, fences, bridges, etc.), sounds, and so on.

- **Power-ups and pickups.** These are items that are often at the core of a game and are meant to be interacted with. Sample items in this category would be coins, gems, weapons, ammunition, health packs, etc.

- **Special effects.** Here we are talking about eye and ear candy. These do have a place in gameplay, but they are often not directly tied to interaction, which is where we should focus our attention first.

- **Miscellaneous elements.** This last category is a grab bag for elements that don't fit anywhere specifically. Some examples are inventory systems, collision detection and response, damage and energy, and general scripting tasks.

Now, armed with an idea of what a game element is, let's list the game elements in our game.

14.2.1 Maze Runner: Game Elements

The finished game has the following elements and attributes.

- **Interfaces.** Splash screen GUI, main menu GUI, credits GUI, and play GUI.

- **Game view.** The game can be played in 3rd POV only.

- **Player.** The initial player will be the Blue Guy that comes with the FPS Starter Kit. We will later design our own player. This player will be an example of the simplest possible player that can be used in a game.

- **Opponents.** There are no opponents in this game, but some suggestions will be provided for adding them if you wish to expand on this game later.

- **The world.** The game world is a simple cauldron-shaped pit. This pit will contain a lake of lava. Our maze will consist of individual shapes that we place using scripts and level-definition files. We will place some environmental objects to spruce the place up. Additionally, there will be a sky box, celestial bodies, clouds, wind, rain, and even lightning. We're going all out on special effects to show how to use as many Torque features as is reasonable.

- **Obstacles.** There are two types of active obstacles and three static obstacles. The active obstacles include level blocks (individual and grouped) that fade, disappear, and reappear over time. There are also blocks that shoot fireballs in any of eight fixed compass directions (N, NE, E, SE, S, SW, W, NW), or down, or any of the prior directions, but randomly. The static obstacles are open horizontal spaces between blocks, vertical spaces between blocks, and blocks themselves.

- **Getting around.** To get around the maze, the player will run and jump. Also, there can be up to three distinct teleport stations; that is, teleport stations can be grouped in sets, and there can be up to three distinct sets of teleport stations in a level. Additionally, if any set contains more than two stations, entering one station will randomly send the player to any one of the other stations in the set.

- **Pickups and power-ups.** The only pickup in the game is the coin. Picking up all coins is the primary goal. A HUD will show the total coins picked up and the number of coins remaining for the level.

- **Inventory system.** We will use the "Simple Inventory" system that comes with this guide and is described in Chapter 7, "Gameplay Classes." It will provide all the mechanics necessary to pick up coins and remove them from the game world.

- **Miscellaneous "glue" scripts.** We will end up writing quite a few scripts to tie the game together, to track the score and our lives count, as well as to load the levels.

14.3 Game Goals, Rules, and Mechanics

Great! Now we know generally what the game is about and what elements it has. The last thing we need to do is describe how the individual game elements interact.

The goal of this game is very simple: score as high as possible by finishing as many levels as possible before losing all of your lives.

The rules and mechanics for this game are as follows.

- **Pick up all the coins.** Picking up all coins on a level ends the level and takes the player to the next level.

- **Stay alive.** Falling into the lava below or getting hit by a fireball kills the player.

- **Gain lives.** To gain more lives, simply complete a level. One new life is gained for each level completed.

- **Teleporting.** We can place up to three sets of teleport stations. Each set may have two or more stations. If there are only two stations in a set, the stations will teleport back and forth between each other. If a set has three or more stations, the spawn point will be randomly selected. Teleporting occurs by running over a station. The destination station will be temporarily disabled to avoid infinite teleport loops. It will not operate again until you walk off the station. Teleporting is not instantaneous, so be careful about fireballs that cross stations, as you are temporarily unable to move when teleporting.

- **Respawning.** When the player is killed, it will respawn in the location where it was first dropped into the game.

- **Level loading.** To make this game easily maintainable, tunable, and modifiable by players, all level loading is controlled by a text file (the level file). Players can add new levels and redefine levels to their hearts' content.

14.4 Setting Up Our Workspace

Before we can work on any lessons, we must first set up a work area. Everything that you need to do this is supplied on the CD that comes with this guide. If you examine the CD, you will find the following directories.

- **"\Appendices".** This directory contains the GPGT appendices.
- **"\Base".** This directory contains data and scripts that are used in the lessons and can also be used later to make new games. Please see the "Lesson Kit Assets" appendix for additional information about the contents of this directory.
- **"\GPGT LessonKit".** This directory contains the GPGT lesson kit. For more information about it, please read the "Lesson Kit User's Guide" appendix.
- **"\MazeRunner".** Excluding the data and scripts in "\Base" and some content we will copy from the TGE demo that you should install using one of the installers found in "\TorqueDemoInstallers", this directory contains all of the unique resources and scripts required to build the MazeRunner prototype.
- **"\MazeRunnerAdvanced".** This directory contains a completed version of MazeRunner with several additional features as suggested in Section 14.10, "Improving The Game".
- **"\TorqueDemoInstallers".** This directory contains installers for TGE.

If you are a Linux user, I must apologize. At the time this book went to print, version 1.4 of TGE for Linux was still being worked on. Please check the GarageGames website to see if it is ready and, if so, download the demo kit. Otherwise, I suggest using one of the other versions of the engine in the interim.

At this time, if you do not have the demo installed on your machine, please do so by running the appropriate installer (based on your computer and operating system type). Once you have finished, please continue reading.

14.4.1 Starting from Torque Demo

First, be sure to install a copy of the TGE demo using one of the installers found in "\TorqueDemoInstallers". Feel free to install this anywhere you please. While writing our game, we will be copying files out of the installed demo to a working directory.

Second, let's make a new (working) directory named "MazeRunner" and place it on a drive with at least 100 MB of free space. We'll want some elbow room while we work. Please note, while we are writing our game (reading the numbered lessons), this is the directory we will be working in. We will be copying materials from the CD to this directory and editing them in some places. Do not confuse this with the GPGT Lesson Kit which is also included on the CD. The GPGT Lesson Kit is a separate application containing several mini-tools and samplers. To learn more about this application you should read Appendix B, "GPGT Lesson Kit Docs."

Third, now that we have a place to work, let's copy the entire contents of the TGE demo directory (from wherever we installed it in step one) into our new directory "MazeRunner".

14.4.2 Write Cleanup Scripts

It is a good idea to have the ability to remove temporary files from a working directory. If we remove all compiled scripts (DSOs) before rerunning the engine, we are insuring that only new script content will be used. Additionally, it is a good idea to occasionally remove terrain lighting files (ML). To accomplish these two tasks, we will write some scripts.

> The demo kit may include a set of cleanup scripts. Regardless, please read this section so you understand the reason for creating them.

The first script (if you are running Windows) will be a batch file called "DELDSO.bat". It is used to delete all compiled script files (DSO cleaning) and contains the following simple line of script.

```
del /S /F *dso
```

In UNIX/Linux/OSX, the file would be "deldso", and the content of the file is the following.

```
rm -rf *dso
```

The second file (if you are running Windows) will be called "DELML.bat". It is used to delete all terrain lighting files (ML cleaning) and contains the following simple line of script.

```
del /S /F *ml
```

In UNIX/Linux/OSX, the file would be "delml", and the content of the file is the following.

```
rm -rf *ml
```

We'll run the DSO cleaner each time we modify our scripts, and occasionally we'll run the ML cleaner to get rid of stale lighting files.

14.4.3 Copy Mod Directory

Although it is possible to modify the demo to create MazeRunner, it will be far simpler to start with a blank slate instead. To that end, a bare-bones mod has been provided. To start with this mod, please copy "\MazeRunner\ A_SettingUp\prototype" from the accompanying disk into "\MazeRunner".

14.4.4 Modify "main.cs"

Next, edit "main.cs" and change line 6 from this:

```
$defaultGame = "demo";
```

to this:

```
$defaultGame = "prototype";
```

This will use our new "prototype" mod instead of the demo mod.

14.4.5 Add Systems Scripts

The accompanying disk comes with a number of scripts that are provided to simplify your game-writing endeavors. We discuss some of these scripts in the guide, and those we do not discuss are documented in the "Scripted Systems" appendix.

From the accompanying disk, please copy the "\Base\Scripts\EGSystems" directory into "\MazeRunner\prototype".

Then, edit the onStart() function in "\MazeRunner\prototype\main.cs" so it looks like the following (bold lines are new code).

```
function onStart() {
  // Maze Runner Changes Begin -->
  exec("./EGSystems/SimpleInventory/egs_SimpleInventory.cs");
  exec("./EGSystems/SimpleTaskManager/egs_SimpleTaskManager.cs");
  exec("./EGSystems/Utilities/egs_ArrayObject.cs");
  exec("./EGSystems/Utilities/egs_Misc.cs");
  exec("./EGSystems/Utilities/egs_Networking.cs");
  exec("./EGSystems/Utilities/egs_SimSet.cs");
  exec("./EGSystems/Utilities/egs_String.cs");
  // <-- Maze Runner Changes End
  //.. leave remaining code alone
```

14.4.6 Add Maze Runner Data

You are not expected to create your own content for this game. I have included all of the models, textures, and sounds you will need.

From the accompanying disk, please copy the following directories.

1. "\Base\Data\GPGTBase" directory into "\MazeRunner\prototype\data", and

2. "\MazeRunner\A_SettingUp\MazeRunner" directory into "\MazeRunner\prototype\data".

14.4.7 Create Maze Runner Scripts Directory

Although we will not be placing anything in it yet, in preparation for our lessons, let's create the directory "\MazeRunner\prototype\server\scripts\MazeRunner".

14.4.8 Test Run

After saving the modified "main.cs" and "prototype\main.cs", run the executable you placed in "MazeRunner", and the prototype should start up. If it does not, please retrace your steps and see if you missed something.

Windows Users

On Windows platforms, some users will get a warning about a missing or wrong sound setup. If, and only if, you get this message, copy the "\Maze-Runner\A_SettingUp\OpenAL32.dll" file (found on the accompanying disk) into your "MazeRunner" directory and try again.

If that does not work, read through the "Getting Help" section in Chapter 1 of this guide.

14.4.8 Ready To Start

OK, if you got the executable to run, you're ready to start.

14.5 90 Percent or 10 Percent?

If we ignore the iterative nature of game creation, we can roughly divide game development into two parts: the first 90 percent and the last 10 percent.

I know, that probably sounds like a bunch of tripe, but bear with me for a moment.

The first 90 percent should be all about planning and implementing. The last 10 percent should be about polishing. If you are doing the polishing first or spending too much time creating polished content, you are simply wasting your time.

The above percentages do not have anything to do with the duration of tasks but rather with the amount of effort that you should put into these two parts when making your *prototype*.

You may have the goal of making games for fun or making them for profit (hopefully for both). In the end, either goal will only be accomplished by focusing on getting your game from the idea state to a playable state as fast as you can.

Without a doubt, nice art, clean interfaces, and special effects are very important to a game and to its ability to sell, but in order to have something to sell, you must first have something to play. Some special effects and artistic elements are critical to the playability of a game, but most are not (this does not negate their value in the final version of a game).

To find out if a game is fun, you must be able to play it. Thus, the only goal you should have is to get the game you are working on to a playable stage.

Often, when you play with your game prototype, you will find that an idea that seemed great doesn't really work or just isn't really fun. Just as often, you may be surprised to find that things you didn't plan on doing turned out to be really fun and/or cool. In either case, you'll never know until you play your game.

In this guide, we do lessons that can be considered either part of the 90 percent or part of the 10 percent. To help you, those lessons that are related to game playability have been marked as "Maze Runner Lesson (90 Percent Step)," and those that are important to the look and feel of the game have been marked as "Maze Runner Lesson (10 Percent Step)." You can safely skip the latter lessons and the game will still be playable.

As a parting note, just remember this when you are tempted to work on 10 percent stuff first:

While a 90 percent is probably a B, 10 percent is definitely an F.

14.6 Returning to Chapter 2?

You may be reading this as a result of having been directed here from the end of Chapter 1. If so, you should now return to Chapter 2, "Torque from 10,000 Feet," and continue from there. Otherwise, feel free to continue here.

14.7 Finishing the Prototype

Thus far, you have probably been working your way through the guide, learning about various features of the Torque Game Engine. Along the way, we have stopped to do little lessons that created one or more game elements to be used in the game.

At this point, we don't really have a playable game. We have just a short distance to go before our game reaches the playable prototype stage. To get our game ready for play testing we must do the following two things.

1. **Finish gameplay code.** At this point, we can start the Maze Runner mission and then manually load a level, but our player doesn't get moved to the right spot on the level, and there is pretty much no interaction. We need to change this. Specifically, we need to make the levels load automatically, have the player die when struck by a fireball or after falling into the lava, load the next level when all the coins are collected, and award our player with a new life on a successful level completion.

2. **Improve feedback.** With the final mechanics in place, we need to provide just a little more feedback to the player. Specifically, we need to update the play GUI to show how many lives we have, how many coins we've collected (score), and how many coins are left for a level. Also, while we are about this, we will add sounds for the fireball firing and explosions and then add some GUI sounds and music to make if feel like a completed package.

14.8 Finish Gameplay Code

By this point, you should be feeling pretty comfortable with TorqueScript and with navigating the prototype directory structure. So, the kid gloves are coming off. In the next few pages, we will run through some terse discussions. We will examine newly added scripts and modifications to scripts we discussed in prior lessons.

14.8.1 Copy Required Files

Before we continue, please do the following.

1. Copy "\MazeRunner\MazeRunner_Post_Finishing_the_Prototype\prototype2" into "\MazeRunner\".
2. Copy "\MazeRunner\MazeRunner_Post_Finishing_the_Prototype\main.cs" into "\MazeRunner\".

The new "main.cs" file points to the newly added "prototype2" mod directory. The directory "prototype2" contains all of the changes we are about to discuss and is ready to play, if you would like to try it before continuing.

14.8.2 Breaking the Law

The first thing we will do is break the law. OK, we're not breaking the law, but we are doing something that I warned you *not* to do earlier. Namely, we are going to make a global variable for tracking the ID of the player. Then, we are going to use it to implement gameplay scripts and later to keep our interfaces up to date.

We are, in effect, ignoring the client-server divide. This is both good and bad. It is good because it makes writing the scripts for our single-player game simple. It is bad because it ties us to a single-player game *only*. If later we decide to make this game support multiple players, we will experience at least some pain modifying our scripts to handle this new mode.

So, why are we doing this? Well, first, I know that in this book we will only ever play this game in single-player mode. Second, the game is simple enough that later, if you do convert this to multiplayer, the pain won't be too bad and it will serve as an excellent object lesson in making good decisions.

Making the Game

Excuses and reason aside, we must implement this change. To do so, I have modified the method `GameConnection::createPlayer()` in "game.cs" to look like the following (bold lines are new code):

```
function GameConnection::createPlayer(%this, %spawnPoint) {
  // Create the player object
  %player = new Player() {
    dataBlock = MazeRunner; // Change this line
    client = %this;
  };
  MissionCleanup.add(%player);
  $Game::Player = %player; // MazeRunner
```

Now, whenever we want the player's ID, we can just reference the global `$Game::Player`.

14.8.3 Automatic Startup

To this point, we have been manually loading missions by typing `buildLevel(0);`. That is just fine for testing purposes, but we really need the game to load when the mission is loading.

Experiments in Loading

If we examine the "game.cs" file closely, we will see that it has a variety of functions and methods. Among these are some promising-sounding places to put a script for automatically loading our first level.

- **onMissionLoaded().** Hmmm... this sounds good. The mission is loaded, so we should be good to go.
- **startGame().** This sounds good, too. I mean, we do want to start the game, right?
- **GameConnection::createPlayer().** OK, maybe you wouldn't think of this one. This is a hint, actually.

Great, we have some possible places to do the level loading, but what are the steps we need to follow in order to load our level?

Can we simply put a `buildLevel()` call in one of these? Why don't we try it? Add the following code to the end of `onMissionLoaded()` (bold lines are new code).

```
  startGame();
  buildLevel(0);
}
```

After restarting the game and reloading the mission, this may work, or it may work partially, or the game may hang. It depends.

At this point in the game startup process, there is some ambiguity in timing due to latencies that can vary from run to run. This means that any of the following actions can occur.

1. The game starts correctly, and the player is on the correct spawn point. This is what we want. Unfortunately, this doesn't always happen.

2. The level loads and the player gets dropped on the safe spawn point—end of story. Now we're stuck.

3. If timing conspires against you, all the resources that need to have been loaded won't be ready, and the loading code will just hang. This is the worst possibility.

So, what is happening here? Well, the mission was loaded, but the player had not been created yet, so our scripts for moving the player can't work. They have no object to move. (If you're curious, you can see the player-moving script by looking at the `playerDrop()` function in "levelloader.cs".)

Since putting `buildLevel()` after `startGame()` didn't work, that pretty much rules out our placing the function call in `startGame()`, too. What about `GameConnection::createPlayer()`, then? Let's try that next.

```
%this.player = %player;
%this.setControlObject(%player);

BuildLevel(0); //MazeRunner
}
```

Perfect! This is guaranteed to work properly every time. The level is always loaded after the player is created, so the scripts have valid object IDs to work with.

14.8.4 Dying

Another problem with our prior revision of this game was that we didn't get killed by the lava or fireballs. Let's remedy that now.

KillZone

To be killed by the lava, we need some way to know we're in it. Now, we could make our water block into a lava block by changing the water type. However, as part of our game design, we chose to make the player invincible, so this won't really help. I mean, we could in theory make our player have a very low damage level, make it damageable, and then maybe, just maybe, falling in the lava would kill him.

The thing is, we don't really want the player object to be destroyed. We just want to decrement a life and move to the spawn point. When a player

Making the Game

object is in the destroyed/dead state (`getState()` returns "dead"), the player will no longer move or take move commands until it is replaced with a new instance. This is by design and is not what we want in this instance.

So, long story short, we get creative. Let's create a really big trigger (named KillZone) and place it in the lava. Then, we can just write an `onEnterTrigger()` callback that will take away a life and move us to the spawn point. Perfect!

```
datablock TriggerData(KillZoneTrigger) {
  tickPeriodMS = 100;
};

function KillZoneTrigger::onEnterTrigger(%DB , %Trigger ,
                                          %Obj) {
  %Obj.loseALife();
}
```

The above code defines the datablock for this trigger, and the callback calls the method `loseALife()` (described below) on the object entering the trigger. But what about placement? The following code will do the placement.

```
function buildKillZone() {
  new Trigger(KillZone) {
    position = "-256 256 40";
    rotation = "1 0 0 0";
    scale  = "512 512 25";
    dataBlock = "KillZoneTrigger";
    polyhedron = "0.0000000 0.0000000 0.0000000 1.0000000
                  0.0000000 0.0000000 0.0000000 -1.0000000
                  0.0000000 0.0000000 0.0000000 1.0000000";
  };
  MissionGroup.add( KillZone );
}
```

Then we can add a call to this code in `onMissionLoaded()` to do the creation (bold lines are new code):

```
function onMissionLoaded() {
  buildKillZone(); // MazeRunner
  startGame();
}
```

So, what about that `loseALife()` thing?

Player::loseALife()

The easiest way to handle removing lives is to make a method scoped to the Player class (so it can be called on the Player object) that handles all of the bookkeeping. This simplifies things greatly. Yes, right now only two things can kill the player, but later you might add more, and having killing code all over the place would be very bad.

Here is the code (located in "mazerunnerplayer.cs").

```
function Player::loseALife( %player ) {
  // 1
  %player.lives--;

  // 2
  if( %player.lives <= 0 ) {
    schedule( 0 , 0 , endGame );
    return;
  }

  // 3
  %player.setVelocity("0 0 0");
  %player.setTransform(%player.spawnPointTransform);
}
```

This code does the following.

1. It decrements the player's life counter. (Yes, we haven't talked about this yet. It's coming up soon.)

2. It checks to see if all of our lives are gone and then schedules a call to endGame() (in "game.cs") to unload the mission, destroy the player, disconnect the client from the server, and get us back into the main menu.

Why not call endGame() directly?

You may wonder why we schedule a call to endGame() instead of calling it directly.

The reason we do this is that, when we call endGame(), we indirectly cause the player to be deleted.

However, the player is the object that the loseALife() method was called on, so when the engine tries to return from the call to endGame(), it will not have anywhere to return to. **This will crash the engine.**

The lesson here is to never delete the current object in a method that is called on that object. Always defer that deletion by using a call to schedule().

Calling schedule() with a time of 0 milliseconds tells the engine to run the function as soon as possible after returning from all nested function calls. In practice, this will always be on the next processing cycle or later.

3. If the game is not over, the player is moved back to its last spawn point. This information is stored in the player by `playerDrop()` in the file "levelloader.cs":

```
$Game::Player.spawnPointTransform = (%actX SPC %actY SPC
                                     $CurrentElevation);
```

Initial Lives

In order to take away lives, we must have lives to take. The best place to add initial lives to the player is either in its `onAdd()` method or at the location where we create it. I chose the `onAdd()` method (in "mazerunnerplayer.cs"; bold lines are new code):

```
function MazeRunner::onAdd( %DB , %Obj ) {
  Parent::onAdd( %DB , %Obj );
  %Obj.lives = 3;
}
```

Fireballs

OK, we got a little off topic there, but we're back now. The next question is: how do fireballs kill?

The projectile object has an `onCollision()` callback that is called for collisions with any world object. So, if we write a version of this callback in the namespace of our projectile, we can have that callback check to see if the player was hit and call `loseALife()`.

```
function FireBallProjectile::onCollision( %projectileDB ,
                                          %projectileObj ,
                                          %collidedObj ,
                                          %fade , %vec ,
                                          %speed )  {
  if (%collidedObj.getClassName() $= "Player") {
    %collidedObj.loseALife();
  }
}
```

In the above callback (located in "fireballs.cs"), the engine is asked to get the class name for the collided-with object. It then compares this to "`Player`". If the comparison returns `true`, `loseALife()` is called on the collided-with object.

Alternate Solution #1

There is an alternate way to write this code that would actually work in more cases (i.e., for Player and aiPlayer).

```
// Alternate implementation
function FireBallProjectile::onCollision( %projectileDB ,
                                         %projectileObj , %collidedObj ,
                                         %fade , %vec , %speed )  {
  if (%collidedObj.getType() $= $TypeMasks::PlayerObjectType ) {
    %collidedObj.loseALife();
  }
}
```

This alternate implementation uses the getType() method to get a bitmask for the collided-with object. The bitmask contains bit settings for all classes from which the object is derived as well as for the class itself. So, as I alluded to, if the collision occurred against an aiPlayer (which is derived from Player), this comparison would still work, whereas the prior code would not. In this game, we don't have that worry, so let's leave it as is.

Alternate Solution #2

Originally, as I wrote this code for the book, I was using a bleeding-edge version of the engine (version 1.4 before release), and I ran into a bug (that has since been fixed) where %collidedObj was always getting "1". For a moment, I thought I was stuck. Then, it occurred to me that there are other ways to solve the identification problem, and I wrote the following code.

```
%Offset = vectorSub( %vec , $Game::Player.getWorldBoxCenter() );
%Len = vectorLen( %offset );
if( %len < 1.7 ) {
  $Game::Player.loseALife();
}
```

This code uses the position of the projectile's collision and then compares it to the position of the player's centroid. If the distance between them is small (1.7 world units or less), in all likelihood the object that was hit is the player, and I call loseALife(). This solved my temporary problem, and in the occasional instance when the player wasn't hit but was just close to the collision point, the difference was not noticeable.

The lesson here is that TGE is very flexible, and you can often solve the same problem in many ways. So, don't let one problem stop you.

Making the Game

Out of Lives

At some time, after all this losing of lives, the player will be out of lives. According to our initial rules list, this means the game is up, time to go home. As we have already seen (above) the `loseALife()` method handles this case and ends the game for us.

14.8.5 Moving On

The last things we need to fix with regard to gameplay are moving on to the next level and getting our extra life.

Last Coin

Our design rules stated that, when the last coin is picked up, the current level should be unloaded and the next level should be loaded. So, how do we do this?

If you recall, the inventory system has a callback called `onPickup()`. When we discussed this callback, I said that you might want to override it to implement special behaviors. This is one of those times.

If you will look in "coins.cs", you will find the following implementation of `onPickup()`.

```
function Coin::onPickup( %pickupDB , %pickupObj ,
                         %ownerObj ) {
  // 1
  %status = Parent::onPickup( %pickupDB , %pickupObj ,
                             %ownerObj );

  // 2
  if (CoinsGroup.getCount() == 0 ) {
    buildLevel($Game::NextLevelMap);
     $Game::Player.lives++;
  }

  // 3
  return %status;
}
```

This callback does the following.

1. It takes advantage of the prewritten pickup code by calling the Parent:: version.

2. It then checks to see if the SimGroup CoinsGroup is empty. In the case that it is empty, `buildLevel()` is called with the stored numeric ID of the next level, and a new life is added to our player.

3. Last, but not least, it returns the return status from the Parent call. This is important because the method/callback that called `onPickup()` in the first place might care if the pickup was successful or not.

14.8.6 Gameplay Scripting Completed

We are officially done with the gameplay scripting now. The game is now in a playable state, and we could define some levels and ship it off to our testers at this point. If this were a business venture, that would be the plan, but since we're learning about Torque and not running a gaming business, let's continue.

14.9 Improve Feedback

To make the game easier to play, we should provide some information to the player about how many lives are remaining, what the score is, and how many coins are left on a level. Also, adding sounds to the fireballs will make them a little easier to detect. Lastly, if we add some sounds and music, we will have a nicely rounded prototype.

14.9.1 Copy Required Files

Before we continue, please do the following.

1. Copy   "\MazeRunner\MazeRunner_Post_Improve_Feedback\prototype3" into "\MazeRunner\".

2. Copy "\MazeRunner\MazeRunner_Post_Improve_Feedback\main.cs" into "\MazeRunner\".

The new "main.cs" file points to the newly added "prototype3" mod directory. The directory "prototype3" contains all of the changes we are about to discuss and is ready to play, if you would like to try it before continuing.

14.9.2 New playGUI HUDs

If you start the game and run the "Maze Runner" mission, you will see that the new and improved playGUI has three HUDS at the top of the screen (Figure 14.1.) The three HUDs are the following.

- **Lives counter (upper-left).** Shows number of lives the player has left.
- **Score (upper-middle).** Shows number of coins thus far recovered.
- **Remaining coins for level (upper-right).** Shows coins left till end of level.

These HUDS should look quite familiar. They are the same counters we discussed in Chapter 13, "Game Interfaces," being put to good use in our prototype game.

Figure 14.1

New HUDs.

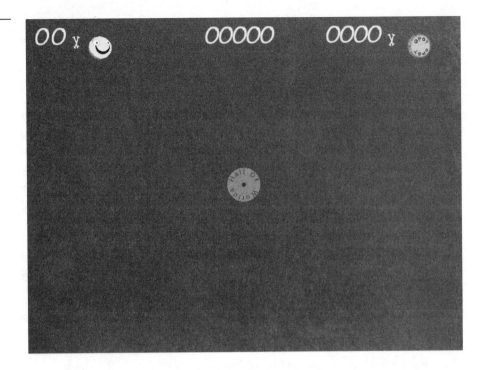

To make your life easier, I have created a completely new playGUI containing these HUDS and placed it and all the scripts and content associated
with it in "~\client\ui\PlayGUIs\". To get this new playGUI interface loaded
instead of the old one, I changed the initClient() function in "~\client\
init.cs" as follows.

```
function initClient() {
    // ...
    //exec("./ui/PlayGui.gui");   // Prior to Maze Runner
    exec("./ui/PlayGUIs/PlayGui.cs"); // MazeRunner (Load My GUI)
    // ...
    //exec("./scripts/playGui.cs"); // Prior to Maze Runner
    // ...
}
```

This change simply tells the function NOT to load the old "PlayGUI.gui" and
"PlayGUI.cs" and to load my "PlayGUIs/PlayGui.cs" intstead. This new script
will automatically load the remainder of the scripts required to build the new
playGUI.

Now, let's talk about how these HUDs are hooked up.

Hooking up the Lives HUD

The lives counter is initialized in the `MazeRunner::onAdd()` callback, from the file "mazerunnerplayer.cs" (bold lines are new code):

```
function MazeRunner::onAdd( %DB , %Obj ) {
  Parent::onAdd( %DB , %Obj );
  %Obj.lives = 3;
  livescounter.setCounterValue(%Obj.lives);
}
```

It is decremented in `Player::loseALife()`, from "mazerunnerplayer.cs" (bold lines are new code).

```
function Player::loseALife( %player ) {
  // 1
  %player.lives--;
  livescounter.setCounterValue(%player.lives);

  // ...
}
```

It is incremented in `Coin::onPickup()`, from "coins.cs" (bold lines are new code).

```
function Coin::onPickup( %pickupDB , %pickupObj , %ownerObj ) {
  // ...
  if (CoinsGroup.getCount() == 0 ) {
    // ...
    livescounter.setCounterValue($Game::Player.lives);
  }
  // ...
}
```

Hooking up the Score HUD

The score counter is initialized in `GameConnection::createPlayer()`, from " ~ \server\scripts\game.cs" (bold lines are new code).

```
function GameConnection::createPlayer(%this, %spawnPoint) {
  // ...
  BuildLevel(0);
  scorecounter.setCounterValue(0);
}
```

Making the Game

It is incremented in `Coin::onPickup()`, from "coins.cs" (bold lines are new code).

```
function Coin::onPickup( %pickupDB , %pickupObj , %ownerObj ) {
    // ...
    scorecounter.setCounterValue(
            scorecounter.getCounterValue() + 1 );
    // ...
}
```

Hooking up the Remaining Coins HUD

The coins counter is initialized at the very end of `BuildLevel()`, from "levelloader.cs" (bold lines are new code).

```
function BuildLevel( %levelNum )   {
    // ...
    coincounter.setCounterValue( CoinsGroup.getCount() );
}
```

It is decremented in `Coin::onPickup()`, from "coins.cs" (bold lines are new code):

```
function Coin::onPickup( %pickupDB , %pickupObj , %ownerObj ) {
    // ...
    coincounter.setCounterValue( CoinsGroup.getCount() );
    // ...
}
```

14.9.3 Adding Sounds

To give the game a little more pizzazz and to make it feel more finished, we need to add a few sounds. As you will recall, in Chapter 11, "Special Effects," we made several audio descriptions and audio profiles. I have included all of these and a few others in two separate places.

The 2D sound descriptions and profiles have been added to a new file named "~\client\scripts\MazeRunnerGUISounds.cs". This includes the following.

- **MazeRunnerNonLooping2DADObj.** A non-looping 2D AudioDescription object for use with AudioProfile objects.
- **MazeRunnerLooping2DADObj.** A looping 2D AudioDescription object for use with AudioProfile objects.
- **MazeRunnerGGSplashScreen.** An AudioProfile object to play music when the GarageGames splash screen is displayed.

- **MazeRunnerButtonOver and MazeRunnerButtonPress.** Two AudioProfile objects used to play button over and press sounds.
- **MazeRunnerLevelLoop.** An AudioProfile object used to play an ambient loop during game play.

This file is loaded by " ~ \client\init.cs" using the following code.

```
/// Load client-side Audio Profiles/Descriptions
  exec("./scripts/audioProfiles.cs");
  exec("./scripts/MazeRunnerGUISounds.cs"); // Maze Runner
```

The 3D sound descriptions and profiles have been added to the existing "fireballs.cs" file at the top and include the following.

- **MazeRunnerNonLooping3DADDB.** A nonlooping 3D AudioDescription datablock for use with AudioProfile datablocks.
- **MazeRunnerFireballExplosionSound.** An AudioProfile datablock that is played for each fireball when it is shot.
- **MazeRunnerFireballExplosionSound.** An AudioProfile datablock that is used by the FireBallExplosion datablock to play an explosion sound.

These sounds will now be loaded when "fireballs.cs" is executed.

Now, let's briefly discuss how each of our new sounds is used.

Adding Sound To Splash Screen

The simplest way to add a sound to the GarageGames splash screen is to play the sound when the splash screen is displayed. If we look in the file " ~ \client\ui\StartupGui.gui", we will find a method named `loadStartup()`. This method is used to display the splash screen. To have the game play a sound when the splash screen is displayed, I made these changes.

```
function loadStartup() {
  // ...
  //alxPlay(AudioStartup); // Before Maze Runner
  alxPlay(MazeRunnerGGSplashScreen); // Maze Runner
}
```

Adding Sound to Buttons

To have the menu buttons play a sound when the mouse passes over a button and when a button is clicked, I needed to define a new GuiControlProfile object and fill in the proper fields.

```
if(!isObject(MainMenuButtonProfile))
  new GuiControlProfile (MainMenuButtonProfile) {
```

**alxPlay()
And Other
Sound Functions**

We did not explicitly discuss the alx*() functions in the guide, but they are all documented in the accompanying "Console Functions Quick Reference" that is part of Appendix A on the accompanying disk.

```
// ...
soundButtonOver = "MazeRunnerButtonOver";
soundButtonDown = "MazeRunnerButtonPress";
};
```

I then made sure that each button in the main menu (" ~ \client\ui\ mainMenuGui.gui") used this new profile.

```
// ...
new GuiButtonCtrl() {
   profile = "MainMenuButtonProfile";
   // ...
```

Adding Ambient Loop to Game

To add the ambient loop to our game, I simply added an `alxPlay()` statement to the `onWake()` callback and a reciprocal `alxStop()` statement to the `onSleep()` callback for the new playGUI. Both of these callbacks are located in " ~ \client\ui\playGUIs\playGUI.cs" and now look like this.

```
function PlayGui::onWake( %this ) {
   $enableDirectInput = "1";
   activateDirectInput();
   // Activate the game's action map
   moveMap.push();
   // Maze Runner
   %this.levelLoop = alxPlay(MazeRunnerLevelLoop);
}

function PlayGui::onSleep( %this ) {
   // Pop the keymap
   moveMap.pop();

   if(isObject ( %this.levelLoop ) )
   alxStop(%this.levelLoop); // Maze Runner
}
```

Notice that I simply store the handle returned from `alxPlay()` into an aptly named dynamic field `levelLoop` created on the fly in the playGUI control object. Later, I check to see if the handle represents a valid handle and stop playing the sound associated with it using `alxStop()`.

Playing Sounds When Fireballs Are Fired

To play the firing sound, we will again use the `playAudio()` ShapeBase method. Although we don't care in this single-player game, by doing this, we insure that every client will hear the sound with no extra effort on our part. To do this, I modified the `StaticShape::shootFireBall()` console method to include the following code.

```
function StaticShape::shootFireBall( %marker,
                                     %projectile ,
                                     %pointingVector ,
                                     %velocity)  {
  // ...
  %marker.playAudio( 0 , MazeRunnerFireballFiringSound );
}
```

If you recall, all fireballs are fired from the center position of a fireball block's world box. Thus, we can approximate the correct location for the firing sound by simply playing the firing sound using the block that marks the origin of the shot itself. In this case I merely called `playAudio()` and played the Maze-RunnerFireballFiringSound AudioProfile datablock in sound slot 0.

Adding Explosion Sounds to An Explosion Datablock

The last sound that was added is the explosion sound. This was accomplished by assigning the new `MazeRunnerFireballExplosionSound` AudioProfile datablock to the existing `FireBallExplosion` datablock's `soundProfile` field.

```
datablock ExplosionData(FireBallExplosion) {
  // ...
  soundProfile = "MazeRunnerFireballExplosionSound";
  // ...
};
```

That's it. We now have a working prototype that we can distribute for testing. What's next?

14.10 Improving the Game

At this point, the game is working and completely playable. However, it is a long way from being a completed, or perhaps even fun, product. This short section is about getting the game from sort-of-boring prototype to fun-to-play finished product.

Also, to show some of the things that can be done to improve this game, an improved version of the game has been supplied on the accompanying disk titled "MazeRunnerAdvanced".

14.10.1 Add More Features

Before you jump into adding new features, I suggest that you play with your final prototype and study the scripts that make it run. Make some sample levels and play them. Then, once you feel confident enough, write down a list of new features and start adding them.

To help your muse, here is a short list of suggested features.

- **Rewrite the level loader.**
  - Get rid of the manual level-editing process and add a visual editor.
  - Write a new level loader to load the files generated by the level editor.
- **Add new gameplay elements.**
  - Gravity chutes.
  - Flaming pipes.
  - Falling blocks.
  - Blocks that disappear (permanently) on contact.
  - Opponents that block the path and kill the player on contact.

14.10.2 Use Missions Instead

As an exercise, consider changing the scripts to dynamically create a mission file then load the mission file instead of generating the level on the fly.

14.10.3 Fix Safe Block

Currently, the player is sent to a "safe" block during level tear-down and build-up. This is kind of weird and not all that pleasant to look at. Come up with a better idea, like the following.

- Overlay the screen with a "loading" GUI while building.
- Fade the screen to black while building.

14.10.4 Cleanup

There are a tremendous number of scripts and assets going unused in the game. Get rid of these to give the game a smaller disk footprint.

14.10.5 Maximize Networking Performance

As a single-player game, you might not think networking code would matter much, but it still does. By default, the networking settings are a bit low. Because our connection is local, we can maximize these settings. This will help decrease the time it takes to build our levels (since all dynamically generated objects are being ghosted on the fly from the local server to the local client). So put the following settings in "game.cs" at the top.

- `$pref::Net::PacketRateToServer = 32;`
- `$pref::Net::PacketSize = 450;`
- `$pref::Net::PacketRateToClient = 32;`

14.10.6 Experiment with Art and Special Effects

Improve the artwork, add more special effects, and tune the ones that are there. Try using blocks that do not self-illuminate.

14.10.7 Features Added To Maze Runner Advanced

Several new features were added and many old features were changed in Maze Runner Advanced.

New Art

The first thing that was changed in Maze Runner Advanced was the art. I had a professional artist replace my ugly programmer art with something that had a lot more style (Figure 14.2).

Figure 14.2
New art.

Added More Splash Screens

Although this is technically new art, too, I want to point out that I needed to allow this product to properly represent all the parties involved, so I added a splash screen for Hall Of Worlds, LLC (my company), and a title screen for the game (Figure 14.3).

Figure 14.3

New splash screens.

Visual Level Editor

Because I realized early on that the method for adding levels was difficult at best and heinously frustrating at worst, I added a visual editor. This editor uses modifications to the old programmer art and some tricky use of data-blocks to supply a greatly simplified level editor (Figure 14.4).

Figure 14.4

Visual editor and resulting level.

Credits and Help Dialog

I added a credits page and a help dialog containing instructions on using the game, editor instructions, a description of the game, etc. (Figure 14.5.)

Figure 14.5
Credits and help.

14.11 Summary

In this chapter, we quickly tied up the loose ends for our gameplay scripts by enabling auto-loading of the mission, scripts to kill the player, more scripts to reward the player with extra lives, and scripts moving us on to the next level or ending the game based on coin and life counts, respectively.

We learned that there are multiple solutions for each problem we face, and we examined a concrete example of a case where a bug (originally) prevented me from writing the game the way I wanted to.

Lastly, we discussed the fact that this game is far from done, and then we brainstormed some ideas for improving it and looked at what some of those improvements entailed.

At this point, you should feel fairly confident that you can in fact make a game, and that the Torque Game Engine will have the power and the features to make that game a reality.

With that said, I wish you good luck and happy Torqueing!

Index